INTERNATIONAL PROJECT FINANCE

Law and Practice

INTERNATIONAL PROJECT FINANCE

Law and Practice

Edited by

JOHN DEWAR

OXFORD

UNIVERSITY PRESS

OXFORD

UNIVERSITY PRESS

Great Clarendon Street, Oxford OX2 6DP

Oxford University Press is a department of the University of Oxford.
It furthers the University's objective of excellence in research, scholarship,
and education by publishing worldwide in

Oxford New York

Auckland Cape Town Dar es Salaam Hong Kong Karachi
Kuala Lumpur Madrid Melbourne Mexico City Nairobi
New Delhi Shanghai Taipei Toronto

With offices in

Argentina Austria Brazil Chile Czech Republic France Greece
Guatemala Hungary Italy Japan Poland Portugal Singapore
South Korea Switzerland Thailand Turkey Ukraine Vietnam

Oxford is a registered trade mark of Oxford University Press
in the UK and in certain other countries

Published in the United States
by Oxford University Press Inc., New York

British Library Cataloguing-in-Publication Data

Data available

Library of Congress Cataloging-in-Publication Data

Data available

Typeset by Glyph International, Bangalore, India
Printed in Great Britain
on acid-free paper by
CPI Antony Rowe, Chippenham, Wiltshire

ISBN 978–0–19–960144–8

1 3 5 7 9 10 8 6 4 2

PREFACE

The purpose of this book is to offer a new framework for the law and practice of international project finance.

My colleagues and I at Milbank approached the task with both excitement and a little trepidation. Our aim has been to write a book which analyses the law and practice of project finance from a different perspective from existing books, which have tended to be rooted in a more domestic focus.

Over the last twenty years, modern project financing techniques have spread rapidly from the US market to Western Europe and then on into emerging markets in Asia, the Middle East, Africa, and Latin America. I have felt for some time that there is a place for a book with a truly international focus, responding to the needs of sponsors, lenders, and practitioners for analysis of the legal and documentation issues of core relevance to the practice of international project finance.

Despite a significant knock during the 'credit crunch', and following the collapse of Lehman, the international project finance market has showed remarkable resilience. It has been sustained by the swelling demand for infrastructure, at a time when governments everywhere are seeking to manage burgeoning fiscal deficits. Therefore, in many countries, private sector-led project finance solutions have come to the fore and many governments are seeking to accelerate the introduction or continued growth of Public Private Partnerships.

Whilst economic growth has, and may continue to be, impacted by the effects of the financial crisis, the quest for oil and gas, minerals, and other natural resources continues unabated across the globe. This has led to the sponsoring and financing in the private sector of a number of 'mega' projects in the gas, LNG, gas transportation, refinery, and mining sectors.

The sustained demand for project finance comes at a time when commercial banks—the institutions which have historically provided the preponderance of project debt finance—have found it increasingly difficult to maintain their position as the core providers of capital. In emerging markets, and in some recent cases, even in OECD countries, the financing of many projects has only been possible with the leadership provided by Export Credit Agencies and multilateral and bilateral funding institutions. The last few years have also seen the increasing application of Islamic financing techniques (particularly in the growing Middle East project finance market). Despite the difficulties faced by the international capital markets, there has also been a resurgent focus on the project bond market. In order to tap this diverse pool of potential sources of liquidity, it is important for both commercial principals and practitioners to have a thorough grasp of the structuring and documentation requirements of these very different funding sources.

In conceiving the book, I also concluded that a book on international project finance would not be complete without presenting and analysing the background and issues arising in the context of projects developed in civil law jurisdictions. I was therefore delighted when Antoine Maffei and Jean-Renaud Cazali of De Pardieu Brocas Maffei agreed to write a chapter analysing practice issues arising in France and other jurisdictions whose jurisprudence is based on the civil code. As project financing techniques have spread throughout Francophone Africa, an understanding of the roots of the relevant legal systems, and the particular issues arising in the context of these jurisdictions, is particularly important.

Our long-standing friend and colleague, Martin Benatar, also agreed to assist us in 'de-bunking' the arcane world of project insurance and re-insurance. For project sponsors and lenders, insurance plays a key part in the overall risk management of projects. Even many seasoned practitioners find the topic both complex and bewildering.

Notwithstanding the recent stresses at play across the global financing markets, the relatively low default rate amongst project financed transactions is a testament to the skills of practitioners in analysing and assessing risk, as well as allocating such risk in the most appropriate manner. Alas, some projects do experience financial distress and, in this context, the book includes a chapter analysing the intricacies of restructuring complex projects.

Last, but by no means least, it appeared to me that there was a need for greater understanding and clarity about the management and resolution of disputes, which regrettably do occur, and raise complex legal issues, particularly in the context of cross-border international project financings.

Many authors from different disciplines have been involved in the writing of this book and many other practitioners at Milbank have been involved in supporting the writing process. I am eternally grateful to all who have contributed and the many others who have lent their time, given their advice and insights, and above all, engaged in analysis and debate which has considerably enhanced the knowledge set forth in the pages which follow.

Apart from the invaluable contributions made by all my colleagues, I have also received tremendous support from my unflappable assistant, Josie, who for some time has had to put up with the combined demands of a busy legal practice, as well as the editing of this book. I have also promised to my wife, Geraldine, and my son, William, that the many weeks of nocturnal activity will diminish following the book's publication!

John Dewar
1 March 2011

SUMMARY CONTENTS

CONTENTS

LIST OF CONTRIBUTORS

Nick Angel is a partner based in the London office of Milbank, Tweed, Hadley & McCloy LLP and is a member of Milbank's Financial Restructuring Group. Nick has particular expertise in complex, international and national corporate reconstruction and insolvency matters and has advised on the restructuring of a number of project financings. Nick regularly acts for all the different types of stakeholder in a restructuring, including debtor companies and their directors, senior secured lenders, junior creditors, government regulators, distressed investors, and insolvency practitioners. Nick is admitted as a Solicitor of the Supreme Court of England and Wales.

Martin Benatar is a recognized market leader in providing insurance advice on behalf of senior lenders with 14 years' experience of working exclusively as an adviser to financiers, primarily in the UK, Europe, and the Middle East but also throughout Asia and the Americas. Martin's 23-year insurance career began as an underwriter for the Commercial Union, a major composite insurer and he took responsibility for the UK construction account and ultimately their property market account. He has provided dedicated consultancy advice to financiers since recruited specifically for that purpose by Sedgwick in 1997. He moved to Miller in 2002 and successfully developed their lender advisory business before joining Jardine Lloyd Thompson Limited (JLT) in 2006, where he was responsible for Financial Insurance Due Diligence until 2010. In 2011, while still a part-time employee of JLT, he has established his own independent advisory business primarily dedicated to the space sector. He has served on a number of market bodies and regularly speaks at conferences and seminars for lawyers, ECAs, and project finance teams. He presented an annual insurance lecture for the project finance course at the London Business School between 2000 and 2006. A graduate in political science, he is ACII qualified and a Chartered Insurance Practitioner.

Alexander K. Borisoff is a senior associate in the Washington, DC office of Milbank, Tweed, Hadley & McCloy LLP and has been a member of the Global Project Finance Group since 2001. His experience includes the representation of project sponsors, financial institutions, export credit and multilateral development agencies, and other project participants in a wide range of cross-border and domestic project and structured financings and investment transactions. Alec is admitted to the New York Bar.

Jean-Renaud Cazali is a member of the Paris Bar and has been a partner with De Pardieu, Brocas, Maffei since 2008. Jean-Renaud started his career with Société

Générale in London and then joined Morgan Stanley, also in London. Jean-Renaud specializes in international banking and project financing and has been involved in the arrangement of numerous national and international projects in the infrastructure, PPP, power, and renewable energy sectors. Jean-Renaud has substantial project finance experience in France and many African countries.

Erin Culbertson is an associate based in the Washington, DC office of Milbank, Tweed, Hadley & McCloy LLP and is a member of the firm's litigation group. She has advised clients on a number of complex disputes, including international arbitration as well as commercial and bankruptcy litigation. Erin is admitted to the Bars of the State of New York and the District of Columbia.

John Dewar is a partner in the Global Project Finance Group and is based in Milbank, Tweed, Hadley & McCloy LLP's London office. John's practice centres on project and structured finance transactions in Europe, Africa, the Middle East, and Asia. He has acted for commercial banks, export credit agencies, Islamic banks, and sponsors in a wide range of industries, including power, oil and gas, petrochemicals, satellites, telecommunications, water, infrastructure (including PPPs), and mining. John also leads the firm's Islamic Finance Business Unit. John has been recognized by *Legal 500, IFLR, Chambers, Legal Experts, Global Counsel 3000,* and *Who's Who Legal* as among the world's leading project finance lawyers and by *Chambers* and *Legal 500* as a leading Islamic finance lawyer. He is admitted as a Solicitor of the Supreme Court of England and Wales.

Daisy East is a senior associate in the Global Project Finance Group based in the London office of Milbank, Tweed, Hadley & McCloy LLP. She advises both lenders and sponsors in international project financings, specialising in power and water, petrochemicals, and mining and metals. Daisy is also a member of the Islamic Finance Business Unit. She has worked on a number of major transactions in the Middle East, Africa, Europe, and Asia and is admitted as a Solicitor of the Supreme Court of England and Wales.

Phillip Fletcher is a partner in the London office of Milbank, Tweed, Hadley & McCloy LLP. He was previously resident in the Milbank's Hong Kong and New York offices and is the chair of the Firm's European Practices. Phill has been a member of the Firm's Global Project Finance Group for more than 20 years. His experience includes representing parties in the development and financing of oil and gas, natural resource, independent power, satellite and other infrastructure projects in Europe, the Middle East, and Africa. Phill has been recognized as a leading project finance lawyer by a number of journals, including *Euromoney* (which has recognized him as among the top thirty projects lawyers in the world), the *International Who's Who of Project Finance Lawyers, Legal 500, PLC,* and *Chambers and Partners.* Phill is on the advisory board of the *International Financial Law Review* and is a member of the Council on Foreign Relations. Phill is admitted at the New York Bar and as a Solicitor of the Supreme Court of England and Wales.

William Fyfe is an associate in Milbank, Tweed, Hadley & McCloy LLP's London office and is a member of the Global Project Finance Group. He has advised lenders and project sponsors on a variety of financings in the power, water, and oil and gas sectors. He is admitted to the New York Bar.

David Gasperow is a senior associate in the Global Securities Group resident in the London office of Milbank, Tweed, Hadley & McCloy LLP. David experience has included offerings of debt and equity securities, representing both issuers and underwriters in IPOs, secondary equity offerings, high yield bond offerings, and investment grade debt offerings. In particular, he has significant experience in both European and Rule 144A and Regulation S capital markets transactions. In addition to transactional work, his practice has included securities regulatory counselling under the US Securities Act of 1933 and the Securities Exchange Act of 1934. He currently serves on the Board of Directors of the *Columbia Business Law Review* and is admitted to the New York Bar.

Alistair Hill is a senior associate based in the London office of Milbank, Tweed, Hadley & McCloy LLP and is a member of the firm's Financial Restructuring Group. Alistair specializes in multi-jurisdictional restructuring and insolvencies, as well as acting for borrowers and lenders on a variety of financing transactions. Alistair's experience in restructuring transactions includes acting for debtors, senior bank lenders, mezzanine and second lien lenders, insolvency practitioners, pension trustees, distressed funds, and monoline insurers. Alistair is a member of the Insolvency Lawyers' Association and is the author of the PLC guide 'Buying the Business and Assets of an Insolvent Company'. He is a Solicitor of the Supreme Court of England and Wales.

Patrick Holmes is European counsel in Milbank, Tweed, Hadley & McCloy LLP's Project Finance Group. He has extensive experience in relation to a wide variety of financings and restructurings in Europe and other parts of the world. He has previously been based in Tokyo, Bahrain, Jeddah, and Moscow. He advises financial institutions, companies, investment funds, and others in relation to limited or non-recourse project and acquisition financings, financial restructurings, and corporate finance. Patrick is admitted as a Solicitor of the Supreme Court of England and Wales.

Mohammad Munib Hussain is a member of the Global Project Finance Group in Milbank, Tweed, Hadley & McCloy LLP's London office. Mohammad has advised both lenders and sponsors in a number of international project financings. Mohammad is also a member of the Islamic Finance Business Unit and has advised on a number of *Sharia'a*-compliant project financings. He has received the Islamic Finance Qualification and is admitted as both a Barrister and a Solicitor of the Supreme Court of England and Wales.

Oliver Irwin is an associate in the Global Project Finance Group in the London office of Milbank, Tweed, Hadley & McCloy LLP. Oliver specializes in advising both lenders and developers on multi-sourced international project financings involving ECAs and multilateral lenders. Oliver has a wide range of experience in a variety of industry sectors such as telecoms, manufacturing, power, and water and renewables and has worked on a number of major transactions in the Middle East, Africa, Europe, and Asia. He is admitted as a Solicitor of the Supreme Court of England and Wales.

Antoine Maffei is a member of the Paris Bar and has been a partner with De Pardieu, Brocas, Maffei since 1993. Antoine started his career with Dewey Ballantine in New York from 1970 to 1972 and subsequently acted as senior counsel with the World Bank in Washington until 1978. Antoine then became senior legal advisor at Banque Française du Commerce Extérieur and subsequently joined the firm of Siméon & Associés as a partner. Antoine was one of the founders of De Pardieu, Brocas, Maffei's Banking & Finance Department and has substantial project finance expertise in both France and Francophone Africa.

Jonathan Maizel is a partner at Milbank, Tweed, Hadley & McCloy LLP and has been a member of the Firm's Project Finance Group since 1989. Jonathan heads the Firm's Washington, DC Project Finance practice. He was the resident project finance partner in the firm's Tokyo Office in 1998–99. He has been named one of the world's leading Project Finance attorneys by numerous publications, including *The Best Lawyers in America, Lawdragon, Who's Who Legal, Chambers USA, Guide to the World's Leading Project Finance Lawyers*, and *Best Lawyers* for the Washington, DC area. Mr Maizel is admitted to the Bars of the State of New York and the District of Columbia.

Cathy Marsh is a partner in Milbank, Tweed, Hadley & McCloy LLP's Global Project Finance Group and is based in the London office. She has extensive experience in project, structured, and acquisition financings in various regions of the world. Cathy has been ranked by *Chambers UK* as a leading projects lawyer for the last two years and as a top-ranked tier mining lawyer. She has also been recognized as a leader in her field by the *Guide to the World's Leading Women* in Business Law and as a leading projects lawyer by *Who's Who Legal* and *Legal Experts*. Cathy is admitted as a Solicitor of the Supreme Court of England and Wales.

Gabriel Mpubani is an associate in the London office of Milbank, Tweed, Hadley & McCloy LLP and is a member of the Global Project Finance Department. Gabriel's experience includes both project finance and other forms of leveraged finance transactions in Europe, North America, Africa and the Middle East. Prior to joining Milbank, Gabriel worked with a magic circle firm in London and with Shonubi, Musoke & Co. Advocates in Kampala, Uganda. Gabriel is a Solicitor of the Supreme Court of England and Wales.

Michael Nolan is a partner in the Washington, DC office of Milbank, Tweed, Hadley and McCloy LLP. Michael is experienced in all phases of commercial litigation and arbitration. He has represented clients in US federal and state courts and before arbitral tribunals in all manner of complex disputes, including general commercial, securities, antitrust, tax, and insolvency cases. His practice has a particular focus on international arbitration and litigation. He has represented clients or served as arbitrator in cases under AAA, ICC, ICSID, UNCITRAL, and other rules. His arbitrations have involved electricity, gas, transportation, and mining concessions; joint-venture agreements; satellite and other insurance coverage; construction; and energy distribution. He has represented both investors and states in arbitrations pursuant to bilateral investment treaties and the Energy Charter Treaty. He has also represented companies and states in connection with court proceedings involving sovereign immunity, acts of state, and the recognition and enforcement of foreign judicial and non-judicial awards. He has substantial experience with compliance issues that arise under the US Foreign Corrupt Practices Act, other anti-bribery laws and sanctions programmes. He is admitted to the Bars of the State of New York and the District of Columbia.

Andrew Pendleton is an associate with Milbank, Tweed, Hadley and McCloy LLP, based in London, and is a member of the Global Project Finance Group. He has significant experience in advising lenders and sponsors on a variety of international project financings. Andrew has also advised on financings involving ECAs and multilateral lenders. He is admitted as a Solicitor of the Supreme Court of England and Wales.

Mark Plenderleith is a partner based in the Tokyo office of Milbank, Tweed, Hadley and McCloy LLP. Mark specializes in multi-source limited recourse financing, reserve based lending, international joint ventures and leveraged finance. His practice and prior representations span a cross-section of financial institutions, energy companies, developers, private equity funds, and agencies. Prior to joining Milbank Mark worked for the Japan Bank for International Cooperation as a member of the project finance transaction team. Mark is a dual-qualified lawyer advising clients in respect of both New York law and English law transactions.

Joanne Robertson is an associate in Milbank, Tweed, Hadley & McCloy LLP's Global Project Finance Department, and a member of the firm's Islamic Finance Business Unit. She has gained extensive experience in advising sponsors and lenders in project financing transactions in Europe, the Middle East, and Asia and is admitted as a Solicitor of the Supreme Court of England and Wales.

Tom Siebens has been a securities and corporate finance partner since 1989 and based in Milbank, Tweed, Hadley & McCloy LLP's London office for over sixteen years. Tom specializes in international transactions and advisory matters. Most recently, his focus has been advising underwriters of project bonds and on restructurings, special situations and opportunity investing and financings in distressed M&A transactions. Historically, his practice has covered a broad range of financings, including IPOs, leveraged buyouts, off-balance sheet transactions, project bonds, and offerings of investment grade, high yield, and structured products. Tom has extensive experience in emerging markets equity and debt offerings; he was based in Singapore for three years in the mid-1990s. Tom is a member of the European High Yield Association. He is also a member of Milbank's European Special Situations Business Unit and its Islamic Finance Business Unit. He is admitted to the Bars of New York and the District of Columbia.

Julian Stait is head of the Litigation & Arbitration practice in the London office of Milbank, Tweed, Hadley & McCloy LLP. Julian specializes in the resolution of large, high-stakes, and complex business and regulatory disputes and has extensive experience of litigation before the English courts (up to and including the House of Lords), the resolution of complaints, disputes and investigations before a number of regulatory authorities, and international arbitration under the auspices of many of the major institutional rules. He has acted in a number of the largest pieces of IT and telecommunications litigation to go before the UK courts and has significant experience in major fraud litigation, international and cross-border disputes, corporate and joint venture disputes, major project disputes, public law and regulatory disputes, and banking litigation. He is admitted as a Solicitor of the Supreme Court of England and Wales.

LIST OF FINANCIAL TERMS, ABBREVIATIONS, AND ACRONYMS

AAU	Agreement Among Underwriters
ALOP	advance loss of profit insurance
BIT	bilateral investment treaty
BLOU	broker's letter of undertaking
BLT	build, lease, transfer
BOAD	West African Development Bank
BOO	build, own, operate
BOOT	build, own, operate, transfer
BOT	build, operate, transfer
BTO	build, transfer, operate
CABEI	Central American Bank for Economic Integration
Capex	capital expenditure
CASDB	Central African States Development Bank
CDB	Caribbean Development Bank
CEAR	construction erection all risk insurance
CIRR rate	commercial interest reference rate
COD	commercial operation date; the date on which the construction phase of a project is completed and the operation phase begins
DBFO	design, build, finance and operate
DEG	German Investment Corporation
DFI	development finance institution
DSCR	debt service cover ratio
DSRA	debt service reserve account
DSU	delay in start up insurance
EAC	East African Community
EADB	East African Development Bank
EBL	equity bridge loan
EBRD	European Bank for Reconstruction and Development
ECA	export credit agency
ECOWAS Fund	Fund for Co-operation, Compensation and Development (Economic Community of West African States)
EEA	European Economic Area
EIA	environmental impact assessment
EIB	European Investment Bank
EIF	European Investment Fund
EITA	Extractive Industries Transparency Initiative
EPCM	engineering, procurement and construction management
EPC	engineering, procurement and construction
ESMP	environmental and social management plan

EURIBOR	Euro Interbank Offered Rate
FCPA	Foreign Corrupt Practices Act of 1977 (15 U.S.C §§ 78dd–1, et seq.)
FMO	Netherlands Development Finance Company
FONPLATA	Financial Fund for the Development of the River Plate Basin
FSA	fuel supply agreement
GCC	Gulf Cooperation Council
GPA	World Trade Organization's Plurilateral Agreement on Governmental Procurement
Hermes	Euler Hermes Kreditversicherungs-AG
IACAD	Inter-American Convention Against Corruption
IADB	Inter-American Development Bank
IBRD (World Bank)	International Bank for Reconstruction and Development
ICMA	International Capital Markets Association
ICSID	the International Centre for the Settlement of Investment Disputes
IDA	International Development Association
IDC	interest during construction
IDEP	United Nations African Institute for Economic Development and Planning
IFAD	International Fund for Agricultural Development
IFC	International Finance Corporation, part of the World Bank Group
IFRS	international accounting standards within the meaning of IAS Regulation 1606/2002 to the extent applicable to the relevant financial statements
IPO	initial public offering
IPP	independent power project
IRR	internal rate of return
ISDA	International Swaps and Derivatives Association
IsDB	Islamic Development Bank
ISO	International Standards Organisation
IWPP	independent water and power project
JBIC	Japan Bank for International Cooperation, the international arm of Japan Finance Corporation
K-Exim	Export-Import Bank of Korea
K-sure	Korea Trade Insurance Corporation
LIBOR	the London Interbank Offered Rate (the reference rate for lending in the London interbank market)
LLCR	loan life cover ratio
LMA	Loan Market Association (London)
LME	London Metal Exchange
LNG	liquefied natural gas
LOI	letter of intent
LSTA	Loan Syndications and Trading Association (New York)
MAC	material adverse change
MIGA	Multilateral Investment Guarantee Agency
MRA	maintenance reserve account

NDF	Nordic Development Fund
NETA	New Energy Trading Arrangement
NEXI	Nippon Export and Investment Insurance
NIB	Nordic Investment Bank
NPV	net present value (of future cashflow)
O&M	operation and maintenance
OECD	Organisation for Economic Cooperation and Development
OHADA	Organisation pour l'Harmonisation du Droit des Affaires en Afrique
Opex	operating expenditure
OPIC	Overseas Private Investment Corporation, an agency of the US government
PD	property damage insurance
PFI	the Private Finance Initiative, a PPP programme promoted by the UK government
PIM	preliminary information memorandum
PPA	power purchase agreement
PPP	public-private partnership
PRI	political risk insurance
Proparco	Promotion et Participation pour la Coopération Économique
PSA	production sharing agreement
PWPA	power and water purchase agreement
SACE	Servizi Assicurativi del Commercio Estero (SACE SpA)
SEC	US Securities and Exchange Commission
SFD	Saudi Fund for Development
SINOSURE	China Export & Credit Insurance Corporation
SPV	special purpose vehicle
SWTI	site wide terrorism insurance
TPL	third party liability insurance
US Exim Bank	Export-Import Bank of the United States
World Bank	the International Bank for Reconstruction and Development

List of Islamic Financial Terms, Abbreviations, and Acronyms

AAOIFI	Accounting and Auditing Organization for Islamic Financial Institutions
A.H.	after Hijri
Akhlaq	moralities and ethics
A'qd	a bilateral contract
Arbun	a down payment
Fatwa	an Islamic legal opinion
Fiqh al Muamalat	Islamic commercial jurisprudence
Gharar	the sale of probable items whose existence or characteristics are uncertain or speculative (*maisir*), the risk of which makes it akin to gambling (*qimar*)
Hadith	each saying, act or approval of the Prophet (PBUH) as complied by the *Sahabah*
IFSB	Islamic Financial Services Board
IIFM	International Islamic Financial Market

Ijarah	lease purchase finance
Ijma	the consensus of the *Mujtahid* on a particular interpretation of or application of the *Sharia'a*
Ijtihad	the individual interpretation of *Sharia'a* principles by *Mujtahids* to infer expert legal rulings from foundational proofs within or without a particular *Madhab*
Istisna'a	commissioned manufacture of a specified asset
Manfa'a	usufruct or other benefit derived from an asset
Mudarabah	investment fund arrangement
Mujtahid	independent Islamic jurists qualified to exercise *Ijtihad*
Murabaha	cost plus financing
Musharaka	joint venture arrangement
Musharaka Muntahiya Bittamleek	Diminishing *Musharaka*
Qard Hassan	an interest-free loan as permitted by the *Qur'an*
Qiyas	the interpretation by analogical reasoning where one situation is measured against another by the *Mujtahids*
Qur'an	Book of Allah (SWT)
Rab al-mal	capital provider
Rahn	mortgage or pledge
Riba	any excess paid or received on a principal amount or an additional return received on the principal which is derived by the mere passage of time
Sahabah	closest companions of the Prophet (PBUH)
Sharia'a	Islamic law as derived from the *Qur'an* and *Sunnah*
Sukuk	trust certificates
Tafsir	exegesis of the *Qur'an*
Takaful	*Sharia'a*-compliant insurance
Wa'd	a unilateral promise
Wakil	an agent

GLOSSARY

concession	an authority to develop, construct and operate a project granted to a project company by a host government for a defined period of time
construction phase	the initial period of a project during which the plant or other project assets are constructed usually by an EPC contractor
drawdown	the borrowing of a loan pursuant to the terms of a facility agreement
EPC contract	engineering, procurement and construction contract (i.e. a 'turnkey' construction contract)
EPC contractor	strictly, the contractor under an EPC Contract, but commonly used in a generic sense to refer to a construction contractor
EPC Delay LDs	the liquidated damages payable by an EPC Contractor to a project company pursuant to an EPC Contract if and when the construction of a project is delayed
Equator Principles	the principles described in 'The 'Equator Principles' – A financial industry benchmark for determining, assessing and managing social and environmental risk in project finance' dated July 2006 and available at <http://www.equator-principles./com/Equator_Principles.pdf>.
finance documents	the agreements that document the financing of a project
Financial Close	the date on which all conditions precedent under a project's finance documents are satisfied or waived
Financial Model	a financial model of a project development using a computer spreadsheet program
Gearing leverage ratio	the ratio of a company's (consolidated) borrowings to its tangible net worth (or adjusted shareholders' funds)
host country	the country in which a project is located
multilateral agency	an entity established by a number of countries to promote the development of particular projects around the world or in certain regions by, for example, direct lending or insuring lenders against political risk
offtaker	a purchaser of the product(s) produced or manufactured by a project
operation phase	the period of a project that follows the construction phase during which the project becomes operational
project company	an entity that develops, owns and operates a project which is ultimately owned by the sponsor(s)
project documents	the documents that relate to the construction, operation and maintenance of a project
security documents	the agreements that document the security taken by the financiers

shareholder	a sponsor which holds the shares in the project company
sovereign immunity	a prohibition preventing the seizure of a government controlled entity and its assets that emanates from a law providing that entity immunity in that regard
sponsor	an entity responsible for promoting and/or developing a project and usually a direct or indirect shareholder in the relevant project company

TABLE OF CASES

ARBITRATIONS

NATIONAL AND INTERNATIONAL CASES

TABLE OF LEGISLATION

TABLE OF INTERNATIONAL TREATIES, CONVENTIONS, AND AGREEMENTS

INTRODUCTION

The Definition of Project Finance

Whilst many attempts have been made to define project finance, the term has been used in many contexts over the years and its meaning has evolved as the techniques which it embodies have been adapted to macro-economic change. Like describing the 'elephant in the room', it is difficult to define, and perhaps not worth the exercise because inevitably you recognize it when you see it.

Accepted definitions focus on the financing of a specific asset in which lenders look principally to the revenues generated by the operation of that asset for the source of funds from which loans will be repaid. The primary security for the loans consists of the assets of the project including, most notably, the cashflow the project generates and the contracts that assure the stability of both its costs and its revenues.

Project finance is deployed most commonly in the development of large infrastructure projects (e.g. power generation, toll roads, telecommunications), social infrastructure (such as hospitals and schools), and the exploitation of energy and other natural resources, but it can be used to finance a broad range of assets and services.

Characteristics

Although each financing is specifically designed to meet the requirements of a particular project and the objectives of its sponsors, the following characteristics are common to most project financings:

(1) the project is developed through a separate, and usually single purpose, financial and legal entity;
(2) the debt of the project company is often completely separate (at least for balance sheet purposes) from the sponsors' direct obligations;
(3) the sponsors seek to maximize the debt to equity leverage of the project, and the amount of debt is linked directly to the cashflow potential of the business, and to a lesser extent the liquidation value, of the project and its assets;
(4) the sponsors' guarantees (if any) to lenders generally do not cover all the risks involved in the project;

(5) project assets (including contracts with third parties) and revenues are generally pledged as security for the lenders; and

(6) firm contractual commitments of various third parties (such as construction contractors, feedstock and other suppliers, purchasers of the project's output and government authorities) represent significant components of the credit support for the project.

1

APPROACHING LEGAL ISSUES IN
A PROJECT FINANCE TRANSACTION

Phillip Fletcher, Milbank, Tweed, Hadley & McCloy LLP

Introduction

Project finance is at its core a form of secured lending. Much of the legal expertise **1.01**
is drawn from the discipline of banking. One who sees the beauty of the perfect
covenant, the joy of an all-encompassing event of default, or the elegance of a multi-
tiered intercreditor agreement has the capacity to excel in the field. But the
inclination to do so comes from never having outgrown the desire to play with big
toys (or for that matter machinery and equipment). The reason for this is that project finance lawyers undertake a greater degree of inquiry into the business of the
borrower, and into the construction and operation of the facilities that it will construct, than do lawyers involved in other kinds of lending. Project finance
transactions entail lenders extending a large amount of credit to a newly formed,
thinly capitalized company whose principal assets at the time of closing are not
physical but rather merely contracts, licenses, and ambitious plans. Hence the focus
on prudent legal analysis.

1.02   Unless a project financing reaches financial close, there are no 'winners'. However, even after the finance documents are signed, the complex relationships among the parties must be sustained through economic, political, and legal change. No matter how comprehensive the legal documentation, virtually every project encounters some form of technical or commercial problem over its life that leads to legal difficulty. Sometimes that difficulty arises because two parties have a legitimate disagreement over the meaning or effect of a few of the words contained within the mountain of documents governing their relationships. In other cases, issues that had not been contemplated at the time of financial close arise with a consequent absence of guidance in the documents as to how to resolve them. Not infrequently, the underlying economics of the project, and the negotiating leverage of the parties, change such that what seemed fair at closing may years later appear to one of the parties as oppressive. In most instances, the parties to a project financing are able readily to resolve such matters, recognizing that their relationships require close cooperation and compromise, but that is not always the case.

1.03   Disputes cannot be avoided on the playground, nor can they be avoided in project finance. When the stakes are high enough, it may be impossible to secure compromise. The frequency with which disputes arise can, however, be limited by a careful initial assessment of the project so that, at a minimum, all parties enter the deal with a common understanding of the rules of the game.

1.04   With the expansion of project finance into new industries and regions, the attendant legal issues have become increasingly complex and the ability to predict where difficulties will arise has become more challenging. Ever-shifting market standards, and the absence of agreed-form project documentation, contribute to the extremely varied nature of project finance transactions. Project finance lawyers must patiently consider the technical, political, and legal risks of each individual project in order to enable parties to reach agreement on how contentious issues should be treated. This process requires familiarity with varied disciplines of law, ranging from civil procedure, contracts, property, trusts, torts, equity, and conflicts of laws, and with a range of financial instruments, such as commercial bank loans, capital markets instruments, multilateral, and domestic government-funded loans, guarantees from export credit agencies, and Islamic *Sharia'a*-compliant instruments.

1.05   By drawing on this variety of disciplines, a project finance lawyer can help the parties structure financings that are robust enough to withstand long-term volatility.[1] There are a range of threshold legal issues and tasks, common to virtually all projects, which must be addressed if the project finance lawyer is to accomplish his or her role effectively.

---

[1] For a discussion of the approach generally to negotiating project finance transactions, see P. Fletcher, 'Rules for Negotiating Project Finance Deals', *International Financial Law Review*, November 2005.

Among these are: **1.06**

(1) identifying the overall legal risks associated with a project;
(2) assessing the laws and regulations of the host states and of the courts and other institutions that implement them;
(3) addressing environmental and social considerations;
(4) choosing the governing law for the finance and project documents;
(5) drafting and negotiating complex credit agreements; and
(6) developing security packages across a range of jurisdictions.

Overall Risk Assessment

Projects inevitably face risk. Although some risks can be structured, contracted, or   **1.07**
insured away, projects, as in the case of all commercial endeavours, are exposed to a
wide range of potential challenges that can have an adverse impact on their economic performance and even their viability. As most projects will not have been
built or even engineered when their financing is implemented, there will inevitably
be differing views on the likelihood and potential impact of future adverse events.
The ultimate assessment in any project is whether the risk profile of the deal, taken
as a whole, is 'bankable'. This is certainly not a science, and to call it an art is perhaps
too kind, but it is a judgment formed by lenders, sponsors, and their advisers every
time a deal closes.

An essential aspect of the project finance lawyer's role in helping the parties reach a   **1.08**
'bankability' assessment involves reviewing the project, and in particular its underlying documentation, in order to identify its potential and fundamental risks and
to determine if, and how appropriately, those risks have been allocated among the
parties. In carrying out this diligence effort, a project finance lawyer must liaise with
a myriad of advisers, including, among others, technical advisers in respect of the
performance of the physical plant, market advisers regarding the availability and
cost of inputs and the value of future revenue streams, environmental advisers on
the social and environmental impact of the project, insurance advisers on the adequacy of the project's insurance programme, and model auditors to assess the
integrity of the financial models. The lawyer also needs to take guidance from the
lenders as to their assessment of the credit standing of each party to a material project agreement. The project finance lawyer will work closely with local lawyers in a
broad range of relevant jurisdictions, and is often responsible for producing a comprehensive due diligence report that pulls together the key risk assessment and
evaluations of each adviser and highlights the potential issues from a documentation perspective.[2]

---

[2] For a more detailed description of the risk identification and allocation process, see Chapter 4.

1.09 The project's risk profile will inevitably lead to a number of assumptions as to how the overall transaction should be structured. For example, power projects are often awarded to sponsors through a competitive tendering process and are thus structured to give rise to the lowest electricity tariffs possible. The consequence is that the returns available to equity investors may be relatively low, and ensuring that the project is funded to the maximum extent possible through debt (being less costly than equity) and that the average maturity of that debt is as long as possible (thereby reducing the debt service burden in any particular year) takes on great importance. Reduced equity funding and low tariffs combine to result in relatively low debt service coverage ratios. These projects thus have limited ability to absorb the risk of increased costs or reduced revenues, and the parties will therefore focus particular attention on the risk allocation effected through the contracts.

1.10 By contrast, a range of other projects may be designed to produce products sold onto global markets where, for well positioned companies, profit levels may be significant. This is often the case with oil and gas and other natural resource extraction and processing facilities, whose 'base case' revenue projections are generally robust enough to sustain the project through periods of revenue volatility or increased costs. Given market uncertainties, the sponsors may be prepared to fund the project with a greater proportion of equity in exchange for contractual flexibility in the management of the business. In these cases, the relevant contracts may be somewhat less comprehensive in addressing all conceivable risks, but the lenders will generally require more robust overall project economics to mitigate these risks.

Assessing the Host Country

1.11 One of the key variables in the legal analysis of a project, and certainly the one that can neither be structured around nor wished away, is its location.

1.12 As a threshold matter, the political and social stability of the host country will be of concern to all investors and lenders. At the extreme, structuring a deal in a conflict zone may be impracticable, but the scope of political risk encountered by most projects is generally broader and more subtle than simply physical violence. There are a wide variety of publicly available measures of the ease of doing business in specific countries,[3] and the credit risk associated with the obligations of most countries is rated by leading commercial rating agencies. If the project's lenders and

---

   [3] The World Bank website publishes rankings of economies based on their ease of doing business, currently from 1–183. See <http://www.doingbusiness.org/economyrankings>. A high ranking on the ease of doing business index means the regulatory environment is conducive to the operation of business. The index averages each country's percentile rankings with respect to ten categories, made up of a variety of indicators, giving equal weight to each topic.

investors have particular concerns as to the stability of the host state, they may seek to address that risk though political risk insurance and other mitigants considered in other chapters of this book.

When the project is located in an impoverished or developing country, multilateral and other public sector lenders, in particular, will focus on the developmental impact of the project. They will seek to confirm that the project benefits a broad spectrum of the host population and not just a limited number of well positioned investors and government officials. They may require diligence to be undertaken to confirm the absence of any corrupt payments in the award of the project's licenses and concessions.[4] They may also seek clarity on how the host government will invest the tax and other revenues derived from the project.[5] In addition to ensuring that these public-sector lenders' developmental mandates are adhered to, this sort of inquiry is designed to ensure that the host state will continue to support the project even after the incumbent government is long out of office. **1.13**

In whatever jurisdiction the project is located, the laws and regulations of the host state will affect virtually every aspect of the project company's activities, and its courts and other governmental institutions will have wide discretion in interpreting and implementing that law. In many cases, the project company will itself have to be organized under the laws of the host state, rendering even its control and management subject to local jurisdiction. **1.14**

Among the legal issues arising under the domestic law of the host state that need to be assessed are: **1.15**

(1) corporate governance;
(2) industrial regulation;
(3) environmental, land use, and other permitting;
(4) taxation;
(5) customs and immigration law;
(6) reliability of local laws and courts; and
(7) changes in law.

---

[4] There is a wide range of international conventions and national statutes to combat corruption. For example, the OECD Anti-Bribery Convention established legally binding standards to criminalize bribery of foreign public officials in international business transactions and provides for a number of related measures that make this effective. See <http://www.oecd.org/document/20/0,3343,en_26 49_2017813_1_1_1_1.00.html>.

[5] The Extractive Industries Transparency Initiative (EITI) is a coalition of governments, companies, and others which set global standards for transparency in the oil, gas, and mining sectors that is focused on, among other things, ensuring transparency in the host state's use of revenues derived from major projects. See <http://eti.org>.

Corporate governance

1.16 If a project company is organized under local law, which is frequently a requirement of host governments, the investors and lenders will need to assess the governance flexibility afforded to them by that law. Of key relevance to investors is to ensure that the ability of the company to distribute profits to shareholders is not unduly constrained by corporate law and local accounting practices. If it is, they may find it preferable to fund the company with debt instruments rather than equity.

1.17 Among the other issues to be considered are whether shareholders benefit from limitations on their individual liability for the obligations of the project company, whether the rights of minority shareholders will be respected, and whether agreed voting, share transfer restrictions, or pre-emption rights, and the like, set out in an agreement among the shareholders will be given effect under local law. It will also be important to the investors that their appointed directors retain the right to direct the company and its management on key issues. This is of particular concern where international investors are in joint venture with local investors or an entity affiliated with the host government.

Industrial regulation

1.18 Many projects operate in regulated industries. The vast majority of countries, whatever their level of economic and political development, impose regulatory oversight on their public utilities (power, water, and telecommunications), transportation and other infrastructure sectors.[6] Many also view their resource extraction industries to be of material importance and extend regulation to them as well. Regulation can encompass a licensing regime, under which permission to operate is granted to specified companies or classes of companies. Licences or concessions (being in effect a more complicated licence, often including undertakings by the host state) may be granted on an application basis, following individual negotiations or on the basis of a competitive tender involving pre-qualified bidders. Regulation may (and often does) extend further to specify the manner in which a project company is to operate and, in many cases, the price it may charge for its services or output.

1.19 Regulation is thus not unusual, but the manner in which it is imposed can vary significantly. For most projects, the analysis of the regulatory environment encompasses two inquiries: (i) what rights are granted to, and what obligations are imposed on, the project company; and (ii) what risk is there that the regulatory regime will change over time to the detriment of the project company or its investors and lenders.

---

[6] For a discussion of how lenders to the early independent power projects in the United States assessed regulatory risk, see P. Fletcher and J. Worenklein, 'Regulatory Considerations in the Project Financing of an Independent Power Production Facility' 8(4) *Journal of Energy & Natural Resources Law* (1990).

Where the regulatory regime is established as a matter of statutory law, project **1.20**
finance lawyers must review the relevant legislation and regulations carefully, in
close consultation with local lawyers. Where those laws are comprehensive and
clear, certainty as to the scope of the regulatory regime can be achieved, but there
will remain the risk that the regime may evolve over time; it is an accepted preroga-
tive of sovereign states to change their domestic laws.

In circumstances where there is an absence of regulation of general application, or **1.21**
where there is significant uncertainty as to the stability of the regulatory regime, it
may be appropriate for the host state to enter into direct undertakings with the
project company and, in some cases, its principal investors, to set out specific investor protections. The scope of these will vary significantly depending on the extent
of investor and lender concern as to the reliability of the host state's investment
regime.[7] The nature of the governmental commitment may vary from providing
legally binding undertakings, a breach of which may entitle the investor or lender
to specific damages, to mere 'comfort letters', which may afford little, if any, certainty of remedy.

The host government might also seek reciprocal undertakings from the project **1.22**
company, including commitments to provide adequate service during the term of
the agreement; observe relevant safety and environmental standards; sell its output
at reasonable prices; and, particularly where the project company is under an obligation to transfer its assets to the host state at the conclusion of the concession
period, to carry out prudent maintenance and repairs so that at the end of the term
the government or state-owned entity will acquire a fully operational project. There
may be specific penalties or termination rights arising by reason of breach of
these undertakings. These agreements also often include a recognition of the role of
lenders, including express notice, cure, and 'step-in' rights.

The commitments of host governments are often implemented into national law **1.23**
through some form of enabling legislation, allowing greater certainty that the relevant undertakings will take precedence over competing, and often inconsistent,
laws and regulations. In other cases they are entered into in the form of bilateral
contracts that may, again, take precedence over competing legislation. In both
cases, it is important to ensure that they were validly entered into and were within
the legal competence of the granting authority. Although on its face there is much
to suggest that a bespoke, bilateral contract is more likely to be certain and reliable
than unilateral legislation of general application, this may not always be the case.

---

[7] For a discussion of the scope and nature of host government undertakings, see P. Fletcher and
J. Welch, 'State Support in International Project Finance', *Butterworth's Journal of International
Banking and Financial Law*, September, 1993.

Permitting

1.24   The construction and operation of a project generally requires the project company to secure a broad range of permits and consents. The subject matter of these range from environmental and social considerations, to land use, to health and safety, to, as noted above, industrial regulation.

1.25   The analysis of the risk arising from the need to secure permits turns, in the first instance, on identifying the consents that will be required and ensuring that they have been issued or will be issued in the ordinary course without undue expense, delay, or conditionality. The risk of permit revocation is also important, as well as a determination as to whether a secured lender, or its transferee, would be entitled to the benefit of the permits were the lender to exercise its remedies under the security documents. In many instances, the granting authority will wish to retain discretion to assess the identity and competence of the transferee, and unless the granting authority provides guidance as to what criteria it will apply in making that assessment, the lenders may be left with a degree of uncertainty.

Taxation

1.26   Virtually all projects are subject to some form of taxation, and the tax regime will generally have a significant impact on the project's economics. Most sponsors assess their return on investment on an after-tax basis, and thus consider clarity and certainty of the tax regime to be a key consideration.

1.27   In assessing the tax treatment of the project company in its host state, the following is usually considered.

Corporate taxes

1.28   The project company is likely to be subject to corporate taxes, often calculated on the basis of the profits arising to it. Occasionally, however, the tax may be calculated by reference to other factors, such as the value of the project company's assets. In some cases, as an inducement to attract foreign investment, the host government may afford the project company with a tax 'holiday' or rate concessions for at least a specified period.

1.29   Where corporate taxes are calculated by reference to profits, the project company will need to be able to deduct expenditure from the payments it receives so that it is liable to tax on its residual profit only. A significant proportion of the project company's expenditure is likely to be interest payments, which as a general rule would usually be deductible. Where the project company is excessively leveraged, however, there may be restrictions on the deductibility of interest payments under thin capitalization and transfer pricing rules.

As an additional category of deductible expenditure, the project company may be **1.30** able to claim depreciation allowances for certain forms of capital outlay—for example, some or all of the cost of the relevant project's plant and machinery.

Other taxes

The project company may be required to account for value added or sales taxes on **1.31** supplies of goods and services it makes. In some cases, it may be obliged to pay royalties to the host government calculated on the gross value of its sales. Stamp taxes, registration taxes, and notaries fees may also be payable on certain transaction documents. Where such taxes and fees are imposed on lending and security documents, the amount payable will often depend upon the amount borrowed or secured. In such circumstances, lenders may be asked to under-secure their loans so as to reduce the cost of the relevant tax or fee.

Subject to relief under an applicable double taxation treaty, certain jurisdictions **1.32** impose taxes on overseas residents who dispose of shares in a company which is incorporated in that jurisdiction. This may be relevant to equity investors in the project company.

Withholding tax

As a general principle, the laws of the host state may require the project company to **1.33** withhold tax on interest and dividend payments it makes to overseas lenders and shareholders, but relief from the withholding may be available under an applicable double taxation treaty. Where withholding tax is due on interest payments a project company makes to its lenders, the project company will usually be required to gross up those payments and compensate the lenders for the withholding.

Customs and immigration law

Whenever goods or individuals cross a border, they become subject to the laws of **1.34** both the country they are leaving and the country they are entering. For projects, the concern is generally focused on the ability of the project to import into the host state key goods and equipment and to employ qualified expatriate managers, engineers, and labour. Customs restrictions may be limited to an import duty, but in some cases may extend to an absolute prohibition on imports. Immigration law may permit some limited employment of expatriates, but may also require the training and employment of local nationals. In some cases, the project company is able to negotiate exceptions to both import and immigration restrictions, but these may be subject to conditions. The other concern that may arise is that the project's revenues may be adversely affected if the target export markets impose customs duties or import restrictions on the project's production or if the host state restricts exports.

Reliability of local law and courts

1.35   Countries with well-developed laws and an established and independent judiciary are often more attractive jurisdictions for investment than countries with little clarity as to their laws or certainty as to their application.

1.36   Countries that achieved independence—and thus a distinct body of law—only recently, or who are unable to afford the cost of an extensive court system, may be at a disadvantage in attracting foreign investment. Emerging economies, in particular, may seek to address this through regional integration and the harmonization of disparate legal systems as an means of attracting foreign direct investment, eliminating barriers to cross-border trade and providing a platform to improve their chances of competing more effectively on the world stage. Integration is perhaps best developed in Europe through the European Union (EU) and European Economic Area (EEA) and is gaining momentum in other regions such as the Middle East through the Gulf Co-Operation Council (GCC) and in Eastern Africa through the East African Community (EAC). However, arguably the most ambitious legal harmonization outside of Europe is the '*Organisation pour l'Harmonisation du Droit des Affaires en Afrique*', better known through its French acronym 'OHADA'. The OHADA Treaty is not new. In fact, it will soon be entering its third decade, having been brought into force on 17 October 1993 in Port Louis, Mauritius. However, its laws have only been in effect from 1998, and it is only recently that investors have begun to take this legal harmonization seriously.

1.37   The OHADA Treaty regime establishes the supremacy and the direct effect of OHADA uniform laws. That it is ambitious is therefore obvious. Whether it is the trigger for any increase in foreign direct investment remains to be seen. However, it is at least not unattractive that a sponsor in Guinea can expect to encounter the same business laws in Benin and seek justice in the same appellate courts. This does not guarantee legal certainty, but at least it brings with it a degree of legal familiarity that can only be good for business confidence.[8]

1.38   Legal certainty will be of concern to all parties, but lenders will focus particular concern on whether local law recognizes the rights of secured creditors and whether their claims will be respected were the project company to become insolvent. Not all countries have express insolvency regimes, and the ones that do vary significantly as to the rights and preferences that they afford to secured lenders.

Changes in law

1.39   Project finance loans are generally repaid over years if not decades. Notwithstanding the initial certainty that may be achieved in assessing the host country's laws, these

---

[8] See also para. 12.182 et seq.

may (and in fact are likely to) change during the life of the project. Public policy evolves in virtually every country as their governments change; where regime change is frequent and policy objectives vary widely, those changes can be volatile. For example, tax rates can be subject to substantial increase as governments manage the competing demands of their spending aspirations and of their budgetary constraints. Governments have tended in recent years to impose increased environmental compliance requirements on companies subject to their jurisdiction in order to comply with new treaty and similar obligations. As their economies develop, host governments are often able to extract more favourable terms from new investors, and agreements reached at an earlier time may begin to appear unreasonable over time. Host governments may be tempted to try to bring older, less favourable, terms in line with current market standards.

In some instances, the risk of changes in law and policy can be addressed through **1.40** the underlying concession agreement, where the host government agrees to freeze the application of laws to the project company or to provide compensation if those laws change. In other cases, the project's off-takers may be prepared to compensate the project company through tariff adjustments to cover increased costs arising from changes in law. At an extreme, changes in law can result in actual or 'creeping' expropriation. In some cases, investors can rely on the protections afforded by bilateral investment treaties entered into by their home jurisdictions and the host state.

Environmental and Social Considerations

The construction and operation of a project invariably have environmental and **1.41** social impacts on the locality of the project. Managing these impacts may help assure the long-term acceptance of the project by affected parties. Lenders will generally require, at a minimum, the project company to undertake to comply with all environmental and social laws and regulations binding on it. They will also likely require the development of, and compliance with, an agreed environmental and social risk management plan. This is both to insulate the project company, and the lenders, from legal risk, but also to preserve the lenders' reputation as responsible parties.

Even in the absence of environmental legislation in a particular jurisdiction, **1.42** national or multinational credit institutions financing a project may require compliance with World Bank or similar standards. The International Finance Corporation, for example, has implemented detailed standards defining a borrower's environmental and social responsibilities in managing its project. Areas of focus include: labour and working conditions; pollution prevention and abatement; community health, safety, and security; biodiversity conservation and sustainable natural resource management; and protection of indigenous peoples and cultural heritage. Standards such as these seek to achieve comprehensive mitigation of environmental impacts and management of the project's impact on local populations.

1.43 A large range of other financial institutions have adopted a voluntary set of guidelines, known as the Equator Principles, that call for such organizations to require compliance with guidelines similar to those of multinational lenders. As a result, virtually every large-scale project seeking access to the financial markets must evidence a high level of environmental and social compliance.[9]

Governing Law Considerations

1.44 Contracts are often quite clear in describing the terms of a transaction, but the manner in which contracts will be interpreted or enforced may differ significantly from those terms. The relevant considerations involve an analysis of: (i) the choice of law to govern the contracts; (ii) the enforceability of contracts under that law; and (iii) the choice of forum for disputes arising from the transaction, including whether judgments or awards from that forum will be enforced in each relevant jurisdiction.

Choice of law

1.45 The knowledge that the transaction is governed by the law of a familiar jurisdiction can be a source of significant comfort to investors and lenders. Choice of law questions inevitably arise in the context of negotiating finance documents and frequently involve an election between English law and New York law.[10] Because the law of each of these jurisdictions relevant to the enforceability of customary finance documents is broadly similar, any preference between the two is perhaps not as substantive as it might appear. Each has well publicized case law precedents that provide clarity as to how the law will likely be applied in specific circumstances. However, lenders may nonetheless have strong views based on familiarity with customary forms and terminology or based on a preference for submission to the courts of one or the other jurisdiction. It is worth noting that both English and New York courts will accept (subject to limited exceptions) jurisdiction to hear disputes governed by English or New York law, respectively, even where there is little connection to either jurisdiction other than the election of the parties.[11]

---

[9] See also para. 4.71 et seq.

[10] For a discussion of the differences between New York and English law governed finance documentation, see R. Gray, S. Mehta, and D. East, 'Debt Repurchases: Easier with the LMA', *International Financial Law Review*, March 2010; R. Gray, S. Mehta, and D. East, 'Similar Objectives, Subtle Differences', *International Financial Law Review*, December 2009/January 2010; R. Gray, S. Mehta, and D. East, 'US and UK Compared: Fundamental Differences Remain Between the Markets', *International Financial Law Review*, October 2009; R. Gray and S. Mehta, 'The Market Disruption Clause', *International Financial Law Review*, December 2008/January 2009.

[11] In respect of New York law, see New York General Obligations Law, sections 5-1401 (*Choice of Law*) and 5-1402 (*Choice of Forum*); in respect of how an English court would treat this issue, see Article 3 of the Rome Regulation on the Law Applicable to contractual Obligations (EC 593/2008).

In relation to a range of commercial contracts, the choice of law can have particular **1.46** significance. For example, parties may find attractive the ability under Article 2 of the Uniform Commercial Code as in effect in the State of New York to leave open for resolution by agreement among the parties (or absent agreement between them, through resolution by a court) key price terms in contracts for the sale of goods and certain commodities. English law, by contrast, may (subject to various exceptions) find that the contract fails for uncertainty in such circumstances.

In some circumstances, there is no real choice of law. Conflict of law principles, **1.47** such as the doctrine of *lex situs* (i.e. the rule that the law applicable to proprietary aspects of an asset is the law of the jurisdiction where the asset is located), may dictate which law is to be applied in relation to certain contracts. For instance, under English conflicts of law rules, ownership of land is determined under the law of the jurisdiction where the land is located, so a contract transferring title to land in (say) France that is invalid because it does not satisfy a particular requirement of domestic French law, will not be valid even if the contract is expressed to be governed by English law and would have been perfectly valid if the land had been in England. Likewise, many governments may require the use of domestic law to govern contracts with national agencies, and in many cases may require that those contracts be written in the domestic language.

Enforceability

Not all contracts are enforceable in accordance with their terms. There may **1.48** be mandatory provisions of law that override the terms of the contract. Many countries have civil or similar codes whose provisions will apply to a contract notwithstanding its terms.[12] Legal uncertainty may be pronounced when the country in which the project is located has no tradition of reported case law (making it more difficult to establish how the rules are applied by the domestic courts in practice) or where domestic law prohibits fundamental aspects of the transaction (for instance, *Sharia'a* principles preventing the enforcement of interest payments). In some cases, mandatory provisions of law will be applied by the courts even if not applicable under the express law stated to govern the contract. Thus, parties need to assess not only the terms of the relevant agreements, but also their consistency with applicable law.

Forum

The selection of a forum for any disputes heard in connection with the project has **1.49** important implications such as:

(1) Will the forum be neutral in its decision-making?

---

[12] For analysis of the application of civil law to project financings, please see Chapter 12.

(2) What law will the chosen forum apply and will the outcome differ as a result?

(3) Which evidential or procedural rules will apply in the forum?

(4) Will judgments or awards be enforced in the home jurisdiction of the borrower or the other project parties?[13]

1.50 One important factor, when considering the choice of forum, is whether the dispute should be litigated or arbitrated. There are advantages to using the courts, particularly in jurisdictions such as England and New York, where long histories of case law precedent, established procedural laws, and unbiased judicial oversight provide comfort for sponsors and lenders that their claims will be duly upheld. In many jurisdictions, courts can compel parties to disclose facts or documents and may be able to order interim relief, such as an injunction. Further, as arbitration is a product of contract, only parties that have consented to arbitration through the contract can be compelled to proceed in that forum. Litigation may thus be necessary in a multi-party dispute in order to join an interested party that is not party to the original contract.

1.51 On the other hand, the speed and privacy of an arbitral process is a benefit, and a specially designated arbitrator may be better equipped to address complex technical issues than a more generalist judge. The parties may view an arbitral forum in a neutral foreign venue as providing certainty of an efficient and reasonable result. Moreover, an arbitral award may, in some cases, be more likely to be recognized and enforced in the relevant party's home jurisdiction without review on the merits than a foreign court judgment. International treaty arrangements, such as the 1958 Convention on the Recognition and Enforcement of Foreign Arbitral Awards (the New York Convention), and regional treaty arrangements, such as the Convention on the Enforcement of Judgments, Disputes and Judicial Summonses in the Arab Gulf Co-Operation Council States (the GCC Convention), call for member states to give effect to arbitral awards made in other member states. Nonetheless, there are often sufficient exceptions to even treaty-based rules to leave open the possibility that the award may be re-opened on enforcement.

1.52 As a practical matter, lenders prefer to use the courts as they typically view arbitration as a less attractive option for disputes under finance documents. This is in part due to the perceived tendency of arbitrators to arrive at compromise positions (so-called 'rough justice'), although lenders may wish to reserve the option of arbitration to address technical issues or where arbitration may have procedural benefits in relation to enforcement of awards. Commercial contracts, on the other hand, far more frequently contemplate arbitration.

---

[13] For a more detailed description of dispute settlement procedures, see Chapter 14.

Sovereign immunity

The host government and its instrumentalities may be immune from being brought **1.53** before the courts of either the host state or of other sovereign countries. In addition, they may be immune from enforcement of judgments, so that even if a court or arbitral panel were to rule against them, it may not be possible to execute that judgment against their assets. This immunity is widely acknowledged as a matter of international law, but there may be exceptions to its application. For example, a state entity acting in a commercial capacity may not benefit from immunity in all circumstances, and it may be possible for a state entity to waive its rights to immunity. Many courts have sought in recent years to subject to their jurisdiction sovereigns for violation of international norms of conduct, but the scope of these decisions remain somewhat narrow and controversial.

Credit Documentation

Once the overall risk of the project has been properly profiled, the parties will need **1.54** to reach agreement on the most appropriate financial structure for the deal. There are some very obvious rules at play: lower risk projects tend to have greater flexibility in their funding sources than projects facing greater risk and are thus able to secure less stringent financing terms; projects with a larger capital cost will need to integrate a broader range of lenders into their finance plan than smaller projects, with the consequent need to satisfy a broader range of credit requirements.

Project finance credit documentation is generally replete with conditions precedent **1.55** to lending, representations, undertakings, and remedies designed to allow lenders to manage the underlying risks of the transaction. As those risks vary significantly across transactions, so does the manner in which they are addressed in credit agreements.

Although most lenders value the comfort provided by relying on precedent transac- **1.56** tions, particularly given the guidance they provide as to what will be accepted in the syndication markets, there is no broad consensus on what model of credit document should be used in the industry. Neither the Loan Market Association (LMA) in London, nor the Loan Syndications and Trading Association (LSTA) in New York, the two leading inter-bank associations charged with developing standard credit documents, has sought to prescribe standard documentation for project finance transactions.

Various categories of lenders have specific and unique requirements. For example, **1.57** export credit agencies may in most circumstances only lend if and to the extent that their funding is expressly applied to finance exports from their home jurisdiction. Capital markets debt can only be accessed if the project company satisfies the requirements of rating agencies and the disclosure and other requirements of listing authorities or other security regulators. *Sharia'a*-compliant transactions must be structured to avoid any of the prohibitions imposed by Islam, including most notably the prohibition on the charging of interest on loans. These disparate and specific requirements must often be blended into a unified set of documents governing the overall transaction.

Security Packages

1.58 Project financings are in essence complex secured lending transactions. The willingness of lenders to extend long-term credit to a project may depend on the degree of comfort they take in the viability of the underlying security 'package'.

1.59 The structuring of security packages across jurisdictions and diverse assets can present numerous and unique challenges.[14] The purpose of a lender's collateral package is to enable it to deprive the borrower of the pledged assets when the loan is in default and to provide the lender with the means to defeat claims that the borrower's other creditors may seek to assert against its assets. Whether a security interest has been validly created and whether it has priority over competing interests are questions of law. As noted above, under English conflicts of law rules, proprietary aspects of an asset are determined by reference to the location of the asset on the basis of the doctrine of *lex situs*. The validity and priority of the security is thus, in most instances, governed by the law in which the charged assets are, or are deemed to be, located. Whilst the bulk of a project company's assets will for these purposes be located in the jurisdiction where its physical plant lies, its bank accounts and receivables may be (or be deemed to be) located elsewhere, as may its shares, which will, in most instances, be the jurisdiction of its incorporation.

1.60 Difficulties arise when dealing with security in jurisdictions where clear procedures for creation or perfection of security (such as registration or filing) are absent or where the enforceability of step-in rights granted to the lenders is uncertain. This may arise in, for example, Saudi Arabia, where the application of *Sharia'a* principles may adversely affect the perfection and/or enforceability of common forms of security. Similarly, lack of clarity as to which country has jurisdiction may adversely affect the certainty of security sought to be taken over satellites in space or cables laid under the sea. Lack of clarity may also arise where the domestic law lacks uniformity. In many countries, the government agency responsible for the registration of security interests varies with the type of asset (e.g. security interests over land use rights may be registered with the local land bureau, and equipment may be

---

[14] For a more detailed description of security packages generally, see Chapter 11.

registered with the commerce and industry bureau). The substantive and procedural requirements for creation and perfection of security interests may be far from
uniform as a result of differing local government agency practices.

In other cases, the cost of filing or registering security may be significant, which **1.61**
sponsors may see as unduly burdensome and resist having to bear. Sponsors may
argue that the practical value of security does not warrant the expense, particularly
in jurisdictions with little experience of complex financings. In some cases, it may
be possible to negotiate reductions in or exemptions from such costs in the underlying concession agreement or enabling legislation.

The efficacy of security interests may be overridden by the relevant insolvency **1.62**
regime, whether this is a court-supervised 'debtor-in-possession' regime (as in the
US) or one whose primary objective is the liquidation of the insolvent debtor.
Whether the court or administrator (or the equivalent) is bound by a grant of security must thus be assessed in light of the applicable insolvency law (or, where the
charged assets are located in a number of jurisdictions, the insolvency laws of all
those jurisdictions). However, many jurisdictions simply do not have an insolvency
law to apply at all, leaving uncertainty as to how security may, as a practical matter,
be enforced.

Process Management

Closing a project finance transaction is often as much about process management **1.63**
as it is legal analysis and drafting. The project finance lawyer is required not
only to analyse the project risks and assess the negotiating leverage of each party,
but also to organize the documentation process and ensure that each of the
parties understands fully the issues in question. With projects often being located
in remote parts of the world, and with sponsors and lenders often being based in a
broad range of countries and time-zones, the challenge of organizing a financing
can be significant. Managing the logistics of complex negotiations across the
globe requires a mastery of both languages and communications technology.
Fortunately, technology is advancing at a pace that allows ever more ambitious
financings to be undertaken. Web based document 'deal rooms' allow parties to
access current drafts of reports, documents and update communications at their
discretion. Although in many respects English is the dominant language of project
finance, it is a significant hindrance to closing deals if the project finance lawyers
are not conversant in at least some of the native languages of the key project
participants.

Of key importance is the ability of the lead project finance lawyer to communicate **1.64**
with local counsel in a broad range of jurisdictions. Local lawyers who have trained

at international firms will often be adept at conveying legal issues in terms that are readily understood by their international counterparts. However, the role of guides in the nature of this book cannot be understated in ensuring that all of the lawyers on all sides of the deal have a common view as to the key legal issues that must be considered by the parties.

2

PROJECT PARTICIPANTS AND STRUCTURES

Cathy Marsh and Andrew Pendleton, Milbank, Tweed, Hadley & McCloy LLP

General Overview

In broad terms, a project financing is characterized by lawyers assisting their clients **2.01** to allocate rights and obligations between the project participants, spreading risks and responsibilities, to create a bankable project. In so doing, complex structures evolve. In the case of the vast majority of project financings, however, such structures are likely to be complex without necessarily being complicated: i.e. though there is likely to be a detailed web of interconnections and relationships between parties (see, for example, figure 2.3), the constituent elements in isolation, or in smaller pieces, rarely fall outside the boundaries of a relatively standard framework. To the inexperienced (and, we should note, on many occasions, to those with much more experience) the complexity of project structures can still be intimidating or, at least, confusing. It is enlightening, therefore, to take a reductionist approach and break-down such structures by examining their most fundamental components: the key project participants.

2.02　An understanding of the objectives and goals of the key project participants is absolutely critical to the successful negotiation of a project financing. The challenge of structuring a transaction lies in reconciling the different objectives of those interested parties to ensure that each stands to benefit from the project and is therefore committed to its success.

2.03　The first part of this chapter will examine the key project participants by addressing the following simple questions: (i) who are they, (ii) what are their roles, and (iii) to a lesser extent, what are their key motivations? The second part of the chapter will give an overview of typical structures employed for a project, in terms of both the ownership structure employed by the sponsors of a project and also the underlying structure of the project as a whole.

2.04　There are, of course, many different types of project so the identity and roles of their respective participants can vary, as can the structures employed, with often great variation even within the same industry sector. However, by considering key project participants in the context of the life cycle of a project, from its origination, through its financing and construction, to its operational phase, and also examining the underlying structures used by these participants in (hopefully) achieving their goal, this chapter aims to provide an accessible and general overview of project financing.

Project Participants: Stage One (Project Origination)

An introduction to project origination

2.05　There is, of course, no single project finance model that is applicable across the entire market. Different models are applicable to each sector, and even within the same sector. While elements of commonality are always identifiable, project finance remains an innovative area wherein bespoke solutions are required on a regular basis. However, the main protagonist in the origination of a project is almost always either a host government or a private sponsor, and both will, normally, have key roles.

2.06　As reflected in figure 2.1, a breakdown of which types of projects are originated primarily by a host government and which by a private sponsors can generally be made on a sector by sector basis.

Figure 2.1 Breakdown of key project originators by sector

Project Sector	Likely Project Originator
Ports	Government
Rail	Government
Roads/tunnels/bridges	Government
Hospitals	Government
Schools	Government
Water/waste water	Government
Power	Government/private sponsors
Leisure amenities	Government/private sponsors
Oil and gas	Private sponsors
LNG	Private sponsors
Mining	Private sponsors
Petrochemicals	Private sponsors
Telecoms/satellites	Private sponsors

A broader theme can also be recognized in figure 2.1: governments are key players **2.07** in encouraging the development of projects to meet the core needs of their communities within the infrastructure sector particularly in less developed countries, while private sponsors are more likely to demonstrate their initiative where there is an opportunity to utilize or exploit resources, as in, for example, the mining sector.

There are, of course, overlaps and exceptions. The power sector is dominated by **2.08** giant utilities companies like GDF Suez and the EDF Group, but many such companies have their origins in state ownership and some continue to be owned, at least in part, publically. The end of the last century and the turn of the millennium were marked, in Europe in particular, by widespread privatization of public utilities and other infrastructure-related entities. Arguably, this reflects that, while governments continue to be good at recognizing developmental needs, the private sector can be better placed to turn ideas into operational projects. An appreciation of some of the same concerns that drove the march of privatization is helpful for the purposes of understanding the roles and actions of host governments and private sponsors during the origination phase of project financings.

The role of host governments

Traditionally, in Europe and beyond, central governments were responsible for the **2.09** planning, financing, construction, and operation of major projects with limited input from the private sector. This approach places a huge weight on the balance sheet of a government. Where developed solely within the public sector, the scale of a major project also weighs heavily in other areas: a wide array of skills and experience is required in spheres such as finance, engineering techniques, and labour.

It is rarely practical, from a cost or logistical perspective, for governments to develop or retain such skills and experience internally. Most countries therefore require a credible alternative to public sector project development.

2.10 The reluctance or inability of host governments to increase their borrowing, together with emerging political will to involve the private sector (including foreign investors), therefore underlie very visible efforts to find ways to involve private capital and private initiative in the promotion of public interest objectives, such as the development of infrastructure.

2.11 Once it decides to involve the private sector in project development, the host government will have at least some of the following objectives.

Objective one: Minimizing costs

2.12 Private participation in the development of infrastructure and other projects can lower overall costs. For example, effectively structured and transparent bidding procedures in respect of projects being proposed by host governments are designed to heighten competition among private sector sponsors and suppliers, thereby encouraging efficiency with a view to lowering overall costs.

2.13 Private participation can facilitate the fulfilment of certain infrastructure needs, such as electricity and water supply, with little or no capital expenditure by host governments. In periods of economic uncertainty, such as that following the 'credit crunch' of 2008, widespread doubts over the serviceability of sovereign debts only increase the desirability of development without substantial capital expenditure funded from the public purse.

Objective two: Risk transfer

2.14 Host governments will, generally, seek to transfer the risk of infrastructure development from the public sector to the private sector. Successfully accomplishing this goal is likely to involve:

(1) no liability for the project;
(2) retaining control over the project; and
(3) limiting the government's undertakings and retaining flexibility.

2.15 A host government will seek to insulate itself from responsibility for the design, construction, development, testing, and commissioning of any project. Fundamentally, it will not wish to be liable to any third parties for cost overruns or accidents in relation thereto.

2.16 Government utilities entities often feature in projects as the purchasers (i.e. off-takers) of project product, particularly in respect of power and water. Under the terms of the off-take agreements governing such purchasing, which are more commonly agreed before the project is developed, a government entity will, often, guarantee payment in respect of a certain level of product output regardless of whether the actual off-taker ultimately takes the relevant output and sells it on to end users.

A guaranteed market acts as credit support inducing private sponsors to develop **2.17** projects to meet the government demand and reassuring lenders that the project will receive income, which can be used to service the repayment of project debt. However, it is then entirely the responsibility of the privately owned company to supply the agreed product. Any technical and financial obstacles to that supply are hurdles for the private sponsors to clear.

Notably, under the terms of, for example, a power purchase agreement, the entity **2.18** controlled by the private sponsors is actually likely to be liable to pay liquidated damages to the government entity purchasing the relevant product in the event that the project does not perform its supply obligations.

Should the original private sponsors fail to provide the required level of service or **2.19** the project runs into insurmountable difficulties, host governments may also want the ability to take control of the project. As a last resort, it may bring the project into public ownership or, more likely, it will offer the ownership or operation of the project to other private sector entities.

Once private sector investors have received an acceptable return on their equity **2.20** investment in a project (and once the project debt has been repaid), a host government may also have an interest in bringing successful projects back into public ownership. A fully operational, efficient project can deliver a healthy revenue stream without the likelihood of significant liability for unforeseen costs, which are much more likely during the construction phase of a project. Ownership and project structures providing for differing levels of ongoing host government involvement, such as 'build-own-transfer' schemes, are discussed in greater detail at 2.142 below).

A host government will seek to limit its own commitments as far as possible. **2.21** However, some undertakings may be essential. For example, certain projects may require the building of access roads and other types of infrastructure, which private sponsors may be unwilling to support. Where the economics of a project are not sufficiently strong to induce private sponsors to participate, particularly in marginal instances, a host government may take more responsibility for peripheral costs that facilitate project development (by, for example, funding new access roads and related infrastructure publically).

Frequently, governments will also be required to exercise powers to purchase com- **2.22** pulsorily land required in connection with a project, while cooperation will normally be required to provide the project with various permits and licenses. Private sponsors may also request further assurances in other areas, such as an agreement not to compete directly or facilitate direct competition with the business of their project.

2.23 As a general rule, a host government will wish to retain as much discretion as possible in passing new laws and regulations dealing with, for instance, taxation, health, safety, and the environment. Sponsors will either wish to constrain this flexibility or include a premium in their pricing to reflect the risk that their return may be subject to changes in law or policy.

Objective three: Demanding a safe, efficiently run project

2.24 A host government will demand that the project be completed to the government's specifications as quickly as possible and seek adequate safeguards and assurances that the project will be operated in accordance with good industry practice and in line with the public's interests.

2.25 Terms relating to, for example, health and safety, the environment, and employment may be set out explicitly in contractual arrangements between a host government and private sponsors, but it is more likely that these matters will be governed by existing laws, rules, and regulations. In certain less economically developed countries, applicable laws, rules, and regulations may also be underdeveloped and major international projects can provide excellent opportunities (and impetus) to address such deficiencies: this process is actively encouraged and assisted by certain international multilateral finance institutions, as further discussed in paragraphs 2.71 and 2.73 below.

Objective four: Attracting new capital

2.26 It is a major goal of all governments to attract new capital investment to their territories from beyond their borders.

2.27 Project financings of new infrastructure facilities, to the extent funded by loans from overseas lenders and equity capital provided by foreign investors, can increase the flow of capital into the host countries substantially. The sums involved will typically amount to many millions, and often billions, of dollars.

2.28 In addition to the creation of new jobs and infrastructure related directly to the relevant project, knock-on benefits are likely to be achieved with potential industrial development in related sectors. For instance, the off-take product of a mining project may be processed at a related project site in the vicinity of the mine. Moreover, it is to be hoped that any project will result in a trickle-down effect involving increased spending in, for example, the shops and bars of local communities.

2.29 The host government will also retain a percentage of the profits generated by a project by way of taxation and various licensing and permitting fees and charges. In less economically developed countries where first-in-country major international projects are proposed, it may actually be necessary for host governments to legislate in respect of areas such as taxation to give private equity and debt investors the necessary comfort to participate. Again, as further discussed in paragraphs 2.71

and 2.73 below, certain international financial institutions will also actively encourage and assist with this process. Promoting such development is the raison d'être of certain publically funded international finance institutions.

Objective five: Technology development and training

Host governments will expect the development of major projects in a variety of sec- **2.30**
tors to promote the innovation and/or introduction of state of the art technology
and the creation of a skilled, well-trained body of professionals and personnel in the
host country. To advance these objectives, the government may require minimum
levels of domestic procurement and employment as conditions of tenders, licences,
and/or permits.

Objective six: Competitive advantage

Looking at project finance from a broader perspective, it may also be hoped that the **2.31**
establishment of private infrastructure facilities by local and foreign investors will
help to generate a more reliable, efficient, and cost effective industrial sector. Such
developments may enhance a country's overall competitive position and promote
economic growth and social development.

Starting a bidding process

Where a host government wishes to procure the development of a project by a pri- **2.32**
vate sponsor, it is likely to publish a request for proposals soliciting bids on particular
terms. Ideally, those terms will be sufficiently detailed and fixed to:

(1) ease comparison of bids; and
(2) with, as discussed above, a key aim of the host government being to encourage
    competition and thereby push down prices, force bidders to compete with
    transparent pricing structures.

However, once a preferred bidder has been selected, there may be further bilateral
negotiations between the host government and the private sponsors to refine the
relevant terms.

The procurement of certain goods and services by public bodies is governed by a **2.33**
variety of supranational rules and regulations, which typically apply to the bidding
process for a major international project. The key international agreement is: the
World Trade Organization's plurilateral Agreement on Government Procurement,
which is known as the GPA and came into force on 1 January 1996.

The parties to the GPA include the EU Member States, the US, Canada, Chinese **2.34**
Taipei, Hong Kong, Iceland, Israel, Japan, Korea, Liechtenstein, Norway, Singapore,
and Switzerland. Other countries that have subsequently become observers of the
GPA include Albania, Argentina, Armenia, Australia, Bahrain, Cameroon, Chile,
China, Colombia, Croatia, Georgia, India, Jordan, the Kyrgyz Republic, Moldova,
Mongolia, New Zealand, Oman, Panama, Saudi Arabia, Sri Lanka, Turkey, and

Ukraine, and, of these countries, Albania, Armenia, China, Georgia, Jordan, the Kyrgyz Republic, Moldova, Oman, and Panama are in the process of negotiating accession to the GPA.

2.35　The key provision of the GPA, Article III, provides that international products, services, and suppliers shall be treated no less favourably than their domestic equivalents and that domestic suppliers in international ownership or providing international goods or services shall not be discriminated against. Similarly, Article IV restricts the application of rules of origin.

2.36　The GPA also contains rules guiding key details of the bidding process. Article VI encourages required technical specifications to be set by reference to performance in the context of international standards rather than design or descriptive characteristics to the extent that this could be an obstacle to international trade. Article VII requires the bidding process to be conducted in an open, non-discriminatory manner to encourage competition. Other provisions provide for inclusive time periods to facilitate international bids and detailed information to be distributed on a consistent, open, and transparent basis. It should then be possible for the winning bid to be chosen on the basis of, chiefly, price, in addition to certain other clear criteria and essential requirements to the extent that they are set out in the request for proposals.

2.37　In light of the GPA and similar requirements, the detailed and fixed terms set out in the request for proposals are likely to focus on the output of the project. For example, in relation to power and water projects, the bid terms should require a certain capacity of power and water output, while the bid terms for a transport infrastructure project, such as a road or port, are likely to require capacity for a certain number and size of vehicles or vessels over a particular time period.

The roles of advisers and consultants

2.38　Before the terms to be set out in a request for proposals are determined (or a project is otherwise developed), a substantial amount of research and development work is always required. Major international projects are typically researched and developed as concepts long before their financing is arranged or construction begins.

2.39　Feasibility and other studies produced by specialist consultants may be required to establish the viability and desirability of a project. Areas to be considered in such studies vary from sector to sector and project to project, but they are a fundamental stage in the life of any project regardless of whether (a) it is the subject of a bidding process and (b) it originates in the public sector or private sector.

2.40　Consultants, who should bring independent and specialist expertise to a project, may be required to:

(1) establish where a resource, such as a mineral deposit, exists and whether it exists in quantities to justify its exploitation;

(2) consider the viability of exploiting a resource or developing a product or service from a cost and other logistics perspective;

(3) develop ideas to facilitate the exploitation of a resource or the development of a product or service;

(4) measure the demand for a particular resource, product, or service;

(5) evaluate the potential to finance the relevant project and, where relevant, help to structure such financing;

(6) advise on the best practice in respect of project insurance and assist arrangement thereof; and

(7) provide legal advice in relation to legal aspects of each of the matters described above and the project in general.

Relevant consultants may therefore be experts in one or more of a wide variety of fields such as engineering, the environment, finance, insurance, or law. **2.41**

The role of private sponsors/equity owners

The principal objective of private sector sponsors and equity investors is to maximize their profits. However, the appetite for risk and the required investment return of each sponsor will vary. Equity investors may have more compelling economic interests in a project than their equity return. For example, they may have another role in the project as a supply, operations and maintenance or off-take contractor. **2.42**

Equity investors typically invest through a project company. The ownership structures applicable to project companies are discussed in greater detail below. The shareholding or other equity interests in the project company may be held by one entity or, as is often the case in large international projects, a consortium of equity investors. Such a consortium may include local participants (often as a condition of bid eligibility), foreign operators and equipment suppliers, and other investors seeking returns sufficient to justify the risks being taken. **2.43**

As discussed in relation to host governments above, infrastructure projects typically have significant funding requirements and entail risks, often in excess of those which an individual sponsors or consortium of sponsors may be willing or able to provide or assume themselves. In this context, the typical project finance structure can be appealing to sponsors for the following reasons: **2.44**

(1) it provides financing that is legally non-recourse to the sponsors (who are likely to be shielded financially by the 'corporate veil', although such a veil offers little protection from a reputational perspective);

(2) it achieves 'off balance sheet' accounting treatment of project debt (as such borrowing for the project does not show among the sponsors's own borrowings in its consolidated accounts);

(3) it allows highly leveraged structures, which often permit a reduction in the cost of capital by way of the substitution of lower cost, tax deductible interest for

higher cost, taxable returns on equity (some projects have been financed on or close to a 100 per cent debt basis, although a level of 60 per cent to 85 per cent is more typical); and

(4) it provides for the allocation of project risks among multiple participants, thereby reducing each participant's individual risk of loss.

2.45 Where participating in project financing, private sponsors are likely to have at least some of the following aims.

Aim one: Maximizing return on equity

2.46 Virtually all sponsors seek opportunities to obtain attractive rates of return on their investment. To attract private foreign investment, host countries may need to afford investors greater returns than are available in other markets internationally. There is, of course, a natural limit to the returns available to investors in that the real cost of a project (manifested in, for example, monthly energy bills) may be a large part of a local consumer's basic cost of living: one can easily imagine the political sensitivity to, for example, increases in domestic retail electricity rates to satisfy the demands of foreign investors. In many cases, host governments, particularly in less economically developed countries, provide more subtly for better equity returns by applying generous taxation regimes to international projects.

Aim two: Strategic expansion

2.47 Sponsors, particularly utilities companies, are very likely to seek to expand into new markets at times when there is limited growth in demand in their domestic markets. As a consequence, national utilities and international private developers may expand into new regions, often by way of successful bids for projects put out to tender by host governments in the manner described in paragraph 2.32 above.

Aim three: The sale of goods

2.48 Certain project participants, such as equipment manufacturers and fuel suppliers, have as one of their principal objectives, securing contracts for the sale of equipment or supplies or for the operation of the relevant facility. Although these parties may be prepared to invest in private projects by way of equity, a significant portion of their profit lies in securing the related supply contracts. They may be willing, therefore, to take risks in relation to their equity investment (which forms only part of their overall return on the project) that other private sponsors may be reluctant to accept.

Aim four: The sale of services

2.49 In addition to selling goods, other project participants, such as utilities companies, may have services and expertise to sell. Again, although these parties may be equity investors, their profits could be supplemented significantly by their fees for the performances of services, such as the operation and maintenance of the project, and this may be more important to them than their equity investment, which may only constitute a small portion of the overall equity investment by a consortium.

In addition to making direct equity investments in a project, we have discussed how **2.50** private sponsors sometimes plan to participate in a project as goods and services contractors. However, their participation is not limited to those matters. They will also typically be involved with all or some of the following.

Credit support

In addition to injecting equity into the project company by subscribing for share **2.51** capital or granting shareholder loans, private sponsors are normally required to provide or arrange related credit support. For example, lenders may require as a condition of providing their debt that the sponsors provide completion or cost overrun guarantees.

To the extent that a relevant sponsor does not have a sufficiently strong long-term **2.52** credit rating from a reputable ratings agency, such as Standard & Poor's, Moody's, or Fitch Ratings, sponsors may, instead of providing a guarantee, be required to procure other forms of credit support, such as letters of credit, from a third party, normally a bank, with an acceptable long-term credit rating.

Private sponsors may also be expected to provide credit support in respect of the **2.53** project company's obligations to pay interest and tax, or in coverage of other shortfalls.

Skills and personnel

An experienced international sponsors will, of course, typically, assist the project **2.54** company by utilizing the skills it has developed on other projects. During the origination and financing phases of a project, it will, in fact, normally, be personnel employed directly by the sponsors who plan and agree the scope of the project and how it is to be financed. The relevant personnel may then move onto assist with other projects in respect of which the relevant sponsors is a participant. Alternatively, they may be transferred to work for the project company directly during the construction and/or operations phases.

Large private sponsors in, for example, the oil, petrochemicals, and power and **2.55** water sectors are also likely to have substantial experience in areas of ongoing relevance to a project such as insurance and marketing.

Specialist insurance teams (who will in most cases be employed directly by a sponsor) **2.56** use their experience to assist the project company in obtaining appropriate cover. Moreover, economies of scale can mean that private sponsors can obtain excellent value when negotiating project insurances for both the construction and operations phases of their multiple projects. Insurance matters are discussed in more detail in Chapter 6.

2.57 Sponsors with long-standing interests in various projects within a sector are also likely to be able to assist with matters such as the international marketing of the project product. In certain cases, care (and legal advice) must be taken to ensure that competition laws and regulations are not breached by such arrangements. There may be relatively small or niche markets for particular products and certain large international sponsors may be dominant players in those markets.

Connected projects

2.58 In many cases, a project will produce a product that is simply purchased on an *ad hoc* basis by a third party who is otherwise unrelated to the project participants. However, other projects are more interconnected. For example, the off-take product of one project may be the feedstock of another. Alternatively, multiple projects, often producing the same off-take product, may be based at the same site or at nearby sites. These projects sometimes share certain facilities, which are often related to the processing, packaging, or transportation of the project product.

2.59 Where a private sponsor has an interest in one project that is closely connected to other projects, it is naturally likely to be involved in some capacity with the other project. The reasons for this include the desirability of having control and certainty in respect of key influences on each project. Moreover, if a private sponsor takes the view that the business case for one project is strong or it has expertise in the area of one project, it is likely to view related business positively.

The role of the project company

2.60 The choice of ownership structure applicable to a project company is very important to the relevant sponsor or sponsors, particularly to the extent agreement must be reached between multiple, independent sponsors or where local laws dictate certain structures. Ownership structures are therefore discussed in greater detail below. However, the relevant structure does not impact significantly on the role of the project company.

2.61 To understand the role played by the project company, it may be helpful to compare a project to a painting: the sponsors are the artists crafting their design onto a blank canvas, which is the project company. The key feature of the project company is that it does not, normally, have any obligations or business beyond the scope of the relevant project. Where a project company is kept 'clean' in this way, investors can best assess the risks involved with their lending: all of the project company's rights and obligations are clearly and exclusively set out in finance documents and commercial contracts, which are each entered into solely for the purpose of developing and operating the one project (and which will each be reviewed by the project company's lenders and their advisers).

2.62 Commercial contracts are analysed in greater detail in Chapter 5 and finance documents are discussed in greater detail in Chapter 7 and the chapters which follow.

Taken together, these contracts should constitute the 'whole world' of the project absent only the various laws and regulations applied to the project by relevant governmental entities. Subject to those laws and regulations, the project company contracts to receive funds from debt and equity investors, which it, in turn, contracts with construction contractors to, primarily, apply to the construction of the project. Because the various investors are repaid from the revenues generated once the relevant project is operational, the project company may also contract from the outset, again subject to applicable laws and regulations, for the operation and maintenance of the project, which is likely to involve arrangements for the purchase of project feedstock, technical equipment and experience, and, often, guaranteed off-take.

Project Participants: Stage Two (Financing the Project)

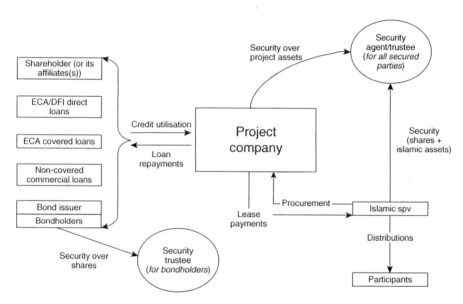

Figure 2.2 **Example financing structure**

An introduction to the financing stage

Through the origination phase of a project, financing costs are typically for the **2.63** account of the project originator, whether such originator is a private sponsor or host government. As discussed above, the origination phase may entail significant research and development in the areas of technical viability and specification, financial and legal planning (including the arrangement of bidding processes), and related matters. The costs involved can be substantial, particularly when you remember that projects are often (and, sometimes, repeatedly) suspended before they can be financed (and sponsors may have other projects that have had to be abandoned following substantial research and investment). Furthermore, private sponsors will also incur significant costs bidding for the right to develop a project in the context of any competitive process and the nature of such processes dictates, of course, that some bids will be unsuccessful.

2.64 The substantial costs involved with originating a project (whether such project is developed successfully, aborted or lost to another bidder) are most easily absorbed by a powerful private sponsor and/or a wealthy host government with other revenue streams. Where host governments retain the ability to raise taxes, well-established private sponsors are likely to have equity interests in multiple projects and can use the revenues from one project to assist the development of further projects. In fact, certain private sponsors opt to finance their projects fully (right through to the operational phase) by way of balance sheet financing. The main advantage of such corporate financing over project financing is that the borrowing is not tied to a particular project. This provides the sponsors with greater flexibility to take whatever action in respect of a specific project it considers to be best in the context of its overall business. In contrast, project finance lenders are, typically, granted security over a particular project and the success of that project is therefore fundamental to their risk analysis. This is reflected in the detailed covenant and information regimes to which the lenders will bind the relevant project company (which regimes are most suitable for financings transacted conservatively in the context of high risk environments such as politically and economically unstable areas, or where cutting edge technologies are being applied). Risk factors in relation to project financings are discussed in more detail in Chapter 4.

The role of equity financing

2.65 Even where debt is secured on the terms of a project financing, the debt lenders usually require that a substantial proportion of the overall project cost, usually in the region of 20 per cent or more, is funded by way of equity investment. Even where private sponsors have the liquidity to provide such equity financing out of their own pockets, they will normally be reluctant to make such an injection from the outset. Equity may be contributed by way of share capital investment in the project company or, more frequently, it is provided via shareholder loans to the project company. The latter approach establishes a simple mechanic enabling the private sponsors to take their equity return by way of repayment, although the main debt lenders will, in most instances, expect such equity repayment to be contractually subordinated to the repayment of their debt.

2.66 As discussed above in the context of ownership structures, private sponsors specializing in the development of a particular type of project will often co-own a project with another equity investor. Although minority share owners are sometimes other private sponsors specializing in the development of the same type of project, they are, frequently, entities with limited specialist knowledge who invest discreetly with a view to achieving nothing other than strong equity returns. Examples of such investors include pension funds and hedge funds investing on an international basis. On other occasions, similar entities, such as regional pension funds, invest with a view to achieving strong equity returns, but also with a view to supporting regional development and/or having some influence on the project in question.

Certain private sponsors prefer to meet their equity funding obligations by way of **2.67** debt financing. This is known as an equity bridge financing as it is bridging the gap that equity investment is meant to fill. Equity bridge financing may be acceptable to the other lenders in a project provided that it is subordinated adequately to the repayment of any senior debt financing. However, certain lenders may be reluctant to participate in a project that involves little balance sheet financing by the sponsors on the basis that this may be considered to demonstrate an absence of equity commitment to the relevant project. As a legal matter, provided that subordination is effective and a suitable guarantee of equity funding obligations is obtained from an entity of substance (i.e. an entity with sufficient assets to support such a guarantee, or a suitable bank demand letter of credit) it is hard to argue that equity bridge financing is inherently detrimental to the interests of other lenders.

The role of debt financing

Who are the lenders?

A variety of commercial banks, export credit agencies, insurance companies, pen- **2.68** sion funds, and other finance entities may participate in a project financing through public or private debt placements. Multilateral and development finance institutions, some of which are global in reach and others regional, may also act as lenders. The identity of the lenders to a particular project will depend on a variety of factors, which will include the extent of any existing commercial relations between a particular sponsor and bank, the political and/or economic/social developmental importance of the relevant project, its location, and its commercial risks.

The Glossary contains a list of export credit agencies as well as national develop- **2.69** ment finance institutions of various countries, and also lists the major multilateral development institutions.

Why do the lenders participate?

In assessing the objectives of lenders, one must bear in mind that debt is priced with **2.70** a fixed or index-linked rate of return. There is little, if any, 'up side' to debt-holders if the project performs beyond expectations. However, with no recourse other than to the assets of the project, the lenders face the full risk of loss if the project fails. Their tolerance for risk, given this skewed risk/reward relationship, will thus be substantially lower than that of equity investors, who can justify accepting risk to achieve the possibility of higher returns. Moreover, notwithstanding the breadth of covenants required by lenders in project finance credit documentation, lenders have only limited practical ability to control their borrower and manage risks. The common question asked in the context of project finance, 'is this risk bankable', reflects the need to assess risk through the eyes of the party least able and willing to assume risk, the debt-holders. However, if all lenders were motivated by purely mercenary values imposed from a short-term perspective, projects would not be bankable and project finance would, frequently, not be practical.

2.71 In a project financing, different types of lenders may have different objectives or, at least, different priorities. For example, export credit agencies may be motivated not only by profit considerations, but also by the aim of promoting the supply of goods and services from the country of origin. Alternatively, multilateral lenders and development finance institutions may have as one of their key missions promoting economic and social development in the host country. A variety of these institutions provide support in the form of loans, political or commercial risk insurance, guarantees or indemnities, or any combination of these, for project financings. Although export credit agencies, development finance institutions and multilateral lenders do not, typically, operate on a charitable basis, the terms on which they lend, insure, guarantee, or otherwise support a project are more favourable than those that may be obtained from purely commercial institutions. Such favourable terms may be absolutely critical to the bankability of more 'risky' projects or, as has been seen in times of international economic downturn, the bankability of any major project when many commercial banks have indicated that they are, even temporarily, closed to new business.

2.72 Co-financing or complimentary financing arrangements among commercial banks and official credit agencies may increase the level of comfort (and debt participation) of commercial banks in project financings. The quasi-governmental nature of official credit agencies and other multilateral institutions may provide some, normally informal and typically political, protection against government expropriation of, or interference with, a project. Moreover, there is also a perception that, again on an informal and political basis, these types of institutions are particularly unlikely to abandon a project to fail and enforce security so they may take action that protects or supports a project to the benefit of the commercial participants without any, or with limited, additional cost to such commercial participants.

2.73 When export credit agencies and multilateral development institutions participate in a project it will be subject to a high level of environmental, employment, and other social standards, which can be expensive to meet. The application of these standards is very important to these institutions from a policy perspective and a key objective is to encourage the use of best practice in the implementation of infrastructure and their projects. A number of leading private sponsors and commercial lenders have begun to incorporate many of these standards such as the 'Equator Principles' and other environmental requirements into project documentation and covenants to have been introduced into finance documentation to ensure compliance during the life of the loans.

The role of alternative financing

As discussed in Chapter 9, additional debt financing for a project may be obtained **2.74** in the bond market. The motivations of bondholders are likely to be, effectively, indistinguishable from commercial banks and financings involving them will be structured as such. The significant documentation and regulatory requirements involved with bond issues is, of course, a not insignificant additional cost to a project. This means that a bond issue is only likely to be undertaken where the margins available are considered advantageous or where a shortage of alternative finance solutions necessitates that the investment net is cast widely.

The Islamic finance market is also becoming increasingly popular as a source of **2.75** project finance. Although the structures used to incorporate *Sharia'a* principles are unique and different from classic debt financing, Islamic finance is, typically, used as a substitute for debt financing. Such structures and the motivations of Islamic finance institutions are analysed in greater detail in Chapter 10.

Hedging products are not an alternative to other sources of project financing, but **2.76** they can complement debt financing. Relatively simple interest rate and exchange rate swaps are undertaken by most project companies in relation to major international projects. The banks involved will, on most occasions, be existing international or local lenders to the project. The terms of the swaps are likely to be negotiated on a purely commercial basis.

The role of other financing participants

As discussed above, various advisers and consultants play a vital role in a project. **2.77** This is particularly true when a financing is being structured and agreed. Experienced commercial banks and financial advisers may be required to help introduce private sponsors to potential equity and debt investors. Moreover, often before such introductions are made or, at least, before commitments are offered, they will participate in the negotiation of documentation, using their market experience to help to structure a deal that is likely to be bankable (i.e. viable for debt investors).

Once a deal is being structured, lawyers for all parties will, of course, be at the centre **2.78** of negotiations, acting as facilitators and recorders of any deal. Although private sponsors are likely to have taken, for example, full technical, engineering, and insurance advice prior to the financing stage, the lenders to a project will require their own advisers to verify that the terms being proposed by the sponsors are consistent with market practice or otherwise appropriate. Around the time of financing, the sponsors' own insurance advisers, typically insurance brokers, are then likely to negotiate actively and independently with insurers and, often, offshore reinsurers for appropriate coverage in advance of construction or amended coverage to facilitate the project financing. Insurance matters are discussed in greater detail in Chapter 6.

2.79 Around the time of financing or commencement of project construction, sponsors are also likely to be formalizing arrangements for various authorizations, consents, permits, and related matters with host governments. This can be a difficult, bureaucratic process requiring significant input from local lawyers. Lenders will expect these matters to be resolved before they make any funds available to the relevant project company.

2.80 Finally, as discussed further below in the context of the operational phase of the project, it can be crucial that off-take arrangements, under which the product of the project may be subject to certain guaranteed purchase terms, are entered into before the financing of the project can be agreed. Where there is no open and developed market for the applicable project product, lenders will need to be able to satisfy themselves that off-take arrangements are in place generating revenues sufficient to cover all, or a portion if there is a limited open market for the surplus product, of the proposed repayments.

Project Participants: Stage Three (Constructing the Project)

An introduction to the construction stage

2.81 The construction phase of a project will, in many instances, commence before the financing for the project is fully agreed. This may be necessary to enable the project to be constructed to a schedule imposed as a condition of a bidding process run by the host government. A shortage of qualified construction contractors may also necessitate that action be taken to secure the services of an appropriate contractor at an early stage. Alternatively, a confident, experienced, and well-resourced sponsor may, simply, opt to proceed with construction as soon as possible on the basis that the project is then likely to become operational, such that it is generating revenues, sooner. In any circumstances where the contracts relating to the construction of a project are agreed before it is financed, there is of course a risk to the project company (quantifiable by reference to its full obligations and liabilities under the relevant contracts), which is typically backed by a payment guarantee from the sponsors or sponsors, who are, therefore, also 'on risk', in the event that financing cannot be obtained on the terms anticipated. In the event of, for example, disruption in global markets in the intervening period, this risk could easily jeopardize the life of the project or, more notably at this stage, the solvency (or, at a minimum, the equity returns) of the relevant guarantor or guarantors.

2.82 Although construction arrangements are, typically, negotiated between the sponsors of a project and the relevant contractor or contractors, and then presented to the project company's lenders as a *fait accompli*, lenders will review the terms of any material contracts that the project company entered into before the financing has been agreed and amendments, usually of a minor nature, may be necessary to ensure bankability.

The role of the construction contractor

Once a project site and purpose has been identified at the origination stage, techni- **2.83** cal advisers will help to identify the specifications of the project and the work required to construct a project capable of producing the relevant product in the quantities and of the quality required to make the project bankable. The sponsors, in consultation with such technical advisers, will then approach the market to negotiate terms with a contractor or contractors for the construction of the project to such specifications. The main construction contract is a key contract because it governs the main costs being financed.

The construction contractor designs and builds the project, often on the basis of a **2.84** 'turnkey' fixed-price contract. The construction contract is generally awarded on the basis of a competitive tendering process, where pricing is likely to be the key consideration. The objective of the contractor will be to complete the construction of the project at a cost that allows it to preserve its anticipated profit margin. The contractor is, usually, liable for delay damages for late completion and may earn an early completion bonus to the extent that the project is completed ahead of schedule. Contractors are also, often, called upon to pay damages in the event that the project does not pass certain performance tests.

The construction contractor generally enters into subcontracts for equipment **2.85** procurement, civil works, and design and engineering services pursuant to which it seeks to pass on many of the risks it is asked to assume under the construction contract entered into with the project company. A contractor will, of course, seek generally to avoid assuming risk (for example, assuming sole responsibility for completing the project) for which it is not compensated adequately or which it is unable to pass through to subcontractors.

Construction contractors and even subcontractors operating on the project site, in **2.86** addition to interacting with each other and the project company's representatives, may also have to join the project company and sponsors in liaising with the host government in respect of licences, consents and approvals.

The role of energy and other infrastructure

Major international projects are constructed in a variety of locations, some of **2.87** which are lacking in every kind of infrastructure. Before a project can, therefore, be constructed, appropriate infrastructure must be developed. Although this may be arranged independently by the host government or other private sector sources as a separate project or projects, the development of appropriate infrastructure may, instead, be fully incorporated within the terms of the project being supported.

2.88 Infrastructure needs of a project are likely to include the following:

Access needs

2.89 Unless the project site is at sea or similar, road and/or rail infrastructure sufficient to support traffic accessing the site for construction and operation of the project is almost certain to be required.

Power and water needs

2.90 The construction contractors and subcontractors are likely to require significant amounts of electricity and water for the construction of a major international project. Appropriate pipelines and cables will be necessary, and must be arranged in coordination with local public or private utilities providers. However, where projects are being constructed in less developed countries, pipelines and cables may not be enough. Additional investment in power generation and clean water supply may be necessary such that there is sufficient supply to guarantee that the needs of the project are met. Where supply is insufficient, arrangements may be made with host governments and/or the private sector to favour supply to the project over alternative end users. This is likely to be a sensitive political issue for certain project participants, such as development finance institutions, who may require that infrastructure is developed to enhance rather than detract from the service being offered to the rest of the local community.

Housing and other social development requirements

2.91 Once work commences on the construction of a project, huge workforces may descend on areas or existing communities without the infrastructure to support them. Their most basic needs will be food and shelter. These may be addressed by the construction of housing and related infrastructure such as restaurants and shops. Over time, these basic needs are likely to be supplemented by a market for entertainment and, if more permanent communities are developing in anticipation of employment being generated by the project during its operational phase, other services relating to health and education needs.

Ongoing roles

2.92 Various advisers and consultants assisting both the project company and its lenders will be involved with monitoring the progress of construction in the context of compliance with the transaction documentation. Expenditure, equity investment, technical specifications, environmental standards, insurance matters, and legal compliance are all likely to be under high levels of supervision through the construction phase.

Certain actions will also be necessary in preparation for the operations phase of **2.93** a project. For example, different insurances will be required for the operation of the project and the lenders will expect that these are in place in anticipation of the commencement of operations.

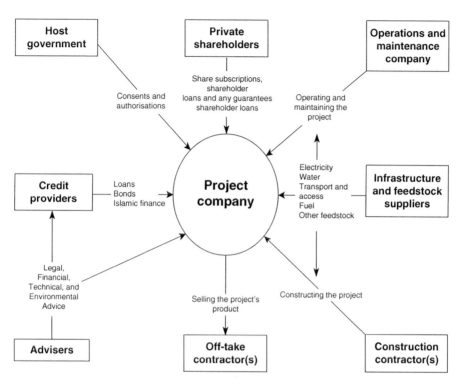

Figure 2.3 **Example Construction and Operations Phase Structure**

Project Participants: Stage Four (Operating the Project)

An introduction to the operations stage

As in relation to the commencement of construction, there is likely to be a timing **2.94** overlap between the completion of construction and the commencement of the operational phase of any project. Early generation revenues may be available if a project can be operated before its scheduled commercial operations commencement date. There may, therefore, be an incentive for a project company to develop operational capability while the construction contractors and/or subcontractors, as applicable, are finishing the building or, more likely, the testing of the project facilities.

The role of the operator

Manufacturing and other facilities are complex and their operation and mainte- **2.95** nance often requires significant skills that a single purpose project company may not have within its own workforce or intellectual property resources. In such circumstances, an independent contractor is often charged with operating and maintaining the project for an extended term. In some cases, separate arrangements, often with an affiliated entity (where a sponsor has industry expertise within its group of companies), will be made to manage ordinary day-to-day operations. To supplement this, major equipment maintenance may be contracted out to an experienced equipment vendor under the terms of a technical support agreement.

2.96 Although operation and maintenance agreements are not always entered into at the time that the financing of the relevant project is agreed, lenders are likely to require comfort that appropriate arrangements have been planned. For example, in the power sector, lenders may want contractual assurances that the operator will be a controlled affiliate of a sponsor where such sponsor is an experienced power developer.

2.97 Strong operating warranties and commitments may mitigate lender concerns as to technology risks. For example, in projects whose economics have been underpinned with assumptions as to the plant's high efficiency or availability, the operator may be called upon to warrant the plant's performance over an extended period to provide assurance as to the attainability of the projected operating standards. However, the fees payable to an operator will often not provide adequate compensation for assuming the significant financial risk posed by impaired operating margins. The debate thus, generally, hinges on structuring the risk/reward relationship to ensure that the operator is properly incentivized.

The role of the operation and maintenance guarantor

2.98 As discussed above, the operator is, often, either the project company or an affiliate of the project company on the basis that there is relevant expertise contained within the relevant group of companies. Neither the project company when acting as the operator of a project nor a separate operating company is likely to be an entity of substance. Lenders will therefore seek additional comfort from an entity of substance, often the senior company within the group or another group company with an acceptable long-term credit rating, in the form of a guarantee of the operator's obligations under the operation and maintenance agreement. Alternatively, a letter of credit may be substituted for such guarantees.

The role of feedstock, fuel, and other suppliers

2.99 Suppliers are critical in providing an assured source of feedstock, fuel, and other raw materials to the project. These inputs will be crucial to the ability of the project to produce its product and, by selling that product, generate revenues with which to repay the project's debt financing. To provide assurance of supply, the project company may enter into long-term supply and transportation arrangements. This arrangement is likely to be mutually beneficial as the supplier thereby also secures an assured market for its resource.

A supplier may be asked to provide warranties of supply and price over a long **2.100** period, which could expose it to substantial risks. The terms of *force majeure* and similar relief provisions, and opportunities for price 'reopeners', will be of significant concern to any supplier.

The role of off-takers

If all the participants discussed above are well chosen and contractually bound to **2.101** perform, a project should be able to produce its target product and offer it for sale. The identity and creditworthiness of any entity that purchases all or any significant proportion of the output from the project and the terms of the purchase or off-take contract are central to most project financings. Only where there is a well developed and reliable open market for a project's off-take product might this not be the most important commercial contract to the credit risk evaluation made by the lenders. Such evaluation of a project will depend upon an assessment of the financial condition of the off-taker or off-takers, since the project's cashflow will be directly dependent upon their ability to perform their obligations.

The objective of the off-taker is generally to secure assured access to the output of **2.102** the project. In most cases, it will be prepared to commit to buy all or a significant portion of the project's output, and in many (if not most) cases it will offer a degree of revenue assurance through a fixed or floor price. The off-taker may have undertakings to others to sell-on the project's output, generally at a price that will afford a margin on those sales. The off-taker will wish to avoid circumstances where there is any price or other mismatch between the primary off-take commitment and its on-sales arrangements. In many cases, such as the distribution of electrical energy, there may be an element of subsidy in those on-sales. The circumstances in which revenues may be curtailed or terminated or, alternatively, increased must be carefully defined. Allocating the risk of *force majeure* events affecting either party, and determining when the obligations of either party may be terminated, are of particular importance.

The off-taker's commitment may be less crucial in mature markets where access **2.103** to purchasers may be certain and price volatility limited or at least predictable. For example, in some countries, regulatory reform has made possible the emergence of 'merchant' power plants. A broad range of energy, natural resource, and petrochemical projects sell their products into mature and liquid markets. In these cases, off-take undertakings may be limited to assurance of access to these markets, sometimes at an indexed price, but not to any specific 'floor' price. In such cases, as in the case of 'merchant' power projects, the underlying economics must be sufficiently robust to withstand cyclical, or even just volatile, price and revenue projections.

Ongoing roles

2.104 As in relation to the construction of a project, various advisers and consultants assisting both the project company and its lenders will be involved with monitoring the ongoing performance of the operational project in the context of compliance with the transaction documentation. Financial covenants, technical specifications, environmental standards, insurance matters, and legal compliance are all likely to be under high levels of supervision throughout the operations phase, although perhaps less than during the construction phase as the inputs and outputs of any mature project should be relatively stable.

Project reincarnation

2.105 Because the inputs and outputs of a project are more stable during the operations phase than before, the risks associated with the project are likely to be commensurately lower. As markets also change, the terms of any financing agreed much earlier in the project's life cycle are unlikely to reflect the terms that might be available to an operational project. The sponsors may therefore consider attempting to refinance the project on improved terms (possibly with the same or many of the same lenders). Alternatively, they may consider whether an agreeable return could be generated by selling some or even all of their equity stake in the project company. The same kind of financial and legal advisers involved with the original financing are likely to be involved in any refinancing or sale.

2.106 As discussed in greater detail below, certain project structures provide for operational projects to be transferred into alternative ownership, possibly by host governments, once operational. Further, in less stable parts of the world, a fully operational and profitable project may be a target for expropriation by a host government, although this is relatively unlikely given the disincentive to further private investment unless fair expropriation compensation is paid.

2.107 In many cases, sponsors will retain their ownership interest in a project company until after the debt financing its construction has been repaid on the basis that it is during this period that it is most straightforward to generate a return on the product. Revenues that were being used to repay lenders can then be used to repay equity loans and pay dividends.

2.108 Where there are, for example, significant mineral deposits in a particular area or there is further demand for power or water, a project that is addressing, but not fulfilling, such demand may be extended, supplemented, or renovated in some way with a view to increasing output and revenues. It is possible that the revenues from the first project will be used to help finance equity investment in further projects or that the first project will be refinanced to provide for debt financing of such parallel projects. Alternatively, where a project is failing, it may still be renovated, extended, or refinanced with a view to generating increased revenues to turn the project's fortunes around.

Wherever a project is reincarnated in any of the ways introduced above, the range **2.109** of project participants is unlikely to include classes of participants fundamentally different from those already introduced in this chapter, even if the individual lenders and contractors will, probably, change. It is to be hoped, therefore, that the first part of this chapter has given the reader a comprehensive introduction to the various players involved in the life of a project.

Ownership and Project Structures

An introduction to ownership and project structures

The premise of a non-recourse or limited recourse project financing is inextricably **2.110** linked to the ability of lenders to assess and, to an extent, control the operations of the borrowing entity. This is most effectively achieved through the use of a single purpose vehicle whose only asset is the project. The first part of this section explores the various considerations that influence, or dictate, the choices made by sponsors in establishing the entity that will implement the project.

All project finance transactions have some level of interaction with their host **2.111** government. At one end of the spectrum this is solely in respect of permitting requirements and at the other may involve a significant degree of government ownership. The second part of this section reviews the most common project structures.

Selecting an ownership structure

General considerations

Although a single sponsors may decide to carry out a project alone, as a matter **2.112** of practice most large projects are jointly owned or jointly controlled. The reasons for selecting a joint structure include: spreading the project risk among a number of participants; maximizing the benefits of a combination of skills, technology, and resources; and allowing participants to act in a project that would otherwise be beyond the capabilities of any of the individual sponsors.

The ownership structure of a project is influenced by the particular financial, legal, **2.113** accounting, and taxation objectives and concerns of the sponsors. Flexibility of management structure, the ease with which profits can be distributed, minimiz- ing tax burdens, achieving off-balance sheet treatment, the scope of minority protection, and considerations regarding dissolution are among the issues that guide decisions about the proper project vehicle.

Particular considerations include:

2.114 **Will the host government be a shareholder?** Generally, any project company that is to be part-owned by the host government will have to be incorporated in the project country. The requirement for government ownership varies across different sectors and host countries and is dependent on the balance between the relevant host government's appetite for risk, its obligation or desire to provide social infrastructure, and its requirement to benefit financially from the project.

2.115 Mining and oil and gas projects often have a minority government stake, paid for by the international shareholders. As a 'carried' interest, the host government bears little financial risk and since such projects do not fall squarely within the category of 'infrastructure', they are not generally within a government's mandate to provide infrastructure. However, they do bring incidental benefits of an infrastructure nature (by way of the construction of roads, railways, and electricity and water networks) and the potential to create significant revenues. The host government typically also requires a royalty under the relevant permitting regime.

2.116 In the United Arab Emirates, the ongoing programme of independent water and power projects is structured so that each project is majority owned by the Abu Dhabi Water and Electricity Authority. The procurement of power and desalinated water is generally considered to be the responsibility of a host government is therefore subject to government regulation. The Abu Dhabi approach to ownership is not the general approach in the power and water sector, within the Middle East or elsewhere. However, it gives the host government considerable control over the provision of a significant segment of infrastructure, augmented by the fact that the power and water is also purchased by the host government. In other countries, such as Oman which is going through a process of privatization of its power and water sectors, no government ownership is required and although the purchaser is currently government-owned, there is the potential for further privatization so that future power and water projects in Oman may, as in the UK and the US, become subject to industry regulation and permitting, but not otherwise be owned by or contract with the host government.

2.117 In the UK and the US, project financing is now most commonly seen in sectors extensively regulated by government and falling within category of infrastructure, such as schools, hospitals, power generation, water and waste projects and roads. Some of these are wholly within the private sector (meaning that they are developed, operated, and financed by independent companies and lenders and their product is bought by an independent purchaser), such as power generation and others, such as schools and hospitals, are financed using the public/private partnerships, in which the government contracts with the developer for the provision of the relevant building and associated services (i.e. teaching or healthcare) but does not take an ownership interest until the expiry (or earlier termination) of the concession arrangement under which the particular facility was developed and built by the private sector.

Will there be more than one shareholder/partner?   Project financing offers devel-   **2.118** opers the opportunity to consolidate resources and expertise to implement a project that none, acting alone, could achieve. This may be a question of finance, technical expertise, or managerial skills. It also enables the shareholders or partners to spread the risk across a broader pool of investors.

What are the requirements of local law?   In some jurisdictions, it may not be pos-   **2.119** sible for a non-local entity to do business, or there may be a requirement for at least one shareholder or partner to be a local entity. Further, it may be that the nature of the project company's business or ownership restricts the types of entity available to the shareholders (for example, a company as opposed to a limited liability partnership).

Are there any relevant lender considerations?   If the financing is to include export   **2.120** credit agencies or development finance institutions, these may have requirements as to the jurisdiction in which the borrowing entity is incorporated.

What are the fiscal implications?   Tax and accounting regulations may signifi-   **2.121** cantly influence the choice of vehicle and jurisdiction for the project company, as may the ability to withdraw shareholder profits.

What are the management implications?   In many cases, the bringing together of   **2.122** several different project shareholders introduces, for example, money from one and experience from another. The potential for an imbalance in ownership proportions means that the ability to have flexible management arrangements that are inde-pendent of ownership interest and to have appropriate protections for minority shareholders.

Types of ownership vehicle

In determining the most appropriate type of vehicle for a given enterprise, as dis-   **2.123** cussed above, the laws of the jurisdiction of organization of the vehicle must be taken into account. Applicable law, or the requirements laid down by the authority that is procuring the project in question, may require incorporation in the country where the project is located and/or dictate the type of vehicle that must be used. Where flexibility is afforded, however, tax and other considerations may lead to the selection of a vehicle organized in another country.

Typically, one of three generic types of vehicle is used as project entities, wherever   **2.124** that particular entity is established: a special purpose company, an unincorporated joint venture, or a partnership.

Special purpose company

2.125 Special purpose companies are often used where the flow-through of tax benefits to the joint venture partners is not critical and where the centralized management control available through a corporate structure is deemed desirable.

2.126 The following are the main advantages of special purpose companies:

(1) they have a separate legal identity, and thus have the ability to enter into contracts and litigate legal proceedings in their own name;

(2) there is generally little restriction on the transferability of interests;

(3) the liability of shareholders will be limited; and

(4) corporations have continuity of life.

2.127 The major disadvantages of special purpose companies are:

(1) equity investors may effectively be exposed to double taxation (at the corporate and shareholder level);

(2) they may be subject to greater administrative complexity; and

(3) a corporate structure may have less operational flexibility than the alternatives.

2.128 There are wide variances in the rules governing companies across jurisdictions and, although it may appear sensible to organize the company in the country where the project is located, investors often wish to organize the company in a jurisdiction that allows flexibility in the management and capitalization of the company (subject to any applicable local law requirements, as discussed above).

Unincorporated joint venture

2.129 An unincorporated joint venture is a form of association between entities that wish to carry out a project together for a particular commercial purpose. This is probably the most flexible form of cooperation between entities in terms of management and has long been used in major oil and gas development projects.

2.130 The following are certain important features of the unincorporated joint venture:

(1) it is an association of persons engaging in a limited common undertaking;

(2) the entitlement of each joint venturer is expressed as a share of the assets not a share of the revenue or profits;

(3) an operator may manage the venture, subject to the direction of an operating committee, which often comprises representatives of each joint venturer (usually voting in accordance with their proportional interests); and

(4) each joint venturer may (depending on the applicable law) owe fiduciary obligations to the others.

2.131 The use of an unincorporated joint venture may pose complexities that render its use impracticable. These include:

(1) because it is not a separate legal entity, it may not be able to borrow or enter into contracts in its own name; and

(2) financing is often more complex to obtain if the joint venturers seek separate, rather than joint, financing as the lenders' security will be limited to an undivided interest in the assets.

Partnership

The partnership is a common form of enterprise in many (but certainly not all) **2.132** jurisdictions because it:

(1) allows tax benefits to flow through directly to the partners;
(2) allows maximum flexibility for the allocation of profits and losses between partners;
(3) affords flexibility for the resolution of management and other business issues; and
(4) has legal personality, allowing it to borrow and enter into contracts in its own name.

The partnership has the following general features: **2.133**

(1) although it may be a separate legal entity, the partners are nonetheless jointly and severally responsible for all liabilities of the partnership;
(2) the liability of each partner to the creditors of the partnership may be unlimited (although recourse to the sponsors can effectively be limited by the use of special purpose corporate partners);
(3) in certain jurisdictions, the number of partners may be restricted; and
(4) transfer restrictions may prevent partners from transferring their partnership interests without the prior consent of the other partners.

Some jurisdictions have constituted hybrid entities, such as a limited liability part- **2.134** nership, that may offer the benefits of partnership tax treatment with the limitation of liability and other attributes of a corporation.

Relationship among equity investors

Whatever the form of the project vehicle, there is often an agreement among **2.135** equity holders that governs their relationship. This may take the form of a development agreement, a joint venture agreement, a partnership agreement, or a shareholders' agreement. Often, depending on the corporate ownership chain, there may be two or more such agreements—the sponsors may invest through a chain of corporate entities, one or more of which may be jointly owned in some manner by two or more sponsors. If that is the case, then one would expect to see a shareholders' agreement or similar between the legal entities that are the direct owners of/investors in the actual project company or other vehicle, together with similar arrangements further 'up the chain' of ownership until such point in the chain as there is no common interest or ownership.

2.136 Whatever 'label' is given to the documentation that ultimately governs the relation-ship between the various equity investors, the following terms, and the manner in which risks are allocated, must be considered (the terms 'joint venturer' and 'venturer' below are used generically to refer to the various parties that have come together to promote the project, via whatever particular vehicle is selected, rather than being used in a restrictive sense):

(1) the nature of the financial obligations to be imposed on the joint venturers;
(2) the allocation of responsibilities, management and voting rights;
(3) the conditions under which distributions may be made;
(4) the restrictions on competition among the joint venturers;
(5) the consequences of default (specifically, whether the venturer will find its ownership share diluted or terminated);
(6) the nature of any restrictions on the assignment or transfer of interests; and
(7) the circumstances under which the venture will be terminated.

2.137 An overview of key provisions of a joint venture, partnership, or shareholders' agreement is set out in Appendix 3.

Dilution and cross-charge mechanisms

2.138 Sponsors will generally wish to address the risk that another equity participant fails to meet its equity funding obligations or otherwise breaches its obligations under the joint venture, partnership or shareholders' agreement. Dilution provisions pro-vide a mechanism to allow the non-defaulting equity participant to reduce the defaulting equity participant's interest by assuming its portion of the funding obli-gation and thereby acquiring a pro rata portion of that equity participant's interest in the project vehicle.

2.139 Many project vehicles also put into place a cross-charge or similar mechanism whereby each of the equity participants grants a charge in favour of the other equity participants over its interest in the project vehicle or the project assets to secure its performance under the joint venture/partnership/shareholders' agreement (includ-ing payment of cash calls). Lenders are frequently asked to permit dilution to occur and to allow such cross-charges to be implemented.

Project structures

2.140 The essential elements of a project financing are the construction or acquisition of a facility by a private sector entity and the sale of the output of that facility to an off-taker or onto the market. There is a wide variety of ways to structure that basic transaction to meet the particular requirements of the parties. The various types of project structures in the international marketplace include the following.

Build, own, operate (BOO)

Under a typical BOO structure, a utility or state entity enters into an off-take **2.141**
agreement with a project company that agrees to build and operate a new manufacturing (or other) plant for a given product. This structure may also be applied
to the development of a 'merchant' plant which has no formal off-take
contracts. BOO projects often involve a consortium consisting of, among other
possibilities, a local developer that brings in local contacts, an equipment
vendor interested in selling its product, and a company interested in operating
the facility.

Build, own, transfer (BOT)

Under a BOT structure, the project company absorbs the risk of completion and **2.142**
then transfers the asset to a public sector entity after repayment of the project debt.
A BOT structure is often based on a concession or development agreement between
a government or a government agency and the project company. The obligation to
transfer the asset back to public ownership may arise at the end of a specified period
of time or, if earlier, upon the occurrence of specified conditions (e.g. material
default by the project company).

Build, lease, transfer (BLT)

In this case, the project company assumes the construction risk. The completed **2.143**
facility is then leased to the government, which assumes the operating risks.
Lease payments, made by the government to the private sector lessor, are
structured to amortise the construction debt and provide a fixed rate of return on
the equity. At the end of the lease term, ownership of the asset is transferred to
the government. This structure allows the government to shift the construction
and financing risks to the private sector whilst retaining operating control over
the facility.

Build, transfer, operate (BTO)

Under this structure, the project company completes the project and transfers it **2.144**
back to the host government for a specified consideration. The government then
contracts with a private company (often related to the project company) to operate
the facility and either pays the operator a fee or receives royalty payments from the
operator during the contract term.

Transfer of operating rights (TOR)

The divesting entity (often, an arm of the government) in this structure transfers the **2.145**
right to use existing assets and, in return, enters into an agreement with the acquiring entity for the purchase of the capacity or output of those assets. Often, the
acquirer must invest significant capital to repair or expand the assets and, in some

cases, must deal with complex issues concerning relations with existing facility employees.

'Within the fence' projects

2.146 In emerging markets, large industrial consumers must often go to considerable lengths to ensure the availability of reliable, cost-effective power or other utilities, even if it means that the consumer must self-generate its requirements. As an alternative to building their own power stations, industrial customers may enter into power purchase agreements with independent power producers. In addition to industrial sales, the independent power producer may sell a portion of its output to a local utility.

Forward sale structures

2.147 In this case, a project company or joint venture will finance the construction of its facilities with, in addition to equity invested by the sponsors, proceeds from selling all or a portion of its anticipated production (oil or gas, for example) during a specified period to an unaffiliated purchaser, often a special purpose company organized offshore and owned by a charitable trust. The sale may be for a lump sum prepayment or for staged payments, timed to meet construction cost liabilities. The special purpose company finances the purchase price payments mainly by borrowing from third party lenders. It on-sells the product in the spot market or pursuant to long-term off-take agreements, often with affiliates of the sponsors, and uses the revenue from the off-take sales to pay the debt service on its borrowings. The primary recourse of the lenders is through security over the special purpose company's purchase agreement with the project company and its off-take sales agreements. By characterizing the structure as a sale of product, rather than as a form of security over project company assets, and ensuring that the debt of the special purpose company is not consolidated as debt of the project company, the forward sale technique is designed to structure around limitations on the ability of the project company to grant liens or to borrow. The key legal and accounting issue with this type of structure is whether the forward sale arrangement is, in fact, effective to transfer title to the future production (generally referred to as a 'true sale') or is merely a disguised loan to the project company, secured by future production.

Privatizations

2.148 Governments often seek to raise capital by selling all or a part of their assets to the private sector. A government may in some instances 'corporatize' the entity that holds the asset and then sell down all or a portion of the equity in that entity. Alternatively, it may 'divisionalize' an entity by selling one or more discrete businesses while maintaining public ownership of others.

2.149 Clearly, the above discussion gives only an overview of the considerations that may be involved in the selection of both the underlying structure of any particular individual project and the nature of the entity that is used as the key project vehicle to pursue a particular project. Hopefully this part of the chapter has provided an overview of the various decisions that may be involved when considering each of these questions, and a flavour of the factors that may underlie the decision to pursue any particular structural direction.

3

SOURCES OF FUNDING

Mark Plenderleith, Milbank, Tweed, Hadley & McCloy LLP

Introduction

From the inception of the development process, sponsors will be minded continu- **3.01** ally to assess the availability and constitution of the likely sources of project capital. A common goal of sponsors is to minimize and delay the funding of the highest cost of capital, the sponsors' equity, and to leverage the project with the cheapest source of external financing which, depending on market conditions and the project, is likely to be long-tenor senior debt from the commercial bank market, eligible financing from public sector funding institutions, or the capital markets.

As has been the case in the wider financial markets, the recent dearth of liquidity in **3.02** the project debt and capital markets has been one of the key factors affecting the achievability of the ambitions of sponsors in terms of transaction scale, pricing, tenor, and gearing of projects.

The project finance market between 2000 and 2010 illustrates the extremes that **3.03** sponsors may face when they approach the capital and loan markets to raise project funds. The dramatic growth in the project finance sector in the years preceding the collapse of the US housing market and the events leading to the September 2008 bankruptcy of Lehman Brothers was in part fuelled by a wealth of options for traditional originating project finance lenders to distribute their exposure, whether through syndication, secondary market sales, or, to a lesser extent, securitization. In the project finance loan market, the traditional model of a commercial lender originating a loan and holding that exposure was replaced with a model which saw the originating lender quickly distributing the booked loan, and thereby creating space on the originator's balance sheet to participate in further financings.

3.04   Primarily in developed countries, the use of credit ratings on loans, in addition to bonds and other securities, expanded the reach of potential investors and allowed the market to move beyond the capacity constraints of the traditional project finance lenders. In the project bond market, the highly developed US and Western European domestic projects' markets were fuelled by the activities of the monoline insurance companies providing guarantees (or 'wraps') of the timely payment of project bond principal and interest for investors wishing to look only to the 'AAA' credit ratings of the monolines, without conducting an in-depth due diligence of the issuer.

3.05   The infrastructure development programmes of both mature and emerging economies and the race for secure access to natural resources generated a highly competitive market for the world's leading export credit agency debt providers. Competition in regional markets was heightened by the rapid deployment of capital in the energy and infrastructure sectors and the boom seen in the Middle Eastern projects market fuelled the development of Islamic financing structures which could be incorporated into more traditional project financing templates in the region. The result of the 'perfect storm' was tremendous competition among lenders and other finance providers and a plethora of competing financing options.

3.06   The global recession, fully felt in 2009 and early 2010, left a firm imprint on deal-flow in its immediate aftermath as the capital markets and project finance debt markets dramatically contracted. Public sector lending provided life support to a limited number of deals, however, the focus of spending was directed at massive governmental intervention through wide ranging stimulus packages in 2009/2010 which strained budgets and the resources of the implementation bodies. During this period sponsors found great challenges in securing sources of project financing as the avenues for arrangers to distribute exposure either tightened or became unavailable and the appetite to originate and hold was at a record low.

3.07   The cycle of the funding market has once again acutely focused participants on the fundamentals of having a well-structured project based on early identification of risks and appropriate allocation and mitigation of such risks. Part of this process, and the subject of this chapter, is the constitution and implementation of the funding structure. This chapter illustrates a variety of sources potentially available to sponsors pursuing a project finance funding plan. The chapter concludes with an overview of the reasons for entering into, and a description of the role of term sheets, letters of interest, commitment letters, and mandate letters. Chapters 8 through 10 discuss three particular funding sources in greater detail, the participation of export credit agencies (ECAs) and multilateral agencies, the use of the international bond markets, and the application of Islamic financing, which has provided additional liquidity predominantly in the Middle East region, Malaysia, and Pakistan.

Sources

Equity capital is the highest risk category in the capital structure. As described in **3.08** Chapter 2, project finance equity providers are willing to accept more risk than debt providers and focus on the return on money invested, the 'up-side'. Debt providers do not share in the up-side. Returns are fixed and relatively low. Debt providers therefore expect to be protected from the 'down-side', and the risks need to be structured such that repayment is, to the maximum extent possible, assured. As discussed further in Chapter 4, re-pricing of the debt alone will not be an acceptable solution to financing a project which has failed to identify, allocate, and mitigate risk correctly.

Sophisticated sponsors dedicate substantial efforts to assessing the financial mar- **3.09** kets in order to identify the optimal sources of funding for a project. A principal determinant of the attractiveness of a project to the financial markets is the robustness of its financial projections. In assessing access to the debt markets, key financial ratios will be considered, including:

(1) the debt-to-equity ratio, which is the ratio of aggregate project debt to the aggregate amount of equity invested in the project;
(2) the average and minimum debt service coverage ratio, which is the ratio of (i) the aggregate net cashflow generated by the project to (ii) the aggregate debt service obligations of the project company for any relevant period; and
(3) the loan life coverage ratio, which is the ratio of (i) the net present value of the projected net operating revenues generated by the project over the term of the project debt to (ii) the principal amount of that project debt.

The sensitivity of the coverage ratios, which are tested through financial modelling, **3.10** to the technical, legal, and political risks associated with the project need to be considered. The outcome of this analysis will be weighed against current financial market conditions to determine the optimal financing plan. The more robust the outcome of this analysis, the greater the project's access will be to deeper and lower cost sources of financing. Sophisticated sponsors will leave their options open until financial close and, even thereafter, will regularly review refinancing options.

The principal sources of finance will change according to the existing state of the **3.11** debt and capital markets. Deal specific factors, such as its geographical location, industry, and identity of the sponsors, and if applicable the procuring government authority, will also be relevant. The most common source of project financing is the commercial bank market, providing senior limited recourse debt to a wide array of projects and sectors across the globe. By contrast, the use of mezzanine and subordinated debt sourced externally, from non-sponsors, remains comparatively rare in project finance funding plans. The use of international and domestic capital markets has been cyclical and in recent years adversely affected by the decline in the monoline insurers.

3.12 Public sector lenders in the form of multilateral, development, and bilateral agencies have long been the key-stone for project financing in developing, countries, where their participation is necessary to mitigate political risks and facilitate access to other forms of co-financing. Export credit agencies (ECA) have provided a deep-pocket, whether in the form of financing which is 'tied' to the export of goods and services from the country of the ECA, or the greater debt funding capacity of their 'untied' loan programmes.[1] However, consideration is first given to the ground layer of the capital structure, the equity or equity equivalent funding of the commercial project participants, the sponsors.

Equity

3.13 Sponsors wish to maximize their profits. However, as discussed in Chapter 2, the methods of achieving a return and the economic interests for participating in a project may be far wider than can be demonstrated by a simple calculation of the projected dividend profile over the life of the project.

3.14 In terms of equity capital, lenders typically require a sponsor or a third-party equity participant (such as an equipment supplier or operator) to contribute a meaningful portion of the capital invested in the project. The level of equity capital is normally driven by the expectations of the project finance market for the relevant sector, and the debt capacity of the projected cashflow of the project. There is a balancing exercise to be performed. As the relative amount of the equity contribution decreases, the rate of return on the equity investment will rise, but the increase in the aggregate debt requirement will affect the project's debt service coverage ratios. For lenders, the injection of equity capital is often perceived to be the investors' commitment to the project through any difficulties that it may encounter. Even when a project's modelled cashflow is strong enough to suggest that the funding could be 100 per cent debt, it is unusual (depending on the quality of the project and the relevant industrial sector) to see projects without a contribution of capital from the equity investors ranging from 10 per cent to 40 per cent of the capital cost.

---

[1] An explanation of the funding programmes of export credit agencies and multilateral development banks can be found in Chapter 8.

Equity investors often prefer to defer making equity contributions until as late as **3.15** possible in order to enhance their return on equity. During the construction period of a green-field project, the lenders may permit pro rata drawdown of debt and equity according to the debt-to-equity ratio, or less commonly, agree to back-end the equity until the senior debt has been fully funded. Senior lenders typically require that any deferred funding of the equity portion of the capital costs will be accelerated if an event of default occurs under the senior financing documents. Credit enhancement in the form of a parent guarantee or letter of credit may be required to support the investors' deferred equity funding obligation.

Equity bridge loans

Sponsors may opt to meet their equity funding obligations by way of debt financ- **3.16** ing. This is known as an equity bridge financing, which has become relatively common in certain markets, particularly the Middle Eastern power market. The loans are typically provided by commercial bank lenders backed by the balance sheets of the sponsors through the provision of sponsor guarantees of the loans on a several basis. The equity bridge loans are commonly funded in one or more draws of debt prior to the funding of the project loans and repaid by the sponsors' equity contributions at the end of the construction period, or if earlier, an agreed long-stop date. At the project level, the loans replace the initial equity investment funding obligations of the sponsors and are designed as a method of improving the equity internal rate of return. Such arrangements are acceptable to the senior lenders if appropriate subordination arrangements are put in place and the equity bridge lenders will need to satisfy themselves that there is sufficient credit behind the guarantee of the relevant shareholder's equity contribution (which will be used to repay the loan). A second ranking security interest over the project assets may be permitted by the senior lenders but the credit for the equity bridge loans is grounded in the sponsor's corporate guarantee.

Subordinated shareholder debt

Subordinated shareholder debt may serve as an alternative or a supplement to equity **3.17** funding of the sponsors' contributions. Sponsors may prefer to make their contributions primarily in debt, rather than equity, for tax and corporate finance reasons.

The advantages of debt instruments over equity, subject to local legal consider- **3.18** ations, are that:

(1) debt can be secured (subject to the senior lenders' priority) and therefore rank ahead of unsecured creditors (subject to the application of doctrines of equitable subordination, which in certain circumstances may, as a matter of the law of some jurisdictions, subordinate debt held by shareholders to third-party claims);

(2) the interest thereon (unlike dividends payable in respect of shares) may be tax deductible;

(3) whilst corporate law often restricts the redemption of share capital, it is unlikely to hinder the repayment of debt; and

(4) as debt, the borrowed amount will eventually be repaid if the project is successful, without tax consequences, whereas a repayment of capital may be more complex from a corporate and tax standpoint.

3.19 If subordinated debt is to be contributed, senior lenders generally will require inter-creditor documentation or a subordination agreement with the providers of the debt to address a number of issues and, in particular, to ensure that:

(1) both the subordinated debt and any security for it are subordinated;

(2) the subordinated creditor's rights of acceleration and enforcement are restricted;

(3) the senior lenders are allowed to advance prior ranking new money if required to address the project's capital requirements;

(4) the senior lenders are permitted to amend their credit agreement and restructure the senior debt without the approval of the subordinated lenders;

(5) the subordinated lenders will agree not to institute insolvency proceedings against the project company; and

(6) the subordinated lenders will agree to cooperate with the senior lenders in any foreclosure or private sale.

Mezzanine debt

3.20 Mezzanine debt provided by third-party, non-equity investors at a higher rate of interest is not a common feature of project finance transactions, but the tightening of liquidity in debt markets following the events of 2008 prompted its appearance in some financing plans. It can be used as a layer of finance between the equity/deeply subordinated debt of the sponsors and senior debt in the capital structure of a project company. Sponsors may look to mezzanine finance to fill a 'financing gap' caused by a shortfall in the amount of senior debt that is available and in the amount of equity that can be raised, or as a way of increasing the leverage of debt to equity. Mezzanine lenders, because they will take and are being remunerated for a greater level of risk, will generally require lower financial cover ratios to be met. This allows an increase in the debt capacity of the project. The project company will have to pay a higher interest rate to compensate the mezzanine lender for its subordination to the senior debt and the mezzanine lender's agreement to finance on comparatively less onerous terms. Mezzanine lenders to project finance transactions expect, at a minimum, consistent interest payments and to share in the security package with the senior debt, but on a subordinated basis. In addition to a relatively high interest rate, the remuneration offered to a mezzanine lender may include an 'up-side' incentive to make a financing sufficiently attractive. Such incentives may be in the form of equity related sweeteners, such as the issuance of cheap stock to the mezzanine lender at the time of the loan, warrants to purchase stock, or rights to call or convert debt to equity at reasonable prices, allowing for up-side potential.

The 'depth' of subordination for both subordinated and mezzanine debt may vary. **3.21** On the one hand, there can be absolute subordination, which precludes, or at least subjects to specific conditions, all payments of principal and interest so long as senior debt is outstanding. This type of debt is generally issued to the sponsors and termed 'deeply subordinated debt'. At the other extreme is subordination that is triggered solely by a bankruptcy proceeding. Between these extremes, there is a wide range of options.

Bank debt

Infrastructure projects have traditionally been financed in the commercial bank **3.22** market, and commercial banks continue to be the main source of project finance debt. In part, this is because commercial banks have substantial experience and appetite for cross-border financings, funding flexibility to manage construction drawdown schedules and multi-currency draws, and the capability to be a positive and responsive force in working with the sponsors to respond to unexpected events affecting a project. The approach of commercial banks is not so different from that in any other form of financing. Many of the large international commercial banks employ a staff of industry and regional experts as well as experienced project financiers. They have the capacity to understand the norms in the industry and appraise the credit risk exposures involved in unusual loan transactions.

Commercial bank loans to a project may involve a single lender, but more typically, **3.23** involve several lenders in a 'club' deal or the loans may be syndicated by one or more arrangers chosen by the sponsors. Project loans are often traded and participated widely, and a number of leading banks have sought to securitize their project loan portfolios. As a result, during the term of the loan the parties exercising voting rights may differ from those who made the original commitment.

Commercial bank loans may take a variety of forms, such as construction, term or **3.24** working capital facilities. The maturity of a term loan rarely exceeds fifteen years, although this may vary from transaction to transaction.[2] Long tenors are less likely to be achievable for riskier projects located in challenging jurisdictions. The loans are generally priced with floating interest rates based on LIBOR (the London Interbank Offered Rate) for US Dollar or Sterling-denominated loans, EURIBOR (the Euro Interbank Offered Rate) for Euro-denominated loans, or similar indices for Yen and other currencies. These interest rate indices are widely used in the syndicated loan markets on the assumption that they approximate most banks' cost of

---

[2] Longer tenors of twenty to twenty-five years have been seen in certain UK PFI projects and tenors of up to twenty years or more were achieved prior to 2008 in certain Middle East power projects.

funding the loans. At times when this assumption is untrue, for example, during financial crises, a customary 'market disruption' clause, which is aimed at ensuring that banks can recover their actual cost of funds, becomes relevant. By comparison, the international bond markets issue and deal predominantly in fixed rate instruments. Commercial banks are required to maintain unallocated capital in reserve against loan exposures, and the ability of banks to extend loans may over time be impaired by increasing capital reserve requirements imposed by central banks and other regulators. The capacity of individual banks may be further affected by that bank's internal country limits or portfolio limits, for example, limits on aggregate exposure to a particular industry sector in the form of limited recourse debt.

3.25 The appetite and experience of international commercial banks to finance a project will in part be determined by the geographical location of the project and their experience in that jurisdiction, the relevant industry, and their relationship with the sponsors. In developing countries, international commercial banks may require political, and sometimes a level of commercial risk coverage provided by the insurance policies of public funding agencies such as ECAs. In such developing countries, local banks are likely to figure prominently in the financing plan. Local banks can play an important role in mitigating certain risks by providing local participation, knowledge of the regulatory system and political environment and local currency financing to provide a natural hedge to currency exposure in the project (for example, a power project in a developing market where the power off-taker has to match its payment obligations with its local currency receipts, but the construction costs and bulk of the financing is denominated in US dollars).

3.26 Commercial banks, whether international or domestic, also often participate in project financings as providers of hedging products. To limit a project's exposure to the risk, for example, of changes in underlying interest rates, the project company may enter into an interest rate swap, cap, collar, or other hedging agreement. Similar hedging arrangements may be put in place to address currency, commodity price, and other risks. The hedging banks' exposure under these arrangements if they were to terminate prior to their term (for example, upon the insolvency of the project company) may be significant, and they will usually require that exposure to be secured *pari passu* with the senior debt.

Islamic project finance

3.27 More than one-fifth of the world's population practices the Islamic faith. In conjunction with the rapid growth in the wealth of many predominantly Muslim Middle Eastern and Asian countries, the project finance market has been affected by an increasing amount of funds from Islamic state-owned investment funds, Islamic financial institutions, and individual Muslims who desire to conduct their commercial and financial activities in accordance with Islamic law. With this increase, Islamic finance has moved from the niche to the mainstream in many project finance markets, particularly in the Middle East, but also in Malaysia and Pakistan.[3]

Capital markets

As discussed in Chapter 9, additional debt financing for a project may be obtained **3.28** in the bond market. Projects have long accessed the bond and commercial paper markets. Standard & Poor's, Moody's and other credit rating agencies regularly rate debt issues by projects. Rating agencies have published details of the criteria they use to rate power and other projects, which are very similar to those used by commercial banks in making their own credit assessments. This significantly expands the sources of capital available to projects by encouraging the participation of investors whose objective is to hold a portfolio of assets without necessarily having to undertake significant due diligence on each investment. Due to the documentary and regulatory burden in effecting a bond issue, its inclusion in a financing plan will commonly be limited to occasions when the cost of funds is significantly lower than the commercial debt market or the search for financing requires that the pool of potential investors has to be as wide as possible.

The investment requirements of insurance companies, pension and mutual funds, **3.29** who often invest through the capital markets, create a deep pool of capital seeking long-term, fixed income assets. Although to date, the vast majority of project bonds have been placed in the US, issuances have also been placed in the European, Asian, and Middle Eastern markets. The participation by a monoline credit insurer in project bond issuances may in some cases enhance access to the market (although these institutions have of late been much less active). A number of government export credit and other official credit agencies have also proposed project bond credit enhancement programmes to help fill the resulting void.

The capital markets have demonstrated an ability to provide attractive economics **3.30** for project financings. Sponsors can more closely match the anticipated life of a project's cashflows using the longer tenors typically available in the bond markets. Sponsors are also attracted by fixed interest rates and the generally less restrictive covenant packages available in the bond market. Large amounts of debt can be raised in a short period of time by relying on exemptions in the US and European securities laws that permit direct sales to institutional investors without a formal regulatory registration process. The capital markets therefore represent a source of funds that, for a project which is properly evaluated and structured, can be competitive with alternative funding sources.

---

[3] A more detailed explanation of the practices and techniques of Islamic finance relating to projects can be found in Chapter 10.

3.31 The depth of the market for a project bond issuance depends in large part on the credit rating given to that issuance. Most issuers seek to achieve an 'investment grade' rating, which is the minimum required level to allow many classes of investors to acquire the bonds. This can be particularly challenging if the sovereign rating of the host country lies below that level. Thus, it is generally only the strongest projects that have ready access to the capital markets. From time to time, market disruptions have resulted in project bond spreads widening and several issues being downgraded, with a number of potential bond deals being cancelled or pushed back to the bank market. Yet, the long-term rationale for using project bonds persists for sponsors that can address the potential structural difficulties of travelling down the capital markets route, some of which are discussed below.

Disclosure

3.32 Securities laws in jurisdictions where project bonds may be sold often require the disclosure, or even display for public inspection, of the material terms of projects agreements. Sponsors and third parties to project agreements may object to disclosure of information they consider to be commercially sensitive.

Waivers and amendments

3.33 Identifying and coordinating all of the bondholders when necessary for consents or waivers can be a challenge if the bonds are widely held. Thus, bond covenants are generally 'looser' than bank covenants, and waivers may automatically be made available where the issuer obtains an affirmation of its credit rating or (in some cases) certifies that the circumstances for which a waiver is sought do not have a material impact on its business or financial projection.

Intercreditor issues

3.34 Integration of a capital markets bond financing for a project with traditional bank debt can present challenges with respect to competing intercreditor interests, particularly in 'work-out' scenarios. Project participants will often find themselves grappling with questions, such as whether credit classes can vote separately in order to exercise remedies and whether all classes should benefit from the same covenants and events of default. However, with the expansion in the number of financings combining both commercial bank and capital markets (and even ECA and Islamic) tranches of debt, there is an emerging consensus as to how these issues should be addressed.

Financing commitment

3.35 The absence of a firm financing commitment by an underwriter up until the time the bond offering is actually priced can be a source of significant uncertainty.

Negative arbitrage

3.36 Capital markets debt, if issued during construction, is generally funded in a single issuance and deposited into an escrow or similar account until required to fund project costs. Interest will accrue on the bonds from the date of issue at a rate which is unlikely to be offset fully by earnings on the escrowed deposit. This is sometimes referred to as 'cost of carry' or 'negative arbitrage'. Thus, capital markets debt may most efficiently be used at a time when proceeds can be applied to significant outstanding project costs or to refinance other debt.

One-time funds

Capital markets are utilized and investors procured on a one-off basis. If arrangers **3.37** of a bond issue agree to arrange a sequential bond issue programme for an issuer, they will do so on an uncommitted basis which is impractical for a project financing unless backed-up by availability of commercial bank debt or implemented as a refinancing of commercial bank debt. The one-time receipt of funds is in contrast to the bank loan market where amounts are drawn over an availability period which in project finance can last a number of years.

Public sector lenders in project financings

The public sector funding sources that provide support to energy, mining, manu- **3.38** facturing, and infrastructure projects around the world comprise four basic categories:

(1) export credit agencies and export and investment insurance agencies;
(2) multilateral agencies;
(3) bilateral and development finance agencies; and
(4) domestic agencies.

Although there are similarities in the agencies' application of credit analysis for **3.39** project financing transactions, the differing development goals of the agencies create unique considerations when contemplating the funding sources for a project.

Export credit finance

Export credit agencies and investment insurance agencies, commonly known as **3.40** ECAs, are typically governmental or quasi-governmental institutions in a variety of guises. Each ECA has a broadly similar objective which is to promote the interests of exporters of goods and services from its home jurisdiction to international markets through the provision of one or more of government-backed loans, guarantees, credits, and insurance. It is the ECAs' primary objective to provide direct support for the national interests of their home countries, which clearly distinguishes them from multilateral financing agencies.

Energy, mining, manufacturing, and infrastructure-related investment in some of **3.41** the less developed regions of the world entail particular political risks that impair the access of these projects to the international capital and commercial debt markets. One of the primary attractions of using ECAs as a funding source is that with their access to diplomatic channels, they are well placed to mitigate certain risks of this nature and thereby facilitate the investment of commercial debt on a co-financing basis. If the project involves the sale of goods and services from the country of origin to a foreign market (or in some cases as further discussed below, the promotion of 'untied' financial investment), the project may satisfy the requirements for ECA participation. Traditionally, the principal cover available to debt and equity investors from export credit agencies has been against political risk; however, most export credit agencies are also prepared to provide more comprehensive guarantees and in some cases, to make direct loans to project companies.

3.42   The slate of products provided by an ECA varies according to the regulations applicable to that ECA, the sector, the structure of the investment and financing, and the country in which the project is located. Typical products include political risk insurance/guarantees, commercial risk insurances/guarantees, interest rate support, and for some ECAs, direct lending on both a 'tied' and 'untied' basis as further described in Chapter 8.

3.43   Within the project finance market, the active ECAs of recent years have included the Export-Import Bank of the United States (US Exim) of the US; Japan Bank for International Cooperation (JBIC) and Nippon Export and Investment Insurance (NEXI) of Japan; Export-Import Bank of Korea (K-Exim) and Korea Trade Insurance Corporation (K-sure) of Korea; COFACE and Direction des Relations Economiques Extérieures of France; Euler Hermes Kreditversicherungs-AG (Hermes) and KfW and its subsidiary IPEX Bank in Germany; and Servizi Assicurativi del Commercio Estero (SACE S.p.A. or simply SACE) of Italy. There is an expectation that non-OECD ECAs, such as the Chinese ECAs, namely the Export Import Bank of China, and China Export & Credit Insurance Corporation (SINOSURE), will increasingly play a more central role in financing, and co-financing with other ECAs, developing country transactions on a project finance basis.

3.44   In addition to the governmental or quasi-governmental export insurance market, there is also a vibrant private export insurance market. The private market is a less liquid market and sponsors may find that sufficient coverage for a commercially acceptable price and tenor may not be available for certain developing country markets.

Multilateral agencies and development finance institutions

3.45   When political risks are significant, or if export content may be insufficient for ECA financing, multilateral or similar regional or national development banks may be instrumental to a sponsor in completing a financing. The social and economic development goals of these agencies may allow them to provide funds when other lenders and investors will not. It is common for these institutions to be 'path-finders' in that they finance the first deals of their kind deals in challenging investment locations.

Multilateral institutions have as one of their primary purposes lending money to **3.46** projects located in the emerging markets. Promoting development and helping host governments legislate in order to create a base of corporate, taxation, and investor laws and regulations to foster international investments are core goals of these institutions. In the project finance context, these development goals do not necessarily mean that the financial terms of the debt offered by these institutions will be on particularly subsidized terms. Development agencies, such as Netherlands Development Finance Company (FMO), Promotion et Participation pour la Coopération Économique (Proparco), German Investment Corporation (DEG) tend to focus their financing in certain regions and like multilateral agencies are capable of participating in many different roles and often in a combination of roles (for example, adviser, equity provider, subordinated/mezzanine debt provider, and senior lender).

In project finance, the participating members of the World Bank group include **3.47** the International Finance Corporation (IFC) and the Multilateral Investment Guarantee Agency (MIGA), which, unlike the International Bank for Reconstruction and Development (IBRD) and the International Development Association (IDA), extend credit principally to non-sovereign borrowers. The IFC promotes growth in the private sector of the economies of developing countries by mobilizing domestic and foreign capital and making loans to private corporations that have projects in such countries. Unlike the World Bank, the IFC does not require direct state support. MIGA provides guarantees against losses caused by non-commercial risks, including currency transfer restrictions, expropriation, war and civil disturbances, and, in same cases, breach of contract.

Other multilateral agencies have similar mandates at the regional level. For exam- **3.48** ple, the European Investment Bank, the African Development Bank, the European Bank for Reconstruction and Development, the Inter-American Development Bank, and the Asian Development Bank each make loans and equity investments and provide technical assistance within the regions to which their respective missions extend. Various individual countries have formed development finance institutions that also regularly participate in private sector financings.

Co-financings of loans among commercial banks and multilateral agencies have **3.49** become standard. The IFC, for example, will in effect syndicate a portion of its loan exposure to commercial banks under its A/B loan structure. In other cases, multilateral agencies and commercial banks will lend side by side. A multilateral lender may not require separate security, but may impose a strict negative pledge and usually will demand to share the benefit of any security taken by the commercial lenders. Further, as in ECA financings, the project may be subject to strict environmental impact assessments and projects must comply with specified guidelines.

Although commercial bank lenders may take substantial comfort from the partici- **3.50** pation of multilateral lending institutions in projects, explicit provisions in the documentation often exclude any inference that the World Bank, MIGA, IFC, or other co-financing agency is acting in a governmental capacity. Indeed, it is likely that commercial banks involved in the project will be required specifically to acknowledge that they have entered into the transaction exercising their own credit judgement and without reliance on the decisions taken by the co-financing agency (similar to the acknowledgement given by the participating banks to an agent bank). Any responsibility or duty on the part of the multilateral agency to the commercial banks is excluded, except for those responsibilities that are expressly set out in the documents.

3.51 For a sponsor, a multilateral or development agency loan may have certain advantages:

(1) As with ECAs, the interest rates tend to be competitive and fixed interest rates may be possible.

(2) The tenor of the financing may be longer than might otherwise be available from the commercial bank market.

(3) The participation of these institutions endorses the credit for other potential lenders and may be a prerequisite for accessing other sources of funds, particularly in jurisdictions with a limited track-record for foreign investment and successful project financing.

(4) A co-financing or complementary financing may be possible with commercial banks.

(5) Funding multiple layers of the capital structure may be possible.

(6) It is generally perceived that these institutions are likely to work with the sponsors to rectify problems in the project as opposed to enforcing over the collateral.

3.52 When considering this source of funding, sponsors need to be mindful of:

(1) the strict compliance required in the fields of environmental and social regulations and non-corrupt practices; and

(2) the potential intercreditor challenges which may be generated by the different policy goals and status of these institutions.

Leveraged and finance lease arrangements

3.53 If a project company or its sponsors cannot utilize the particular tax benefits derived from ownership of the project assets, the financing may be structured as a traditional leveraged lease. Under a lease structure, an equity investor holds legal and tax ownership of the project and leases it to the project company. This structure separates ownership of the project for tax purposes from control over it, thereby enabling the project company to reduce its cost of capital by, in effect, transferring tax benefits to an equity investor. The project company, as lessee of the project, retains the right to the residual cashflow from the project during the term of the lease, after provision for lease rental payments. The lessee often negotiates a purchase option at the conclusion of the lease term.

The typical lessor in a leveraged lease becomes the owner of the leased equipment **3.54** by providing a minority percentage of the capital necessary to purchase the equipment. The lessor borrows, on a non/limited recourse basis, the remainder of the capital and to secure the loan, a first priority collateral interest is provided to the financier over the lease, the lease rental payments, and the equipment. The amortization of the debt will be based off the lease term and principal and interest shall coincide with the rental payments. The intent of a leveraged lease is that the lessor can claim the tax benefits of the leased asset and the residual value notwithstanding that it is providing a certain minority percentage of the capital.

Letters of Intent, Term Sheets, Commitment Letters, and Mandate Letters

Showing interest without a commitment—the letter of intent

A letter of intent (LOI) provides a sponsor with an initial indication of whether a **3.55** lender is interested in the project based on the terms proposed by the sponsor. An LOI may be an alternative to procuring a legal commitment to provide financing, or a precursor to agreeing a more detailed and legally binding commitment in the form of a commitment letter or mandate letter.

Whether an LOI is perceived to provide value will depend on the preferences of **3.56** the project participants. An LOI may be procured for a number of purposes, for example:

(1) as a type of preliminary loan application, where the sponsor and the lender agree on the basic terms for a financing and the sponsor wishes to formalize the expression of interest through an LOI;[4]
(2) to provide evidence to a procuring state authority or other project participants that financing for the project will be available; and
(3) an LOI may be the only form of commitment a financial institution is capable of providing at an early stage in the development of the funding plan, for example, commitments provided by ECAs and development agencies tend to be in the form of a non-legally binding LOI.

The commercial comfort a sponsor may take from receiving an LOI will vary **3.57** according to the type and reputation of the lender, the relationship between the lender and the sponsor, and the internal approval process and due diligence that has

---

[4] The commercial assumption may be that the signing of an LOI implies a moderately higher level of internal approval than would otherwise be the case.

been conducted by the lender prior to the issuance of the LOI. For example, many ECAs only issue an LOI after a certain level of due diligence and a rigorous management approval process, so the fact that an LOI has been issued lends great credibility to a sponsor's expectation that financing will ultimately be available from that institution.

3.58 If an LOI references financing terms and conditions, it will start to look more similar to a commitment letter. The distinguishing factor is that, in an LOI, the lender does not, through the signing of the LOI, intend to legally commit itself to providing funds even on a conditional basis.

The term sheet

3.59 A term sheet provides the terms of the financing in a level of detail which is driven by its intended use, and the requirements and preferences of the lenders and the sponsors.

3.60 A term sheet has a number of uses:

(1) as a proposal of the sponsors to test the debt capacity of a project, whether as a stand-alone document or as part of a preliminary information memorandum (PIM) which will form the basis of a funding competition;[5]

(2) recording the terms and conditions of the financing for the purpose of preliminary approvals of the lenders; and

(3) it may form an attachment to a commitment letter or a mandate letter identifying the terms upon which a lender's commitment or obligation is based.

3.61 Unless the term sheet is a short-form commercial term sheet, the sponsors typically work in conjunction with their advisers, particularly their legal adviser, to prepare the first draft of a term sheet. Term sheets are not intended as legal commitments unless otherwise stated, or attached to a commitment or mandate letter as further discussed in the succeeding paragraphs below.

3.62 There is no firm requirement for a term sheet to be comprehensive (including, for example, fully drafted and exhaustive lists of conditions precedent, representations and warranties, covenants, and events of default).[6] The sponsors may wish to focus the potential lenders'/arranger's attention on the commercial terms and not attempt to assess competing mark-ups of detailed documentary points. However, a number

---

[5] A PIM is prepared by the lead sponsor often in conjunction with its financial and legal advisors and distributed to prospective arrangers or lenders as part of a funding competition. The contents of a PIM for a commercial bank project financing typically contains a description of the project and the key project agreements, an overview of the sector or market for the product, an indicative financing plan, a description of the borrower and the sponsors, and commonly contains an analysis of the risks and a set of financial projections.

[6] A checklist of conditions precedent, representations and warranties, covenants, and events of default typically found in term sheets is set out in Appendix 1.

of sponsors prefer to provide a detailed term sheet in order to streamline the preparation of the financing plan. To facilitate this strategy, the sponsors may pre-appoint lenders' advisers so that the form of term sheet circulated to prospective leaders is based on realistic commercial, legal and tax assumptions.

Commitment letters and mandate letters

Commitment and mandate letters record the relationship of the lender/arranger **3.63** and the borrower/sponsors prior to signing the full-form financing documentation. In the case of many project financings, the selection of lenders and arrangers and agreement of terms is often organized as a competitive bidding process or series of bilateral negotiations with a number of competing financial institutions.

The terms of a lender's individual commitment to fund, and the terms in a mandate **3.64** letter which require a lender to arrange or underwrite an amount in addition to the participation in the facility it intends to retain as its committed amount, will be a product of these negotiations. It is common in a bidding situation for a prospective lender/arranger to be asked to agree the material terms of the commitment or mandate letter in addition to providing its indicative financing terms based on the project and financial information supplied by the sponsors.

The commitment letter

A commitment letter is one form of document under which a lender makes a bind- **3.65** ing offer to its customer to lend money, subject to stated conditions. A commitment may be provided in a number of guises, and may be packaged with other material terms governing the relationship between the sponsors and a lender in the proposed project (for example, if the financial institution will also have a role as an underwriter or arranger of the facility, its commitment will commonly be packaged in the form of a mandate letter as discussed in paragraph 3.69 et seq below).

Not surprisingly, the key element in a commitment letter is the statement of a **3.66** lender's commitment to provide a specified level of participation in a facility. The commitment will be conditional and should be read in conjunction with the conditions that apply. For project finance transactions, where the variables and due diligence are greater than a corporate financing transaction, a project lender may condition its commitment on the basis of further or full due diligence on the underlying project, and that the terms of the commitment are subject to change based on that due diligence and the negotiation of final loan and security documentation. In the commitment letter provisions, this expectation will be translated to the conditions to closing which govern whether, and if so, when, the lender is obliged to fund the relevant facilities. If the project company satisfies the conditions to the commitment, the lender is legally bound to close the financing. The sponsor's interest is in binding the lender to the stated commitment amount on the referenced terms. A description of frequently negotiated exclusions to a lender's commitment is provided in the discussion of mandate letters below.

3.67 The commercial terms of the proposed financing, together with the material representations, covenants, and events of default required in the definitive loan documentation are typically included, often by attaching a form of term sheet to the commitment letter. Many documentary provisions in project finance transactions are customary in nature, but the use of catch-all phrases, such as 'customary in a project financing', can result in subsequent disputes as parties may disagree as to what is actually customary, and it may unnecessarily lengthen future negotiations. The sponsors may be incentivized to provide a detailed term sheet and pre-packaged advisers' reports detailing the results of their due diligence in order to more securely bind a lender to its commitment.

3.68 One of the provisions will contain a date by which the terms of the commitment letter are required to be accepted by the project company, and an expiration date by which all of the lender's conditions to closing must be satisfied. If closing has not occurred by that date, the commitment obligations and the letter will terminate, and the lenders will have no further obligation, absent some action to the contrary, to continue to work towards a closing. From a lender's perspective, it is important for the commitment letter, or an ancillary fee letter, to provide that the lender's costs and expenses remain payable notwithstanding the cancellation of the commitment.

The mandate letter

3.69 As mentioned in the preceding section, a mandate letter records a legally binding relationship between an arranger and the project company/sponsors prior to signing the core financing documentation. A mandate letter has features not found in a commitment letter as the financial institution is agreeing to be responsible for syndicating a portion of the facilities, which may be on a 'best-efforts' basis or by way of an underwriting commitment to fund any participations left unsyndicated by a stated date. A combination of both concepts is also possible and may be termed a partially underwritten commitment.

3.70 The structure of a typical mandate letter would include some or all of the features mentioned in paragraphs 3.71–3.84 below.

3.71 The mandate letter will provide for appointment of, and for reasons primarily related to the marketing requirements of the relevant financial institutions, the title of the participants (for example, mandated lead arranger, underwriter, and bookrunner).

3.72 Any restrictions on the sponsors appointing, awarding titles to or agreeing to terms and fees with other financial institutions will be included. The arrangers will not want to expend time in furtherance of the financing plan if the sponsors have the ability to exclude them from the financing of the relevant facility. The arranger will also wish to ensure a level playing-field so that it is not disadvantaged when approaching the syndication market to find participants.

3.73 The obligations and levels of commitment the arranger assumes typically range from a 'best-efforts' commitment to arrange the syndication to a commitment to fully underwrite the facilities and thereby assume the risk of having to take-up the unsyndicated funding commitment on its own balance sheet. The degree of commitment and the terms of any conditionality to those commitments are the fundamental provisions of the mandate letter.

If the facilities are underwritten, the portion which is underwritten will be stated. **3.74** If the arranger is under a 'best-efforts' obligation, the intended hold amount of the arranger will be recorded, with the remainder made up of the portion of the facilities it is obliged to syndicate on a 'best-efforts' basis. In the wake of the financial crisis of 2008, the number of underwriting commitments in project finance transactions was dramatically reduced. This was a reflection of the lack of confidence of arrangers in their syndication capability at such time, due to the lack of new-lending and the limited liquidity in the secondary markets.

Any carve-outs to the commitment of the arranger will be recorded, including an **3.75** exclusion if a material adverse change (MAC) occurs in relation to the project or the financial health of specified major project participants, or any MAC occurs in the relevant syndicated loan or other credit markets. As a key provision for negotiation in any commitment letter or mandate letter, the MAC clause is further considered in paragraph 3.85 et seq. A condition requiring the completion of full-form documentation is common, however, the sponsors will wish to confine its scope to completion of documentation on commercial and financial terms attached in the form of a term sheet to the mandate letter. Extending the conditionality to the satisfactory conclusion of due diligence is not uncommon but on its face, from a sponsor's perspective, provides an uncomfortably wide level of flexibility to the arrangers. Breaches by the project company or the sponsors of the material terms of the mandate letter is another customary condition which may give the arranger a right to terminate the mandate letter. Sponsors will be well advised to be as specific as possible as to the scope of the conditions; and may be incentivized to provide to prospective arrangers, pre-packaged due diligence reports from advisers appointed on behalf of the lenders. Whether the mandate letter is governed by English or New York law, prudent arrangers should not treat conditions expressed as 'completion of satisfactory due diligence' or 'subject to final board approvals' as unfettered rights to withdraw from their commitment.

Subject to the extremes of the financial markets, mandate letters for project financ- **3.76** ings commonly include 'market flex' terms, whereby the commercial pricing, and potentially other important terms of the financing, may be amended by the arranger to the extent necessary to achieve a successful syndication. Further discussion of market flex, together with an example of a lender's starting point for a market flex provision, is further considered below.[7]

---

[7] Market flex is discussed below in paragraph 3.101 et seq.

3.77 Clear market provisions are also a standard feature in a mandate letter and are designed to regulate competing approaches to the relevant debt market to raise finance which may adversely affect the chances of a successful syndication or increase the costs for an arranger to successfully syndicate its portion of the facility.

3.78 'Front-running' restrictions may apply so that each arranger agrees not to take actions to encourage any person to take an interest in the facilities prior to an agreed date in order that the arrangers' approach to the market is coordinated.

3.79 References to the obligation to pay costs, expenses, boiler plate language in respect of payments (including make-whole provisions in respect of taxes), and non-reliance provisions are also typically included in a mandate letter. The timing of payment of upfront fees in project finance transactions (which may be documented in a separate fee letter) is often an issue for discussion as sponsors usually prefer to delay payment from signing of the finance documentation to first drawdown. Arrangers commonly ask sponsors to credit-enhance the project company's obligation to pay fees (although not always successfully).

3.80 A non-disclosure provision is often included to prevent the project company from revealing the arranger's confidential pricing and terms.

3.81 Provisions regulating the process for the acceptance and allocation of participations may be included; however, in practice, an arranger will have a level of discretion in terms of the amount of the participations and distribution of a portion of its fees to other lenders who join in syndication.

3.82 The sponsors usually agree to assist the arranger with the preparation of any information memorandum which will be provided to potential syndicate participants, and to contribute management personnel and time to any syndication road-show, etc.

3.83 Representations are made by the sponsors as to the accuracy and completeness of the information provided, and an indemnity will be included, for the benefit of the arranger, against any liability or cost arising out of the arrangement, use of the facilities or entering into the mandate and financing documents.

3.84 Termination provisions are often negotiated in some depth and the arranger is usually able to terminate the letter if the project company and/or a sponsor has withheld information material to its decision to arrange, manage, or underwrite the facilities, or if a stated condition to its obligations is not achieved. The letter will terminate if the project company does not take up the offer by a stated date.

Material adverse change

3.85 A MAC clause may be required by a lender under a commitment letter, or by an arranger underwriting a commitment, so that it can decline to close the financing if a MAC occurs, or can renegotiate the terms of the financing. In the latter situation, there may be a certain amount of overlap with the market flex provision in a mandate letter, however, the triggers for invoking the provision have subtle but important differences.

A MAC clause in the context of a commitment to participate or underwrite may, **3.86** for discussion purposes, be divided into two, a business MAC and a market MAC:

(1) The business MAC focuses on:

 (i) the financial health of the project company, and may extend to other major project participants, which will include the sponsors, contractors or offtakers, etc.;

 (ii) the ability of the project to be constructed in accordance with the construction plan;

 (iii) matters affecting the expected coverage under the financial ratios, key project documents or the available collateral package; and

 (iv) the project itself.

(2) As the name implies, the market MAC looks primarily at adverse conditions in the relevant debt markets (and depending on the financing structure, the capital markets) and for projects in emerging markets, the ability of the relevant project company to continue accessing the international markets.

The interests of a lender in allowing flexibility not to fund or extract itself from its **3.87** underwriting commitment are directly opposite to the interests of the sponsors in binding the lender to provide the conditionally committed financing.

A sample MAC clause

A typical London market lenders' starting point for a market and business MAC **3.88** condition to a bank's commitment to arrange or underwrite a corporate financing might read as follows:

> The obligations of each Mandated Lead Arranger and each Bookrunner under the Mandate Documents are subject to the absence, in its opinion, of any event(s) or circumstance(s) (including any material adverse change or the continuation of any circumstance(s)) which, in its opinion, has (have) adversely affected or could adversely affect:
>
> (a) the business, condition (financial or otherwise), operations, performance, assets or prospects of [any Obligor] [since the date as at which [its latest / the latest consolidated] audited financial statements were prepared];
>
> (b) [the ability of the Company or any other Obligor to perform its obligations under any Mandate Document or Facility Document;] or
>
> (c) the international or any relevant domestic syndicated loan [, debt, bank, capital or equity] market(s) [which in the opinion of the relevant Bookrunner could prejudice Syndication], during the period from the date of [this letter / the Term Sheet] to the date of signing of the Facility Documents.[8]

---

[8] Sample taken from the Loan Markets Association form of mandate letter entitled, 'Mandate Letter—Best Endeavours'.

3.89 In the project financing context, paragraph (a) of each sample provision is commonly adapted to refer to the business and prospects set out in the Financial Model since the project company in a green-field development will be a special purpose vehicle with no trading history and limited assets.

3.90 A typical New York market lenders' starting point is similar:

> The arranger's commitment hereunder is subject to:
>
> (a) the absence of (A) any material adverse change in the [business, financial condition or operations] [or prospects,] of the borrower since __, ____, and (B) any circumstance, change or condition (including the continuation of any existing condition) in the loan syndication, financial or capital markets generally that, in the judgment of the arranger, could reasonably be expected to materially impair syndication of the facility;
>
> (b) the accuracy and completeness of all representations that the borrower makes to the arranger and all information that the borrower furnishes to arranger; [and]
>
> (c) the borrower's compliance with the terms of this Commitment Letter, including, without limitation, the payment in full of all fees, expenses and other amounts payable under this Commitment Letter.

Issues for consideration

3.91 For a lender or an arranger, a key goal of the drafting of the conditionality to a commitment letter or mandate letter is to mitigate the risk that it may remain liable for its commitment in circumstances where it did not expect to be. Borrowers and sponsors are similarly incentivized to have predicable interpretation of the MAC provision to avoid unexpected losses of anticipated or underwritten funding commitments, and would commonly expend great effort in negotiating as narrow a definition as possible, particularly in underwritten financings.

3.92 Litigation in the US has provided lenders and underwriters with indications of the potential treatment by courts of MAC clauses, but there continues to be debate among market participants. Across the Atlantic, in England, there is limited judicial authority in the English courts which leaves a myriad of untested arguments potentially available to an aggrieved borrower.

3.93 Each sponsor and arranger will need to consider the matters mentioned in paragraphs 3.94 through 3.100 below.

3.94 How it wishes to treat pre-existing and known circumstances: absent specific drafting, it will be difficult for the arranger, and against the borrower's expectations, to invoke the condition on the basis of such adverse circumstances.

3.95 The intended criteria for determining whether a MAC has occurred, particularly in respect of known conditions, for example, if there is a pre-existing condition, is the commercial understanding that the materiality determination be made in the context of the state of the deteriorated market or business condition. It should also be clarified whether only an incremental additional deterioration may be deemed material. For example:

> The arranger may not invoke this [MAC] paragraph solely with respect to event(s), development(s) or circumstance(s) which are generally known to be in existence on the date of this letter in the absence of any change (including worsening) therein,

or, the reverse:

> It is understood and agreed by each of the parties hereto that circumstance(s) and condition(s) in [state market conditions or business conditions] referred to above have deteriorated significantly prior to the date of this letter and that therefore even a small further change or worsening of such circumstance(s) or condition(s) or the occurrence of new event(s), development(s) or circumstance(s) that might not otherwise be regarded as materially and adversely affecting such markets could be materially adverse to such [state markets or business conditions] in the context of the transactions contemplated by this letter.

In many cases, at the time a commitment letter is signed, a bank does not expect to **3.96** be able to withdraw its commitment on the basis of pre-existing circumstances, i.e. absent any adverse change. Accordingly, the other changes above to the MAC provision are designed to achieve a solution which may be acceptable to a borrower, whilst preserving the bank's rights in case of a further deterioration.

An arranger would commonly seek to extend the market MAC wording to contem- **3.97** plate adverse changes to the ability of that borrower to continue to access the international markets. For projects with a strong nexus to developing countries, an arranger may also suggest to the borrower that adverse changes in the political risks faced by the project in relevant countries can constitute a MAC.

For certain projects, an arranger may wish to specifically contemplate within the **3.98** business MAC, adverse movements in the price of key supply materials or offtake prices, if supply and market price risk is not assumed by a participant other than the borrower; however, the borrower may argue this is already sufficiently addressed by the traditional business MAC wording.

In making a determination of whether a MAC has occurred, in the New York law **3.99** context, a general duty of good faith is applicable which would not be imposed under English contract law. However, where a determination is crucial as to whether or not the bank will be obliged to perform its principal obligation, for example, under a commitment letter (i.e. to lend), an English court is likely to require that such a determination be made on a *bona fide* basis.

Parties should be aware of the potential for pre-contractual statements and negotia- **3.100** tions about the MAC clause being relevant to a determination as to the invocation of the clause. An arranger may be well advised to consider a robust 'entire agreement' clause, for example:

> Subject to any fraudulent misrepresentation, the borrower acknowledges that it has not relied on, or been induced to enter into the Mandate Documents by, any

representation, warranty, collateral contract or other assurance other than those (if any) expressly set out in the Mandate Documents [and any other documents incorporated into the Mandate Documents] made by or on behalf of any other party before the date of the Mandate Documents. The borrower waives all rights and remedies that, but for this clause, might otherwise be available to it with respect to any such representation, warranty, collateral contract or other assurance.

Market flex provision

3.101 As pervades each aspect of the creation of the financing plan and the decisions to be made as to the sourcing of funds, the state of the financial markets, in this case the relevant syndicated debt market, has to a large part driven the acceptability of, and coverage of, market flex provisions in mandate letters. During the run up to the 2007/2008 crisis, arrangers' attention was focused on winning mandates in a very competitive lending market. The high levels of liquidity in the debt markets, including for project financed assets, allowed arrangers to gain favour with borrowers in bidding scenarios by pairing back or entirely deleting provisions designed to protect syndication strategies, including the market flex and clear market protections. The collapse in liquidity that followed the financial crisis resulted in lenders giving acute attention to these provisions. Market flex and clear market provisions, contemporaneous with a dearth of underwritten as opposed to 'best efforts' commitments, once again became embedded into mandates for international, and a large proportion of wholly domestic US and UK, project financings. Exceptions can be identified in the project finance market, but these tend to be only with respect to highly active, strong investment grade sponsors with an ability to bring to bear a wealth of corporate banking influence on their project finance banking relationships.

3.102 Whenever the economic background increases the likelihood of arrangers having to invoke market flex provisions due to thin syndication markets and unpredictable credit committees of potential lenders, sponsors and arrangers alike will focus great attention on the coverage of the provision. Although there are many forms of market flex provisions in use, a sample lenders' starting point assuming an arranging group may read as follows:

> During the period from the date of [this letter / the Term Sheet] to the date, following close of Syndication, on which all the Syndication Lenders become party to the Facility Documents, the Majority Bookrunners shall be entitled, after consultation with the Mandated Lead Arrangers [and the Company] [for a maximum period of [ ] days], to change the pricing, terms and/or structure [(but not the total amount)] of the Facility/ies if the Majority Bookrunners determine that such changes are advisable in order to enhance the prospects of a successful Syndication.[9]

---

[9] Sample taken from the Loan Markets Association form of mandate letter entitled, 'Mandate Letter—Best Endeavours'.

A successful syndication will commonly be defined as the arranger achieving a **3.103** stated amount of subscriptions or the underwriter reducing its participation to a pre-agreed level. The mandate letter should be clear whether syndication is a single-step syndication, or if more than one step, whether the syndication referred to is a primary syndication where additional co-arrangers will be added, or runs through to a general syndication to the initial lending base of the facility.

A number of themes in the negotiations are often encountered, in particular those **3.104** mentioned in paragraphs 3.105–3.107 below.

Which parts of the commercial terms of the referenced facility are subject to 'flex'—a **3.105** sponsor will prefer a narrow scope as by the end of primary syndication or general syndication, as the case may be, significant expenditure may have been incurred by the sponsor and there will be limited scope to renegotiate a reallocation of risk or pricing to any other project participant. Many sponsors will seek to clarify that neither the total amount of the facility nor the amount of on-balance sheet sponsor support can be amended since the total equity amount required and the extent of the balance sheet support for the limited recourse financing will be fundamental parts of their existing corporate authorities to continue with the transaction. The sponsors may negotiate to confine the application to 'pricing' flex, and perhaps within certain caps in order to avoid the erosion of the required return on equity of the sponsors. The ability to 'flex' the 'structure' will raise a concern from the sponsors that the required changes may unravel what is likely to be a highly structured risk allocation between the project participants. Amendments to the 'terms' raise the spectre for the sponsors that major commercial terms, such as the draw-down conditions, financial ratio coverage, amortization profile, reserve amounts, or conditions to releasing sponsor distributions, may change.

Whether it is a subjective determination of the arranger to invoke the clause, with **3.106** or without consultation with the sponsors, or whether there is an objective element to the trigger right—unlike the MAC clause, it is unusual for an arranger to have to show an objective problem arising in the financial markets since the date of the commitment is given; if any reference is made to the state of the financial markets it will be to the 'condition' at such time, without requiring any comparative deterioration. A sponsor may feel aggrieved at this standard formulation if the arranger has been permitted to actively test the market appetite for the facility at the time of entering into the mandate, but the point is rarely conceded by an arranger who is seeking a requirement for market flex.

Whether the benchmark is a standard more challenging than 'advisable in order to **3.107** enhance the prospects of a successful syndication'—it is rare for sponsors to persuade the arrange to materially raise this low and unspecific evidentiary hurdle.

The question as to whether a flex provision is included or not remains a matter of **3.108** negotiation, however, the arranger will be well aware that the sponsors' expectation, even if included, will be that the arranger would only call on the flex terms as a last resort. This will be particularly acute if the definition of successful syndication extends past the signing of the finance documents, which will commonly mean the vast majority of material project contracts will also have been finalized by virtue of their signing. Since the sponsors will have projected their own return on equity based on the debt terms committed by the arranger, it is not surprising that the sponsors will likely be resistant to attempts by the arranger to invoke a market flex provision.

4

PROJECT RISKS

John Dewar and Oliver Irwin, Milbank, Tweed, Hadley & McCloy LLP

General Overview

Introduction to project risks

The business of project financing is founded upon the identification, assessment, **4.01** allocation, negotiation, and management of the risks associated with a particular project. Indeed, as project finance lenders look to the revenues generated by the operation of the financed project for the source of funds from which that financing will be repaid, the whole basis for project financing revolves around an understanding of the future project revenues and the impact of various risks upon them.

Projects face a variety of risks, and not all of these risks can be easily identified. One **4.02** power developer has said that his projects, on average, are documented through 30,000 pages of tightly drawn contracts, but they inevitably face difficulties never contemplated by the draftsmen. Risk cannot always be mitigated or contracted away, but it can be assessed, allocated, and managed so that it is commercially reasonable. The first step is to identify the material risks and the second is to decide how they should be addressed.

Risk Identification—Due Diligence

4.03 A project's value is based principally on its ability to generate revenue during its operating phase. Therefore, both the sponsors and the lenders require assurances that the project is technically and economically feasible and that it will be built and operated according to the agreed specifications and in compliance with the laws and regulations of all relevant governmental authorities. This can be determined initially by having a competent technical adviser undertake a feasibility study. Such a study should address a number of issues, including:

(1) whether the facility can be constructed and operated within the projected budgets;

(2) whether the project company has the requisite skills and experience to operate and maintain the project;

(3) the acceptability of the facility site;

(4) the environmental and social impact of the project;

(5) the availability and cost of utilities such as gas, water, electricity, and waste treatment and disposal; and

(6) whether the project can meet the terms and conditions of operating licenses, environmental approvals, and construction permits.

4.04 The technical adviser is typically the primary consultant responsible for analysing the viability of design, engineering, and other related technical issues. It is not, however, the only expert whose opinion will be solicited. In the case of power plants, fuel consultants may assess the pricing and feasibility of the project's fuel supply and transportation arrangements. In the case of mining or oil and gas projects, experts may be called upon to assess the adequacy of dedicated resource reserves. Insurance, environmental, geotechnical, and, in some cases, security experts, among others, may also be called upon to address significant issues of concern to the lenders. Where the project's output is to be sold onto a market without the benefit of long-term sales contracts, an evaluation of the market projections by a qualified consultant may be required.[1] An auditor may also be retained to validate the project's Financial Model.

4.05 Legal counsel, often in conjunction with the technical and other advisers, will review the project's contractual structure to assess the proposed allocation among

---

[1] In the power sector, this would apply to uncontracted or part-contracted merchant power plants. Many petrochemical and refinery projects also sell their products through marketing agreements rather than firm off-take contracts. Some liquefied natural gas (LNG) projects sell their LNG under sale and purchase contracts which may provide for volume off-take, but pricing is linked to a gas market bench mark such as, in the US, Henry Hub. Concession based projects, such as certain toll roads, bridges, tunnels, and airports may also be heavily reliant on consumer linked demand for all or a proportion of their revenue stream.

the project's participants of the principal construction, operating, and other risks identified through the due diligence process and to identify the residual risks remaining with the project company.

The lenders will also conduct their own due diligence process, ensuring that such **4.06** matters as their assessment of the credit standing of each key project participant or of the overall political risk associated with the project are properly considered.

General Issues For All Projects

Completion risk

Completion risk, also known as development, delay, cost-overrun, or construction risk, **4.07** addresses the possibility that the project will not be constructed on time, on budget, or to the required specifications. A project finance lender's focus on completion risk is understandable, since the project company's cashflow is all (or predominantly) outgoing during the construction or pre-completion stage and its security over the project assets is of limited (or no) value before the project is completed.

The degree of completion risk inherent in a project is a function of three factors: **4.08**

(1) the level of technical risk involved in the project (projects with simple and well-proven designs and technical requirements carry lower risks);
(2) the technical capability and financial strength of the construction contractor; and
(3) the level of guarantees and sureties provided by the construction contractor or other third parties and their respective capacity to perform under those obligations.

Construction contract structures

In a number of projects, completion risk is allocated to a contractor through a 'turn- **4.09** key' construction contract. In such an agreement, the contractor undertakes to build a fully operational facility for a fixed (subject to limited exceptions) price by a specified date certain.

Where the market for construction work is competitive, with enormous costs **4.10** and great attention to bidding detail, when tenders are called for projects, a pre-committed project financing package[2] will often be required by the relevant procuring authority. In many sectors a turnkey construction contract by itself will

---

[2] Bid packages submitted by sponsors to procuring authorities or utilities customarily include a complete technical package detailing the design and engineering specifications, full form project contracts or detailed term sheets and a fully (or as has been the case during the 'credit crunch') a partially underwritten financing of the project by the relevant lenders.

be accepted by banks for known sponsors, familiar equipment and systems, and safe locations without further sponsor support for delay or cost overruns.[3] These structures are commonly seen in the context of independent power projects (IPPs) and a number of public private partnerships (PPPs).

4.11 In many project financings, however, contractors are not willing to build projects on a turnkey basis at a commercially acceptable price because there may be too many risks (including the reliability of the local work force, 'local content' requirements, political instability, import restrictions and customs controls, or commodity price instability) to enable the contractor to have confidence that the project can be built for a specified price. In other projects, including in many process industries, the various components to be constructed are distinct, with significant differences in the required skills and technology, and thus no single contractor can provide the full range of technology or skills required to construct the project. In such instances, it may only be possible for a project financing to proceed with some form of completion support.[4]

4.12 Construction contracts should be structured to incentivize timely completion and include appropriate liquidated damages for delay. The construction expertise and credit quality of the main contractors will of course be an important factor in considering completion risk. Multinational scale of operating capacity (for large projects), previous experience with the technology and the type of project, as well as experience in the country where the project is located, are all desirable. 'Name' recognition will often play a large part in a project finance lender's assessment of completion risk. Certain construction companies (and sponsors) have excellent track records in project delivery and their involvement in a project will be likely to be regarded as lowering completion risk.[5]

Completion guarantees

4.13 To avoid the incurrence of a 'turnkey' premium that might render the project uneconomic, completion risk may be directly assumed by either the sponsors or a government entity (or both) through completion guarantees issued to the lenders. These guarantees may be limited to ensuring physical completion of the project or may extend, for example, to ensuring the maintenance of all financial projections at the time of completion, or even a full repayment of all project financing debt in the event completion is not achieved by an agreed date certain.

---

[3] For example, for over a decade, power and water procuring authorities in a number of countries have had great success in tendering for power and/or water desalination plants in the Middle East, Asia, Latin America, and elsewhere. These have included highly successful programmes tendered in Abu Dhabi, Saudi Arabia, Oman, and Bahrain.

[4] See para. 4.13.

[5] For more analysis of the participant risk associated with construction contracts, see Chapter 2 and for more analysis as to how completion risk may be allocated under a construction contract and the minimum requirements for construction contract bankability, see Chapter 5.

Delay risk

There are many factors that could delay the scheduled completion of a project, **4.14** including the strength and experience of the contractors, the length of the projected construction period, the availability of building material and supplies, the terrain over which the project is being constructed, the risk of not receiving permits as and when required, the exposure to labour problems, the connection of required infrastructure, dispute resolution, and political risks. Many of these risk factors will also have cost implications for the project.

Cost overruns

In assessing the risk of compliance with the project budget and the incurrence of **4.15** cost overruns, the project company may consider advance placement of orders for commodities necessary for construction (such as steel) or equipment which can lower the likely project costs, or even commodity hedging arrangements. In recent experience, commodity markets have been extremely volatile and these strategies can significantly reduce the risk of cost overruns where, for example, an engineering, procurement, and construction management (EPCM)[6] (rather than a turnkey) contracting structure is proposed. Similarly, to mitigate cost overrun risk, lenders may require that a certain amount of cost overrun support is procured by the project company either by way of allocated debt facilities and/or equity contribution commitments from the sponsors.

Technology risk

Technology risk will contribute to the overall matrix of both completion and **4.16** operating risks. Problems with the application of the proposed technology during construction may contribute to delays in completion and, during operation, may result in lower performance, leading to diminished operational cashflows. The completion risk for projects that employ proven technology is considered lower, particularly if proven in similar terrain, climate, and scale.

A good example of relatively high technology risk can be found in the field of telecoms **4.17** projects, which by their technical nature require very expensive sophisticated equipment and software that is often new to the market. The technology underpinning such projects is constantly evolving and, because such projects will involve the connecting of many points to fashion a network, they generally require a large amount of equipment often from several different sources which gives rise to compatibility risk.

In the growing offshore wind sector, where contractors have been reluctant to pro- **4.18** vide EPCM turnkey wraps, lenders have had to analyse carefully the new techniques used for piling and constructing the civil works which support the turbine towers and this has necessitated the structuring of appropriate completion support.

---

[6] See para. 5.27 et seq.

4.19 While the risks associated with unproven technology are largely self-evident, even proven technology used on an unprecedented scale, can significantly increase project risk. For example, in the petrochemicals and refinery sectors, scale-ups of more than 25 per cent over and above existing and proven facilities may be the cause of concern to lenders, unless the technical evidence is very persuasive.

4.20 There are a number of ways in which operational phase technology risks can be managed and minimized. A contractor skilled in the operation of the relevant technology may be appointed as the operator under an operation and maintenance contract or other operational support can be contracted from an established technology provider. A sponsor, or the party supplying the relevant goods or services, may guarantee a certain performance level from the relevant technology. Failure to achieve such performance level may result in liquidated damages becoming payable by that party. Alternatively, guarantees may be given to cover any shortfall in operational cashflows resulting from technology failure. These types of involvement by a manufacturer or operator, either operationally or through warranties or guarantees, are particularly positive if supported by appropriate financial capacity.

4.21 Where technology risks exist, lenders are likely to place reliance on the opinions of an independent engineer, who will likely be required to confirm, prior to the lenders committing to finance, that the project can be completed to the required standards on the basis of a reasonable completion test.

Completion testing

4.22 The conditions to end any pre-completion support required by the lenders are customarily set forth in the finance documents in a completion test, or through some progressive release mechanism. Usually, post-completion, the lenders expect to rely on the project's ability to perform, which can be demonstrated through a reliability test run. When such testing is completed, the performance risk is usually mitigated through manufacturers' and/or contractors' warranties for a specified period after the commencement of operations.

Off-take (revenue) risk

4.23 The revenue that a project can generate will underpin its cashflows. The key risk to revenue generation is that, over the life of the project, the demand for its output will diminish or that the price it can achieve for its output will be reduced, whether by other, less costly suppliers entering the market, or a particular off-taker deciding to reduce its purchases.

4.24 For that reason, the off-take contract may be central to the financeability of a project. A long-term sales contract with an entity that has an acceptable credit standing, extending for at least the term of a project's loans, may offer a level of assurance to lenders in respect of these 'market' risks. Particularly where there is only one or perhaps a few off-takers, the credit strength of that party or parties will be a key consideration. If a government owns or controls an off-taker which itself lacks an acceptable credit standing, it may be necessary that the government itself guarantee or otherwise assure the off-taker's performance under the contract.

Off-take arrangements can range from availability or capacity-based revenue struc- **4.25**
tures, which afford higher predictability of cashflows (i.e. projects in respect of which the market risk has been contracted), to arrangements where revenues are a function of volume and/or the price of the output, where cashflows will be less predictable (i.e. in respect of which the project is taking market risk).[7]

Typically, availability based payment structures appear in the context of projects **4.26**
entered into by one or a limited number of procurers (for example, in Private Finance Initiative (PFI) social infrastructure, such as school and hospital projects, or power projects in markets which have yet to be deregulated). Such projects are often less exposed to demand risk. Generally, take-or-pay agreements or some other form of arrangement with limited conditionality (such as an availability payment under a concession agreement) will provide a high degree of comfort in respect of off-take risk.

In the case of power purchase agreements, for example, the tariff will often comprise **4.27**
a capacity and an energy charge. The capacity charge is generally sized to cover fixed charges (such as debt service, equity return, fixed operating charges, taxes, insurance premiums, and administrative overheads), while the energy charge covers the variable operating costs and fuel charges. Other tariff structures may combine the two components into a single unitary charge (often with a minimum purchase obligation) and others may reflect a cost reimbursement or pass-through structure.[8]

Many projects operate in markets in which long-term sales contracts are not avail- **4.28**
able at economic prices. Petrochemicals, natural resources, oil and gas, telecoms, and, in some cases, electric power, are often sold on spot or short-term markets. These markets may be mature and deep, providing assurance that the project's output can be marketed. However, projects operating in these markets are likely to face significant price instability in response to market conditions. The project's ability to withstand market volatility will determine its ability to raise financing and lenders will expect projects with significant market risk to have the capacity to survive tougher 'sensitivity' analysis in the Financial Model than those without such exposure. Market forecasts will be essential, which may be supported by historical information, if relevant, and such projects may require significant levels of equity or contingent equity support or funded reserves. Financing documentation for these types of projects may also contemplate flexible repayment profiles, with

---

[7] For example, this may be the case in mining, petrochemical, refinery, telecom, and some infrastructure projects.

[8] For further analysis as to how market risk may be contracted either completely or partially under sales contracts, see Chapter 5.

provision for some principal repayment deferment, as well as, in certain cases, debt prepayment requirements during periods where revenues exceed the original projections. Project companies may seek flexibility to enter into a wide variety of short and medium term sales contracts to allow them to manage market conditions. Issues which need to be considered in this regard include the applicable regulatory environment, the reliability of access to the market, and the transparency of pricing.

4.29 An example of how the regulatory environment can drastically impact upon market risk, is illustrated by the introduction of the New Energy Trading Arrangement (NETA) in the UK in 2001, which intensified competition between electricity generators, leading to a collapse in merchant power prices as it became clear there was too much supply in the market. Following the introduction of NETA, the existing off-take agreements between the distributors and generators had to be renegotiated, which raised a number of issues. Under the previous pooling and settlement system, generators would hedge against price volatility through 'contracts for differences', referencing the universal pool price. However, under NETA, such hedging was no longer effective and agreement had to be reached between the distributors and generators themselves. With wholesale prices in free-fall, long-term power purchase and tolling agreements were no longer commercially sustainable. These regulatory changes in the UK placed considerable stress on a number of project financed power plants, which resulted in lenders becoming very circumspect about financing power projects on a partial or uncontracted basis.

Operating risk

4.30 Operating risk includes the possibility that:

(1) the cost of operating and maintaining the project will exceed budgeted forecasts;
(2) the facility will be unable to perform consistently at a level sufficient to meet the required performance criteria; and/or
(3) the project's operation will be interrupted by the acts or omissions of the operator.

4.31 The operator must have the financial and technical expertise to operate the project in accordance with the cost and production specifications that form the basis of the project's original feasibility study. The necessary skills extend not only to routine operations, but also to undertaking or supervising major overhauls of complex equipment (which may be separately contracted to the relevant equipment supplier). The operator may be an independent company or an affiliate of one of the sponsors. The ability to operate the project efficiently and effectively is usually evidenced by past experience with the same type of project and technology, ideally in the same country and region, together with adequate resources, such as appropriately qualified staff.

Although operators generally resist underwriting the full operating risk of a project, **4.32** a well-structured operating agreement will provide sufficient incentives to ensure compliance with industry standards of performance. So, for example, contracts which appear underpriced may be regarded unfavourably by lenders as this might lead to delay or reduced expenditure on repairs and maintenance. To the extent that the operator does assume at least some material portion of the risk of operational cost overruns, the sponsors and the lenders will be able to place greater reliance on the certainty of the project's financial projections.

In addition to skilled operators, a good management team is crucial to the success **4.33** of a project. The management personnel are required to make basic policy decisions, arrange financing, provide information to lenders and investors, and take responsibility for administrating the project company. The management must also control the ability of the project to maintain production levels and to comply with legal and regulatory requirements. Thus, the management team needs to be experienced, reliable and serve as a bridge among the sponsors, the operator, the government authorities, and the lenders.

Supply risk

A project's inputs or supply requires just as much investigation as its off-take. The **4.34** particular supply risks which will apply to a project will be determined by the nature of the project itself. For example, a toll road project will depend upon sufficient traffic; telecoms projects will require handsets; water projects will depend upon sufficient water supply; oil and gas and mining projects must have sufficient reserves; a processing plant must have sufficient raw materials and energy; and a power project must have sufficient fuel.

Each project must have a guaranteed and steady supply of feedstock, fuel, or other **4.35** necessary resources at a cost that does not significantly exceed the provision for those costs in the project's financial forecasts.

To enable the project to access those materials, it is often necessary that new pipe- **4.36** line, rail, or road infrastructure be constructed, generally by parties other than the project company. The risk that the necessary infrastructure will not be completed in a timely manner must also be addressed.

The choice of materials or fuel gives rise to various concerns in respect of supply and **4.37** transportation. For example, if a power facility is gas-fired, adequate reserves of gas must be available and sufficient pipeline capacity must exist to satisfy transportation needs during the entire term of the financing. Many gas-fired power facilities have the capability to burn oil on a temporary basis, so that if gas becomes temporarily unavailable due to the occurrence of a *force majeure* or other event, the project will be able to continue operating until supply is restored. However, to the extent that the project relies on a single source of supply, as may be the case, for example, with plants fuelled by LNG sourced from abroad, the lenders will focus attention on the political or technical risk of the project's LNG sources.

4.38 For projects that are extracting and/or processing oil and gas or other natural resources, the lenders will focus particular attention on the sufficiency of the relevant reserves. The inquiry focuses both on the extent of the resource in the ground and also on whether it is economically recoverable. Volumes of resource are generally classified in accordance with the degree of uncertainty associated with their existence. The level of uncertainty is highest before the prospect is bored or drilled, and is reduced with the increase in data available as the resource area is mapped and assessed. A reserves audit report may provide a comprehensive tabulation of volumes at any stage of exploration or development, assigning appropriate risk classifications to the existence of those volumes.

4.39 The other variable, relevant to oil and gas reserves, is whether they can economically be recovered. When commodity prices are high, the project company can afford to extract higher cost resources. When prices are low, reserves that are physically available may nonetheless prove uneconomic to exploit.

4.40 Lenders naturally prefer to finance oil and gas projects with sufficient proven, economically recoverable reserves. Although probable or possible reserves may be accorded value, these reserves are given less weight and lenders may require a significant margin of such reserves over the life of the project. In most cases, lenders will require a 'reserve tail', providing assurance that sufficient levels of resource will remain available to be exploited beyond the scheduled maturity of the debt. Lenders may require accelerated repayments (i.e. cash sweeps) if such probable or possible reserves are not converted to proven status at the rate anticipated in the exploitation plan or if reserves are no longer appropriately classified either due to technical or economic criteria. Lenders may also require accelerated repayments of the debt if the reserve is exploited by the project company at a faster or higher rate than was originally forecast in the financial model, so as to avoid debt remaining outstanding should the relevant reserves become depleted.

Currency risk

4.41 Projects derive their revenues either from domestic sales (as in the case of power, water, and infrastructure projects) or exports (as is the case of most natural resources projects), or a combination of both. Domestic revenues may be denominated in (or may be indexed to) a freely transferable currency, but are also frequently earned in the local currency. This is perhaps unavoidable as local consumers will expect to pay for their utilities and public services in the currency in which their own incomes are earned. Export sales, by contrast, are frequently priced in US dollars or another freely transferable currency.

The project's finance (i.e. debt service), capital, and operating costs are likely to be **4.42** incurred at least in part in international currencies. The liquidity of credit markets is generally deeper in US dollars and euros than it is in many domestic currencies, and thus debt is often incurred in those currencies. Large scale capital assets are also generally priced in internationally traded currencies. Local labour expense, rental costs, and taxes are, by contrast, generally payable in the domestic currency.

The risks associated with differing currencies include: **4.43**

(1) revaluation;
(2) convertibility; and
(3) transferability.

Revaluation

If revenues are earned in one currency, but costs (including debt service) are incurred **4.44** in another, then the project is exposed to the risk that either the relative value of its costs increase (because the value of the relevant currency increases) or that of its revenues diminishes (because the value of the relevant currency depreciates). Although foreign exchange rates may be regulated or 'pegged' at the direction of the host government or central bank, no government can long ignore the effect of financial markets. Foreign exchange risk can, to some extent, be hedged in the market, but generally not for a period as long as the tenor of the loans. Even if available, the cost of hedging can be substantial, particularly if one of the currencies in question is thinly traded.

Convertibility

To help manage limited access to foreign exchange, host governments may restrict **4.45** access to foreign exchange. In such circumstances, the project company may earn revenues in one currency, but may be prohibited from converting it into another, even if its costs (including debt service) are denominated in that other currency. Most cross-border credit agreements expressly prohibit borrowers from submitting payment of principal or interest in an alternate currency, and convertibility restrictions will thus result in default. It may be possible, but perhaps expensive, to insure against this risk through political risk coverage.[9]

Transferability

In some cases, the project company may in fact hold foreign currency, but is pro- **4.46** hibited from transferring it abroad, whether to satisfy lenders or other creditors or to pay dividends. To mitigate against this risk, many project financings call for the payment of all receivables due to the project company into an account pledged for

---

[9] See para. 4.60.

the benefit of the lenders offshore, generally in a financial centre such as London or New York. This risk is also frequently insured against through political risk cover.

4.47 A project company may be able to hedge much of its currency risk through swaps or hedges. However, the market for such instruments may be limited both in terms of aggregate amounts that can be placed and for the length of period for which hedging is available. This is particularly the case where the local currency market may be relatively small and volatile. A thin currency hedging market may result in the unavailability of hedging or a material impact on hedging cost where banks' swaps desks take full advantage of a captive project to price front-end fees and additional margin into their swap rates.

4.48 An example of a limited currency swap market can be seen in the Indian power sector, which has been dominated by rupee denominated financings. With many Indian banks close to reaching their sectoral exposure limits and with India's significant desire to increase electricity generation, developers are actively considering the US dollar lending market. However, due to the very high pricing of rupee to US dollar hedging, international debt has not hitherto been competitive with local rupee debt.

Financing risk

4.49 In order for a sponsor to fund the development of a project it will need to obtain finance.[10] Traditionally, sponsors will take the risk of procuring the finance required to develop the project, and their ability to obtain financing commitments may be critical in a bid for a project that is being put out for competitive tender by a procuring authority. This is not, however, always the case: for example, in recent projects in Qatar the procuring authorities have solicited proposals from bidding sponsors in a competitive tender situation where the procuring authority assumes the risk of procuring the base financing for the project, and in other cases the procuring authority has tendered a project with a portion of the required base financing already committed and required bidders to utilize that 'stapled financing' as part of the financing plan when bidding for the project.

4.50 A sponsor's ability to source financing on acceptable economic terms will have a significant impact on the profitability (and in some cases viability) of a project. Financing costs (which typically comprises of costs such as interest on the debt and fees payable to lenders and the professional advisers) can have a huge impact on a project's economics. Whilst some of these financing costs are within the project company's control, some are not. By far the most significant of these costs is the interest cost of the debt package.

---

[10] For further discussion on this subject, see Chapter 3.

In the majority of cases, the financing available to a special purpose project vehicle **4.51** will attract a floating rate of interest (which will typically comprise of a LIBOR[11] or EURIBOR[12] rate plus a margin). If the interest payable on a project company's financing is floating, the project company is at risk that there will be a potential mismatch between its income (which it should hopefully be able to predict with a relative degree of certainty) and its interest payments (which will fluctuate in accordance with the daily changes in the rate of LIBOR and EURIBOR). Historically, as has been seen in recent years, there can be significant fluctuations in LIBOR and EURIBOR rates, which exposes the project company to significant risk.

There are two ways that a project company can mitigate the risk of interest rate **4.52** fluctuations. The most straightforward of these is simply to obtain financing with a fixed rate of interest. However, other than in the case of multilateral agencies, development finance institutions, and ECAs,[13] many lenders are unwilling to provide fixed rate debt to special purpose project vehicles and even if a lender will offer this type of financing the project company will invariably pay a premium for its fixed rate financing as the lender passes on the cost of hedging its own variable internal financing costs. Furthermore, there are usually high costs associated with the early prepayment of a fixed rate financing and sponsors will wish to keep open the possibility of refinancing the project on more attractive terms once the project is fully operational and lenders are no longer taking a project's construction risk into consideration when pricing debt.

The second, and most commonly used, way of mitigating the risk of interest **4.53** rate fluctuations, is for a project company to enter into interest rate hedging agreements. Interest rate hedging agreements, commonly referred to as 'interest rate swaps', play a crucial role in a project company's risk management, so much so that it will normally be a condition to a lender providing financing that the project company enters into an interest rate swap programme set out in an agreed hedging strategy. A typical hedging strategy will require higher levels of debt, and hence floating rate interest exposure, to be hedged in the early years of a project, when debt levels are at their highest and so the economics are the most sensitive to increases in the overall interest burden, decreasing over time as the debt burden, and thus the project's sensitivity to the cost of debt, declines.

An interest rate swap is a derivative contract that will involve an exchange of cash- **4.54** flows analogous to interest payments on an agreed notional amount of principal. The project company will pay to the hedging counterparty a fixed rate (of notional interest) and receive from that hedging counterparty a payment which will fluctuate in parallel with the floating interest rates of the project company's financing

---

[11] For sterling or US dollar rates.
[12] For euro rates.
[13] For further discussion, see Chapter 3.

arrangements. The project company will then use the payment from the hedging counterparty to service its floating rate financing. The principal amounts are not usually exchanged and (as noted above) are expressed to be notional.

4.55 In the early days of interest rate swaps, individual transactions were documented as tailor-made, 'full-blown' contracts which would be negotiated in detail between each party's lawyers. In 1985, an organization which is now called the International Swaps and Derivatives Association (ISDA) was formed to set about the task of creating standard forms of documentation. The accepted practice in today's market is for the parties to an interest rate swap to enter into a preprinted ISDA 1992 or 2002 'master agreement' and negotiate a 'schedule' to this master agreement. The master agreement and the schedule, along with a transaction 'confirmation' together form the interest rate swap. In the case of any conflict between the schedule and the confirmation, the confirmation prevails, both of which prevail over the master agreement. The contractual effect of these arrangements is that the master agreement is signed between the parties in its standard form, with any variations to its terms, or particular provisions individual to the specific project, being set out in the schedule. The master agreement and the schedule must therefore be read together to determine the commercial terms applicable to a particular swap transaction.

Political risk

4.56 Political risk may arise from actions by the host government (whether or not arbitrary or discriminatory) that have a negative impact on the financial performance or commercial viability of a project (as is the case with acts of expropriation or the imposition of restrictions on the repatriation of a project's foreign currency earnings). Political risk also arises from other events, such as war and civil disturbance, which may not be initiated by the host government but nonetheless also have a negative impact.

4.57 As a threshold matter, the nature of political risk in a host country can be evaluated through its sovereign credit rating. 'Soft' indicators, such as education levels and the scope of religious and political freedoms, may provide a more nuanced picture for the purposes of understanding the longer-term potential risks faced by a project.

4.58 There are a wide variety of means which may assist in the mitigation of political risk. In many circumstances, the involvement of local investors in the sponsors consortium may be seen as helpful, and the role of multilateral lenders is seen by many as a deterrent to adverse governmental action. Projects whose output may require further processing offshore, or whose access to the market may depend on an international sponsors, may also be able to negotiate away governmental intrusions. However, economic cycles will shift the relative negotiating balances as between investors and host governments, and changes are likely to occur over time in the standing of the political party that negotiated the original investment terms. As most projects have a long life, they are likely to face changes in the overall environment in which they operate. Hence, many projects will rely on a variety of direct governmental undertakings, treaty arrangements and insurance products to help mitigate political risk.

In some cases, sponsors may rely on bilateral investment treaties, which afford **4.59** nationals of a contracting state treaty protection from specified actions (for example, expropriation or discriminating treatment) by the government of another contracting state, to mitigate certain types of political risk. These so-called bilateral investment treaties (BITs) may afford an investor access to international arbitration (often before the International Centre for the Settlement of Investment Disputes (ICSID)) to resolve investment disputes with the host state.[14] In some cases, foreign investors may seek direct and legally binding commitments from the host state to address a range of concerns. In other cases, the sponsors and lenders may be content with a comfort letter given by the government, although it is worth noting that whilst comfort letters may give rise to enforceable obligations, depending on their terms, the remedy nonetheless may be quite uncertain.

The losses that can result from political risk events are not generally covered under **4.60** customary property/casualty insurance policies. Separate political risk insurance (PRI) markets may provide coverage, for both equity investment and debt, against political risk. Providers of PRI include export credit agencies, multilateral organizations, and specialized sectors of the private insurance markets.[15] Many lenders, often including commercial banks, are able to assess a broad range of commercial risks, but are often unable to assume the risks associated with political developments, particularly in countries where there is a history or probability of civil unrest or political instability. For such lenders, political risk insurance is often a prerequisite to their internal credit approvals.

Other lending institutions do not require the protection of political risk cover. **4.61** Development finance institutions and ECAs, for example, are known as 'political risk absorbing entities' because they will lend without PRI cover and, indeed, may themselves provide political risk guarantees or insurance policies.

The scope of political risk insurance differs across insurance providers. As a general **4.62** matter, most political risk guarantees or insurance will cover at least the general categories mentioned in paragraphs 4.63, 4.64 and 4.65 below; many include the category mentioned in paragraph 4.66 as well.

---

[14] For further discussion see para. 14.25 et seq.
[15] See Chapter 8.

Expropriation

4.63 Expropriation insurance offers protection against loss of the project site or assets as a result of acts by the host government that may impair or eliminate ownership of, control over, or rights to the project or its assets.[16] Such policies will cover the expropriation of the entirety of the project as well as so-called 'creeping expropriation' (i.e. losses attributable to a series of acts that, over time, have an expropriatory effect). *Bona fide*, non-discriminatory measures taken by a host government in the exercise of its legitimate regulatory authority are generally not considered expropriatory. However, there is frequent debate as to whether governmental changes in regulation, such as reductions in tariffs required to be paid to the project company by consumers, constitute expropriation. In some instances, in the context of expropriation claims, it may be necessary to make use of contractual dispute resolution mechanisms to benefit from insurance protection due to the requirement that covered investors take all reasonable measures to prevent expropriatory action.[17] Examples of a covered investor commencing contractual arbitrations with political risk insurance in mind are the *Himpurna* and *Patuha* arbitrations in Indonesia.[18]

Currency transfer restrictions

4.64 Transfer restriction insurance protects against losses arising from the borrower's inability to convert funds that are available to it in local currency into foreign exchange for transfer outside the host country or against other prohibitions on the repatriation of foreign currency earnings. The coverage may also insure against excessive delays in acquiring foreign exchange caused by the host government's actions or failure to act. Currency devaluation is generally not covered.

---

[16] See Alliant Techsystems, Inc. (Belarus: 1997), in 1997 Alliant Techsystems, Inc was paid US$6 million by its political risk insurers on the grounds that its business was expropriated by the government of Belarus.

[17] See MidAmerican Energy Holdings Company (Indonesia: 1999); but see Continental Milling Company (Zaire: 1980(I)) (stating that in the context of an inconvertibility decision that 'requiring Continental to take the extreme measures of threatening to exercising either its Art. 22 or Art. 23 prerogatives [the arbitration clause] is not considered a "reasonable step" which the Investor must take').

[18] See M. Kantor, 'International Project Finance and Arbitration with Public Sector Entities: When Arbitrability is a Fiction' (2001) 24 *Fordham Int'l L. J.* 1122, 1132; see also MidAmerican Energy Holdings Company (Indonesia: 1999). The underlying project concerned the development of geothermal fields in Indonesia. Later, the government of Indonesia issued Presidential Decree 39/1997, which divided Indonesia's independent power projects into three categories: (i) those that would be continued; (ii) those that would be reviewed; and (iii) those that would be postponed. Several sub-parts of each of the insured's projects fall under each of these categories. Based on their stage of development, there was no basis for the classifications to be applied to sub-parts of each project. The various classifications caused various lenders to withhold loan disbursements until the issues were resolved with the government of Indonesia. Such resolution never occurred. In May and October 1999, the insured investor received favourable arbitral awards against the government of Indonesia's wholly owned subsidiary. No payment, however, was ever made in accordance with such awards. Subsequently an Indonesian court enjoined the enforcement of the award against the government-owned subsidiary and any further arbitration proceedings against the government of Indonesia.

War and civil disturbance

War and civil disturbance insurance protects against loss due to the destruction, **4.65** disappearance, or physical damage to tangible assets caused by politically motivated acts of war or civil disturbance, including revolution or insurrection. War and civil disturbance coverage also extends to events that result in the total inability of the project to conduct operations essential to its overall financial viability. It should be noted that this may not cover commercially motivated sabotage against the project and will generally not cover the effect of wars occurring outside the host country.

Breach of contract or denial of justice

Breach of contract insurance protects against losses arising from the host govern- **4.66** ment's breach or repudiation of a contractual arrangement with the project company. If such a breach or repudiation is alleged, the covered party must be able to invoke a dispute resolution mechanism (for example, arbitration) set out in the underlying contract and obtain an award for damages. The covered party may make a claim under the policy if the project company's damages award is not discharged within a specified period. Breach of contract coverage is sometimes substituted or supplemented with 'denial of justice' coverage which protects against losses resulting from acts by the host government which prevent the project company effectively invoking the contractual dispute mechanism (or which unreasonably hinder its progress) or enforcing a resulting decision in its favour.

Political risk insurance providers vary in their approach to defining each of the **4.67** above categories and in their requirements as to causality (i.e. their requirements concerning the extent to which a particular insured consequence is the result of the occurrence of a particular event), an issue that is of particular importance where there are multiple causes for the loss in question. The customary causality standards range from a direct, to a proximate or even an immediate consequence. Some providers focus on the effect that a political risk event has on the guaranteed parties, such as non-receipt by lenders of their scheduled debt service payments. Others focus on whether the event is such as to prevent the borrower fulfilling its debt service obligations.

Political risk may also arise outside of the host country. For example, there is a risk **4.68** that a sponsor or a project may be, or become, subject to some form of international sanction as a result of the deterioration of relations between the home jurisdictions of the lenders or the investors and the host jurisdiction. Both the US and countries in the EU have enacted legislation that authorizes their respective governments to impose sanctions on foreign nationals consistent with specified foreign policy objectives. Such sanctions extend to prohibiting persons subject to their jurisdiction (which may be interpreted quite broadly through 'extraterritorial' assertions of jurisdiction) from engaging in trade and other transactions with persons falling within the scope of the sanctions regime. In recent years, sanctions have been applied to Iran, Iraq, and North Korea, and, by the US, to Cuba. A project company affected by the imposition of sanctions may find itself without access to key equipment and technology from particular countries may also face financing difficulties as lenders invoke illegality clauses in their credit agreements and cancel credit facilities.

4.69 The nature of political risk is often debated in the context of political risk exclusions to completion support guarantees or undertakings provided by sponsors. Sponsors may be prepared to accept responsibility for achieving completion, but may wish their undertakings to be excused to the extent that completion cannot be achieved due to political events beyond their control. This view may be expressed particularly in circumstances where the project company has paid a premium for PRI to protect the lenders or where there is significant participation in the lending group by political risk absorbing entities. The scope and nature of political risk exclusion regimes vary across transactions, but the material variables are typically as follows:

(1) the definition and scope of what constitutes an 'allowable' political risk event (customarily addressing the political risk events described above);

(2) the events (known as 'bad act exclusions') that preclude a sponsor from claiming the benefit of a political risk carve-out; and

(3) the causality standard between the political risk event and the result (being in most cases a direct and immediate or proximate cause of a default or material adverse effect of some sort).

4.70 Governing law and forum considerations becomes important when approaching political risk exclusions. For example, on the one hand, the completion agreement may specify that the agreement is governed by, say, English law, and that all disputes arising from it will be heard before the courts of England. On the other hand, the PRI policy covering the lenders may be governed by the laws of a different jurisdiction, and all disputes arising from it will be heard before the courts of that jurisdiction. Difficulties could arise where, although the covered parties may have ensured that, on the face of it, the PRI policy provides coverage for the political risk exclusions contained in the completion support agreement, the laws of the relevant jurisdictions interpret the political risk exclusions differently.

Environmental and social risk

4.71 Most industrial facilities emit at least some waste and pollutants into the environment and require permits and other authorizations to construct and operate those facilities. Environmental concerns have become more prominent as a result of increased public and lender awareness, more stringent environmental, health and safety laws, and permitting requirements and heightened liability for the management, identification, and clean-up of hazardous materials and wastes. Regulations to moderate harmful emissions usually exist on a national level and sometimes also exist at international and local levels. These regulations often require studies of the impact of project construction and operation on the natural and social environment and restrictions on the project's harmful emissions and impacts. Multilateral and bilateral treaties and other agreements often regulate the manufacture, use, and release of certain hazardous chemicals and substances. In addition, increasing emphasis is being placed on the broader impacts of a project, including labour and working conditions for those employed by the project and the preservation of local biodiversity.

These legal requirements give rise to five primary risks to a project: (a) liability **4.72** for the discharge of contaminants into the environment; (b) liability for non-compliance with environmental, health and safety laws, and permits; (c) uncertainty in environmental permitting; (d) changes in laws and enforcement priorities that tend to make environmental requirements more stringent over time; and (e) potential exposure to challenges brought against the project by affected populations or interested non-governmental organizations (NGOs) on their behalf. Most countries regulate contamination under a 'polluter pays' regime. Contamination at a project site could give rise to liability and requirements that the polluter investigate and remediate the contamination. Non-compliance risk arises when a project fails to comply with the terms of issued permits or applicable environmental, health and safety laws and regulations. Non-compliance with these requirements can give rise to governmental action to rescind or terminate permits or authorizations or impose monetary fines and penalties or criminal sanctions. Permitting risk arises from concerns about whether a project will be able to obtain permits to construct and operate on terms that are not unduly burdensome or unfair. Permitting risk also arises under regimes that allow NGOs to challenge or appeal the issuance of permits to a project. Change in law risk acknowledges that environmental laws tend to become more stringent over time, often requiring capital upgrades for additional pollution controls or the acquisition of pollution credits. Of particular concern is the regulation of greenhouse gases that are thought to give rise to global climate change, which has given rise to international treaties and host county laws that regulate emissions of greenhouse gases from industrial operations. Social and biological risk arises from actions taken by affected parties, or those acting on their behalf, to object to the project's potential impacts. This risk can often be significant in developing counties where indigenous populations may be displaced by a project, biodiversity may be threatened by project construction and operation or local labour laws may not meet international guidelines and standards.

In many developing countries, environmental, health and safety laws are generally **4.73** under development or have only recently been enacted. The government officials responsible for the administration of such laws are sometimes uncertain about how to apply or enforce the laws. Many governments lack the resources to administer environmental regulations effectively and enforcement is often inconsistent or even non-existent. In order to understand the risks related to environmental regulation, it is necessary to understand how the environmental regulatory system works in practice both currently and as it may work (usually more stringently) in the future.

4.74 Much of the regulatory uncertainty stems from how environmental and social laws are administered and enforced. Local authorities often administer the national laws and, in some countries, may impose their own regulations and project authorization requirements. Such regulations and authorization requirements may exist within a legal system that often differs from that to which the lenders or the sponsors are accustomed, and it may be administered in an inconsistent manner even within a single country. The regulatory system may or may not provide for public notice and hearings. It may provide for administrative or judicial appeals of project approvals. Legal action by an individual may be permitted to enforce provisions of the law, to challenge project permit issuance or requirements, or to recover damages from personal injuries or property damage. With the support of international environmental groups, the citizens of many developing countries are becoming more sophisticated in using available legal means for opposing projects.

4.75 Lenders and sponsors generally seek assurance that their involvement in projects will not expose them to liability for hazardous discharges or any type of environmental problems or give rise to reputational risk for environmental issues. For example, in some jurisdictions, the owner or operator of a project (which could be the lenders following foreclosure) may face liability for cleaning up soil contaminated by waste discharge committed by prior owners or operators. If the project site is acquired or leased the project company may seek the benefit of an appropriate indemnity from the seller or lessor for any past or existing environmental problems. If a project gives rise to environmental and social issues during construction and operation the lenders can face a risk to their reputations for financing a project that has environmental problems.

4.76 The involvement of multilateral agencies and ECAs in financing projects generally means that strict environmental and social guidelines will be imposed upon the project. Entities such as International Finance Corporation (IFC) in conjunction with the World Bank, the US-Exim Bank, the Japan Bank for International Cooperation, and the African Development Bank have developed their own stringent environmental and social guidelines. Thus, even if the host country does not have well-established environmental regulations, the project company, at the lenders' request or simply in order to protect itself, will often have to comply with the IFC, World Bank, or other applicable environmental and social guidelines. These extend not only to the assessment and management of environmental risks posed by a project and the moderation of emissions but also to an assessment of the social impact of the project on local populations.

4.77 In 2003 a group of international financing institutions adopted the 'Equator Principles'[19] to govern categorization, identification and management of

---

[19] The Equator Principles are a voluntary set of standards for determining, assessing, and managing social and environmental risk in project financing based on the IFC performance standards

environmental and social risks of a project. The goal of the Equator Principles is to identify and manage the environmental and social risks of a project. The Equator Principles have since been adopted by over sixty international financing institutions. A majority of lenders in the project finance market have adopted the Equator Principles. Therefore, the arranger of a project financing will find it very challenging to syndicate a financing unless it is able to confirm to potential syndicate lenders that the Equator Principles have been complied with by the project company. It is worth noting that although the Equator Principles are primarily a set of principles to be followed by lenders, it will not be possible for the lenders to comply with the Equator Principles unless the project company carries out certain steps (for example, completing an environmental and social risk impact assessment and environmental and social management plan). The Equator Principles also mandate that certain environmental and social covenants become part of the finance documentation.

The Equator Principles require projects to be divided into three categories which **4.78** identify a project's environmental and social risk (projects are categorized in Exhibit I of the Equator Principles[20] as A, B, or C, with category A projects having the greatest risk). The Equator Principles also require the performance of an environmental and social impact assessment from which action items and an environmental and social risk management plan are developed. The environmental and social risk management plan is the key document that dictates how the project company will abate and manage environmental and social risks throughout its construction and operation (a list of the potential social and environmental issues to be addressed is set out in Exhibit II of the Equator Principles[21]). These plans typically impose IFC and World Bank pollution prevention and abatement guidelines on a project, require compliance with international labour, health and safety standards, and mandate appropriate resettlement of displaced indigenous populations.[22]

International environmental laws now also offer opportunities to encourage the **4.79** development of certain projects in developing counties. Under various treaties and protocols (both existing and proposed), renewable energy projects in developing nations may be used to generate carbon credits for sale in developed countries. These clean development mechanisms are one example of market-based solutions

on social and environmental sustainability (<http://www.ifc.org/ifcext/sustainability.nsf/Content/PerformanceStandards>), and on the World Bank Group's Environmental, Health and Safety general guidelines (<http://www.ifc.org/ifcext/sustainability.nsf/Content/EnvironmentalGuidelines>). The Equator Principles serve as a framework for the implementation by each adopting financial institution of its own internal social and environmental policies, procedures and standards related to its project financing activities.

[20] <http://www.equator-principles.com/documents/Equator_Principles.pdf>.
[21] <http://www.equator-principles.com/documents/Equator_Principles.pdf>.
[22] Note that under the Equator Principles host countrie's laws apply in lieu of IFC and World Bank guidelines in countries that are classified as 'high income' by the Organisation for Economic Co-operation and Development (OECD).

that are gaining popularity in many countries as a means of confronting global environmental issues.

4.80 Appendix 2 provides a checklist of material considerations that should be addressed in assessing the overall environmental and social risks posed by a project.

Insurance

4.81 All companies engaged in industrial activities face the risk of adverse physical events that can delay or interrupt revenue generation and impose the cost of repairs or even of rebuilding the project. These may include fire, storms, earthquakes, and the like. To address these risks, lenders place significant emphasis on the insurance policies taken out by or on behalf of the project company. Commercial insurance arrangements in project financings are considered in further detail in Chapter 6.

Supervening events affecting contractual performance

4.82 In assessing risk allocation, a risk factor which should be borne in mind is the possibility that a supervening event or combination of events or circumstances may have a material and adverse effect on the ability of a contracting party to perform its obligations under the relevant project agreement. Many project agreements are governed by the law in which the relevant project is located and these laws would be applicable when assessing the possible impact on risk allocation arising from the effects of any supervening events. We set forth below the relevant analysis under English law.[23]

Force majeure

4.83 The underlying principle of the concept of *force majeure* is that no party to an agreement should be held to its performance obligations to the extent that performance is prevented by unexpected circumstances outside that party's control. The *force majeure* concept is a common feature of most commercial agreements including those which form the basis for any project financing.

4.84 Despite the ubiquity of this concept in commercial agreements, '*force majeure*' is not a term of art under English law. The term itself, meaning 'superior force' in French, derives from continental legal systems and has no recognized meaning in English law. Subject to the doctrine of frustration (discussed below), generally English law will impose strict liability for breach of contract. English law places a great emphasis on the certainty and sanctity of contract. The House of Lords has held that:

---

[23] An analysis of *force majeure* under civil law can be found at para. 12.138 et seq.

... the parties to an executory contract are often faced, in the course of carrying it out, with a turn of events which they did not at all anticipate—a wholly abnormal rise or fall in prices, a sudden depreciation of currency, an unexpected obstacle to execution or the like. Yet this does not of itself affect the bargain they have made.[24]

So, if commercial parties wish to ensure that their agreement is subject to the *force majeure* principle, the usual practice is to expressly exclude strict liability in such circumstances.

4.85 The expression '*force majeure* clause' is normally used to describe a contractual term by which one or both parties is excused from performance of the contact in whole or in part or is entitled to suspend performance or claim an extension of time for performance upon the happening of a specified event or events beyond its control. The effect of a *force majeure* clause will depend on how it is drafted, but for the most part, *force majeure* clauses are suspensory, that is, the affected obligations are not brought to an end, but are simply suspended while the *force majeure* event is continuing (unless the parties agree otherwise). Once the *force majeure* clause is triggered, the non-performing party's liability for non-performance or delay in performance is removed, usually for as long as the *force majeure* event continues.

4.86 Although many *force majeure* clauses go no further than to suspend the parties' obligations so long as the *force majeure* event continues, this may be unsatisfactory if it becomes commercially unfeasible for the parties to resume performance of the agreement once the *force majeure* event ceases. To address this, some *force majeure* clauses allow either or both parties to serve a notice terminating the agreement after a specified 'wait and see' period. Termination can be without liability (except in respect of previous breaches), which preserves a neutral position.

4.87 Unless otherwise agreed between the parties, it will be the party which seeks to rely upon a *force majeure* clause who will bear the burden of proving that the relevant circumstances fall within the ambit of the clause. Such party must therefore prove the occurrence of one of the events referred to in the clause and that it has been prevented, hindered or delayed (as the case may be) from performing the contract by reason of that event. The affected party also needs to demonstrate that its non-performance was due to circumstances beyond its control and that there were no reasonable steps that it could have taken to avoid or mitigate the event or its consequences.[25] Even though an affected party is required to take steps to avoid or mitigate the event under English law (unlike in other jurisdictions) a *force majeure* clause can apply even though the obstacle to performance is not insurmountable.[26]

---

[24] *British Movietonews Ltd v London District Cinemas* [1952] AC 166, cited by G. H. Treitel, *Frustration and Force Majeure* (2nd edn, Thomson/Sweet & Maxwell, London 2004).

[25] *Channel Islands Ferries Ltd v Sealink UK Ltd* [1988] 1 Lloyd's Rep 323, CA.

[26] See G. H. Treitel, *Frustration and Force Majeure* (2nd edn, Thomson/Sweet & Maxwell, London 2004) 12.021, which cites *Peter Dixon & Sons v Henderson, Craig & Co Ltd* [1919] 2 KB 778 at 789.

4.88 Where one party seeks to rely on a clause which relieves it of liability if it is 'prevented' from carrying out its obligations under the contract, the affected party will need to demonstrate that performance has become physically or legally impossible, and not merely more difficult or unprofitable. For example, where the intended method of performance is prohibited by government embargo, but a party is nevertheless able to perform in an alternative manner, it is a question of construction of the clause, and of the facts surrounding the case, whether its performance has been effectively prevented by the embargo. Also, if an embargo is not absolute but subject to certain exceptions, the affected party may be obliged to show that it cannot perform its obligations under the contract within the exceptions to which the embargo is subject. Although one might assume that the courts would seek to construe a *force majeure* clause narrowly against a party wishing to rely on it, there is no rule of law to this effect.[27]

4.89 A typical *force majeure* provision will describe the events which constitute *force majeure* for the purposes of the particular project agreement in some detail. Sometimes, *force majeure* may be described as falling within separate categories such as: acts of nature (sometimes called acts of God); acts of man (such as war, industrial action, etc.); acts of government (usually addressed in a project financing under political risk);[28] and impersonal acts. Each type of disruption may be addressed separately with the consequences, associated solutions and remedies and cures differing markedly.[29]

Frustration

4.90 As noted above, English law does not recognize a legal concept of *force majeure*, however, the English law doctrine of frustration will operate to discharge a contract when something occurs after the formation of the contract which renders it physically or commercially impossible to fulfill the contract or transforms the obligation to perform into a radically different obligation from that undertaken at the moment of entering into the contract. It is important to note that the doctrine of frustration is a narrow one largely because of the prevalent use of *force majeure* clauses, which reduce the effect of the doctrine.

4.91 A subsequent change in the law or in the legal position affecting a contract is a well-recognized head of frustration. Similarly, supervening illegality is also treated as an instance of frustration. As such, an event such as the imposition by the UN of sanctions which has the effect of making performance illegal, could give rise to frustration by illegality, which cannot be excluded by any agreement between the parties.

---

[27] See G. H. Treitel, *Frustration and Force Majeure* (2nd edn, Thomson/Sweet & Maxwell, London 2004) 12.021.

[28] See also Chapter 8 and para. 14.25 et seq.

[29] For further discussion of *force majeure* clauses, see Chapter 5.

Where a contract governed by English law is to be performed abroad and that performance becomes illegal by the law of the place of performance, the contract will not be enforced in England. Such a restriction would only affect obligations arising after the illegality. A contract governed by English law is not frustrated where the law of the place of performance, without making performance illegal, merely excuses a party from performance in full, nor is an English contract frustrated because the party liable to perform would, by its performance, contravene the law of the place of its residence, or of which it is a national (if that law is neither the applicable law of the contract nor the law of the place of performance).

A contract is also not discharged by frustration where: **4.92**

(1) the parties have made express provision for the consequences of the particular event which has occurred (for example, where the parties have included a *force majeure* provision in their agreement which covers the situation);
(2) the event is brought about through one of the parties' own conduct (but note that it is for the party seeking to avoid the legal consequences of frustration to demonstrate that the event happened as a result of the negligence or default of the other party);[30]
(3) an alternative method of performance is possible;[31] or
(4) the contract is merely more expensive to perform.[32]

Accrued rights under a contract which has been frustrated are not extinguished,   **4.93**
though the right to sue for such rights may be suspended for the duration of the frustrating event. If the event in question was in existence at the time of making the

---

[30] *J Lauritzen AS v Wijsmuller BV (the 'Super Servant Two')* QBD (Commercial Court) 1988 and Court of Appeal 1989 involved a contract for carriage by sea of the plaintiffs' drilling rig using Super Servant One or Super Servant Two as transportation. The defendants proposed to use Super Servant Two which sank. The defendants told the plaintiff they would not be carrying out the contract using either Super Servant One or Two. The *force majeure* clause was held not to apply because its subject matter was events which were not under the reasonable control of the defendants. It was held that the essence of frustration is that it should not be due to the act or election of the party seeking to rely on it. The case of *Bank Line and Arthur Capel* [1919] AC 435 was quoted: 'It is now well settled that the principle of frustration of an adventure assumes that the frustration arises without blame or fault on either side. Reliance cannot be placed on a self induced frustration; indeed such conduct might give the other party the option to treat the contract as repudiated.'

[31] Impossibility was also ruled out in the case of *J Lauritzen AS v Wijsmuller BV (the 'Super Servant Two')* QBD (Commercial Court) 1988 because where a promisor has alternative modes of performing the contract and one becomes impossible, that does not make it impossible for him to perform the contract. If the impossibility only comes about because the promisor makes some choice or election, then it is that choice or election which causes the alleged impossibility, not any antecedent event. The court held that the submission that 'frustration should not be excluded by a party's election where his only choice was of which of two contracts to frustrate' was unacceptable as it is 'within the promisor's control how many contracts he enters into and the risk should be his'.

[32] Courts will not apply the doctrine of frustration to relieve contracts which are the result of bad commercial bargains or which would be commercially unprofitable. In *Davis Contractors Ltd v Fareham UDC* [1956] AC 696, which involved a breach of a building contract, it was held by the Court of Appeal that 'it is not hardship or inconvenience or material loss which calls principles of frustration into play'.

contract or was foreseeable by both parties, it will not (except in the case of illegality) frustrate the contract as English law will imply (as prima facie evidence) that the parties considered the risk and allocated it between them.[33]

4.94　When a frustrating event occurs the contract is automatically discharged and the parties are excused from their future obligations. Because no one party is at fault, neither party may claim damages for the other's non-performance. The general rule is that the 'loss lies where it falls' so no claim can be made for the value of a partially completed contract. If a party incurred obligations before the time of frustration, it remains bound to perform them.

4.95　The ability of a party to recover money paid under a contract before the occurrence of the frustrating event depends on the applicability of the Law Reform (Frustrated Contracts) Act 1943 (the 1943 Act). This statute only applies to contracts governed by English law and in respect of which performance has become impossible or been otherwise frustrated. The 1943 Act provides that money paid before the frustrating event can be recovered and that money due before the frustrating event, but not in fact paid, ceases to be payable.[34] The court may require a party who has gained a valuable benefit under the contract before the frustrating event occurred, to pay a 'just' sum for it. This is so whether or not anything was paid or payable before the frustrating event.[35]

4.96　If the contract is one to which the 1943 Act does not apply, then the parties must rely on the common law rules. These provide that money paid before the frustrating event is recoverable only if there is a total failure of consideration. If failure of consideration is only partial, money is not recoverable and any expenditure incurred in performing the contract is also not recoverable.

Procurement rules

4.97　Many jurisdictions require public authorities and utilities, and in some cases suppliers to public authorities and utilities, to comply with public procurement rules. These rules may arise under treaty obligations, domestic law of general application, or specific regulations adopted by the relevant regulatory authority. The primary focus is to ensure that the procuring authority (such as a national utility) contracts with parties only after complying with a public and transparent tendering process. In some cases, losing bidders may challenge and seek to invalidate a contract award to a competitor if the procurement rules were not properly complied with.

---

[33] In the case of *Davis Contractors Ltd v Fareham UDC* Lord Reid said that the doctrine of frustration did not apply because: 'the delay was greater in degree than was to be expected. It was not caused by any new and unforeseeable factor or event; the job proved to be more onerous but it never became a job of a different kind from that contemplated in the contract.'

[34] See s 1(2) of the 1943 Act.

[35] See s 1(3) of the 1943 Act.

These rules have led to the emergence of public tendering procedures for the provision of services such as power and water, with bidders being required to provide legally binding commitments to deliver the project (fully financed) as bid, often backed by significant bid bonds. These tendering procedures will only be successful in attracting sufficient market interest if the project, as tendered, meets market standards of 'bankability', placing a significant burden on the tendering authority and its advisers to structure both the project and the tendering procedures carefully.

Procurement rules can also directly affect the project company's activities. The EU, **4.98** for example, has adopted a number of directives governing procurement by companies furnishing power or similar services to the regulated networks. These rules are designed to ensure that such companies are required to procure equipment and services pursuant to public and transparent procedures. Many sponsors find of concern that these procurement rules extend to contracts between the project company and its affiliates (requiring the sponsors to compete in a public proceeding to be awarded a construction or operating contract for a project company in which it is an equity investor). Certain multilateral credit institutions may impose similar requirements. In each case, the objective is to ensure that the project is developed at a reasonable and market-tested cost. Failure to comply with tendering rules may result, in some jurisdictions, in civil and criminal penalties and even in the invalidation of the underlying concession or contract.[36]

Competition law

Projects may find that they run foul of national or international competition law **4.99** and treaties. For example, in the European Union, Art. 81 (formerly 85) of the 1957 Treaty of Rome prohibits all agreements that have as their object or effect the prevention, restriction, or distortion of competition between member states. This can affect various aspects of a project.

For instance, selling exclusively to one off-taker prevents other potential purchasers **4.100** from buying the product of a project, which might be regarded as restricting competition depending on the importance of the project in the relevant market. In the case of power, a contractual requirement that the utility must purchase a substantial portion of its capacity and energy needs from a particular facility might be regarded as restricting competition by limiting the ability of the utility to purchase electricity from other facilities. Projects which breach these rules could be required by the European Commission or the courts to amend the contract at a later stage and may find themselves at risk of significant fines and liability to those damaged by the restrictions.

---

[36] See also para. 12.13 et seq.

4.101 Similarly, the use of destination clauses in typical off-take arrangements for oil and gas and related products has been heavily scrutinized by the European Commission. Under these arrangements, buyers will commit to taking a minimum volume of product which the supplier will sell at a competitive price, such price to be determined by a formula linked to the pricing of energy in the buyer's end-user market. The supplier will often want to include a clause which prohibits the buyer from on-selling their oil/gas to other markets without the prior approval of the supplier (or which requires the buyer to share any profit made in doing so). The European Commission has taken the view that such provisions may be unlawful on the basis that they restrict competition within the EU. As a consequence, these provisions have been removed in certain contracts or adapted in others. For instance, some suppliers have responded by delivering gas on an ex-ship basis—thus remaining the owner of their oil/gas cargo until it is unloaded in the intended market. However, the European Commission's approach to the lawfulness of these provisions has yet to be tested before the courts.

4.102 If agreements are deemed to restrict competition then they can still be permitted provided the restrictions are outweighed by the pro-competitive effects of the agreement, such as improving the production or distribution of goods or promoting technical or economic progress. In the past, operators were required to notify the European Commission if they believed they could benefit from this exemption. However, the burden of assessment now lies on the operators and will be highly dependent on the specific facts of each case.

4.103 Another issue may arise where a project benefits from unlawful subsidies or state aid. Article 87 (formerly 92) of the 1957 Treaty of Rome, for example, prohibits state aid (including subsidies, tax concessions, and grants) that distorts intra-European trade (subject to limited exceptions (which require approval by the European Commission)). The recipient of unlawful state aid will be required to repay it. Numerous international and regional treaties similarly prohibit subsidies that distort, subject to limited exceptions, international trade. Thus, an export-led project benefiting from grants or subsidized inputs or funds may also find its access to the international markets barred or subject to countervailing duties, which might prejudice the economic viability of the project.

Corrupt practices and money laundering

4.104 Although European and North American markets are not free from corruption, 'grease' payments and direct payments to governmental officials to secure business or other commercial advantage are common in many developing countries. Governments may seek to invalidate contracts on the basis that a predecessor government was induced into imprudent conduct. Whether or not a payment is proscribed by applicable law, lenders will often conduct due diligence to be certain that the underlying concession or other project documents were not procured through corruption or fraud and will require that representations and warranties in respect of specific corrupt practices be included in the project and financing documents. In addition, many official credit agencies will require confirmation of an absence of corrupt payments as a condition to participating in a project.

For a number of years, the US has been vigilant in addressing such forms of corruption. The US has, for example, adopted the Foreign Corrupt Practices Act (FCPA),[37] which renders it illegal for persons subject to the FCPA to engage in specified practices. The FCPA prohibits any payments or gifts, directly or indirectly, to any foreign public official or employee. FCPA enforcement guidance released by the US Department of Justice has clarified the 'long-arm' jurisdictional reach of the FCPA, noting that any act committed in the territory of the US in furtherance of a violation, such as physical participation in a meeting or use of the US publicly switched communications infrastructure, to plan or approve a prohibited 'grease' payment, is sufficient to establish jurisdiction over the parties involved, regardless of their nationality. FCPA violations may result in civil and/or criminal liability, including disgorgement of any revenues or profits associated with the underlying project and additional penalties. **4.105**

Significant steps have also been taken at a regional level to facilitate a coordinated response across countries. The Organization of American States sought to address the issue when member states adopted the Inter-American Convention against Corruption (IACAC)[38] in 1996. The IACAC recognizes the importance of corruption as an international issue and creates a legal mechanism to promote inter-country cooperation to combat it. The IACAC identifies specific acts of corruption and creates binding obligations under international law. The 1997 Convention on Combating Bribery of Foreign Public Officials (the OECD Convention) adopted by the OECD obligates the signatory parties (being the OECD members plus a number of additional countries) to adopt legislation criminalizing acts of bribery of government officials in international business transactions. In Europe, the Council of Europe's Criminal Law Convention on Corruption and Civil Law Convention on Corruption requires signatory countries to adopt legislative and other measures to criminalize passive and active bribery in both the public and private sectors. **4.106**

For many years the UK was the subject of criticism by the OECD for its failure to bring its anti-bribery laws in line with the OECD Convention. This was rectified with the introduction of the Bribery Act 2010, which was due to come into force in April 2011, however, this implementation date has subsequently been delayed. **4.107**

---

[37] The Foreign Corrupt Practices Act of 1977, as amended, 15 USC §§ 78dd.
[38] The Inter-American Convention against Corruption was adopted in March 1996 in Caracas, Venezuela, and came into force on 3 June 1997.

4.108 The Bribery Act 2010 represents a long-awaited overhaul of the UK's (previously antiquated and fragmentary) anti-corruption legal framework and is part of a renewed effort by the UK government to bolster the approach to anti-corruption. As part of this effort, in recent years the UK Serious Fraud Office has demonstrated a more robust approach to the investigation of corruption.

4.109 The Bribery Act 2010 sets out three main offences:

(1) a 'basic offence' of offering, promising or giving of a bribe and requesting, agreeing to receive or accepting a bribe either in the UK or abroad, in the public or private sectors;

(2) a 'bribery of foreign public officials' offence if the intention is to influence the official in the official's capacity as a foreign public official in order to obtain or retain business; and

(3) a 'corporate offence' in relation to relevant commercial organizations which fail to prevent a bribe being paid by those who perform services for or on behalf of the organization.

4.110 Critically for international organizations, the corporate offence has extra-territorial effect as the Bribery Act 2010 grants the UK jurisdiction to prosecute 'relevant commercial organizations' regardless of whether the 'acts or omissions which form part of the offence take place in the UK or elsewhere'. A 'relevant commercial organization' includes, in addition to companies incorporated in the UK, 'any other body corporate (wherever incorporated) which carries on a business, or part of a business, in any part of the United Kingdom . . .'. This offence is one of strict liability. The corporate offence is subject to a defence where an organization can prove that it had 'adequate procedures' in place to prevent its associates (including employees, agents and subsidiaries (whether domestic or foreign)) from paying bribes and that essentially the bribe was paid by a rogue element within the organization, acting independently rather than at the direction or with the (even tacit) approval of management.

4.111 Certain industries have adopted voluntary transparency-enhancing measures intended to reduce corruption and improve governance. For instance, the Extractive Industries Transparency Initiative (EITI)[39] identifies a number of 'validation' indicators, which serve as the basis for determining a country's compliance. Such criteria include, among others, the publication of material payments received by governments from oil and gas and mining projects, the application of accepted auditing standards to the payments and revenues generated by projects, and the involvement of civil society in the design and monitoring of projects. The phased approach

---

[39] <http://eiti.org/eiti>. The EITI is a coalition of governments, companies, civil society groups, investors, and international organizations.

adopted by the EITI allows countries to advance to a compliant status through the achievement of targeted milestones on a specified timeframe.

The home jurisdictions of most lenders have implemented anti-money laundering **4.112** legislation[40] that requires such lenders to undertake detailed 'know-your-customer' (kyc) procedures with respect to each borrower and other material project participants These are designed to ensure that the lenders have undertaken sufficient due diligence to ensure that such persons are not funding the project through the proceeds of unlawfully gained money.

Participant risk

As discussed in Chapter 2, a project finance transaction will involve many partici- **4.113** pants. Lenders and investors will have to assess the creditworthiness of each of these participants and whether specific structures are required to mitigate the relevant contracting parties' participant risk.

These risks will extend from the structuring of the project's special purpose vehicle **4.114** as described in Chapter 2, to consideration of the credit position of the sponsors providing completion guarantees. The contractual structures which may be used to mitigate sponsors' participant risk, including cross collateralization, performance guarantees, and other agreements to provide support for a project company are discussed in further detail in Chapter 11.

---

[40] For example, s 326 of the US Patriot Act imposes stringent kyc obligations on US financial institutions and in the UK the Proceeds of Crime Act 2002 and the Money Laundering Regulations 2007 imposes kyc obligations on UK financial institutions.

5

ALLOCATION OF RISKS IN PROJECT DOCUMENTATION

*Cathy Marsh, Daisy East, and William Fyfe, Milbank,
Tweed, Hadley and McCloy LLP*

General Overview

Many of the project risks discussed in the previous chapter are allocated to stake- **5.01**
holders in the project through the project documents. At the outset, the aim of risk
allocation is to meet market standards of financeability, or 'bankability'. The agreements embodying the risk allocation should be assessed as a whole, with a view
to: (a) providing that significant risks are allocated to those parties that are best
able and most motivated to assume them; and (b) reducing the residual risks in the
project to a level that the sponsors and lenders can prudently manage.

It is important to structure the project contracts as a whole, with consistent alloca- **5.02**
tion of risk throughout. If, for example, the power purchase agreement allocates
unusual completion risks to the project company, those may need to be 'passed
through' to the construction contractor. 'Pass through' means simply that the project company requires some other party, for example, the construction contractor,
to assume a risk that would otherwise be a risk of the project company. Thus a concession agreement may require the project company to build the particular project
facility by a given date certain, and impose upon the project company a liability
to pay pre-determined levels of delay damages for each day of delay past that

date certain.[1] However, where the project company has contracted with an engineering, procurement, and construction (EPC) contractor for that contractor to build the project facility in question, the project company will 'pass through' the liability for delay damages to the EPC contractor, rendering the EPC contractor liable under the terms of the EPC contract to pay to the project company delay damages in an amount at least equal to the level of delay damages to which the project company would be liable under the concession agreement.

5.03 It is also important to address consistently the circumstances in which the parties can be relieved of their contractual obligations. In England and other common law countries, the parties to a contract may be relieved of their obligations to perform the contract where the contract is found to be frustrated. This is where an event occurs that is beyond the parties' original contemplation and outside their control, with the result that performance of the contract becomes impossible, illegal, or radically different from that undertaken when the contract was made. In many civil law countries, relief is afforded by statute if the ability of the affected party to perform the contract is prevented or impaired by virtue of specified events beyond its control, generally referred to as '*force majeure*'.[2] Each of these concepts has already been described in detail in Chapter 4.[3]

5.04 In most commercial contracts, these legal concepts are dealt with expressly through provisions in the contract that seek simply to relieve the affected party of its obligations in such circumstances or otherwise expressly to allocate the risk of such events. In allocating the risk of such events across contracts and parties, it is important to ensure that categories of *force majeure* events are treated consistently across all of the principal project contracts and that, as far as possible, adequate assurance is provided through insurance or other means to address these risks.

5.05 *Force majeure* provisions in project contracts can be the subject of intense negotiation, as these provisions will operate in a contract so as to relieve the affected party of its obligation to perform under that contract. A 'typical' *force majeure* provision would apply where there is an event or circumstance that affects a party's ability to perform its obligations under the particular contract (other than obligations to pay money) to the extent that the event or circumstance:

(1) is beyond the reasonable control of that party;
(2) is not the result of any act, omission, or delay of that party; and
(3) could not have been anticipated, avoided, or reduced by the exercise of reasonable precautions or measures.

---

[1] See para. 5.17.
[2] For further discussion about '*force majeure*' in civil law jurisdictions, see para. 12.138.
[3] See para. 4.82 et seq.

The provision will usually also contain a list of events that may constitute *force majeure*, which list is typically cast in a non-exhaustive manner and would include strikes or other labour disputes (usually, excluding those of the workforce of the party seeking to rely on the *force majeure* relief), fire, acts of God, drought, flood, earthquake, unusually severe weather conditions for the relevant locality, epidemic, war, riot, civil disturbance or commotion, sabotage, explosions, embargoes, governmental interference, and change in law.

In some project contracts,[4] the *force majeure* events may be subdivided into two **5.06** categories, comprising 'natural' *force majeure* and 'political' *force majeure*. Usually, this subdivision will result in differing relief for the affected party under the contract should a particular event occur; for example, a natural *force majeure* event (act of God, fire, explosion, and similar events) would relieve the affected party of its obligation to perform, but have no other consequence, whereas a political *force majeure* event (governmental interference, change in law and, sometimes, war and similar events) might not only relieve the affected party of its obligation to perform, but also afford that party some further benefit such as an extension of the overall concession period or compensation for increased costs arising by reason of that event occurring. In contracts where this split approach is adopted, typically the natural *force majeure* events will be drafted so as to be a non-exclusive list, while the political *force majeure* events will be drafted as an exhaustive list.

In either case, the sponsors and lenders will go to great efforts to try and achieve a **5.07** full 'back to back' treatment of *force majeure* relief provisions across the suite of project contracts. This 'back to back' exercise may even go so far as to state that a party to which the project company has passed through various risks, such as an EPC contractor, may only claim *force majeure* relief under the relevant contract to which it is party if and to the extent that the project company can similarly claim *force majeure* relief under the primary project contract (for example, the concession agreement or the off-take contract). In other cases, the back to back exercise may be limited to seeking to ensure that the universe of circumstances in which *force majeure* relief may be claimed under, for example, the EPC contract is drafted in such a way that it is no wider than the corresponding circumstances under which the project company can claim relief under, for example, the concession agreement. In this latter case, however, care must be taken to ensure that all parties are clear as to the effect; *force majeure* relief afforded to an EPC contractor pursuant to the terms of an EPC contract will not, in and of itself, relieve the project company of its obligation under the concession agreement that it has passed through to the

---

[4] For example, concession agreements with public authorities or power purchase agreements with state owned or controlled utilities.

EPC contractor, unless there is express provision to this effect in the concession agreement itself.

5.08 There are obvious trade-offs in negotiating project contracts. Commercial counter-parties will often object to the comprehensive risk allocation called for by the sponsors. Such counterparties may respond by increasing the price of their partici-pation in the project or even by declining to play a role. However, by persuading counterparties to assume such risk, sponsors better position the project company to raise financing on attractive terms.

5.09 In many cases, by the time lenders are involved in a project, the project company may have already allocated risks in the underlying project contracts. Accordingly, the lenders are requested to assess whether the project, as structured, meets their risk threshold and then to provide pricing for the relevant financing—a customary approach in project bond issuances. In other cases, the project may not be fully developed when it approaches the financial markets, and the lenders may be more deeply involved in the risk allocation process.

5.10 Where the lenders' technical feasibility study or other due diligence identifies risks that were not addressed in the project contracts, the process of risk allocation can be complicated. When such risks are central to the successful construction and operation of the project, their resolution may delay financial closing as amend-ments to the contractual structure are negotiated. Alternatively, lenders may not be prepared to limit their recourse to the project company until key milestones have been met. For example, in projects (such as petrochemicals, refineries, LNG plants) where the construction risks are not capable of being assumed under a full turnkey contract, the sponsors may remain liable for the debt until completion of construc-tion and, in some cases, confirmation of key financial ratios.[5]

5.11 When the relevant risk may have a direct impact on the project's operating margins, but is not considered by the lenders to be a fundamental threat to the viability of the project, resolution of key project risk allocation issues can sometimes be postponed until after financial closing to the extent that the project company and the lenders agree a satisfactory solution and covenants are incorporated in the credit agreement to implement that solution within a specified time frame. For example, if addi-tional off-take contracts are required to ensure the full marketing of the project's production, the lenders may insist that all or a percentage of a sponsor's develop-ment fee and equity distributions be placed in a reserve account until such contracts have been entered into. This is intended to provide the project company with sufficient incentive to resolve outstanding issues while giving protection to the lenders through an ability to draw on the reserve to repay the loans if the project company does not implement the agreed solution by a date certain.

---

[5] For further discussion of project completion support, see para. 11.31 et seq.

A significant number of commercial contracts may be required to facilitate a **5.12** project. These can broadly be classified into:

(1) the principal project agreements, such as the concession agreement, the construction contract, the operation and maintenance contract, and the project off-take contract;

(2) the secondary project agreements, such as power and water connection agreements with the local utility, shared facilities agreements (perhaps with other projects or ventures affiliated with the sponsors), and subsidiary feedstock agreements with local suppliers; and

(3) project subcontracts (such as a long-term turbine maintenance contract, which a turbine supplier may enter into with the project's operation and maintenance contractor).

While the primary focus of sponsors and lenders will be on the principal and **5.13** secondary project contracts, some of the subcontracts may also be key to the overall contractual risk allocation. Thus, for example, it may be important for the project company and/or the lenders to have direct rights with key subcontractors (such as a long-term maintenance subcontractor) in the event that the relevant principal project agreement is terminated following a material default by the relevant counterparty.

Risk Allocation in Project Agreements

Whilst the secondary project agreements and some of the subcontracts need to be **5.14** structured carefully, the principal project agreements will naturally be key to the bankability of the project. The principal agreements in a project financing, and the risks that they seek to address, often include the following.

Shareholders' or joint venture agreements

Shareholders' or joint venture agreements govern the relationship among the proj- **5.15** ect's equity investors. The handling of potential conflicts of interest, in particular where the equity holders include a private sector sponsors and a host government, are particularly important in project financings. These have already been discussed in Chapter 2, and we refer the reader also to the checklist set out in Appendix 3, which describes some of the more significant provisions and issues that should be considered in negotiating and drafting a shareholders' or joint venture agreement. Applicable law may require that some of these issues be resolved in the project company's constitutional documents rather than in a shareholders' or similar agreement. As the contents of the constitutional documents of the project company are dependent upon the jurisdiction of incorporation of the company, it is important to seek the advice of local counsel in this regard.

Construction contracts

General provisions

5.16   Many projects[6] are built on a turnkey basis, commonly by way of an EPC contract. As such, the sponsors will generally seek to shift as much completion-related risk as possible onto the turnkey, or EPC contractor.

5.17   The contractor is generally called upon to agree to damages provisions tied to delays and to facility performance, with performance guarantees relating to such factors as plant output and efficiency, as well as, in some instances, emissions levels. The use of specified, commonly referred to as 'liquidated', damages provides the project company with an enhanced degree of certainty as to the level of damages that the contractor will in fact pay to compensate for any delay or impaired performance. The English courts are predisposed to seek to uphold liquidated damages provisions in a contract, and have rarely struck down such provisions as constituting a penalty and therefore being unenforceable;[7] however, not all jurisdictions will take the same approach, and in certain jurisdictions liquidated damages may not be enforceable to the extent they are seen as punitive and not a reasonable projection of actual damages. The contractor will often seek pre-agreed termination payments in circumstances where the sponsors abandon the project, or the lenders cease funding, during construction (in many cases these payments may be insured through ECA coverage).

5.18   Perhaps the most critical element of a turnkey construction contract is the scope of work, which should be broad enough to ensure that the contractor will furnish a complete facility capable of meeting the project's projected operating standards and

---

[6] This is particularly the case in power and water projects and projects procured by public authorities (such as public private partnerships) but less common in oil and gas, LNG, process industry, and mining projects.

[7] The English courts will generally seek to uphold liquidated damages clauses, particularly where the contract in question was made between parties of comparable bargaining power—see, for example, Jackson J in *Alfred McAlpine Capital Projects Ltd v Tilebox Ltd* [2005] BLR 271 at 280: 'Because the rule about penalties is an anomaly within the law of contract, the courts are predisposed, where possible, to uphold contractual terms which fix the level of damages for breach. This predisposition is even stronger in the case of commercial contracts freely entered into between parties of comparable bargaining power.' The leading case in English law remains *Dunlop Pneumatic Tyre Co Ltd v New Garage & Motor Co Ltd* [1915] AC 79, in which Dunedin LJ set out (at 86–8) the criteria to apply in determining whether to strike down a contractual provision for being a penalty. Note also that, as a matter of English law, a liquidated damages provision will be upheld even where the true amount of damages is uncertain and difficult to assess—*Clydebank Engineering and Shipbuilding Co v Yzquierdo y Castaneda* [1905] AC 6 at 11, and a pre-estimate of damages does not have to be right and perhaps even not genuine in order to be reasonable—see Jackson J in *McAlpine* at 280. As Lord Woolf put it in the Privy Council case of *Philips Hong Kong Ltd v A-G of Hong Kong* (1993) 61 BLR 41 (at 59): 'The court has to be careful not to set too stringent a standard and bear in mind that what the parties have agreed should normally be upheld. Any other approach will lead to undesirable uncertainty, especially in commercial contracts.'

contractual obligations. Appendix 5 contains a checklist of the other key provisions in a turnkey construction contract.

Compensation

Most of the contractor's base compensation is routed through a milestone payment   **5.19** schedule, which usually includes the entire turnkey price. Payment of the final instalment, as well as bonus payments, usually related to early completion and to performance above the guaranteed levels, are often withheld until final completion. The contract price may also be offset by penalties for late or unsatisfactory performance.[8]

The payment of performance-related damages may be secured by retaining a   **5.20** percentage of the contractor's monthly progress payment (usually in the range of 5 per cent to 10 per cent). On the date of final completion, the contractor receives the amount retained, sometimes with interest, minus any damages resulting from failure to meet performance guarantees. As an alternative to direct retention, contractors may in some instances post bonds or letters of credit in satisfaction of their retention obligations.

Scheduling guarantees

The contractor's scheduling guarantees usually relate to the timely achievement of   **5.21** certain milestones in the construction schedule. Mechanical completion (or a similarly defined term) occurs when the project is completed in accordance with the design specifications, but has not yet undergone any performance tests. Substantial completion (or a similarly defined term) occurs on the date on which the project successfully passes performance tests related to, for example (in relation to a power plant), electricity output, steam output (for cogeneration plants), heat rate levels, and emissions levels. The performance tests are usually carried out simultaneously and are of sufficient duration to assure that the plant is able to meet the guaranteed performance levels with appropriate reliability. Following substantial completion, the project company will assume care, custody, and control of the plant. Final completion (or a similar term) marks the close of the follow-up phase, during which any remaining work is finalized by the contractor.

Delay damages

Delay damages are typically tied to the target date of substantial completion.   **5.22** Projects will begin to sell their output and generate revenue following substantial completion. Therefore, delay damages are structured to replace revenue that is

---

[8] These will usually be expressed as liquidated damages. Note that the use of the word 'penalty' in a contract in respect of such payments will not be conclusive as to whether the provision is in fact a penalty—see Dunedin LJ in *Public Works Comr v Hills* [1906] AC 368 at 375–6 and *Dunlop Pneumatic Tyre Co Ltd v New Garage and Motor Co Ltd* [1915] AC 79 at 86.

foregone during this time as a result of the missed target date for substantial completion and are usually sufficient to cover debt service and other costs, including fixed operation and maintenance expenses and delay damages which may be payable by the project company to a concession authority or product off-taker. The contractor generally will seek relief from damages obligations if the delay is caused by the project company or an event of *force majeure*. Accordingly, the sponsors and lenders will insist that the scope of *force majeure* is drafted as narrowly as possible.

Performance damages

5.23   Performance damages are tied to the contractor's performance guarantees. To the extent that guarantee levels are not demonstrated by the performance tests which are carried out as a condition to substantial completion, and still are not achieved by the contractor during subsequent retesting before final completion, performance-related damages may be paid to compensate the project company for the difference between the project's actual performance levels and the guaranteed performance levels. Such damages are often designed to 'buy-down' the amount of the debt to a level at which the project can meet its debt service obligations in light of the reduced revenues resulting from the impaired levels of performance.

Warranties

5.24   The construction contract typically contains a warranty by the contractor to repair or replace defective equipment or re-perform services (including design) for a period of one year or more following final completion. It is best if this warranty period is 'evergreen' (i.e. if there is a defect within the warranty period, a further warranty is given by the contractor from the date of rectification, although it is common for such evergreen provisions to include an eventual back-stop date). Additional warranties or guarantees of operating standards (for example, availability and heat rate) may be required for some period where the applicable technology is unproven. In some civil law jurisdictions, there may be further liabilities under statutory law on the contractor for certain hidden defects in the completed works.

Liability caps

5.25   The contractor will often seek to limit its liability for damages under the construction contract (whether with respect to liquidated damages, warranty obligations, or otherwise) to a specified level, generally expressed as a percentage of the contract price. Depending on the nature of the project or market practice, the limit on liability may range from 20 per cent to 100 per cent of the contract price, with higher limits on liability customary in power projects and lower limits often agreed in process and natural resources projects (in which sponsor completion support is more prevalent). Typically, there are exceptions considered to be 'fundamental' to the stated limit for certain instances of liability, such as a failure to deliver good title to equipment or for gross negligence or wilful misconduct.

Credit support

If the contractor itself is not viewed by the sponsors and/or the lenders as **5.26**
sufficiently creditworthy fully to perform its obligations, a parent company guarantee may be required. In addition, performance, retention, and warranty bonding
is customary in construction contracts and provides significant performance
incentivization on contractors.

Multiple procurement contracts

In some industries, the use of multiple technologies may be required to facilitate a **5.27**
project and, as such, the cost of a turnkey 'wrap' may be economically prohibitive
because no single contractor or consortium is prepared to take responsibility for the
design, construction, testing and commissioning of the entire project facility.
In such circumstances, the project company may wish to enter into multiple procurement contracts with individual suppliers, in some cases contracting with an
engineering firm for the management of the overall construction process. This is
often referred to as an engineering, procurement, and construction management
(EPCM) structure. It differs from a turnkey or EPC arrangement by virtue of the
fact that the EPCM contractor provides a professional service but does not itself
take direct and sole responsibility for the overall execution of the construction
process. Although it may be paid bonuses or be subject to penalties determined
by reference to the schedule or performance of the plant, these are generally modest
in relation to the overall capital cost of the project.

Whilst entry into an EPCM structure might avoid prohibitive construction costs, **5.28**
such an arrangement is not without its risks. As the EPCM contractor will not take
sole responsibility for overseeing the works, it will not be liable to the project
company for the overall cost or performance of the project. Consequently, there is
risk associated with the interface between the roles of the various contracting parties under which impaired performance by one contractor (whose individual
liability may be quite limited) may adversely affect the performance of the plant as
a whole.

In light of the risks posed by a multi-contract, EPCM structure, the lenders may **5.29**
require a completion guarantee or undertaking from a creditworthy sponsor[9] or
the provision of other completion risk mitigants, such as significant oversight by
the lenders' technical adviser and the commitment of substantial debt and equity
contingencies.

'Split' contracts

In certain projects, a 'split' arrangement may be entered into. This is typically **5.30**
employed for tax reasons; for example, a particular jurisdiction may impose

---

[9] See para. 11.31 et seq.

withholding tax on payments for services rendered by a foreign company. In such a case, it may be beneficial to the overall economics of the project for the construction contract to be split into component parts.

5.31 A split EPC structure will usually comprise three separate contracts:

(1) an onshore contract, pursuant to which a locally incorporated company con-trolled by a parent construction contractor provides certain services that are required as part of the EPC package, such as the procurement of equipment and materials from within the country in which the project is located, design services, supervision and management required for the construction itself, site clearance, and, usually, the actual construction of the facility;

(2) an offshore contract, pursuant to which the parent construction contractor provides the remainder of the services, such as offshore procurement and technical expertise that resides in the parent company, including developing environmental management plans and general and detailed engineering and design work; and

(3) a coordination agreement, to which both the onshore contractor and the offshore contractor are party, under which the two contractor companies assume full responsibility for the entire EPC package.

5.32 A split EPC arrangement can be distinguished from the EPCM arrangement described above, since under a customary EPCM arrangement no one contractor or consortium takes overall responsibility for the delivery of the project on time and to specification. Under a split EPC arrangement, the split is essentially merely a device employed for (usually) tax reasons, and the intention of the parties remains that the 'contractor' as a whole, in other words the onshore contractor and the offshore contractor, will together be liable on the same basis is if there had been no split of the actual contractual arrangements.

Operation and maintenance agreements

5.33 Key provisions of a typical operation and maintenance agreement (O&M agree-ment) are set out in Appendix 8. As noted in Appendix 8, there are a wide range of arrangements used to structure O&M agreements.

5.34 In a fixed-price structure, the operator assumes risks related to operating costs and makes a profit only to the extent that actual costs fall below the contract price. There are likely to be adjustments for a broad range of factors, including changes in the cost of spare parts or consumables. This type of arrangement nonetheless affords a project company substantial certainty as to its costs, but the operator may charge a significant premium to assume the risk which is entailed.

5.35 Alternatively, a cost pass-through structure may be adopted, in which the operator receives a fixed fee and performance bonuses, while passing operating costs directly back to the project company. In this structure, it is critical that the operator be provided with sufficient incentive, usually in the nature of:

(1) a performance bonus, to maximize plant performances or production (in a power project, for example, these would typically comprise such categories as electricity output, heat rate, and plant emissions levels); and

(2) adequate adverse consequences, in the form of liquidated damages, if the appropriate performance levels are not achieved.

Furthermore, provisions regarding scheduled major overhaul and maintenance programmes and formal review by the project company of the annual operation and maintenance budget to ensure that costs and expenses are kept within projected levels, may also be included in the O&M agreement.

There should also be sufficient remedies (i.e. indemnities) for all acts or omissions **5.36** of the operator that result in loss to property or third-party liability. Operators generally seek to cap their total contract liability, arguing that, given their limited potential return under an O&M agreement, exposure to potential liability should not be unlimited. In that situation, the project company's general insurance programme should address potential loss or liability in excess of the operator's limitations on liability.

It is not uncommon in project financings for the operating company to be a special **5.37** purpose vehicle formed specifically to perform the O&M agreement. In such instances, a parent company guarantee is usually put in place to guarantee at a minimum the operator's payment obligations under the O&M agreement.

Site purchase or lease agreements

In many respects, project financings are simply complex property transactions. The **5.38** project company and its lenders must consider all of the customary real property issues, such as certainty of title to land and assurance that the lender's mortgage will be first in priority, as well as issues of environmental liability. An assessment will need to be made as to whether the host jurisdiction has implemented a property or mortgage registration system that facilitates certainty of title, or whether some form of alternative arrangement is implemented.

Particularly where the project site is in an industrial zone, the project company **5.39** should obtain environmental indemnification from the site seller or lessor so that it is responsible for the clean-up of any contamination on the site that can be traced to the period before construction of the facility. Even if there is no current legislation addressing clean-up, it is best to anticipate the adoption of laws during the life of the project that address the discharge of hazardous substances.

Power and cogeneration plants are often sited on land owned by and adjacent to the **5.40** plant site of the purchasing utility or the industrial steam user. The lease is usually negotiated as a package with the power purchase agreement or the steam sales agreement and may involve only nominal compensation. To avoid affording the lessor/off-taker too much leverage, the lease should be structured to prohibit termination even if the related power purchase agreement or steam sales agreement is terminated by reason of the impaired performance of the project.

Off-take agreements

5.41 In any projects, the principal means to manage revenue risk is through off-take agreements. The nature of these agreements, and the scope of undertakings that they customarily envisage, depends principally on the market into which the project's output is to be sold. If the project is to sell, for example, electric power in a country where there is a single or dominant purchasing utility, the terms of that contract are likely to be critical as, absent a creditworthy commitment from that utility to purchase the plant's output, there may simply not be a market for the project to sell its product into. Where, at the other extreme, the project produces a high quality commodity that is commonly traded on an exchange (such as London Metal Exchange (LME)-grade metals), the issue of market access is limited to a question of whether the project can manage the logistics of getting its output to the market. This range of circumstances leads to a wide variance in the type of contract appropriate for each project.

5.42 Among the categories of off-take agreement commonly encountered are:

(1) take or pay contracts;
(2) tolling contracts;
(3) marketing contracts; and
(4) power purchase agreements.

Take or pay contracts

5.43 This type of agreement sets out the terms on which a purchaser agrees to take for a specified period a minimum level of output, often at a price based on a pre-agreed formula. If the purchaser does not take delivery of the product, it may nonetheless be liable to pay for it, provided that the actual product was available for delivery. These contracts are commonly used in oil and gas, metals, and other commodity markets, as well as being the basis for power purchase agreements (PPAs) in developing markets.[10] At the extreme, they require the purchaser to pay for the product even if it is not tendered for delivery, but the more customary variant is a 'take if delivered' commitment, which places the risk of production and delivery on the seller.

5.44 Minimum volume commitments can impose significant burdens on the buyer, particularly when coupled with a fixed or floor price. If the buyer commits to paying

---

[10] See para. 5.48 et seq.

more than the then current market price, it may be put under financial stress that leads it to look for ways of avoiding the stipulations of the contract. The disputes that arise in such circumstances often end up in court or before an arbitral panel. The buyer may rely on the express terms of the contract, such as price 're-openers' or *force majeure* clauses, or domestic legal doctrines that may afford relief as a matter of law where performance is frustrated or rendered impossible.

While, as a matter of English law, a well-drafted take or pay provision will be upheld, **5.45** a poorly drafted provision may constitute a penalty and thus be unenforceable.[11] Similar concerns may arise under the laws of other jurisdictions, and the off-take contract may be governed by, for example, the laws of the jurisdiction in which either the project company or the off-taker is incorporated. Care should therefore be taken to confirm if any penalty type concerns, or other reason for which a take or pay provision may be struck down, arise under the governing law of the relevant contract, or (if different) the laws of the jurisdiction of incorporation of the parties to the contract in question. Thus, the express terms affording relief to the purchaser, the enforceability of the agreement, and the credit-worthiness of the purchaser will all be of relevance to the lenders.

Tolling contracts

This type of agreement is similar to a take or pay commitment in that it places the **5.46** risk of fluctuating demand for the project's output largely on the purchaser. It goes beyond that by also placing the risk of availability and, in many cases, price of fuel or other feedstock on the purchaser. In effect, the project company is simply paid a

---

[11] In *M&J Polymers Ltd v Imerys Ltd* [2008] EWHC 344 (Comm), a buyer that was subject to a 'take or pay' obligation in a supply contract argued that, where it had failed to order the product in the quantities required by the contract, it should be liable in damages for breach of that contractual obligation and not liable under the 'take or pay' clause in the contract (which stated that the payment obligation applied for the minimum quantities of products required to be ordered even if those quantities were not ordered), on the basis that the take or pay clause amounted to a penalty and was thus unenforceable. Although Burton J found in favour of the supplier on the point, he nonetheless suggested in his judgment that, in certain circumstances, a take or pay clause could constitute a penalty. In *M&J Polymers*, the purchase contract provided that it was a contractual obligation of the buyer to order the minimum stated quantities of product, and the take or pay provision was drafted such that it applied if the buyer had not ordered those required quantities. Burton J found that the claim for payment of money arising under the take or pay provision arose from a breach of the contractual obligation to place the minimum order, thus allowing an argument for penalty to be entertained; conversely, where a claim for payment of money arises other than by reason of breach of contract, a penalty argument will not apply—see Roskill LJ in *Export Credits Guarantee Department v Universal Oil Products Co* [1983] 1 WLR 399. If a claim that a take or pay provision could constitute a penalty was arguable on the basis that the liability under the provision arises as a result of a breach of contract, the usual considerations regarding the determination of whether the provision did in fact constitute a penalty would apply—see footnote 7 above. A well-drafted take or pay provision should therefore be cast as an election of the buyer, such that the buyer may elect to take the stated quantity of product at the required time or, if it does not so elect, it will pay for that stated quantity of product.

fee for processing feedstock into a marketable product. Similar arrangements, referred to a 'throughput agreements', are often used in the financing of pipeline, power transmission and similar projects. In most cases, tolling contracts and throughput agreements will ensure the project company a minimum level of revenue by specifying a minimum level of use or by paying it a capacity charge for merely being available for use by the toller or transporter.

Marketing contracts

5.47 In projects where there is a sufficiently deep and transparent market for the output of the project, and where the lenders are prepared to accept the risk of price volatility, the lenders may be prepared to place reliance on a commitment by the purchaser simply to market the project's output at the then current market price or at the best price available to the purchaser (which may be different). In these cases, the commitment is generally one of 'best endeavours' or a similar standard, and not of absolute assurance, of performance. Although a marketing agreement may be entered into by the project company with a sponsor or an affiliate of a sponsor, there is customarily scope to replace the marketer if it is unable to perform. As part of their due diligence, the lenders will generally want to assess the availability of replacement marketing arrangements. In most cases, the availability of alternative marketing arrangements means that the credit standing of the marketer is less critical than it is in relation to other forms of off-take commitment.

Power purchase agreements

5.48 A PPA is often the foundation of a power project's 'bankability'. It is generally analogous to both a take or pay or tolling contract. It is typically entered into by the project company, as the seller, and a utility company, as the buyer, which will often be owned or guaranteed by the host government. The rate, or 'tariff', paid for energy under the agreement must be sufficient to cover both fixed costs, including debt service, and variable costs, including fuel costs and operation and maintenance expenses. In most cases, the responsibility to procure fuel is placed on the project company, but in countries where there is a single, government-owned supplier, a tolling structure under which the purchasing utility takes responsibility for fuel supply is common. With the revenue stream so established, the remaining primary objective of the lenders is to ensure that the PPA remains in force during the entire term of the project loans and that the risk of *force majeure* and other adverse events is appropriately allocated. Appendix 7 sets out a checklist of provisions that are often addressed in a PPA.

5.49 Lenders generally focus particular attention on the termination provisions of the PPA and require that both the project company and the lenders themselves, as assignees of that company, be afforded a reasonable opportunity to cure defaults under the agreement before the off-taker is permitted to exercise termination rights.

The lenders may seek a payment obligation by the purchasing utility were the PPA to be terminated, and the amount of that payment may vary depending on the circumstances under which the termination occurs.

The credit standing of the purchasing utility generally, and in relation to the termination liability specifically, will be of significant importance to both the sponsors and the lenders.   **5.50**

Power generation may afford an opportunity concurrently to produce efficiently   **5.51**
other outputs, such as desalinated water or steam. As a consequence, a PPA may also envisage the sale of those other outputs, often to the same purchaser, but in some case to different entities through separate agreements. In such cases, coordination over such matters as despatch of the plant to address variable demand for these separate outputs is required.

In some cases, the project may rely on long-term sales arrangements with a vari-   **5.52**
ety of industrial end-users. For example, in less developed countries a power generator may find it preferable to secure firm contracts from industrial power consumers whose capacity to pay fixed charges may be better than a national utility that is required to serve a broad range of often non-paying consumers. In other cases, electricity purchasers have sought to enhance their credit by offering to dedicate the payments by their best customers, secured through escrow arrangements, to satisfy or support their obligations under the power purchase agreement.

In countries with an open electricity market, energy may be sold to a power pool   **5.53**
through which the generator has access to regional distribution companies or directly to consumers. Although in this type of structure the generator can gain assured access to the market, it has no certainty as to the price it will receive for selling its electricity. This uncertainty can be overcome by a project company and a consumer entering into what is essentially a hedging arrangement or 'contract for differences'. The typical contract for differences compensates both sides against a strike price. When the price paid by the pool goes above the strike price, the generator pays the consumer; when the pool price goes below the strike price, the consumer pays the project entity. This two-way contract operates in a similar fashion to an interest rate swap agreement. It otherwise may have the practical effect of a more standard PPA.

Fuel and other feedstock supply and transportation agreements

The sensitivity to fuel supply arrangements will vary depending on the fuel used by   **5.54**
a project. A checklist of customary provisions in feedstock supply contracts is set out in Appendix 6. A principal objective in any fuel supply agreement is to ensure that the price provisions, including any escalation indices or other price adjustment

mechanisms, match the terms of the project's off-take agreement or other revenue projections.

5.55 For coal-fired power generation facilities, there should be certainty as to the availability of sufficient reserves of adequate quality coal, a long-term supply contract, and viable transportation arrangements from the coal mine to the project site. Complexity may be reduced where the coal supplier is obliged to deliver coal directly to the project site and secure its own transportation arrangements. Consideration should also be given to ash and other waste disposal, including the availability and cost of land fill or disposal sites.

5.56 For power projects fuelled by natural gas, the sponsors and the lenders will require assurance that the project has access to sufficient natural gas reserves to fuel its operations for the term of the loans. Such assurance may take the form of dedication of specified reserves or a corporate 'warranty' of supply. Natural gas transportation arrangements must also be subject to close scrutiny; sponsors and lenders will want to be assured of firm pipeline capacity from the wellhead to the plant site. Projects fuelled by LNG pose additional concerns related to the reliability of liquefaction, shipping, and regasification arrangements.

5.57 Other projects, such as petrochemical plants, smelters, refineries, or LNG liquefaction plants, that rely on the supply of feedstock from third parties, may have very similar concerns. These projects will also need assurance of access to adequate resource reserves, certainty of transportation arrangements, and, in many cases, stability in relation to the cost of the resource.

5.58 In the event long-term fuel supply arrangements are not available, the project company may have to adopt complex and innovative fuel supply and storage strategies. Often, because the fuel supplier and the fuel transporter are separate entities, care is required to ensure that all fuel risks are properly addressed in the various fuel-related agreements.

Development agreements/concession agreements

5.59 Sponsors must focus attention on the particular risks posed by governmental involvement in projects. Governments, in turn, must be sensitive to the need for a consistent commitment, across all levels of government, to private infrastructure development. For example, if a government's ministry of finance or national development agency endorses the concept of private infrastructure projects, but the relevant utility regulator refuses to approve tariff rates that allow full recovery of costs, then the project will not prove 'bankable' despite the commitment of key elements of the national government. Where host country governments enter into a comprehensive development agreement with the project company before the procurement of financing, sponsors and lenders are afforded a degree of certainty with respect to issues of concern and can rely on an efficient, 'one stop' agreement addressing government-related issues.

There are a wide range of agreements used to document the relationship between the **5.60** sponsors and the host government. These range from concession agreements (which are regularly used in the natural resource extraction and processing sectors), to production sharing agreements (widely used in the oil and gas sectors), to licensing regimes, which may afford the benefit of detailed investment promotion legislation to authorized licence holders. The terms used may depend on the domestic legal tradition or the market in which the project is to operate. In some cases, the agreements may allow the project company to hold legal title to land and natural resources, in other cases it may only authorize the project company to operate in the relevant sector, with the project company obtaining legal title only to processed resources or assets.

Although most arrangements with host governments set out the terms of the royal- **5.61** ties or other economic benefits to be paid to the host government, the extent to which they address specific sponsors protections will vary significantly depending on the extent of the sponsor and the lenders concerns as to the reliability of the host state's investment regime. The nature of the governmental commitment may vary from providing legally binding undertakings, a breach of which may entitle the sponsors and/or the lenders to specific damages, to mere 'comfort letters', which may afford little, if any, certainty of remedy.

In projects where the project company is providing a service to a government entity **5.62** (for example, producing electricity), the contract governing that provision may address many of the relevant issues, rendering the need for other direct agreements with government less critical. In export-based projects (for example, in the mining or oil and gas sectors), where the project company does not otherwise have a direct contractual relationship with the government, the concession agreement may need to address a broader range of issues. These agreements are often implemented into national law through some form of enabling legislation, allowing greater certainty that the relevant undertakings will take precedence over competing, and often inconsistent, laws and regulations.

Development agreements and concession agreements with the host government **5.63** generally address issues such as:

(1) The rights granted to the project company to exploit natural resources or otherwise to carry out its business.
(2) Confirmation of the sponsor's right to repatriate capital and profits.
(3) The means by which the project will be assured access to foreign exchange.
(4) Whether the project will be afforded grants, subsidies, or concessions on taxation.
(5) Whether the central government will provide credit enhancement for the obligations of national utilities or other public-sector entities.

(6) Relief from import restrictions: since private infrastructure developers often need to import components of the plant and other equipment during the construction phase and import spare parts on an ongoing basis, the host government may assure that such items are not subject to import restrictions and even waive, as an added incentive, any import tariffs that may otherwise be incurred.

(7) Compliance with the host country's labour laws: the sponsors may require that qualified expatriate personnel necessary to construct and operate a project be granted work permits for the entire period during which their skills are required; if a host country government is eager that its own citizens have access to skilled positions within the project, agreements may be negotiated to balance the project's requirement for experienced, skilled personnel with the need to create opportunities for host country nationals on a gradual but accelerating basis.

(8) License or permitting issues that may be outstanding, including any obligation to obtain central bank approval for financing relating to the required investments.

(9) A recognition of the role of lenders, often including express notice, cure, and 'step-in' rights.

(10) Any assurances that the host government might seek that the project company will provide adequate service during the term of the agreement; observe relevant safety and environmental standards; sell its output at reasonable prices; and, particularly in a BOT structure, carry out prudent maintenance and repairs, so that at the end of the term, the government or state-owned entity will acquire a fully operational project (there may be specific penalties or termination rights arising by reason of breach of these undertakings).

5.64 Appendix 4 sets out a checklist of key provisions, including those listed above, which should be taken into consideration when drafting or reviewing a concession agreement.

5.65 Each of the checklists of key provisions set forth in Appendices 3–8 is intended as guidance only, and should not be taken as being comprehensive lists of all provisions that would or should appear in a particular contract. In addition, in many project financings, the commercial contracts will likely be governed by a variety of governing laws; for example, a concession agreement will usually be governed by the laws of the host jurisdiction, supply contracts may be governed by the laws of the jurisdiction in which the relevant supplier is located, off-take agreements may be governed by the laws of the jurisdiction in which the relevant off-taker is located, and the construction contract may be governed by English law or the laws of the host jurisdiction (or a combination of the two, in the case of a split EPC structure). The above discussion is thus intended as guidance only, rather than a comprehensive legal review of the effects of any particular provision that may be found in a commercial project contract. We hope, however, that the discussion above, and the appended checklists, will assist in guiding the practitioner or other interested party in their consideration of the contractual means by which a number of the risks described in Chapter 4 are typically addressed in the commercial documentation that underpins any project financing.

6

INSURANCE

Martin Benatar, Jardine Lloyd Thompson Ltd, and William Fyfe,
Milbank, Tweed, Hadley & McCloy LLP

Introduction

The importance of project insurances

The approach taken by financiers to insurance in project financed transactions is oner- **6.01**
ous, requiring a comparably more robust insurance programme than would be adopted
in a project that is financed on balance sheet alone. This is a reflection of the fact that
until the project company has established a reliable revenue stream, it will have a low
level of capitalization and be highly leveraged. This means that any reduction in its
cashflow or call on its capital as a result of material loss or damage to the project's assets,
or an interruption or delay in achieving its revenue generating capability, will have a
detrimental impact on its ability to maintain adequate debt service cover ratios.

While insurance does not remove risk, it does offer some financial security to the **6.02**
project company by providing financial assistance should it suffer the effects of such

risk becoming manifest. The primary function of insurance is to act as a risk transfer mechanism. In return for a known cost (the premium) the uncertainty associated with both the frequency and severity of loss is transferred to the insurer. The project company's premium is its contribution to the 'pool' or fund of all premiums received by the insurer from all the insured parties it acts for and out of which all losses are paid. In other words, the project company, and all other contributors to the pool, make up-front payments of their known share of losses for the period of the contract of insurance. Ideally, the contributions to the pool should be fair and equitable, taking into account the likely frequency and severity of claims that may be made on the pool by the insured parties.

6.03   In theory, the cost and availability of finance should reflect the risk profile of a project. Therefore, in order to attract funds, the cost of such finance will be determined by how much risk the project company retains and to what extent these residual risks are mitigated. Although the interests of lenders and sponsors should converge, if the project suffers from significant financial stress, the lenders need the insurance to continue to operate in the event they exercise step in rights and replace key project parties including, potentially, the project company itself. In such a situation, the lenders may directly assume the full array of liabilities that until that point had been carried by the project company and will need to have all residual risks and liabilities mitigated to the optimal extent which is commercially feasible. Where such mitigation is provided by transferring risk to the commercial insurance market, the integrity of the insurance programme protecting the project must be guaranteed to the fullest extent possible in order to ensure that it will respond as designed when it needs to be relied on. And this itself is one of the key areas of risk to which any project is exposed: the risk of relying on the insurance programme to operate as required. It should be borne in mind that insurance is by definition not a guarantee and as such its operation is subject to express and implied terms and conditions that must be understood by lenders and project company alike.

A 'bankable' insurance programme

6.04   The objective of the lenders is to ensure that the project company puts in place a 'bankable' insurance programme. Central to doing this are risk management and control strategies, which generally fall into two categories: physical and financial control of risk. Physical control of risk may be achieved through the elimination or minimization of the uncertainty associated with loss both before and after such loss has occurred. Financial control may be achieved through retention (for instance, by way of a captive insurance company[1] which the insured party creates in the event

---

[1] Many of the leading oil and gas companies have incorporated captive insurers to assist in the risk management of their portfolio of exploration projects and downstream ventures. In some project financings these captives have been used to place insurances and lenders generally apply the same credit assessment principles to such captives as they would to any other insurer or reinsurer.

risk cannot be controlled or covered via the commercial insurance market, thus effectively insuring itself or collectively with other affiliated entities); by transferring such risk to other parties, usually by way of contract; or for residual risks, by way of insurance. Against certain risks that cannot be eliminated or reduced by technical means to manageable dimensions or transferred commercially under contract, transferring the risk to the commercial insurance market may represent the sole available solution. This is particularly the case for catastrophic consequences of natural *force majeure* events such as earthquake, tsunami, or volcanic eruption.

Design

A bankable insurance programme should be designed to provide the types of cover **6.05** that lenders expect and that the project company requires. The first and most important cover is for the costs of reinstating loss or damage to the project's assets, which is typically covered by either construction 'all risks' (CEAR) insurance or 'property damage' (PD) insurance. Further cover will be required to protect against any delay or interruption to the project's revenue stream that might arise from loss or damage to the project's assets and, in certain circumstances, damage to assets not even owned by the project but on which the project is dependent. This cover can be achieved by way of 'delay in start up' (DSU) and 'advance loss of profit' (ALOP)[2] insurance or 'business interruption' insurance. Lenders will also insist on 'third party liability insurance' against the cost of funding obligations owed to third parties stemming from an accident or occurrence that results in a third party's bodily injury or loss of property for which the project company would be held legally liable. All of these insurances are so crucial to the bankability of the project that the lenders will take security over them in the event they exercise 'step in rights'. The lenders will also expect the insurance programme to cover insurance contracts required by a 'prudent developer' or operator as well as those such as 'personal accident insurance', 'employers' liability insurance', and 'directors' and officers' liability insurance' that are required by law in the jurisdiction in which the project is operating.[3]

Project company control

The fundamental starting point of a bankable insurance programme is that, in **6.06** almost all circumstances, it should be under the exclusive control of the project company rather than any individual sponsors, contractor, operator, or an authority.

---

[2] Also referred to as 'advanced loss of revenue' insurance.
[3] See para. 6.27 et seq.

To allow control to another party presents significant issues for the lenders, since it prevents them from regulating the insurance programme via the finance documents. For example, if revenue protection insurance was procured by an entity other than the project company it would be difficult for the lenders to rely on this insurance.[4]

Breadth and scope

6.07 The insurance programme should respond efficiently by covering against the largest possible quantum of loss that could be suffered by the project due to any particular risk becoming manifest as well as against as comprehensive an array of risks as is available on commercially reasonable terms. Although that is a subjective criterion, in practice the programme should protect at least against the traditionally insurable perils the project is exposed to, particularly if such risks have not been mitigated by technical or contractual means. Such risks would embrace both *force majeure* events such as earthquake, storm, flood, or terrorism as well as non-*force majeure* events like machinery breakdown, damage caused by any defects in design, plan, specification, materials or workmanship, burst pipes, or accidental damage.[5]

Integrity

6.08 The usefulness of the insurance package naturally depends on the integrity of the insurance placement. The lenders will want to have assurances as to the financial security of the insurance and reinsurance underwriters. This is often difficult as the insurance programme must be procured and maintained in accordance with applicable legislation, which in some emerging markets entails using local insurance carriers that have inadequate financial standing. In such cases, the lenders will seek comfort that the use of facultative reinsurance with acceptably rated counterparties and incorporating mechanisms, such as assignments of reinsurance, will protect their ability to access reinsurance proceeds directly.[6] However, this practice of requiring insurance placements with local insurers creates insolvency risks (and in some jurisdictions, corruption risks) that cannot be completely avoided.

Restrictions

6.09 The lenders will seek to include a number of clauses in the insurance contracts intended to ensure the integrity of the insurance contracts is maintained. These clauses will restrict the impact of certain undesirable terms and conditions that are

---

[4] See para. 6.32 et seq.
[5] See para. 6.37 et seq.
[6] See para. 6.45 et seq.

expressly or implicitly contained in all the project company's insurance contracts to provide the optimum comfort to the lenders that the integrity of the insurance will be maintained so that it will respond when called upon.[7]

Insurance Programme Design[8]

Whilst there are a myriad of labels categorizing the risks which are typically insured **6.10** against, insurance contracts in project financed transactions may be split into three distinct categories:

(1) those that protect against the direct costs, and to some extent, indirect costs to reinstate, repair, or replace assets that have been lost or damaged;

(2) those that protect against a loss of revenue or a loss of anticipated revenue that would have been earned but for the loss or damage that delayed or interrupted the generation of revenue; and

(3) those that protect against a claim by a third party for indemnity as a result of an occurrence or accident for which the project company is held to be legally liable, whether under applicable law or in negligence.

A further distinction should be drawn between those parts of an insurance pro- **6.11** gramme that constitute material insurances over which the lenders will need to take security, and those that the lenders require to be in place, but over which they do not intend to take security. The material insurances contain covers that the lenders would expect to see effected on a project financing regardless of sector or location and are also required to benefit from clauses commonly known as 'the lenders' clauses'.

Material insurances—material damage insurance

Construction erection all risk, builders' risks, and construction all risks insurances

Construction erection all risk (CEAR) insurance provides cover against material **6.12** loss or damage to any permanent or temporary works, the completed project, and any materials incorporated, or due for incorporation, in the project. In addition to the project company, insured parties will include the project operator and the secured lenders as well as contractors, subcontractors, professional consultants, and architects to any of the insured parties, although they will only be covered in relation to their activities on the project site.

---

[7] See para. 6.56 et seq.
[8] See figure 6.1 for a chart detailing the insurance participants in a typical project financed transaction.

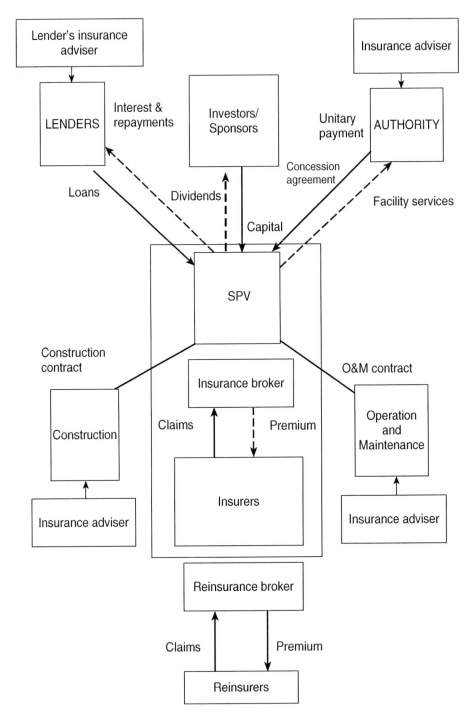

Figure 6.1 Insurance participants in a project financing

During the period of cover, which lasts until the project's commencement of opera- **6.13** tions, a broad range of assets are covered even if they are not situated at the site of the project. The policy will respond to loss or damage suffered to the insured property anywhere in a specified territory that typically includes the entire jurisdiction in which the project operates. With respect to offsite storage and temporary removal, this coverage is extended to anywhere worldwide. The range of works and related materials covered by CEAR is similarly broad, including free issue materials, spare parts, fuels and oils, and other consumables. Any material or property for incorporation into the project should be covered against loss or damage. Free issue materials will, by definition, include any property or equipment that is to be incorporated into the permanent works and plant, the property of the insured or for which the insured is responsible whilst at the project site and, in the case of locally supplied materials, whilst in transit other than by air or sea. Limitations to CEAR cover may include contractors' and subcontractors' temporary buildings, as well as their construction related plant, tools, and equipment.

Although construction insurance will have the widest amount of defects cover rea- **6.14** sonably available on stand-alone projects with respect to loss or damage to the project assets, there will be limits to the cover. It will not cover the costs to repair or replace (or respond to a delay in start-up) arising from any insured property being in a defective condition. However, if insured property is damaged *as a result* of defective property, then this insurance may respond.

The policy will also provide a number of extensions that include automatic increases **6.15** in the sum insured, provisions to allow for the expediting of expenses and accounting for extra expenses, as well as fire fighting, inland transit, offsite storage, and temporary removal expenses. Unexpected expenses related to the loss of plans and drawings, professional fees, public authorities, removal of debris, and reproduction of computer records may also be contained in the policy as extensions. In the event construction materials and plant are transported by sea (for instance, for the construction of an oil rig or an offshore wind park), a 'sue and labour' extension would be included that requires the insurer to compensate an insured party for expenses related to extraordinary efforts made to preserve any insured cargo or property.

Marine transit, aviation transit, transit 'all risks', and 'goods in transit' insurances

Insurances covering the transit of goods required for the construction of the project **6.16** is crucial to a project financing. Such a policy typically includes coverage of all materials, equipment, and supplies (excluding the contractors' plant and equipment) against all risks of physical loss or damage while in transit by sea, air, land, or inland waterway. The geographical scope of coverage is worldwide and the insurance is in effect from the time the insured items leave the suppliers' premises for shipment or transit to the moment they are unloaded at the laydown area at the project site.

6.17   Usual underwriting clauses provide cover that is broad and comprehensive, including war, charges of general average sacrifice,[9] as well as any contribution and salvage expenses for relevant materials, equipment, spares, and supplies that are lost or damaged in transit. Lenders customarily insist that coverage is the widest available meaning institute cargo clauses (A),[10] as well as institute war clauses and institute strike clauses.[11] A '50/50 clause' will also be added to increase the efficiency of the insurance programme by ensuring that when a loss occurs that is covered by both marine cargo all risks and CEAR insurances, 50 per cent will be covered by each policy.[12]

Property damage 'all risks', material damage/industrial all risks insurances

6.18   Property damage insurance provides cover against 'all risks' of loss or damage to the property insured during a specified period. The sum insured will often be set at the full reinstatement value of the project although lenders will allow a first loss limit on larger projects, as long as it is set at a level adequate to cover the absolute worst case event of loss or damage or, if lower, the limit of availability at commercially reasonable terms. A 'first loss basis' of insurance will thus be acceptable provided that it represents sufficient protection to ensure the project will be indemnified for the full reinstatement costs of the perceived worst possible event of loss or damage.

6.19   There tends to be confusion as to the meaning and purpose of 'first loss' insurance. It typically means that the insurers are liable for the 'first part' of the amount of loss or damage claimed in the period of insurance, up to the 'first loss limit' for each occurrence. When it is considered unlikely that the entire value of the property of a project will be impacted by a single event, the lenders may become comfortable with the PD all risk policy covering only a given amount of the total value of the project. Therefore, as long as the protection will cater to the worst case loss event with a reasonable margin of safety (using the benefit of a post-September 11 hindsight) it is difficult to sustain an argument for a greater amount of cover. However, it is a common fallacy that a first loss limitation will reduce the cost of any premium

---

[9] Parties to a common maritime adventure must cover any expenses or damages incurred during the course of that adventure in proportion to the amount of their interests exposed to the danger.

[10] This is the widest cover available under such standard clauses developed by the Institute of London Underwriters and Lloyd's. These clauses generally regulate marine cargo ((B) and (C) cover are respectively more restrictive).

[11] Institute war and strike clauses were similarly developed by Lloyd's and the Institute of London Underwriters and cover perils such as capture, seizure, arrest or restraint by a belligerent power, and, in the case of the institute strike clauses, loss caused by strikes, locked out workers, and labour disturbances.

[12] A 50/50 clause divides cover between marine cargo all risks and construction/erection all risks insurance. When a loss occurs and it is unclear under which insurance the loss was suffered, 50 per cent will be covered by each insurance policy. For example, if a container is opened on site and its contents are found to have been damaged, it would be difficult to determine whether the damage occurred on the vessel or whilst being handled at the site and thus the 50/50 clause would apply.

payable. It will only do so if the first loss limitation also reduces the insurers' liability, meaning that the limit to the coverage purchased is set below the worst case loss, in which case it is likely that the relevant insurances are in fact inadequately covering the project.

Sabotage and terrorism and site-wide terrorism insurance

Prior to September 2001, unless the territory involved had a meaningful history of **6.20** terrorism (for instance, Spain, Bahrain, or the UK) insurers tended to provide protection against terrorism and sabotage as part of the standard fire cover under a property damage or construction 'all risks' insurance. Following the September 11 attacks, separate and specifically underwritten insurance has been required.

Sabotage and terrorism insurance provides indemnity against the costs to repair or **6.21** replace insured property damaged by an act of terrorism. Such an act is defined along the lines of:

> . . . an act, including, the use of force or violence, of any person or group(s) of persons, whether acting alone or on behalf of or in connection with any organization(s), committed for political, religious, or ideological purposes including the intention to influence any government and/or to put the public, in fear for such purposes.

This dovetails with the exclusion in the construction all risks and property damage insurance policy wordings. The insurance indemnity is usually provided to cover 'any one occurrence and in the annual aggregate' and may be extended to cover business interruption following loss or damage caused by an act of terrorism. If commercially available, lenders may insist on site wide terrorism insurance (SWTI) as a means of providing coverage across a number of separate projects at the same site rather than requiring that each project be insured separately. Sabotage and terrorism insurance (including SWTI) may be based on the Insurance Market Association's standard T3 policy.

Material insurances—consequential loss insurance

Construction delay in start up, marine delay in start up, advance loss of profits, and advance loss of revenue insurance

This insurance provides protection against a loss or reduction in revenue as well as **6.22** any increased costs of activities designed to avoid such a loss. As their names suggest, such insurance covers loss sustained following delay to the scheduled achievement of revenue from the project as a direct result of physical loss of or damage to the contract works during construction, testing, or commissioning. For example, in power projects, the policy might cover loss of capacity payments which would otherwise be payable to the project company under the power purchase agreement arising from a delay caused by damage during construction or compensate the project company for increased costs associated with actions taken to avoid loss of capacity payments. The scope of coverage will typically only apply during the period of insurance cover provided by CEAR or marine cargo insurance and may be extended to include suppliers. The duration of marine delay in start up cover will be slightly different and begin on the date the first shipment of equipment and material for the construction of the project leaves port and continue until the final consignment is delivered.

Business interruption, loss of revenue/machinery, and consequential loss insurance

6.23 Once the project is operational, insurance will be required to provide protection against a loss of revenue, and increased costs of working capital sustained to avoid loss of revenue, where such loss is caused by interference of or interruption to commercial operation and where such interference or interruption is caused by physical loss or damage indemnifiable under the property damage insurance. The sum insured will be set at the longest period the project is estimated to require to reinstate its revenue stream (the 'maximum indemnity period') and will be subject to a time deductible or waiting period.

Material insurances—liability insurance

Comprehensive general liability (construction and operation) and third party liability insurance

6.24 Third party liability insurance (TPL) provides cover against all sums that the insured parties may become legally liable to pay in respect of liabilities to third parties. This will include liability for bodily injury to a third party, which is broadly construed to include death, disease, injury or illness, mental injury, mental anguish, shock, false arrest, false detention, false imprisonment, invasion of right of privacy, false eviction, malicious prosecution, wrongful dismissal, and defamation of character. Material damage to property owned by a third party is defined in a similarly broad manner to include loss of, physical injury to, damage to, or destruction of tangible property. Other covers include compensation for interference, trespass, and nuisance that occurs during the period of insurance. Cover will also respond to indemnify legal costs and expenses as well as costs to minimize bodily injury or damage to third party property. To ensure that each insured party is protected against liabilities owed by other insured parties, the policy will contain a 'cross liabilities' clause.

6.25 Insurers usually insist that cover be provided subject to a limitation of liability that will apply per occurrence, as long as the occurrence arises from an act or omission that took place during the periods of insurance. Sometimes, particularly in North America, cover is provided to apply as long as *the claim* is made within the period of insurance coverage. Cover will be further limited to liability that arises out of activities of the insured parties that are connected to the construction or ownership, operation, maintenance, and occupancy of the project arising in a given territory (and worldwide in relation to non-manual business trips). There will also be limitations to comprehensive liability or third party liability coverage; for instance, there will be no protection against liabilities arising from pre-existing contamination or a gradual release of contaminants, although this may be obtained by way of a separate 'environmental impairment liability' insurance.

The insurance may respond to liabilities brought in any jurisdiction in the world **6.26** although certain limitations would apply with respect to claims brought through the courts of a North American jurisdiction.[13] Cover will also typically respond to defend the insured parties against liabilities under relevant consumer protection legislation and health and safety at work legislation.

Mandatory but non-material insurances

Finally, there is a further category of insurance that is not usually viewed as 'material **6.27** insurance' and is solely required by the lenders in order to satisfy statutory legal requirements or as part of the project company's obligation to act as a prudent developer or operator. In most jurisdictions this includes automobile liability insurance and workmen's compensation insurance.

Automobile liability

Automobile liability insurance provides cover against liability for claims of bodily **6.28** injury (including personal injury and death) and property damage resulting from the operation or use of an owned, leased, non-owned, or hired motor vehicle. Typically, cover will only apply if the vehicle was used in relation to the building, operation, and maintenance of the project. The premiums and scope of coverage associated with automobile insurance can vary significantly depending on the jurisdiction in which the project is located. For instance, jurisdictions with no-fault automobile insurance regimes will limit the amount recoverable by both parties following an accident, which results in lower premiums. Other considerations, such as the nature of claims in tort in the US, will also be a factor in determining cost.

Workmen's compensation and employers' liability

Workmen's compensation and employers' liability insurances generally cover the **6.29** insured for the cost of injury or illness suffered by an employee. They differ in that most jurisdictions have workmen's compensation regimes that require employers to take out minimum levels of insurance so as to ensure that employees who are injured or become ill while employed by the insured receive certain benefits. Employers' liability is available to provide coverage in excess of the requirements of the workers' compensation regime including, for instance, coverage of the employer for injury caused by its negligent acts.

The exact scope of workmen's compensation insurance is, like automobile liability **6.30** insurance, dependent upon the jurisdiction in which the project is located. As such, the lenders will require that the project company procure that such insurance is in

---

[13] This is to account for the higher damages awards in most North American jurisdictions.

compliance with the laws of the jurisdiction in which the project will be operating and will cover all relevant employees. This will usually extend to employees of the project as well as those of any construction and operations and maintenance contractors.

Directors' and officers' liability

6.31 Under English law, companies (but not directors or officers themselves) are able to purchase insurance that covers their officers and directors in respect of their acts (including negligent acts) which may arise in the course of performing their duties to the company.[14] A failure to procure directors' and officers' liability insurance is considered evidence of poor corporate governance and lenders would, for instance, typically expect a European project company to carry such cover.

Project Company Control

6.32 Best practice in project finance transactions (in the absence of a strong completion guarantee from creditworthy sponsors) is to require that all the insurance necessary for the lenders' protection (the 'material insurance') be procured and controlled by the project company. It is central to the lenders' interests and their ability to place reliance on the material insurances that they are, if not effected, at least controlled by the project company rather than the main contractor or their suppliers and that such insurance is to be as completely ring-fenced as far as possible from any insurance placed by the sponsors or related entities. There are numerous benefits to the insurances being centrally organized and controlled by the entity over which the lenders have the most control. This consolidation ensures that the insurance programme will provide comprehensive coverage while limiting disputes between the various insurers as well as between the insured parties. It will also lower costs for the project company and facilitate the taking of security over the material insurances by the lenders.

6.33 The ability of the project to effect a comprehensive risk management strategy will be aided by the consolidation and control of insurance by the project company. The project company is responsible for the entire cover and thus has a powerful incentive to ensure that its scope of coverage is adequate and costs are reasonable. In addition to allowing for the effective management of risks in their entirety, this approach will provide for consistent coverage of the various risks being managed by ensuring that there is a lower likelihood of 'gaps' which are more likely to occur if a project's insurance programme is put in place in a piecemeal fashion. In addition to reducing risk, this also reduces the likelihood of project participants having to enter into costly one-off 'top up' and 'in fill' insurance policies.

---

[14] N. Legh-Jones (ed.), *MacGillivray on Insurance Law* (Sweet and Maxwell, London 2003) 28–95 ('MacGillivray').

This approach will also help ensure potential areas of conflict can be addressed **6.34** in advance, reducing the risk of disputes. For instance, project company control ensures commonality of interest between material damage and business interruption insurers. Similarly, insurance costs are more definite and transparent which will have the effect of limiting disputes between the insured parties and the insurers. In the event disputes do arise, consolidating the insurances in the project company will facilitate better resolution of conflicting claims arising out of the insurance programme by allowing a more streamlined risk management approach. For instance, contentious disputes arising in respect of claims made by different suppliers and contractors who damage each other's works will be less likely.

The project insurance approach also reduces cost and promotes a longer and more **6.35** mutually beneficial relationship between the project company and the insurers. Funding of premiums is simplified as a schedule of premium payments throughout the project period may be arranged to ensure optimum cashflow. Insurers will also provide more advantageous terms to the project as a whole through more specific consideration of the project's risk exposures. The insurance programme administration costs will also be lower as the project company will no longer need to vet the policies of individual suppliers and contractors.

The most important incentive from the point of view of the lenders is that this **6.36** approach facilitates the creation of security over the insurance programme. The proceeds of claims will be paid directly to the project company's accounts, as required under the finance documents, which reduces delays in payment and administration. For the project company, this approach allows control over the levels of cover, within the terms of the insurances prescribed in the finance documents, and permits the project company to select insurers provided they meet adequate credit rating requirements.

The Breadth and Scope of the Insurance Programme

Insurance is required to respond against losses arising from risks that may be split **6.37** into four main categories: natural *force majeure* events, political *force majeure* events (including sabotage and terrorism), non-*force majeure* events (including testing and commissioning risks), and risks that concern liabilities to third parties, including environmental risks. The scope of cover for each of these risks will ideally be for 'full value', although this will depend on the location of the project in question.

Full value coverage

Lenders in project finance transactions customarily seek an insurance package **6.38** which covers the full reinstatement value of the project assets. This coverage includes physical damage and DSU protection triggered by all the classic natural *force majeure* events such as flood, windstorm, lightning, and seismic risks (including volcanic eruption). It should be in place, or procured to be in place, at the commencement of construction and be maintained until completion or, in the case of marine transit and marine delay in start up cover, from the first consignment of critical path plant and equipment ex-works until the date the project is completed. The physical location of the project will determine the availability and cost of insurance against the major catastrophe perils such as flood, windstorm, and earthquake. For example, major infrastructure projects in a seismically active territory such as the Sakhalin Islands, Colombia, or Turkey may struggle to obtain full reinstatement value cover against earthquake, whereas projects of similar scale located in relatively asiesmic territories such as Saudi Arabia, the UK, or French Guyana should be able to obtain cover to full value without significant difficulty or incurring excessive cost.

Natural force majeure

6.39 Depending on the location of the project, the risk of it being adversely affected by natural *force majeure* events may be greater during the process of manufacturing key items at the manufacturer's premises and whilst in transit to the site rather than at the actual site of the project. Thus, a natural *force majeure* event that has limited potential for causing damage at the project site may nevertheless pose a significant threat to the construction schedule. Any such delay, at best, is insurable only to a limited extent.

Political force majeure

6.40 *Force majeure* events arising from 'political' or 'non-natural' occurrences such as strikes, riots, civil commotion, political violence and terrorism, or any general amendment of the law affecting all private corporations, may be significant risks depending on the location and nature of the project. As is the case with natural *force majeure*, it is possible that a political *force majeure* event, which is only a remote risk while the project is being structured, may pose a more significant threat to the construction schedule depending on the location of suppliers' premises and the routes of supply. For instance, the project may be exposed to strikes, industrial disputes, actions of environmental or political protest groups, and riot, civil commotion, and terrorist acts that affect the project infrastructure directly and indirectly. Whilst terrorism is insurable in most territories of the world, with capacity constraints only in areas subject to high terrorism risk (at the time of writing, this included countries such as Iraq, Somalia, Afghanistan, and Pakistan), it is universally the case in all project financed transactions that there are a number of 'fundamental' political *force majeure* events that are considered uninsurable by the private commercial insurance market. These commercially uninsurable *force majeure* risks (if they occur within the territory of the project itself) include violent conflicts such as outbreak of war (whether declared or undeclared) or any other armed conflict within or affecting the territory of the project. Risk associated with revolutions or insurrections are similarly uninsurable within the territory of the project as are nuclear explosions and radioactive or chemical contamination. National strikes or national lockouts are also uninsurable in the event that they affect the entire territory of the project. With respect to political risks such as war, contract frustration, expropriation, and nationalization, the insurance market will not be prepared to write these risks for a project company if the perceived risk is located within the project company's territory.

Insurability of force majeure risks

The table below summarizes typical heads of *force majeure* risks and the degree to which insurance solutions can be found to mitigate against such risks in the context of a project financing.

6.41

Force Majeure Event	Available Insurance Solutions
Lightning, fire, earthquake, flood, cyclone, tornado, tsunami, typhoon, or other natural disaster or act of God.	During construction, the project is protected against the costs of repair or reinstatement of damaged property under the marine transit and CEAR insurance.
	Revenue protection insurance will be available for a delay in achieving completion is provided by marine delay in start up and construction delay in start up insurance.
	Delay due to unusually severe weather without loss or damage would not be conventionally insurable.
	Once operational, the project will be covered by PD insurance.
	Interruptions to operation will be insured by business interruption insurance. Most events that result in loss or damage will be insured against, including, landslip, subsidence, heave and collapse, etc., causing damage to the project insured under the CEAR and any resulting delay under the DSU insurance. Contamination or damage to the project from an accident off the site are insured subject to not being caused by gradual pollution. Loss or damage caused by falling debris is fully covered.
	If *force majeure* is considered to embrace perils of the sea, (accidents of navigation or breakdown or injury to vessels, accidents to harbours, docks, canals or other assistance to or adjuncts to shipping or navigation) then marine transit delay in start up insurance will respond.
Epidemic or plague.	Not usually insured against.
Accident, explosion or chemical contamination.	Explosion (unless due to nuclear reaction) will be fully insured against (including pressure explosions).

(continued)

Force Majeure Event	Available Insurance Solutions
	There is generally no insurance available for loss or damage arising from nuclear explosion or radioactive contamination unless from isotopes used on site for medical, surveying or similar purposes. Similarly, chemical, biological and radioactive contamination is generally uninsurable.
Strikes, works to rule or go-slows (other than solely by employees of the affected party or its affiliates).	Most events that result in loss or damage will be insured against by the project company.
Acts of war (whether declared or not), invasion, armed conflict, act of foreign enemy or blockade in each case occurring within the territory, acts of rebellion, riot, civil commotion, strikes of a political nature.	Covered by marine transit and marine consequential loss and CEAR and DSU (probably subject to inner limits). Cover for loss or damage from strikes, riot and civil commotion may be limited on a first loss basis under the CEAR insurance.
Act or campaign of terrorism, or sabotage of a political nature, in each case, occurring within the territory.	Terrorism cover for material damage and business interruption is available.
Boycott, sanction, embargo penalty, or other restriction imposed directly on the territory by the government of the main equipment country(ies) of origin during the period up to and including the latest of: (1) the project commercial operation date; or (2) the expiration of the relevant warranty period stipulated in the EPC contracts.	Protection may be provided by multilaterals and export Credit Agencies. Stand-alone political risks insurance is typically available from the commercial insurance markets to offshore contractors, offshore sponsors and lenders who may insure the value of the outstanding principal and interest due against a payment default by the project company that would be triggered by confiscation, expropriation, or nationalization. This would typically cover 'creeping' expropriation. Insurance could also be obtained against inconvertibility of the currency of the host country due to restrictions on exporting capital.
Any action or failure to act by a competent authority, including any action or failure that results in any approval ceasing to remain in full force and effect despite the project company having taken all steps to re-apply for the same; or not being issued or renewed in a timely manner upon due application having been made.	If it leads to expropriation, requisition, confiscation, nationalization, or export or import restrictions by any governmental authority then a stand-alone political risks insurance is available from the commercial insurance markets to offshore EPC contractors, offshore sponsors and lenders. To the extent not covered by multilateral agencies and ECAs, the lenders may insure the value of the outstanding principal and interest due against a payment default by the project company that would be triggered by confiscation, expropriation or nationalization. This would also cover 'creeping' expropriation. Insurance could also be obtained against inconvertibility of currency due to restrictions on exporting capital.
Change of law	No insurance protection available.

(continued)

Force Majeure Event	Available Insurance Solutions
Discovery of archaeological remains or hydrocarbons, underground man-made objects or constructions, any pre-existing toxic or hazardous material or contamination on or within the site of the project.	No insurance protection available unless such events result in loss or damage to the project's assets.

Standard exclusions from insurable risks

A project insurance programme will not cover loss or damage due to 'fundamental' **6.42** risks that are so extreme and severe that the commercial insurance market would be unable to survive if they were covered. Such fundamental risk events include war, civil war, and any rebellion or insurrection. However, certain exceptions apply and coverage is available for loss caused by munitions of war[15] as well as loss or damage arising from a strike, riot, and civil commotion. Other exclusions include losses caused by radioactive contamination and nuclear risks (but not consequent fire damage), as well as asbestos and electronic date recognition losses.

There are also limitations on coverage relating to losses that arise from 'inevitable **6.43** causes' such as losses related to routine maintenance and making good defects to project equipment. Other inevitable causes include gradual wear and tear, deterioration, the normal settling and shrinkage of walls and floors, rust, erosion, and corrosion. Subsequent damage caused to insured property free of such defects would be covered as would defects that are not 'inevitable', such as mechanical and electrical breakdown. Cover is not extended to damage caused to the project resulting from experiments or overloading or similar tests requiring the imposition of abnormal conditions unless they are carried out with the approval of the manufacturer or by normal rules of operational practice. There will also be exclusions where the insurer believes coverage should be the responsibility of manufacturers or suppliers, for example, with respect to certain defects or series losses.

Certain risks are expected to be covered by way of specialized insurance policies. In **6.44** a project financing, these risks will include loss to watercraft, aircraft, and motor vehicles or transmission and distribution lines, towers, poles, pylons, and cables in excess of 1,000 feet from the project site. Other risks that will be specifically underwritten will include terrorism, latent defects, consequential loss, and loss of cash, bank notes, and monetary instruments.

---

[15] This includes residual munitions left unexploded after an armed conflict has ended.

Legal and Commercial Influences on Procurement

6.45 An insurance programme needs to be procured and maintained in accordance with applicable legislation, which in many territories entails using local insurance carriers that have inadequate financial standing to satisfy the lenders. This necessitates the use of facultative reinsurance with acceptably rated counterparties and using mechanisms, such as assignments of reinsurance, to allow the lenders adequate comfort with respect to their ability to access reinsurance proceeds directly.

6.46 Placement is also determined by commercial considerations. Ideally, the insurance provisions in the project documents should satisfactorily regulate the relationships of the key project parties with regard to the insurance programme by setting out the duties and obligations of the various parties as well as the rights and duties of the parties when the insurance programme is to respond to indemnification for loss, damage, or liability. Relevant provisions would include those that address disclosure obligations of counterparties (at the inception of the insurance and also on an ongoing basis) as well as counterparty compliance with policy terms, risk improvements, warranties and requirements, allocation of liability for deductible funding, and claims notification and handling.

Creditworthiness of the risk carriers

6.47 The lenders will almost always insist that the project company only place insurance with an insurer that possesses a given minimum required credit rating. However, this may not be possible in jurisdictions in which local law requires the regional placement of insurance and in which such insurers are not rated, or have particularly low ratings. To control the primary insurer in such cases, the lenders will often have rights to approve any proposed insurance placement both with respect to the identity of the insurer and the amount of exposure the project has to that insurer. The lenders often also require that a certain percentage of the insurances be reinsured and that the reinsurers meet the minimum required ratings test.

6.48 Where the insurance programme is governed by English law, the financing documents will typically include a provision requiring an endorsement on the terms of insurance through which the reinsurers consent to an assignment of reinsurance.

Reinsurance

Credit issues

6.49 As mentioned previously, because governments in certain markets seek to promote their domestic insurance industry, it is not uncommon for them to require that a certain amount of the project's risk is insured locally. In such circumstances, lenders will seek to control the amount of risk that remains with local insurers via a clause that requires a given percentage of risk be reinsured with international insurers having an acceptable credit rating. The actual percentage varies depending on the market, but often will be as high as 90 per cent or 95 per cent, meaning that very little of the insured risk will remain exclusively in the domestic insurance market in which the project is located.

Security—cut through clauses versus reinsurance assignments

The purpose of both cut through clauses and assignments of reinsurance is to pro- **6.50** tect the insured party against the risk of the insolvency of the primary insurer. It is important to note, however, that they do not necessarily achieve the same result in all jurisdictions. In particular, as noted below, although cut through clauses continue to be used in relation to insurance programmes governed by New York law, they are not now used where the insurances are placed in London.

Claims under a reinsurance policy are claims that the primary insurer has against **6.51** the reinsurer as a result of the occurrence of an insured event under the primary policy of insurance which is reinsured under the reinsurance policy. Moneys payable under the reinsurance policy will therefore ordinarily be payable to the primary insurer either to enable him to pay the corresponding claim that has been made by the insured under the primary policy or to reimburse him for having paid that claim. The problem that this presents for both the insured (i.e. the project company) and the lenders is that in an insolvency of the primary insurer the reinsurance proceeds that were intended to be available (albeit indirectly) to meet the claim under the primary policy may well be become trapped in the insolvency. This would leave the project company (and the lenders as assignees) with a claim against the primary insured under the primary policy and (at worst) nothing more, and (at best) nothing more than an argument that they have a specific entitlement to the proceeds of the reinsurances.

A cut through clause included in the reinsurance policy is (in theory, if not always **6.52** in practice) designed to avoid this potential problem because it requires that, in the event of the insolvency of the primary insurer, payment of all proceeds payable under the reinsurance policy direct to the insured to the extent that the proceeds are attributable to a claim by the insured as opposed to the primary insurer, as would normally occur. In effect, this means the insured under the primary policy becomes an insured under the reinsurance policy in the event of the insolvency of the primary insurer. However, it should be noted that the *quid pro quo* for a reinsurer agreeing to include a cut through clause in the reinsurance policy is often the imposition of a requirement that the insured assume at least some liability for the payment of premiums under the policy.

As the name suggests, an assignment of reinsurances involves the assignment by the **6.53** primary insurer of its rights under the reinsurance policy as security for the primary insurer's liabilities under the primary policy. The assignment is either in favour of the insured (i.e. the project company) or the lenders' security agent. Where the assignment is in favour of the project company, it will then be further assigned to the security agent pursuant to the terms of the general assignment of insurances that the project company will grant as part of the overall security package in favour of the lenders. Either way, with this approach, if the primary insurer becomes insolvent, the project company or the lenders will he able to assert a proprietary claim over the reinsurance proceeds and therefore defeat an argument from the officials overseeing the insolvency that the proceeds should be distributed amongst all the primary insurer's unsecured creditors.

New York and London market practice

6.54 While cut through clauses are used in New York-governed insurance programmes, they are no longer used in their English law-governed counterparts; and indeed their use is on the wane in many other jurisdictions. The underlying concern in relation to the cut through clause, as a matter of English law, is that in its operation it offends one of the basic principles of insolvency law, which is that the unsecured creditors of an insolvent company should be treated equally (unless their claims are preferred by law). This is the so-called *pari passu* or anti-deprivation principle and provisions in contracts which offend it are void as a matter of public policy.[16] Since the function of the cut through clause is to ensure the reinsurer's obligations are owed to the insured in the event the primary insurer becomes insolvent, it is likely that the provision would be held to fail as an attempt to avoid the anti-deprivation principle. The problem is avoided if the primary insurer assigns the reinsurance policy because there is no reason why the primary insurer cannot agree to create security over his assets (the reinsurance policy) to secure his obligations under the primary policy.

6.55 It is also perhaps worth noting that until the enactment of the Contracts (Rights of Third Parties) Act of 1999, another potential barrier to the efficacy of cut through clauses (depending on the specific provisions of the reinsurance policy and in particular the cut through clause) was the fact that there might be no privity of contract between the reinsurer and the ultimate insured. The common law doctrine of privity stipulates that a person who is not party to a contract may not make a claim for its enforcement. The Contracts (Rights of Third Parties) Act of 1999 introduced a new regime overriding the privity doctrine and allows third parties that are expressed to have rights under a contract (but who are not parties to it) to enforce those rights. While this removed a significant hurdle facing insured parties wishing to make use of cut through clauses, it does not address the risks associated with the primary insurer's insolvency, so the normal practice in financings where English law is the applicable governing law, is to use assignments.

---

[16] *British Eagle International Airlines v Compagnie Nationale Air France* [1975] 2 All ER 390.

Insurance Risk itself and Lenders' Clauses

It has become customary practice in project financings to incorporate a number of **6.56** provisions intended to restrict the impact of a number of explicit and implicit terms and conditions contained in a project company's insurance contracts. After first considering the general legal principles applying to the insurances in a project finance context, the conditions and the clauses that are customarily endorsed on project insurance policies to mitigate the risks they present will be considered.

General insurance law principles

Utmost good faith and the duty of disclosure

Under English law, contracts of insurance differ from ordinary contracts in that they **6.57** are based on the legal principle of *uberrimae fidei* or 'utmost good faith', which creates a duty both not to make untrue statements with respect to any material fact and to disclose all material facts. According to s 17 of the Marine Insurance Act 1906, a failure to act in good faith means that 'the contract may be avoided by the other party'. This obligation primarily exists in relation to the party seeking insurance coverage since (in theory) it should have the greatest access to the information needed to assess the risk being insured against. However, the obligation technically must be observed by both parties and, according to the Marine Insurance Act, not only at the time of formation of the contract of insurance but also on a continuing basis, although the scope of the duty differs slightly in post-contractual situations.[17]

To understand the principle of utmost good faith and its related duty of disclosure, **6.58** it is necessary to consider the concept of materiality. Under s 18(2) of the Marine Insurance Act, information is considered material if a prudent insurer would take it into account when assessing the risk. The Court of Appeal in *St Paul Fire* further delineated the scope of what is material information by affirming that information may be material even if it has not had a decisive effect on the decision taken by the insurer ultimately to accept a risk.[18]

The duty to disclose material information has existed under English law since *Carter* **6.59** *v Bohem* was decided in 1766 as a positive duty to divulge all material facts relating to the risk against which insurance is being sought, regardless of whether such information is requested by the insurer.[19] The scope of the duty is now wider than actual knowledge. Under s 18(1) of the Marine Insurance Act, the insured is deemed

---

[17] MacGillivray , 17-6, citing *London Assurance v Mansel* (1879) 11 Ch. D. 363, 367.
[18] *St Paul Fire and Marine Insurance Co (UK) Ltd v McConnell Dowell Constructors Ltd* [1996] 1 All ER 96, citing *Pan Atlantic Insurance Co Ltd v Pine Top Insurance Co Ltd* [1995] 1 AC 501. Also see H. Beal (ed.), *Chitty on Contracts* (Thompson Reuters, London 2008) 41–031 ('Chitty').
[19] *Carter v Bohem* (1766) 3 Burr 1905, 1 Wm Bl 593.

to know every circumstance which, in the ordinary course of business, it ought to know.[20] This includes the knowledge of agents working on behalf of the insured, even if the insured does not actually possess or share in this knowledge.[21] Unless specifically requested to do so by the prospective insurer, the obligation to disclose material facts does not, for instance, include an obligation to disclose circumstances that decrease risk or circumstances that are known, or should be known, to the insurer.[22] Although this obligation is principally borne by the insured and owed to the insurer, certain information is material to the insured. This includes conflicts of interest of the insurer with respect to the insured and any information in the possession of the insurer that might assist the potential insured assess the probability of an insured peril occurring.

6.60 Unlike the duty to disclose, which starts when the proposer begins to negotiate its insurance and ends when the contract is formed, the duty of utmost good faith continues to apply throughout the life of the contract of insurance.[23] A separate contract is created every time the contract of insurance is renewed and the duty of good faith applies to each such contract. If the policy is renewable, then the duty of disclosure is revived at renewal. Insurers may on occasion seek to add a clause to the policy that similarly extends the duty of disclosure throughout the policy period.

6.61 It should be noted that general insurance law principles in the US are often different from those under English law. Under US law, for example, as a general principle, the duty of utmost good faith applies to reinsurance contracts, but does not apply to insurance policies (or even to commercial insurance policies). Although there are disclosure duties on every insured in the US, and material misrepresentations can form the basis for rescinding insurance policies, this will occur not by way of application of the principle of utmost good faith, but rather under the policy wording itself. Under US insurance law (which varies from state to state) there is a duty of good faith and fair dealing in insurance contracts, but breaches of that duty are most typically found against the insurer, not the insured. In some jurisdictions in the US, tort damages are actually available to policyholders for breach of this duty,

---

[20] MacGillivray 17-13; Marine Insurance Act 1906, s 18(1).

[21] There are exceptions to this rule, for instance, if agents have withheld information by way of fraud etc. See MacGillivray, 17-13 and 17-14.

[22] According to s 18(1) of the Act:

    (a) Any circumstance which diminishes the risk;

    (b) Any circumstance which is known or presumed to be known to the insurer. (The insurer is presumed to know matters of common notoriety or knowledge, and matters which an insurer in the ordinary course of his business, as such, ought to know);

    (c) Any circumstance as to which information is waived by the insurer;

    (d) Any circumstance which it is superfluous to disclose by reason of any express or implied warranty.

[23] Chitty 41-030, citing *Manifest Shipping & Co Ltd v Uni-Polaris Shipping Co Ltd (The Star Sear)* [2001] UKHL 1, [2001] 2 WLR 170. The nature of the duty changes in post-contractual situations.

but they are not available to the insurer for breaches by the insured, in contrast to the principle of *uberrimae fidei* which is a mutual concept.

Joint insurance, composite insurance and severability of interest

An insurance contract covering more than a single party will be considered to be **6.62** a 'joint' insurance' or 'composite' insurance. Courts make this determination as a matter of construction when considering allegations, or the consequences, of a breach of duty or misconduct by one or more of the co-insureds. In a project finance context in which lenders are seeking to protect their investment in the project by way of the project insurance programme, it is in their interest to ensure that the insurance will not be prejudiced by one of the co-insureds.

Joint insurance will exist if: (1) there is more than one insured party under a single **6.63** contract of insurance; and (2) such parties have the same insurable interest. It is not enough, for instance, that multiple parties are insured under the same policy. It is necessary that all parties actually have the same underlying interest and will thus suffer the same loss in the event that the insured peril occurs.[24] This has a number of important consequences for all parties. For instance, because loss suffered by the parties under the policy is shared, any insurance proceeds received as a result of that loss will similarly be shared. However, any act by either of the joint insureds that would serve to vitiate a contract of insurance (for instance, the non-disclosure of a material fact) could allow the insurer to avoid the entire contract, meaning that the joint insured who did not commit the vitiating act will nevertheless lose its rights under the contract of insurance.[25]

Having more than one insured on the same policy does not mean that it is a policy **6.64** of joint insurance. The moment that the interests of the multiple insured parties differ, even if the underlying property being insured is the same, the policy will be one of composite insurance. This position attaches when a loss affects each of the insured in a different way. A composite policy is typically seen as a series of separate contracts of insurance meaning that, unlike joint insurance, any vitiating act on the part of one of the co-insured will not allow the insurer to avoid the entire insurance policy. Provided that the nature of the parties' insurable interests differ, and even if one or more of the parties might be entitled to recover the full amount of the loss sustained, the party will be characterized as composite.[26] This distinction is particularly relevant in the context of the vitiation and invalidation of insurances.[27]

---

[24] MacGillivray, 1-194.
[25] See para. 6.79 et seq.
[26] Chitty, 41-011 citing *State of Netherlands v Youell* [1997] 2 Lloyd's Rep 440.
[27] See para. 6.79 et seq.

Insurable interest

6.65 Under English law, to be able to procure insurance, the policyholder must have an insurable interest, or a 'legal or equitable' relationship with the subject matter of the insurance.[28] The subject matter of the insurance policy must also be identified. Insurance does not protect an object per se, but rather insures a person against the pecuniary loss that arises from damage to or destruction of the object or interest in the object. Thus, in the case of business interruption insurance, it is effectively the loss of revenue from the destruction of the object that is being covered.

6.66 The legal relationship between the insured and the subject matter of the insurance is usually found to exist because of ownership or a financial interest, but courts in England have been reluctant to articulate a single set of criteria applicable to all circumstances.[29] An insurable interest can also be created or amended by business practice (being a bailee, executor, trustee, agent), under contract (by borrowing money, renting premises, issuing an insurance policy), and by statute—creating or limiting liability to specific persons. The existence of an insurable interest also depends upon the type of insurance in question. An insurable interest under a contract of life insurance must exist when the policy is taken out whereas an insurable interest under maritime law must exist when the claim is made.[30] For all other insurances, an insurable interest must exist both when the policy starts and when the claim is made.

6.67 Finding its roots in English common law and statute, the law of New York will find a valid contract of insurance exists only if the insured party has an insurable interest in the subject matter of the insurance.[31] The law of New York differs in that the notion of an insurable interest is more expansive than that currently in existence in England and Wales. As is the case under English law, the existence of legal and equitable interests in property are accepted as evidence of an insurable interest in that property. However, both courts and the state legislature have adopted the position that a person who has an 'economic interest' in a property also has an insurable interest.[32]

---

[28] Section 5(1) of the Marine Insurance Act 1906.

[29] Chitty, 41-006.

[30] MacGillivray, 1-70, citing the Life Insurance Act 1774 and *Dalby v India and London Life Assurance Co.* (1854) 15 CB 365.

[31] Donald S. DiBenedetto, *1-3 New Appleman New York Insurance Law* § 3.01 ('DiBenedetto').

[32] DiBenedetto, § 3.01 citing s 3401 of the Insurance Law and *Meyers v Norwich Union Fire Insurance Society* 47 Misc 2d 353, 262 NYS2d 579 (Sup Ct Ulster Co 1965). The statute states that: 'No contract or policy of insurance on property made or issued in this state, or made or issued upon any property in this state, shall be enforceable except for the benefit of some person having an insurable interest in the property insured. In this article "insurable interest" shall include *any lawful and substantial economic interest* in the safety or preservation of property from loss, destruction, or pecuniary damage.'

Valuation of the subject matter of the insurance

Because the premium payable by the insured is calculated based on the potential **6.68**
quantum of any claim (along with the perceived risk of such a claim being made),
undervaluing the subject matter of the insurance could undermine the financial
position of the insurer. In such cases, the insurer will look to see whether the insured
breached its duty to disclose. However, in the event that (in the case of a non-
marine insurance policy) there was no breach of the insured's duty of utmost good
faith, the insured will be allowed to recover up to the maximum sum agreed.[33] For
this reason, it is common in practice for the insurers to consider the insurance 'subject to average'. This is accomplished by including an 'average' clause which reduces
the amount payable in the event the subject of the insurance is undervalued. The
claim settlement will be reduced according to the average clause in proportion to
the amount of underinsurance by applying the following formula: the product of
the sum insured divided by the value at risk, multiplied by the amount of loss,
equals the settlement.

The amount provided as an indemnity can be amended by additional clauses added **6.69**
to the policy. For example, when there will be no deduction for wear and tear
throughout the life of the insurance, the policy is referred to as 'reinstatement'
when applying to commercial insurances. 'Agreed values' or 'valued policies'
mean that the amount to be paid in the event of a total loss has been agreed at the
inception of the policy. This will be paid in full despite variations in the actual value
of the insured item at the time of the loss.

There are additional legal principles which ensure that the insured cannot recover **6.70**
more than the indemnity. In the event that more than one policy is insuring against
a loss, the remedy of contribution may apply. Similarly, if a third party is responsible
for all or part of a loss, the insurer may be subrogated to the rights of the insured
against that third party.

Contribution

When more than one policy covers the same item, the legal principle of indemnity **6.71**
will apply to prevent the insured receiving indemnity from both policies and therefore recovering for more than the loss suffered. Contribution is an equitable remedy
so that a proportion of a paid claim can be recouped from other insurers who have
also received premium for the same risk.[34] In a project finance context, lenders
require that the project company's insurance be treated as the primary protection
without contribution from any other insurance. The requirement for this clause
stems from the fact that the lenders will have, through the due diligence process,
agreed the insurance policies including not just the scope of cover but also the terms

---

[33] MacGillivray, 22-33.
[34] MacGillivray, 23-32.

and conditions and the adequacy of the counterparties acting as risk carriers. It is in the interests of both the insureds and the lenders to ensure that, if a claim is to be made there will be no uncertainty regarding whether the insurers will deny liability for a portion or all the loss citing the existence of another insurance that may be brought into contribution for its rateable proportion. The 'other' insurance may be poorly constructed and entered into with a less creditworthy insurance counterparty. At best, the project company would be faced with delays in receiving loss proceeds due to the need to progress the claim and agree liability and quantum with another set of insurers and at worst, it could find that a portion of the loss lies with an entity lacking the financial strength to pay. Therefore, this clause is intended to maintain the integrity of the intention between the insured and the insurer to have the designated insurance cover in place.

6.72 To establish whether contribution will apply, it is necessary to establish whether or not the following factors exist between the policies. First, do they cover the same subject matter? A policy covering the buildings and a policy covering both the buildings and their contents would contribute in the event of damage to the buildings but not the contents. Secondly, do they cover the same peril causing the loss? This must be the same under both policies meaning that a policy covering property on a fire and perils basis would not contribute with a policy covering theft only, whereas a policy covering 'all risks' will contribute with a fire policy. Thirdly, are they both policies of indemnity? Contribution only applies to contracts of indemnity and not to contracts that provide benefits. Fourthly, do they both cover the same insurable interest? Different persons can have an interest in the same property, for example, a senior lender and a project company, a landlord and a tenant, a mortgagor and a mortgagee. If each takes out insurance to protect their own interest there will not be contribution. However, if both insure their own interest but one includes the interest of the other party then there will be contribution with respect to the overlapping cover. Finally, do they both provide liability for the claim? Both policies must establish that the claim is covered by its terms and conditions and therefore is liable to pay the loss. If one policy has more strict terms that mean the relevant insurer is not liable, then it will not contribute to the loss.

Subrogation

6.73 Sometimes the insured event is the responsibility of another party. This could have two undesirable consequences: first, the insured could claim under their policy, then pursue the guilty party and so recover more than they had lost, which would breach the principle of indemnity.[35] Secondly, the insured who suffered the loss and is indemnified by insurers may suffer a further loss because the cost of maintaining

---

[35] MacGillivray, 22-2. An insurer may not avoid liability on the grounds that the insured has a right of action against a third party just as a third party may not avoid liability to the insured based on the existence of insurance covering the loss suffered.

its insurance coverage (for instance, at the renewal of the policy) will have increased to reflect the loss experienced by the insured. To prevent these situations from occurring, the courts have developed the principle of subrogation. This allows insurers to recover their outlay for claims settled under a contract of indemnity from the third party in the name of the insured and this also ensures that the premiums of the insured will not rise.

Under English law, there are four ways in which the rights of subrogation may arise. **6.74** The first is in tort, and most commonly subrogation arises after an insured loss is caused by a negligent third party who remains liable for the loss caused. Because the damages are also insured, the insurers can recover what they pay out from the negligent party. Subrogation may also arise by way of contract, meaning that if a contractual term makes another party responsible for the damage which has been sustained, then the insurers can recover the amount they pay out in the event of a claim. Thirdly, under statues like the Riot (Damages) Act 1886 the police are responsible for keeping the peace as well as for damage caused by rioters if they fail to do so. Fourthly, where a constructive total loss has been paid by an insurer the insurer becomes the owner of the undamaged property and can raise funds by selling it. Insurers can only recover their liability under the insurance contract. Therefore, if the claim has been settled with reductions because of, for example, an excess applying, the insured can still recover this uninsured amount from the party responsible.

When subrogated to the rights of the insured, the insurer has both a right of action **6.75** in money against the third party that caused the loss, as well as an equitable proprietary interest in any money received by the insured from that third party as compensation. An insurer who has paid under the insurance therefore benefits from all rights possessed by the insured relative to the loss insured against.[36] In the event the insured receives compensation both from the insurer and from the third party who caused the insured loss, and the total amount of compensation exceeds the quantum of the insured loss, the insured must account to the insurer for any excess amount.[37]

Mitigation of the risks presented by general insurance law principles—lender endorsements

Lenders as insured parties and severability of interest

By being a named insured, the lenders obtain a degree of control over the relevant **6.76** insurance policy. It provides protection to the lenders in their own right against any

---

[36] Chitty, 41-091, citing *Castellain v Preston* (1883) 11 QBD 380; *Lord Napier and Ettrick v Hunter* [1993] 2 WLR 42; Marine Insurance Act 1906, s 79.
[37] Chitty 41-094.

liabilities that may arise from their activities related to the project as well as allowing them to bring claims in respect of their own insurable interest.

6.77 By insuring their interest it means that there is a 'severability' of insurable interest that facilitates protection in the event another insured voids the policy. For example, if the project company voided a policy in a situation where the lenders were not also a named insured, cover would be withdrawn as there was only one insured involved and no other insurable interest that could be indemnified. There would therefore be no protection of the project company's ability to maintain its debt service obligations in situations where insurance acts as the sole source of revenue protection, for example, following a natural *force majeure* event.

6.78 With insured party status, the lenders may exercise their rights over the policy, particularly in a 'step in' situation whereby they would need not only to take possession of the policy in order to control its benefits, control premiums, return of premiums, and negotiation of claims, but also to protect themselves against any liabilities or risks that arise following the taking over of the project assets, as well as prevent the cancellation of the insurances by the insurers following the demise of the project company. Customarily, the lenders are named as additional insureds on all material insurance policies of the project company except with respect to the employer's liability and motor vehicle liability insurances.

Vitiation and invalidation

6.79 'Non invalidation' and 'non vitiation' are generally used as synonymous terms. An invalidating or vitiating act occurs where an insured fails to make a proper disclosure of material information to the insurers or otherwise misleads them by way of a misrepresentation, whether innocent or deliberate. This would entitle the insurers to declare the policy void or give them grounds to vitiate a given contract of insurance. Similarly, if an insured breaches a term, condition, or warranty contained in a contract of insurance, the insurer is entitled to invalidate cover with respect to the loss.

6.80 Under English law, where the insurance has more than one insured party and also includes a severability of interest clause, insurers will accept liability for losses where one insured party has been at fault for breaching policy terms and conditions. The protection obtained by the 'non invalidation' wording is that insurers will not declare the policy void with respect to the other insured parties who have not made a false disclosure or breached any term or condition of the contract of insurance. Therefore, the position of the other insured parties is always protected, provided they themselves do not fail to make a material disclosure to insurers or otherwise mislead the insurers or breach a condition or warranty of the insurance.

6.81 The purpose of the 'non-vitiation clause' or 'non invalidation clause' in a project financing is to prevent the insurer from using such a vitiating event as a means of declaring the contract of insurance to be void and thus circumventing its obligation to make payment to the lenders as loss payees. To ensure the optimum level of protection, the project company needs to be protected in the insurance policies by:

(1) a provision that expressly sets out that each insured party operates as a separate and distinct entity and cover applies in the same manner and to the same extent as if individual policies had been issued to each insured party in respect of its own interest;

(2) a provision that clearly states the liability of the insurers to any one insured is not conditional on the due observance or fulfilment by any other insured party of the terms and conditions of the policy or duties imposed; and

(3) an express 'non invalidation' insurance protection in the insurance policies that states a vitiating act committed by one insured party shall not prejudice the right to indemnity of any other insured party.

A further issue with respect to such clauses in project financed transactions centres, **6.82** not on the invalidating act itself, but rather on the insurers' right to subrogate to the rights and remedies available to the party they indemnify, against any party that was responsible for an invalidating act that contributed to the loss for which the insurance indemnity was made. There are two aspects to this:

(1) First, if a lender is found to have committed an invalidating act that in some measure contributed to the amount of indemnity payable under the insurance programme to another project party, the insurers seeking to recover from them to the extent of the lender's culpability should not expose them to a right of action. Not surprisingly, insurers can be very resistant to waiving rights against a party that is culpable of a vitiating act. In practice, it is highly unlikely that a lender will ever be in a position to invalidate the insurance and therefore the risk to the lenders in not obtaining this 'protection' is not considered significant. It is fairly standard (although not universal) for insurers to retain rights against the party that vitiates. However, insurers will also often agree to waive rights of subrogation in favour of the lenders in this regard.

(2) Secondly, the insurers should not as a rule have the ability to assume the rights of the lenders under the finance documents against the project company. Insurers, when requested, commonly agree to this. Therefore, if the insurers pay a claim to the lenders in circumstances where the project company may have committed a vitiating act, the insurers would not then be able to seek recovery of their outlay to the lenders by pursuing the project company using the lenders' rights under the financing documents.

Assignment of insurances

In project finance transactions, the key element that is used to create security for the **6.83** lenders in the insurance programme is a legal assignment of the insurance. The project company will issue a notice of assignment in respect of the marine transit, construction, physical damage, delay in start-up, operational physical damage, and business interruption, and other material policies of insurance and reinsurance and acknowledgements of such assignments are customarily obtained.

6.84 It is crucial to the lenders' ability to rely on and take security over the insurance programme that the project company assigns to the security agent or trustee all its rights, title, benefits, interests, and claims, whether existing now or in the future, under and in respect of the material insurances (the insurer will do likewise in respect of the reinsurances) and all insurance proceeds in respect of material insurances and reinsurances. The assignment will not include any material insurance in respect of liabilities to third parties to the extent that the assignment of that right, title, benefit, interest, or claim is unlawful or impossible as a matter of law, or would constitute a breach of the terms of any contract or agreement regulating or creating such right, title, benefit, interest, or claim. Additionally, the assignment will have to be structured to ensure that it will not render the insurance or reinsurance contract void or voidable or unenforceable by the project company or any other insured or reinsured party as a result of the deed of assignment. Finally, assignment is not typically required with respect to the non-material insurance such as employers' liability or motor vehicle liability insurance. In the event that the lenders exercise step-in rights these insurances would need to be effected in respect of the substitute company's directors, employees, and motor vehicles.

6.85 One of the key differences between New York and English law-governed financings relates to the manner in which security is taken over the project insurances. Unlike in England, assignments of insurances or reinsurances are rarely used in financings governed by New York law. Rather, security is granted by way of a pledge and security agreement that serves to attach the policy of insurance and, under the New York Uniform Commercial Code, art. 9-203, also provides for the perfection of the security interest. This will often be complemented by a separate acknowledgement or endorsements whereby the insurer agrees that proceeds are to be paid into project accounts over which the lenders have security.

Loss payee provisions

6.86 Under the finance documents, the project company is typically required to open and maintain an insurance and compensation account for receipt of insurance proceeds (other than delay in start-up, business interruption, and/or third party liability proceeds) and other compensation amounts. The insurance policies will contain loss payee provisions that treat the project company as the sole loss payee but will direct that proceeds be credited to different accounts depending on their nature. Material damage insurance proceeds (all proceeds of insurance received by or payable to the project company under the 'material damage' policies of marine transit, CEAR, and PD insurance) and third party liability proceeds (not paid directly to third parties) will be credited to a compensation account along with any other compensation amounts that are not expressly directed elsewhere. Proceeds from loss of revenue insurance (including proceeds received in respect of a delay in start up) will be credited to the project company's offshore operating or revenue account. Any proceeds payable directly to a third party in settlement of third party liabilities will be paid directly to the third party claimant unless the payment is to indemnify a payment already made by the project company, in which case those funds will be paid into the insurance account. The lenders are granted security over the project company's accounts and any disbursements to be made from those accounts are regulated by the provisions of the finance documents. Typically, the notices of acknowledgement of the reinsurance assignment contain loss payee provisions that direct the reinsurers to pay insurance proceeds directly to the project company's accounts.

Waiver of rights of subrogation

In the context of a project financing, policies of insurance will frequently cover **6.87** multiple parties. These parties, in the event a loss occurs, could have valid claims against one another and the insurer might be entitled to subrogate itself to these rights. For instance, if the project company and a subcontractor are both insured parties under the same policy, any loss caused by one to the other could result in the insurer subrogating itself to the rights of the injured party against the party that caused the loss. To avoid the numerous problems that this would pose, the insured would typically insist on the inclusion of a waiver of rights of subrogation in which the insurer waives any right of subrogation it has against certain defined parties. While the parties against which this right is waived might be explicitly named, in other circumstances a group may be defined generally to include, for example, all subcontractors or the secured lenders.

Ability to amend insurances and market availability

Since risk is variable, the initial insurance may cease adequately to cover the project **6.88** and the lenders. For this reason, the finance documents may allow the lenders' agent or trustee, acting reasonably or on the instructions of the majority lenders and in consultation with the lenders' insurance advice, to require that the project company seek an amendment to an existing policy within a given time period.

Like many markets, the insurance market is subject to cyclical movements and **6.89** changes in risk appetite. As a result, an insurance programme agreed between the project company and the lenders at financial closing which reflects the availability and terms of insurance available at that time may not be deliverable by the project company throughout the term of the loans. Certain types of cover may become unavailable (as was the case with terrorism insurance in the immediate aftermath of the events of September 2001). More commonly though, some specified insurances may cease to be available on 'commercially reasonable terms', such that a prudent company would not consider it appropriate (based on a reasonable risk-reward balance) to place such insurance. Alternatively, certain deductible levels or endorsements required by the lenders may cease to be available or insurers may decline to provide such endorsements containing the required wording. In such instances, it is not unusual for the finance documents to contain a mechanism to allow for a suspension or amendment of the relevant insurance obligations until such time as the project company is able to resume such obligations.

Broker's letter of undertaking

Purpose

6.90 The role of an insurance broker is to act as an intermediary between the insured and the insurer or, in the context of reinsurance, between the insurer and the reinsurer. It thus becomes necessary that material information passes from the broker to both parties to ensure that a valid contract of insurance is formed. In the case of primary insurances, the broker acts as the agent of the project company and so the lenders typically wish to ensure they can control the scope of the grant of authority that the broker receives from the project company and commit the broker to act appropriately. This is done by way of a broker's letter of undertaking (often referred to as a BLOU) which is included in the schedule of insurances set forth in the finance documents. It is signed by the broker and addressed, as appropriate, to the onshore or offshore security agent or trustee.

Customary provisions

6.91 The provisions included in a BLOU vary significantly depending on the nature of the project as well as the state of the insurance market. Generally, it will require that the broker provide material information to the project company and the lenders and contain provisions ensuring that payments be made to specified project accounts. The broker will also confirm that the insurances entered into are in full force and effect and are substantially in form required by the relevant finance documents and the schedule of insurances. As is crucial to ensure the validity of the insurances, the BLOU will also confirm that the broker made adequate disclosure to insurers and reinsurers and that no such disclosure was inaccurate, incomplete, or misleading.

6.92 The BLOU will often include specific undertakings to give notice to the lenders that any insurance to be entered into, renewed, or renegotiated will comply with the requirements of the relevant finance documents. The broker will also undertake to give similar notice in the event premiums due are not paid and that all premiums received from the project company will be appropriately paid to, as relevant, the insurers or reinsurers. Information regarding any act, omission, or event that any insurer or reinsurer advises may have a material impact on the cover provided by the project's insurances will need to be notified to the lenders. Any change to the insurances that the lenders require be put in place will also need to be notified. In particular, this includes notice of any assignment or purported assignment or the creation of any security interest over any of the insurances. Since the insurance market is not static, changes to the terms of insurance or reinsurance may be necessary and the broker will be obliged to give notice of any alteration of material terms of insurance or reinsurance, including changes to any premiums that are payable, as well as the expiry of coverage. Of course, notice must also be given if the broker ceases to act in that capacity.

Broker's letter of undertaking in the context of reinsurance

As mentioned previously, because certain jurisdictions require that insurance be **6.93** purchased in the domestic insurance market, and because of the scope and nature of the risk being insured in an international project finance context, a certain percentage of the insurance is required by the lenders to be reinsured. The crucial difference in respect of the broker, in the context of reinsurance, is that it is acting as an intermediary between the primary insurer and reinsurer. As such, it has no obligation to the insured parties or the lenders in much the same way the primary insurance broker would not normally have an obligation towards the lenders. Otherwise the BLOU serves much the same function as under the primary insurances, and must be executed by any broker acting as agent of the insurers.

7

PRINCIPAL LOAN FINANCE DOCUMENTATION

Gabriel Mpubani, Milbank, Tweed, Hadley & McCloy LLP

Introduction

Project financings can be document-heavy transactions due to the elaborate risk **7.01** allocation and mitigation measures they engender. A particularly complex financing will generate copious amounts of documentation addressing the project's construction and operation, the financing that supports it, and the security that in turn underpins the financing. The financing arrangements between the project company and the lenders will typically be memorialized in a suite of documents that reflect the idiosyncrasies of the particular transaction. Needless to say, great care must be taken faithfully to reflect the parties' actual commercial bargain; the consequences for not doing so are considerable.[1]

7.02 This chapter will analyse the key loan documentation typically encountered in a project financing and a selection of the key documentation issues therein that most often arise in practice.

Credit Agreements

7.03 The credit agreement is the principal legal document that formally records the express terms[2] agreed by the borrower and lender to govern their contractual relationship. At its core, the lender will lend or agree to lend a sum of money to the borrower in return for the borrower's promise to repay that sum either on demand or at the agreed time, usually with interest.[3] This foundation will be supplemented by protective and administrative provisions, such as representations and warranties, covenants, events of default, agency mechanics, and dispute resolution clauses, among others. Market practice and the desire on the part of arrangers and originating lenders to syndicate or sell down all or part of the loan will often dictate the form, if not the substance, of the credit agreement. Potential syndicatees and transferees will baulk at participating in agreements that contain material provisions seen to be unusual or 'off market'. There is therefore merit in reserving adventurous or novel ideas for the genuinely bespoke and complex transaction. For this reason, a number of English law governed project finance credit agreements are based on the London Loan Market Association's (LMA's) leveraged form credit agreement, duly adapted to suit the relevant circumstances of the particular transaction, and are readily recognisable in the lending market.

---

[1] This is particularly important under English law, where pre-contractual negotiations will, as a general rule, be superseded by the written agreement of the parties. But not, it appears, under continental civil law regimes. Art. 4.3 of the UNIDROIT Principles of International Commercial Contracts, UNIDROIT, 2004 and Art. 5.102(a) of the Principles of European Contract Law (1999) allow recourse to prior negotiations in ascertaining the 'common intention of the parties', as does the United Nations Convention on Contracts for the International Sale of Goods (1980). See also C. Valcke, 'On Comparing French and English Contract Law: Insights from Social Contract Theory', 16 January 2009 at <http://ssrn.com/abstract=1328923>, mentioned favourably by Lord Hoffmann in *Chartbrook Ltd v Persimmon Homes Ltd* [2009] UKHL 38, which case also reviews the English case law authorities on the point.

[2] In addition to other terms that may be implied by the applicable general law.

[3] Certain jurisdictions, such as Saudi Arabia, do not enforce the payment of interest on the basis that it is contrary to *Sharia'a* law. In those cases, other fee or profit-sharing structures may be employed. These are more fully explored in Chapter 10.

In a multi-sourced financing where a number of lenders are advancing different **7.04** tranches of debt, it has become customary for the provisions that are common to the various debt tranches to be set out in a 'common terms agreement'. This allows the commercial and operational features unique to each debt tranche to be set out in a more streamlined agreement, which incorporates the common terms by reference. This approach saves time and cost in avoiding multiple bilateral negotiations over substantially similar provisions, ensures lender parity, at least to the extent of the common terms, and, perhaps most importantly, reduces the risk of terms being construed inconsistently across tranches, particularly where they are governed by different laws.

The project financing credit agreement is broadly similar to the agreement seen in **7.05** other financings, with a few (but critical) differences, some of which are explored below. Detailed checklists of the typical conditions precedent, representations and warranties, covenants, and events of default customarily set out in project financing credit agreements are outlined in Appendix 1.

Purpose clause

Most credit agreements will set out the purpose for which loans advanced under the **7.06** agreement are to be applied. Lenders will want to ensure that the borrower does not divert the borrowings away from the project and to demonstrate compliance with their lending eligibility criteria. In most cases, actual misuse will trigger an event of default. Furthermore, the purpose clause evidences the intention of the parties in advancing the money, which helps protect the lender on the borrower's insolvency if the money has either not yet been applied or has been misapplied. Under English law, a loan to a borrower for a specific purpose, where the borrower is not free to apply the money for any other purpose, gives rise to fiduciary obligations on the part of the borrower which a court of equity will enforce.[4] When the money is advanced, the lender acquires an enforceable right in equity, rather than in contract, to prevent its application for any other purpose.[5] This prevents the borrower from obtaining any beneficial interest in the money while the designated purpose is still capable of being carried out. If for any reason the purpose cannot be carried out, for instance, on abandonment of the project, a resulting trust would prevent the money from falling within the general fund of the borrower's assets so as to pass to its trustee-in-bankruptcy in the event of its insolvency; the money would not become part of the assets of the borrower.[6]

---

[4] Per Lord Millet in *Twinsectra Ltd v Yardley* [2002] 1 AC 384.
[5] Most credit agreements will state that the lenders are not obliged to monitor the application of the funds, thus making clear that the equitable right is not burdened with a policing obligation.
[6] See *Quistclose Investments Ltd v Rolls Razor Ltd* [1970] AC 567; *Twinsectra Ltd v Yardley* [2002] 1 AC 384.

Conditions precedent

7.07 Upon signing the credit agreement, the lenders become committed[7] to lend the agreed sums of money to the borrower, subject to the conditions specified in the agreement itself. There will usually be two sets of conditions precedent: those which are common to all debt tranches and are therefore set out in the common terms agreement; and those which are specific to a particular debt tranche and are therefore set out in the individual loan agreement applicable to that tranche. Each set of conditions precedent will usually be divided into two parts: one being those conditions precedent that apply only to the initial drawdown of loans and the other applying to both the initial and subsequent drawdowns.

7.08 Conditions precedent to the initial drawdown are designed to ensure that:

(1) the borrower is duly authorized to borrow the loans and grant the relevant security;
(2) the project has satisfied the lenders' due diligence requirements and verification by their advisers;
(3) the project complies with applicable laws and governmental permits;
(4) all material project and finance documents have been entered into and are binding and enforceable against the parties thereto; and
(5) the security arrangements are adequate and effective.

7.09 Conditions precedent to each subsequent drawdown are designed to ensure that there is no material deterioration in the risk profile of the project or the borrower and that the lenders do not lend into a distressed project on terms designed for benign conditions. Thus, these conditions precedent will help the lenders to:

(1) ensure that agreed construction milestones are being met as scheduled and on budget;
(2) identify emerging problems such as environmental or technical complications; and
(3) confirm that no other material adverse events have arisen since the last drawdown.

Loan drawdowns are often directly tied to progress under the construction contract, and many credit agreements may require a technical adviser's certification that certain 'milestones' have been achieved or that a prescribed degree of construction has been completed.

---

[7] However, under English law, an order for specific performance would not be available to compel the lender to honour its obligation to lend under a loan contract nor will the borrower be able to maintain a debt claim for the unadvanced moneys; the borrower would only be entitled to damages for its actual loss caused by the lender's non-performance, which may, depending upon the circumstances, be minimal. See *South African Territories v Wallington* [1898] AC 309.

Usually, the initial conditions precedent will have to be met to the satisfaction of, **7.10** or waived by, each lender while subsequent conditions precedent (other than those in respect of which a particular lender may insist on a veto right[8]) will commonly only be fulfilled to the satisfaction of a prescribed majority of the lenders. This means that a single lender could prevent an entire syndicate from making the initial (and perhaps even subsequent) advances of the financing. Some borrowers attempt to secure the lenders' prior agreement on the form and content of as many of the documentary conditions precedent as possible prior to signing the credit agreement, but this is often resisted as lenders do not want to commit the required resources until they have firm assurances that they will definitely participate in the financing and have completed their due diligence. Neither the lenders' agent nor counsel will be willing to certify unequivocally that the conditions precedent comply with the terms of the credit agreement. However, it is not uncommon for a letter to be furnished by one of them to the lenders stating that documents have been provided by the borrower which appear to comply with the required conditions precedent.

Where ECAs are either guaranteeing or directly providing 'tied' lending to a project, **7.11** there will be additional conditions precedent requiring the borrower to deliver documentation evidencing the eligibility of the costs being funded. Such documentation would typically include the relevant goods or services supply contracts to which the funding is tied; documents certifying the eligibility of the goods or services, together with supporting documentation, such as bills of lading and certificates of origin; and, where funding is being made available on a reimbursement basis, certification that the relevant invoices in respect of the eligible goods or services have been paid.

Drawdown of loans

If the conditions precedent have been met, the project company will be entitled to **7.12** request loans to be advanced to it by delivering written requests in accordance with the procedures set out in the credit agreement. The loans may be drawn in their entirety at once or in installments during the availability period. Lenders always require a minimum period of notice to raise the funds in the interbank market. This notice period is negotiated, but will largely be driven by the customary practice of the relevant interbank market. However, such notice period should be sufficient to allow a reasonable time for the lenders' agent to fulfill its obligations and enable the lenders to take the necessary steps to fund before any proposed date of drawdown. Development finance institutions (DFIs), micro finance institutions (MFIs), and export credit agencies (ECAs), usually require longer notice periods, particularly where the loan is to be disbursed in a currency other than dollars, euro, or sterling.

---

[8] For instance, in relation to compliance with its environmental standards or, in the case of an ECA, its official credits eligibility criteria.

7.13 A drawdown notice will usually be stated to be irrevocable and the borrower is typically liable to pay the lender's breakage costs if it does not proceed with a borrowing after delivering a drawdown notice. However, whereas the borrower may not withdraw from the drawdown without penalty, lenders will typically be entitled to stop an advance at any point prior to wiring the funds, if they became aware of a 'draw-stop' event, typically a default or other occurrence such as supervening illegality or market disruption, entitling the lender to withhold funding.

7.14 In a multi-sourced financing, the borrower will usually request that funding be made through a single lenders' agent for logistical convenience, a practice which, albeit normally accepted, exposes the lenders to a risk of the agent's insolvency for the duration that the disbursed loans are in the agent's possession.

Repayments

7.15 Project finance loans typically have long tenors to reflect the credit profile of the relevant project, with the loan amortizing over time. The repayment profile of a project finance loan will usually reflect the revenue generating characteristics of the relevant sector; thus, where revenues are cyclical and volatile, the credit agreement could allow the borrower to defer principal repayments during the lean cycles and then 'catch-up' with the repayment schedule when the project's revenues permit. Sculpted repayment profiles are increasingly common, but will only be agreed where the business case is clearly made. Also, where the project generates excess cash in certain periods, the lenders may require that all or part of the surplus is applied to make prepayments, thereby reducing the average life of the loan.

7.16 Repayments will usually be made to the lenders' agent for distribution to the lenders, usually on a pro rata basis. As a function of the law of agency, the borrower's obligation to pay is, as a general rule, discharged upon paying the agent even if the agent then fails to pay the lenders.

Prepayments and cancellation

7.17 Most credit agreements will expressly permit the borrower to repay all or part of the loan early. It is widely thought that no such right can exist in the absence of an express prepayment clause. Prepayment can be either mandatory, upon the occurrence of certain prescribed events (for example, illegality, change of control, or damage to the plant), or at the borrower's volition.

7.18 Voluntary prepayment will usually be conditional on the borrower giving the lenders a minimum amount of notice and prepayment being made at the end of an interest period. If the borrower requests the right to prepay other than at the end of an interest period, it will usually be granted on the basis that the break costs indemnity is applicable and that any costs of unwinding interest rate hedges are for its account.

Some lenders occasionally request a prepayment fee or premium on the basis that **7.19** they have incurred costs and agreed margins on the expectation of a return over a longer period. Borrowers maintain that the flexibility to make prepayments is central to the efficient management of a project's finance plan and will, if relevant, point to prepayment as being a key justification for preferring bank loans over a less flexible capital markets debt issuance. However, borrowers also recognize that certain DFIs, MFIs, and ECAs are required by their internal policies to demand a prepayment premium upon a voluntary prepayment.

Prepayments can either be applied rateably to reduce all scheduled repayments or **7.20** chronologically to reduce the earliest scheduled repayments. Lenders prefer prepayments to be made rateably in inverse chronological order (i.e. the latest scheduled payments being prepaid first) to shorten the average life of the loan and avoid effectively giving the borrower a repayment holiday.

Prepayments or cancellations of commitments proposed to be made during the **7.21** availability period will usually be an indication of 'over-borrowing'. However, lenders will customarily insist on a certification that there will be sufficient committed funding after the prepayment or cancellation to complete the project without the borrower having to incur additional debt.

There are a number of events, most of them outside of the direct control of the **7.22** borrower, which will, upon their occurrence, trigger an obligation enjoining the borrower to mandatorily prepay the outstanding loans. These typically include:

(1) Illegality, although the borrower will usually have the option of requesting the affected lender to sell its participation to another unaffected lender, switch the location of its lending office to the extent possible, or allow a grace period within which to make the prepayment, being the maximum period permitted by applicable law.
(2) Change of control, usually to guard against unsavoury or inexperienced sponsors taking over the project; this obligation will sometimes fall away after a prescribed minimum retention period, but will usually only be contemplated if the sponsor has no material obligations to the project.
(3) Deterioration of the borrower's credit rating below a prescribed level, particularly in relation to rated project bonds, where certain lenders are prevented by internal policy from lending other than to an investment grade credit.
(4) Recoveries, such as insurance and compensation realizations for damage or loss to the project above a specified threshold, or liquidated damages paid under the construction contracts.
(5) Failure to meet prescribed financial ratios, including those which form part of a completion test.
(6) The realization of excess cash, in which case the lenders may wish to share all or part of it to shorten the loan life.

Interest

7.23 Most credit agreements not structured as Islamic financings[9] will charge interest on the loans advanced to the borrower, either on a floating or a fixed rate basis. Floating rate lending is based on the notion that lenders fund their loan participations through short-term deposits in the interbank market for each interest period at an interbank rate usually provided through a screen service such as Telerate or Reuters. If a screen rate is not available, an arithmetic mean of rates quoted to the lenders' agent by pre-named reference banks will be used instead. The rate will therefore reflect the lender's cost of funds, and a margin, the latter being the lender's return for accepting the borrower's credit risk. This will be in addition to other fees charged on the loan.

7.24 During the construction period, a project will not be revenue generating. As such, interest will either be paid from debt drawdowns (for which reason financing costs will be included in the definition of project costs) or will be capitalized and added to the principal amount.

7.25 A failure to pay interest when due will trigger a payment default but also cause a higher, default rate to apply, usually in the range of 100 to 300 basis points.

Market disruption

7.26 Most credit agreements recognize that LIBOR or the relevant interbank offer rate may not accurately reflect a lender's funding cost and consequently will contain a so-called 'market disruption clause' to protect lenders accordingly. A minimum threshold of lenders will usually be required to trigger this clause,[10] to rule out disruption that is unique to a few lenders, rather than being truly reflective of the state of the market. If the market disruption clause is triggered, each lender would be paid interest at a rate calculated by reference to that lender's cost of funding its participation in the loan from whatever source it may reasonably select.[11]

7.27 Despite its ubiquity in credit agreements, the market disruption clause will only be invoked very rarely as demonstrated in the recent 'credit crunch' when LIBOR was severely criticized but abandoned in only a relatively small number of cases. Reasons for this reticence are manifold: lenders are reluctant to be seen to have higher than average funding costs as it is a reflection on how the market perceives their credit risk. Also, some banks are unwilling to disclose their cost of funds for competitive and reputational reasons and will absorb the mismatch rather than disclose their

---

[9] In respect of which see Chapter 10.

[10] In the London market, the required threshold is typically a simple majority or 35 per cent, while the US market tends to retain the same percentage that would apply to normal amendments and waivers under the credit agreement, typically 66.67 per cent.

[11] In the US market, the interest rate would begin to be calculated by reference to the 'base rate', a domestic US pricing option that historically has often exceeded US dollar LIBOR.

internal calculations. Thus, the continuing importance of this clause is in practice limited to those relatively rare circumstances where loans are being advanced in less convertible currencies.

Yield protection

Credit agreements will invariably set out a cluster of provisions intended to safe-guard the yield that the lenders expect to receive from lending to the borrower. **7.28**

The borrower will be required to preserve the lenders' profit margin from tax impositions and the mandatory costs arising from changes in law or compli-ance with the requirements of a central bank or other monetary authority, generally regardless of whether or not the occurrence existed on signing the credit agreement. **7.29**

In most cases, if the borrower becomes obliged to make a yield protection payment, it may elect to prepay the affected lender's loans instead, an exception to the equal treatment paradigm that underpins most credit agreements. Lenders are also usu-ally under an obligation to take reasonable mitigation measures, including transferring their loans to an affiliate or other lending office. Also, assignments and transfers by lenders must not increase the borrower's obligations to protect the lenders' yield. **7.30**

Tax gross up

Lenders very rarely agree to take withholding tax risk, and as such, the inclusion of a tax gross-up clause is usually a non-negotiable prerequisite. The gross-up clause will shield lenders from the effects of withholding taxes on interest payments by requiring the borrower to make payments in full as if there had been no deduc-tion; it usually takes no account of the ability on the lender's part, to obtain tax credits for the deduction in due course, as this would in itself impose a time and administrative cost and expose the lender's tax affairs to potential scrutiny by the borrower. Where the financing structure features an A/B loan structure,[12] the tax gross up may be extended to deductions on payments to the B loan participants. **7.31**

Borrowers will also be required to indemnify the lenders against any tax (other than normal profit tax) imposed on or in relation to sums received under the credit agreement. The indemnity will not, however, extend to taxes on net income imposed by the lender's jurisdiction of incorporation or residence or the location of its lending office. **7.32**

---

[12] See para. 8.35 et seq.

7.33 In cross-border transactions, the laws of the borrower's jurisdiction of incorpora-tion, and those of other jurisdictions through which payments are made, are relevant, and local counsel should, as a matter of good practice, be consulted.

Increased costs

7.34 The increased costs clause is designed to protect lenders against changes in law or official regulation that increase their underlying costs, such as those deriving from central bank reserve, capital adequacy, and liquidity requirements and will custom-arily feature in domestic or eurocurrency loans. The increased costs clause usually excludes existing requirements or costs caused by a lender's willful non-compliance with relevant regulations.

Representations and warranties

7.35 A lot of time is spent negotiating representations and warranties, which in project financings, are extensive and are repeated often. The set of representations and war-ranties will typically be based on market standard forms such as the LMA leveraged form, with additional representations added to reflect the policy requirements of certain lenders, such as ECAs and DFIs, as well as the specific characteristics of the borrower and the project. Appendix 1 sets out a list of representations and warran-ties typically encountered in project finance transactions.

7.36 Borrowers will seek to restrict the scope of representations and warranties, particu-larly by using materiality or knowledge qualifications in respect of commercial warranties. Each representation and warranty will be deemed to be made on the date of signing the credit agreement. Selected representations and warranties will be deemed to be repeated at important stages, including on financial close, the first and each subsequent drawdown (if different) and in some financings, at the begin-ning of each interest period.

Covenants

7.37 The project finance covenant package is one of the broadest in the financing world, extending beyond the borrower to include the sponsors and other counterparties to material project contracts whilst they owe obligations to the project (most often during the construction period, but also, for example, in the case of product off-take, during the operating period). Due to the limited or non-recourse nature of the credit, the project lender's basic instinct is to assert a far-reaching control over the project and its revenue-generating capacity, recognizing that the debt advanced by it will be recoverable from that source alone. In negotiating the covenant package, the lenders will therefore, as a starting point, discount the strength of the sponsor as there may be little to prevent the latter from walking away from the project. Naturally, the sponsors will seek as light a covenant package as they can credibly make a case for, largely arguing that an overly strict covenants package interferes with their ability to run the project profitably. A balancing act is therefore inevitable, and the lenders will draw on the advice of their various advisers in finding the appropriate equilibrium.

The negotiation surrounding the covenant package will, in many cases, be driven **7.38** by precedent. Many an adviser is at a loss to explain the rationale for a particular provision beyond it having featured in a transaction that was successfully financed. Barring such instances where precedents become an article of faith, there are sound reasons for a full complement of covenants in the typical project financing: information covenants will provide data to evaluate the ongoing soundness of the project; financial covenants will serve as early warning signs of the project's inability to service its debt obligations; negative undertakings will ensure that the borrower does nothing to materially undermine its creditworthiness and the project's risk profile, while positive undertakings will require the borrower proactively to maintain or enhance its credit. At this basic level, project financing is no different to any other financing. It is in the detail of the various covenants, however, that the project financing loan makes a firm departure from the corporate or leveraged buy-out loan.

The reader is referred to Appendix 1 for a checklist of the typical covenants which **7.39** are customarily found in a project financing credit agreement.

Financial ratios

Project financings, like most other leveraged financings, invariably feature financial **7.40** ratios which will not only frequently test the lawyers' patience but also, on an ongoing basis, the debt capacity of the project and its ability to generate revenue in amounts that are sufficient to meet its operating costs and repay the debt on a current basis. The types of ratios used will vary depending on the project and its sensitivities, but certain ratios have become almost standard in the typical limited recourse financing. These are: (1) the debt to equity ratio; (2) the backward-looking DSCR;[13] (3) the forward-looking DSCR; and (4) the LLCR.[14] In mining projects, a reserve tail ratio will also be relatively common.

The debt to equity ratio is a snap shot test to assess the dependence of a project on **7.41** debt. Customarily, a cap will be imposed on the leverage of a project, usually ranging from 50 per cent to 80 per cent, depending on a number of factors ranging from common sector benchmarks to the revenue profile of the project company. The DSCR and LLCR seek to test the ability of the project company's cashflows adequately to cover its debt service obligations. The backward-looking DSCR is calculated on the basis of the project company's actual performance, usually

---

[13] Debt service cover ratio.
[14] Loan life cover ratio.

over a prior twelve-month period; the forward-looking DSCR and LLCR are based on projected revenues and costs during the relevant testing period (in the case of a forward-looking DSCR, often relating to the succeeding twelve-month period and in relation to the LLCR, from the testing date through to final maturity of the debt).

7.42 In projecting the forward-looking DSCR and LLCR, the project company will typically use an updated banking case applying, in all cases, the then current technical and cost assumptions. In certain circumstances, the credit agreement will call for the use of the then current economic (including pricing) assumptions whilst in others, the economic (including pricing) assumptions used in the original banking case at the time of financial close will be applied.

7.43 Procedurally, the project company usually proposes the new technical assumptions, which may then be disputed by the lenders using customary contestation procedures (often referring the matter to an appropriately qualified expert).

7.44 The financial coverage ratios will be tested in a number of circumstances. These include:

(1) as a condition precedent to financial close and perhaps even to drawdowns;
(2) passing the relevant completion test;
(3) permitting shareholder distributions;
(4) incurring additional debt; and
(5) as a default trigger.

7.45 The tables below set out examples of how different ratios could be used in different circumstances and the relationship with the assumptions used in the base case Financial Model.

Table 7.1

(a) Backward-looking DSCR

Purpose	Ratio level
Distributions to shareholders	1.[•]:1 (12 months prior to the testing date).

(b) Forward-looking DSCR

Purpose	Nature of assumptions	Ratio level
Distributions to shareholders	Updated.	1.[•]:1 (12 months following the testing date).

Purpose	Nature of assumptions	Ratio level
Incurrence of replacement debt	Original (but amended to take into account the proposed replacement debt).	Is at least equal to the forward-looking DSCR for each testing date through to final maturity in the banking case delivered at financial close.
Conditions precedent (if applicable)	Original.	For each testing date through to final maturity of not less than a specified minimum.
Completion (testing)	Original (but amended to take into account the actual technical parameters demonstrated during the completion test, if less than the minimum requirements assumed at financial close).	Is at least equal to the forward-looking DSCR for each testing date through to final maturity in the banking case delivered at financial close.

(c) LLCR

Purpose	Nature of assumptions	Ratio level
Incurrence of replacement debt	Original (but amended to take into account the proposed replacement debt).	Is at least equal to the LLCR in the banking case delivered at financial close.
Conditions precedent (if applicable)	Original.	For the period from the testing date through to final maturity of not less than a specified minimum.
Completion (testing)	Original (but amended to take into account the actual technical parameters demonstrated during the completion test, if less than the minimum requirements assumed at financial close).	Is at least equal to the LLCR in the banking case delivered at financial close.

7.46 It is important that the ratios used in the credit agreement accurately reflect the ratios set out in the official version of the financial model and are reviewed, as appropriate, by the documentation bank or technical adviser. The definitions should follow the appropriate accounting convention used by the borrower, and if necessary, with changes being made to the IFRS-based[15] definitions used in, for example, the LMA standard form financial covenant definitions.

---

[15] IFRS are the international accounting standards within the meaning of IAS Regulation 1606/2002 to the extent applicable to the relevant financial statements.

Events of default

7.47 Only a credit agreement in which the debt is repayable on demand of the lender is complete without events of default. If they were absent from loan agreements, lenders would have to look to general contract law for remedies, which is not ideal. On the other hand, the inclusion in the credit agreement of events of default gives lenders the ability to bring the lending relationship to a premature end, should a change in circumstances make this appropriate, with clear pre-agreed remedies, without the need to head for the law courts. Their occurrence will also normally automatically suspend the ability of the borrower to request further advances under the credit agreement whilst simultaneously preventing distributions to the sponsors or, where they exist, more junior creditors. Lenders will also usually become entitled to receive enhanced information and site visit access rights. The lenders will also customarily acquire a freer hand to transfer their loan holdings to third parties without reference to the borrower, an action that could bring more aggressive or non-relationship lenders into the project. But the biggest threat posed to the borrower by the event of default is the ability that lenders then acquire to accelerate outstanding loans; acceleration will typically cross-default all of the borrower's debt and almost certainly lead to insolvency. It is therefore an option that lenders would exercise only if no further assistance can be found in working out of the distressed scenario.

7.48 The events of default in a project financing will mirror those in other financings, including in respect of:

(1) the failure to repay principal or to pay interest and fees when due;
(2) breach of financial covenants;
(3) breach of general undertakings;
(4) misrepresentations by the project company and other obligors;
(5) impairment of the transaction security; and
(6) the insolvency or bankruptcy of the borrower.

7.49 The credit agreement will also contain events of default that address any material adverse effect on the project by reason of:

(1) misrepresentations and breaches of covenants by counterparty to a material project contract;
(2) material adverse changes in law or governmental authorizations;
(3) the bankruptcy or insolvency of counterparties to the project contracts;
(4) loss of regulatory licenses, permits, or exemptions;
(5) failure by the shareholders to fund any equity support arrangements or to comply with share retention covenants;
(6) expropriation by governmental authorities; and
(7) failure to complete the project or commence operations by a date certain.

Clearly, the most controversial of these relate to defaults triggered by the conduct of persons or conditions beyond a borrower's control. The reader is referred to

Appendix 1 for a checklist of events of default which are typically included in a project financing credit agreement.

Remedies

Following an event of default, the credit documentation generally sets out the **7.50** remedies afforded to a lender, including the right to:

(1) cancel the commitment to advance funds;
(2) declare the loans to be due on demand or to accelerate the maturity of the loans; and
(3) exercise the rights of a secured creditor under the security agreements.

Additional remedies may allow the lenders to assume the construction and operation of the project or to cure defaults by the project company under any of the project contracts. It is advisable, however, for the lenders to consult with counsel to ensure that these remedies do not result in liability to third parties. For example, liablility may attach to lenders and other persons exercising control over a thinly capitalized project company.

To exercise the remedies, the credit agreement will usually require the lenders' agent **7.51** to deliver a notice to that effect, sometimes only while the relevant event of default is continuing, i.e. has not been cured or waived. It is important that any such notice is given in accordance with the terms of the contract.[16] Occasionally, the borrower will successfully negotiate the inclusion of a procedure to be followed in the giving of such notice, such as a notice period; in that event, that procedure must be observed, particularly where it is capable of being construed as a condition precedent to taking enforcement action. The agent will usually, even where it is given the power to accelerate, request to be authorized to deliver the notice of acceleration by a majority of the lenders.

Accounts Agreements

Since a true project financing is non-recourse to the sponsor's balance sheet, with **7.52** cashflows from the project's assets and operations being the only source of debt service and repayment, the project accounts and the cashflow will be jealously guarded by the creditors via elaborate, and occasionally onerous, restrictions regulating the flow of cash and its allocation. The lenders will insist on having access to virtually all available cashflow in the forward years of the project and will use the

---

[16] *Re Berker Sportcraft Ltd's Agreements, Hartnell v Berker Sportcraft Ltd* (1947) 177 LT 420.

loan financing documents to impose covenants on the use to which the project's revenues must be applied.

7.53 The creditors will exert control through a 'waterfall' of accounts, so called because funds initially go into the receipt or revenue account at the top and then cascade through the operating account, the debt service account (for the payment of current principal and interest) and various reserve accounts (generally including a debt service reserve account (DSRA), into which a reserve for future debt service payments, often calculated on the basis of six months' debt service, will be set aside). The cascade defines the priority of uses for the project's cashflow, which will take on significance when actual revenue falls below operating cost requirements. At the bottom of the waterfall is an account from which dividend distributions will be permitted to be paid to the shareholders of the project company.

7.54 The project company is typically permitted to withdraw funds from the operating account solely to cover approved operating expenses, from the reserve accounts to fund specified costs, and from the project company's distributions account to fund distributions to its shareholders, so long as the conditions for withdrawal set out in the credit agreement have been satisfied. The lenders will generally have security over the accounts and the balances contained within them, and they will often seek the right to assert broader control over the use of the funds held in the accounts upon the occurrence of a default or other adverse conditions.

7.55 The waterfall and other accounts operating mechanics, as well as provisions governing the relationship between the account bank, the other finance parties, and the project company, will be detailed in the common terms agreement or in a stand-alone accounts agreement. The latter is likely to be more appropriate where the account bank is not also lending to the project and prefers not to be party to the common terms agreement or where a different governing law applies to the accounts, particularly in relation to the onshore accounts. The accounts agreement will also be useful in disapplying certain rights that the account bank enjoys, either under the normal banker-customer relationship, or pursuant to its normal bank mandates. Lord Cottenham LC's statement in *Foley v Hill* describing the features of the banker/customer relationship makes plain why express account provisions are needed to counteract the effects of the normal banker-customer relationship:

> Money, when paid into a bank, ceases altogether to be the money of the principal . . . it is then the money of the banker . . . ; he is known to deal with it as his own; he makes what profit on it he can, which profit he retains to himself, paying back only the principal, according to the custom of bankers in some places, or the principal and a small rate of interest, according to the custom of bankers in other places. The money placed in the custody of a banker is, to all intents and purposes, the money of the banker, to do with it as he pleases; he is guilty of no breach of trust in employing it; he is not answerable to the principal if he puts it i/nto jeopardy, if he engages in a hazardous speculation; he is not bound to keep it or deal with it as the property of his principal, but he is of course answerable for the amount because he

has contracted, having received that money, to repay the principal, when demanded, a sum equivalent to that paid into his hands. That has been the subject of discussion in various cases, and that has been established to be the relative situation of banker and customer.[17]

In a financing involving international lenders and in cases where there are concerns **7.56** about political risk in the host country or the enforceability of local security, the project accounts will, subject to applicable local regulatory requirements, typically be maintained in one of the principal financial centres, usually London or New York. Debt and equity proceeds as well as project revenues will be paid into and maintained in the offshore accounts, with transfers made periodically (usually monthly) to a local account in an amount sufficient to meet budgeted expenditure until the next scheduled transfer.

The key provisions in the accounts agreement will address the following: **7.57**

(1) *Acknowledgment of security*: The accounts agreement will generally be used as the means by which the project company gives notice of the security created over the project accounts (and any monies paid into such accounts from time to time). The account bank will also usually be required to undertake not to claim or exercise any rights of set-off, combination or consolidation of accounts, or any other rights over the project accounts or investments purchased out of account balances. Without this clause, the account bank could, under the normal banker-customer relationship, appropriate the money in the accounts against liabilities owed to it by the project company, ahead of the lenders.

(2) *No other accounts*: The project company is usually prevented from establishing any other accounts beyond those prescribed in the accounts agreement without the prior written consent of the lenders. Such consent would typically only be given if the additional accounts are regulated by the accounts agreement (usually achieved by being opened with the account bank or accession by the new account bank) and are charged to the same extent as the existing project accounts for the benefit of the secured parties.

(3) *Instructing party*: The borrower will usually retain full access to the project accounts prior to the occurrence of an event of default and the account bank will usually be entitled, without further verification, to allow the project company to operate the project accounts in accordance with the provisions of the accounts agreement until such time as it is notified by the finance parties that an account blocking event has occurred or that the finance parties have voted to enforce their security over the accounts. Upon the lenders taking enforcement action, the account bank will be obliged to honour only the instructions given by the finance parties. Access is sometimes restricted progressively, initially through a 'lock-up' that prevents distributions being made to the

---

[17] *Foley v Hill* (1848) 2 HL Cas 28 at 36, 37, [1843–60] All ER Rep 16 at 19.

sponsors if a potential event of default occurs. When the potential event of default matures into a full event of default, the borrower's powers to operate the accounts are often further curtailed, ranging from preventing it from being able to operate certain accounts, to altogether losing the ability to manage the accounts.

(4) *Waterfalls*: The principal demarcation as to the application of account balances (and therefore the applicable 'waterfall' structure) will be informed by whether the use occurs during the construction phase or operations phase; and/or before or during the occurrence of a default. Each such phase will normally have a specific priority waterfall that can be summarized as follows:

(a) *During the construction phase*: Subject to local regulatory requirements, the debt and equity proceeds will be deposited into a single account, usually, out of which funds will be drawn periodically to pay project costs as they fall due. During this phase, the payment cascade will be quite limited. Project costs will be given priority. Separate accounts will be maintained for contingency based receipts such as insurance recoveries. An issue that some-times engenders discussion is the application of revenues generated during the start-up phase of the project where project completion has not occurred, but the project has in fact become revenue generating. Where the amounts generated are significant, the lenders usually insist on exercising some con-trol over such proceeds, either by requiring that they be applied towards prepaying the senior debt or funding senior debt service reserves. Commonly, the answer lies in the lenders sharing the pre-completion revenues with the shareholders. At the end of the construction phase, the balance on the account will be transferred into a revenues account, into which the project's revenues will also be paid.

(b) *During the operations phase*: After project completion, the typical waterfall will allow operating costs to be paid out first ahead of senior debt service in order to maintain the ability of the project to generate cashflows while per-mitting distributions to be made to the project owners if all other cash requirements are addressed. A simplified cash waterfall during the period from project completion might be structured to include the following priorities:

(i)   *firstly*, to pay operating costs and taxes;
(ii) *secondly*, to pay the lenders' agents' fees, costs and expenses;
(iii) *thirdly*, to pay debt service due on the next repayment date;
(iv) *fourthly*, to pay mandatory prepayments, if any;
(v)   *fifthly*, to fund the DSRA up to the required balance;
(vi) *sixthly*, to fund other reserve accounts up to the prescribed balances;
(vii) *seventhly*, to pay voluntary prepayments, if any; and
(viii) *finally*, if the distribution conditions are met, to make distributions to the equity parties.

(c) *During an event of default*: The project company will customarily be prevented from making payments to the equity parties where on event of default is continuing. The rest of the waterfall will usually remain intact, until such time as the lenders choose to take enforcement action.

(5) *Distribution and dividend restrictions*: The accounts provisions usually restrict the project company's ability to make dividend payments or distributions of any kind unless the prescribed preconditions have been satisfied, which include, for example, requirements that:

(a) the sponsors have made their equity contribution in full;

(b) there are no outstanding defaults;

(c) the specified financial cover ratios continue to be met; and

(d) all reserve accounts (for example, maintenance and debt service reserve accounts) are fully funded.

(6) *Cash traps*: Project finance credit agreements sometimes also require the project company to use excess cashflow to make mandatory prepayments of loans or to fund special reserves if circumstances occur that increase the project's risk profile from the lenders' perspective. For example, projects that are exposed to market risk for fuel or output may require reserves to be established if market conditions indicate that fuel costs may be rising above, or that output prices may be falling below, projections or assumptions made in the financial model. The lenders may also require cashflow capture if, for example:

(a) the project fails to obtain an important contract or a governmental permit by a given date;

(b) operating costs exceed budgeted amounts; or

(c) in the case of oil and gas or mining projects, the project depletes its fuel or mineral reserves at a faster rate than projected in the financial model.

By capturing cashflow, the lenders reduce their immediate exposure and improve the economics of the project.

(7) *Acceptable credit support*: It is common for the project company (or the sponsors) to be permitted to substitute the cash balances in certain reserve accounts (including the DSRA and any maintenance reserve accounts) with acceptable credit support, usually taking the form of a letter of credit or guarantee issued by an acceptable entity with a suitable credit rating. Lenders tend to require that the issuer or provider of any acceptable credit support may not have recourse to the project company or its assets and is fully subordinated to the senior creditors. Sponsors with credit ratings which are acceptable to the lenders may be able to put in place a corporate guarantee instead of a letter of credit. Where the sponsors are acting through a joint venture and one or more is not able to fund its proportional share of acceptable credit support at the same time as the other sponsors are providing acceptable credit support, they may insist on transferring their proportional share to a separate account in the name of the

non-funding sponsor so that they can have the benefit of any interest accruing on such accounts. Lenders usually accept this provided that the separate account is secured to them and the relevant sponsor is entitled only to receive interest (on a post-tax basis) accruing on amounts standing to the credit of the account.

(8) *Access to books and records and confidentiality.* To enable the finance parties to police the accounts, the project company will authorise the account bank to give access to the books and records held by it on the accounts to the finance parties and authorise the account bank to waive any general duty of confidentiality that it may owe to the project company.

Shareholder Senior Facilities

7.58 Occasionally, a sponsor or its affiliates may provide debt to the project company to fill funding gaps arising from a shortfall in the amounts raised from the other senior lenders. Strong sponsors, particularly in the oil and gas sector have been successful in procuring that that debt ranks *pari passu* with the other senior debt, subject to the commercial terms of each tranche of the shareholder senior facilities being no more favourable than the corresponding tranche being bridged on the basis of the base case financing plan. For instance, if the shareholder senior loan is bridging a commercial bank tranche, it would be expected to bear the same (or a lower) margin. Similarly, the tenor of each affiliated senior debt tranche would be equal to (or greater than) the tenor of the corresponding tranche being bridged as reflected in the base case financing plan.

Mezzanine Facility Agreements

Introduction

7.59 The reader will have been introduced to mezzanine debt in Chapter 3.[18] While mezzanine structures can often plug gaps in a financing plan and have been seen in the straitened times that have affected the market since the credit crunch, mezzanine finance is rarely encountered in project financings and is more readily associated with the leveraged buy-out market. However, mezzanine debt structures in project financings do exist, as seen in the Worsley multi-fuel cogen project in Western Australia which featured mezzanine debt in the form of preferred return instruments. Mezzanine facilities have also been incorporated in a number of renewable energy project financings and infrastructure projects.

---

[18] See para. 3.20 et seq.

Mezzanine debt is a type of subordinated debt that ranks below senior debt and **7.60** above equity, or in more complex financings, above junior debt. Mezzanine debt will sometimes allow the mezzanine lenders to convert all or part of their debt into equity where the project is unable to service the debt on time but remains fundamentally sound on a longer-term outlook. Specialist lenders will typically provide mezzanine funding that more traditional lenders are not able or willing to underwrite, either because the specialists lenders see opportunities in the enhanced margin or convertible aspects that enable them to share in the equity upside or because they have a strategic policy reason for taking on the enhanced risk. A number of ECAs and DFIs have chosen to participate in both senior and mezzanine or other subordinated debt tranches, particularly in the mining sector in the recent past, thus spreading pricing and risk across facilities. Sponsors and owners might also view mezzanine debt as a means of optimizing their financing plan, and rather than seeing the increased risk as a threat, they will focus on the debt characteristics of mezzanine finance that present important advantages over equity, such as tax deductibility, lower funding costs, and higher returns on investment. Traditional mezzanine lenders have largely avoided exposure in emerging markets because of concerns surrounding legal codes and greater operating risks. Mezzanine finance as a product is therefore more prevalent in jurisdictions with stable and predictable legal frameworks, particularly those recognizing debt subordination and having less interventionist insolvency regimes.

Mezzanine debt may also involve extending credit to the sponsors, with the mez- **7.61** zanine lenders taking a charge over the sponsors' equity interests. The need to take such security could therefore lead to a multi-tiered shareholding structure to enable the mezzanine lenders to have exclusive share security at the level that is above the senior lenders. This would enable the mezzanine lenders to take over the equity interests without interfering with the underlying project financing or having to find cash to buy out the senior lenders. Alternatively, the mezzanine debt could be advanced at the project company level, with the mezzanine lenders agreeing to rank behind the senior lenders in the project's cash waterfalls, but ahead of the more deeply subordinated creditors and the equity.

This form of financing may include subordinated/junior debt, preference shares, **7.62** and convertible notes. A mezzanine facility will reflect the fact that the mezzanine lenders are being compensated for accepting an enhanced level of risk relative to the senior creditors. Thus, the mezzanine facility agreement will generally reflect lower financial cover ratios and a higher interest rate to compensate the mezzanine lender for its subordination to the senior debt.

Key features of mezzanine facility agreements

The return: Mezzanine financings encapsulate a variety of structures which are **7.63** shaped by the financing objectives of the parties. However, it is possible to identify characteristics that will at least be given some consideration by the parties in developing a mezzanine facility agreement. Mezzanine lenders look for a certain rate of return which will reflect the longer maturity profile that defines mezzanine debt and which usually results in its full retirement after the senior debt has been paid in full. This means that these aspects of mezzanine debt will not be suited to the lenders whose internal requirements do not permit this level of deferral:

(1) *PIK interest*: In addition to the traditional cash interest, mezzanine finance will typically feature a 'payment in kind' interest element that allows accrued interest to be capitalized rather than being paid in cash.

(2) *Equity interest*: Mezzanine capital will often include an equity stake in the form of attached warrants or a conversion feature.

7.64 *The borrower*: Mezzanine financings can be made at either the project company level or at a holding company level above the project company, depending on the type of subordination required by the senior creditors and other interested constituents.

7.65 *Passive rights*: The rights of the mezzanine lenders in the project finance/PFI/PPP market are narrower than those they are accustomed to enjoying in, for instance, the leveraged buy-out debt market, where they typically are actively involved in decision-making and taking enforcement action, subject only to temporary standstill periods. In a number of project financings and PFI/PPP transactions, the senior lenders have required a 'silent' mezzanine tranche, i.e. the ability of the mezzanine lenders to take or initiate enforcement action will be heavily curtailed, while being permitted intercreditor rights with respect to a very limited universe of matters, usually those that would directly affect their debt. In effect, the senior lenders have regarded and treated the mezzanine tranche as another slice of the equity. However, this is usually accepted by mezzanine lenders in relation to project financings, not least because they may also hold senior debt and will choose to exercise their influence at that level. In rated transactions, the major credit rating agencies generally express concern about the ability of mezzanine lenders to interfere with the senior lenders' debt and security package. To address their concerns, creative structures have been developed to subordinate the mezzanine debt structurally by interposing a mezzanine borrower holding company at a level above the borrower of the senior debt with the mezzanine lenders being given exclusive security over a limited range of assets, such as accounts at the holding company level and share security over the mezzanine borrower holding company. The senior lenders will then be less concerned with the mezzanine lenders having rights to make decisions or take enforcement action at that structurally subordinated level, since their actions would be less likely to interfere with the senior debt. There are a number of reasons why the senior lenders in the project finance/PFI/PPP market take a more aggressive stance against the more junior or mezzanine tranches in the finance structure. These range from the relatively lengthy tenors of the senior debt, to the fact that mezzanine lenders are seen as potentially short-termist, a view that some consider to be unjustified.

Cashflow waterfall priority: Mezzanine debt service customarily ranks below senior **7.66** debt service and the funding of the senior debt service reserve account, but above more junior, subordinated debt. It will also be subject to a lock-up test akin to that applicable to the payment of dividends. In a contractually subordinated structure, negotiations on the waterfall priority tend to focus on whether other reserve accounts, such as maintenance and capital expenditure reserve accounts, should rank ahead of mezzanine debt service. Parties also strongly debate the levels of the lock-up tests, with the senior lenders looking to set them at the same level as those that apply to the equity participants.

Exclusive security: Where the mezzanine lenders are given exclusive security, they **7.67** will take a first ranking security interest over the:

(1) mezzanine debt service reserve account;
(2) mezzanine lock-up account; and
(3) (if the mezzanine lenders are lending to a holding company above the project company) shares of that holding company.

In respect of common security (if any), they will either hold second ranking security (behind senior lenders) over the assets of the borrower, or share first ranking security with the senior lenders, but with an entitlement to recoveries only to the extent that the senior lenders are paid in full. Shares in the project company may form part of the common security.

Selected mezzanine facility agreement issues

The mezzanine facility agreement will usually be drafted only after the senior facil- **7.68** ity agreement has been advanced to a reasonable degree. This is because the two agreements will be substantially similar, with only a few sections being altered to give the mezzanine facility agreement its distinguishing features. The following are some of the sections that will customarily be adjusted:

(1) *The purpose clause*: This will allow the mezzanine debt proceeds to be applied towards the payment of mezzanine fees and debt service.
(2) *Drawdown provisions*: The agreement will clarify whether the mezzanine lenders can influence the determination as to the satisfaction of conditions precedent, particularly in relation to those disbursements that occur after financial close, and whether proceeds are paid into a dedicated proceeds account (over which the mezzanine lenders may have exclusive security) or whether the debt proceeds are intermingled with the senior debt proceeds, and therefore come within the common security package. Where the commercial understanding is to regard the mezzanine debt as equity, the senior lenders may insist on the mezzanine debt being available to be drawn to repay accelerated senior debt.

(3) *Repayment clause.* The key debate here will be seen in determining the circumstances in which the senior lenders will be entitled to prevent the project cashflow reaching the mezzanine lenders through the lock-up tests in the senior facility agreement (or any common terms agreement). The mezzanine facility agreement will similarly set out lock-up tests that restrict payments to more junior debt and the equity.

(4) *Yield protection.* Mezzanine lenders may require prepayment fees to compensate them for loss of expected realizations due to an early retirement of all or part of their debt. This is by no means a feature that is unique to mezzanine debt (for example, ECA debt tranches may also provide for prepayment premia), but whether or not the mezzanine lenders are able to secure this would be determined by the relative bargaining strength of the parties.

(5) *Covenant package:* The mezzanine covenants will typically follow the senior covenant package. However, additional covenants and different ratio thresholds will be required to reflect the mezzanine debt's position behind the senior tranche. The mezzanine facility will also set out restrictions to avoid cash leakage to more junior debt or the equity in much the same way as the senior facility.

(6) *Mezzanine enforcement rights:* These will typically be set out in the intercreditor agreement and are discussed in more detail below.[19]

Subordinated and Equity Bridge Facility Agreements

7.69 A number of sponsors are increasingly using subordinated and equity bridge loans (EBLs) to make their equity contributions to the project company in order to maximize their return from the project and will often champion their use up to the tolerance permitted by applicable thin capitalization rules and the credit requirements of the senior lenders. EBLs are traditionally short-term loans with a tenor of up to three years[20] and a bullet repayment profile. The use of EBLs to maximize equity returns has become prevalent in the water and power sectors (particularly with respect to projects benefiting from creditworthy long-term off-take contracts). EBLs may be priced to encourage a refinancing ahead of schedule through devices such as upward margin ratchets. The senior creditors will usually be content to accept such devices but will seek to ensure that:

(1) at least a portion of total project costs (usually 10 per cent) is funded by share capital;

(2) the shareholder subordinated debt to equity ratio is capped, primarily to address thin capitalization requirements and to preserve the efficacy of subordination provisions in an insolvency;

---

[19] See para. 7.116 below.
[20] Although prior to the credit crunch, longer tenors stretching beyond project completion were seen in the project finance market.

(3) the EBLs are replaced with share capital on a date certain as an undertaking by the sponsors; and

(4) the EBLs are fully first drawn prior to the first drawdown of the senior debt tranches.

Credit risk: Except where all of the equity is contributed up-front, the sponsors' **7.70** credit-worthiness will have to be satisfactory to the lenders; alternatively the sponsor will be required to provide acceptable credit support, usually in the form of letters of credit, from an acceptable rated provider, including where the sponsor's rating deteriorates below an acceptable threshold. In this instance, the parties will need to assess the margin payable on the equity bridge loan against the cost to the sponsor of paying the fees to the provider of the acceptable letter of credit. Occasionally, the senior lenders will accept a corporate guarantee from a sponsor with a particularly strong credit rating. From time to time, sponsors will also seek to provide credit support only where their own credit rating falls below a prescribed level. This is normally only applicable in the case of the very strongest credits. Once the EBL lenders are comfortable with the credit of, or credit support provided by, the sponsors, the issue of whether an equity bridge is funded prior to the senior debt or whether equity will be 'back-ended' is largely a mechanical one.

Subordination: Lenders providing an equity bridge loan will usually do so without **7.71** taking any security over the project's assets and with no recourse to the project company. EBL lenders will either accede to the intercreditor agreement or enter into a separate subordination deed to confirm the junior, non-recourse nature of their debt but they will not usually take part in any voting, nor will they receive the proceeds of any enforcement action.

Drawdowns: It is likely that equity bridge loans will be drawn before the senior **7.72** facilities because they usually have lower margins (thereby maximizing the equity returns). However, for example, where even lower funding costs are available from other sources (for example, 'soft loans'), it may be possible to substitute the usual requirement that the EBLs be fully drawn prior to the drawdown of the senior debt tranches, with an undertaking to make the EBLs available pro rata with the senior debt, with the result that at any given time (and absent the occurrence of any particular events that entitle the senior lenders to require the sponsors to fund their equity contributions in full) the funded exposure of both sponsors and lenders as a proportion of their respective commitments is the same. Indeed, with the increased use of equity bridge loans in project financings, particularly within the water and power sector, it is often now the case that the sponsors do not actually fund their equity contributions to a project until project completion or later (although of course the fact that they have guaranteed the equity bridge loan means that their credit exposure to the project is essentially no different to that which it would have been had they made their equity contributions to the project company in the usual way).

7.73 *EBL debt service*: EBL debt repayment obligations are usually non-recourse to the project company; thus, neither the proceeds of senior debt nor the project company's cashflows may be applied to retire the principal of the EBL. However, current interest payments on the EBLs are usually payable out of the project cash waterfall up to a capped amount, unless a default of some sort occurs; the sponsor credit support provider will guarantee the obligations of the project company to pay such financing costs on a non-recourse basis, with the result that if the project company fails to pay the financing costs or another event of default relating to that sponsor arises under the EBL, the EBL lenders will be entitled to accelerate the EBL facilities (and in turn to take steps to exercise their rights against the sponsor credit support provider), but would not otherwise be able to take any action against the project company, including in its insolvency.

7.74 *Cross-default to senior loan*: It is generally the case that a breach under the EBL will not trigger a default under the senior credit agreement. Senior lenders generally take the view that:

(1) during the construction period, once the EBL loan has been injected into the project and suitably subordinated, it is of little moment that the EBL loan is in default; and

(2) following project completion, any failure to pay interest on (or, indeed, principal of) the EBL is simply akin to a shortfall in dividends.

Clearly, if the EBL is to be funded pro rata to the senior debt, such that an EBL default will trigger a drawstop under that facility, the senior lenders will have a greater concern with the existence of the default, particularly as the drawstop will likely result in a shortfall of funds needed to meet total project costs. A common solution in that case is for the senior loans to default, and therefore cease to be available to be drawn.

7.75 *EBL lender protections*: To protect their position, the EBL lenders will:

(1) require a hedging programme in respect of any interest rate or currency risk;

(2) in recognition that it represents their sole recourse for the recovery of the principal amounts advanced to the project company, ensure that their ability to call on the credit support is unfettered by any other party (including the senior lenders);

(3) require that any payments due to the EBL lenders from a credit support provider are made directly to the EBL lenders;

(4) agree to a cap on the level of the sponsor credit support. However, the EBL lenders in these circumstances are likely to wish to ensure that the cap:

(a) has a significant LIBOR-based buffer to take into account both interest over an agreed period beyond the repayment date of the EBLs and any enforcement costs; and

(b) does not extend to hedging (i.e. if the EBL hedge providers are to benefit from a guarantee, it should be a separate guarantee designed exclusively to cover hedging liabilities).

Documentation: The inclusion of an EBL in a financing plan usually necessitates a **7.76** separate loan agreement between the project company, the relevant sponsors and the EBL lenders. Due to the intercreditor issues which may arise, separate counsel may also be required to advise the EBL lenders.

ECA Covered Facilities

As discussed in Chapter 8, many ECAs will, in their official export credit support **7.77** role, act under the aegis of the OECD Arrangement on Officially Supported Export Credits.[21] ECA support may be provided by way of export credit guarantees or insurance or through direct credit/financing and refinancing or interest rate support. Thus, in a project financing, ECAs may provide insurance cover to exporters or lenders or guarantee payments to the lenders that are making advances to an overseas borrower. Such insurance cover or guarantees may be comprehensive (i.e. provide commercial and political cover) or provide only political risk cover.

Documentation

There is no standard form of documentation across the ECA universe and each **7.78** entity will have its own preferred forms. However, in international syndicated transactions, an LMA-based form is often used as a starting point for the documentation.

The OECD Arrangement[22] allows ECAs to provide flexible loan repayment terms **7.79** to match a project's revenue stream and transactions can be structured with sculpted repayment profiles and flexible grace periods within the rules and subject to market practice in the relevant industry sector. This is particularly beneficial to projects in, for example, the petroleum refining and telecommunication sectors which see seasonal volatility in their cashflows and for whom temporary deferral of principal repayments is critical to avoid breaching their financial covenants (even where the overall project economics remain robust).

Eligibility criteria

A number of ECAs have gradually relaxed their eligibility rules as they seek to **7.80** become more competitive in the market place.[23] Most ECAs are enjoined only to

---

[21] See para. 8.20 et seq.
[22] See para. 8.20 et seq.
[23] See also para. 8.11 et seq.

support projects that have a sufficient nexus with their own countries, whether that nexus is a local off-taker, equipment supplier, or EPC contractor. The purpose clause of most facility agreements will therefore require that the proceeds from the ECA facilities are applied towards payment or reimbursement of project costs incurred in purchasing eligible goods and services under eligible construction and supply contracts. Increasingly, what constitutes a local component in a project is given a liberal interpretation in an effort to support a country's industry and exports.

Bribery and corruption—OECD Guidelines

7.81 ECAs are encouraged to combat the bribery of foreign public officials in international business transactions benefiting from official export credit support by the OECD Recommendation on Bribery and Officially Supported Export Credits, which was adopted by the OECD Council on 14 December 2006. Recommended best practice includes looking for red-flags by verifying whether the exporters and applicants are blacklisted by international financial institutions or have been indicted for bribery in the previous five years. Even where the transaction passes the ECAs' initial due diligence, the ECAs are urged to:

(1) require that exporters and applicants provide an undertaking or declaration that neither they nor anyone acting on their behalf have been engaged or will engage in bribery in the transaction; and

(2) take 'appropriate action' (such as denial of payment, indemnification or refund of sums provided) if bribery is subsequently proved.

7.82 It is therefore now standard practice for the common terms agreement or the relevant facility agreement to contain a representation to the effect that neither the project company nor its representatives have paid or sanctioned the payment of a bribe or similar payment in relation to the project (coupled with a covenant that they will not make such payment at any time in the future). A breach of this representation or covenant and the potential reputational damage that could ensue gives the ECAs the right to accelerate their debt.

Policing environmental covenants

7.83 Another feature that has become a fixture in ECA finance documentation is a package of measures designed to ensure that the ECA-supported project does not endanger local communities or the environment. This derives from the adoption in 2001 by the OECD of the Recommendation on Common Approaches on the Environment and Officially Supported Export Credits (the Common Approaches) for evaluating the environmental impact of ECA supported infrastructure projects to ensure that they meet established international standards. The Common Approaches were strengthened in December 2003 shortly after the private sector-focussed Equator Principles came into force, and again in 2007 when they were further revised and expanded. Adherence to the Common Approaches is intended to increase transparency in official ECAs' environmental review processes to ensure consideration of the environmental effects of projects on a consistent basis.

The Common Approaches are not legally binding but are adhered to very firmly in **7.84** practice and are viewed as capable of impacting the bankability of a project. They require that both new projects and projects undergoing significant change in output or function are evaluated against the environmental standards of the host country or international standards against which the project has been benchmarked, which-ever are the more stringent. The relevant international standards tend to be those of the World Bank Group or of regional development banks.[24]

With regard to the most sensitive projects: **7.85**

(1) the environmental standards to be applied must be reported and monitored by the OECD's Export Credit Group (the ECG)[25] and exceptional deviations from the international standards will have to be justified; and

(2) ECG members will seek to make environmental information, particularly environmental impact assessment reports, publicly available before final commitment.

Most official ECAs have established internal procedures to assess the potential ben- **7.86** eficial and adverse environmental effects of goods and services for which support is requested and will only grant board approval for financing support after such an assessment. A number of ECAs have also borrowed a leaf from leading regional development banks and issued their own environmental guidelines, with the result that they will usually require that the loan financing documentation takes into account such procedures and guidelines.

For environmentally sensitive projects, ECAs will require the development of an **7.87** environmental and social impact assessment that accords with minimum standards and will require that the assessment is publically disclosed to interested parties for a minimum period[26] or direct interested parties to a source, such as a publicly acces-sible website, where it can be reviewed. This disclosure requirement can have a timing implication on a proposed signing or closing and should always be taken into account in structuring the transaction schedule.

---

[24] These include the African Development Bank, the Asian Development Bank, and the European Bank for Reconstruction and Development.

[25] As of the date of writing, the ECG includes the following OECD countries: Australia, Austria, Belgium, Canada, the Czech Republic, Denmark, Finland, France, Germany, Greece, Hungary, Ireland, Italy, Japan, Korea, Luxembourg, Mexico, the Netherlands, New Zealand, Norway, Poland, Portugal, Slovak Republic, Spain, Sweden, Switzerland, Turkey, the UK, and the US.

[26] This period ranges from thirty days to 120 days depending on the ECA involved.

7.88 Upon signing the financing documents, a number of ECAs will summarize or disclose in their entirety the material environmental requirements associated with their financial support, including a list of the environmental reports required of the borrower, on their website.

7.89 Projects are expected to be designed, constructed, and operated in a manner that will enable them to maintain compliance, on an ongoing basis, with the environmental guidelines pursuant to which the ECA evaluated the project. If a project does not meet the applicable environmental guidelines, the ECA may reject the funding proposal or provide financial support that is conditional on the implementation of measures to mitigate the project's adverse environmental effects.

7.90 ECAs will seek to police compliance with the prescribed environmental and social guidelines and ensure that the project is constructed and operated in accordance with the relevant host-country and applicable international environmental guidelines throughout the term of their support. Monitoring is usually conducted through a desk-top review of information provided by the sponsor and regular site visits paid for by the sponsor.

7.91 In finance document negotiations, ECAs usually defer discussion on environment-related covenants pending receipt and review of the environmental and social management plan (ESMP). Nevertheless, they will invariably require:

(1) quarterly and semi-annual reporting on compliance with the construction phase ESMP;
(2) semi-annual and annual reporting on compliance with the operations phase ESMP; and
(3) mechanisms with respect to the transition of the ESMP from the construction to the operations phase and public disclosure of that ESMP on the project company's website.

Other documentation issues of interest to ECAs

Stapling

7.92 In a multi-sourced financing involving ECAs and commercial lenders, it is not unusual for the ECAs effectively to club together to ensure that they have a greater influence on the structure of the transaction and that their interests are communicated effectively. Increasingly, commercial lenders find this influence helpful, as it means that commercial lenders do not have to advocate positions that the ECAs are already espousing. To maintain their influence throughout the transaction, ECAs will often require a degree of pro rata drawdown and prepayment across all ECA facilities.

7.93 In cases where an ECA is both a direct lender and a risk policy provider or where another official institution from the same country is providing cover alongside an ECA lending directly to the project company, the ECA may insist on drawdowns being made pro rata between the direct facility and the covered facility in a pre-scribed ratio, subject to a carve-out for capitalization of interest and the payment of relevant premia. Where the two institutions are financing different EPC packages in the same project, they may relax these stapling requirements, but may require the borrower to endeavour to maintain the proportionate exposures of the institutions, subject to the eligibility criteria of each ECA.

The ECAs may therefore require pro rata prepayment or cancellation of commit-ments across, and replacement of, all ECA facilities, but permit non-pro rata prepayments, cancellation of commitments, or debt replacements across other senior facilities. Clearly, this requirement may limit the project company's flexibil-ity in managing its financing plan, but many view this disadvantage as outweighed by the pricing and other advantages that ECAs bring to a project. **7.94**

Voting

ECAs usually insist on directing the manner in which the lenders benefiting from their cover exercise their voting rights under the financing documentation. As such, the relevant ECA facility agreement will tend to provide for the relevant ECA to control the voting behaviour of the lenders covered by its guarantee or insurance. It is reasonable to give the covered lenders an independent vote once they have ceased to have the benefit of the ECA cover or where the vote is in respect of a change that would fundamentally alter the commercial structure originally agreed to by those lenders. Thus the right to control the voting is rarely absolute. It will also be limited, for instance, in respect of the waiving of initial conditions precedent and proposed variations to provisions capable of affecting the yield to those lenders, such as the margin and repayment dates. ECAs providing direct loans to a project company would obviously be granted full voting rights. **7.95**

Conditions precedent

ECAs also usually require, as a condition precedent to the initial drawdown under a covered facility, evidence that the eligible contracts have been entered into. In some cases, ECAs will require that a notice to proceed has been issued under such contracts to ensure that the project company is fully committed to sourcing content from the relevant countries. **7.96**

Mandatory prepayment upon termination of contracts

Some ECAs require mandatory prepayment upon termination of the relevant export contract or a pro rata prepayment in the case of a termination of one of a number of export contracts being supported by ECA loans. **7.97**

Fees and premium

ECAs will usually charge a premium for their products. Where the ECA is provid-ing a direct loan as well as insurance or guarantee coverage, it may charge two kinds **7.98** of premium: one for the direct loan and the other for the risk policy. The direct loan premium can be included in the margin, in which case the direct loan facility agreement will not have a separate provision for that premium.

Ineffectiveness of risk policy

7.99 It will usually be an event of default under an ECA covered facility agreement if the relevant risk policy becomes ineffective. If that event of default appears in the relevant ECA facility agreement, the covered lenders will usually be entitled to cancel their commitments and accelerate the indebtedness under their facility (thereby entitling, but not obliging, all other facilities to accelerate their indebtedness as well), but they would only be entitled to call for enforcement action against the common security following a full intercreditor vote across all facilities.

Subrogation rights

7.100 The financing documentation will usually contain an acknowledgement by the borrower and the other finance parties of the right of subrogation by an ECA providing a guarantee or insurance policy to the extent that that ECA has discharged a debt obligation owed by the borrower to an ECA covered lender pursuant to such guarantee or insurance policy. The documentation usually provides that the ECA will, on being subrogated, be deemed to be an ECA lender for all purposes of the finance documents to the extent of the relevant payment. The obligation of the borrower to that ECA as subrogee will constitute an unpaid senior debt obligation of the borrower (and an event of default under the finance documents will be continuing), until that obligation is fully paid. The documentation will also make clear that this right of subrogation is in addition to any right of indemnification or subrogation that may be available to the ECA risk policy provider as a matter of general law. This provision is usually uncontroversial, but the relevant ECA will wish to ensure that it is included, to counter any argument that the ECA impliedly waived its subrogation rights by accepting other indemnities (if any) from the borrower in lieu of those subrogation rights.[27]

Intercreditor Agreements

Introduction

7.101 The desirability of an intercreditor agreement begins the moment that a project's finance plan features two or more consensual creditors. This desirability quickly turns to necessity when those creditors have differing perspectives on the risk/reward equation presented by the project company's credit. Most creditors having assessed the borrower's creditworthiness and the economic viability of a project,

---

[27] See e.g. *Cooper v Jenkins* (1863) 32 Beav 337. For a more detailed and useful discussion on subrogation, see C. Mitchell, *The Law of Subrogation* (Oxford University Press, Oxford 2007).

will consider the bankability standard to be met only if they are able to recover the loans advanced to the project company at least *pari passu* with other creditors. However, while some creditors will be prohibited by their internal rules from participating in a project financing on other than senior terms, others will seek to realise a better return by accepting a relatively less senior ranking. For many years, a market has developed around lenders that see opportunities in being junior, albeit secured, creditors, in the hope that the correspondingly higher margin paid to them will reflect the increased risk being assumed, both in the normal course of events and upon an enforcement of security or the insolvency of the borrower.

It is in addressing the various, often conflicting, creditor interests and priorities that **7.102** the importance of an intercreditor agreement lies. As its name suggests, the intercreditor agreement is a compact among creditors, the *raison d'être* of which is the orderly re-prioritization of creditors who would, without more, rank equally at law. Thus, at the core of an intercreditor agreement will be found provisions providing for the contractual subordination to the senior debt of all other debt tranches and the application of the proceeds of the enforcement of the project security so that the claims of the senior creditors are discharged ahead of the claims of the other finance parties. But the role of the modern intercreditor agreement has grown beyond this primary function to encompass many other mechanics, largely because it is one of few documents to which each present and future project finance party is or will be a party. It is now generally accepted that such provisions are binding on the parties to the intercreditor agreement, a liquidator or administrator of any party thereto, and a liquidator or administrator appointed under the Insolvency Act of any creditor of any party thereto in accordance with their terms and will not be set aside under the rule in *British Eagle v Air France*.[28]

Secured creditors are not affected by the *pari passu* principle and the assets that **7.103** constitute the collateral are not part of the insolvent's estate and are therefore not available to the unsecured creditors or to the liquidator. As amongst the secured parties, the general proposition under English law is that they should be free to

---

[28] The decision of the House of Lords in *British Eagle v Air France* [1975] 1 WLR 758, [1975] 2 All ER 390 makes it clear that transactions may be cut down on grounds of public policy where they are intended to avoid basic insolvency principles such as mandatory set-off and *pari passu* distribution amongst unsecured creditors. However, the contractual subordination provisions in the typical intercreditor agreement would not be set aside under the rule in *British Eagle*. The judgments of Vinelott J in *Re Maxwell Communications Corporation plc (No. 2)* [1994] 1 All ER 737 and Lloyd J in *Re SSSL Realisations (2002) Ltd (formerly Save Service Stations Ltd) (in liquidation); Manning v AIG Europe (UK) Ltd; Robinson v AIG Europe (UK) Ltd* [2004] EWHC 1760 (Ch) support the proposition that, in the context of considering the validity of the contractual subordination of the claims of unsecured creditors, the courts may not strike down an agreement between a creditor and his debtor which contracts out of the requirements for *pari passu* distribution, if that contract does not seek to provide for the relevant creditor to enjoy some advantage in a bankruptcy or winding up which is denied to other unsecured creditors. See also *Re Maxwell Communications Corporation plc (No. 2)* [1994] AER 737 and *Re SSSL Realisations (2002) Ltd (formerly Save Service Stations Ltd) (in liquidation); Manning v AIG Europe (UK) Ltd; Robinson v AIG Europe (UK) Ltd* [2004] EWHC 1760 (Ch) in para. 21(e) of Sch. 3).

allocate the assets contractually as they see fit, as an incident of their proprietary rights to the security, subject only to the terms of that security.

7.104 The modern intercreditor agreement will therefore also seek to subordinate certain classes of debt, outline payment priorities both before and after a project has gone into default, oblige creditors to turn over payments received or recoveries made out of turn, regulate the ability to take, and set forth procedures governing the taking of, enforcement action against the borrower or its assets, and the voting rights of the various creditor constituencies.

Drafting and negotiation considerations

7.105 Negotiations around the intercreditor agreement do not directly concern the borrower although it will often insist on being party to the intercreditor agreement in order to prevent amendments to the agreed voting thresholds and to certain defined terms without its consent.

7.106 During the negotiation process, the most senior creditors usually generate the first draft of the intercreditor agreement, which will be reviewed and commented upon by the subordinated creditors. The intercreditor agreement is not usually finalized until the full complement of finance documents has been largely settled. Only then can the draftsman really know what to prescribe for. However, for complex financings, it is advisable, and indeed increasingly common, to agree a summary of the key intercreditor features—the intercreditor principles—as part of the term sheet negotiations to ensure that the main commercial aspects of the intercreditor relationship are negotiated (or at least noted). Failure to do so will likely result in delay or, worse, a hastily drafted intercreditor agreement that does not properly address all the material issues.

7.107 Given the inherent conflict of interest with senior creditors, subordinated lenders often retain separate counsel (or a separate legal team at the firm appointed to act as common lenders' counsel) to advise them on intercreditor matters.[29] In any event, subordinated creditors should ensure that, as much as is possible, the intercreditor agreement contains protective provisions which, in a distressed scenario, will both preserve value and allow the subordinated creditors some influence in a restructuring situation. Needless to say, the ability of the subordinated creditors to negotiate

---

[29] Acting for different tiers of lenders (for example, senior lenders and mezzanine lenders) entering into a financing transaction where there is already an agreed or commonly understood structure with regard to the ranking of their respective claims, the content of their respective obligations and associated commercial issues, is one of the examples, specifically cited by the Solicitors Regulation Authority, where it may be permissible for a solicitor to act despite a conflict under rule 3.02, subject to the relevant safeguards, recognising that 'this will facilitate efficient handling of the matter (taking into account amongst other things the desire to complete the transaction quickly, the availability of necessary experience/expertise and the overall costs)'. See para. 6(a)(iv) of the Guidance to rule 3 (Conflict of interest) of the Solicitors' Code of Conduct 2007 at <http://www.sra.org.uk/solicitors/code-of-conduct/rule3.page>.

a robust intercreditor arrangement will depend on their relative negotiating strength. This cannot always be assured, such as where a rating for the senior debt is being sought and prevailing market conditions present ready alternatives to a subordinated creditor seen as being overly activist. In such circumstances, the subordinated creditors will likely find themselves being deeply subordinated as a 'silent' tranche (attractive to equity but not to others), not least because credit rating agencies charged with rating senior debt paper will take into account the ability of subordinated creditors to interfere with the senior creditors' enforcement and recovery entitlements and processes.

In March 2009, the LMA launched a standard form intercreditor agreement **7.108** designed for use with the LMA leveraged facility agreement, to add to its growing arsenal of negotiation starting points. The initial version was revised six months later, to address a number of concerns raised within the London mezzanine lender community, that the initial LMA form was overly favourable to senior lenders and hedging counterparties, to the detriment of more junior creditors. In any case, it is worth noting that the LMA intercreditor agreement is designed to address the issues arising in a classical European leveraged buyout structure and, while it can be adapted to the project finance market, it may be quicker and more familiar, at least in the short-term, for experienced project finance parties to base the drafting on recent market precedent.

The typical project finance creditor classes

Unlike corporate or leveraged buyout financings, project financings have tradition- **7.109** ally featured a relatively simple intercreditor profile, in which most, if not all, the finance parties (bar those affiliated with the sponsors) are categorized as senior creditors. As more and more sponsors and lenders in varying and wide-ranging sectors have turned to project finance, the structuring has become increasingly complex and intercreditor agreements have had to adapt to this complexity. The project finance practitioner will rarely, however, see the multi-tiered structures prevalent in the acquisition finance market. A typical project finance intercreditor arrangement might involve the following classes of creditors.

(a) Senior creditors

The senior creditor category will, in project finance transactions, typically be the **7.110** broadest creditor class. The senior creditors will usually, but not invariably, be third party debt providers and hedge providers, as well as the account banks and agents under the project finance documents. The concomitant definition of senior debt will not only include all moneys advanced under the original senior facility agreements and hedging liabilities, but also permitted supplemental, additional, or replacement senior debt. Occasionally, the sponsors will insist on a senior *pari passu* ranking to the extent that they (or their affiliates) are providing senior debt (over and above their equity commitments) or where they, for example, are supplying feedstock or lifting project production on generous credit terms. In some of the largest oil and gas financings, these credit terms can be significant, perhaps even exceeding the external senior creditors' commitments. For the benefit accorded to the project company through these terms, the external lenders may agree to share their senior status with the sponsor (or its affiliate) up to a prescribed limit subject, additionally, for example, to the sponsor or its affiliate agreeing (to the extent permitted by applicable law) to waive its set-off, retention of title and enforcement rights. Also, the affiliated senior creditor will usually only have the right to vote in respect of decisions requiring unanimity or which are capable of directly and adversely affecting its rights in its capacity as a senior creditor.[30]

(b) Subordinated creditors

7.111 Ranking immediately below the senior creditors and above the equity providers[31] is the more junior class of creditor, variously called the mezzanine or junior creditor, depending more on the features of their financing than their rights under the intercreditor agreement. In the acquisition financing market, a more defined characterization exists to differentiate the mezzanine from the junior, and the mezzanine from any 'second-lien' creditors; whatever the nomenclature, these are usually finance providers that, for a higher margin, accept a lower position in the priority of payments and recoveries. In a project financing, the subordination of these creditors is only relative to the senior creditors; they will still rank ahead of the unsecured creditors and the equity providers. DFIs have been seen to take subordinated debt tranches to plug funding gaps in the finance plan of strategically important projects.[32] Sponsors or their affiliates may also invest debt on a subordinated basis, and will usually do so for at least a part of their equity commitments, subject to restrictions imposed by any relevant thin capitalization requirements. Affiliated subordinated creditors will usually not be entitled to vote on any decision under the intercreditor agreement.

---

[30] For example, any amendment affecting its priority status.

[31] This work does not explore structurally subordinated debt incurred by a direct or indirect holding company of the borrower of senior debt on the basis that such structures are relatively rare in project financings, and will be more likely to arise where legal doubts exist locally as to the efficacy of contractual subordination. If structural subordination is envisaged, it is important to require that the relevant holding company is the sole borrower of the subordinated debt to protect the integrity of any senior lock-up tests and cash distribution or up-streaming restrictions within the senior loan documents or the intercreditor agreement.

[32] The EIB, for example, which took a subordinated debt position in the Moma titanium mine in Mozambique. See EIB's press release at <http://www.eib.europa.eu/projects/news/eib-financed-mine-project-in-mozambique.htm>.

Selected intercreditor issues

The more complex a project's finance plan, the more complex its intercreditor **7.112** agreement will be. This section discusses some of the key issues that a practitioner may encounter in drafting and negotiating a moderately complex intercreditor agreement. The issues must of necessity be viewed from all the contrasting perspectives: the senior and subordinated creditors' and the equity parties' view points are all relevant. In a transaction with a rated debt tranche, the rating agencies will also review the arrangements for the purposes of making their ratings affirmations.

Below, we discuss, among other things: **7.113**

(1) the priority of payments in respect of any money recovered by the security agent or creditor other than in the normal course of events;
(2) the universe of actions that creditors can or cannot take to enforce their rights or security in a distressed scenario;
(3) the value protective measures, if any, of which the more junior creditors can avail themselves as against more senior creditors;
(4) the voting rights enjoyed by the various creditor classes, common voting structures, and the voting thresholds; and
(5) the unique intercreditor provisions affecting hedge providers and ECAs.

Intercreditor restrictions

The intercreditor agreement will generally restrict the right of any particular lender **7.114** to accelerate its debt, enforce security, initiate bankruptcy or insolvency proceedings or take other independent action that may prejudice the project, without the agreement of at least a designated percentage of the senior creditors. Following an event of default, a particular lender may, at a minimum, be restrained from exercising remedies for a specified period in order to afford other more senior lenders the opportunity to cure the default or to exercise their own remedies. The agreement will also contain provisions relating to the sharing of the proceeds derived from the enforcement of security.

The rights of subordinated creditors will generally be further restricted. The subor- **7.115** dinated creditors will usually only be entitled to receive debt service payments on a subordinated basis in accordance with the project revenue cash waterfall set out in the finance documents, with such payments in most cases being locked-up on the occurrence of an event of default. A different waterfall will often apply upon enforcement of security to allocate the distribution of the resulting enforcement proceeds.

The rights of subordinated lenders to accelerate and take other enforcement action **7.116** against the borrower will usually be subject to a 'standstill period' during which the senior creditors are given free rein to decide how to proceed. The duration of the standstill period is negotiated but a pattern has emerged. Commonly seen are durations of sixty to ninety days for payment defaults, ninety to 120 days for breach of financial covenants and 120 to 180 days for all other defaults. These standstill periods are disapplied in the case of exclusive security (if any), against which the subordinated lenders can take action at any time, since that action should have no impact on the senior creditors. As such the more junior creditors may be permitted to take enforcement action provided that no senior debt or security is thereby compromised or disturbed, and if such enforcement action results in a change of control, that such action has no material adverse effect on the project's permits or prospects.

Subordinated creditor value protections

7.117 The senior lenders will invariably restrict the subordinated creditors' ability to take any action that could interfere with the senior lenders' ability to take enforcement action. However, the subordinated creditors and equity parties will be particularly interested in influencing the ability of the senior creditors to initiate enforcement action or alter the template on the basis of which the financing was closed. The senior creditors will be receptive to such influence only if it improves prospects for new investment or assures the senior creditors of a better chance of recovery than is otherwise available through enforcing security. The subordinated creditors will also recognise that they are unlikely to make significant recoveries if they are not proactive in influencing, as far as is feasible, the course of events. Thus, taking a view on the hold-out value of a project may result in a less passive subordinated creditor class. The following provisions in an intercreditor agreement are designed to preserve value at the subordinated levels:

(1) *Restrictions on amendments to senior documents*: The senior lenders will require the subordinated lenders' consent to amend or give any waiver or consent under any senior finance document which would:

   (a) increase the senior debt at all or by more than a prescribed amount;
   (b) increase the margin and other amounts payable in respect of the senior debt at all or by more than a prescribed amount;
   (c) change the repayment profile of the senior debt; or
   (d) change the basis on which interest is calculated.

   The ability of subordinated creditors to block amendments to the senior documents will assist syndication of the more junior debt but, from an equity perspective, will undermine the flexibility to restructure the senior debt.

(2) *Option to purchase*: Subordinated creditors will often be granted an option to purchase the senior debt in full at par after a senior default.

(3) *Subordinate exclusive security*: Where subordinated creditors have exclusive security (usually where they are structurally subordinated or where they have the benefit of credit support from parties other than the project company), they would usually expect to have the ability to enforce that security at any time

without limitation. However, such enforcement action will not be permitted if it would impede any enforcement action by the senior creditors.

(4) *Narrow standstill*: Subordinated creditors will typically be subject to a 'standstill' obligation preventing them from taking enforcement action for a fixed period whilst the senior creditors consider their options. Subordinated creditors will focus on keeping the standstill period as short as possible and may seek exemptions from it if the senior creditors commence enforcement action against the project company (in which event the subordinated creditors will be permitted to take equivalent enforcement action). Subordinated creditors may also have the right to match terms proposed by a buyer in the context of a proposed enforcement by the senior lenders. The exercise by the subordinated lenders of such matching rights is effectively a step-in right on identical terms to those of that offer.

Voting rights and structures

Often the most complexity in a project finance intercreditor agreement is found **7.118** within the voting framework. It is advisable to adopt a formulaic structure based on the type of decision required to be made and the voting threshold needed to pass the relevant decision. There are a number of voting structures which creditors may adopt. To determine the appropriate voting arrangement for a particular project, one needs to assess the size of each debt tranche as this obviously has a direct effect on the proportionate voting strength of each lender group. Other considerations which need to be taken into account include whether there are differences in the maturity of the various tranches of debt, whether the financing incorporates debt with both fixed and floating interest rates, and involves risk policy providers who are likely to seek to control the votes of the lenders benefiting from their risk cover. For a number of lenders, the key consideration will be to maintain the 'day one' balance of power for as long as possible, particularly where institutions with different commercial or policy drivers are involved. In certain financings, it may be appropriate for there to be 'block voting', whereby a majority vote within a particular lender group is deemed to be a unanimous vote of that particular group when the votes of all the relevant facilities are aggregated (usually by the intercreditor agent).

Variations to loan financing documentation, waivers, and consents or determina- **7.119** tions must usually be agreed to by a prescribed majority of the creditor group. However, matters of a purely administrative or routine nature are often delegated to a facility or intercreditor agent without the need for referring such matters to a vote by the lenders. Whether or not these agents feel able to exercise these discretions is another matter altogether and many will be reluctant to do so in the absence of a satisfactory indemnity from the lenders.

Certain decisions will, however, be seen as affecting the basis on which credit **7.120** approval for a particular project was originally obtained or as having the potential fundamentally to alter the economics of the project. In such cases, there will be a requirement for the approval of each creditor class. Such decisions customarily include:

(1) confirming satisfaction of, or waiving, initial conditions precedent to funding by the lenders;
(2) variations to the cash waterfall;
(3) changes to applicable interest rates or principal amounts owed to the lenders;
(4) the release of security;
(5) changes to the priority ranking of debt tranches;
(6) amendments to voting thresholds and related definitions;
(7) material changes to the intercreditor provisions; and
(8) extensions to the availability period of the facilities or increases in a creditor's commitment.

7.121   There is no standard approach to setting voting thresholds required to pass a particular creditor decision. A number of transactions adopt three thresholds: simple majority, super-majority, and unanimous consent. The simple majority is usually either over 50 per cent or 66.67 per cent, whilst super-majority thresholds range from 66.67 per cent to 85 per cent. Occasionally, a fourth level may be interposed between the simple majority and super-majority thresholds. The key drivers for determining the thresholds will be precedent transactions in the relevant sector and the identity and character of the creditor group. Clearly, setting a threshold too high for a routine matter that then ends in impasse, to the detriment of the project, is in no one's interest. Equally, setting the bar too low will be unattractive as it could alter the commercial parameters on which the lenders' original credit approvals were based without due scrutiny. If unanimity is required, waivers may prove impossible or expose a borrower and the other lenders to the risk of being taken hostage (in commercial terms) by an intransigent or rogue creditor. If a simple majority is adopted, individual lenders may be concerned that their views will be rendered to be of no consequence.

7.122   Figure 7.1 below sets out an example of a four-tier threshold decision matrix and identifies the type of decisions within each category.

7.123   *Calculation of voting entitlements*: Voting rights are usually determined by the exposure that a particular creditor has to the project, the so called 'skin in the game' test. This will usually be predicated on the amount of money each creditor stands to lose and which is readily identifiable. Thus, most financings will use the yard stick of the principal amount of loans outstanding owed to each lender plus, before the debt is fully drawn (i.e. during the availability period), each lender's undrawn commitment. However, if enforcement action is to be taken during the availability period, the undrawn commitments will be ignored in recognition of the fact that such commitments will not give rise to further losses. In any post-enforcement situation,

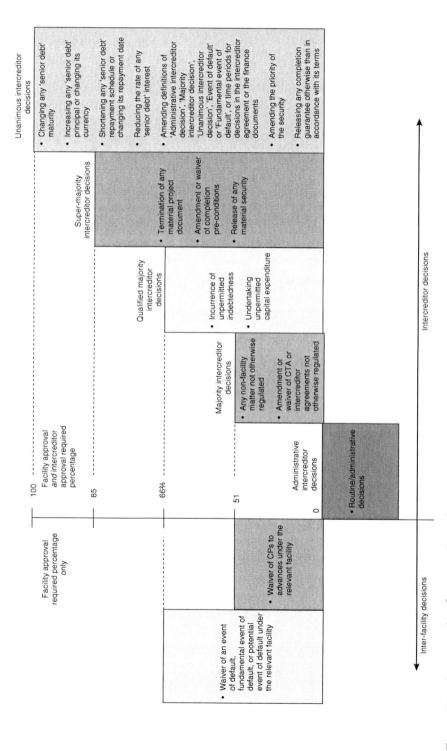

Figure 7.1 An example of intercreditor decision thresholds

voting entitlements will usually also include the crystallized termination amounts owed to each hedge provider.

7.124 *Regulation of voting entitlements*: A number of borrower friendly refinements to voting and intercreditor mechanics that have developed in the leveraged buy-out and high yield bond markets have now found their way into the more conservative project finance market and, in projects with strong sponsors, appear to have become regularly used. The most recognizable of these are the so called 'yank-the-bank' and 'snooze-you-lose' clauses. The former enables the borrower to buy out a lender who does not consent to a particular voting request where the majority are otherwise in favour. The latter enables the relevant lender agent to exclude from the tally the vote of any creditor which does not respond to a voting request in a timely fashion, effectively disenfranchising them. A more aggressively drafted snooze-you-lose clause may provide that a creditor would be deemed to have consented to a voting request if it did not signify its acceptance or objection to that request within a prescribed period.

7.125 Another measure is the stepped voting structure. Borrowers will want to ensure that enforcement action is very much a last resort and that as broad a spectrum of creditors as possible is involved in a decision to enforce the security (thereby reducing the chances of being held hostage by a rogue lender). An increasing number of voting provisions therefore make a distinction between 'fundamental' events of default (such as non-payment, insolvency, or loss of concession rights) which entitle the lenders to take enforcement action at a lower voting hurdle more quickly, and other, less cardinal defaults. Thus, the documents could require that for the first sixty days following the occurrence of a fundamental event of default, a 'supermajority' voting threshold would be required to commence enforcement action before dropping down to a less exacting threshold. On the other hand, the supermajority requirement might apply for twice as long in the case of less material defaults, before stepping down. These mechanics are likely to be heavily negotiated and the occurrence of defaults that bring third party creditors into the equation, such as the insolvency of the borrower, will entitle a simple majority to insist on enforcement. Ability to block the project accounts will usually be automatically triggered by an event of default, or require a simple majority vote.

7.126 Common voting structures include:

(1) *One dollar, one vote*: Usually, each lender's voting power will be directly proportionate to its monetary exposure and votes will be determined by the percentage of all commitments or outstandings. This approach is popular for its user-friendliness and fairness.

(2) *Block voting*: Another commonly employed voting structure is 'block voting' where lenders within a particular debt tranche are assigned a vote equal to the amount of the debt in the tranche as a group but, within each tranche of debt will vote on the basis of their individual exposure. Under this structure, passing a measure requires the vote of a majority of the lenders in each of the various

debt tranches, thus requiring a high degree of consensus among the lending group as agreement will be necessary both within each tranche and also across all tranches. This system may delay decision making.

(3) *Golden vote*: A variant to the exposure vote system is to require the consent of particular lenders within the group over and above the absolute voting thresholds. Thus a minority group could exercise a disproportionately greater decision-making power than would otherwise be possible under other structures. Moreover, determining which lenders should hold a golden vote and when the golden vote should apply is often challenging. Each lending group and each lender will tend to view itself as deserving of special recognition, given their particular market or political position and many will likely resist conceding the special treatment afforded to a co-lender/lending group. The golden vote is also commonly employed by governments in particular strategic industries.

(4) *Consultation*: Occasionally, the borrower will push for inclusion of a consultation period before a vote can be taken, particularly with respect to taking enforcement action. The usefulness of this device is, however, doubtful as most reputable lenders will, in any event, only take enforcement action as a last resort and consultation will occur as a natural part of the deliberations leading to such action.

If a project becomes distressed, the subordinated lenders will be the first to quickly **7.127** lose any value, particularly if the senior creditors take enforcement action against the project assets. Warrants and equity held by mezzanine or other subordinated lenders will at that point become virtually worthless (if they are not already so) unless they can take steps to protect long-term value. Forming a view of where value breaks, and carefully reviewing the underlying transaction documents to uncover strategies that may have hold-out value, can ultimately improve recovery rates. In *Barclays Bank Plc and others v HHY Luxembourg SARL and another* (Rev 1) [2010] EWCA Civ 1248, the Court of Appeal held that the release on disposals clause in an intercreditor agreement in relation to a company's liabilities would apply equally to the subsidiaries of the company whose shares are being sold by way of enforcement.

Senior lenders' right to release subordinate security

Once they become entitled to take enforcement action, the senior lenders will wish **7.128** to be free to instruct the security agent: (1) to release all the subordinated debt upon an enforcement of security; and (2) if they enforce security over an asset which is subject to mezzanine security, to release mezzanine security over that asset.

Considerations affecting hedge providers[33]

Voting rights: Hedge providers will usually only be entitled to vote in a default or **7.129** enforcement situation and then only in respect of crystallized termination amounts.

---

[33] For analysis of hedging in project financed transactions, see para. 4.49 et seq.

If a sponsor-affiliated entity is acting as hedge provider, it will rarely have any voting rights. Hedging liabilities usually 'crystallize' when the hedges are terminated upon a specified event, commonly the occurrence of a default or acceleration by the senior lenders or the passage of a given period thereafter following which the hedging bank may unilaterally terminate. The postponement of a hedge provider's voting rights is a pragmatic reflection on the difficulty and potential delay in calculating closeout amounts in the time available to make a decision as well as a recognition of the fluctuating nature of such amounts.

7.130 *Drag along*: Where a hedge provider has the benefit of the undertakings in the senior facility agreements, it is commonly the case that they are deemed to waive or modify such undertakings to the same extent as senior lenders may waive or modify them.

7.131 *Information rights*: Consideration is sometimes given as to whether hedge providers should be entitled to receive all information delivered to senior lenders under the senior facility agreements, including notices of repayments and prepayments or whether to restrict such information rights prior to default or the occurrence of an enforcement event. This is usually not controversial where the lending or sponsor group is also providing the hedging.

7.132 *Hedge provider undertakings*: A hedge provider will typically covenant not to:

(1) terminate (or close out any transaction under) any hedging document prior to its stated maturity otherwise than:

(a) upon the occurrence of a specified default; or
(b) if it (or its relevant lender affiliate) is prepaid in full as a lender or is subject to a mandatory transfer in full (pursuant to 'yank the bank' provisions in the finance documents to avoid the spectre of 'orphan hedges'); and

(2) transfer its rights under any hedging document other than to a person that accedes to the intercreditor agreement.

ECA covered loan voting mechanics

7.133 ECAs may require a veto right in respect of representations, covenants and/or events of default relating to such matters as corrupt practices and environmental undertakings, including compliance with environmental laws and any environmental and social management plans. These rights are seen as critical to avoiding reputational damage that could arise as a result of such breaches and to ensure compliance with the applicable OECD guidelines.

7.134 In addition, as noted above, ECAs providing insurance or guarantee cover will, as a general rule, direct the manner in which voting rights held by lenders benefiting from their cover are exercised; however, if the relevant guarantee or insurance policy is terminated or is invalid or unenforceable, the lenders cease to be under such direction. The covered lenders will nevertheless have a vote on a limited number of matters, including amendments or waivers to the terms of the covered facility agreement to which they are a party or which are capable of adversely affecting their rights thereunder.

Considerations affecting project bonds

Bondholders will typically rank *pari passu* with the senior bank lenders but the 7.135
latter will usually have the benefit of a considerably more conservative covenant and events of default package. Over the life of the project loan, the borrower is likely to seek, and the bank lenders are likely to grant, a number of amendments, waivers, and consents in respect of that package. On the other hand, a bond financing typically features a very large constituency of usually passive investors, making the process of obtaining amendments or waivers from bondholders expensive and laborious. Bond covenants consequently are usually structured as 'incurrence' as opposed to 'maintenance' covenants (i.e. covenants capable of being breached by the borrower's positive action).

However, a multi-sourced project financing featuring both bank and bond financ- 7.136
ing poses a 'cross-contamination' challenge because the bondholders will, through the common finance documents, such as the intercreditor agreement, gain indirect access to the bank lenders' broader covenant package and maintenance covenants. Previously, bondholders would cede decision making to a monoline insurer, thereby ensuring a more streamlined decision making process irrespective of the nature of the decision required to be made. With the collapse of the monoline insurance market, the natural successor would be the bond trustee. However, bond trustees rarely take decisions without consulting with, and being indemnified by, bondholders.

Current practice is to minimize the circumstances in which the bondholders' 7.137
consent is required. As such, intercreditor agreements commonly provide that bondholder consent need not be obtained if an independent consultant certifies that the required amendment or waiver would not adversely affect the bondholders in a material respect. The intercreditor agreement also typically allows the borrower to obtain routine waivers and consents without the bondholders' approval if a prescribed threshold of bank lender approval (usually between 20 and 30 per cent) is obtained, with the effect that a vote by the bank lenders in those circumstances is binding on the bondholders. Obviously, these devices will not apply to more fundamental decisions that affect the common security or the economics of the project and the bond debt.

8

OFFICIAL FUNDING SOURCES: EXPORT CREDIT AGENCIES AND MULTILATERAL DEVELOPMENT BANKS

Jonathan Maizel and Alexander Borisoff, Milbank, Tweed, Hadley & McCloy LLP

General Overview

Export credit agencies and multilateral development banks are an essential source **8.01** of capital for the financing of cross-border trade, including for the financing of major infrastructure projects worldwide. Historically, the role of these institutions in capital-intensive project financings has been to facilitate sponsors' access to capital in regions where commercial and political risks were deemed to be the greatest and where commercial credit providers were either unwilling or unable to make loans without some element of political or country risk mitigation. As might be expected, the primary goal of providing these credits was (and remains), in the case of export credit agencies, to support exporters in the home country of the relevant export credit agency and, in the case of multilateral development banks, to support economic and social development goals in the country or region targeted for investment. While these lending institutions have always played a major role in facilitating cross-border investment, the recent upheavals in the global markets arising from the 2008–2010 economic crisis (and the resulting constriction of available capital to project developers from traditional commercial funding sources) has served to enhance the importance of export credit agencies and multilateral development banks in global commerce and international development. For these reasons, it is important to understand the differences between export credit agencies (ECAs) and multilateral development agencies (multilaterals), and to understand how these types of institutions fit into the spectrum of financing alternatives available to project developers.

ECAs and Multilaterals Generally

8.02 ECAs and multilaterals are—at the most intrinsic level—government-backed suppliers of financing and other credit support. The fact that these types of institutions find their roots in politics, rather than commerce, means that they possess a variety of tools that are not available to commercial entities alone. Among the most important of these tools are the ability to offer financial terms that are more generous than their commercial counterparts, as well as the ability to provide both 'hard' and 'soft' political protections for the projects in which they invest. These agencies have of late also been recognized for their ability to provide a stable flow of fresh capital during both good and bad times, making them attractive market participants in all types of credit environments.

Export credit agencies defined

8.03 An ECA is an arm or agency of a national government, created for the purpose of promoting or facilitating exports from that nation to other countries, and by so doing, contributing to national employment and overall national economic well-being in the ECA's home country.[1] Consistent with these objectives, an ECA might also be empowered to promote or facilitate national investment overseas and/or the exchange of commodities between its home country and other nations. ECAs are generally funded by the national treasury of their home nation, and virtually every nation in the world that is active in the global economy has its own ECA. Figure 8.1 gives a global list of ECAs.

---

[1] See, for example, s 2(a)(1) of the Export-Import Bank Act of 1945, as amended ('The objects and purposes of the Bank shall be to aid in financing and to facilitate exports of goods and services, imports, and the exchange of commodities . . . and in so doing to contribute to the employment of United States workers. The Bank's objective in authorizing loans, guarantees, insurance, and credits shall be to contribute to maintaining or increasing employment of United States workers.'); see also Art. 1 (Purpose) of the Export-Import Bank of Korea Act ('to promote the sound development of the national economy and economic cooperation with foreign countries by providing financial assistance required for export, import, overseas investment and the exploitation of overseas natural resources').

Figure 8.1 List of Export Credit Agencies (By Country)

Country	Name	Abbreviation
Argentina	Banco de Inversión y Comercio Exterior	BICE
Australia	Export Finance and Insurance Corporation	EFIC
Austria	Oësterreichische Kontrollbank AG	OeKB
Belgium	Office National du Ducroire	ONDD
Brazil	Banco Nacional de Desenvolvimento Econômico e Social	BNDES
Canada	Export Development Canada	EDC
China	China Export and Credit Insurance Corporation	SINOSURE
	The Export-Import Bank of China	CHEXIM
	China Development Bank	CDB
Colombia	Segurexpo de Columbia	Segurexpo
Croatia	Croatian Bank for Reconstruction and Development	HBOR
Czech Republic	Export Guarantee and Insurance Corporation	EGAP
	Czech Export Bank	CEB
Denmark	Eksport Kredit Fonden	EKF
Ecuador	Corporación Financeiera Nactional Fondo de Promoción de Exportaciones	CFN
Finland	Finnvera plc	Finnvera
	Finnish Export Credit Ltd	FEC
	Finnfund	Finnfund
France	Compagnie Française d'Assurance pour le Commerce Extérieur	COFACE
	Direction des Relations Economiques Extérieures (Ministere de L'Economie)[2]	DREE
	Promotion et Participation pour la Coopération Économique[3]	PROPARCO
Germany	Deutsche Investitions–und Entwicklungsgesellschaft mbH	DEG
	Euler Hermes Kreditversicherungs-AG	Hermes
	KfW IPEX Bank[4]	KfW
Greece	Export Credit Insurance Organization	ECIO
Hong Kong	Hong Kong Export Credit Insurance Corporation	HKEC
Hungary	Hungarian Export Credit Insurance Ltd	MEHIB
	Hungarian Export-Import Bank	Eximbank
India	Export Credit Guarantee Corporation of India Ltd.	ECGC
	Export-Import Bank of India	I-Eximbank

[2] This entity may more appropriately be classified as a bilateral agency rather than an ECA.

[3] This entity may more appropriately be classified as a bilateral agency rather than an ECA.

[4] While still nominally tied to the German government, this entity operates more as commercial bank rather than as an ECA.

Figure 8.1 List of Export Credit Agencies (By Country)—(*Cont'd*)

Country	Name	Abbreviation
Indonesia	Asuranski Ekspor Indonesia	ASEI
Iran	Export Guarantee Fund of Iran	EGFI
Israel	The Israel Export Insurance Corporation	ASHRA
Italy	Servizi Assicurativi del Commercio Estero (SACE SpA)	SACE
Japan	Japan Bank for International Cooperation	JBIC
	Nippon Export and Investment Insurance	NEXI
Korea	The Export-Import Bank of Korea	KEXIM
	Korea Trade Insurance Corporation	K-sure
Luxembourg	Office du Ducroire	ODD
Malaysia	Malaysia Export Credit Insurance Berhad	MECIB
Mexico	Banco National de Comercio Exterior	BANCOMEXT
Netherlands	Nederlandse Financierings-Maatschappij Voor Ontwikkelingslanden N.V.	FMO
	Atradius	Atradius
New Zealand	Export Credit Office	ECO
Norway	The Norwegian Guarantee Institute for Export Credits	GIEK
Oman	Export Credit Guarantee Agency	ECGA
Philippines	Philippine Export-Import Credit Agency	PhilEXIM
Poland	Korporacja Ubezpieczén Kredytów Eksportowych	KUKE
Portugal	Companhia de Seguro de Créditos, S.A.	COSEC
Romania	EXIMBANK Romania	EximBank
Russia	Export-Import Bank of the Russian Federation	Eximbank
Singapore	Export Credit Insurance Corporation of Singapore Ltd.	ECICS
Slovak Republic	Export-Import Bank of the Slovak Republic	Eximbank SR
Slovenia	Slovene Export Corporation	SEC
South Africa	Credit Guarantee Insurance Corporation of Africa Limited	CGIC
Spain	Compañía Española de Seguros de Crédito a la Exportacion, S.A.	CESCE
	Secretaría de Estado de Comercio (Ministerio de Economía)	MCX
Sri Lanka	Sri Lanka Export Credit Insurance Corporation	SLECIC
Sweden	Exportkreditnämnden	EKN
	Svensk Esportkredit	SEK
Switzerland	Swiss Export Risk Insurance	SERV
Thailand	Export-Import Bank of Thailand	Thai Exim
Trinidad & Tobago	Export-Import Bank of Trinidad & Tobago	Eximbank
Turkey	Export Credit Bank of Turkey	Türk Eximbank

Figure 8.1 List of Export Credit Agencies (By Country)—(*Cont'd*)

Country	Name	Abbreviation
Ukraine	State Export Import Bank of Ukraine	Ukreximbank
United Kingdom	Export Credits Guarantee Department	ECGD
United States	Export-Import Bank of the United States	US Exim Bank
	Overseas Private Investment Corporations	OPIC
Uzbekistan	Uzbekistan National Export-Import Insurance Company	Unic

While significant overlap exists, the range of ECA mandates differs widely depend- **8.04**
ing on the home country and the policy objectives the applicable ECA was created
to further or promote. Whereas resource-constrained countries may seek to empha-
size the securing of raw materials, other countries may focus singularly on the
promotion of domestic producers, and yet others may view national objectives in a
broader light and instead focus on encouraging an environment of global trade that
is conducive to the over-arching goal of promoting national economic well-being.
By way of example, the Export-Import Bank of the United States (US Exim Bank)
focuses primarily on the promotion of US exports,[5] with each of its primary credit
products being strictly tied to the US content of the goods being acquired.[6]
Conversely, Export Development Canada (EDC) provides funding that is not strictly
tied to exports, with a focus that is more related to the potential benefit of the applicable investment to Canada (as measured by research and development potential,
market share maintenance or growth, and the number of primary/lead contractor
designations for projects).[7] Other ECAs have a dual existential purpose—to serve
the home economy through the promotion and facilitation of trade and investment
(the 'pure' ECA purpose) while at the same time also having a developmental mission more akin to that of a multilateral (even if such developmental mission is
ultimately tied to fostering a trade environment that is intended to support the
domestic economy). An example, of this is the Japan Bank for International
Cooperation (JBIC), which represents the amalgamation in 1999 of the former

---

[5] This focus was recently confirmed through President Obama's stimulus package, whereby the
US has committed—through US Exim Bank—to doubling US exports over the next five years. See
'Ex-Im's Day' in *Congress Daily*, 13 May 2010 (available at <http://www.usaexport.org/data/upload_
articles/Exim's%20Day%20-%20Congress%20Daily.pdf>).

[6] See mission statement of US Exim Bank, available at <http://www.exim.gov/about/mission.cfm>
('Ex-Im Bank's mission is to assist in financing the export of US goods and services to international
markets. Ex-Im Bank enables US companies—large and small—to turn export opportunities into real
sales that help to maintain and create US jobs and contribute to a stronger national economy.').

[7] See mandate and role of EDC, available at <http://www.edc.ca/english/corporate_mandate.
htm> ('EDC's mandate is to grow and develop Canada's trade, and the capacity of Canadian companies to participate in and respond to international business opportunities. EDC provides trade
finance and risk mitigation services to Canadian companies to help them compete internationally.').

Export-Import Bank of Japan and the Japanese Overseas Economic Fund. Covering both policy goals, JBIC has the purpose of 'contributing to the sound development of Japan and the international economy and society', and its credit products may either be tied to exports (to support Japanese industry) or imports (to obtain commitments of strategically important materials to Japan), or be altogether untied (to support overseas business environments to facilitate Japanese trade).[8]

Multilateral development banks defined

8.05 Multilateral development banks are bodies or agencies created by international agreement among multiple nations whose purpose is to promote development among all or certain member states.[9] These development goals focus primarily on the economic and social benefits to be achieved through the investment, as well as corollary matters such as protection of the environment and sustainability. Unlike ECAs, multilaterals are generally funded or financed by contributions from member states party to the multilateral agreement or other arrangement creating such multilateral.

8.06 As described in further detail below, multilaterals function both globally and regionally. The World Bank Group is the principal globally active multilateral, providing private sector financing through the International Finance Corporation (IFC) and political risk insurance through the Multilateral Investment Guarantee Agency (MIGA). Other multilaterals function on a more regional basis. Examples of regional multilaterals include the European Investment Bank (EIB), the European Bank for Reconstruction and Development (EBRD), the African Development Bank (AfDB), the Inter-American Development Bank (IADB) and the Asian Development Bank (ADB).[10] Common among each of these multilaterals is a desire to leverage their capital with that of the private sector, through co-financings or otherwise, while at the same time taking care not to displace or 'crowd out' private capital which might be available for a given use or project in the absence of multilateral participation.

---

[8] See Art. 1 of the Japan Finance Corporation Act, Act No. 57 of 2007, available at <http://www.jbic.go.jp/en/about/company/law/pdf/japan-finance-corporation-act.pdf> ('The Japan Finance Corporation . . . has the purpose of contributing to the sound development of Japan and the international economy and society and to the improvement of the quality of national life, by taking responsibility for (i) the financial function to provide for procurement assistance to the general public . . . and (ii) the financial function to promote the overseas development and securement of resources which are important for Japan'). Note that, to maintain brand awareness, the international finance arm of the Japan Finance Corporation continues to use the name of JBIC.

[9] See e.g. Art. 1, s 1 of the Agreement Establishing the Inter-American Development Bank, as amended ('The purpose of the Bank shall be to contribute to the acceleration of the process of economic and social development of the regional developing member countries, individually and collectively.').

[10] See Figure 8.2 for a global list of multilaterals.

Figure 8.2 List of Multilateral Development Institutions

Name	Abbreviation
African Development Bank	AFDB
African Development Fund	ADF
Andean Development Corporation	CAF
Arab Bank for Economic Development in Africa	BADEA
Arab Fund for Economic and Social Development	AFESD
Arab Investment & Export Credit Guarantee Corporation	DHAMAN
Arab Monetary Fund	AMF
Arab Organization for Agricultural Development	AOAD
Asian Development Bank	ADB
Caribbean Development Bank	CDB
Central American Bank for Economic Integration	CABEI
Central African States Development Bank	CASDB
East African Development Bank	EADB
European Bank for Reconstruction and Development	EBRD
European Investment Bank	EIB
European Investment Fund	EIF
Financial Fund for the Development of the River Plate Basin	FONPLATA
Fund for Co-operation, Compensation and Development (Economic Community of West African States)	ECOWAS Fund
International Bank for Reconstruction and Development	IBRD (World Bank)
Inter-American Development Bank	IADB
International Development Association	IDA
International Fund for Agricultural Development	IFAD
Islamic Development Bank	IsDB
International Finance Corporation	IFC
Multilateral Investment Guarantee Agency	MIGA
Nordic Development Fund	NDF
Nordic Investment Bank	NIB
OPEC Fund for International Development	OECD
Saudi Fund for Development	SFD
United Nations African Institute for Economic Development and Planning	IDEP
West African Development Bank	BOAD

Other governmental and quasi-governmental funding sources

8.07 While not the primary focus of this chapter, it is worth noting the existence of other 'official' funding sources that cannot cleanly be categorized as ECAs or multilaterals. A good example is the Overseas Private Investment Corporation (OPIC), a development finance institution that is an agency of the US government whose purpose is to promote economic development in new and emerging markets through US private sector investment in a manner that is complementary with US foreign policy objectives.[11] By its authorizing statute, OPIC is limited to participating in projects that meet specific eligibility criteria, including substantial US person participation in the relevant project. Much like an ECA, OPIC provides two primary forms of support to projects: (1) financing support, where OPIC provides either a loan guaranty or a direct loan; and (2) political risk insurance. In France, the mission of Promotion et Participation pour la Coopération Économique's (PROPARCO) is to be a catalyst for private investment in developing countries which target growth and sustainable development. PROPARCO is a bilateral agency partly owned by Agence Française de Développement (AFD) and private shareholders. It finances operations which are economically viable, socially equitable, environmentally sustainable, and financially profitable, and it tailors its operations to the level of a country's development, focusing on infrastructure and equity investments. PROPARCO's products include a range of financial instruments for private investors in developing countries, including direct loans and equity guarantees.[12] Another example of a development finance institution is the Millennium Challenge Corporation (MCC), whose purpose is to provide large-scale grants to less developed countries to fund projects aimed at reducing poverty.[13] Grants given by MCC fall into two categories: 'compacts', which are five-year grants for countries meeting MCC's eligibility requirements,[14] and 'threshold programs', which are generally smaller sized grants awarded to countries that substantially

---

[11] See Title IV, s 231, Foreign Assistance Act of 1961 (P.L. 87-195) (establishing OPIC and stating that the purpose of it is to 'mobilize and facilitate the participation of United States private capital and skills in the economic and social development of less developed countries and areas . . . thereby complementing the development assistance objectives of the United States').

[12] See generally PROPARCO's website, <http://www.proparco.fr> (providing mission statement and background information of PROPARCO).

[13] See Millennium Challenge Act 2003 (P.L. 108-199) (establishing the Millennium Challenge Corporation and stating that the purpose of it is to provide 'assistance in a manner that promotes economic growth and the elimination of extreme poverty and strengthens good governance, economic freedom, and investments in people').

[14] See Selection Criteria for Countries Eligible for MCC Assistance, available at <http://www.mcc.gov/mcc/selection/index.shtml> (indicating that: 'for a country to be selected as eligible for an MCC assistance program, it must demonstrate a commitment to policies that promote political and economic freedom, investments in education and health, the sustainable use of natural resources, control of corruption, and respect for civil liberties and the rule of law as measured by 17 different policy indicators.').

meet MCC eligibility requirements (and undertake to fully meet those requirements).[15]

Similarly, domestic loan incentives, subsidies and loan guarantees are available **8.08** in certain countries for both domestic and foreign-owned investors. An example is the US Department of Energy's Loan Guarantee Program, established under Title XVII of the Energy Policy Act of 2005, which provides a mechanism for US federal support of clean energy projects that use innovative technologies as well as investments in new innovative technologies. Under this program, the Secretary of Energy is authorized to make loan guarantees to support qualified projects. In Japan, the Ministry of Economy, Trade and Industry (METI) helps foster foreign direct investment into Japan. METI supports foreign companies by matching them with Japanese companies interested in establishing business partnerships, and by inviting and assisting individuals from abroad in establishing companies in Japan.[16]

These programmes and entities, while not directly tied to exports or development, **8.09** do provide project developers with other options for officially backed credits where the requirements for ECA or multilateral funding may not otherwise be met.

Funding Considerations

Sponsors and project companies have much to gain by considering ECAs and mul- **8.10** tilaterals in their mix of funding sources, since these institutions are generally perceived as being able to offer more competitive cost of funds and longer tenors than might be available, if at all, in the commercial lending market for projects being developed in more challenging markets. The remit of these institutions is also to promote best practices, and so sponsors need to be prepared to face higher levels of scrutiny, increased documentary and sourcing requirements, and stricter covenant packages when negotiating the terms of their credit. Understanding the different products that are available and the limitations that may apply when working with an ECA or a multilateral is critical to the decision as to whether to access guarantees or financing from entities of this type.

---

[15] See Millennium Challenge Threshold Program, available at <http://www.mcc.gov/mcc/panda/programs/threshold/index.shtml> (stating that MCC selects countries for the Threshold Program based on: (1) the country's overall performance on all 17 MCC policy indicators; (2) the country's commitment to improving their scores on each of the 17 MCC policy indicators that they have failed; and (3) the country's ability to undertake reform).

[16] See generally METI's website, available at <http://www.meti.go.jp/english/index.html> (providing history of METI, organizational charts, and a listing of the agencies that make up METI).

Credit alternatives with export credit agencies

Guarantees and direct loans

8.11 ECAs generally offer credits in support of trade or investment that are 'tied' credits—meaning that the amount and required use of the credit are limited to a percentage of the value of the exported goods and services from the ECA's home country and related finance charges (i.e. interest during construction), or to the value of the supported home country private sector investment overseas, as the case may be. ECAs typically offer these types of credits in the form of guarantees of third party debt and/or in the form of direct loans. Such home country 'sourcing' requirements are in most instances the key factors when deciding which ECA to approach.

8.12 The calculation of eligible 'tied' content of goods and services requires detailed preparation in conjunction with the exporters of goods and services sourced from the country of the relevant ECA. Commonly, a sponsor will be assisted in the preparation of an the application to the relevant ECA, by the relevant exporters of such goods or services and by a financial adviser with working knowledge of the procurement rules and documentation of that ECA. The criteria for eligibility for 'tied' content is specific to each ECA. However, common factors include the source of the content; the timing of the shipping of content compared with the application process; the national flag of the vessel shipping exported content; whether the content is sourced from a related party to the sponsors and, if so, whether such sourcing is on arms' length terms; and the nature of the goods or service (for example, whether it is a capital cost, a finance charge, a contingency built into the contract value relating to the service or goods to be financed, etc.). In addition to goods and services sourced from the country of the ECA, a percentage of eligible local costs can typically also be co-financed by the same ECA.

8.13 The distinctions between direct loans and debt guarantees are exactly as the names imply. ECAs that are able to make direct loans are able to fund directly to project companies, in the case of 'tied' facilities, upon confirmation that the proceeds of such loans will be used to satisfy (or reimburse the borrower for) the above-described sourcing requirements. For other ECAs, due to internal liquidity restrictions, direct funding of a loan is not an option—for these entities, the mechanism for providing official funding credits in support of exports is through the provision of debt guarantees (as further described below) to third party commercial lenders who provide loan advances directly to the project company. The Italian ECA—Servizi Assicurativi del Commercio Estero (SACE)—is an example of the latter type of ECA, insofar as its primary mechanism for providing export credits is by guaranteeing loans granted by commercial banks to foreign borrowers to finance Italian exports or civil works executed overseas by Italian companies or their foreign subsidiaries.[17]

---

[17] Other forms of credit support offered by SACE include political risk insurance policies and the issuance of surety bonds on behalf of Italian suppliers. See Profile of SACE, available at <http://www

Political and comprehensive risk coverage

ECA debt guarantees include both guarantees against political risks as well as guar-   **8.14**
antees against all risks—commercial and political (i.e. 'comprehensive guarantees').
Historically, political risk guarantees were the staple long-term credit product of
many ECAs. This is because so many ECAs supported private sector transactions
involving the sale of goods and/or services from the developed country of origin to
a developing and emerging market, where private sector capital has historically
been unavailable due to its inability to absorb political or country risks perceived to
be greater in such markets than in the developed world. While there are important
differences among individual ECAs, such political risk debt guarantees generally
cover private sector lenders against loss resulting from:

(1) expropriation or nationalization of the project or its assets;
(2) currency conversion or transferability restrictions (including cancellation of
     export rights); and
(3) war and politically motivated violence.[18]

In certain cases, such coverage also includes breach of contract or contract repudiation coverage where the counterparty to a key agreement or contract in the particular
ECA-supported transaction is an instrumentality of the host government in which
a project may be located (such as a power purchase agreement with a state-owned
electric utility or a concession with state agency). Political risks that are not typically
covered include:

(1) currency devaluation;
(2) increased taxes (except for breach of contract coverage of the type described
     above in cases where an 'implementation agreement' or 'investment agreement'
     between a sponsor and a host government exists and 'freezes' a taxation regime
     applicable to the relevant investment);
(3) legal system risk; and
(4) strikes that are not country or industry-wide.

In the context of major international project financings, some ECAs used to com-   **8.15**
bine their political risk debt guarantee product with a direct 'take-out' loan made at
'project completion', with the effect that the ECA would take political risk during
the project's construction period and comprehensive risk thereafter. While still an
important product, stand-alone ECA political risk debt guarantees have become
much less prevalent in large international project financings since the Asian

---

.sace.it/GruppoSACE/content/en/corporate/sace_group/profile/index.html> (providing general
background information on the forms of credit support offered by SACE).

   [18] MIGA defines political risks generally as risks that: 'are associated with government actions
which deny or restrict the right of an investor/owner: (i) to use or benefit from his/her assets; or
(ii) which reduce the value of the firm. Political risks include war, revolutions, government seizure
of property and actions to restrict the movement of profits or other revenues from within a country.'
See <http://www.pri-center.com/directories/glossary.cfm>.

economic crisis of the late 1990s. Increasingly, in such transactions, ECA debt guarantees are taking the form of comprehensive cover against all risks.

8.16 ECA debt guarantees (whether against political or comprehensive risks) generally provide for payment by the ECA guarantor if a borrower cannot pay scheduled interest or principal on the guaranteed debt as a result of any of the covered risks. In certain cases, the guarantee may be triggered by other, unscheduled payment failures resulting from a covered risk (such as a failure to make a mandatory prepayment), although this is less common and it is generally the rule that such guarantees extend only to the stipulated covered percentage of scheduled principal and (non-default) interest thereon. Increased costs, funding losses, and general indemnification obligations are almost universally never covered by ECAs. When a borrower defaults in the payment of a covered amount, such guarantees will generally (although not always, and often with waiting periods before payments may be made) provide for the payment by the ECA to the guaranteed lender of the specific covered amount which the borrower failed to pay, rather than for a one-time, lump-sum payout by the ECA of the entire guaranteed debt.

Political risk insurance

8.17 As discussed in Chapter 4,[19] political risk insurance (PRI) is another mechanism whereby political risks can be mitigated to support the need of international investors. Although a commercial market for PRI does exist, it has historically been (and remains) an important product for many ECAs and other official credit providers in developing world infrastructure projects, although many government providers encourage investors to look first to commercial markets before seeking to obtain policies from official sources. These policies are quite similar to political risk debt guarantees in terms of the covered 'political' risk events, and the existence of such a policy can often facilitate equity investors' ability to obtain financing—whether from commercial or official funding sources—on more favourable terms. As with their direct loan and debt guarantee products, the policy goals of the ECA providing a PRI policy will dictate the extent to which such policies can be made available to the relevant investor, and many of the same policy requirements (i.e. compliance with environmental and social standards; anti-corruption, etc.) that apply to direct loan and debt guarantee products are applicable to PRI policies issued by ECAs.

Working capital facilities

8.18 In addition to direct export credits, ECAs will sometimes offer credits for working capital facilities intended to be made available to potential exporters. The EDC Supplier Financing Program is a good example—under this program, EDC will buy promissory notes issued to a small- or medium-sized exporter by a foreign buyer related to the sale of Canadian goods and services. Doing so reduces the risk

---

[19] See para. 4.56 et seq.

of non-payment and increases access to cash, and is available for contracts with relatively simple payment terms and with repayment terms of up to two years. The Export-Import Bank of Korea (K-Exim) offers a similar program through its Technical Service Credit that is extended to Korean companies for the export of technical services abroad, including overseas construction products. Repayment terms are two years or more, and repayment of principal typically occurs in instalments or in a lump-sum. Yet another example of an ECA support program is US Exim's Working Capital Guarantee Program. These working capital loans, made by commercial lenders and backed by US Exim Bank's guarantee, enable US exporters to obtain loans that facilitate the export of goods or services. Generally, US Exim Bank guarantees 90 per cent of the bank loan (including principal and interest) and typically loan terms are from one to three years. Exporters may use the guaranteed financing in a variety of different ways, including to: (i) pay for raw materials, equipment, supplies, labour, and overheads to produce goods and/or provide services for export; (ii) cover standby letters of credit; (iii) finance foreign receivables; or (iv) purchase finished products for export.

Rules applicable to ECAs

One area of concern related to ECA financing is the risk that government provided **8.19** export credits have the potential to create significant distortion of global trade as a result of subsidies in the form of favourable or concessionary ECA financing terms. To address this concern, agreements have been entered into among certain ECAs that regulate the terms pursuant to which ECA funding may be provided.

The Arrangement

In order to provide for a common framework for the orderly use of ECA credits, and **8.20** specifically to provide for a level playing field whereby international trade competition is based on price and quality of the exported goods and not on the terms and conditions of related country ECA support, certain member countries[20] of the Organisation for Economic Cooperation and Development (OECD) in 1978 adopted the 'Arrangement on Export Credits' (the Arrangement), which is often referred to as the 'OECD Consensus'. The Arrangement is a voluntary 'gentleman's agreement' among its participants, with provisions for information sharing and monitoring among such ECAs being intended to promote transparency and ensure compliance. A participating ECA may deviate from the Arrangement rules to match financial and other terms offered by another ECA, or the participants can collectively agree to offer a 'common line' in relation to a specific transaction. In such cases, the Arrangement includes procedures to ensure consultation and agreement. Although the Arrangement does not have the force of law, it is generally credited

---

[20] As of February 2011, the participants to the Arrangement are: Australia, Canada, the European Community (all 27 member states), Japan, Korea, New Zealand, Norway, Switzerland, and the US.

with having introduced discipline into the marketplace and most commentators agree that it has been successful in avoiding many of the more severe international trade distortions resulting from government subsidy. The Arrangement applies to ECA credits with a maturity of two years or more and establishes, among other things, minimum down payment requirements on supported sales of goods and services, maximum permitted levels of support for export and local costs, maximum principal repayment periods, required commencement dates for repayment of principal, minimum interest rates, and minimum risk-based premium fees. The basic rules of the Arrangement require that:

(1) the first principal repayment and the first payment of interest occur within six months of the 'starting point of credit';

(2) interest ceases to be capitalized after the 'starting point of credit';

(3) equal instalments of principal in respect of the credit be repaid no less frequently than semi-annually (although 'mortgage-style' amortization involving fluctuating principal repayments is allowed for lease transactions and nuclear power plants);

(4) interest be repaid no less frequently than annually (semi-annually for nuclear power plants); and

(5) the credit have a maximum weighted average life not to exceed:

   (a) in the case of exports to sovereign buyers (or exports guaranteed by a sovereign), four years where the export destination is a high income country and five-and-a-quarter years where the export destination is a non-high income country;

   (b) in the case of exports to non-sovereign buyers which are not guaranteed by a sovereign, five years where the export destination is a high income country and six years where the export destination is a non-high income country;

   (c) in the case of non-nuclear power plants (regardless of whether a sovereign is involved and regardless of the country of destination), six-and-a-quarter years; and

   (d) in the case of nuclear power plants (regardless of whether a sovereign is involved and regardless of the country of destination), nine years.

8.21 Additionally, the Arrangement allows 'on an exceptional and duly justified basis' export credits to be provided on terms different from those described above.[21] An imbalance in the timing of a borrower's revenue stream relative to a semi-annual, equal principal payment debt service profile is specifically identified as such an 'exceptional and duly justified' basis.[22]

---

[21] See Arrangement on Officially Supported Export Credits, January 2010 Revision, s 14(d) (available at <http://www.oecd.org/officialdocuments/displaydocumentpdf/?cote=TAD/PG(2010)2&doclanguage=en>).

[22] In such cases, ECAs may offer credits having the following terms: (1) principal shall be repaid no less frequently than every twelve months, with the first repayment of principal being made no later

The Arrangement requires a minimum 15 per cent down payment on supported **8.22** sales of goods and services, limits the covered percentage of an export to 85 per cent of the related export contract value (exclusive of local content) and allows for support of local costs associated with the export (up to 30 per cent of the value of the export contract, with prior notification to other Participants if such support for local content exceeds 15 per cent of the export contract value). The Arrangement stipulates that the maximum principal repayment period is five years for exports to high income countries (with the possibility of extending to eight-and-a-half years if prior notification requirements are followed) and ten years for exports to non-high income countries, except that for exports relating to non-nuclear power plants the maximum principal repayment period is 12 years and for exports relating to nuclear power plants the maximum principal repayment period is 18 years.[23]

Over the course of the years, the OECD ECAs have come to recognize that certain **8.23** of the Arrangement rules were not readily applicable to limited recourse project financings (i.e. financings where the ECA looks primarily to a special purpose, non-sovereign project company's cashflows for repayment are not guaranteed by a sovereign and are limited recourse to the sponsors). As a consequence, revisions to the basic Arrangement rules described above have been implemented in order to allow an OECD ECA more flexibility in structuring each of the first principal repayment date, the maximum principal repayment term and the overall principal repayment profile, in each case better to match the cashflow requirements of a limited recourse project financing. The limited recourse project financing regime allows an OECD ECA to offer a project company a maximum repayment term of 14 years, together with repayments of principal that are less frequent than

---

than twelve months after the starting point of credit and no less than 2 per cent of the principal sum of the credit shall have been repaid twelve months after the starting point of credit; (2) no single repayment of principal or series of principal payments within a six-month period shall exceed 25 per cent of the principal sum of the credit; (3) interest shall be paid no less frequently than every twelve months with the first interest payment being made no later than six months after the starting point of credit; (4) the maximum weighted average life of the repayment period shall not exceed: (a) four-and-a-half years for transactions with sovereign buyers (or with a sovereign repayment guarantee) in Category I countries and five-and-a-quarter years for Category II countries, (b) five years for Category I countries and six years for Category II countries where the transaction is with non-sovereign buyers (and with no sovereign repayment guarantee), and (c) notwithstanding (1) and (2) above, six-and-a-quarter years for transactions involving support for non-nuclear power plants. Further, the applicable ECA must give prior notification explaining the reason for not providing support that doesn't fall into the 'exceptional and duly justified basis' category.

[23] The rules for nuclear power plants were added to the Arrangement in 2010. The maximum repayment period for credits extended in respect of the initial nuclear fuel load is four years from delivery, with credits in respect of subsequent re-loads having a maximum repayment period of two years. Additionally, the maximum repayment term for credits relating to spent fuel disposal is two years, and the maximum repayment term for credits in respect of fuel enrichment or other fuel management is five years.

semi-annual and are in uneven amounts (such that mortgage style amortization would be permissible), so long as:

(1) the weighted average life of the export credit is no longer than seven-and-a-quarter years;

(2) the first repayment of principal due is within two years of the starting point of credit; and

(3) no single principal repayment or series of principal repayments within any six-month period is more than 25 per cent of the principal sum of the credit.[24]

Starting point of credit

8.24 The 'starting point of credit' referred to in the Arrangement will vary depending on the nature of the transaction being financed. For instance, in 'pure' export transactions, the credit period generally starts at the time of delivery of goods. In the case of projects involving a turnkey construction arrangement, the 'starting point of credit' may be the day on which care, custody and control of the project is handed over to the project company. In projects where the importer is obliged to assemble and commission the equipment, the starting point of credit may be the day the equipment is ready for commissioning.

Commercial interest reference rate

8.25 The Arrangement additionally sets minimum interest rates to be charged by OECD ECAs. In general, OECD ECAs providing fixed rate export credits are required to fix interest rates at a level not less than the applicable 'commercial interest reference rate' (the CIRR rate) applicable to the currency in which the ECA credit is denominated. The CIRR rate is established for each currency of the participants to the Arrangement and is re-set monthly. A CIRR rate may also be established for a non-participating country currency. According to the Arrangement, the CIRR rate should represent the current fixed rate of interest which corresponds, as closely as possible, to the fixed rate charged by commercial lenders to 'first-class' borrowers in

---

[24] Certain of the special Arrangement rules relating to limited recourse project finance transactions (specifically those relating to maximum repayment term and minimum weighted average life in high income countries) will expire at the end of 2010 unless they are affirmatively renewed by parties to the Arrangement. If they are not renewed, then the fourteen-year maximum repayment term will remain applicable except where the aggregate credit support provided by the OECD ECAs to any project in a high income country exceeds 35 per cent of the 'total syndication', in which case the maximum repayment term for such project will be ten years. Similarly, the current rules applicable to the minimum weighted average life of a credit in a limited recourse project finance transaction will remain applicable except where the aggregate credit support provided by the OECD ECAs to any project in a high income country exceeds 35 per cent of the 'total syndication', in which case the weighted average life for such project may not exceed five-and-a-quarter years.

the country in question. Each OECD ECA is required to designate one of two base rates for its CIRR rate-either:

(1) the three-year government bond yield for credits having a repayment term of up to five years, the five-year government bond yield for credits having a repayment term of up to 8-and-a-half years and the seven-year government bond yield for credits having a repayment term in excess of eight-and-a-half years; or
(2) the five-year government bond yield for credits of all maturities. A 100-basis point margin is added to the applicable base rate in order to arrive at the applicable ECA's CIRR rate.

Additionally, for repayment terms in excess of twelve years, a surcharge of twenty basis points is added. OECD ECAs are not precluded by the Arrangement from offering support for floating rate export loans, and frequently do so, but may not offer support based on the lower of a fixed CIRR rate and a short-term floating rate. Finally, the Arrangement sets minimum risk premia which may be charged by OECD ECAs based on objective criteria relating to the country that is the export destination.

It should be noted that although the Arrangement is designed to ensure level pric- **8.26** ing across participating ECAs, those ECAs that are able to provide direct lending have a potential advantage over those who simply issue loan guarantees that support loans from banks with higher funding costs than the sovereign cost of funds of the ECAs themselves.

Helsinki Package

In 1991 the participants to the Arrangement agreed to the 'Helsinki Package' of **8.27** rules regarding the use of 'tied' aid. Generally speaking, 'tied' aid is governmental support that is 'tied' to trade and may take the form of financing provided by ECAs or their governments on concessional terms that oblige the recipient to procure goods or services from the provider country, whereas 'untied aid' is aid which includes loans or grants whose proceeds are fully and freely available to finance procurement from any country, the use of which is outside the terms of the Arrangement (as further described below). Such 'tied' support may take the form of credits or grants. Although part of the overall Arrangement, the Helsinki Package of rules deals specifically with 'tied' aid or government support. There are two keys tests of project eligibility for tied aid. First is whether the project is financially non-viable (i.e. whether the project lacks capacity to generate cashflow sufficient to cover operating costs and to service the debt). The second key test is whether it is reasonable to conclude that it is unlikely that the project can be financed on market terms. The Helsinki Package also established baseline rules precluding the granting of any tied aid to high income nations and established minimum levels of 'concessionality'.[25] Under the Agreement, the Participants are prohibited from providing tied aid that has a concessionality level of less than 35 per cent, or 50 per cent if the beneficiary country is a 'least developed country'.[26]

8.28 In 2005 the Participants clarified in the 'Ex Ante Guidance for Tied Aid' (the 'Ex Ante Guidance') the two tests of project eligibility for tied aid originally established in the Helsinki Package.[27] In addition to the two keys tests of project eligibility for tied aid described above, the Ex Ante Guidance provides specific guidance and recommendations for various types of projects, including power plants, transmission facilities, transportation projects, and manufacturing facilities. For example, to determine whether a project is financially non-viable, the Ex Ante Guidance states, the:

> ... general characteristics of financially non-viable projects include projects whose principal output is a public good, capital-intensive projects with high per unit production costs and slow capacity update, and/or where the beneficiary group (normally household consumers) is deemed unable to afford the output at the appropriate market-determined price.[28]

Whether a project is feasible, such that it is reasonable to conclude that it is unlikely that the project can be financed on market terms, is a more nuanced question. The Ex Ante Guidance provides a checklist intended to assist in the preparation of 'Feasibility Studies' for the evaluation of individual projects subject to the Helsinki process.[29]

---

[25] The concept of 'concessionality' relates to the value of the subsidy being provided for any individual loan. For example, if a country receives a grant of $100 million for a $100 million project, the 'concessionality' level would be 100 per cent, whereas a grant of $35 million combined with a traditional export credit for the remaining $65 million would have a 'concessionality' level of 35 per cent. See <http://www.exim.gov/products/policies/appendix-g-03.pdf>.

[26] Two exceptions may apply: (1) technical assistance: tied aid where the official development aid component consists solely of technical cooperation within certain defined limits; and (2) small projects that are funded entirely by development assistance grants.

[27] In agreeing to the original tied aid rules under the Helsinki Package, the participants fully expected to revisit the topic of tied aid once a body of experience had developed over time that 'would more precisely define, both for export credit and aid agencies, *Ex Ante* guidance as to the line between projects that should be financed with tied aid or with commercial terms'. See Arrangement on Officially Support Export Credits, 'Ex Ante Guidance for Tied Aid', 2005 Revision, available at <http://www.oecd.org/officialdocuments/displaydocumentpdf?cote=TD/PG(2005)20&doclanguage=en>.

[28] See ibid.

[29] For example, the 'Feasibility Study' asks specific questions about: (1) the justification for and objectives of the project (including how it is expected to contribute in the long run; (2) the level of development in the economy of the country where the project is to be located; (3) information on the financial capacity of the implementing organizations, including their profitability, their relations with the borrower, and the impact the project will have; (4) a description of the consumers of the products of the project, including GNP per capita; (5) various financial appraisals (including cashflow calculations and sensitivity analysis); and (6) development aid aspects relevant to the project. See ibid.

Berne Union and the Prague Club

Of less direct and visible relevance to the funding and sourcing of finance from **8.29**
ECAs are the principles formulated under the umbrella of The International Union
of Credit and Investment Insurance, otherwise known as the Berne Union. The
Berne Union, is made up of members from both the public and private sectors of
export credit and investment insurance providers and the association works closely
with the OECD and the World Bank.[30] It is an international, non-profit organization dedicated to facilitating worldwide cross-border trade and investments by
fostering international acceptance of sound principles in export credits and investments insurance, and by providing a forum for professional exchanges among its
members.[31] The Berne Union promotes uniform principles for export credit and
investment insurance through organized meetings of members, ad hoc seminars
and workshops, and the exchange of the information and experiences among the
insurers. In accordance with the message included in its 'Value Statement', members of the Berne Union declare their commitment to operate in a financially
responsible manner, to be respectful of the environment, and to demonstrate high
ethical values.

The Prague Club is another ad hoc group of relevance. It is made up of certain insur- **8.30**
ers in the public sector who do not meet the entrance requirements for the Berne
Union but broadly share the same goals.[32] The aim of the Prague Club is to work out
an information exchange forum for newly established credit and investment agencies as well as encouraging the international trade development by supporting
unified rules both for export credit insurances and foreign investments. A number
of Prague Club members have gone on to meet the requirements for full Berne
Union membership, but remain active members of the Prague Club.

---

[30] See Members of Berne Union, available at <http://www.berneunion.org.uk/bu_profiles.htm>
(listing private insurers, for example, Chubb and Chartis, alongside ECAs such as SACE, COFACE,
and US Exim Bank).

[31] See Value Statement of Berne Union, available at <http://www.berneunion.org.uk/value
-statement.html>.

[32] The five membership requirements for Berne Union members: (1) institutions should be underwriters carrying out actual and direct export credit and/or investment insurance business as their core
activity; (2) institutions must have been effectively in operation in the field of credit/investment insurance for a period of at least three years; (3) institutions should meet certain thresholds for premium
income or business covered; (4) if the applicant is engaged in export credit insurance, its operations
must include insurance of both commercial and political risks and it must underwrite political risks in
a global and general sense; and (5) if an institution is engaged in the insurance of outward investment,
it must be providing direct insurance against the normal political risks, including expropriation, war
and transfer difficulties). Membership in the Prague Club is open to: (1) organizations engaged in
insuring or guaranteeing export credit transactions and in underwriting the political risks in such
transactions and/or in insuring outward investments; and (2) organizations that are not yet legally
established but that are in development.

Credit alternatives for multilaterals

8.31   Where political risks are significant, or where export content may be insufficient for ECA financing—for example, where a project entails a substantial civil works component[33]—multilaterals or similar regional or national development finance institutions may be instrumental in financing a project.

8.32   The principal multilateral, the World Bank, comprises the International Bank for Reconstruction and Development (IBRD) and the International Development Association (IDA). The IBRD focuses on middle income and creditworthy poor countries, whereas the IDA focuses on the poorest countries in the world. Each of the IBRD and the IDA provides low-interest loans to developing countries for a wide range of purposes, including infrastructure projects. The World Bank also offers private sector lenders a variety of guarantee products against commercial risks. 'Partial risk' guarantees cover private sector lenders against loss resulting from default by a sovereign under one or more key project documents between the sovereign and a private sector project, such as a concession agreement, a power purchase agreement, or any sovereign guarantee of the same. One significant condition to a partial risk guarantee is that an indemnity agreement between the project's host country and the IBRD will be required. Pursuant to such an indemnity agreement, the host country sovereign agrees to indemnify the IBRD against payments made under the partial risk guarantee.

8.33   Other members of the World Bank group include the International Finance Corporation (IFC) and the Multilateral Investment Guarantee Agency (MIGA), which, unlike the IBRD and IDA, extend credit principally to non-sovereign borrowers. The IFC promotes growth in the private sector of the economies of developing countries by mobilizing domestic and foreign capital and making loans and equity investments to private corporations or investment funds that have projects in such countries. Unlike the World Bank, the IFC does not require direct state support. MIGA provides both debt and equity guarantees against losses caused by non-commercial risks, including currency transfer restrictions, expropriation, war and civil disturbances, and, in certain cases, breach of contract.

8.34   While multilaterals have traditionally been in the business of extending or supporting financing to borrowers, more recently certain multilaterals have focused on expanding their efforts to include assistance with equity investments. These investments typically focus on providing start-up capital, early stage capital, and/or expansion capital, in each case where equity funds are needed to assist companies with their product development and commercialization efforts. Examples of multilaterals that provide this type of assistance include the IADB, the AfDB, and the ADB.

---

[33] For example, hydroelectric dam projects.

A/B loan structures

Co-financings of loans among commercial banks and multilaterals have become **8.35** standard in the project finance market. While in many cases multilaterals and commercial banks will lend side by side, certain multilaterals have developed A Loan/B Loan structures that allow such multilaterals to leverage available liquidity from commercial banks while acting as lender-of-record on the loan. Both the IFC and the IADB, for example, have structured their B-loan programs such that they will enter into a loan agreement with the borrower for the entirety of the loan, but then enter into a participation agreement with a syndicate of commercial banks that will provide liquidity for the B portion of such loan. Under this type of structure, the IFC/IADB administers the loan and collects all payments from the borrower, while also committing to distribute payments pro rata among itself and the commercial banks. This structure has the benefit of allowing the multilateral to commit more funds to a project in order to achieve its development priorities, while also providing participating banks the ability to hold an economic interest in loans that are effectively being administered by the multilateral.

Nonetheless, while commercial bank lenders may take substantial comfort from **8.36** the participation of multilaterals in the financing of a project, explicit provisions in the documentation often exclude any inference that such multilaterals are acting in any type of governmental capacity. Indeed, commercial banks involved in the project are often required specifically to acknowledge that they have entered into the transaction exercising their own credit judgment and without reliance on the decisions taken by the co-financing agency (similar to the acknowledgement given by the participating banks to an agent bank); any responsibility or duty on the part of the multilateral to the commercial banks is excluded, except for those responsibilities that are expressly set out in the documents.

Preferred creditor status

Multilateral agencies that have 'preferred creditor status' enjoy preferential access to **8.37** foreign exchange by member governments in the event the host country experiences a foreign exchange crisis. Such multilaterals are excluded from general country debt restructurings and are not subject to new money obligations under any such restructurings. Preferred creditor status also typically exempts the relevant multilateral from in-country taxation, including in respect of withholding taxes. In most cases, preferred creditor status is recognized as a matter of practice, rather than as a matter of law. The involvement of multilaterals with preferred creditor status can be a source of comfort to lenders in a multi-sourced financing, because the host government is likely to prioritize loans made by multilaterals so as to maintain access to financial support. Other lenders take the view that the involvement of multilaterals with preferred creditor status leaves them at a disadvantage to the extent that the multilateral does not pass along the benefit of its preferential access to foreign exchange to the other lenders in the financing group.

Common funding issues

Documentation

8.38 As a conceptual matter, much of the documentation for an ECA or multilateral-funded loan will seem familiar to those that are experienced with traditional project financing structures. In a direct loan context, the lending institution will enter into a credit agreement with the borrower which will set forth the basic terms and conditions relating to the loan. Most institutions have their own 'form' agreement or heavily rely on precedents from prior loans, although the documentation requirements and reliance on precedent may differ substantially from institution to institution. Additionally, the extent to which ECAs and multilaterals will agree to covenant packages that are common among commercial lending institutions in their loan documents will vary, although (as further discussed below) there has recently been a trend where certain agencies have become more and more comfortable looking to the commercial markets for guidance on appropriate levels of loan oversight.

8.39 Most multi-sourced financing facilities will be structured around a common terms agreement, where each of the agencies (and commercial banks, where applicable) involved will negotiate common conditions, representations, covenants, and other loan terms and conditions that will apply to each of the loans being extended to the project company. Each agency (and again, each group of commercial banks, where applicable) will then issue their loans under a separate loan agreement, which may include terms and conditions that are specific to such facility, including in respect of pricing, tenor, yield protection, and other specific covenants and events of default that may apply to such lending group. Often one of the most complicated aspects of documenting these types of multi-sourced loans is harmonizing the different requirements of each loan facility and ensuring that each individual agency's requirements have been addressed in a manner that is satisfactory to not only the project company, but also the other lenders in the transaction. Where A Loan/B Loan structures are being used, negotiations often occur between the B lenders and the relevant agency to ensure acceptable voting rights for each of the applicable credit providers. In general, ECAs and multilaterals will share in any project security on a *pari passu* basis, except for any proceeds available to a multilateral as a result of its Preferred Creditor Status.

Pro-rata lending

8.40 One issue that can arise in multi-source financings—particularly where 'tied' loans are being provided by more than one institution—is the potential that loan drawdowns may not be able to occur on a pro rata basis across all facilities insofar as certain loans may only be permitted to be used for specific eligible costs. In these types of financings, project companies and their advisers need to pay close attention to drawdown schedules as well as construction and or delivery schedules to ensure that loan proceeds can be sourced from the appropriate lender or group of lenders in a timely manner while also satisfying each applicable ECA's sourcing requirements. Project companies additionally need to monitor the impact any such non-pro rata drawdown schedule may have on loan repayment schedules. In general, ECAs have come to accept non-pro rata drawdowns necessitated by sourcing requirements and the timing of acquisition of disparate project components.

Voting rights and other intercreditor matters

Transactions involving more than just a single ECA or a single multilateral will often involve intercreditor arrangements that need to be designed to contemplate special ECA/multilateral rights on key issues. Such special rights may relate to issues such as environmental and social matters, minimum off-take requirements (for example, where an ECA may require that a minimum percentage of project production be sold to companies based in such ECA's home country, which is often a requirement in mining and commodities projects), minimum equity ownership requirements (for example, where an ECA requires that a minimum threshold of the project company's equity be owned by companies from such ECA's home country), or continued membership in the applicable multilateral by the country in which the project is being developed. Where applicable, parties also need to agree as to the impact of the Preferred Creditor Status (described above) that may be available to some, but not all, of the agencies involved in the transaction. Special veto rights may also be considered where the applicable ECA or multilateral has identified 'core' or 'fundamental' events (often relating to matters such as political risks or developmental goals) that could conflict with such institution's policies or cause substantial political embarrassment for the applicable institution. **8.41**

In addition, significant intercreditor issues often arise in the context of multi-source financings that include ECAs, multilaterals, and commercial lenders as a result of the different policy goals that influence the investment decisions made by these entities. Given the different credit perspectives of the various institutions that may be involved in a single financing, project companies and lenders must focus on structuring intercreditor rights in such a way as to address the needs of the different lending entities that are involved, and to anticipate that lender perspectives may differ when it comes to addressing major transactional issues. An example of this arises in the context of events of default—depending on the institution involved, certain lenders may favour efforts to work out any issues with the project company and enable the project company to take steps to rectify the circumstances leading to the default; other lenders, particularly commercial lenders, may seek to extract high waiver fees from the project company or to enforce rights against the project company in a much more aggressive manner. Both lenders and project companies need to be cognizant that these credit and policy perspectives will colour the respective rights being required by commercial banks, ECAs, and multilaterals. Where A loan/B loan structures are being used, these issues may become more pronounced **8.42** in the context of negotiating participant rights for those commercial banks providing liquidity under a B loan package, where participants may request voting and/or oversight rights that the fronting multilateral may not be prepared to grant.

Environmental and social considerations

8.43 Environmental and social considerations play a large role in financings undertaken by institutions providing official credits. Most multilaterals and ECAs adhere to some variation of the performance standards developed and implemented by the IFC. In developing its performance standards, the IFC's objective was fourfold:

(1) to identify and assess social and environmental impacts, both adverse and beneficial, in the project's area of influence;
(2) to avoid or, where avoidance is not possible, minimize, mitigate, or compensate for adverse impacts on workers, affected communities, and the environment;
(3) to ensure that affected communities are appropriately engaged on issues that could potentially affect them; and
(4) to promote improved social and environmental performance of companies through the effective use of management tools.

8.44 To meet these objectives, the IFC has come up with a 'Social and Environmental Management System' (the Management System) applicable to projects with social or environmental risks and impacts that need to be managed, beginning in the early stages of project development and continuing on an ongoing basis through project completion. The Management System incorporates the following elements:

(1) social and environmental assessment that considers in an integrated manner the potential social and environmental risks and impacts of the project;
(2) creation of a management program consisting of a combination of operational policies, procedures, and practices, effectively to mitigate negative externalities and improve performance;
(3) establishment of an organization structure that defines roles, responsibilities, and authority to implement the management program;
(4) training of employees and contractors with direct responsibility for activities relevant to the project's social and environmental performance;
(5) community engagement, including discourse on the project's risks to and adverse impacts (if any) on the affected communities;
(6) monitoring and measurement of the effectiveness of the management program, including site inspections and audits; and
(7) reporting, consisting of periodic assessments of the effectiveness of the management program.[34]

---

[34] See IFC Performance Standard 1, 'Social and Environmental Assessment and Management Systems', 30 April 2006, available at <http://www.ifc.org/ifcext/sustainability.nsf/AttachmentsBy Title/pol_PerformanceStandards2006_PS1/$FILE/PS_1_SocEnvAssessmentMgmt.pdf>.

Monitoring requirements

Monitoring requirements are mandated by multilaterals to ensure compliance **8.45**
with environmental action plans throughout the course of the project, from
inception through project completion. For instance, the Environmental Policy
of the EBRD states that: 'operations are monitored on an ongoing basis by an
operation team . . . throughout the Bank's relationship with the project.'[35] EBRD
uses a host of monitoring mechanisms for projects that it finances, including 'review
of periodic environmental reports and other progress reports, monitoring visits by
the Bank's environmental specialists or consultants and periodic third party audits
to ensure that the sponsor is implementing agreed programs, policies, and actions'
as set forth in the underlying legal documents.[36] Although broadly applicable,
EBRD defines a specific monitoring program for each project, based upon due diligence and public consultation. The negotiation and implantation of these programs
often require significant negotiation and documentation to ensure that the standards being applied are properly enforced throughout the term of the loan. Other
multilaterals similarly require comprehensive monitoring of projects in order to
assess social and environmental impacts, including, for example, the IADB,[37] the
AfDB,[38] and the EIB.[39] ECAs often apply similar standards, although monitoring
requirements can differ substantially from institution to institution.

---

[35] See EBRD Environmental Policy, available at <http://www.ebrd.com/downloads/research/
policies/policy.pdf>.

[36] Ibid.

[37] 'The ESMP [environmental and social management plan] must include: . . . the framework for the monitoring of social and environmental impacts and risks throughout the execution
of the operation, including clearly defined indicators, monitoring schedules, responsibilities
and costs. The ESMP should be ready for, and reviewed during, the analysis/due diligence mission.'
See Inter-American Development Bank, 'Environment and Safeguards Compliance Policy',
19 January 2006, available at <http://idbdocs.iadb.org/wsdocs/getDocument.aspx?DOCNUM=
665902>.

[38] 'The project implementation phase involves that the Borrowers ensure the implementation
of ESMPs and monitor project impacts and results . . . supervise the Borrowers' work and verify
compliance through supervision missions and/or environmental and social audits, whenever necessary.' See African Development Bank, 'Environmental and Social Assessment Procedures for African
Development Bank's Public Sector Operations', June 2001, available at <http://www.afdb.org/
fileadmin/uploads/afdb/Documents/Project-related-Procurement/ESAP%20for%20Public%20
Sector%20Operations.pdf>.

[39] 'The EIB [European Investment Bank] monitors the environmental and social performance
of the projects it is financing, especially the fulfilment of any specific obligations described in the
Finance Contract. The extent of monitoring is a function of the characteristics of the project, the
capacity of the promoter and the country context. Monitoring by the Bank is based on reports from
the promoter. It may be supplemented by site visits by the bank and other sources of information,
including that provided by affected communities.' See The European Investment Bank, 'The EIB
Statement of Environmental and Social Principles and Standards', 2009, available at <http://www
.eib.org/attachments/strategies/eib_statement_esps_en.pdf>.

Recent Trends

8.46 While global commercial markets have suffered recently, a number of recent developments have indicated the staying power of ECA and multilateral funding sources as part of the project finance landscape for the foreseeable future.

Non-OECD ECAs and 'cooperation' agreements

8.47 Although ECAs have traditionally been based in OECD and other developed countries, recent growth in a number of developing countries have encouraged the development of ECAs in places that have historically been the target, rather than the sourcing of ECA funding. While this development evidences growth in these regions and should be encouraging from a development perspective, it is worth noting that many of these 'newer' ECAs often do not adhere to common agreements such as the OECD Arrangement that are intended to ensure that ECA funding does not constitute unfair subsidization of home country exporters. In order to effectively compete with ECAs that do not adhere to the Arrangement, certain ECAs have established funds to enable them to offer additional financing options in order to prevent market distortions that may occur when official funding is offered to projects on terms that are not consistent with consensus protocols. US Exim Bank's Tied Aid War Chest, for example, is a program that was designed to counter situations where there is a reasonable basis for determining that a foreign government is unfairly supporting home exporters in a manner that does not comply with the Helsinki Package. Part of the purpose of the program is to defend US exporters from foreign government financing that may create long-run trade advantages for foreign exporters to the detriment of US exporters.

8.48 Another recent trend relating to non-OECD ECAs has been the initiation of cooperative arrangements between different agencies. The Brazilian ECA BNDES and US Exim Bank recently concluded a cooperation agreement allowing both entities to work together to identify projects of interest for both Brazilian and US companies. Similar arrangements have been entered into by JBIC, IFC, and ADB, as well as by K-Exim and the IADB, the latter which will focus on infrastructure development in Central and South America. These cooperation agreements, while a new trend and (as of now) limited to a finite time period, enable these entities to work together to both identify mutually beneficial opportunities while leveraging the support they are ultimately able to provide to their domestic exporters.

Local currency funding options

8.49 Given recent turmoil in currency markets and investor's demands to limit the potential for currency risk exposure, certain multilaterals have begun to provide local currency funding options. The IADB, for example, has recently begun offering local currency facilities to project companies, which not only helps mitigate the risk of currency shocks and potential mismatches between asset values and project liabilities, but also acts to strengthen local capital markets by encouraging local currency investments in projects that have all the traditional stability of multilateral support. The participation of local investors can also help mitigate political risks, as local governments may be less inclined to interfere in investments where local participation has provided crucial funding for project development.

Credit crisis of 2008–2010 and beyond

While ECAs and multilaterals have always constituted a major source of potential **8.50** financing for investors and developers, recent events have thrust these institutions into an even more central role in the funding of major projects. Simply put, over the past few years there have been virtually no major project financings in non-OECD countries that have not involved at least one ECA or multilateral, and a substantial portion of what has been financed has included two or more of these types of entities. In addition to providing a constant source of liquidity and credit protection, the presence of ECAs and multilaterals has proven to be a major attraction for commercial banks, as these institutions have been perceived to provide stability in an otherwise unstable market. Without even considering the 'hard' and 'soft' political support an ECA or a multilateral can bring to the table, commercial lenders have grown comfortable with the extensive diligence and technical expertise that these entities offer, and given the prevalence of these funding sources over the past few years, many in the commercial market have come to not only invite agency participation but also to expect it.

On the agency side, after numerous years of developing their expertise working **8.51** side-by-side with commercial lenders in a variety of projects markets, many have become accustomed to their role of not just providing competitive economic terms but also of leading negotiations in respect of the general terms and conditions for the multi-source transactions in which they are involved. More and more often, these covenant packages reflect standards that have been commonplace in the commercial project finance market for many years. Indeed, many ECAs have not only embraced these standards, but have also taken structural steps to adopt commercial bank covenant standards as their own and to participate in financings in regions that were not traditionally designated for official credits. An example of this is the 2008 spin-off of KfW Ipex-Bank, which effectively created a fully independent subsidiary of KfW Bankengruppe that was designed to function in a primarily commercial capacity, while still supporting its parent company's primary mission of supporting exports and promoting development. This fusion of official ownership with a commercial mandate has been welcomed by the market, as borrowers and other lending institutions have recognized the value of merging the strengths of a public institution—with the ability to coordinate with international institutions and foreign governments—and the commercial perspectives necessary to address many complex financing issues. Other public institutions have also expanded their mandates to address demand for ECA-style funding in developed as well as developing nations. Both JBIC and COFACE have recently made forays into the US domestic PF market in support of Japanese and French exporters, respectively. These institutions are able to provide a full spectrum of support for the companies they seek to promote, from initial investment structuring to analysis of funding alternatives, all the way through to financial closing.

8.52 ECAs and multilaterals have, in short, become key financing providers to the projects marketplace. As the market continues to rely on the levels of diligence and technical capability—not to mention the attractive loan terms—offered by these official funding sources, it is to be expected that both ECAs and multilaterals will continue to play a leading role as credit providers to the project finance market for many years to come.

9

DOCUMENTATION OF PROJECT BONDS

Tom Siebens and David Gasperow, Milbank, Tweed, Hadley & McCloy LLP

Introduction

Bonds issued in the international capital markets to raise financing for projects— **9.01** commonly referred to as 'project bonds'—have been a well-known source of project capital since the 1980s, though less commonly used than traditional sources of project financing debt such as export credit agencies, banks, and other financial institutions, as well as loans from the sponsors. The attractiveness of the bond market tends to fluctuate depending upon the comparative cost and availability of funding from these other sources, the willingness of the sponsors to undertake the additional effort to incorporate a bond offering into a project's capital structure and the relative difficulty of implementing a bond financing at any given stage of a project's development (for example, bonds issued early in a greenfield project entail more risk for investors, compared with bonds issued to fund the expansion of a project that is already producing revenue and, therefore, entails less risk).

9.02 Documenting a project bond involves a number of elements not found in more common forms of project finance. This difference is primarily due to the way bonds are marketed and the fact that, unlike loans, bonds are 'securities', making them subject to various legal regimes governing the offering and trading of securities, to which traditional loans are not subject. From a documentation standpoint, the most significant additional element is the need to prepare an offering document, or prospectus,[1] and to comply with the attendant disclosure requirements, as well as the need to document the relationship with the underwriters who are responsible for the sale and distribution of the bonds to investors while complying with restrictions on where and to whom the bonds may be marketed.

9.03 This chapter summarizes the legal framework for securities offerings, recognizing of course that various jurisdictions may impose different requirements. After describing the general legal context, the chapter explains the due diligence and underwriting processes for project bonds, followed by a discussion of the various project bond offering documents and how they relate to the legal framework. Finally, there is a brief discussion of bond listings.

History of project bonds

9.04 Accessing capital markets to fund projects and infrastructure arguably dates back to the 1800s, with bond offerings used to back railroad expansion in the US. The US also has a long history of state and local government bonds to fund infrastructure projects, with bond debt service being covered by revenues from those projects. The first modern private sector project bond offerings date to the late 1980s and early 1990s, encouraged in part by changes in the US securities regulatory regime that facilitated bond offerings to institutional investors. The first wave of project bonds financed independent power projects (IPPs), notably the $800 million project bond offering for Sithe/Independence Funding Corporation of a 1,000 MW cogeneration facility in New York State, which was the first capital markets transaction in which the debt securities of a project under construction received an investment grade rating. Project bonds also provided refinancing for completed IPPs, such as the $600 million project bond for IEC Funding Corp. to refinance debt incurred in the development of two 300 MW cogeneration projects in the US, which helped to demonstrate the burgeoning role of project bonds as a key portion of projects' capital structures.

9.05 Capital markets financings of projects have evolved rapidly, covering a broad range of electric, oil and gas, water, and other power-related assets; toll roads, railways,

---

[1] An offering document may also be referred to as an 'offering circular' or 'offering memorandum'. These terms should not be confused with an 'information memorandum', a document that is less comprehensive than a prospectus and used to syndicate bank facilities or to assist in a private placement of bonds with institutions who conduct their own due diligence rather than relying on a prospectus.

rolling stock, and other infrastructure-related assets; as well as more esoteric assets such as hospitals, schools, and prisons (as a result of private financing initiatives in places such as the UK).

Further afield, project bonds have played critical roles in financing oil and gas and **9.06** other energy-related projects in the Middle East, Africa, and the former Soviet republics of Central Asia, presenting opportunities to connect international institutional investors seeking to diversify their portfolios with interesting new projects and geographic regions. As new markets focused on green energy sources continue to emerge, project bonds are likely to find a place in the financing of a variety of new project classes.

Securities Regulation and Legal Framework

Generally speaking, bonds are financial instruments that can be sold to a wide range **9.07** of investors who do not have direct access to information about the issuer of the bonds, unlike a bank lender or ECA that deals directly with a project borrower and its sponsors. In addition, as securities, bonds can be traded in the capital markets more readily than other types of debt, such as bank loans. However, in order to protect investors and the integrity of the capital markets against abuses such as fraud, insider trading, and market manipulation, securities laws are extensive and complex, particularly in countries with mature capital markets. The requirements of the securities laws in particular jurisdictions drive decisions as to which geographic markets and types of investors to target for a project bond offering and, consequently, decisions about the form and substance of the bond documentation.

In this regard, the most significant aspects of securities laws are those directed at **9.08** assuring adequate disclosure to investors and preventing offers and sales of securities to unsophisticated investors unless the offering has been vetted by a regulatory authority for distribution to the general public.

Disclosure

A more specific discussion of the process for preparing a project bond offering **9.09** document and its contents is set out later in this chapter. These aspects of documentation will be easier to understand if one first has an overview of how securities laws shape the disclosure process.

United States

Extensive regulation of securities markets began first in the US in the 1930s, **9.10** leading to one of the most developed bodies of regulatory and case law in this area currently. The US also is important because it was the first, and is today the largest, market for project bonds. This is no surprise, given the size and liquidity of US markets, the sophistication of the US investor base for project bonds, and the long-standing and well-understood US regulatory environment for securities. US and foreign issuers alike regularly structure their project bond offerings to allow offers and sales in the US markets as one of the best ways to assure sufficient investor demand and competitive funding terms for those bonds.

9.11 In the US, as in other jurisdictions, raising new capital from public markets is more heavily regulated than capital raising in the institutional or private markets where investors are viewed as more sophisticated and, therefore, less in need of regulatory protection. For example, public offerings in the US are subject to the Securities Act of 1933 (the Securities Act)[2] which requires that such offerings be registered with the US Securities and Exchange Commission (the SEC), unless an exemption from registration is available. The registration process essentially requires disclosure in accordance with SEC rules in an offering document (the prospectus) filed in a registration statement with the SEC. A filing is required before the relevant securities may be offered to the public. The registration statement must be declared 'effective' by the SEC before actual sales may be completed. Once securities are registered and publicly traded, an issuer must provide ongoing disclosure in periodic reports filed publicly with the SEC under the Securities and Exchange Act of 1934 (the Exchange Act). The Exchange Act also regulates the subsequent trading of securities in the secondary market.[3]

9.12 Exemptions from the SEC registration and reporting process are available in the US for offerings to large institutional investors (so-called 'Rule 144A' offerings[4]) and private placements to accredited investors. These exemptions (discussed further below under 'Selling Restrictions') have become the preferred choice for foreign issuers wishing to issue debt securities—including project bonds—to US investors. By employing these exemptions, issuers can avoid SEC registration and reporting. As a result, the preparation of the offering is not delayed by the SEC registration process, the prospectus disclosure and ongoing reporting requirements are less burdensome for the issuer and, in the event of defective disclosure, the liability exposure under securities laws is somewhat less for the issuer. Regulatory regimes in other jurisdictions are similar in that they impose less stringent disclosure requirements,

---

[2] This section discusses securities laws at the federal or national level in the US. Issuers of securities and their offerings in the US are subject to securities regulation at the state level as well under the so-called 'blue sky' laws. These should be considered in connection with any securities offering into the US.

[3] A variety of other federal laws may also be relevant to a US bond offering, including the Trust Indenture Act of 1939, which imposes a standard of independence and responsibility upon the bond trustee and requires that certain protections for debt holders are included in the terms of the bonds or notes. Generally, these requirements are not burdensome for issuers.

[4] Rule 144A promulgated under the Securities Act.

prospectus review procedures and ongoing reporting requirements for securities that are not distributed into retail investor markets.[5]

Regardless of whether a bond offering will be registered with the SEC or exempt from registration, the anti-fraud provisions of US securities laws impose potential liability on bond issuers, underwriters, and, potentially, their 'control persons'[6] if disclosure in the offering document is deficient in a material respect. The most relevant statutory provision in this regard is Section 10(b) of the Exchange Act, which provides that it is unlawful to use, in connection with the purchase or sale of any security, whether registered or not, any manipulative or deceptive device in contravention of rules adopted by the SEC.[7] Rule 10b-5, promulgated by the SEC under Section 10(b) of the Exchange Act, provides that in connection with the purchase or sale of a security it is unlawful: 'to make any untrue statement of a material fact or to omit to state a material fact necessary in order to make the statements made, in the light of the circumstances under which they were made, not misleading.'   **9.13**

This regulatory approach seeks to protect investors primarily through mandating adequate disclosure, thereby allowing investors to make properly informed investment decisions. Note that this approach does not leave it to a regulatory authority to rule or comment on the actual merits of an investment in the securities being offered or the creditworthiness of the issuer. In other words, the US regulatory regime is designed to ensure full and complete disclosure of all material information to investors in order to enable investors to make their own investment decisions. Hence, potential liability under this regime is directly tied to defective or deficient disclosure.   **9.14**

Parties that can be liable for defective disclosure under Section 10(b) and Rule 10b-5 include the issuer and the underwriters of a bond offering. An underwriter (and the issuer, for unregistered offerings) may avail itself of the 'due diligence defence', which basically allows the underwriter to avoid liability where it can demonstrate that it properly undertook due diligence with respect to the information contained in the prospectus. Specifically, the due diligence defence requires a showing that the defendant 'had, after reasonable investigation, reasonable ground to   **9.15**

---

[5] In the EU, for example, Article 3 of the Prospectus Directive (Directive 2003/71/EC) does not require an issuer to publish a prospectus fully compliant with the disclosure requirements of the Prospectus Directive for: (1) an offer of securities solely to 'qualified investors'; (2) an offer of securities to fewer than 100 individuals per EU member state (excluding qualified investors); (3) an offer of securities with a minimum investment threshold of €50,000; (4) an offer of securities with a minimum denomination of €50,000; and/or (5) an offer of securities with a total consideration of less than €100,000.

[6] 'Control persons' can include, among others, senior executive officers, directors, and controlling shareholders of an issuer or underwriter.

[7] There are various other statutory provisions imposing liability. For example, in the case of a registered offering, the issuer faces strict liability, for which there is no defence, with respect to any material misstatement or omission from the registration statement (Section 11, Securities Act).

believe and did believe . . . that the statements [in the prospectus] were true and that there was no omission to state a material fact required to be stated therein or necessary to make the statements therein not misleading'.[8] Control persons can also be held liable.[9]

9.16 What is deemed to be 'material' varies with the specific facts and circumstances of the particular situation. The basic test is whether there is a substantial likelihood that a reasonable investor would consider the misstatement or omission to be important in deciding whether or not to purchase a security. The US Supreme Court has ruled that a fact is material if there is: 'substantial likelihood that the . . . fact would have been viewed by the reasonable investor as having significantly altered the "total mix" of information made available.'[10] The SEC has indicated that the following factors, among others, can contribute to the determination of whether a misstatement or omission is material:[11]

(1) whether the misstatement arises from an item capable of precise measurement or whether it arises from an estimate and, if so, the degree of imprecision inherent in the estimate;

(2) whether the misstatement masks a change in earnings or other trends;

(3) whether the misstatement hides a failure to meet analysts' consensus expectations for the enterprise;

(4) whether the misstatement changes a loss into income or vice versa;

(5) whether the misstatement concerns a segment or other portion of the issuer's business that has been identified as playing a significant role in the issuer's operations or profitability;

(6) whether the misstatement affects the issuer's compliance with regulatory requirements;

(7) whether the misstatement affects the issuer's compliance with loan covenants or other contractual requirements;

---

[8] Section 11(b)(3)(A) of the Securities Act. The burden of proof rests with the defendant (i.e. the issuer or underwriter). Note that this section refers to 'non-expertised' information in the prospectus (i.e. information that has not otherwise been vetted by experts such as the issuer's auditors), which requires 'reasonable investigation' by the underwriters. However, with respect to expertised information, case law suggests that underwriters cannot blindly rely on experts where 'red flags' suggest a flaw in the disclosure. See generally *In re WorldCom, Inc. Securities Litigation*, 346 F Supp 2d 628 (SDNY 2004). Further, what constitutes a 'reasonable investigation' varies with the relevant facts and circumstances, though courts have held that a reasonable investigation requires 'more effort on the part of the underwriters than the mere accurate reporting . . . of "data presented" to them' by the issuer, concluding that 'the underwriters must make some reasonable attempt to verify the [issuer's] data'. *Escot v BarChris Construction Co.*, 283 F Supp 643 (SDNY 1968).

[9] The control person may raise a defence of having acted in good faith and not having directly or indirectly induced the act or acts constituting the violation or cause of action.

[10] *TSC Industries v Northway, Inc.*, 426 US 438, 449 (1976).

[11] SEC Staff Accounting Bulletin: No. 99—Materiality, 12 August 1999.

(8) whether the misstatement has the effect of increasing management's compensation—for example, by satisfying requirements for the award of bonuses or other forms of incentive compensation; and

(9) whether the misstatement involves concealment of an unlawful transaction.

These points are merely guidance, however. The issuer together with the underwriters and their legal counsels, and perhaps the auditors and/or other experts and advisers, will collectively have to take a view on specific points as to whether or not they are material in the particular context of the bond offering and the project. **9.17**

As the market regulator, the SEC has the authority to bring enforcement actions for violations of Rule 10b-5. In addition, the securities laws in the US recognize a private right of action under Rule 10b-5 such that investors themselves may bring their own claims under Rule 10b-5 for damages against the participants in a offering, asserting that the seller acted intentionally or recklessly in preparing a misleading offering document and that the claimant relied on a material misstatement or omission in making its purchase. Often these claims are brought collectively as class actions by groups of investors and, as a result, an extensive body of case law exists in the US with respect to liability for disclosure documents. This system of, in effect, enforcement through private litigation is somewhat unique to the US. Accordingly, issuers and underwriters have to take the due diligence process and contents of the disclosure document seriously when offering bonds in the US. **9.18**

Moreover, even in a Rule 144A offering which is exempt from SEC registration, the disclosure requirements for an SEC-registered offering will be followed as closely as possible for the content of a prospectus, including a project bond prospectus, being used in the US. Although the specific disclosure rules applicable to registration statements for a public offering do not apply in an exempt offering, the rules are viewed as guidance as to what is material to investors for purposes of Rule 10b-5. **9.19**

The scope of disclosure in a Rule 144A offering can deviate, however, from strict compliance with SEC requirements, as long as all material information is disclosed. For example, where a project company is not able to produce financial statements that meet requirements for an SEC-registered offerings, a Rule 144A offering may still be possible. (Similarly, under EU legislation, where a company does not prepare financial statements that satisfy the requirements for a prospectus that complies with the Prospectus Directive,[12] an offering may still proceed with institutional investors in markets that are exempt from such compliance requirements.) **9.20**

In any event, when drafting a prospectus, one should bear in mind that its function is twofold. First, it is needed to provide investors with sufficient information to make an investment decision whether to purchase the bonds. Secondly, it is often **9.21**

---

[12] Directive 2003/71/EC.

characterized as a 'defensive' document, meaning that, in the event of litigation if the bond's value collapses for any reason, the project company, its sponsors and the underwriters can point to the prospectus as evidence that they met their legal obligations to disclose all material information to investors. Drafting the prospectus is, in that respect, a liability management exercise. In other words, liability will not necessarily stem from a collapse in value of the bond or the underlying project. Rather, liability can emanate from a failure adequately or accurately to disclose information that would have enabled an investor to understand a particular risk or aspect of the project that related to the subsequent cause of such loss.

9.22 Alternatively, in order to avoid the disclosure burdens and risks in the US, it is not uncommon for an issuer to elect not to offer its securities there, even if, by excluding the large capacity of the US market, the issuer limits the amount of capital markets financing it can raise.

European Union

9.23 Comprehensive securities regulation exists in many other jurisdictions and continues to evolve with globalization of capital flows. For example, during the past decade, the EU adopted both the Prospectus Directive and the Transparency Directive,[13] now part of national law of the EU member states, as part of a general reform and harmonization of securities regulation in that region.

9.24 In Europe, as in the US, project bonds generally are not marketed as a retail investor product. Accordingly, project bonds can be documented in a manner that exempts them from the disclosure requirements of the Prospectus Directive and are listed on the 'exchange-regulated' markets,[14] which are largely self-regulated and accessible only by mainly institutional investors, rather than on the 'regulated' markets[15] where retail instruments are listed and which are subject to more extensive governmental regulation. Issuers listed on certain exchange-regulated markets can also avoid being subject to the ongoing disclosure requirements of the Transparency Directive.

9.25 Project bonds listed on exchange-regulated markets are subject to the disclosure requirements of those markets and whatever ongoing disclosure requirements are dictated by market practice and agreed in the terms of the bonds themselves.

9.26 However, given the common practice of offering at least a portion of a project bond issuance in the US under Rule 144A, as a matter of market practice the more

---

[13] Directive 2004/109/EC.

[14] For example, the Euro MTF market of the Luxembourg Stock Exchange or the Global Exchange Market of the Irish Stock Exchange.

[15] For example, the Bourse de Luxembourg, the main market of the Luxembourg Stock Exchange, the Main Securities Market of the Irish Stock Exchange, or the Main Market of the London Stock Exchange.

extensive disclosure required for the US determines the scope of disclosure in the prospectus. Even where project bonds are not offered in the US, investor expectations often are that the disclosure will be based, more or less, on market practice for Rule 144A offerings.

Other jurisdictions

Emerging markets have generally adopted new legislation or modernized existing **9.27** legislation as the globalization of capital flows has brought foreign investors, including bond investors, into those countries. Given that these jurisdictions are relatively new sources of international capital, they have less developed histories of disclosure regulation. A prospectus that complies with the requirements for a Rule 144A offering generally will satisfy the requirements in these jurisdictions but for, perhaps, some local technical requirements.

Selling Restrictions

Typically the documentation for a project bond will contain restrictions on the **9.28** types of investors to whom the bonds may be offered or transferred upon resale. These restrictions are designed to ensure that the bonds are offered and sold only to investors permitted by relevant legislation in each country where the bonds will be distributed.

United States

In the US, unless a project bond offering has been registered with the SEC, it must **9.29** be distributed in a manner that fits within one of the available exemptions from registration. As mentioned above, the exemption most commonly used for project bonds is Rule 144A, promulgated by the SEC in 1990, essentially to create a securities market limited to large institutional investors, known as 'qualified institutional buyers' or 'QIBs'.[16]

In a Rule 144A offering, an issuer will sell its securities in a private placement **9.30** (explained below) to one or more underwriters who, in turn, resell the bonds in the US to QIBs, such resales being exempt from SEC registration under Rule 144A,[17]

---

[16] To be eligible as a QIB, an investor must own or invest in, on a discretionary basis, a least $100 million of securities and must be one of the types of institutions specified in Rule 144A, including certain types of insurance companies; an investment company registered under the US Investment Company Act of 1940; certain types of small business investment companies; certain types of employee benefit plans; any broker-dealer registered under the Exchange Act; and any US or foreign bank or savings and loan or equivalent institution that has an audited net worth of at least $25 million.

[17] Rule 144A has fairly minimal requirements. The securities cannot be of the same class or otherwise fungible with a class of securities that is SEC-registered (i.e. already publicly traded in

and outside the US to other investors, in resales exempt, under the SEC's Regulation S,[18] from SEC registration.

9.31 An alternative to a Rule 144A offering for project bonds targeted at the US is available in so-called 'US private placements'. The private placement exemption allows an issuer to place its bonds directly with accredited investors in a transaction that does not involve an underwriter. From a documentation perspective, private placements are simpler to execute because a prospectus is not required. A placement agent[19] and the issuer prepare a relatively simple information memorandum and term sheet to approach institutional investors, who are responsible for conducting their own due diligence on the issuer. No underwriting agreement is used. The placement agent has a simple engagement letter. The bonds themselves are documented in a form note purchase agreement between the issuer and each investor.

9.32 However, although simpler from a documentation and execution standpoint, the disadvantage of a US private placement is that the investor base is significantly smaller than for a Rule 144A offering or a registered public offering, so the market is inevitably capacity-constrained, resulting in relatively small deal sizes, and bonds that are less liquid for trading purposes.

European Union

9.33 In the EU, bonds that have a minimum denomination in excess of €50,000 are exempt from the requirement for a prospectus that complies with the Prospectus Directive in a public offering. The Prospectus Directive also exempts from its prospectus requirements bonds that are offered only to 'qualified investors' somewhat like the exemption in the US for offerings only to QIBs under Rule 144A.

---

the US). Investors must be notified that the seller may be relying on the Rule 144A exemption (i.e. the securities being sold are not SEC-registered and the issuer may not be a public reporting company). The issuer must undertake to provide basic information to QIB investors or potential investors (i.e. a brief description of the issuer's business and the product and services it offers, as well as its most recent balance sheet, profit and loss statement, or similar financial information for the periods during the two latest fiscal years that the issuer has been in operation).

[18] Regulation S under the Securities Act confirms a territorial approach to US securities laws by establishing an exemption for non-US transactions. Generally speaking, in order to fit within the Regulation S exemption safe harbor, an offer or sale of securities must occur in an 'offshore transaction' and must not involve any 'directed selling efforts' in the US. An offshore transaction is one in which the seller reasonably believes that the buyer is offshore at the time of the offer or sale or one which occurs on certain 'designated offshore securities markets' and the transaction is not pre-arranged with a buyer in the US. 'Directed selling efforts' are any activities made in the US by the issuer, a distributor, any of their respective affiliates, or any person acting on behalf of any of the foregoing that could reasonably be expected to condition the US market for the securities.

[19] As opposed to an underwriter. The placement agent acts as an agent for the issuer and does not actually purchase and resell the bonds. See the discussion at para. 9.41 et seq.

Other jurisdictions

Generally speaking, exemptions similar to those in the US and the EU are available **9.34** in other jurisdictions for offerings of securities to the institutional markets. Project bond documentation will include offering and transfer restrictions for the principal jurisdictions where the bonds will be offered. One point worth noting, however, is that offers and sales of the bonds in some jurisdictions may be prohibited for tax or other regulatory reasons.

Governing Law

The securities laws of the relevant jurisdictions (for example, the US, the EU, **9.35** or individual EU member states) where the bonds will be offered regulate the securities offering process and related issues of liability. However, contractual project bond documents—the underwriting agreement, the indenture or trust deed, and the bonds themselves (as opposed to the regulatory regime governing the offering process) generally will be governed by either New York or English law, regardless of the jurisdictions in which the offering is undertaken. This practice has developed over time because the contract law in these two jurisdictions is well established and familiar to investors. The governing law of the project bond contracts will be agreed between the issuer and the underwriters at the commencement of planning for the project bond offering. Note that although it is common for project bond contracts for Rule 144A offerings to be governed by New York law, there is no reason that English law could not be used even for offerings into the US, and vice versa for transactions targeted at European investors.

Security documents will usually be governed by the law of the jurisdiction in which **9.36** the collateral is located.

The Due Diligence Process

Given the importance of the due diligence defence for various parties in both **9.37** registered and Rule 144A offerings, establishing the grounds for such a defence, along with ensuring accurate and adequate disclosure, is the objective of the extensive due diligence process that characterizes securities offerings involving the US markets. The objective of the due diligence process is to create a record that the potential defendants undertook significant and reasonable due diligence efforts to ensure the accuracy of disclosure in the offering materials.

A foreign issuer contemplating a bond offering to US investors is expected to **9.38** comply with the due diligence process, including opening its books and records to its own legal counsel, the underwriters, and the underwriters' legal counsel.

For example, underwriters and the respective legal counsels will seek to review material documents that have been prepared by the issuer or its affiliates including, among other things:

(1) the issuer's constitutional documents;
(2) minutes of board of directors, board committee, and shareholders' meetings;
(3) material agreements with major suppliers and customers;
(4) agreements regarding credit facilities and other significant sources of financing for the project;
(5) licences, intellectual property, and permits material to the project;
(6) documents relating to insurance and liability management;
(7) employment agreements with senior executives and other key employees, labour union contracts, and employee medical, retirement, and stock option plans;
(8) research reports about the project prepared by financial analysts;
(9) press releases by the project;
(10) financial statements and management accounts;
(11) tax returns;
(12) internal management reports relating to the adequacy of the issuer's accounting procedures and controls; and
(13) documents relating to regulatory issues and ongoing litigation.

9.39 The issuer is also expected to facilitate aspects of the underwriters' due diligence that involve discussions with various parties, such as key officers, board members, and outside auditors. In particular, the issuer is expected to facilitate the following:

(1) a review of operations with the issuer's chief operating officer (or equivalent) and heads of major business divisions and material subsidiaries;
(2) a review with the chief financial officer and the issuer's external accountants (often in separate meetings) of the issuer's financial condition, accounting standards, and internal controls;
(3) a review with internal and external counsel of existing and potential litigation or governmental proceedings; and
(4) additional discussions to the extent the issuer's business and financial condition is dependent on a few important key customers, suppliers, or lenders.

9.40 In addition to the legal imperative to avoid material misstatements in, and omissions from, the information contained in the prospectus, due diligence procedures followed in preparing for Rule 144A offerings are often designed with business and reputational issues in mind for both issuers and underwriters. This means that, while the scope of due diligence may vary depending on the circumstances of a particular offering, the underlying rationale for conducting a thorough due diligence review (that is, the need to avoid defective disclosure, liability and litigation) remains the foundation on which the due diligence process is based.

The Underwriting Process

One of the key distinctions between a bond transaction and a bank loan transaction **9.41** is the offering process itself. Most bond transactions are undertaken through an underwriting process whereby investment banks, acting as underwriters, purchase the bonds from the issuer at closing and then resell the bonds to investors. This intermediate step of sales through underwriters encourages the offering process both in terms of facilitating marketing and also assisting with securities regulatory compliance, particularly in the US. As a practical matter, the underwriters receive funds from investors prior to funding their own purchase of the bonds and sell the bonds on to investors immediately upon receipt of the bonds from the issuer. This also makes the process easier for the issuer, as the issuer only has to receive funds from one or a few underwriters, rather than separately from all investors. Figure 9.1 illustrates the underwriting process in simplified form.

Many transactions, particularly higher value bond issuances, tend to have several **9.42** underwriters.

Types of underwritings

There are three basic types of underwriting commitments, which are as follows: **9.43**

(1) Firm commitment underwriting—also known as a 'hard underwriting', whereby the underwriters assume all risk by purchasing a pre-agreed principal amount of bonds at a pre-agreed price, after which the underwriters sell the bonds on to investors. If the underwriters fail to sell the bonds on to investors successfully, the underwriters must retain the bonds, making this the riskiest underwriting arrangement from the underwriters' perspective (and conversely the safest form for the issuer). As a result, firm commitment underwriting is the most expensive type of underwriting for the issuer because underwriters demand the highest fees for this arrangement.
(2) Standby underwriting—whereby the underwriters agree to purchase the portion of the bond issue that remains unsold to investors. As a practical matter, this form of underwriting is not fundamentally different from a firm commitment.
(3) Best efforts underwriting—whereby the underwriters agree to use their best efforts to sell as much of an issue as possible. However, the underwriter is obliged to purchase only the amount required to fulfil investor demand. If the underwriters are unable to sell the total principal amount of bonds sought to be issued by the issuer, the underwriters do not have to purchase the shortfall.

Figure 9.1 The Bond Underwriting Process

9.44 Regardless of which underwriting arrangement is followed, the underwriters are expected to advise the issuer in the pre-marketing stage about how best to structure and market the transaction to appeal to investors and then assist in the roadshow process to present the issuance and the project to investors. Investment banks often have teams specializing in different industries and asset classes and it is common to select underwriters based on their industry and/or asset class expertise and their relative access to investors who are interested in that industry or asset class.

Roadshow

9.45 After completion of the preliminary offering circular (described below), the underwriters will organize a 'roadshow' whereby senior members of the issuer's management team will meet with potential investors in a series of presentations scheduled over a period of anywhere from one to two days to several weeks. These meetings are usually scheduled in multiple cities, usually at least in New York (assuming the offering is targeted at US investors) and London, and often encompassing other major financial centres such as any of Hong Kong, Frankfurt, Dubai, Abu Dhabi, Milan, Paris, Los Angeles, Tokyo, Singapore, Shanghai, and Beijing, depending on the size of the deal and the number and type of investors being targeted.

9.46 At these meetings, the issuer's management presenters will use a slide presentation, prepared in conjunction with the underwriters, that summarizes the project and its financial prospects. The information contained in the roadshow presentation should be consistent with the information included in the offering circular. Hard copies of the presentation should not be left with investors.

9.47 During the roadshow process, the underwriters will be undertaking a 'bookbuilding' process, whereby the underwriters assess demand from potential investors to determine what size investment the investor might be willing to make and at what price. Through this process, the underwriters can work towards optimizing the deal size and price for the issuer.

9.48 Throughout this period, it is likely that the underwriters will keep the issuer apprised of market conditions and how activity in the markets might impact the offering. At the time of pricing, the underwriters will advise the issuer as to their views on appropriate deal size and price. Once the deal size and price are agreed with the issuer, the underwriting agreement will be executed and the parties will move towards issuance and funding of the bonds.

Typical Project Bond Documentation

9.49 Numerous documents comprise the suite of materials for a project bond offering. Together they encapsulate:

(1) materials and information used to market the bond offering;

(2) part of the foundation for establishing the underwriters' due diligence defence; and

(3) the contractual terms with respect to the initial marketing and sale of the project bonds by the underwriters and the terms and conditions of the project bonds themselves.

Figure 9.2 shows the primary bond documentation, described in detail below. Obviously each transaction and each project is different, and the commercial and disclosure issues that present themselves in each transaction will vary. In addition, the documentation governing the project bonds will vary depending on governing law and specific market practice.

Offering circular

As mentioned above, the bond offering process requires that the project bond issuer **9.50** produce an offering circular or prospectus. Given the disclosure liability and due diligence obligations described above, the offering circular has evolved into a critical transaction component for conveying all material information about the project to investors. As mentioned above, although the specific disclosure rules applicable to a public offering do not apply in exempt offerings, those rules are viewed as guidance as to what is material to investors, and therefore what needs to be disclosed, in an exempt offering. For this reason, market practice has developed to the point where Rule 144A offerings adhere generally to public disclosure guidelines (often even in non-US offerings).

Similarly, although disclosure tends to be less extensive for transactions that are **9.51** done entirely outside the US (i.e. without seeking US investors), the stringent US

```
┌─────────────────────────────────────────────┐
│  Primary project bond documentation         │
├─────────────────────────────────────────────┤
│   • Offering circular                       │
│                                             │
│   • Subscription/underwriting agreement     │
│                                             │
│   • Bond trust deed/indenture               │
│                                             │
│   • Global note                             │
│                                             │
│   • Intercreditor arrangements              │
│                                             │
│   • Security documents/collateral deed      │
│                                             │
│   • Auditor's comfort letter                │
│                                             │
│   • Agreement among underwriters            │
│                                             │
│   • Legal opinions                          │
└─────────────────────────────────────────────┘
```

Figure 9.2 The Primary Bond Documentation.

requirements provide a good checklist or reference point for assessing the adequacy of a disclosure document. However, the scope of disclosure can depend on a variety of factors, including:

(1) the customary scope of inquiry in the international market and, if it is well developed, the issuer's home market;
(2) the type of securities being offered;
(3) the financial strength of the issuer and its credit standing; and
(4) technical disclosure requirements of regulatory regimes where the bonds will be offered or of stock exchanges where the bonds will be listed.

9.52 In other words, while the level and type of disclosure required for a US public offering is usually relevant in a Rule 144A offering, in practice the necessary disclosure may be more extensive or less so, depending on the particular circumstances and marketing objectives.

Categories of information in the offering circular

9.53 Regardless of how closely the offering circular disclosure adheres to US public offering disclosure requirements, there are broad categories of information that will almost always be included. These include, inter alia, a description of the project, a description of the project's other financing arrangements, descriptions of upstream and downstream contractual relationships, and the terms and conditions of the project bonds. If the sponsors are providing financing, completion guarantees, construction services, or off-take arrangements for the project, disclosure about the sponsors will likely be necessary as well. Similarly, if other third parties are providing material support for the project or credit support for the project bonds, disclosure about them and those arrangements will be appropriate.

9.54 Typically, the issuer and its legal counsel will take the lead in drafting the sections of the offering circular specifically related to the issuer, such as those mentioned in paragraphs 9.55 through 9.66 below.

9.55 *A technical description of the project.* Disclosure regarding a project normally begins with a description of the material details of the project itself—its development history, physical location, facilities and operations, the technology involved and its supporting infrastructure. If a project is based upon the extraction of natural resources—an energy or mining project, for example—a description of the size of the resource, often based on an engineer's or geologist's report annexed to the prospectus, will be essential.

9.56 *Descriptions of material project agreements.* For a project still under construction, the prospectus will include summaries of the material terms of the significant construction agreements, including EPC contracts, completion guarantees, and construction services agreements. Contract descriptions for a project, whether completed or not, will cover concession agreements, land use rights, agreements with key suppliers to the project (including raw materials, power and other utilities, and transportation), key customers (particularly if a project depends on one or a handful of major off-takers) or the nature of the customer base if it is diffuse. Note that a major consideration when planning for contract disclosure in a bond offering is that contracts with third parties may contain commercially sensitive information such as pricing, quality, quantity, duration, take-or-pay features and the like. These provisions can be quite material to investors when trying to model the project company's ability to generate cashflow to service the bonds and other project debt. Yet, a confidentiality clause in a material agreement may prohibit disclosure without the consent of all parties to the contract. If a party refuses to consent to disclosing terms that are material to bondholders, financing through a project bond will not be possible.

Competitors: If a project faces current or likely future competition for markets or customers, the offering circular should describe the sources of competition and management's view of the relative strengths and weaknesses of competitors. **9.57**

Risk factors relating to the project and/or industry: These can include geographic risks, political and jurisdictional risks, environmental and safety risks, and competitive risks, among others. This section is an area that issuers initially may find troublesome, as it may seem counter-intuitive to include negative information in the document that will be used to market the project bonds to investors. However, for the disclosure-related liability reasons explained above, it is critical to disclose potential pitfalls that could materially impact the issuer and/or the project. **9.58**

A description of the issuer's industry: This will include typical supply and sales frameworks, domestic and international considerations and industry performance and outlook. The underwriters are often also deeply involved in drafting this section, with input from their internal industry analysts. It is important that the underwriters help 'position' this section from a marketing perspective to focus investors on critical industry drivers and expectations. If appropriate, industry specialists or consultants may also be separately engaged to produce reports to assist in drafting this section or to support the data and conclusions included. Ideally, all statistics and data included in the industry section will be cited from independent sources, which may involve seeking permission to reprint information, such as data included in industry reports published by trade associations or other industry publications. **9.59**

A description of the project's other financing/indebtedness: This description should include a reasonable level of detail on the overall financing of the project, credit support, and intercreditor provisions such that bond investors have sufficient information on all sources of funds for the project and all material obligations of the project. The ranking of different groups of creditors, whether senior, *pari passu*, or subordinate in relation to the bonds, also must be described. Such a description will contain detail as to the material terms of the intercreditor arrangements that affect the bonds, as well as bondholders' relative position in the project's overall capital structure. **9.60**

9.61   *The 'MD&A':* This is the management's discussion and analysis of financial condition and results of operations.[20] This section should go into significant detail about the factors that affect the project's results of operations, such as market pricing mechanisms, interest or exchange rate fluctuations, types of costs unique to the project, and occurrences or trends that could impact revenues or expenses. This section should also describe the critical accounting policies—those policies followed by management for which management must use discretionary judgment. To the extent that historical financial statements exist, income statement, balance sheet, and cashflow line items should be compared over a historical period (usually two or three years), with detailed commentary explaining movements and trends in each line item.[21]

9.62   *A description of the issuer's management team and board of directors:* Usually, this section includes short biographical descriptions of the senior management, including age, educational background, and professional experience. Note that in a deal registered with the SEC, specific details of management and director compensation would need to be disclosed.

9.63   *Description of shareholders/sponsors:* Depending on the transaction structure, where a project is heavily dependent upon sponsors' shareholders, disclosure about those shareholders may be necessary to ensure a fulsome description of the entire project. In particular, financial guarantees, completion guarantees, and any other credit support provided by a sponsor will need to be described. For further details about completion guarantees, see Chapter 11.

9.64   *Related party transactions:* Related parties to a project company include its controlling shareholders—the sponsors—and its senior management and directors. This section is intended to disclose relationships that may exist between the project company and these related parties in addition to their primary roles. For example, a sponsor may be a controlling shareholder but also have other roles such as that of a supplier of construction or operating services, a supplier of raw materials and utilities, or an off-taker. The disclosure of these additional roles is necessary given that they represent potential conflicts of interest such as additional ways in which a project relies upon a sponsor's performance, opportunities for a sponsor to extract revenue from the project ahead of debt service payments on the bonds, or the potential for below-market sales to the sponsors. As another example, if a director is also part of the management for a services provider to the project, a potential

---

[20] The SEC has published detailed guidance as to the purpose of the MD&A, which describes at length the types of disclosure that should be considered for inclusion in this section. SEC Release Nos. 33-8350, 34-48960. A copy of the release is available on the SEC website at <http://www.sec.gov/rules/interp/33-8350.htm>.

[21] Note that for a greenfield project, no historical financial information will exist. Historical financial information should be available for an existing project where expansion financing is sought in the capital markets.

conflict of interest arises. Features like this, if they exist, will be material to investors and need to be disclosed.

Regulatory, tax and accounting matters: To the extent material to a project or the conse- **9.65** quences of holding a bond, the offering circular will include sections on regulatory requirements affecting the project, currency exchange controls (particularly if the project generates its revenues in a different currency from that of the bonds), foreign investment controls in the country where the project is located, special tax benefits on which the project relies, and the tax treatment of the bonds (withholding tax on interest payments, for example).

Use of bond proceeds: Normally, this is a brief section explaining how the bond **9.66** proceeds will be applied, whether to a specific aspect or for general purposes of the project.

At the same time as the issuer and its legal counsel are working on the sections **9.67** described above, the underwriters and their legal counsel will be working together to produce drafts of the sections of the offering circular specifically related to the terms and conditions of the bonds and the underwriting process, such as:

(1) Risk factors relating to the project bonds. These can include any enforcement or insolvency risks related to the issuer's jurisdiction of incorporation or the location of the project, risks related to intercreditor arrangements or subordination provisions vis-à-vis other project indebtedness and risks associated with floating interest rates or currency exchange, if applicable.

(2) The 'description of the notes' or the 'terms and conditions of the notes'.[22] In particular, this section sets forth the covenants to which the issuer will be bound and the events of default under the project bonds (see discussion below at 9.83).

(3) The 'plan of distribution' or 'subscription and sale' description, explaining the terms of the underwriting arrangements. This section provides information about the size of each underwriter's commitment, special terms of the underwriting arrangements such as restrictions on the issuer issuing other securities for a period after the bond issuance, and securities law compliance procedures to be followed in certain specific jurisdictions where the project bonds are to be offered.

(4) Bond mechanics. Several sections of the offering circular will deal with administrative details of the securities, such as transfer restrictions and clearance and settlement mechanics for trading the bonds.

---

[22] Practice in transactions governed by New York law is to describe the terms of the bonds in a section entitled 'Description of the Notes', the terms of which will be contained in the New York law-governed indenture. For transactions governed by English law, the terms are included in a section entitled 'Terms and Conditions', which is usually appended in its entirety to the English-law governed trust deed.

9.68 Throughout the drafting process, the issuer, the underwriters and their respective legal counsels will meet on multiple occasions for 'drafting sessions' where questions are raised and comments and suggestions are provided. Drafting sessions serve not only to improve the disclosure, but also as another form of due diligence, given that specific aspects of the issuer's business will be discussed at length. Drafting an offering circular is an iterative process that requires ongoing consideration and input and it is likely that the final draft will be very different from (and better than) the first draft.

Financial information

9.69 The offering circular generally will include,[21] to the extent they exist, two to three years of financial statements of the issuer (and sometimes those of guarantors of the bonds). These will be included at the end of the offering circular in a separate section known as the 'F pages', short for financial pages. The auditor's report on those financial statements also will be included, consent for which may be required from the auditors. If the accounts are not prepared under IFRS or US GAAP, the offering circular often will include a qualitative description of the material differences between the accounting standards under which the issuer's financial statements are prepared and either IFRS or US GAAP.

9.70 Depending on the transaction structure and, potentially, the listing requirements of any stock exchange on which the bonds may be listed, historical financial statements for the same periods may need to be included with respect to any guarantors of the bonds.

Preliminary and final offering circulars

9.71 Generally, the offering circular is completed in two stages. First, the deal team completes the preliminary offering circular, often referred to as the 'red herring'.[23] The preliminary offering circular should be complete in all respects, except that pricing-related information—total aggregate principal amount, issuance date, maturity date, interest payment dates, and yield—is not yet included.

9.72 After a roadshow and marketing (described above), the underwriters will be in a position to 'price' the deal—literally, the determination of the final offering price. Immediately after pricing, the underwriters and their lawyers will produce a final pricing term sheet, the form of which will have been pre-agreed with the issuer and attached as a schedule to the underwriting agreement.

9.73 This pricing term sheet and the preliminary offering circular together comprise the 'time of sale' information, which is considered the package of marketing materials

---

[23] So named because the front cover typically has a legend in red ink indicating that the offering circular is not an offer to sell securities; before inclusion of the final terms, the document cannot be considered to be the offer to sell securities, since material information is missing.

on which an investor's decision is based. The time of sale information concept has developed under US law to acknowledge the fact that the completion and circulation to investors of the final offering circular lags behind the time of pricing and, therefore as a practical matter, is not the document on which an investor makes its final investment decision. As such, disclosure liability attaches under US law to the combination of the preliminary offering circular and the pricing term sheet, and any other supplementary data used up to the time of pricing to market the bonds to investors.

After pricing, the underwriters' and issuer's lawyers will work together to insert all **9.74** of the pricing-related data into the preliminary offering circular in order to create the final offering circular.[24]

Subscription/underwriting agreement

The underwriting agreement[25] is the principal contract between the bond issuer **9.75** and the underwriters, pursuant to which the underwriters commit to purchase the securities from the issuer at a particular price. It will be executed after the roadshow has been completed. Until the agreement is signed, the underwriters are not legally obligated to purchase the bonds. Even after the agreement is signed, the underwriters' obligations will be subject to representations and warranties given at closing and the satisfaction of various conditions, described further below.

The agreement will establish the underwriters' commission for underwriting the **9.76** transaction, which the underwriters usually recover by simply retaining the commission from the proceeds of the bond offering that are paid over to the issuer when the bond are issued. In other words, the underwriters' commission is derived from the price difference between the price they pay the issuer and the higher price paid by investors who purchase the bonds from the underwriters.

The agreement typically contains representations and warranties by the issuer **9.77** regarding the business and other matters. Depending on the issuer, its industry, and its geographic location, these representations and warranties can be quite extensive and cover a broad range of topics, including, among others:

(1) the accuracy of financial statements;
(2) the efficacy of internal controls;
(3) the due incorporation of the issuer and any material subsidiaries;
(4) the due authorization of the underwriting agreement and all of the transaction agreements;

---

[24] For a certain period of time after the closing of the bond offering, dealers must deliver a final offering circular to 'after-market' purchasers of bonds.
[25] Often referred to as the 'subscription agreement' when governed by English law or the 'purchase agreement' when governed by New York law.

(5) the due authorization of the securities and the bond offering;

(6) the absence of defaults and conflicts of law;

(7) the absence of labour disputes;

(8) the ownership of material properties;

(9) the ownership of material intellectual property;

(10) the possession of necessary licenses and permits;

(11) environmental liabilities;

(12) off-balance sheet transactions;

(13) adequate insurance;

(14) compliance with relevant securities laws and any distribution restrictions;

(15) compliance with relevant anti-money laundering and corruption laws;

(16) compliance with 'OFAC' rules (i.e. no dealings with or in jurisdictions or parties subject to US sanctions); and

(17) related party transactions.

9.78 Also included in the representations will be the '10b-5 representation', wherein the issuer will represent that the offering circular does not contain any untrue statement of a material fact or omit to state a material fact required to be stated therein or necessary to make the statements therein not misleading. This representation is critical because it is designed to ensure that the issuer has considered the disclosure in its entirety to make certain it is complete and accurate in all material respects before publishing the offering circular.

9.79 If there is more than one underwriter, their obligations will be several and not joint, meaning each underwriter is responsible only for the share of the securities it is committed to purchase, and does not have an obligation to cover defaults by other underwriters.[26] Under the agreement, the issuer also will have to indemnify the underwriters for, among other things, losses arising from material misstatements in, or material omissions from, the disclosure in the offering circular. Such losses will also include the indemnified party's litigation expenses and legal fees.

9.80 The underwriting agreement will include customary 'MAC' and 'market-out' clauses that will entitle the underwriters to terminate the agreement (during the period between pricing and closing the bond offering as described below) if an event occurs that causes a material adverse change in the business or if a negative event, such as a banking crisis that has caused banks or stock exchanges to close temporarily in key financial centres such as New York City and London, has occurred. In practice, these termination clauses are rarely, if ever, exercised but will nonetheless be required by the underwriters.

---

[26] However, see the discussion at para. 9.93 below for circumstances where non-defaulting underwriters may have responsibility for the obligations of a defaulting underwriter.

The underwriting agreement will be signed at the time of the pricing of the bonds. **9.81** Closing, which entails the actual issuance of bonds against payment of funds, will occur a few days later. Typical timing is to close three, five, or seven business days after pricing. In addition to the MAC and market-out clauses described above, the underwriting agreement will set forth the other conditions precedent to the underwriters' obligations at closing. These conditions precedent customarily include the following items, among others:

(1) delivery of an officer's certificate of the issuer confirming that the representations and warranties in the underwriting agreement remain true and correct at the time of closing and that no 'MAC' has occurred since the time of signing the underwriting agreement;

(2) delivery of a secretary's certificate of the issuer certifying that attached copies of the issuer's charter documents and resolutions of the board of directors approving the transaction are accurate, valid, and binding;

(3) delivery of legal opinions (as discussed below);

(4) delivery of the auditor's comfort letter (as discussed below); and

(5) all filings necessary to perfect the security package being completed (except as otherwise agreed).

As a practical matter, most of these items will have been confirmed, and drafts **9.82** produced, prior to signing the underwriting agreement.

Bond trust deed/indenture and global note

Although the terms and conditions of the bonds will be set forth in the offering **9.83** circular, the contractual documentation that actually binds the issuer to the terms and obligations of the bonds are contained in the indenture[27] or trust deed[28] and the note itself. The note is the formal security reflecting an obligation to repay a certain principal amount at a future date. Sometimes, specific terms of the bonds are included within the note itself. Other times, most of the terms will be included in the indenture or trust deed under which the note is constituted (and therefore the terms of which the note is subject).

Global note

An investor in a bond will not receive a physical bond certificate. Instead, the bonds **9.84** will be issued in the form of a global note and holders will have individual interests in the global note which are held through an electronic book-entry system. The global note itself will be issued as a physical instrument, registered in the name of a nominee for a bank that acts as the depositary for the institution or institutions

---

[27] As the document is known under New York law.
[28] As the document is known under English law.

that provide clearing and settlement services—normally, The Depository Trust & Clearing Corporation ('DTC') in the US and Euroclear or Clearstream outside the US. When the bonds are traded, changes in ownership will be recorded through the electronic book-entry systems of the participants in the clearing systems and the entities for whom the participants hold interests in the global note.

Trust deed/indenture

9.85 The trust deed or indenture is a contract between the issuer (and any guarantors), on the one hand, and a trustee who represents the bondholders, on the other hand. In addition to including the basic terms of the bonds, such as principal, interest rate, interest and principal payment dates, and the maturity date, the indenture will also include, where applicable, provisions regarding optional or mandatory redemption, covenants, events of default, and amendments and waivers, as well as certain administrative provisions such as notice requirements and procedures, indemnities for the trustee and the issuer's consent to jurisdiction in the relevant court system (New York or England and Wales).

9.86 The covenants and events of default will vary with each transaction and will be impacted by the overall credit rating and position of the project. Often, project bonds will benefit from the covenants and obligations of the issuer that are contained in the 'common terms agreement'. For further details about common terms agreements, see Chapter 7. In other cases, the bonds may be completely separate from the covenant structure of the rest of the project financing.

9.87 Some bonds may contain covenants/restrictions with respect to any or all of the following:
(1) the future incurrence of additional indebtedness;
(2) the making of certain kinds of investments or 'restricted' payments, such as dividends or certain other types of distributions;
(3) ongoing reporting to bondholders of financial and operational results;
(4) mergers and acquisitions;
(5) asset disposals; and
(6) operational covenants, such as maintenance of the project and its assets, compliance with applicable laws and regulations, maintenance of insurance coverage, and maintenance of supply and off-take agreements.

9.88 In addition, some bonds may require the issuer or the project group to meet certain financial ratios based on leverage or interest cover thresholds.

Intercreditor arrangements

9.89 Depending on the transaction structure, it is likely that the bond trustee will be party to the intercreditor agreement, which governs interactions and the relative positions among the project's various groups of lenders, in particular with respect to their respective rights to exercise remedies if the issuer breaches its obligations or other events of default occur. For further details about intercreditor agreements, see Chapter 7.

Security documents/collateral deed

As with other types of project finance, project bonds are usually secured by the **9.90** underlying project assets. In addition, the shares of the issuer usually will be pledged to the bondholders. For further details about project finance security arrangements, see Chapter 11.

Auditor's comfort letter

The comfort letter is a document provided by the issuer's auditors at the time of sign- **9.91** ing of the underwriting agreement and again at the closing of the bond offering. The comfort letter is addressed to the underwriters and often to the board of directors of the issuer. This letter provides 'comfort' that certain financial information contained in the offering circular has been audited and that certain tests and procedures have been undertaken by the accountants with respect to the period subsequent to the date of the latest financial statements (whether annual or interim) included in the pro- spectus. Based on these procedures, the auditors essentially confirm that they have compared certain financial information in the prospectus with the books and records of the issuer and that the numbers agree. The auditors also will provide 'negative assurance' that their procedures have not uncovered any undisclosed specified events, such as the incurrence of material new debt or material losses or other events affecting stockholders' equity, since the date of the last published financial statements.[29]

The comfort letter is one critical element for underwriters in building a due dili- **9.92** gence defence, as it helps to demonstrate that due diligence was performed on the financial information disclosed in the offering circular. As mentioned above, and related to the comfort letter process, the underwriters will often request a due dili- gence meeting with the issuer's auditors to inquire about matters such as the quality of the issuer's internal control structure, the openness of management in the audit process, any disagreements between management and the auditors about account- ing treatment, and prior audit adjustments. Recently, auditors have become reluctant to participate in such sessions due to concerns about liability. In some cases, the auditors will only participate if the underwriters sign a 'hold harmless' letter absolving the auditors of legal liability in connection with statements made by the auditors in such a session.

---

[29] For a Rule 144A deal, the standard form of comfort letter is dictated by Statement on Auditing Standards 72 (better know as SAS 72) as promulgated by the Auditing Standards Board of the American Institute of Certified Public Accountants. Another common form, used sometimes for transactions wholly outside the US, is the form of comfort letter published by the International Capital Markets Association (ICMA).

Agreement among underwriters

9.93 As mentioned above, many transactions, particularly higher value bond issuances, tend to have multiple underwriters. In such cases, it is common for a subset of the underwriters to be responsible for underwriting a larger proportion of the overall transaction and, therefore, to take the lead in managing the transaction on behalf of the other underwriters. In such circumstances, the underwriters often enter into a formal 'Agreement Among Underwriters' or AAU. This agreement sets the parameters of responsibilities, effectively delegating authority to the lead underwriter or underwriters to manage the transaction. The AAU may also provide for 'defaulting underwriter provisions', which set forth the extent to which the underwriters may have to cover the individual underwriting commitment of an underwriter who defaults on such commitment.[30]

Role of legal counsels and legal opinions

9.94 On a typical transaction, the issuer and the underwriters will each be represented by international counsel (usually with US and/or English law capability, as most international project bonds are issued under New York or English law). In addition, the issuer and the underwriters will have counsel in the project jurisdiction, which will take the lead on, among other things, security governed by local law, non-English due diligence, and domestic corporate matters. To the extent the transaction has other requirements, such as multiple jurisdictions, or the need for special counsel on, for example, tax issues, additional sets of legal counsel may be required.

9.95 As part of the bond offering process, the counsels will issue legal opinions at the time of the closing of the bond offering, which together will cover corporate matters such as enforceability of the bonds, the indenture, the subscription agreement and the security, corporate authorizations for the transaction, and validity of the choice of law (i.e. New York or English), as well as any other legal matters specific to the transaction.

9.96 In addition, for a Rule 144A bond offering into the US, the underwriters will require both their US counsel and the issuer's US counsel to issue '10b-5 disclosure letters' as part of fulfilling their own due diligence defence requirements.[31] Often mentioned in shorthand as '10b-5 opinions', such letters are not actually opinions of law. The 10b-5 disclosure letter will cite the work performed by the law firm as part of its due diligence and then state that nothing has come to the attention of that law firm that causes it to believe that the disclosure contained or contains an

---

[30] Usually the lead underwriter(s) will have twenty-four hours to find replacement purchasers to cover the defaulting underwriter's commitments. If the lead underwriter is unable to make any such arrangements, and if the defaulted securities commitment does not exceed 10 per cent of the total, then the other underwriters are usually obliged to purchase the defaulted commitment in an amount proportionate to their share of the total underwriting.

[31] See the discussions above regarding Rule 10b-5 and the due diligence defence.

untrue statement of a material fact or omitted or omits to state a material fact necessary in order to make the statements therein, in the light of the circumstances under which they were made, not misleading.

This 10b-5 statement will speak as of the time of the final offering circular and usu- **9.97** ally as of the earlier date of the 'time of sale' information, which refers to the time at which an investor had all information in order to make an investment decision. As described above, this point in time generally occurs when the investor has received the preliminary offering circular plus the pricing term sheet, as the investment decision is completed before receipt of the final offering circular. Note that law firms will usually carve out from coverage under the 10b-5 statement any financial, accounting, statistical, and other information that is provided by other professional experts such as auditors and engineers.

Listing

Often, bonds will be listed on a stock exchange. Such listings are undertaken **9.98** primarily to accommodate certain large institutional investors, such as pension funds, that, as a matter of regulation or corporate governance provisions, are restricted in their ability to invest in unlisted securities. Listing the bonds therefore can facilitate their placement with a wider range of investors. Listings are not undertaken to facilitate trading and few project bonds actually trade over exchanges. Such listings are often referred to as 'listings of convenience'. Project bonds may be listed on many different exchanges, though commonly they are listed on one of the markets of the London Stock Exchange, the Luxembourg Stock Exchange, or the Irish Stock Exchange.

The listing rules of the relevant stock exchange will impact the disclosure required **9.99** to be included in the offering circular. As a general matter, though, offering circulars that follow US-style disclosure requirements should cover disclosures required by the relevant exchange. Certain 'unregulated' exchanges in Europe permit issuers who are targeting only sophisticated institutional investors (as are most project bond issuers) to opt-out of the more rigorous disclosure requirements under European regulations, such as the Prospectus Directive, that are aimed at protecting small-scale retail investors.

Depending on which exchange a listing is sought, the issuer may need to engage a **9.100** listing agent to help navigate the listing application process through the exchange. The listing agent can provide guidance as to the more mechanical and administrative requirements that need to be met in order to facilitate a smooth application process. In conducting their review of the offering circular in advance of approving the bonds for listing, most exchanges will not comment on the quality of the disclosure included in the offering circular, but rather will focus only on whether or not specific technical requirements of the exchange's listing rules have been satisfied.

10

ISLAMIC PROJECT FINANCE

*John Dewar and Mohammad Munib Hussain, Milbank, Tweed,
Hadley & McCloy LLP*

Introduction

With approximately 1.5 billion adherents, the global population of Muslims **10.01** equates to over 22 per cent of the world's population.[1] This, in conjunction with the rapid growth in the wealth of many Middle Eastern countries and the trend of a significant number of governments, financial institutions, and individual Muslims of investing in a manner which is consistent with Islam, means Islamic finance has now moved from the niche to the mainstream. Islamic finance is concerned with the conduct of commercial and financial activities in accordance with Islamic law.

In the Middle East and parts of Asia, a growing proportion of the financing for **10.02** projects is sourced in accordance with Islamic finance principles. With traditional

---

[1] 'Mapping the Global Muslim Population, A Report on the Size and Distribution of the World's Muslim Population' October 2009, Pew Research Centre.

project finance structures being rooted in conventional interest-based systems, the manner in which risks are allocated and transaction structures are implemented needs to be reassessed as the investment of the Islamic-compliant participant will no doubt be conditional on compliance with Islamic finance principles. Structuring the investment of such capital therefore requires a comprehensive understanding of Islamic finance principles, knowledge of international and domestic laws and documenting such arrangements in a manner that satisfies the priorities of all the project participants including those not necessarily constrained by Islamic finance principles.

10.03 This chapter analyses how these priorities are accommodated and how Islamic finance techniques are applied in project financings. Context is paramount to achieve this aim, and so by way of introduction, the sources of Islamic finance are discussed, followed by a brief analysis of the principles and financial techniques that underpin Islamic finance. For those unfamiliar with Islamic finance principles, this will enable a better understanding of the ensuing discussion of the issues that commonly arise in a project financing that is entirely or in-part financed with Islamic compliant funding. Then, the focus is turned to assess how Islamic project finance techniques are utilized in practice, including how such arrangements are documented.

Sources of Islamic Finance[2]

10.04 Islamic finance is concerned with the conduct of commercial and financial activities in accordance with Islamic law. Islamic law is a manifestation of the divine will of Allah (SWT) and finds its expression in the *Qur'an* (Book of Allah (SWT)) and *Sunnah* (words or acts) of the Prophet (PBUH). The *Qur'an* is the most sacred canonical text in Islam and perceived by Muslims as the word of Allah (SWT) for which reason it is a primary reference for Muslims and is inviolable.[3] The *Sunnah* is comprised of all the sayings, acts and approvals (tacit or otherwise) of the Prophet (PBUH)[4] as compiled by the *Sahabah* (closest companions of the

---

[2] Throughout this chapter, the term 'SWT' follows the name of Allah (SWT) (which means 'praise and exaltation') and the term 'PBUH' (which means 'Peace be upon Him and His Family') follows the name of the Prophet Muhammad (PBUH). Also, following the names of other venerable Muslims, the term 'RA' (which means 'May Allah (SWT) be pleased with him') is used. These are terms used by Muslims as a mark of veneration and respect.

[3] The *Qur'an* must be interpreted in light of the exegesis (*Tafsir* and plural *Tafasir*) of the *Qur'an*, the most notable being Imam as-Suyuti's (RA) *Tafsir, Ad-Durr al-Manthur Fi't-Tafsir Bi'l Ma'thur*.

[4] Each saying, act, or approval of the Prophet (PBUH) is called a *Hadith* (singular of *Ahadith*) and these have been collated according to stringent rules most of which are documented in the six canonical collections (*as-Sihah as-Sittah*) which include *Sahih Bukhari, Sahih Muslim, Sunan al-Sughra, Sunan Abu Dawood, Sunan al-Tirmidhi*, and *Sunan Ibn Majah*.

Prophet (PBUH)).[5] The law contained in both of these primary sources is known as the *Sharia'a* which means 'the road to the watering place [and] the clear path to be followed'. Reflecting the *Qur'an* and *Sunnah*, *Sharia'a* is therefore a compilation of the values, norms, and rules which govern all aspects of a Muslim's life (such as family life and economic activities). *Sharia'a* is pervasive in that a Muslim is obliged to comply with *Sharia'a* at all times and in all respects:

> Then We placed you on the right road [*Sharia'a*] of Our Command, so follow it. Do not follow the whims and desires of those who do not know. (*Qur'an, Surah Al-Jathiyah* 45:18)

Notwithstanding its breadth (as exemplified in figure 10.1), *Sharia'a* is not amply **10.05** codified to rule on every matter that may arise in contemporary scenarios since the *Qur'an* and *Sunnah* were settled over 1,400 years ago. *Sharia'a* has, however, remained relevant and addresses the myriad of original situations through the use of secondary sources that are based on *Ijtihad*[6] namely:

(1) *Ijma*: consensus of the independent jurists qualified to exercise *Ijtihad* (a *Mujtahid*) on a particular interpretation of the *Sharia'a*; and
(2) *Qiyas*: interpretation by analogical reasoning where one situation is measured against another by the *Mujtahids*, in each case subject to and in accordance with the *Qur'an, Sunnah* and *Ijma*.

The principles derived from the application of *Ijma* and *Qiyas* to the *Sharia'a* form the body of jurisprudence known as *Fiqh* (understanding and knowledge applied to any branch of knowledge). The body of rules that underpin the derivation of *Fiqh* is referred to as *Usul al Fiqh*.[7]

Certain *Sharia'a* principles may be ambiguous not least because of the numerous **10.06** *Tafasir* of the *Qur'an* and the voluminous *Ahadith* as well as the *Mujtahids* involved in the practice of *Ijtihad*, interpreting the *Sharia'a* in different yet equally permissible ways because of the interpretation methodologies they may apply. This means that often there can be different legal opinions (*fatawa*) on the same aspect of the *Sharia'a*. This difference of methodology for interpreting the *Sharia'a* and the body of *fatawa* derived thereby, is one reason why there have developed several schools of

---

[5] Of the *Sahabah*, Imam Ali ibn Abi Talib (AS) has contributed significantly to the development of the *Tafasir* of the *Qur'an, Fiqh, Usul al Fiqh* and the Islamic normative sciences. The contributions of Imam Ali (AS) have been such that the Prophet (PBUH) was reported to have said in the *hadith* narrated by Ibn Abbas (RA) as is documented in *Al-Mustadrak alaa al-Sahihain Hakim*, that 'I am the city of knowledge and Ali is its gate'.

[6] *Ijtihad* means the individual interpretation of *Sharia'a* principles by *Mujtahids* to infer expert legal rulings from foundational proofs within or without a particular *Madhab*.

[7] For a general discussion on *Usul al Fiqh*, see Prof Ahmad Hasan, *The Principles of Islamic Jurisprudence, the Command of the Sharia'ah and Juridical Norm* (Adam Publishers & Distributors, 2005).

thought/*Fiqh* (*Madhabs*) to which a *Mujtahid* would ordinarily be aligned. The renowned *Madhabs* are:

(1) *Hanafi*, founded in Kufa, Iraq by Imam Abu Hanifa Nu'man Ibn Thabit (RA)[8] and based largely on logical deduction by the *Mujtahid*s;
(2) *Maliki*, founded in Medina, Saudi Arabia by Imam Malik ibn Anas (RA);[9]
(3) *Shaf'i*, founded by Imam ash-Shaf'i (RA);[10] and
(4) *Hanbli*, founded by Imam Ahmed Bin Hanbal (RA)[11] which is predominate in the Arabian peninsula and is perceived as the more doctrinal of the *Madhabs*.

As *Fiqh* is law derived by *Mujtahid*s interpreting the *Sharia'a* in accordance with the methodology ascribed by a *Madhab*, differences on a matter relating to *Fiqh* is inevitable but there can be no difference on the *Sharia'a* itself, as this is law derived from the *Qur'an* and *Sunnah*.

10.07 With respect to these differences, the Prophet (PBUH) was reported to have said, 'My community's differences of opinion (*ikhtilaf*) are a blessing'[12] and evidently this process has derived a comprehensive corpus juris providing guidance on almost every facet of a Muslim's life (see figure 10.1). For commercial organizations, however, the various methodologies of interpreting the *Sharia'a* and the different *fatawa* derived as a result mean that in order for them to determine the legitimacy

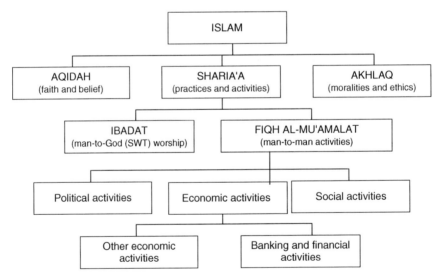

Figure 10.1 Islamic Construct

---

[8] (80-150 AH / 699-767 CE). Imam Abu Hanifa (RA) is known in the Islamic world as 'The Greatest Imam' (*al-imâm al-a`zam*) and his school has assisted with the development of the principles of Islamic finance not least because of its application of *Qiyas*.
[9] (93-179 AH / 712-795 CE).
[10] (150-204 AH / 767-820 CE).
[11] (164-241 AH /780-855 CE).
[12] *Al-Jami as-asghir*, Jalal ad-Din as Suyuti.

of a particular commercial activity with the *Sharia'a*, they may need to seek expert guidance.

The role of Sharia'a scholars and regulators

This has led to the role of specialist *Sharia'a* scholars and *Sharia'a* advisory firms **10.08** rising to prominence. Most banks, sponsors and *Sharia'a*-compliant funds retain independent *Sharia'a* scholars (who are usually renowned in the relevant domestic market) and who sit as a *Sharia'a* board to issue *fatawa* certifying the compliance of a transaction structure or a financial product, for example, with the *Qur'an*, *Sunnah*, and typically a specific *Madhab*. The duties of the *Sharia'a* board include:

(1) assisting in the development of products and structuring transactions;
(2) issuing *fatawa* relating to certain activities, products, or transactions having reviewed their legitimacy from a *Sharia'a* perspective;
(3) day-to-day oversight of the operations of the institution to ensure *Sharia'a* compliance; and
(4) providing a letter on an annual basis to indicate *Sharia'a* compliance by the institution for inclusion in its annual report.

This approach of retaining independent *Sharia'a* scholars became the subject of **10.09** some criticism since it appeared to result in a lack of harmonization and hampered the development of common principles across international and even domestic financial markets. This had the ancillary effect of undermining regulatory confidence in Islamic finance. In order to mitigate this, bodies of interpretation such as the *Sharia'a* Supervisory Board and the Islamic *Fiqh* Academy, endeavour to issue *fatawa* to deal with contemporary issues that may arise in the Islamic finance context. And in order to systematize and regulate Islamic finance with the intention one day to have globally accepted *Sharia'a* standards for Islamic finance transactions, the Accounting and Auditing Organization for Islamic Financial Institutions (AAOIFI), the International Islamic Financial Market (IIFM), and the Islamic Financial Services Board (IFSB) are playing a prominent role. Their issuance of practice directions and standards for accounting have gone some way towards becoming global standards and thereby instilling investors with confidence to invest in *Sharia'a*-compliant products. This chapter will consider Islamic project finance structures that are compliant with the core consensus of Islamic scholars and these leading regulators.

Islamic Finance Principles

Akin to Western legal systems, in Islam there is a presumption that everything **10.10** is permissible (*halal*) unless there is an express law which rebuts that presumption by declaring it as forbidden (*haram*). Financiers are therefore expected to carry out their activities subject to and in accordance with *Sharia'a* principles. The perti-nent *Sharia'a* principles that relate to Islamic finance are that the following are avoided in any transaction: *riba* (excess or increase); *gharar* (uncertainty); *maisir* (speculation); and *qimar* (gambling). Two other general *Sharia'a* principles that apply are the prohibition on investing in or being involved with *haram* products and activities (such as alcohol and gambling establishments) and the prohibition of becoming unjustly enriched.[13]

10.11 *Riba* has been declared *haram* on numerous occasions in the *Qur'an*[14] and *Sunnah*.[15] *Riba* means any excess paid or received on the principal or an additional return received on the principal derived by the mere passage of time.[16] There are two types of *riba*; *Riba al-Naseeyah* (a pre-determined premium on the principal received by a lender solely due to the passage of time) and *Riba al-Fadal* (excess compensation received by one party from an exchange or sale of goods without adequate consid-eration). Interest paid on a conventional loan is a form of *Riba al-Naseeyah* and certain exchange of commodities contracts may contain *Riba al-Fadl* if on an exchange of commodities of similar value, one party pays excessive compensation to the other party. The philosophy behind the absolute prohibition of *riba* (which has the effect of rendering any contract harbouring *riba* as being void), is that *Sharia'a* regards money as having no intrinsic value in itself (unlike commodities such as gold, silver, dates, and wheat) and is merely a means of exchange to procure goods and services. Money cannot therefore derive a profit either from the exchange of money of the same denomination or due to the passage of time as is the case with interest.

10.12 *Sharia'a* by no means prohibits the making of profit, but it does scrutinize the basis upon which profit is made as, for example, charging interest could exploit the client in a time of hardship whilst the financier's wealth is increased by no effort of its own. Islam instead empowers the financier to derive a profit by investing its money or other consideration directly (or indirectly through a joint venture arrangement, for example) in real assets using one or more of the Islamic finance techniques dis-cussed below.[17] The financier will then generate a profit and recoup the principal sum invested in the asset by exercising its rights as an owner; using, leasing, or sell-ing the asset. Here, unlike conventional finance, the money itself has not yielded the profit; instead the assumption of the risks and responsibilities as owner of the

---

[13] For example, if a financier charges a late payment fee when their client is in default, this is not typically retained by the financier and is instead donated to charity.

[14] *Qur'an, Surah Al Baqara* 2:275, *Qur'an, Surah Al Baqara* 2:276-280, *Qur'an, Surah Al-Imran* 3-130, *Qur'an, Surah An-Nisa* 4:161, and *Qur'an, Surah Ar-Rum* 30:39.

[15] *Majma al-Zawa'id*, Ali ibn Abu Bakr al-Haythami (vol 4, 117).

[16] For a detailed study of *riba* and a discussion of the related *fatawa* of the various *Madhabs*, see Wahbah Al-Zuhayli, *Financial Transactions in Islamic Jurisprudence* (tr. Mahmoud A. El-Gamal; rev. Muhammad S. Eissa) (Dar Al-Fikr, 2003), Vol. 1, Chapter 10 ('Al-Zuhayli').

[17] See paras 10.14–10.22 below.

asset or as a partner in the venture has yielded the profit made by the financier. This depicts the preference of Islamic finance for equity over debts and seeking to deal in tangibles and explains why Islamic finance is often referred to as a form of asset-backed financing. Therefore, in facilitating financing arrangements, if the client requires money for a profit-seeking venture, the client and the financier enter into an equity-sharing arrangement and if the client requires money for an asset, rather than simply loaning the money, the financier purchases the asset outright from the supplier and sells it on to the client for a profit.

Gharar can be defined as the sale of probable items whose existence or characteris- **10.13** tics are uncertain or speculative (*maisir*), the risk of which makes it akin to gambling (*qimar*).[18] The rationale for prohibiting *gharar* and *maisir* stems from the belief that bargains should be based upon contractual certainties as far is possible in order to bring about transparency and avoid conflict over key terms of a contract such as the object, the quality of goods, the time for delivery, and the amount payable. Contemporary examples of *gharar* include: the sale of an object prior to it coming into existence, which subject to certain exceptions,[19] would render the contract as void; where the object is unknown; where the specifications of the object are unknown; and where the price or rent cannot be ascertained with certainty.

Islamic Finance Techniques

Profit and loss sharing forms the bedrock of Islamic finance since Islam perceives **10.14** that the ideal relationship between contract parties should be that of equals where profit and losses are shared. *Mudarabah* (investment fund arrangement) and *Musharaka* (joint venture arrangement) are two finance techniques which facilitate this priority. With the need for diversity in risk/return profiles and conventional lender reluctance to enter into a profit and loss arrangement where the lender would otherwise expect the client to remain liable for the principal and interest regardless of how the venture performs, certain traditional Islamic trading techniques have been adapted which, to an extent, are *Sharia'a*-compliant versions of conventional finance products. These include *Murabaha* (cost plus financing), *Istisna'a* (commissioned manufacture of a specified asset), and *Ijarah* (lease purchase finance). Finally, a key source of *Sharia'a*-compliant financing is the *Sukuk* (trust certificates), which have similarities to conventional bonds. The focus of this chapter will be on the *Istisna'a* and the *Ijarah* structures as these techniques form the building blocks of

---

[18] For a detailed discussion of *gharar*, see Al-Zuhayli 82–7.
[19] Examples of Islamic forward contracts include *Bai Salam* and *Istisna'a*. On the other hand, conventional forward contracts and futures are not permitted as the object of the sale may not exist at the time the trade is to be executed and are therefore also considered akin to *qimar*.

the single tranche and the multi-tranche *Sharia'a*-compliant transactions which are discussed below.

Mudarabah

10.15 A *Mudarabah* is an investment fund arrangement under which the financiers act as the capital providers (*rab al-mal*) and the client acts as the *mudareb* (akin to an investment agent) to invest the capital provided by the *rab al-mal* and manage the partnership. The profit of the venture, which is based on the amount yielded by the fund that exceeds the *rab al-mals'* capital investment, can be distributed between the parties at a predetermined ratio but with any loss (subject to whether the loss is caused by the *mudareb*'s negligence) being borne by the *rab al-mal*. The fund is controlled by the *mudareb* with the *rab al-mal* as a silent partner. In practice, however, conventional investment agency arrangements are used instead of the *Mudarabah* enabling the *rab al-mal* to exercise further control over the fund and potentially to limit the discretion of the *mudareb* when it comes to investing the capital, for example.[20]

Musharaka

10.16 In a *Musharaka*, the financing arrangement is similar to a *Mudarabah* except that the losses are borne in proportion to the capital invested by both the client and the financier. Each party to the *Musharaka* has the right to participate in the affairs of the enterprise but each can also choose to waive that right and instead be a silent partner as in a *Mudarabah*.[21] However, the silent partner will then only be entitled to profits in proportion to its capital investment and not more. Under a 'Continuous *Musharaka*', each partner retains its share of the capital until the end of the project or in the case of a 'Diminishing *Musharaka*' (*Musharaka Muntahiya Bittamleek*), it is agreed at the outset that one of the partners will purchase units in the *Musharaka* from the other partner at a pre-agreed unit price.

Murabaha

10.17 A simple *Murabaha* transaction involves the purchase of an asset by the financier (on behalf of the client) who then sells the asset to the client for the cost of the asset plus a pre-stated margin on a deferred payment basis which may be pegged to a benchmark such as LIBOR.[22] The profit margin earned by the financier is legitimate profit and not interest because the financier acquires ownership of the asset (and therefore the risk associated with ownership of the asset) before on-selling it to

---

[20] For a detailed discussion of *Mudarabah*, see Al-Zuhayli, Chapter 28.
[21] For a detailed discussion of *Musharaka*, see Al-Zuhayli, Chapter 21.
[22] Where the financier does not disclose the cost of the asset and the value of the margin charged, such a transaction is called a *Musawama*. The *Musawama* has recently been adopted in the context of *Sharia'a*-compliant hedging.

the client. The client is also not bound to accept delivery of the asset, although in practice, the financier will mitigate this risk by seeking a letter of credit, a good faith down-payment (such as *arbun*),[23] or a unilateral purchase undertaking from the client. This transaction is effected through a *Murabaha* contract which reflects a conventional sale and purchase agreement. Upon acquiring ownership of the asset, the client may go a step further and sell the asset to a third party for cost price so that the client now has the money it may have always wanted (rather than the asset) whilst it remains liable to the financier to pay the cost-price of the asset plus a pre-stated margin on a deferred payment basis. In this case, the underlying asset could be a base metal such as copper, but not commodities which were originally used as a means of exchange or money such as gold, silver, and wheat. For larger transactions, it may not be possible to purchase the required amount of commodity on, for example, the London Metals Exchange and so an alterative is to acquire shares in a publically trading company since shares represent an ownership interest in the relevant company. This variation of the simple *Murabaha* is commonly referred to as 'Commodity *Murabaha*'.[24] In the project financing context, there has been a recent trend to utilize the Commodity *Murabaha* to provide both working capital funds required by a project company and equity contributions that a sponsor is obliged to make to a project in a *Sharia'a*-compliant manner.[25]

Istisna'a

An *Istisna'a* is a construction and procurement contract for the commissioned man-**10.18** ufacture of a specified asset and can be used during the construction phase of a project financing. Here, following a request from the client, the financier procures the contractor to manufacture an asset which meets the specifications of the client for delivery by a specified date. The financier will in practice appoint the client as its *Wakil* (agent) (which can be facilitated pursuant to a *Wakala* agreement) to enter into the EPC contract with the contractor. *Sharia'a* requires that the price payable for the asset is fixed at the outset (but not necessarily paid in full at this point) and only altered if the specification of the asset is amended by the client. The date on which and the proportion of the price payable will usually be the same as the

---

[23] Note, however, that the majority of the *Mujtahids* have ruled that an *arbun* is a forbidden type of sale for contradicting the *Sunnah* and containing *gharar* as the buyer of the asset may or may not purchase the asset at a future date (see Al-Zuhayli, 99–100). Recently, *arbun* has been used to mirror conventional covered call options giving the holder the right to buy a fixed quantity of an underlying asset on or before a specified date in the future.

[24] A variation of Commodity *Murabaha*, which is referred to as *Tawarruq*, is where the intention of the client is not to own the commodity but to sell it instantaneously and obtain the required funds using one single transaction where the bank buys from, and sells the commodity back, to the broker as the client's agent. *Tawarruq* is considered to be a *makruh* (reprehensible) sale in the opinion of Imam Malik (RA); however it has been accepted as a financing technique by contemporary *Sharia'a* scholars in the absence of a viable alternative.

[25] See para. 10.63 below.

milestone payments due under the EPC contract. Although the client will contract under the EPC contract as a *Wakil*, there will not be privity of contract between the client and the contractor once the asset has been constructed, so the warranties given by the contractor to the financier in respect of the asset in respect of defects to the assets, for example, will be assigned to the client. The manufactured asset must be accepted by the client if it meets the given specifications. Once the asset has been constructed, title to the asset must be transferred by the contractor to the financier, who will then either sell the asset to the client outright or alternatively lease the asset to the client pursuant to an *Ijarah*.

Ijarah

10.19 The *Ijarah* is a form of lease financing pursuant to which the usage (*usufruct*) of an asset or the services of a person are leased by the lessor to the lessee for rental consideration.[26] The nature of the asset or service must be precisely defined in the lease. Under the *Ijarah*, the lessor (the financier) will purchase the asset from the supplier and then transfer possession to the lessee (the client) with the profit margin built into each lease payment over the term of the lease. The lessee may act as the lessor's agent to purchase the assets from the supplier. It is also possible for the lessee to own the asset which it sells to the lessor who, in turn, will lease it back to the lessee. The lease can take effect as an operating lease, with the asset returning to the lessor at the end of the lease term, or akin to a finance lease, with title to the asset being transferred to the lessee at the end of the lease term or ownership units being transferred to the lessee during the term of the lease (an *Ijarah-wa-iqtina'a*). The lease will commence immediately upon execution of the *Ijarah* if the assets have sufficient economic value and substance so that it can and is used for the purpose intended. If the assets do not have sufficient economic value at the time the lease is executed, then the rent will only become payable when such value and substance does exist. In any event, although *Sharia'a* does not permit a forward sale, the *Ijarah* can become effective at a future date provided the rent is only payable after the leased asset is delivered to the lessee.[27] This type of forward lease is called an *Ijarah Mawsufa fi al-Dhimma* and is most prevalent in the project financing context.

10.20 As will be explored further below, it is useful to note that the *Ijarah* has become the mechanism by which the principal and the profit margin are returned to the financier during the post-construction period of a project financing as rental consideration comprising the purchase price of the asset as well as a fixed and/or floating profit margin calculated by reference to LIBOR.

10.21 Although the lessor can claim compensation from the lessee for misuse of the leased assets, akin to an operating lease, the lessor remains responsible for all maintenance

---

[26] For a detailed discussion of *Ijarah* see Al-Zuhayli (Chapter 13).
[27] This is subject to the payment of advance rentals: see paras 10.46 and 10.47.

and repair incidental to ownership, including structural maintenance of the leased assets.[28] In practice, the lessee will be appointed as an agent of the lessor to ensure adequate insurance is in place for the leased assets through the service agency agreement (see para. 10.58 below). The lessee is only liable to pay the rent so long as the asset exists, so if the asset is destroyed and therefore cannot be used by the lessee, the lessee can then terminate the lease without further liability and the lessor's only recourse will be to pursue a claim under the insurances.

Sukuk

Although *Sukuk* (plural of *sakk*) are often referred to as 'Islamic bonds', they are **10.22** more akin to Islamic trust certificates representing an undivided beneficial ownership interest in an underlying asset where the return is based on the performance of that underlying asset. The key attributes of *Sukuk* are that they are asset-based securities and any profit or benefit derived from the *Sukuk* must be linked to the performance of a real asset and the risks associated with ownership of that asset. *Sukuk* are therefore distinguishable from conventional bonds which are bearer negotiable debt securities that pay the holder fixed or floating interest on a periodic basis during the term of the bond. *Sukuk* do share certain features with conventional bonds, such as being in certificated form, being freely transferrable on the secondary market if the *Sukuk* is listed, paying a regular return, and being redeemable at maturity, but conventional bonds are also tradable debt which *Sharia'a* prohibits. Therefore, *Sukuk* have to be linked to an underlying asset using, for example, an *Ijarah* or *Musharaka* arrangement to generate revenues that mirror the coupon payments received under a conventional bond. The return generated is justified as the *Sukuk* holder has an ownership interest in the underlying asset as represented by the *Sukuk* and is therefore assuming ownership risks.

Islamic Project Finance Techniques

As mentioned above, a reassessment of how risks associated with the construction, **10.23** operation, ownership, and financing of a project are allocated and how transaction structures are implemented will need to be undertaken in order to contemplate the priorities of all the project participants in the most commercially acceptable manner. Conventional project finance structures have evolved to take into account these risks by apportioning the risk to the participants according to their role and who is best able to assume the risk. Such structures have, however, been developed in Western *riba*-based financial systems and as a result have not contemplated

---

[28] The lessee will remain responsible for any routine maintenance and repair of the Islamic assets.

certain additional priorities that an Islamic participant possesses, most notably, compliance with the principles of *Sharia'a*. These priorities have been accommodated in two types of *Sharia'a*-compliant project finance transactions: a single tranche transaction comprising only *Sharia'a*-compliant funding with no conventional *riba*-based financing; and a multi-tranche transaction where conventional and *Sharia'a*-compliant tranches of funding are integrated in a single financing. The former type of transaction is not common, especially in large project financings since the liquidity of Islamic banks and the capitalization requirements of such banks means that they cannot alone finance such projects. What follows, therefore, is a brief discussion of conventional project finance structures in order to visualize how such structures need to be adapted to a *Sharia'a*-compliant model. Then there follows an analysis as to how the multi-tranche project finance transaction is facilitated in practice, including how such arrangements are documented.

Conventional Project Finance Structures

10.24 In a conventional project financing, the sponsors will incorporate a single-purpose project company to build and operate the project. A syndicate of banks and other financial institutions (such as ECAs) will finance the construction of the project pursuant to one or more interest-bearing facility agreements. There will be a common terms agreement (the CTA) to govern the rights between the lenders and the project company and an intercreditor agreement or coordination deed to govern the rights, obligations and priorities of the lenders as between themselves. During the construction phase, the project company will ordinarily be obliged to pay interest on the loan which will typically be based on an inter-bank lending rate (such as LIBOR) plus a specified margin. During the operating phase, the project company will then begin to repay the principal monies borrowed according to a repayment schedule in addition to interest payments.

10.25 The project company will enter into a series of project contracts, including, the construction contract between the project company and the contractor to construct the project and deliver ownership of the same to the project company upon completion. In return, the project company will make stage payments to the contractor upon achieving certain milestones.

Multi-tranche Sharia'a-compliant Financing

10.26 Most project financings source the monies required to construct and operate the project from various sources, for reasons that include, accessing a broader pool of funding and using local banks or international financial institutions for geopolitical reasons. Apart from the commercial lenders, who provide a *riba*-based loan facility to the project company, one or more tranches of financing can be provided by other financial institutions, such as ECAs, development banks, and Islamic financial institutions (referred to herein as the IFIs). Each tranche may serve different purposes in the financing. An ECA, for example, may have a separate facility agreement from the commercial lenders stating that its facility is to be used for the acquisition of certain equipment or services provided to the project by a company of the same national origin as that ECA. Likewise, because the priority of an IFI is to invest in accordance with the *Sharia'a*, such IFIs will expect their investment to be made in the project in accordance with Islamic finance principles. The IFIs cannot lend, akin to the conventional lenders, directly to the project company as one of the many *Sharia'a* issues that would arise includes the return on the investment being deemed as *riba*. Therefore, as is the case with the needs of the ECAs, the priorities of the IFIs are accommodated by adapting the structure of the project, as manifested through separate documentation, comprising the IFI tranche.

There have been many instances in practice, where a single project financing **10.27** comprises more than one IFI tranche.[29] The reason for this may, perhaps in part, be due to irreconcilable differences between the investment criteria of certain IFIs which arise because:

(1) the investment criteria of the IFIs may be based on a specific *Madhab* and so may mean one IFI accepts a particular Islamic finance technique, but another IFI does not;
(2) a *Qur'anic* ruling is interpreted differently;
(3) an IFI may not accept a particular *hadith* or does not assign it particular credence because the conditions applied to collate that *hadith* were contrary to the methodology applied by a particular *Madhab*; or
(4) the *fatwa* of a *Mujtahid* or *Sharia'a* scholar authorizing a particular Islamic financial technique is not accepted.

Such marked differences generally arise in cross-border financings where an IFI may be aligned with the more doctrinal *Hanbli Madhab*, which has a more stringent investment criteria than an IFI based elsewhere and who abides by the more liberal *Hanafi Madhab*. In order to resolve this issue, separate documentation for each Islamic tranche will need to be entered into by the IFIs to suit their respective *Sharia'a* requirements. Regardless of the number of IFI tranches, the structure of each IFI tranche will in practice be, for the most part, the same, although their manifestation in the documentation will differ.

The Islamic financing strategies adopted in recent project financings are now **10.28** explored to discuss the structural considerations and documentation involved in

---

[29] PP11 IPP located in Saudi Arabia (June 2010) is an example.

projects with one or more IFI tranches, as well as the issues that arise when integrating the conventional tranches and the IFI tranches in a single project financing.

10.29   Recent Islamic project financings have included one or two Islamic structures, such as a *Wakala-Ijarah* tranche and an *Istisna'a-Ijarah* tranche, which are two of the most prevalent, commercially accepted and *Sharia'a*-compliant structures for an Islamic tranche in a multi-tranche project financing.[30] The structure and documentation applied to implement a *Wakala-Ijarah* tranche is depicted in figure 10.2. The structure for an *Istisna'a-Ijarah* tranche largely reflects the *Wakala-Ijarah* structure and any variation is analysed further below.

10.30   During the construction phase, the *Wakala* agreement in the *Wakala-Ijarah* tranche and the *Istisna'a* agreement in the *Istisna'a-Ijarah* tranche provide the construction financing for certain assets (referred to as the Islamic assets), isolated from the overall project, up to the value of the financing to be provided under the relevant Islamic tranche. The remainder of the project assets are financed using the monies from the conventional tranches. Upon a phase payment request from the project company (for an amount equivalent to the EPC milestone payments payable by the project company to the EPC contractor pursuant to the EPC contract), the IFIs provide the required funding to the Islamic facility agent who disburses the same to the project company. During the construction period, the project company makes advanced rental payments to an agent for the IFIs which mirrors the interest payable by the project company to the financiers under the conventional tranche. Upon construction of the Islamic assets, on or before the scheduled commercial operation date, the operations phase begins and the *Ijarah Mawsufa fi al-Dhimma* becomes effective to lease the usage of the Islamic assets to the project company. The project company pays lease payments during the course of the lease and at the end of the lease (as is the case in the *Wakala-Ijarah* tranche), ownership of the Islamic assets will, be transferred to the project company. An alternative is that units of the IFIs' ownership interest in the Islamic assets are transferred to the project company during the course of the lease, as is the case in the *Istisna'a-Ijarah* structure.[31]

10.31   Prior to embarking on a discussion of the Islamic documentation used in recent financings, it is useful to note that the Islamic facility agent or Investment Agent acts as agent for the IFIs. The Islamic facility agent is appointed for the *Wakala-Ijarah* tranche pursuant to the terms of an asset agency agreement and the investment agent is appointed for the *Istisna'a-Ijarah* tranche pursuant to the terms of an investment agency agreement. The advantage of appointing an agent is that: (i) the agent

---

[30] The *Wakala-Ijarah* tranche structure was introduced in the *Shuaibah* IWPP located in Saudi Arabia (December 2005) and subsequently also applied in the Marafiq IWPP located in Jubail, Saudi Arabia (May 2007), the Al Dur IWPP located in Bahrain (June 2009), and PP11 IPP. An Istisna'a-Ijarah structure was applied in Qatargas 2 LNG project located in Qatar (December 2004), in the Rabigh refinery located in Saudi Arabia (March 2006) and also in PP11 IPP.

[31] See also para. 10.19 above.

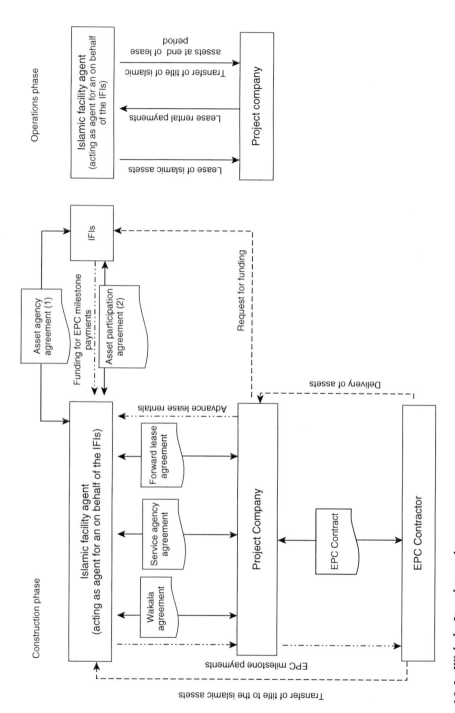

Figure 10.2 *Wakala-Ijarah* tranche

acts as a liaison between the project company and the IFIs during the course of the project; (ii) the agent can if required, sign the Islamic documentation on behalf of all the IFIs; and (iii) the agent would also be involved in receiving and disbursing monies received from the IFIs and the project company in accordance with the finance documents. The agent may also receive from the EPC contractor title to the Islamic assets upon their construction. It is usual, in practice, to appoint an IFI who is participating in the Islamic tranches and, therefore, familiar with the transaction, as the agent.

Wakala-Ijarah tranche

Wakala agreement

10.32   Under the *Wakala* agreement, the IFIs appoint the project company to act as their *Wakil* in respect of the procurement of the Islamic assets from the EPC contractor pursuant to the EPC contract, but subject always to the terms of the *Wakala* agreement. The EPC contract effects the *Istisna'a* arrangement (commissioned manufacture of the Islamic assets) between the IFIs and the EPC contractor. The parties to the *Wakala* agreement will be the project company, as the *Wakil*, and the Islamic facility agent, acting on behalf of the IFIs.

10.33   The *Wakala* is an agency contract that has been applied in many project financings. It is preferred by IFIs, as the *Wakil* assumes the responsibilities for project execution and completion and supervision of the construction of the Islamic assets. The *Wakil* will also be responsible for negotiating the terms of the EPC contract, based upon the specifications required by it, as the eventual lessor of the Islamic assets; this is a key requirement of *Sharia'a*. The *Wakil* will also indemnify the IFIs and the Islamic facility agent against all claims, losses, and liabilities incurred by them as a result of the negligence or wilful misconduct of the *Wakil*. From the perspective of the project company, the *Wakala* arrangement does not adversely impact on its management of the project, since it can continue to deal with the EPC contractor with little involvement from the IFIs, so long as it acts in accordance with the terms of the *Wakala* agreement.

10.34   The Islamic assets, together with their cost, are specifically identified in a schedule to the *Wakala* agreement in order to avoid *gharar*. During the construction period, as is depicted in figure 10.2, upon a drawdown request from the *Wakil* for an amount equal to an EPC milestone payment under the EPC contract, the IFIs pay the equivalent amount as a phase payment under the *Wakala* agreement to the Islamic facility agent for onward disbursement to the *Wakil*. A key requirement of *Istisna'a* is that the asset price is fixed at the outset and therefore such contracts are either fixed-price or capped. A schedule to the *Wakala* agreement specifies the date and the amount of the phase payments in order to, inter alia, avoid *gharar* as to when payments are made. There is flexibility as to amending the phase payment schedule, if required. The maximum amount of the total phase payments is expressed in the agreement as being the cost of constructing the Islamic assets, which is the total facility amount to be contributed by the IFIs. In some financings, on or before each phase payment date, the *Wakil* is obliged to deliver a promissory note up to the value of the phase payment to the IFIs. The *Wakil* is also entitled to a one-off *Wakil* fee payable by the Islamic facility agent which is usually set-off against the monies owed by the *Wakil* as lessee under the *Ijarah*.

Upon construction of the Islamic assets, the *Wakil* agrees to accept delivery of the same from the EPC contractor, whilst acknowledging that title to the Islamic assets will pass automatically to the Islamic facility agent. It is critical that ownership is transferred directly from the EPC contractor to the Islamic facility agent as depicted in figure 10.2, as certain *Sharia'a* scholars do not favour ownership of the Islamic assets being transferred via the *Wakil*, prior to being transferred to the Islamic facility agent and then being leased back to the project company pursuant to the lease agreement.[32] Although uncommon in project financings, as an alternative to leasing the Islamic assets to generate a return, the Islamic facility agent may instead sell the Islamic assets by way of a parallel *Istisna'a* that is entered into at the time of the original *Istisna'a* for the construction of the Islamic assets. The sale of assets not in existence or owned by the seller at the time the contract is entered into is ordinarily prohibited by *Sharia'a*, but the *Istisna'a* is an exception to this prohibition. This does not, however, permit the Islamic facility agent to sell the Islamic assets to the project company as *Sharia'a* prohibits a sale and buyback. The sale could, however, be to a special purpose vehicle owned by a corporate service provider, which is not related to the project company, or to a third party on an arm's length basis. Upon delivery of the Islamic assets, the *Wakil* will also be responsible for ensuring that all licenses and permits are in place and all filings have been made to protect the ownership interest of the Islamic facility agent.

10.35

The *Wakala* agreement ends on the date on which title to all the relevant Islamic assets is received by the Islamic facility agent from the EPC contractor. Upon the occurrence of an event of default under the *Wakala* Agreement, the lease agreement, and/or the finance documents, the Islamic facility agent may be entitled to terminate the *Wakala* agreement subject always to the terms of the intercreditor agreement. Upon termination, the *Wakil* will be liable for all losses, liabilities, and damages resulting from such termination, which will be equal to the aggregate of the phase payments disbursed by the IFIs.[33]

10.36

---

[32] Some *Sharia'a* scholars have not favoured a mechanism where the project company would hold title to the assets on behalf of the IFIs as one effect of this is that the IFIs become insulated from ownership risks in respect of the Islamic assets.

[33] On a termination of the *Istisna'a*, the IFIs will be responsible for repayment of any advance rentals received from the project company as further discussed below.

10.37   When structuring an Islamic project financing, a pertinent consideration that needs to be settled at the outset is the governing law that applies to the agreement and the forum for settling any disputes arising thereunder. Although the principal determinant as to the validity of the Islamic finance documents will be based on compliance with the *Sharia'a*, there are no internationally recognized *Sharia'a* courts applying universally settled principles of *Fiqh* that have developed with respect to issues, such as insolvency, that arise in the context of complex cross border project financing. Project participants will require a level of certainty as to interpretation of law and the remedies available to be able to anticipate how courts may deal with project related issues so that, inter alia, the lenders can determine whether to lend to the project and so that risks can be apportioned appropriately amongst the participants. For these reasons, the finance parties will insist on specifying a governing law which is accessible, has a developed jurisprudence covering issues that arise in a complex cross border financing and which has a consistent law which is not subject to different interpretation methodologies, as is the case between the *Madhabs*.[34] English law is often chosen as the governing law in many complex cross-border financings because of its globally renowned creditor-friendly approach, established system of precedent and the willingness of the English courts to accept jurisdiction to hear disputes governed by English law even when there is little connection to the jurisdiction other than the election of the parties.

10.38   Using English law as the governing law raises several conflict of laws issues because the law of the jurisdiction in which the project is located may have automatic jurisdiction or the agreement may not be enforceable in the jurisdiction in which the project is located as the agreement may be inconsistent with its laws. Another issue, which *Sharia'a* scholars are more concerned with, is whether English law or *Sharia'a* law takes precedence in the event of a conflict between the two sets of legal principles. From this flow the related issues of whether an English qualified judge is qualified to adjudicate on a dispute relating to an Islamic agreement; whether *Sharia'a* law or English law will be applied and if *Sharia'a* law, then which particular *Madhab* will be applied. The approach of the English courts, in the main, has been to distinguish between the *Sharia'a* and the contractual governing law of an Islamic agreement by ruling that *Sharia'a* issues are not justiciable in the English courts. That element of the agreement is deemed as forming part of the commercial agreement (which English courts will rarely interfere with) and not the legal agreement. Instead the dispute will be dealt with applying the ordinary principles of English law and an English court will avoid ruling or commenting on the compliance of the agreement with *Sharia'a*.[35] In practical terms, the parties to the Islamic documentation must

---

[34] The Convention on the Law Applicable to Contractual Obligations 1980 (the 'Rome Convention') also requires that a governing law of an agreement must belong to a country and the *Sharia'a* does not belong to a particular country although it has been adopted by countries such as Saudi Arabia.

[35] See *Shamil Bank of Bahrain v Beximco Pharmaceuticals Ltd* [2003] 2 All ER (Comm) 849.

satisfy themselves as to their validity and compliance with the *fatwa* giving legitimacy to those documents, as being in accordance with *Sharia'a*, prior to entering into the agreements. The Islamic documentation will usually contain a provision where each party acknowledges that it is satisfied with the legitimacy of the *fatwa* and the compliance of the Islamic documentation with the *Sharia'a*.

However, for a number of reasons, which may include the participation of domestic **10.39** lenders, a legal necessity of the jurisdiction in which the project is based or where there is no real choice of law as a result of the applicable principles of conflict of laws such as the doctrine of *lex situs*,[36] there is a trend for Islamic documentation to be governed by the relevant local law, especially where the project is based in the Middle East. *Sharia'a* scholars in a number of Saudi project financings have required that the governing law of the Islamic agreements be the laws of Saudi Arabia (which has a *Sharia'a* legal system) instead of English law and that the parties submit to the jurisdiction of the Saudi courts or a special committee established to deal with banking disputes. This is to ensure that any dispute is settled before a Saudi judicial forum that applies *Sharia'a* which will no doubt, however, be guided by the *fatawa* and interpretation methodology of the *Hanbli Madhab*. This may mean that a *fatwa* as to the legitimacy of an Islamic transaction given by a scholar aligned with the *Hanfai Madhab*, for example, may be declared invalid by a Saudi court if that *fatwa* contradicts an equivalent *Hanbli fatwa*.

Asset participation agreement

The asset participation agreement is an agreement between each IFI to participate **10.40** in financing the acquisition of and ownership of the Islamic assets in pre-agreed proportions. Each IFI will be obliged to pay its participation upon the project company serving a drawdown notice to the Islamic facility agent pursuant to the *Wakala* agreement as depicted in figure 10.2. The asset participation agreement will also contain provisions in relation to an IFI transferring its participation to another IFI.

Asset agency agreement

The asset agency agreement documents the terms upon which the IFIs appoint **10.41** the Islamic facility agent as their agent in connection with the project. The Islamic facility agent is authorized to enter into the finance documents on behalf of the IFIs as well as to hold title to the Islamic assets if this has been agreed. Aside to this, the obligations of the Islamic facility agent do not differ markedly from that of a facility agent to the conventional lenders.

---

[36] The rule that the law applicable to proprietary aspects of an asset is the law of the jurisdiction where the asset is located.

Istisna'a-Ijarah tranche

Istisna'a agreement

10.42 As an alternative to the structure documented in the *Wakala* agreement, the IFIs will appoint the project company to procure the Islamic assets on the terms of the *Istisna'a* agreement. The project company (as Procurer) then takes the necessary steps to construct the Islamic assets, including contracting with the EPC contractor by entering into the EPC contract. In return the IFIs agree to purchase the Islamic assets and pay the agreed amount to the project company in order to fund the construction of the Islamic assets in phase payments. The main difference between the *Istisna'a* agreement and the *Wakala* agreement is that there is no agency arrangement between the IFIs and the Procurer to procure the Islamic assets; the Procurer is simply contracted to procure the construction of the Islamic assets and the IFIs act as purchasers of those Islamic assets. This may be preferred by the IFIs since the project company at all times remains responsible for procuring the Islamic assets and so, for example, the IFIs will not be liable for any delays in the construction of the Islamic assets. In other respects, the *Istisna'a* agreement operates in much the same way as the *Wakala* agreement with the Procurer making requests to the Investment Agent for phase payments reflecting the EPC milestone payments under the EPC contract. It is to be noted that although the project company is not appointed as a *Wakil*, similar obligations are imposed on the project company in respect of entering into the EPC contract with the EPC contractor and maintaining the licenses and permits for the Islamic assets upon their delivery.

10.43 The parties to the *Istisna'a* agreement are the project company, as the Procurer, and the Investment Agent, acting on behalf of the IFIs. In certain projects where an *Istisna'a* agreement has been entered into, instead of the Investment Agent contracting with the Procurer, the IFIs have incorporated a special purpose vehicle company (SPV Co) owned by the IFIs in proportion to their respective investments. The SPV Co acts as purchaser of the Islamic assets from the project company, which in turn procures the construction of the Islamic assets from the EPC contractor pursuant to the EPC contract. An advantage of this SPV Co structure is that the IFI interest in the Islamic assets becomes insolvency remote and asset-risk remote. Certain *Sharia'a* scholars have, however, not favoured the Islamic assets being held by an SPV Co, preferring the Islamic facility agent, who is usually a reputable IFI in the jurisdiction where the project is situated, to hold title to the Islamic assets for and on behalf of the IFIs. The rationale for such an approach is that the IFIs should be seen to take risk on the assets and not be shielded from liability by the SPV Co.

Investment and investment agency agreement

10.44 This agreement contemplates the terms of both the asset participation agreement and asset agency agreement whereby the IFIs agree to participate in the financing of the acquisition of the Islamic assets and the Investment Agent is appointed to hold title to the same. This agreement also documents the decision making procedure between the IFIs, conduct of business between the IFIs, the payment mechanics for the IFIs pursuant to the terms of the finance documents, and the treatment of any late payment fees levied on the project company.

Wakala-Ijarah tranche and Istisna'a-Ijarah tranche

Lease agreement (Ijarah Mawsufa fi al-Dhimma)

Once constructed, the IFIs lease the usage of the Islamic assets to the project com-   **10.45** pany by way of an *Ijarah* pursuant to the lease agreement. The *Ijarah*, in practice, has become the mechanism by which the principal and the profit margin are returned to the IFIs during the post-construction period of a project financing, as rental consideration. Rental consideration comprises the purchase price of the Islamic assets as well as a fixed and/or floating profit margin which, in a conventional project financing, would be equivalent to the debt service payable by the project company. The profit margin can be structured as variable rentals which are adjusted according to agreed terms so that the rate of return can be benchmarked against LIBOR, for example, but in each case, the basis for determination and adjustment must be disclosed to the lessee prior to the execution of the lease agreement. Benchmarking the variable rental against LIBOR has the advantage that the *Ijarah* tenor can be longer, as the rate of return takes into account market conditions which a fixed return would not contemplate. Most *Sharia'a* scholars agree that benchmarking against LIBOR is acceptable, since although typically LIBOR is used to calculate interest, here LIBOR is being utilized as a benchmark alone and no *riba* is present in the lease agreement itself, as the lessor is taking risk in the ownership of the asset, and therefore entitled to a profit. Certain scholars have held that benchmarking the variable rental against LIBOR can impute *gharar*, since any fluctuations in LIBOR are not foreseeable, and therefore, an element of the rental payable is not foreseeable. *Gharar* can be resolved here by renewing the lease agreement each time LIBOR is revised, or providing that the variable rental amount can only be up to a certain percentage above or below LIBOR.[37]

Although the lease agreement will be executed at the same time as the other finance   **10.46** documents, the rental consideration will only be payable once the Islamic assets have sufficient economic value and substance that they can be used for the intended purpose. This will be the scheduled date on which the operations phase of the project begins, as will have been forecasted by the technical advisers. This scheduled date will be expressed in the lease agreement in order to avoid *gharar* as to when the

---

[37] This approach has been supported by Mufti Taqi Usmani in *An Introduction to Islamic Finance* (Maktaba Ma'ariful Quran, 2007) 168–71.

rental consideration becomes payable.[38] Whilst the lease period only commences from this date, the forward lease has an essential use for the IFIs during the construction phase by obliging the project company to pay advance rentals during the construction phase (equivalent to the debt service amount that a lender would receive during the construction phase under a conventional financing). The lease agreement will contain a schedule of dates on which advance rental payments are to be made.

10.47 There has been debate as to whether accepting advance rentals is permitted by *Sharia'a* law, since the IFIs are generating a return from the Islamic assets prior to their construction, and therefore prior to the same being available to the IFIs to lease to the project company. Such a return has been perceived by certain *Sharia'a* scholars as *riba*; the IFIs making a return on monies they disburse to the project company (as *Wakil* under the *Wakala* agreement or as Purchaser under the *Istisna'a* agreement) for the construction of the Islamic assets, rather than the return being generated by the project company making use of the Islamic assets. This has been resolved by providing for the deduction of the aggregate amount of the advance rentals paid during the construction phase from the first rental payment that is due once the operation phase has begun, or on a pro rata basis during the term of the *Ijarah*. The lease agreement usually contains a gross-up clause whereby the project company will pay a supplemental rent reflecting the advance rentals deducted during the operations phase, as otherwise, the rationale for the IFIs obtaining a return during the construction phase would be thwarted. However, if during the construction phase an event of default results in the termination of the *Wakala* agreement or the *Istisna'a* agreement (as the case may be), the IFIs will be obliged to refund the aggregate of all the advance rentals already paid by the project company. An amount equal to the refunded amount would then be incorporated within the termination sum payable by the project company under the *Wakala* agreement or *Istisna'a* agreement.

10.48 With respect to events of default, the project financing will need to be structured so that any event of default under the lease agreement (and the other Islamic documentation) constitutes an event of default under the CTA. This is achieved by including the Islamic events of default in the CTA to the effect that any default under the Islamic documentation will constitute a CTA event of default. Conversely, *Sharia'a* scholars look unfavourably on treating a CTA event of default as an Islamic event of default. This is because cross-referring to the conventional finance documents in this manner may taint the Islamic tranche, especially since the rationale

---

[38] The Lease Agreement may contain a mechanism to adjust the first rental payment date if the scheduled operation date is postponed for certain reasons up to a long stop date. An alternative is for the lessor and lessee to enter into an 'Agreement to Lease' which operates during the construction phase and obliges the lessor and lessee to enter into the Lease Agreement once the operations phase actually begins.

for having separate documentation for the Islamic tranche is to keep it distinct from the conventional tranches to the extent possible. Several techniques have developed to keep the Islamic tranche separate from the conventional tranches. These include the use of an Islamic common terms agreement which mirrors the terms of the conventional CTA.[39] An alternative approach which has grown in prevalence because of its simplicity and inexpensive nature, is for the Islamic facility agent (acting on behalf of the IFIs) to be a party to the relevant finance documents including the CTA and the intercreditor agreement. These approaches ensure that to the extent possible, the Islamic tranche is kept distinct, whilst with respect to events of default, the exercise of remedies, and the project's revenue and enforcement cash waterfalls, there is coordination between all the tranches and a *pari passu* relationship (where this has been agreed) between the conventional senior lenders and the IFIs.

It is useful specifically to outline some of the pertinent features of a lease agreement **10.49** which enable the *Ijarah* to be applied as an effective Islamic finance technique by which the principal and the profit margin are returned to the IFIs during the post-construction phase of a project financing.

(a) Voluntary prepayment

Under a conventional financing, the project company has a right to make voluntary **10.50** prepayments of the facility on terms specified in the facility agreement. Likewise, the project company can, subject to the terms of the CTA and intercreditor agreement, make voluntary prepayments of the IFI tranche either by the exercise of a call option (referred to as a sales undertaking), as is the case in an *Istisna'a-Ijarah* tranche, or by making early rental payments pursuant to the lease agreement, as is the case in a *Wakala-Ijarah* tranche.

The sales undertaking, which is documented separately, is a unilateral promise **10.51** (*wa'd*) granted by the IFIs to the project company to sell all or some of the Islamic assets at their outstanding value on specified lease payment dates (to avoid break costs) during the term of the lease. Exercising the sales undertaking in respect of all the Islamic assets is akin to voluntarily prepaying the entire conventional facility and exercising the sales undertaking in respect of certain Islamic assets is akin to making a partial voluntary prepayment of the conventional facility. Where several Islamic assets have been leased, the sales undertaking will be exercisable (by the service of an exercise notice) against specific Islamic assets, and go towards satisfying the total outstanding value of such Islamic assets. The sales undertaking may provide that the prepayment applies to all the Islamic assets on a pro rata basis so that the project company purchases an interest in all the Islamic assets in accordance

---

[39] The definitions used in the Islamic common terms agreement will be revised so that 'Interest' is replaced with 'Commission' or 'Profit Return', for example. The parties to this agreement will also only include the IFIs and the Islamic facility agent.

with their value. This will result in the project company owning a beneficial interest in the Islamic assets in accordance with the proportion of interest in the Islamic assets it has acquired, with the remainder of the beneficial interest remaining with the IFIs. Although the beneficial interest will not entitle the project company to an equivalent proportion of future rentals payable under the lease agreement, the return of the IFIs will decrease, as their ownership interest in the Islamic assets will have been reduced. At the end of the lease term, the IFIs will, pursuant to the sales undertaking and a sales agreement (a form of which will be appended to the sales undertaking), transfer their legal interest in the Islamic assets to the project company for a nominal amount, or on a cashless basis, since at the end of the lease agreement term, the IFIs have recovered the cost of acquiring the Islamic assets and their profit margin thereon.[40]

10.52 The alternative, as is the case in a *Wakala-Ijarah* tranche, is for the project company to make early rental payments (on specified payment dates in order to avoid break costs) which are applied pro rata to reduce all the remaining rental payments due under the lease agreement. If the project company wishes to acquire all of the Islamic assets prior to the expiry of the lease agreement term, then it will need to pay the termination sum, which is the aggregate of the outstanding principal amount that the IFIs paid to acquire the Islamic assets and any rental consideration due but unpaid. At the end of the lease term, the IFIs will transfer the ownership of the Islamic assets to the project company (pursuant to a transfer of ownership instrument) for a nominal amount or on a cashless basis.

(b) Termination and mandatory prepayment

10.53 Upon the occurrence of an event of default and the issuance of an enforcement notice, the conventional lenders and the IFIs will accelerate the monies paid under the various tranches. Under the conventional tranche, the lenders would call in the loan in accordance with the terms of the facility agreement and the intercreditor agreement. Under an IFI tranche, the IFIs may accelerate by requiring the project company to pay a termination sum by exercising a put option (referred to as a purchase undertaking) as is the case in an *Istisna'a-Ijarah* tranche, or obliging the lessee to pay the termination sum pursuant to the lease agreement as is the case in an *Wakala-Ijarah* tranche.

10.54 The purchase undertaking is a *wa'd* granted by the project company to the IFIs to purchase all the Islamic assets upon the issuance of an enforcement notice subsequent to an event of default. Following payment of the termination sum,

---

[40] The Sales Undertaking will also cover the circumstance where the project company elects to replace or repay a single IFI in specified circumstances, such as where the relevant IFI requires the project company to increase the rental consideration payable to take account of a tax deduction payable in respect of that payment by the project company.

ownership in the Islamic assets is transferred to the project company pursuant to a sale agreement, a form of which will be appended to the purchase undertaking. The alternative, as is the case in a *Wakala-Ijarah* tranche, is that upon the issuance of an enforcement notice subsequent to an event of default, the project company will be obliged to pay the termination sum following which the IFIs will assign the ownership of the Islamic assets to the project company. If the lessee fails to pay the termination sum, then the lessor will have the right to take possession and sell the Islamic assets.

It should be noted that the purchase undertaking will also cover mandatory prepay- **10.55** ment events or 'early settlement events', as is the case where there has been a change of law which adversely affects the economics or legality of the project as a consequence of which the conventional lenders and/or the IFIs may desire, or be required by law, to cease their participation in the project. In such circumstances, upon the IFIs serving an exercise notice upon the project company pursuant to the purchase undertaking, the project company will generally be obliged to prepay the outstanding amount contributed by the relevant IFI affected by the mandatory prepayment event, by acquiring that IFIs beneficial interest in specific Islamic assets. The lease agreement in a *Wakala-Ijarah* tranche also contains similar provisions, but rather than acquiring a beneficial interest in specific Islamic assets, the rental amounts thereunder are reduced pro rata in proportion to the interest of the relevant IFI that has been prepaid.

(c) *Total loss of the Islamic assets*

If an event causes a total or partial destruction of the Islamic assets as a consequence **10.56** of which the Islamic assets cannot be used by the lessee to generate a return, the IFIs will not have a right to receive further rental payments from the project company, with the IFIs' only recourse being to the insurances they are obliged to maintain as owners in respect of the Islamic assets. As owners, the IFIs will be assuming the risk of a total loss of the Islamic assets as well as risks associated with renewal payments under the policies, together with any delay in the processing and payment of claims under the insurance policies. Where the loss or damage to the Islamic assets arises from the wilful misconduct or gross negligence of the lessee, then the lessee will continue to remain liable for the rental consideration in addition to reinstating the Islamic assets. In practice, the IFIs will appoint the project company as the service agent pursuant to the terms of the service agency agreement to, inter alia, maintain the appropriate levels of insurance. Should the service agent not maintain the appropriate levels of insurance, the service agent will be obliged to indemnify the IFIs to cover the outstanding amounts under the *Ijarah* not covered by the insurance proceeds. Where a total loss of the Islamic assets is not a CTA event of default, but only an Islamic event of default, the conventional lenders may decide against accelerating the financing, and so the service agent will ordinarily be required to replace the Islamic assets with other assets that are designated as Islamic assets, and then lease the same to the project company pursuant to a new or replacement lease agreement. This ensures that the pari passu treatment of the conventional and Islamic tranches is maintained.

(d) Late payment fees

10.57   Under a conventional financing, where the project company fails to comply with its payment obligations under a facility agreement, default interest is levied on the unpaid sum. Lenders justify this additional rate as compensation for the increased risk of lending to the defaulting project company so long as the rate of default interest is reasonable as a matter of English law, i.e. the default interest is not deemed a penalty offending the rules laid down in *Dunlop Pneumatic Tyre Co Ltd v New Garages & Motor Co Ltd*.[41] *Sharia'a* law, however, regards such additional compensation which adds to the income of an IFI after a debt has become payable, as *riba*. Therefore, under the lease agreement, the lessor cannot charge the lessee a late payment fee for payment of the rent consideration after the due date where such a fee, once paid, would form part of the income of the lessor. In order to avoid a situation where the lessee takes advantage of this prohibition, the lease agreement will stipulate that the lessee pay the late payment fees directly (or through the lessor for onward payment) to a registered charity or charitable fund maintained by the lessor. As a consequence, the late payment fees do not form part of the income of the lessor whilst the lessee is deterred from delaying rental payments under lease agreement. As is the case in an *Istisna'a-Ijarah* tranche, certain scholars also permit a deduction from the late payment fee of any actual costs (excluding opportunity costs and funding costs) incurred by the IFIs due to the lessee making a late payment. The remainder of the late payment fee is then paid to charity.[42]

Service agency agreement

10.58   As outlined earlier, the IFIs as owner of the Islamic assets remain responsible for insurance, structural maintenance, settlement of ownership taxes and maintenance of consents in respect of the Islamic assets. The project company will be appointed as the IFIs' service agent pursuant to the service agency agreement, since it is best placed to undertake these obligations. The project company, in turn, passes through some of these obligations and associated costs, to the O&M contractor pursuant to an O&M agreement. The IFIs will remain responsible for each of these obligations and will indemnify the service agent for the costs incurred by the service agent in undertaking its obligations under the service agency agreement. The IFIs will, however, usually be counter-indemnified by the project company (as lessee under the lease agreement) for such costs by way of supplemental rent. In addition, as discussed earlier, where there is a total loss of the Islamic assets and the service

---

[41] [1915] AC 79
[42] For a critique of the reasons given by such scholars, see Mufti Taqi Usmani, *An Introduction to Islamic Finance* (Maktaba Ma'ariful Quran 2007) 131–40.

agent has failed to maintain adequate insurance cover in respect of the same, the service agent will be required to indemnify the IFIs for any shortfall between the amount of the insurance proceeds and the aggregate amount of the remaining rental consideration due under the lease agreement. The IFIs will pay the service agent a service agency fee which will usually be netted off against the amounts the project company owes to the IFIs.

Other techniques utilized in a multi-tranche project financing

Sukuk

Having outlined the nature of *sukuks* earlier in this chapter, it is useful to note **10.59** how *sukuks* are increasingly being considered as a means of sourcing additional *Sharia'a*-compliant financing as they provide an opportunity for a wider investor base to participate in the financing of a project. The most commonly used *sukuk* structure is the *Sukuk al-Ijarah* (as illustrated in figure 10.3). The structure involves the acquisition by a special purpose vehicle (the SPV Issuer), as agent and trustee for the investors (the Certificate Holders), of assets from the seller using proceeds generated from the issuance of the *sukuks* to the Certificate Holders. Each Certificate Holder will have a joint and undivided property interest, together with the other Certificate Holders, in the assets. The SPV Issuer then leases the assets to the lessee in return for the rent which equates to the purchase price of the assets plus a fixed and/or variable margin, which may, akin to the margin payable under a lease agreement entered into by Islamic banks, be benchmarked against LIBOR. Using the rental proceeds, a return is then paid to the Certificate Holders, in proportion to their investment, periodically or as may otherwise have been agreed between the Certificate Holders and the SPV Issuer. At the end of the term of the *sukuk*, the SPV Issuer will exercise a purchase undertaking requiring the lessee to acquire the assets; the price payable under the purchase undertaking will be the balance of the fixed rent that has not yet been paid and all other rental amounts that are then outstanding under the lease. The proceeds of the sale will then be distributed to the Certificate Holders in repayment of the capital contributed by the Certificate Holders.

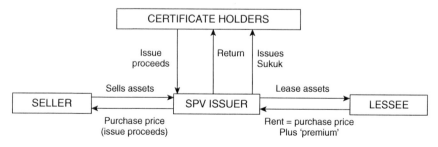

Figure 10.3 *Sukuk al-Ijarah*

Commodity Murabaha

10.60 As outlined earlier in this chapter, recently there has been an increasing use of the Commodity *Murabaha* to provide both the working capital funds required by a project company, as well as to fund the equity contributions that a sponsor is obliged to make to a project, in accordance with the *Sharia'a*. As illustrated in figure 10.4, the project company (as the Purchaser) requests the Investment Agent (appointed pursuant to a separate *Murabaha* facilities investment agency agreement) to purchase certain commodities from a supplier for the cost-price with funds made available by the IFIs. The Investment Agent then sells the purchased commodities to the Purchaser for the relevant deferred price (which includes the cost-price of the commodities plus a pre-stated margin) on deferred payment terms. The Purchaser then sells these commodities to a third party for the cost-price so that at the end of this process, the Purchaser (as the project company) receives an amount equivalent to the equity contributions of the sponsors. The obligations of the Purchaser to repay the deferred price to the IFIs is set forth in the equity subscription agreement.

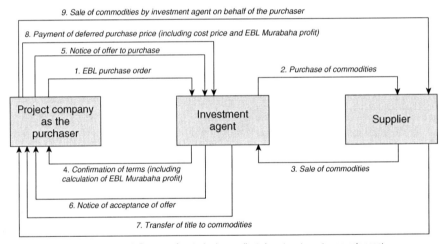

Figure 10.4 Commodity *Murabaha*

Musharaka

10.61 During the construction phase of a project, an alternative to the *Wakala* and *Istisna'a* is the Diminishing *Musharaka*, as documented in a *Musharaka* agreement.[43] Although the *Musharaka* is not often applied in project financings, it is a useful

---

[43] The *Musharka-Ijarah* structure was adopted in the Al Waha project located in Saudi Arabia (December 2006).

mechanism by which the IFIs and the project company can agree to procure and enjoy joint ownership of the Islamic assets with the profits being shared in pre-agreed proportions and losses being borne according to the capital contributions made to the venture. The Islamic facility agent enters into a separate *Istisna'a* agreement with the project company to procure the Islamic assets, which does so by entering into an EPC contract with the EPC contractor. Title to the assets will, however, first transferred to the project company by the EPC contractor, following which the project company transfers the IFIs' proportion of the Islamic assets to the Islamic facility agent pursuant to the *Musharaka* agreement. The IFIs generate a return during the operating phase by leasing their ownership interest to the project company pursuant to an *Ijarah* and receiving the principal amount they invested in the *Musharaka*. The IFIs transfer a portion of the Islamic assets to the project company by selling ownership units in the Islamic assets on each principal payment date.

Integrating the Conventional and Islamic Tranches

It is essential that the issues and tensions that arise when integrating the conven- **10.62** tional tranches and each IFI tranche in a single project financing are resolved (or at least mitigated) at the outset. Most of these matters have been discussed earlier in this chapter, and it will have become apparent that the most pertinent issues to resolve relate to the complex intercreditor arrangements between the conventional lenders and the IFI. It is paramount that the events of default and the exercise of remedies in a default scenario between the conventional tranche and the Islamic tranche are harmonized. This is because the project is an indivisible whole and, as an intercreditor matter, it would not be acceptable for one tranche to be accelerated as a result of an event of default, whilst others are unable to because there is no corresponding event of default in the documents relating to that tranche.

Furthermore, conventional banks and IFIs need to be paid from the project's **10.63** cash waterfall on a pari passu basis. So there is a need to ensure that scheduled payments, as well as mandatory or voluntary prepayments are coordinated in a commercially acceptable manner. Usually, prepayments are distributed pro rata to both the senior conventional lenders and the IFIs in the pre-enforcement payment waterfall pursuant to the intercreditor agreement. Issues may arise, however, if the *Sharia'a* scholars do not permit proceeds from the sale of the Islamic assets or early lease payments to be distributed to the conventional lenders. It is for this reason that the IFIs and the senior conventional lenders will need to agree: (i) when the IFIs will jointly make decisions with the conventional lenders under the CTA and the intercreditor agreement; (ii) whether acceleration under an IFI tranche can be undertaken without consulting the senior conventional lenders so that accelerating

the IFI tranche does not necessarily mean the other tranches also have to be accelerated; and (iii) what voting threshold applies if a process of consultation does need
to take place, noting that if the threshold is high, it will be unlikely the IFIs will
obtain the requisite consent for the prepayment to proceed, since the IFI tranches
have traditionally been smaller in proportion to the aggregate amount of the
conventional tranches.

10.64 Although project security is covered in detail elsewhere in this book, an important
issue to consider when structuring an Islamic project financing is whether the
security granted by the project company will be in respect of the project company's
obligations under just the conventional tranches, or will it also directly cover any
Islamic tranche. Furthermore, as the proposed security package would usually cover
the project as a whole, the impact on the Islamic assets will need to be considered as
well as the extent to which security will be shared with the conventional lenders.

11

ANCILLARY FINANCE DOCUMENTATION

Joanne Robertson and Patrick Holmes, Milbank, Tweed, Hadley & McCloy LLP

General Overview

Chapter 3 provides an overview of a number of the sources which may provide **11.01** funding for a particular project, including equity funding, subordinated and other debt funding of one sort or another; Chapters 7 to 10 consider the principal contracts pursuant to which such other debt funding is made available to a project and identify the main requirements associated with documenting the different financing arrangements that are encountered most frequently.

As discussed in Chapter 3, where a project is being financed by a combination of, **11.02** on the one hand, debt and equity provided by the sponsors and, on the other, debt provided by third party lenders, the claims against the project company in respect of the debt advanced by the third party lenders will invariably be classified as being 'senior' to both the debt and the equity claims of the sponsors, their claims as shareholders being subordinate as a matter of law in most jurisdictions and their claims as lenders being subordinate by agreement.[1] Even in projects where the third party lenders are divided into senior and non-senior categories (the latter usually being labelled as junior or mezzanine lenders), the rights of the lenders providing the non-senior categories of debt will be classified as 'senior' to the rights of the sponsors, both as providers of equity capital and as providers of debt.

11.03 The simplest financing arrangement for a project might involve the provision of debt finance by a single lender pursuant to a single credit agreement the terms of which require that the sponsors' equity contributions are made in full (by way of the subscription for shares in the project company) before the lender advances any funds to the project. However, the sheer scale of the costs involved in the development of a major project necessitates the ever-wider syndication of credit facilities and the tapping of ever-more diverse sources of funding. The result of this is that financing arrangements have become increasingly complicated as more and more parties become involved. The combination of this multiplicity of parties and an ever increasing need to balance the diametrically opposed demands for, on the one hand, the minimization of costs (to make a project economically competitive) and, on the other, the generation of adequate financial returns to investors, means that the principal credit documentation for most projects is anything but simple. The complexity, however, comes not so much from what the different stakeholders are doing (each is essentially providing money for the development of the project on terms such that the money, and some sort of return on it, will be paid back over time from the revenues generated by the project once it has been completed) as from the fact that the different stakeholders have different ways of doing things (often necessitated by particular political considerations and legal constraints) and different attitudes to risk.

11.04 This chapter examines:

(1) some of the myriad types of financial support that is given to the project by its sponsors and the way that that support is provided (Equity Support, paragraphs 11.05–11.46 below);

(2) the types of assets over which security is taken to ensure that, to the extent possible and practicable, the senior lenders' claims against the project are indeed senior to the claims of the sponsors (Security Arrangements, paragraphs 11.47–11.104);

---

[1] For the purposes of this chapter, and indeed this book, we are assuming that contractual subordination works from a legal perspective in the relevant jurisdiction. Where there are doubts as to the efficacy of contractual subordination (as may be the case in some countries), and if the circumstances justify the incremental costs and complexities, the financing arrangements may be structured so that the subordinated creditors have no debt claims against the project company at all. Instead, they make their loans to the project company's holding company which then uses the loan proceeds to subscribe for shares in the project company. This achieves so-called 'structural subordination' because the claims of the subordinated lender are necessarily subordinated to the claims of the project company's creditors (which will include the 'senior' lenders).

(3) the contractual documentation between the senior lenders and the counterparties to the principal commercial contracts in relation to the project which allow the senior lenders to step into the project company's contractual shoes and thereby take control of the project in order to protect their commercial interests (Direct Agreements, paragraphs 11.105–11.114); and

(4) the way in which formal legal opinions are used in relation to a project financing as a means of confirming the extent to which the contractual arrangements for the project operate as the different parties and groups of parties intend (Legal Opinions, paragraphs 11.115–11.128).

Equity Support

Introduction

The equity support for a project will take essentially one of two forms—financial **11.05** and non-financial—and all projects will be dependent on both. Non-financial support for a project can, and does, take the form of virtually any sort of obligation to provide things that the project will need other than money.

Money is of course necessary if a project is ever to get beyond the stage of being **11.06** simply an idea, but in relation to many projects money is less important in terms of determining the identities of the sponsors of the project and ensuring its success than the non-financial support that the sponsors are able to offer. Indeed, it may well be the strength of a particular sponsor's non-financial support that dictates which of the competing bidders is awarded the project in the first place.

There are almost as many examples of non-financial support from sponsors for **11.07** projects as there are projects, but some of the classic examples of non-financial support that sponsors will provide to a project include:

(1) the contribution of their know-how and other expertise, including the technical and organizational skills needed for the efficient construction and operation of comparable projects, wherever located;

(2) the application of their specialist knowledge of the commercial and political environment in which the project will operate and the legal regime to which it will be subject (recognizing that in most instances these issues will involve international considerations as well those in the jurisdiction in which the project is located);

(3) the dedication of natural resources that constitute the feedstock or fuel for the project, whether because they own these resources or because they are able to obtain access to them in preference to others (or on more favourable terms than others);

(4) the provision of specialist marketing services to the project in order to gain access to a potential customer base for its products that would otherwise take a considerable time to establish; and

(5) the provision of, or of access to, port, pipeline, or other transportation facilities that the project will need, whether for its fuel and feedstock or for the product that it produces.

11.08   Our concern in this chapter is not, however, with the many types of support that sponsors provide to a project but with the financial support that the senior lenders will require them to provide to the project and the financial interests that the senior lenders will require them to maintain in the project.

11.09   It is perhaps worth making an obvious comment here, that being that even where a promise to provide funds for a project is, to quote a phrase adopted in countless legal opinions, 'legal, valid, binding and enforceable', a promise is only as strong as the person that makes it. It is often the case that the 'real' sponsors of a project are not the companies that sign the contractual documentation regulating the sponsors' equity contribution obligations. Tax considerations, in particular, frequently mean that the sponsors' obligations are in fact obligations of special purpose, and minimally capitalized companies established in jurisdictions selected more for their tax treaties than for their links to the business interests of the sponsors. In such cases (and also in cases where the creditworthiness of different sponsors is particularly unequal, which is often the case as between international sponsors and the local sponsors for a project), it is likely that another important part of the contractual arrangements relating to the provision of the sponsors' equity contributions will be a credit enhancement agreement such as a guarantee issued by the ultimate sponsor (or one of its affiliates) or a letter of credit issued by an unrelated creditworthy institution such as a bank.

Equity capital contributions

11.10   The simplest form of financial equity support that the sponsors will provide for any project will be in the form of the subscription for shares in the project company or (or, more probably, and) the making of long-term subordinated shareholder loans to the project company. Chapter 7, whilst ostensibly focusing on the differences between the various types of credit agreement encountered in project financings, also emphasizes the fact that, despite the differences, the various ways in which lenders provide credit to a project have many elements in common. Indeed, they are essentially the same in that ultimately the relationship between the project company and the lenders is that of debtor and creditor.

11.11   The fact that equity support is usually provided by means of two fundamentally different routes (one giving rise to an ownership interest in the project company and one giving rise to a debtor-creditor relationship with the project company), coupled with the fact that tax considerations will inevitably drive different sponsors to adopt different ownership and financing structures for projects in different jurisdictions, means that there will always be considerable diversity in relation to the

contractual arrangements for the provision of equity support for projects in different countries. As a result, and also because different host countries have their own
preferences for the ownership arrangements for projects in particular sectors (which
may or may not involve an element of state ownership), it is difficult to discuss the
contractual arrangements in relation to the provision of equity support otherwise
than in rather general terms. This being so, the main thing to note about the contracts regulating equity support arrangements is that they are diverse. They often
involve a shareholders' agreement (which is designed to regulate the sponsors' commitments *inter se*) and a separate equity support agreement (which is intended to
benefit the project company and the lenders). Some equity support agreements
provide a framework for the support to be provided pursuant to other contracts
(such as share subscription agreements, partnership agreements, or subordinated
loan agreements), while others themselves contain appropriate legally binding
undertakings to make moneys available to the project company.

Ultimately, there will be contracts (probably governed by the laws of a mix of juris-   **11.12**
dictions) pursuant to which the sponsors are bound to provide their support to the
project (these contracts being the subject of this chapter) and further contracts that
deal with the rights of the sponsors to extract their investment returns from the
project. A discussion in relation to the continued support the lenders may require
from the sponsors after completion is included in paragraphs 11.42–11.45.

Quantum

The extent of the total equity (whether constituted by share capital or subordinated   **11.13**
loan capital) that will be invested in a project over its construction phase as a proportion of the total capital cost of the project will be influenced in particular by the
extent of the risk associated with the project: the greater the degree of predictability
associated with the project once it is in operation the lower the amount of equity
that the project lenders will insist be contributed to the project. Conversely,
increased volatility in relation to a project's cashflows will, as a rule, mean that the
project lenders will wish to see a lower ratio of debt to equity. The basic logic for this
is simply that the more equity that is invested in a project, the lower the risk that
interruptions in the project cashflows will lead to a failure by the project company
to meet its debt service obligations. This is because the effect of the cash waterfall[2]
is such that the first casualty of any cashflow disturbance will be the distributions
payable to the sponsors. The greater the equity investment, the greater the level of

---

[2] As discussed in Chapter 7, the cash waterfall is the contractual provision that (by agreement
among the project company, the lenders, and the sponsors) stipulates the sequence in which the
moneys for the time being available to the project company are applied in or towards the discharge of
its payment obligations. Broadly speaking, the sequence ensures that operating costs are paid before
obligations owed to the senior lenders and hedge providers, which in turn are paid before moneys are
paid to junior lenders or are available for distribution to the sponsors.

distributions available for the sponsors and so, necessarily, the larger the 'cushion' protecting the senior lenders.

11.14 The high proportion of equity to debt in relation to mining projects as compared with power projects, for example, reflects the fact that unforeseen geological and hydrological problems, whilst not irrelevant in the context of the development of a power project, could have a far greater impact on the development of a mine and, more significantly, its operation. The extent of the equity contribution requirement for any given project is thus almost an irrelevance from a legal perspective—the legal objective is simply to provide an effective contractual framework that specifies the circumstances in which the sponsors are obliged to make their agreed contributions (including 'standby' contributions[3]) available.

Shares or subordinated loans?

11.15 Although the sponsors' equity investment in the project will invariably consist of a combination of share capital and subordinated loan capital, in most jurisdictions there are minimum capitalization requirements in relation to the formation of companies, often for tax reasons because interest payments on loans are deductible in calculating income for tax purposes while dividend payments are not. These so-called 'thin capitalization' rules will necessarily prevail over the preferences of the parties to the transaction. In particular, they will prevail over the sponsors' general preference to maximize the extent to which their contributions are constituted by the making of loans, a preference which, as well as usually being more tax efficient, is driven by the fact that loans provide them with greater flexibility than shares when it comes to the extraction of funds from the project company.[4] This enhanced

---

[3] As with any financial projection, the capital budget for a project will be prepared on the basis of certain assumptions. Inevitably, things will happen over the construction phase of the project that prove the assumptions were wrong. As a result, estimates in the budget will usually be conservative, with cash outflows generally being, if anything, overstated (and assumed as being required to be made sooner rather than later) and cash inflows being, if anything, understated (and assumed as arising later rather than sooner).

In addition, the lenders will require that the project company will have available to it funds that it might need to meet 'contingencies' (i.e. funds to meet project costs that have not been anticipated or to meet incremental project costs attributable to unexpected (or longer than expected) delays in the development of the project). Such 'standby' funding arrangements usually involve funding commitments from both lenders and sponsors which are only available for drawing by the project company once it has exhausted its other sources of funding. Because these facilities are by definition not expected to be utilised, the fees which the project company will be required to pay for them is often structured on two bases: a fee of x% if the facility is not used and a fee of x + y% if the facility is used.

Standby debt and equity facilities are usually drawn proportionately. However, it is not uncommon for the sponsors to make their standby contributions available first and for there to be a 'true-up' advance made by the lenders at the time of completion which will bring the overall debt to equity ratio back to an agreed level.

[4] The sponsors' rights to extract funds from the investment will, of course, be subject to the terms of the finance documents, which will regulate both the timing and the extent of payments to the sponsors (whether by way of the payment of interest on, or the repayment of, amounts they have provided

flexibility derives from the fact that the laws relating to the formation and operation of companies in most jurisdictions include maintenance of capital rules which, and independently of any minimum capitalization rules that may be applicable in that jurisdiction, operate to impose constraints on a company's rights in relation to the repayment of its share capital.

Maintenance of capital rules

In England, maintenance of capital rules are basically designed to protect a company's creditors.[5] Although it is logical to assume that, to a greater or lesser extent, this is also the case elsewhere, it may well be that the reasons for the rules in particular jurisdictions are different to the reasons for them in others in the same way that the rules themselves will differ from jurisdiction to jurisdiction.   **11.16**

As well as restricting the redemption of issued shares, rules on the maintenance of capital also restrict the ability of companies to make distributions to shareholders out of capital by requiring that dividends are paid out of profits, which in this context means (a) undistributed profit for prior accounting periods to the extent they have not been offset by subsequent losses and (b) undistributed profit for the current accounting period after they have been reduced to offset losses in earlier accounting periods.   **11.17**

Although the actual operation of maintenance of capital rules will vary from jurisdiction to jurisdiction, their very existence means that a project company and its board of directors will not be free to decide to make payments to the project company's shareholders merely because, for example, the project company has cashflow (as opposed to profit) that is surplus to its immediate operating requirements. If the project company's payment to its shareholders involves a reduction of capital, then before the payment may lawfully be made the applicable rules must be satisfied. The rules could range from the very stringent in a jurisdiction which requires that the payment is sanctioned by the court or approved by a governmental department (or both), to the more relaxed in a jurisdiction that will allow the payment subject to the delivery of an auditor's certificate satisfying particular criteria. However, irrespective of the specific tests, the end result is that the project company will not be able to pay money to its shareholders as and when its board of directors elects to do so.   **11.18**

---

to the project company in the form of loans or by way of the payment of dividends on amounts they have provided by way of share capital).

[5] *Trevor v Whitworth* (1887) 12 App Cas 409. In the words of Lord Watson (at 423, 424): 'Paid-up capital may be diminished or lost in the course of the company's trading; that is a result which no legislation can prevent; but persons who deal with, and give credit to, a limited company, naturally rely upon the fact that the company is trading with a certain amount of capital already paid . . . and they are entitled to assume that no part of the capital which has been paid into the coffers of the company has been subsequently paid out, except in the legitimate course of its business.'

Shareholder loans

11.19 Since a company's obligations to repay loans that have been made to it by its shareholders (and to pay interest thereon) are not necessarily within the scope of the rules on the maintenance of capital, the simplest way that shareholders can avoid the constraints of such rules in relation to their investment in a project is to make loans to the project company instead of subscribing for shares. As well as providing the shareholders with greater flexibility in terms of the withdrawal of cash from the project, in most jurisdictions interest paid on loans will constitute an expense which is deductible from the project company's income in the determination of its income for tax purposes. As a result, both the lenders to the project and the authorities seeking to collect tax revenues from the project have their own reasons for controls that have much the same effect as the rules on the maintenance of capital.

(1) Lenders are creditors of the project company and as such will want to ensure that the project company does not make payments to its shareholders (or the sponsors) if to do so might operate to their potential detriment (by leaving the project company in a position such that it is less likely to be able to meet its future obligations (and, most importantly, its obligations to the lenders)).

(2) The tax authorities will want to minimize the amounts that are deducted in the computation of taxable income because their tax revenue will necessarily be reduced by every such deduction.

11.20 The lenders protect their interests by (a) insisting on the subordination of the loans to the project company which are made by the shareholders and the sponsors to the loans which are made by the lenders (so that in the project company's insolvency the lenders, the shareholders, and the sponsors are all in the respective positions in which they would have been had the loans made by the shareholders and the sponsors constituted share capital) and (b) prohibiting the project company from making payments in relation to the loans made to it by its shareholders or the sponsors (whether by repaying the principal thereof or paying interest thereon) unless it meets specific financial criteria that demonstrate that the project company is healthy (and then only so long as the project company is not in breach of any of its obligations under its finance documents).

11.21 The tax authorities protect their interests through 'thin capitalization rules' of one sort or another that limit the amount of interest that a company can deduct on loans made to it by its shareholders (or others) to the level of the loans that (when expressed as a proportion of the project company's total share and loan capital) could be expected to be provided by third party commercial lenders on normal arm's length terms (which in this context can be taken to mean on terms that are not directly influenced by the profitability of the project company).

To whom should the promise of equity be made?

11.22 For a variety of reasons (some of which, on detailed analysis, have less validity than others), the contractual arrangements pursuant to which shareholders undertake to subscribe shares in, or make loans to, the project company are often quite different.

One of the reasons that there may be a divergent approach to the contractual **11.23** arrangements regulating the shareholders' obligations for equity funding is that, in the course of the commercial debate between a project's potential lenders and its potential shareholders regarding the extent of the relative amounts of debt and equity to be contributed to the project, the fact that the project will necessarily involve a third party (namely the project company) does not always remain fully in sight. As a result (and even though the credit agreement will include a requirement that the shareholders must have entered into a suitable contribution agreement (and, at any given time, to have made a prescribed level of contributions pursuant thereto) as a condition precedent to the entitlement to make drawings thereunder), the parties to the relevant contribution agreement may not include the project company. On the assumption that, as is usually the case, the contribution agreement contains a provision to the effect that a person that is not party to it will have no right to enforce any of its provisions by virtue of the Contracts (Rights of Third Parties) Act 1999, the shareholders' promises to make their agreed contributions are thus promises made to the lenders alone.[6]

Given that the project company will be the recipient[7] of all equity contributions **11.24** (whether in the form of the subscription moneys for shares or in the form of shareholder loans), it is important that the contractual undertaking to provide the contribution is made to the project company. Apart from anything else, the project company is the natural person to whom the promise of making the money available should be made because it is the project company that needs the money. The lenders are obviously interested in the promise but their interests can be adequately served by means of a security assignment of the project company's rights to call for, and receive, the shareholder's equity contributions.[8] On this basis, therefore, there is no

---

[6] Even where the project company is a party to the relevant equity contribution agreement, it is often the case that the shareholders' promise to make funds available to the project company is specifically given to the lenders rather than to the project company (or to both the lenders and the project company, a hedged approach which rather suggests indecision more than clear analysis).

[7] Even if the proceeds of the contribution are paid to a third party such as the EPC Contractor, the project company should be treated as the recipient of the contribution because the contribution gives rise to a liability on the part of the project company.

[8] It may be that in some jurisdictions a company cannot effectively assign or otherwise encumber its uncalled capital. Where this is the case, there would seem to be no objection to providing for the capital to be credited to a bank account which has been made the subject of appropriate security interests in favour of the lenders. However, it must be questionable whether (irrespective of the jurisdiction) such an arrangement could be effective to ensure that a contribution paid after the onset of insolvency could be claimed by the lenders to the exclusion of the project company's liquidator on the basis that there must logically be a moment between the time at which the moneys are paid by the shareholder and the time that they are credited to the relevant bank account when they are 'owned' by the company but not subject to any encumbrance.

need for the lenders to be the direct beneficiaries of the shareholders' promise, which can thus be made to the project company alone.

11.25 Quite apart from the fact that the project company is the natural recipient of the promise of funds from the sponsors, where the equity contribution agreement is governed by English law this approach is also preferable from a technical legal perspective because the project company will be able to establish its claim for damages against a sponsor that fails to make its contribution available in accordance with the requirements of the contribution agreement more readily (and, more importantly, sooner) than a lender would be able to do so. The reason for this is that, unlike the lenders, the project company will have contractual obligations to make payments to third party suppliers in connection with the project works and needs the funding from the sponsors (as well as that from the lenders) to enable it to meet these payment obligations. If, therefore, a shareholder fails to make its contribution available, the project company will be forced[9] either to obtain replacement funds (probably at significantly greater cost) to enable it to make the relevant payments or to default on its own obligations to its suppliers (and so become liable to pay them damages for breach of contract). In either case, however, to the extent the project company is able to demonstrate a causal connection between the shareholder's failure and the costs it has incurred, the project company will probably be able to recover the costs from the shareholder by way of damages for breach of contract.

11.26 If the defaulting shareholder's promise of funding is made to the lenders, then damages are more difficult to establish. What damage does the lender suffer if the shareholder fails to make a loan to the project company? On the face of it, none. The project company may as a result end up in default of an obligation to a third party supplier because he has insufficient funds to pay the supplier, but that is not a loss suffered by the lender. Nor can the lender say his damage is that he himself had to lend the project company the money—he does not have an obligation to lend if the shareholder does not lend and if he elects to do so the amount lent is not (of itself) a loss in respect of which he is entitled to be compensated by the shareholder.[10] Ultimately the lender will only suffer a loss to the extent that the lack of funding can be demonstrated to have resulted in a failure by the project company to repay the lender's loan.[11]

---

[9] The example is overly simplistic for illustrative purposes. The project company will inevitably have more options open to it in these circumstances.

[10] The lender could, perhaps, procure that a third party make the requisite funds available to the project company, but the damages it would be able to claim from the shareholder if it does so would be limited to the incremental costs charged by the third party (and even then only to the extent they are not reimbursed by the project company). Moreover, a payment by the lender under its guarantee to the third party is akin to the making of a loan by the lender to the project company to enable it to repay the moneys owed to the third party and so would not of itself represent a loss in respect of which he is entitled to be compensated by the shareholder.

[11] This, of course, means that there can be no loss to the lenders unless the project has collapsed. Whilst this may provide the lenders with a degree of comfort, it will in practice be difficult for them

Whether in these circumstances the lenders would be able to persuade a court to **11.27** make an order for specific performance requiring the sponsor to make its equity contribution available on the basis that damages for the breach would not be an adequate remedy is debatable. On the face of things, one might well (and in many ways reasonably) conclude that the shortcomings of a mere damages claim (as discussed in paragraph 11.26 above) are clearly such that an order for specific performance would be the more appropriate remedy in these circumstances. However, although it may eventually prove to be the case that this is the correct conclusion, it is in direct conflict with (among other authorities) the decision of the House of Lords in *The South African Territories, Limited v Wallington*,[12] in which Lord Macnaghten observed:

> That specific performance of a contract to lend money cannot be [specifically] enforced is so well established, and obviously so wholesome a rule, that it would be idle to say a word about it. [13]

---

to establish that the shareholder's failure to make its equity contribution available was anything other than one of many factors that contributed to the collapse of the project (which means that at best the shareholder will be required to compensate them for only a part of their losses).

[12] [1898] AC 309.

[13] The reason that, notwithstanding the decision in *The South African Territories, Limited v Wallington*, there may be scope for a different conclusion comes in part from s 740 of the Companies Act 2006, which provides: 'A contract with a company to take up and pay for debentures of the company may be enforced by an order for specific performance.' This section (which stems from the Companies Act 1907) reverses *The South African Territories Ltd v Wallington*, but only applies to a contract with a company formed and registered under the Companies Acts (or treated as so formed and registered), with the apparent result that *The South African Territories, Limited v Wallington* still applies to contracts with other companies (and to simple contracts to lend money to companies formed and registered under the Companies Acts). There is some authority for the proposition that in certain circumstances specific performance should be available for an obligation to lend money notwithstanding *The South African Territories, Limited v Wallington* (a) In his dissenting judgment in *Loan Investment Corporation of Australasia v Bonner* [1970] Privy Council 724, Sir Garfield Barwick said (at 742): '*No doubt the general assumption is that damages for breach of a mere promise to lend money adequately compensates the would be borrower. But, in my opinion, that assumption of fact is not necessarily of universal validity and, again in my opinion, must yield in any case when in fact in the particular circumstances damages would not do justice between the parties. So it seems to me that equity in the more complicated situations of the modern world may well yet find an occasion when justice can only be done in relation to a contract merely to lend money by ordering its specific performance*; (b) In *Wight v Haberdan Pty Ltd* [1984] 2 NSWLR 280, the New South Wales Supreme Court (Kearney J) granted an order for specific performance of an obligation to lend money; and (c) In *Lee v Standard Chartered Bank (M) Bhd* [2004] Part 4 Case 15 HMC, the High Court of Malaya (HG Kang J following *Wight v Haberdan Pty Ltd*) also granted an order for specific performance of an obligation to lend money. It is perhaps worth commenting here that, in the same way that a contract to buy a share would not ordinarily be specifically enforceable against the purchaser (because in theory the share could always be sold to someone else), a contract to subscribe for shares will not usually be specifically enforceable. Nor does an obligation to subscribe for shares in a company formed and registered under the Companies Acts fall within the scope of s 740 of the Companies Act 2006. This is because for the purposes of that section debentures are defined (in s 738) to include 'debenture stock, bonds and any other securities of a company, whether or not constituting a charge on the assets of the company', a definition that contemplates only securities evidencing debts and which therefore would not include shares.

Timing of equity contributions

11.28 It used to be the case that lenders could (and would) insist on the sponsors of a project making the whole of their equity contribution to the project company before the lenders would disburse any of their project loans. The logic for this approach was that it was consistent with the proposition that, as between equity investors and lenders (and irrespective of the fact that, as discussed in the Completion Support section below, the sponsors would also be providing completion support), the equity investors should always take the bigger risk (a) because they stand to make the greater return and (b) because (indirectly at least) they are in control of managing the construction and operational risks associated with the project. This logic is sound and is consistent with the accepted proposition that the sponsors should only be entitled to a return on their investment if the project has been completed and is operating at an agreed level of performance (with the result that the project company is discharging its obligations to the lenders in a timely fashion), but things have changed.

11.29 Today, sponsors increasingly make use of equity bridge loan arrangements[14] for the purpose of making their equity contributions to the project company.[15] It is likely that equity bridge loans will be drawn before the senior facilities because they usually have lower margins. However, even in cases where the respective contributions of the sponsors and lenders to the capital costs of a project are made available

---

[14] As discussed in Chapter 7, an equity bridge loan is a loan made to the project company under the guarantee of the sponsor on terms such that:

(a) the lender's only recourse with respect to the loan is to the sponsor under the guarantee (i.e. specifically without recourse to the project company and its assets (although equity bridge liabilities are sometimes included in the cash waterfall 'below' liabilities owed to the senior lenders but 'above' distributions to be paid to the shareholders, which means that technically there is recourse to the project company but on a subordinated basis)); and

(b) all claims that the sponsor might have against the project company in relation to amounts paid out under the guarantee (whether the claims arise under a contract of indemnity or by operation of law, thus including rights of subrogation) are subordinated to the claims of the project lenders in the same way as shareholder loans would have been subordinated.

In cases where a sponsor's credit rating does not meet the minimum rating required by the equity bridge lenders, it may still avail itself of the benefits of an equity bridge loan arrangement by procuring that an appropriately rated bank issue a standby letter of credit under which the equity bridge lenders can make drawings if the project company fails to discharge its obligations in relation to the equity bridge loan. This approach will, however, increase the overall cost of the arrangements to the sponsor because it will have to bear the cost of procuring the letter of credit in addition to indirectly bearing the cost of its equity bridge loan.

It is also worth noting that if a sponsor's credit rating drops below an agreed minimum, the equity bridge lenders are likely to require that it procure the issuance of a standby letter of credit by an appropriately rated bank in substitution for the sponsor's guarantee within a specified (and reasonably short) period after the downgrade.

Any 'standby' equity contributions required to be made available by the sponsors will be required to be supported by a guarantee or letter of credit in the same way.

[15] Sponsors generally prefer to use equity bridge loans because doing so improves their return on capital and so enables them to offer more competitive prices when tendering for the project.

pro rata, the equity support and financing documentation will include provisions pursuant to which the lenders will be entitled to require the sponsors to fund their equity contributions in full upon the occurrence of particular events.

It is now often the case[16] that by using an equity bridge loan a sponsor will not actu- **11.30** ally fund its equity contributions to a project until a year or two after the project has been completed, although of course the fact that it has guaranteed (or arranged a letter of credit to support) the loan means that its credit exposure to the project is essentially the same as it would have been had it made its equity contribution to the project company in the usual way.

Completion support

Completion support is simply a label for whatever contractual undertakings are **11.31** required of the sponsors over the course of the development phase of the project in order to help mitigate completion risk, completion risk essentially being that the project will not be constructed on time on budget and to the required specification:

(1) *On time*: A delay in completion means (in particular) that the project company will have more interest to pay, particularly where delays arise towards the end of the construction period when debt levels are at their highest.

(2) *On budget*: Expenditure which exceeds that contemplated by a project's capital budget (whether because there has been an unexpected need to purchase equipment or materials or because the cost of equipment and materials is simply higher than anticipated) and other unbudgeted expenditure still needs to be funded. It will therefore either give rise to increased interest costs because of the need for additional debt or result in a reduced equity return because of the need for additional equity.

(3) *To specification*: A project which for some reason is not built to specification will be incapable of operating at the level necessary to produce the income that was anticipated it would produce. If the project is less efficient than it should be it will use more feedstock or energy to produce a given quantity of output. If the quality of the output from the project is not as high as it should be it will command a lower price when it is sold. If a project is unreliable and so cannot maintain appropriate levels of production it will both cost more to maintain and be less attractive as a source of supply to purchasers and as a source of revenue to suppliers. Essentially, if a project does not work as intended it will be likely to cost more to run or earn less (or both).

---

[16] The collapse of Lehman Brothers in September 2008 and its aftermath saw even strong sponsors struggling to put equity bridge loans in place. It took a number of months for lenders to feel sufficiently secure to return to lending to sponsors on the basis of their balance sheets. Even then, the loans available tended to have shorter tenors than they had had in the past and were being made by core 'relationship' banks rather than large syndicates.

11.32 As with other projects risks, it is the potentially damaging financial consequences associated with completion risk that are of particular concern to lenders and sponsors because damage to the project economics will mean (at best) the sponsors will enjoy a reduced financial return on their investment (if not the loss of their investment), which in turn increases the risks faced by the lenders, first, because of the erosion of the financial cushion that the equity provides and, secondly, because a sponsor facing a small or no return on his investment has nothing to provide him with an incentive to do all that he can to ensure that the project will be as successful as it can be in the circumstances.

11.33 As discussed in Chapter 4, project finance is really all about risk and its allocation between the stakeholders involved in the project, with different stakeholders assuming the risks they are best placed to manage, mitigate, or (having regard to the benefits that they will derive from the project) simply accept. The level of support that will be required of the sponsors in any given case will be part of the project's overall risk matrix, the only real rule that can be said to apply in this context being that there is no hard and fast rule that applies: the level of completion support that will be provided by the sponsors of a specific project will depend on the different interests of the different stakeholders.

11.34 At one extreme, there are projects with very high development risks—perhaps because they rely on the use of new (and thus unproven) technological processes—in relation to which the lenders may insist that their loans are unconditionally guaranteed by the sponsors until completion (a requirement that is an anathema to sponsors because it counts against the borrowing capacity reflected by their own balance sheets). At the other extreme are projects where the lenders require that the sponsors commit to do no more than make their agreed equity contributions available to the project company, perhaps coupled with an obligation to use 'reasonable endeavours' to achieve completion within a particular time frame.[17] There are then the projects somewhere in the middle, where the sponsors' completion support might consist of (for example) undertakings to ensure that the project company has the necessary funds to enable it to:

(1) meet all project cost overruns (i.e. costs for which the project company has no other available sources of funds) up to completion;

(2) meet all project cost overruns up to completion on condition that the project lenders make a contribution to the funding thereof as well (which is the effect of the 'standby' equity contributions and loan facilities discussed in footnote 4 above);

(3) meet all incremental interest costs incurred by the project company before completion as a result of delays in achieving completion (and, perhaps, also to

---

[17] In other words, ultimately without having a substantive obligation to ensure that completion occurs.

meet any scheduled debt repayments that fall due before completion, a less attractive proposition from the sponsors' perspective because undertakings to ensure that principal is repaid begin to look more like guarantees of the debt); and/or

(4) meet the capital cost of making modifications to the project to bring it up to specification in order to avoid price reductions that would otherwise occur or the imposition of penalties (or to fund the payment of 'buy-down' amounts to an off-taker by way of the price for its agreement to a reduction in the project company's contractual obligations with respect to the output from the project so that the guaranteed output matches the actual output capacity of the project), in each case to the extent that there are no other funds available for the purpose.

Completion

The moment at which the construction phase of a project is completed and the **11.35** project, whatever it is, is doing whatever it has been developed to do, is one of the most significant milestones in the life of the project, and in many cases is the most significant one because thereafter completion risk is no more (or, perhaps more accurately, is a known quantity). Completion marks the watershed for the project's cashflows, with the replacement of the rapid cash outflow that occurs during the development phase by the rather more modest income stream that, over time, should both discharge the project company's liabilities to its lenders and provide a return to its investors. Going forward, the project's cashflows, whilst still variable, are far more predictable; there are still risks that need to be managed, but by and large once a project is complete both lenders and sponsors can breathe a collective sigh of relief in the knowledge that they have survived the biggest hurdle they faced when they started the project.

Although self evident, completion will also mark the moment at which any com- **11.36** pletion support from the sponsors will fall away, leaving the lenders in the position in which (as between the sponsors and the lenders) they will be shouldering more project risk than before.[18]

The definition of completion in the contracts that regulate the financing and equity **11.37** support arrangements for a project is therefore of major importance to both lenders and sponsors. It is critical that the definition is as precise as possible and that it deals with everything that each party considers necessary to enable it conclude that the project is complete. The definition, of course, has to be agreed at the time the contracts are signed and although the fact that the interests of the lenders and the

---

[18] The operation of the cashflow waterfall will leave the sponsors bearing a degree of risk in relation to post completion cashflow problems on a 'first loss' basis because the cash that they are entitled to receive by way of distributions in respect of a given trading period will always be reduced to zero before the amounts payable to the senior lenders will be reduced.

sponsors are in direct conflict in this context (often making negotiations in this area both protracted and acrimonious), it is important from all perspectives to avoid the soft option of including some sort of 'to be agreed at the time' formulation. It is a truism that if it is difficult to agree a definition of what constitutes completion before the relevant contract is signed, it will be virtually impossible to agree the definition when the sponsors have concluded that completion has occurred and the lenders have concluded that it has not.[19]

11.38　The completion definition will involve the project passing a battery of technical tests that measure whatever the engineers conclude it is appropriate to measure for the particular type of project, with details of outputs per input and inputs per output and all manner of other things that lawyers may (or, more likely, may not) fully understand. Some of the tests that will need to be satisfied to establish completion for the purposes of the finance documents will be the same as the tests that establish completion for the purposes of the EPC contract for the project.

11.39　Whether a project passes the various tests will therefore depend in large part on expert technical analysis. Although the tests themselves will be objective (so that it should not matter who conducts them), a frequent commercial issue that needs to be resolved in this context is whether the analysis and resulting technical certification that triggers completion should be that conducted by the technical consultants advising the sponsors or the technical consultants advising the lenders. For the purposes of the EPC contract (i.e. as between the sponsors and the EPC Contractor), it should probably be the sponsors' consultants that confirm completion. For the purposes of the finance documents, however, the fact that, as between the sponsors and the lenders, completion can be said to be disadvantageous to the lenders, there is a good argument to support the proposition that the lenders' technical consultants should be responsible for providing the primary confirmation that completion has occurred, or at least confirming that they agree with the views of the sponsors' consultants. In most instances, therefore, it would be unreasonable for the sponsors not to agree that the lenders' consultant should be required to confirm completion for the purposes of the finance documents, whether independently or in conjunction with the sponsors' consultants.[20]

11.40　It goes without saying that the contracts should provide for all applicable tests to be conducted on a coordinated basis with oversight rights being given to the parties

---

[19] It is also the case that under English law an agreement to agree an essential term of a contract could mean that in fact there is no contract between the parties at all. (See, for example, *Willis Management (Isle Of Man) Ltd & Willis UK Ltd v Cable & Wireless Plc & Pender Insurance Ltd* [2005] EWCA Civ 806.)

[20] The sponsors would generally protect themselves against an impasse in these circumstances by including in the relevant contracts provisions that allow disputes of this nature to be resolved through some sort of 'expert' determination arrangement rather than by means of the usual dispute resolution process (which would usually involve an arbitration), the idea being that the expert will look at the relevant data and make an independent assessment whether completion has occurred.

that are interested in the outcome of the tests even though they may not be parties to the contracts pursuant to which the tests are being conducted. Completion tests will also usually be used for establishing the level of liquidated damages that are payable under the applicable contract in cases where performance, whilst below the agreed specification level, is not sufficiently far below to cause the project to fail the completion test.[21] The key point to note about the use of completion tests in relation to the release of the sponsors' completion support is that the tests, whatever they are, should be comprehensive and produce a clear positive or negative result in a timely manner.

In addition to the technical tests that need to be passed to achieve project comple- **11.41** tion, the financing documents and the equity contribution agreement will include other conditions that must also be satisfied. These will vary from project to project, both as to type and as to scope, but are likely to include:

(1) the requirement that there are then no continuing Events of Default or Potential Events of Default;
(2) the delivery of a set of financial projections for the project prepared on a basis that reflects:
   (a) the actual capital costs incurred in connection with the project (and the mix of debt and equity contributions that have financed those costs); and
   (b) the actual operating capacity of the project as completed (rather than its design capacity, which may or may not have been achieved),

   and that demonstrates compliance with the agreed financial covenants;[22] and

(3) to the extent relevant, evidence that the project company has entered into marketing and transportation arrangements with respect to the production from the project (as well as transportation arrangements for fuel and raw materials) to the extent that these were not concluded at or before the time of financial close.

Post-completion support

Although it is unlikely that the sponsors of a project will have obligations to make **11.42** additional equity contributions once completion has occurred, it is normal for

---

[21] See Chapter 5 for a fuller discussion on how liquidated damages provisions work in this context.

[22] On occasion, there may be negotiations between the sponsors and the lenders as to whether the 'economic' assumptions made at financial close (particularly assumptions as to raw material prices and the price of the product of the project) should be updated for the purposes of the financial tests that must be met in order to achieve completion. The sponsors will maintain that the lenders should take risks of this nature because their due diligence should provide them with sufficient background data to enable them to structure mitigation arrangements that they regard as appropriate in the circumstances.

lenders to require them to seek the lenders' approval to a disposal of their equity interest after completion.

11.43 Shareholding retention covenants do not, of course, oblige the sponsors to do anything other than retain their shares. However, whilst this may be so, lenders can and do take considerable comfort from the sponsors' continued involvement in the project as mere investors. This is because the lenders, quite reasonably, can assume that the sponsors will monitor their investment and, where necessary, take steps to protect it. Those steps may or may not include making further equity contributions, but given that the sponsors (or at least one of them) will have a degree of industry expertise or political connections that are likely to be of benefit to the project company (both in terms of seeing problems that might arise in the future and dealing with problems that may have arisen), there is value in the retention of shares covenants. This reduces over time as the project company develops its own expertise and political connections and its own trading and operating record, which is why the share retention covenants are often (but not invariably) written so that in time they fall away entirely.

11.44 As with the extent of the completion support that the lenders may require from the sponsors, the structure and duration of the 'lock-in' arrangements to which the lenders will wish to subject the sponsors will vary from project to project. It may be, for example, that provision is made for a step-down mechanism whereby the required minimum holding reduces over time or as and when the project achieves further milestones or satisfies more stringent financial ratio tests. However, it is unlikely the sponsors will have unfettered rights to sell their interests in the project until after somewhere between three and five years following completion, and even then the lenders may specify criteria that potential new investors must satisfy before a sponsor is entitled to dispose of its investment. These criteria often include positive requirements such as having appropriate financial standing and technical credentials, but may also include negative requirements such as not being under the direct or indirect control of the public sector entities that control or have interests in the project.

11.45 One of the principal types of post-completion support that sponsors provide in relation to many projects will be the supply of the project's raw materials or fuel or the purchase of the project's output. Indeed, the *raison d'être* of many projects is to enable a sponsor to sell its products to the project company for some sort of specialized downstream processing or refinement (or to create a captive supplier of a particular product or service that the sponsor requires for purposes connected with one of its own facilities). Where this is the case, of course, the viability of the project (and so the financial health of the project company) is heavily dependent on the continued need of the sponsor to supply the relevant raw materials or fuel (or to purchase the relevant products or services).

11.46 The extent of a project's dependence on the business that the project company will conduct with the sponsors will dictate both the level of interest that the lenders will have in ensuring that the relevant supply or off-take agreements remain in place and also the strength of any minimum supply or off-take obligations that the sponsors will need to assume thereunder. The more difficult it would be for the project company to set up an alternative supply of raw materials or fuel (or an alternative arrangement for the sale of its products or services) on terms comparable to those offered by the sponsor, the more likely it will be that the lenders will insist on the supply, off-take or throughput contracts with the sponsors (a) remaining in place for as long as the project loans remain outstanding and (b) containing 'supply-or-pay' or 'take-or-pay' obligations discussed in Chapter 5.

Security Arrangements

Introduction

The contractual arrangements that deal with the creation of security for different **11.47** project financing transactions are more varied than most other elements of the documentation for different transactions for the simple reason that how security is taken varies from jurisdiction to jurisdiction. There are often similarities (and indeed sometimes striking similarities) between the approaches to the creation of security interests that need to be followed in different jurisdictions. However, even where the principles that apply to the creation and perfection of security interests in different countries are similar (because both countries are 'common law jurisdictions' or 'civil law jurisdictions'), it cannot be assumed that a security arrangement that works in one of the countries will also work in the other.

It is not just the fact that the project being financed is located in a particular 'foreign' **11.48** jurisdiction (which to the English lawyer means anywhere outside England and Wales, including in particular jurisdictions such as Scotland and Northern Ireland). Relevant jurisdictions when it comes to taking security can include the countries in which the sponsors (and the SPVs that they may have established for the purpose of holding their interests in the particular project), the Offtakers, Insurers and EPC and O&M Contractors are incorporated and in which the project company's bank accounts are maintained. When this multiplicity of jurisdictions is coupled with the interaction of different legal systems and conflicts of laws principles, issues relating to security and the parties that are granting it can get particularly complicated from the legal perspective.

Chapter 12 provides an overview of the creation of security interests in civil law **11.49** jurisdictions which will be of particular interest to lawyers with a common law background and who are generally unfamiliar with civil law principles. This chapter proceeds on the assumption that the reader is either familiar with the English law terminology applicable to the creation of security interests or has access to materials that provide more than sufficient general and specific guidance on the subject.

11.50 Despite the fact that the title of the chapter suggests otherwise, this section does not seek to focus on the documents that will constitute the security under discussion. Nor does it seek to provide an exposition of the types of security that might be included in a typical all-singing, all-dancing debenture granted in a domestic English financing, a definitive explanation of the differences between fixed and floating charges, details of the ins and outs of preferences and transactions at an undervalue, or the distinction between legal and equitable charges and assignments. There are more than enough publications that do all these things and more.

A digression

11.51 Notwithstanding what is said in the preceding paragraph, it is perhaps useful to make a brief mention here of one particularly useful provision that is (and should always be) included in security documents governed by English law. The clause in question is the lowly further assurances clause,[23] a straightforward provision the purpose of which is clear from its terms: it simply obliges the person granting the security to do everything that needs to be done to carry out the basic intent of the security document. It is not a clause that excites many people. It is not a clause that is often negotiated with much in the way of vigour (by any of the parties to the security document or even their lawyers). It is, however, a clause that can create problems for the unwary.

11.52 The pitfall associated with the further assurance clause is more strictly a problem associated with another provision that should also be included in security documents governed by English law, the power of attorney clause, but the two are inextricably linked because it is the power of attorney clause that ensures the further assurance clause is as effective as it can possibly be in all circumstances.

11.53 The power of attorney clause in a security document authorizes the person in whose favour the security is granted to execute any instrument or document which the security provider is obliged, but fails, to execute. The beauty of such a power of attorney clause is that if the power is expressed to be irrevocable and is given to secure a proprietary interest of the donee or an obligation owed to the donee, then (so long as the donee has that interest or that obligation remains undischarged) it will indeed be irrevocable by the donor and will not be revoked by the donor's winding up or dissolution.[24] The sting in the tail in relation to a power of attorney

---

[23] A typical further assurance clause in a security agreement would read something like: 'The Company shall, at its own expense, promptly execute all such deeds and other documents and otherwise do all such things as the security agent may reasonably require: (a) for the purpose of enabling the security agent to exercise its rights, powers and remedies hereunder, to create, perfect or protect the security hereby intended to be created and to vest title to the Charged Property or any part thereof in the security agent or its nominee(s); and (b) to confer on the security agent security over any property and assets of a Chargor located in any jurisdiction outside England and Wales equivalent or similar to the security intended to be conferred by or pursuant to this Deed.'

[24] Section 4(1) of the Powers of Attorney Act 1971.

is that for a power of attorney to be valid the instrument pursuant to which it is created must be executed as a deed.[25]

Other secured parties

Contractors, off-takers, major suppliers (such as a fuel supplier), and other project **11.54** participants (including in some cases the sponsors and their affiliates as providers of mezzanine debt or even junior subordinated debt) may also require that the project company's liabilities to them be secured or that they be given rights to assume responsibility for the operation of the project in specified circumstances. Although ultimately there is no reason why requirements of this nature should not be accommodated, they can only be accommodated if the relevant participants enter into intercreditor arrangements with the senior lenders which identify the circumstances in which the different security interests and other rights held by the various interested parties can be enforced. Such intercreditor arrangements will obviously add another layer of complexity to the financing documentation (and a particularly complicated and contentious layer at that), but should not cause insurmountable problems.

The lenders' approach to security

The lenders to a project almost always insist on being granted a security package for **11.55** their loans which is as comprehensive as possible, yet it is surprisingly unusual for them to get to the point where they enforce their security. Moreover, whilst taking and perfecting security over virtually any type of asset (be it tangible or intangible, moveable or immovable, current or fixed, real or personal, present or future, or of some other type) is straightforward, inexpensive, and effective in jurisdictions with a well-developed legal system with experience of catering for complex and innovative financial and commercial transactions, it is often the case that the laws of the jurisdiction in which projects are located are such that, at least in certain respects or as regards certain assets, the security package is of doubtful or limited efficacy or difficult or expensive to enforce.

It is important, however, not to conclude from this that security is of little real **11.56** value from the lenders' perspective, particularly in relation to projects in jurisdictions where the accepted view is that the security being granted probably does not work.

Ordinarily, the security for a project financing will comprise: **11.57**

(1) security created by the sponsors over their interests in the project company; and
(2) security created by the project company over all its assets.

---

[25] Section 1(1) of the Powers of Attorney Act 1971.

11.58 We consider a number of points in relation to these two basic categories in paragraphs 11.66–11.69 and 11.70–11.104 below, but before doing that it is worth first answering the following question.

Why take security?

11.59 Although stating the obvious, it is perhaps worth emphasizing that taking security does not provide a creditor with the assurance that the claim thereby secured will be discharged in full; it merely provides him with the assurance that his claim will be paid to the extent of the value of the assets over which the security has been granted (and then only after the payment of all costs he may incur in the enforcement of that security).

11.60 From a legal perspective, the fact that the lenders' claims against the project company are secured means that, when the security becomes 'enforceable' in accordance with its terms (as to which see paragraph 11.62 below), the lenders will be entitled to exercise their rights under the security documents, their ultimate right being to take control of the assets over which the security has been granted and sell them, applying the net proceeds resulting from the sale in the full payment of their claims before any part of such proceeds are available for satisfying the claims of any of the project company's other creditors. In rather more commercial terms, the grant of security for the loans made to finance a project will assure the lenders that, when it matters most (which is to say when the project company is the subject of an insolvency proceeding), their claims are senior to the claims of the project company's unsecured creditors as well as to the claims of its shareholders.

11.61 However, the fact that security gives the project lenders a preferred standing in an insolvency of the project company is not itself the driver for taking security. The real driver is the fact that their security will give the senior lenders the right to control any workout or restructuring that may be needed to survive any difficulties the project has encountered.[26]

11.62 As we have seen in Chapter 7, credit agreements include all manner of provisions designed, essentially, to ensure the success of the project and to enable the lenders to monitor the financial and commercial health of the project so that they have early warnings of problems that could result in their loans not being repaid in accordance with their original amortization schedules. Why then do we need security as well? The answer really lies in the distinction between what is meant by

---

[26] This is perhaps an overly simplistic statement because it suggests that the claims of other parties can be ignored in a restructuring, which is not the case. It is likely that at least some of the claims of the unsecured creditors to a project will need to be paid in full in order to make a restructuring a success. The most obvious claims that fall into this category are the claims of creditors that supply goods or services to the project which it will be difficult (or more expensive) to source from alternative suppliers.

the enforceability of security, on the one hand, and the enforceability of a contract, on the other. The distinction is important because saying security is 'enforceable' in accordance with the terms of the security document pursuant to which it is constituted is fundamentally different to saying that a contract is enforceable in accordance with its terms:

(1) Security is said to be 'enforceable' if (but only if) (a) a particular state of affairs has arisen and (b) the terms of the relevant security document (or general law[27]) provide that the existence of that state of affairs gives the holder of the security the right to exercise (whether or not under judicial or other official supervision) rights in relation to the property over which he holds security. Where security is enforceable, the rights of the holder of the security will override the rights that the owner of that property may have in relation thereto (subject to the owner's right to redeem his property by discharging the liabilities thereby secured).

(2) A contract, on the other hand, will (assuming the criteria necessary to create a binding contract have been satisfied) be 'enforceable' from the moment it is concluded. (Indeed, if an arrangement that purports to be a contract is for some reason not 'enforceable', it is not properly called a contract at all.) It is thus more accurate to say that a contract is 'effective' rather than 'enforceable'.[28]

Thus, whilst on its own the credit agreement provides the lenders with the right to demand repayment of their loans (against a back-drop which invariably includes a right as a matter of general law to institute insolvency proceedings if the demand is not met), in the final analysis,[29] the security documents will provide that if the project company fails to perform its obligations and the security becomes enforceable, the lenders will be entitled to seize the project assets to protect their own interests despite the protestations of the project company. Security can therefore be said to be the mechanism that provides the lenders with the most effective sanction underpinning the basic proposition that the rights of lenders in relation to the project should always be 'senior' to the rights of the project company's shareholders (and of the project company's other creditors). **11.63**

Notwithstanding that it is the antithesis of security (and as such seems out of place in a chapter dealing with security), it is worth observing here that a negative pledge from a project company (which is to say an undertaking that it will not grant **11.64**

---

[27] If a company that has granted security enters a formal insolvency proceeding, it is likely that the creditor will be entitled to enforce his security even if the security document does not specifically so provide.

[28] See also para. 11.127 below.

[29] This is something of an oversimplification because as well as being subject to the debtor's right to redeem his property mentioned in para. 11.62(1) above, a creditor's rights to enforce security may also be subject to constraints imposed by insolvency legislation (which, of course, differ from jurisdiction to jurisdiction).

security over its assets in favour of any other creditors) should not be seen as a substitute for security. A negative pledge in a credit agreement does not, of course, constitute security in favour of the lenders. More to the point, however, it does not prevent the project company from creating security in favour of others. Although negative pledges without security have their place (in credit agreements and bond issues for so-called 'investment grade' borrowers who will (rightly) assume that a breach of the negative pledge is likely to be regarded by lenders as a major breach of trust), they do not make sense in a project financing where their breach could ultimately leave the lenders with nothing more than a valid (but worthless) claim against a shell company that has been lawfully stripped of its assets and revenues by the actions of its secured lenders. The taking of security by the lenders minimizes the risk to the lenders that flow from the breach of a negative pledge and so serves an important defensive purpose that cannot be served by a negative pledge alone. The taking of security by the lenders also makes it more difficult for other creditors who may have overdue claims against the project company to satisfy their claims by seizing the project company's assets, though of course in most jurisdictions it is usually open to creditors with unsatisfied claims to initiate proceedings for insolvency as a means of ensuring that their claims are met (or at least discussed on a sensible basis).

11.65 Security should therefore always be treated as being of critical importance to the lenders' interests in the context of project financing. However, there will always be a need to balance the lenders' preference for obtaining the strongest security possible, on the one hand, with the security that it is practicable to give them in the particular circumstances, on the other. Considerations that might be relevant in relation to this particular debate include, for example:

(1) *The cost of providing the security*: Where mortgage registration fees or stamp duties on a particular security document are linked to the amount of the debt secured by the mortgage, the cost of registering or paying the stamp duty may be so high that to incur the cost would increase the capital cost to the point where the project becomes uneconomic.[30] However, even where the extent of the relevant fees appears to be prohibitive, there can be a logical reason for them to be incurred. Where, for example, the relevant Offtaker is a public sector entity in a particular country, the government of the country might prefer the Offtaker to pay a slightly higher unit price for the whatever the project

---

[30] A registration fee of $3.50 per $100 is a significant item in the context of a transaction where the fee is calculated by reference to a capital sum of $1,000,000 (the fee being $35,000). Where the capital sum is increased to $1,000,000,000 (which is by no means unheard of) the fee jumps to $35,000,000, which is not the sort of sum that anyone would willingly pay if it could be avoided by the simple expedient of not giving the lenders a mortgage to secure the whole debt. A pragmatic lender is likely to regard a suitably enhanced front end fee or interest rate on his loan (perhaps coupled with the right to insist on the grant of the mortgage in the future in certain circumstances) as an acceptable substitute for a mortgage in these circumstances.

produces over the life of the Offtake contract project in return for the one-off capital payment that will be paid to the authority responsible for collection of the applicable registration fee (probably at the time of financial close).

(2) *The practicality of providing the security*: It may be that security can only be taken over an asset by taking possession of the asset. Even if possession can be achieved by taking control of documents of title rather than the assets themselves, a cost benefit analysis of taking security over (say) stockpiles of oil or coal is likely to lead to the conclusion that the security is better not taken at all, perhaps as long as there are some controls imposed on the level of the stockpiles.

(3) *Contractual limitations that might be relevant to the creation of security interests in favour of lenders*: Although the terms of the financing agreements to which most commercial sponsors are party will probably not restrict the creation of security by a project company in which they have a shareholding interest (or even in their shares in that company), it may be that restrictions imposed on the government in a particular country (notably restrictions such as the World Bank negative pledge) could mean that a government-owned sponsor would need special dispensation before a project company in which it held a significant number of shares could encumber its assets.

Security over the sponsors' interests

Much of what has been said in the preceding section has been said from the perspective of a lender taking security over the project company's assets. This is the natural perspective in relation to the taking of security because (a) the project company is the borrower of the moneys that the lenders have advanced, (b) the project company's assets actually constitute the project, and (c) the project company's revenues will provide the cashflows needed to repay the loans that the lenders have made. This being so, there is clearly a case for restricting the security package for a project financing to the security that the project company is able to create over its own assets and revenues. However, in most cases, the lenders will seek and receive security over the sponsors' shares in and loans to the project company in addition to the security granted by the project company. There will always be three main reasons for this: **11.66**

(1) As discussed in paragraph 11.42 above, the lenders will wish to see the sponsors maintain their equity interest in the project. The creation of a security interest in those interests protects the lenders against the risk that a sponsor concludes that the commercial advantages he might gain by selling his interest in breach of his covenant to retain them outweigh the commercial disadvantages (being his liability in damages to the lenders for breach of his covenant) of the breach.[31]

---

[31] Although a purchaser is unlikely to be particularly keen on buying the shares in circumstances where he knows that the sale is being made in breach of the terms of a contract, he might be prepared to buy them despite the breach if the price is right and he is given a suitable indemnity by the seller.

(2) If the project encounters problems and the lenders find that they have to enforce their security, then having the ability to take control of the project company's shares gives the lenders the ability to take control of the management of the project company (because as shareholders they will be entitled to appoint the project company's board of directors) and so leaves them with greater flexibility in relation to any work-out arrangements that might become necessary.

(3) Again where the lenders find themselves in a position where they have to enforce their security, a sale of the project company's shares is the best way to ensure that the purchaser becomes entitled (albeit only indirectly) to all the project company's rights and interests. More specifically, a sale of the shares in the project company may facilitate the transfer of rights and interests which are not transferable as a matter of law (as is often the case with operating licences and other governmental approvals) or which may only be transferred with the consent of a third party (which may or may not be readily forthcoming, even where the third party has agreed that its consent 'will not be unreasonably withheld or delayed').[32] A sale of shares is also almost invariably quicker, simpler and cheaper than a direct sale of the project company's assets.

11.67 To the extent that a shareholder has agreed to provide financial support to the project by way of a guarantee of the project company's indebtedness to the lenders, there will be a fourth reason for taking security over the shareholders' interests in the project company, and that is that by doing so the lenders' claims under the guarantee will be secured claims in any insolvency of the guarantor.

11.68 It is impossible to even attempt to produce a set of rules that need to be followed with respect to the creation of security over the shareholders' interest in a project company. That said, there are a number of things that should be considered in most, if not all, cases (but always with advice from counsel in all relevant jurisdictions):

(1) What law should govern the applicable security document? It is usually the law of the jurisdiction in which the project company is incorporated because that is usually the *lex situs* of the shares, although the law in some jurisdictions will give effect to a security document expressed to be governed by a foreign law.[33]

He will not, however, be prepared to do so where the shares are the subject of security in favour of the lenders.

[32] It should be noted, however, that a sale of the project company's shares may be indirectly restricted by the terms of 'Change of Control' provisions in contracts to which it is a party or in the licences and governmental authorisations that it needs in order to operate.

[33] Security documents that create charges over the shares of companies incorporated in a number of Commonwealth countries are often expressed to be governed by English law on the advice of counsel in those countries. This is counter-intuitive because an English court considering such a security document would look to the *lex situs* of the shares to determine the effect of the charge. Arguably, it would be better not to have an express choice of law at all because its absence simplifies

(2) What is the effect of the security document as regards the voting rights that attach to the shares? If it operates to transfer title to the shares (as would be the case, for example, where shares in an English company are the subject of a legal mortgage, but not where the mortgage is equitable and not where the shares are only subject to a charge), the voting rights will likewise be transferred. As a result, with a legal mortgage it is necessary to oblige the lenders to vote as directed by the sponsors (at least unless an Event of Default has occurred). It is perhaps worth commenting here that there is often much discussion between lenders and sponsors as to the point at which the lenders rather than the sponsors should control the voting rights in relation to the shares. Although there is no right or wrong on the point, it seems reasonable to provide that votes should be exercisable (a) by the sponsors until the occurrence of an Event of Default, (b) by the sponsors subject to the lenders' approval thereafter unless the security has become enforceable, and (c) by the lenders thereafter.

(3) What is the effect of the security document in relation to future dividends that might be paid on the shares? Again, if the security document transfers title to the shares it will necessarily operate to transfer the dividend rights associated with them, with the result that the lenders should be required to turn over any dividends they may receive to the sponsors.[34]

(4) What should the security document be called?[35] In many jurisdictions security over shares is created by means of pledge, and for some reason it is this terminology that is most widely used (and understood) to refer to the charging instrument that creates security over shares whatever the applicable governing law. This notwithstanding as a matter of English law it is technically incorrect to describe shares as being 'pledged' pursuant to 'pledge' agreements because a pledge involves the bailment of a chattel as security (and a share in a company—even a bearer share—is not a chattel).

(5) Will liabilities attributable to the shares be transferred to the lenders when the security is created (thereby, for example, making the lenders liable to pay the balance of the moneys due in respect of any partially paid shares)? Ordinarily one would expect that liabilities attaching to shares would only be transferred where legal title to the shares is transferred upon creation of a security interest. Whilst this may be so, the analysis needs to go further. It is quite possible, for example, that there will be provisions in the project company's constitutive

---

the analysis. New York law is also often expressed as the governing law of security packages relating to Latin American projects which often leads to expensive and cumbersome perfection requirements.

[34] The terms of the credit agreement or common terms agreement with the project company will invariably specify the conditions that must be satisfied before the project company is permitted to pay dividends. If the specified conditions have been satisfied, dividends paid to the lenders because they are the legal owners of the shares would therefore always be required to be paid over to the sponsors.

[35] This question is not a particularly important one because it will be the operative provisions in the document, rather than its title, that will determine its effect.

documents that allow it to refuse to recognize a transfer of a partially paid share (whether or not the project company has made a call on the share). Even if this is not the case, a sale of the shares upon an enforcement of the security would necessarily involve a transfer of the liability for future calls, which will inevitably make the shares less attractive to potential purchasers. (The answer of course is for the lenders to insist that the shares be fully paid before they take security.)

(6) Should the shareholder deliver the originals of his share certificates to the lenders at the time the security is created? If the project company is incorporated in a jurisdiction in which share certificates evidence title to the relevant shares, counsel in that jurisdiction will almost certainly advise that the share certificates should be entrusted to the lenders (or a custodian acting on their behalf) as part of the process of perfecting the lenders' security interest. Even in jurisdictions (such as England) where share certificates are not evidence of title, it is likely that (unless title to the shares has been transferred to the lenders or someone acting on their behalf) counsel will make this recommendation, but in these jurisdictions it will not be to perfect the lenders' security interest so much as to make it more difficult (but not impossible) for the shareholder to deal with his shares in breach of his covenants in the finance documents.

(7) Should the shareholder provide the lenders with share transfer forms executed in blank when the security is created? Charges and equitable mortgages of shares governed by English law ordinarily include provisions that entitle the chargee or mortgagee to 'upgrade' his security interest in the relevant shares by converting it into a legal mortgage. Coupled with a power of attorney in his favour, this will give him the necessary authority to do whatever needs to be done to register the shares in his own name or the name of his nominee. Where this is the case, blank stock transfer forms do not need to be delivered at the time the security is created.

11.69 Even where a security document pursuant to which a sponsor creates security over its shares in the project company constitutes security over any dividends and voting rights attributable to them, it will not (without more) create security over the sponsor's interest in any shareholder loans that may be outstanding from time to time. Shareholder loans are an integral part of the sponsor's commercial interest in the project and as such (and for the same reasons that the shares are made the subject of security in favour of the lenders) should be charged in favour of the lenders pursuant to appropriate security documentation.

Security over the project company's assets

11.70 This section considers the types of security that a project company will typically grant over its assets to secure the loans from the senior lenders. Although the actual security that will be granted in any given case will depend on the nature of the particular project and the assets concerned (from an English law perspective the *lex situs* of a tangible asset being of fundamental importance in the determination of the efficacy of any security over the asset), most project financings will involve security over:

(1) the principal physical assets that constitute the project (i.e. the project site and the buildings that house the items of plant and equipment that produce whatever the project produces);

(2) stockpiles of raw materials and fuel, spare parts, and other items of inventory such as unsold production from the project;

(3) the project company's rights under the contracts to which it is a party (notably the contract pursuant to which the project is being constructed, any supply contracts for fuel and raw materials, any off-take contracts pursuant to which the project's output is sold, operation and maintenance contracts, and marketing agreements) as well as under any applicable operating licences and permits and the like (to the extent applicable law permits them to be made the subject of security);

(4) the project company's intellectual property rights (in particular any licences that it may have been granted for the purpose of using particular manufacturing processes in the project);

(5) cash from time to time held by the project company in its bank accounts, as well as cash equivalent investments that the lenders may have agreed it may hold in order to generate a better return than it would earn on simple cash deposits; and

(6) any claims the project company may have under the policies of insurance that it maintains in connection with the project.

English law (like the law of many other jurisdictions, both civil and common law **11.71** based) looks to the *lex situs* of tangible assets in order to determine how (as a legal matter) security over the asset should be created (because it is the *lex situs* that determines the applicable rules as to title to the asset and its transfer). However:

> The choice of law rules which govern the assignment or transfer of intangible property are not easy to state with certainty . . . It is unrealistic for a single choice of law rule to govern all issues relating to the assignment of all such property.[36]

This being so, it is therefore not possible to do more than make general observations in relation to the sort of security interests that are created over the various types of asset described in paragraph 11.70 above. However, it is worth observing that even in cases where a project is located in a jurisdiction having a legal system which is less sophisticated than that of, say, England or some other Western European country, many of the project company's assets will not in fact be located in, or otherwise subject to the laws of, the jurisdiction in which the project itself is situated. As a result, even though some of the security that the lenders may require might be of

---

[36] *Dicey, Morris & Collins The Conflict of Laws* (14th edn) para. 24-051.

limited or doubtful efficacy, much of the security package will be as good as it would be if the project was located in a jurisdiction with a more developed legal system. Thus with an oil refinery project in Yemen, any security over the refinery and the site on which it is located may well not be as effective as comparable security over a refinery in Germany, but security over the project company's offshore bank accounts and offshore insurances, as well as the security over its rights under sales and other contracts with parties outside Yemen, will not be limited by the fact that the project is in Yemen.

11.72 The primary question to be answered in relation to the creation of security over a tangible asset is therefore: 'Where is the asset that is to be made the subject of the security located?' The same question may also become relevant in relation to the creation of security over an intangible asset, but in that context the answer is more complicated because its 'location' will be derived from legal rules and the application of these rules often result in the asset being 'located' in more than one place at the same time.

11.73 Deciding on the location of land and buildings is straightforward. Deciding on the location of items of moveable property such as trucks, trains, and aircraft is also straightforward but the fact that such items of property can be in one jurisdiction one minute and in another jurisdiction moments later can have surprising consequences, as is apparent from the recent decision of the High Court (Beatson J) in *Blue Sky One Limited v Mahan Air*,[37] in which the court considered the validity of a mortgage expressed to be governed by English law over an aircraft that was registered in England. At the time the mortgage was created, the aircraft was physically located in the Netherlands. Had the aircraft been in England at the time the mortgage was created, it would have been valid. However, because the *lex situs* of the aircraft at the time of creation of the mortgage was the Netherlands, the validity of the mortgage was (as a matter of English law) a question that fell to be determined as a matter of Dutch law. Under domestic Dutch law the mortgage was invalid. However, under Dutch conflicts of laws rules the mortgage would have been treated as valid if it was valid under the law of the jurisdiction in which the aircraft was registered (i.e. England). The English court's conclusion? The mortgage was invalid because in applying Dutch law to determine the issue of the validity of the mortgage the English courts should apply only Dutch domestic law without reference to its conflicts of law rules (and in particular taking no account of the principle of *renvoi* whereby Dutch law would determine an issue by reference to some other system of law). (Whether this decision, which was not welcomed by aircraft financiers, will be overturned on appeal remains to be seen.)

---

[37] [2010] EWHC 631 (Comm).

Land and buildings/plant and equipment

Whatever security can or cannot be taken over the site on which the project is **11.74** located and the buildings, plant, and machinery on the site will be a matter of the law of the country in which the project is located. Although most of the more general questions that it is important to consider in this context are reasonably obvious (and will be asked as part of the general due diligence exercise in relation to the whole project), it is perhaps worth noting a few of them here:

(1) Does the security over the site automatically include the buildings and the plant and equipment that will be built on site or moved to the site having been built elsewhere? In some jurisdictions[38] it is not possible to take security on an asset until the asset exists. In such cases, the financing arrangements may be structured so that the lenders' security is only put in place at the time of Project Completion (perhaps on the basis that until then the loans to the project company will be guaranteed by the sponsors).[39]

(2) Does the security include all rights of access and easements that the project will need in order to operate? If the security is ever to be enforced, a potential purchaser of the project would be more than a little troubled if in buying the site he was not also buying all rights that will enable him to cross adjoining properties in order to get all his fuel, power, and raw materials to the plant (and to remove all his production and waste materials from it).

(3) Does the project company own the site outright or does it simply have an entitlement to occupy it under a lease, and if the latter:

    (a) In what circumstances does the lessor have the right to terminate the lease?

    (b) Are the lessee's rights under the lease freely transferable?

    (c) Is the lease term longer (by some margin) than the economic life of the plant that is being built on the site?

    (d) Will the plant need to be decommissioned and dismantled when the lease term comes to an end so that the site can be returned in the state it was in when the lease was granted?

(4) Does the security over the site include (for example) stockpiles of fuel and raw materials or of the output from the plant? If not, can these items of inventory be made the subject of a security interest? The English answer to the creation of security over stockpiles and inventory is the floating charge, a somewhat mysterious (and some would say remarkable) creature of English common law which allows a creditor to be granted security over a class of assets owned by a company

---

[38] For example, Norway and Brazil.

[39] It may be that security could be taken over moveable assets—such as earth-moving and transportation equipment used in a mining project—in the jurisdiction in which that equipment is manufactured. The question will then become one of the efficacy of the security in the jurisdiction in which the project is located. However, even if such security is effective in the local jurisdiction, this sort of solution is only likely to be practicable where the particular assets have a relatively high unit value.

from time to time on terms which, until the moment at which the charge 'crystallizes' (and thereby becomes a fixed charge on such of the assets within the relevant class as are then owned by the company), allow the project company to sell the assets free and clear of the creditor's interest without the need for the consent of, or even the giving of notice to, the creditor. However, despite its flexibility, a floating charge governed by English law will still look to the *lex situs* of the relevant assets to determine whether the charge is effective.[40]

Contract rights

11.75 The security package for any project financing will invariably include assignments by the project company of the benefit of all the contracts which it has entered into in connection with the project. Indeed, until the project is complete and the project company is the proud owner of a brand new, state of the art plant for doing whatever the project does, the project company will in reality own nothing much else over which it can grant security for the debt that it is incurring.

11.76 The actual assignment of the relevant contract rights is unlikely to be anything other than straightforward, although it is worth bearing in mind that rights under some contracts may not be assignable as a matter of law.[41] It is also worth bearing in

---

[40] Security documents in relation to project financings in jurisdictions where the effectiveness of the security agreements governed by local law is uncertain sometimes include a charging instrument governed by English law pursuant to which, in addition to granting fixed security interests over its offshore assets, the chargor grants a floating charge over all its other assets, wherever situated (and therefore including its assets in its home jurisdiction). Given the fact that, at least as regards tangible assets, English law looks to the *lex situs* of the assets to decide whether the security is effective, it is difficult to see how this approach can actually achieve anything more than a security agreement governed by the law of the local jurisdiction.

[41] Government licences and permits required for the operation of a project are often incapable of assignment except with the approval of the authority that granted the relevant licence; sometimes the applicable enabling legislation will not even allow assignments with an approval. Whilst this may appear to be a potential problem that can arise in the course of the process of producing the financing documents for the project, these sorts of assignability issues should come to light in the course of the initial due diligence exercise for the project, with the result that appropriate mitigation provisions will be built into the contractual structure in some way. The point is noted here more for the sake of completeness. As a general rule the benefit of a contract governed by English law will be assignable as long as 'it can make no difference to the person on whom the obligation lies to which of two persons he is to discharge it'. (*Tolhurst v Associated Portland Cement Manufacturers Ltd* [1902] 2 KB 660 at 668; affirmed [1903] AC 414). The question is an objective one, but the court would not, for example, distinguish between persons on the basis that they would probably have differing attitudes towards defaulting debtors (*Fitzroy v Cave* [1905] 2 KB 264). Contractual rights that involve personal qualifications or skills of the creditor are not assignable, so even though an author can assign his right to be paid royalties under a publishing contract, neither the publisher nor the author may assign his rights to the other's performance under the contract (*Stevens v Benning* (1855) 6 De GM & G 223; *Hole v Bradbury* (1879) 12 Ch D 886; *Griffiths v Tower Publishing Co* [1897] 1 Ch 21; *Don King Productions Inc. v Warren* [2000] Ch 291).

It is assumed that where a particular project agreement includes restrictions on the assignment by the project company of its rights thereunder the restrictions will make a specific exception for the assignment of the agreement to the security agent in connection with the financing arrangements. Restrictions on onward assignments by the security agent should it have to enforce its rights under

mind whilst the assignment itself might be straightforward enough, complications inevitably arise when the time comes to negotiate the terms of the related direct agreements (as to which see paragraphs 11.105–11.114 below).

As with tangible property, an important preliminary question that will need to be **11.77** considered in the context of creating security over contractual rights is the governing law that should be chosen to govern the contract pursuant to which the assignment is effected (the 'assignment agreement').

More specifically, does the governing law chosen to govern the assignment agree- **11.78** ment need to be the same as the governing law of the contract being assigned (the 'assigned contract')? In relation to contracts signed on or after 17 December 2009, the answer to this question as a matter of English law (and the law of the other states in the EU other than Denmark) is provided by Article 14 of Regulation 593/2008EC on the law applicable to contractual obligations (Rome I) and is surprisingly simple. The effect of Article 14 (coupled with the other provisions of the Regulation) is essentially[42] that:

(1) the parties' choice of the governing law of the assignment agreement will be effective; and
(2) the law so chosen need not be the same as the governing law of the assigned contract (because, under Article 14(2), whatever the governing law of the assignment agreement, the governing law of the assigned contract will 'determine its assignability, the relationship between the assignee and the debtor, the conditions under which the assignment . . . can be invoked against the debtor and whether the debtor's obligations have been discharged ').

Although on the basis of Article 14 of Rome I there is no reason not to use English **11.79** law as the governing law of the assignment agreement relating to contracts governed by (say) the laws of the Sultanate of Oman, in many (and probably most) cross-border financing transactions where some of the project documents are governed by the law of the jurisdiction in which the project is located ('local law')

---

the relevant security document will be dealt with in the relevant direct agreement, as discussed in para. 11.112 below.

[42] There are exceptions to the general rule. Articles 3(3) and 3(4) of Article 3 of Rome I provide: '3.   Where all other elements relevant to the situation at the time of the choice are located in a country other than the country whose law has been chosen, the choice of the parties shall not prejudice the application of provisions of the law of that other country which cannot be derogated from by agreement. 4. Where all other elements relevant to the situation at the time of the choice are located in one or more Member States, the parties' choice of applicable law other than that of a Member State shall not prejudice the application of provisions of Community law, where appropriate as implemented in the Member State of the forum, which cannot be derogated from by agreement.'

Article 9 of Rome I makes provision whereby Rome I can be overridden by 'mandatory overriding provisions' of (a) the law of the forum in which a dispute on a contract is being conducted and (b) of the country where the obligations arising out of a contract are to be or have been performed (insofar as those overriding provisions render performance of the contract unlawful), mandatory overriding provisions being essentially matters of public policy.

while others are governed by English law (or the law of some other jurisdiction), the practice has been (and continues to be) to use the governing law of the assigned contract as the governing law of the assignment agreement. Thus:

(1) the benefit of the project agreements governed by local law will be assigned pursuant to an 'onshore' security assignment (i.e. an assignment agreement governed by local law);

(2) the benefit of any project agreement governed by English law will be assigned pursuant to the main 'offshore' security document (which will be governed by English law); and

(3) the benefit of any project agreement governed by the law of some other jurisdiction will be assigned pursuant to an assignment agreement expressed to be governed by the law of that other jurisdiction.

11.80 There is one very good reason why this approach should continue to be adopted: if it ever becomes necessary to institute any legal proceedings in connection with the lenders' security interest in the relevant project agreements in the local law jurisdiction, having both the assignment agreement and the assigned contract governed by local law means that the proceedings should be simpler (and in consequence both quicker and cheaper) because there will be no need to complicate matters by reference to the conflicts of law rules that apply in that jurisdiction.

11.81 Generally speaking, from the moment at which a party to a contract assigns 'all its rights' under that contract to another, as between the assignee and the assignor the assignee will be entitled to exercise all those rights. In the same way, once a party to a contract has (a) assigned 'all its rights' thereunder and (b) given notice of such assignment to the relevant counterparty, as between the assignee, the counterparty, and the assignor, the assignee will be entitled to exercise those rights to the exclusion of the assignor. Two straightforward, but critical, points arise from this in the context of a security assignment:

(1) In order to ensure that the assignment by the project company to the security agent is effective as between all relevant parties, notice of the assignment will need to be given to the relevant counterparty.

(2) In almost every case it will be necessary to include provisions in the assignment agreement (and corresponding provisions in the notice of assignment) that allow the project company to continue to exercise some or all of its rights under the contract as if the assignment had not occurred (and so without reference to the security agent) until something happens (the 'something' invariably being linked in some way to the occurrence of an Event of Default)[43] which makes it appropriate to curtail the project company's authority.

---

[43] Whether the project company's rights should be terminated sooner rather than later will depend on the circumstances and the negotiations between the parties. From a practical perspective, however, using the concept of a 'Declared Default' to define the time at which the project company ceases to

The particular rights that the project company will be permitted to exercise as if the **11.82** assignment had not occurred will vary from project to project, though it would be more than a little surprising if a project company was permitted to amend (at least in a material way) or terminate any of the key project contracts without reference to the lenders. To some extent, the rights that the project company will be left free to exercise will also vary with the type of contract being assigned, primarily because some contracts require the project company to perform a more active monitoring role than others. An assignment agreement relating to an EPC Contract, for example, will need to give the project company extensive rights to continue to exercise the rights thereunder subject to a specific list of 'reserved discretions' (which the project company is not entitled to exercise without the consent of the security agent) because this ensures that the lenders only get involved where a particular decision could be expected to affect the security value of the contract. The flexibility that will be given to the project company in relation to an EPC Contract will not generally be mirrored in an assignment agreement relating to an Offtake Contract (except perhaps as it relates to purely operational matters such as shipping and delivery schedules), the general rule here being that most decisions affecting the Offtaker's performance thereunder will be decisions with which the lenders will wish to be involved.

Receivables, bank accounts, and permitted investments

Receivables

An assignment by the project company to the security agent of its rights under a **11.83** project agreement will necessarily include its rights to receive moneys paid under that agreement.[44] In the absence of an instruction to the contrary, therefore, once notice of the assignment has been given to the relevant counterparty, amounts payable by the counterparty thereunder will be required to be paid to the security agent. This is perfectly logical, not least because once an amount payable under a contract has been paid in accordance with the requirements of the contract, the security value of the contract is necessarily diminished by that amount: the fact that the security value of the contract is diminished is of no consequence if the arrangements are such that the security agent comes into possession of a cash fund (in the

---

be entitled to exercise any of the rights under the contract produces a sensible compromise between the interests of the lenders and the interests of the project company. There is no real need to change the *status quo* simply because an Event of Default has occurred (though it might be, for example, that whilst an Event of Default subsists the project company should be required to give a minimum period of notice to the security agent of its intention to exercise particular rights in order to give the security agent an opportunity to object to the action). On the other hand, leaving the project company free to continue without the imposition of some level of additional control by the lenders until the point at which the security becomes enforceable is in reality leaving it too late.

See also the discussion in para. 11.85 below.

[44] The discussion in para 11.78 above applies to receivables payable under a contract as it does to other rights under the contract.

form of the credit balance on its bank account) which replaces the receivable under the contract. However, whilst this may be logical because it preserves the lenders' security position, it does not produce a practical result because it means that the money is inaccessible to the project company except to the extent the security agent actually takes steps to transfer the money from its account to the project company's account.

11.84 In order to give the project company access to the funds paid under the project agreements that it will need for its day to day operations and at the same time preserve the lenders' security position in relation to the project revenues, the normal practice is for:

(1) the notices of assignment that are given to the counterparties to the various project agreements to stipulate that, notwithstanding the assignment thereof:

(a) unless the security agent otherwise directs, moneys of a revenue nature[45] payable to the project company thereunder should be paid by credit to a specified account in the name of the project company;[46] and

(b) moneys of a capital nature payable to the project company thereunder should be paid by credit to a specified account in the name of the security agent; and

(2) the account in the name of the project company referred to in sub-paragraph (1)(a) above to be charged in favour of the security agent as part of the general security package for the financing.[47]

11.85 In the same way that the project company will normally be expressly authorized to exercise its rights under an assigned project agreement until something happens that makes it appropriate to limit its authority in this respect,[48] the Security

---

[45] The notice of assignment should not, of course, simply refer to 'moneys of a revenue nature' or 'moneys of a capital nature'. It should specify which particular payment obligations fall into which category by reference to the particular clauses under which those obligations arise.

[46] The moneys could be paid into the account of the security agent who could then set up a standing instruction on the account requiring that all moneys paid into the account are automatically transferred to the project company (or give the project company signing authority on the account (exercisable as agent for the security agent)) and therefore the right to withdraw moneys therefrom without reference to the security agent. However, this sort of approach rather obscures what is actually happening and so has the potential disadvantage of leaving it open to interested parties (notably a liquidator of the project company) to argue that the project company has some sort of interest in the security agent's account (but without necessarily being effective to avoid the problems of control associated with *Spectrum Plus* (as to which see paras. 11.91–11.95 below)).

[47] The creation of security over the project company's bank accounts is complementary to the detailed account management provisions which will be included in the principal financing documentation in order to specify the bank accounts to which the project company's different sources of income must be credited and then to regulate the expenditure that may be funded with the moneys in the different accounts (an exercise which is primarily intended to simplify the process of monitoring the financial health of the project).

[48] See para. 11.81 above.

Document pursuant to which moneys payable to the project company are assigned will usually allow the security agent to direct the counterparty to make payments direct to the security agent at any time after the occurrence of an Event of Default (or perhaps a Declared Default). A point to note in this context is that it is preferable (from the perspective of both the lenders and the counterparty)[49] for the notice of assignment not to state that the security agent is only entitled to give contrary instructions regarding the payment of money if a default, Event of Default, or Declared Default has occurred or similar circumstance arisen. This is because to do so exposes the security agent to the risk that when it gives the contrary instructions the counterparty will want some evidence of the occurrence of the relevant event before it will make payments in accordance with the new directions for fear that if in fact the event has not occurred, it could be compelled to pay an amount to the project company that it had already (but wrongly) paid to the security agent.[50]

Bank accounts

A bank account is nothing more than a means of recording the extent of a bank's liability to its customer (in which case the account will be in credit and the customer will have an asset in an amount equal to the amount of the debt constituted by the credit balance) or the liability of a customer to its bank (in which case the account will be in debit and the bank will have an asset in an amount equal to the debt constituted by the amount of the debit balance). Creating a security interest over the project company's money in any of its bank accounts therefore involves creating a security interest in its claim against the bank with whom the account is maintained. This being so, Article 14 of Regulation 593/2008EC on the law applicable to contractual obligations (Rome I)[51] applies to the creation of security interests in relation to bank accounts as it does to other contractual claims. **11.86**

It is reasonable to assume that if the terms and conditions that apply to the relationship between a bank and its customer in relation to a bank account specify that their respective rights and obligations are governed by the law of a particular jurisdiction, the jurisdiction specified will be that in which the branch of the bank at which the **11.87**

---

[49] From the point of view of the project company, the position should be regarded as neutral. If the terms of its contract with the security agent stipulate that the security agent can only give a notice in certain circumstances but it gives the notice notwithstanding that those circumstances have not arisen, the project company has a claim for breach of contract against the security agent. There is no justification for the project company insisting on more than this, particularly as anything more could in practice be used by the counterparty to the contract in a way that could operate to the detriment of the lenders.

[50] There is also the risk that the security agent may be unwilling to write a letter to the counterparty stating that an Event of Default has occurred without suitable indemnification from the lenders. Even if the indemnification is forthcoming, it will not be forthcoming very quickly, with the result that the relevant moneys will not necessarily be paid to the security agent in the circumstances in which, as a commercial matter, it has been agreed that the project company should not be receiving them.

[51] See para 11.78 above.

account is maintained is located.[52] It is probably also reasonable to assume that, if the terms and conditions that apply to the relationship between a bank and its customer in relation to a bank account do not specify that their respective rights and obligations are governed by the law of a particular jurisdiction, then under the law of the jurisdiction in which the branch of the bank at which the account is maintained is located (and the law of most other jurisdictions to the extent they may be relevant), the governing law applicable to those rights and obligations will be that of the jurisdiction in which the branch of the bank at which the account is maintained is located.[53]

11.88 It is likely that there will be bank accounts located both in the jurisdiction in which the project itself is located and, where the financing arrangements are governed by English law, in England. As a result, the bank accounts in England will certainly be charged pursuant to a security document governed by English law but (as was the case with contracts governed by the law of the jurisdiction in which the project is located)[54] the onshore bank accounts (which is to say those in the jurisdiction in which the project is located) will usually be charged pursuant to a security document governed by the law of that jurisdiction.

Problem areas

11.89 There are two principal issues in relation to the creation of security over bank accounts in England. The first of these (which is also an issue when it comes to creating security over receivables) is whether the charge is fixed or floating. The second is whether the charge falls within the ambit of the EU Directive on Financial Collateral Arrangements (Directive 2002/47/EC).

11.90 There is also a related issue which is not so much a question of the efficacy of security in relation to bank accounts as a question as to how best to deal with 'permitted investments' in a way that protects the lenders' security position and at the same time gives the project company (and indirectly the sponsors) a reasonable opportunity to earn a better return on funds that are surplus to the project's immediate cash needs than can be earned by maintaining them as simple cash deposits with the

---

[52] Certainly it would unusual if the terms and conditions were to specify that the laws of some other jurisdiction should regulate these rights and obligations.

[53] This would be the position throughout the EU other than Denmark on the basis of the rules in Article 4 of Regulation 593/2008EC on the law applicable to contractual obligations (Rome I). Article 4(2)–(4) provides:

(2) . . . the contract shall be governed by the law of the country where the party required to effect the characteristic performance of the contract has his habitual residence.

(3) Where it is clear from all the circumstances of the case that the contract is manifestly more closely connected with a country other than that indicated in paragraphs or 2, the law of that country shall apply.

(4) Where the law applicable cannot be determined pursuant to paragraphs 1 or 2, the contract shall be governed by the law of the country with which it is most closely connected.

[54] See the discussion in para. 11.79 above.

account bank for the project. Both the issue of whether a charge will be characterized as fixed or floating and the issue of whether the EU Directive on Financial Collateral Arrangements (Directive 2002/47/EC) will apply to such a charge are relevant in the context of charges on permitted investments.

Fixed or floating?

In his judgment in *National Westminster Bank plc v Spectrum Plus Ltd*,[55] Lord Scott of Foscote described the essential characteristic of a floating charge to be: **11.91**

> . . . the asset subject to the charge is not finally appropriated as a security for the payment of the debt until the occurrence of some future event. In the meantime the chargor is left free to use the charged asset and to remove it from the security.[56]

On the basis of this definition, any arrangement that allows a chargor to deal with its book debts or their proceeds[57] (or amounts equal thereto) will necessarily mean that a charge over those book debts is a floating charge. To create a fixed charge, the holder of the charge must actually (and actively) control the process of releasing funds to the chargor. **11.92**

The test is reasonably clear: are the arrangements so structured that the book debts (and their proceeds) are appropriated to the charge holder's security, or is the chargor permitted to deal with them and so use the proceeds as a source of cashflow (whether the permission be until further notice or the occurrence of an Event of Default or for a limited period of time)? In the former case, the charge will be fixed, whilst in the latter it will be it will be floating.[58] **11.93**

In practice, the extent of the rights that are normally retained by a project company in relation to its receivables and the credit balances on its bank accounts is such that it is difficult to see that a charge on these assets will be anything other than floating. **11.94**

---

[55] [2005] UKHL 41.

[56] At 111.

[57] This is the case both where amounts payable to the project company under a project agreement that has been assigned to the security agent are dealt with as described in para. 11.84 above and where the project company is permitted to withdraw moneys from a charged bank account as described in para. 11.85 above.

[58] The *Spectrum Plus* debenture purported to create a fixed charge over book (and other) debts and then restricted the chargor's ability to deal with those debts in the following terms: 'with reference to book and other debts hereby specifically charged [Spectrum] shall pay into [Spectrum's] account with the Bank all moneys which it may receive in respect of such debts and shall not, without the prior consent in writing of the Bank sell factor discount or otherwise charge or assign the same in favour of any person or purport to do so and [Spectrum] shall if called upon to do so by the bank from time to time execute legal assignments of such book debts and other debts to the Bank.' The book debts were paid into an overdrawn account with the bank, but Spectrum remained free to draw on the account until the overdraft limit was reached. The House of Lords concluded that Spectrum's continuing contractual right to draw out sums equivalent to amounts paid in to the account was 'wholly destructive' of the argument that there was a fixed charge over the uncollected proceeds of the book debts, and so held the charge was a floating charge.

11.95 Does it matter? There are disadvantages with a floating charge[59] but these really only present themselves in an insolvency. In the context of cross-border project financing transactions where financial problems suffered by the project are in almost every instance dealt with by means of some sort of consensual restructuring, the answer is that in truth it matters not whether a charge in favour of the lenders is fixed or floating.

Financial collateral

11.96 The EU Directive on Financial Collateral Arrangements (Directive 2002/47/EC) establishes a degree of harmonization in the method and legal effect of entering into financial collateral arrangements, its purpose being to remove obstacles to the use of 'financial collateral' and to minimize the formalities required to create or enforce security over it. The directive has been implemented in the UK by way of the Financial Collateral Arrangements (No 2) Regulations 2003 (SI 2003/3226) (the 'Financial Collateral Regulations'), which, among other things, seek to:

(1) remove almost all the formal requirements with respect to creation, validity, perfection (including registration), admissibility in evidence, and enforcement of financial collateral arrangements (the only formalities to be satisfied being, as discussed below, that the arrangements must be in writing and that there must be a transfer of possession or control of the financial collateral); and

(2) establish clear conflict of laws rules for the treatment of book-entry securities that are used as collateral.

11.97 There are thus distinct advantages afforded to the parties to a financial collateral arrangement that falls within this legislation, and in particular to those in whose favour security over the financial collateral is granted.

11.98 The Financial Collateral Regulations only apply to 'financial collateral', which is defined as 'cash or financial instruments', although this definition is to be extended to cover the taking of security over 'credit claims' (these being 'pecuniary claims arising out of an agreement whereby a credit institution . . . grants credit in the form of a loan').[60]

11.99 In order to fall within the scope of the Financial Collateral Regulations:

(1) the collateral must be in the possession or control of the collateral-taker;

---

[59] The most notable disadvantages are a longer 'hardening' period, the postponement of the claims of the holder to certain claims of employees and the costs of the relevant insolvency proceedings and the fact that a prescribed part of the proceeds realised on enforcement of the charge will be earmarked for the benefit of the company's unsecured creditors.

[60] The Financial Collateral Regulations are to be amended to implement EU Directive 2009/44/EC on settlement finality and financial collateral arrangements (which, among other things, amends the EU Directive on Financial Collateral Arrangements) by 30 December 2010.

(2) both the collateral-taker and the collateral-provider must be non-natural persons (which is to say that neither may be an individual);

(3) the arrangement must be evidenced in writing (rules which require that the collateral instrument be signed or that the arrangement be entered in a register being disapplied); and

(4) there must be a connection with the EU, whether through a choice of law provision or through the location of the asset or performance of a contractual obligation.

The fact that the Financial Collateral Regulations require the collateral to be in the **11.100** possession or control of the collateral taker means that assets the subject of a floating charge will be excluded from their scope unless it has crystallized (because the essence of a floating charge is that until then the chargor is free to deal with the assets thereby charged) and the collateral-taker has then taken appropriate steps to exercise control over the assets. This is so (and whether the charge is a floating charge by its express terms or virtue of being characterized as such as discussed in paragraphs 11.91–11.95 above) because notwithstanding the fact that Financial Collateral Regulations expressly include floating charges within the definition of security financial collateral arrangements, they do not elaborate on what constitutes possession or control of collateral beyond recognizing that substitutions or withdrawals of excess collateral will not of themselves prejudice the control of a collateral-taker.[61]

Permitted investments

Whilst it is ultimately the sponsors of a project that benefit most from good cash **11.101** management in relation to the project's cashflows (because there is obviously a direct correlation between their equity return and the profitability of the project company), the lenders are also interested in good cash management because it means that the financial tests of the project's performance provide a more accurate picture of underlying business of the project. Although funds standing to the credit of a project company's bank accounts can be expected to earn interest, with interest on term deposits and larger balances accruing at more favourable rates than on current account balances, it is unlikely that the rates of interest offered by a bank with whom the project company is obliged to maintain its bank accounts will be higher than those offered by other banks or other creditworthy institutions. This being so, it is likely that good cash management will make it appropriate to use funds standing to the credit of the project company's bank accounts in the making of investments that generate a higher return than can be obtained by simply leaving the cash in its

---

[61] In Chapter 3 of its consultation paper published in August 2010 on the implementation of EU Directive 2009/44/EC, HM Treasury discusses the possibility of modifying the Financial Collateral Regulations so that they extend to all floating charges, but recognises specifically that such a change raises concerns because it would operate to the disadvantage of unsecured creditors who would be unaware of the existence of floating charges over financial collateral (because such floating charges would not be registrable).

bank accounts. As a result, the finance documents will usually contain provisions that allow the project company to invest moneys it believes to be surplus to its immediate needs.

11.102   One of the risks in any project is the risk associated with the creditworthiness of the creditors and potential creditors of the project, including the banks through whom the project company's revenues flow and with whom its positive cash balances are maintained. As a result, it is normal for the financing documentation to stipulate that the project company is not permitted to open or maintain bank accounts with banks without a minimum specified credit rating. In the same way, the definition of the investments in which the project company is permitted to invest will look to (among other things[62]) the creditworthiness of the relevant obligor.

11.103   In addition to the question of whether a charge over permitted investments is fixed or floating,[63] there is an inherent difficulty in knowing whether the security document pursuant to which the security over the bank account containing the money used to purchase the investment is appropriate to create effective security over the investment, whether this is because of the nature of the investment itself or because of conflicts of laws rules that apply in the particular circumstances (or both).[64] Although it is possible to deal with both these issues by introducing appropriate limitations in the definition of permitted investment, in order for this approach to work from the lenders' perspective, it will either need to be overly prescriptive (which is not necessarily a straightforward exercise) or it will need to allow the lenders the right to determine whether they are happy that their security arrangements apply to any given proposed permitted investment.[65] Perhaps surprisingly, it is more

---

[62] Permitted investments will invariably be restricted to reasonably short-term, publicly quoted debt obligations issued by governments and bank and other corporate issuers having a minimum specified investment grade credit rating. The currency of the obligations will also be restricted so that the investment does not give rise to any foreign exchange risk.

[63] See paras. 11.91–11.95 above.

[64] Investments in publicly quoted securities are more often than not held through intermediaries (by credit to 'investment accounts' of some sort) rather than directly. Indeed, in most instances securities are held through tiers of intermediaries, with the investor having an account with one intermediary and that intermediary having an account with another in a different jurisdiction (Euroclear in Belgium or Clearstream in Luxembourg, for example) in which are recorded all the relevant securities held by the first intermediary for all its customers (including, in particular, the ultimate beneficial owner of the investment, i.e. the project company).

Under English common law and conflicts of laws rules, the law that will determine the efficacy of a security interest granted in relation to registered securities credited to an investment account with an intermediary will be the law of the jurisdiction where the account is maintained. Coincidentally, EU law on this point (the relevant EU Directives being 02/47/EC (Financial Collateral Arrangements), discussed in paras. 11.96–11.100 above, and 98/26/EC (Settlement Finality in Payment and Security and Settlement Systems)) is the same, the rule being generally referred to as the PRIMA rule (the 'place of the relevant intermediary approach').

[65] Neither of these approaches will be particularly attractive to the project company or the sponsors. However, given the fact that the point goes to the heart of one of the fundamental terms of the financing, the point is not one in relation to which the lenders have much scope for making concessions.

common for the financing documents to adopt the latter approach. This is certainly simpler from the point of view of the documentation and the legal analysis that would otherwise have to be undertaken, and whilst in effect it leaves the lenders with a right to approve permitted investments that the project company might wish to make, it can be regarded as a sensible result, not least because at the time the financing agreements are being negotiated the actual investment opportunities that will be available to the project company when its project becomes cashflow positive are unknown.

Insurances

The security for a project will include assignments of the project company's interest **11.104** in the insurances that it is required to take out in connection with the project as well as (where applicable) assignments of any offshore reinsurance policies that the primary insurers are required to maintain. Chapter 6 considers all aspects of the insurance and reinsurance arrangements in relation to projects, both from the perspective of the project company and its shareholders and the perspective of the lenders.

Direct Agreements

The idea of a project company granting security over its assets for its borrowings so **11.105** that, if circumstances are such that the project company is unable to meet its liabilities as and when they fall due, the lenders to whom that security has been granted can sell the assets and apply the proceeds to recoup the moneys that are owed to them (accounting to the project company for any surplus funds that may exist following that application) is quite straightforward. A degree of complication arises where the assets being used as security consist of contractual rights because when creating security over contractual rights it will be necessary to involve third parties in the security arrangements, if only to give them notice of the assignment by the project company of its claims against them and to request them to confirm that they have received the notice.[66] Even then, however, the basic idea is simple.

However, notwithstanding the simplicity of the theory, as can be seen from the **11.106** discussion in the section on security taken over contract rights in paragraphs 11.75–11.82 above, the reality is that the complexities of the project contracts themselves

---

[66] As discussed in paras. 11.81 and 11.83–11.85 above, an assignment of a party's rights under a contract can only be binding on the counterparty to the contract once he has been given notice of the assignment. Quite apart from being perfectly obvious, this is also the position under English law, both in equity (*Stocks v Dobson* (1853) 4 De GM & G 11) and also at law (under s 136 of the Law of Property Act 1925, which stipulates that in order to be effective at law an assignment of a debt or other thing in action must be an absolute assignment and in writing under the hand of the assignor and written notice of the assignment must be given to the debtor).

means that the simple model of an assignment of the contracts coupled with notices of the assignment to the relevant counterparties requires considerable refinement if it is to work in a way that protects the interests of the lenders without adversely affecting the ability of the project company and the counterparties to the various contacts to exercise their respective rights and perform their respective obligations thereunder.

11.107 Although it is something of an over-simplification, in practice the lenders will end up having to enforce their security interests (and therefore look to direct agreements) only in cases where the problems that the project company has encountered are such that it cannot continue to discharge its obligations to its creditors as and when they fall due. So long as the project company is able to continue to trade (even if that requires some sort of work-out and a restructuring of the project company's finances), it is unlikely that the lenders will wish to enforce their security.

11.108 Security over the project agreements to which the project company is a party coupled with a direct agreement should not be seen as a luxury in cases where the lenders also hold security over the shares of the project company. Whilst the share security would enable the lenders to take control of the project by replacing the project company's directors and senior management, there could be legal impediments to doing this in the relevant jurisdiction. This approach might also be both politically difficult (because, for example, it could involve the seizure of shares owned (directly or indirectly) by a government, a pension fund or individual employees) and commercially unattractive (because the project company is likely to be burdened with liabilities that would obviously continue notwithstanding a change of the project company's management).

11.109 Whilst direct agreements can be regarded as ancillary to the main project agreements, they should not be regarded as of secondary importance. If a project has encountered problems of a magnitude that they have resulted in the lenders having to take steps to enforce their security, particularly before the project is complete, the various stakeholders in the project will all be looking at ways to minimize the losses they are likely to suffer in the circumstances, if at all possible at the expense of the other parties. Recriminations will abound and everyone will be looking at the contractual documentation with microscopes. The result? Everything in the documentation that works to the advantage of one of the parties will first be magnified and then exploited to the fullest extent possible.

11.110 This being the case, whilst a 'good' direct agreement (which is to say one that has been properly thought through from both commercial and legal perspectives) will not actually improve the situation for any of the parties, one that is anything less than good for some reason has considerable potential for making matters far worse for at least one of the parties than they should be.

From the lenders' perspective, there are two key benefits to a direct agreement: **11.111**

(1) It provides a pre-agreed route that the lenders[67] can use as a means of 'stepping into the shoes' of the project company under the contracts over which they have security so that they can take day to day control of a project which has run into trouble in order to protect their own interests.
(2) It provides them with a legally binding promise from the counterparty to the relevant project agreement that it will not exercise its rights of termination thereunder except as and when, and to the extent, specified in the direct agreement.

From the perspective of the counterparty to the relevant project agreement (except, **11.112** of course, where the counterparty is itself the cause of the project's problems), there are three key benefits to a direct agreement:

(1) In all probability[68] it will provide the counterparty with a pre-agreed route to extricate itself from the contract with the project company (which is what it would be doing if it were to exercise its termination rights) in return for a promise to do what it would have been obliged to do had the project company performed its obligations under the contract.
(2) It will (again in all probability), provide the counterparty with a promise by the lenders that all overdue amounts owed by the project company to the counterparty (or at least an agreed proportion of them or, perhaps, those overdue by more than an agreed period) will be paid on an agreed basis, so that, for example, some of the arrears are payable only out of any future positive cashflows that the project is able to generate.
(3) It will include restrictions on the exercise by the lenders of their rights to assign the rights under the project agreement that have been assigned to them by the project company. The relative importance of these restrictions obviously varies from project to project, but in the case of projects with new or proprietary technology, defining the restrictions can be both time consuming and difficult because there will be a considerable divergence of interests on this point between the lenders (who will want to have minimal restrictions in order to maximize the pool of potential purchasers should they opt to sell the project as part of the

---

[67] As a practical matter it will never be the lenders themselves (or the security agent) that actually 'steps-in'. The person that actually steps in will be a special purpose company of some description established for the purpose. Irrespective of how this vehicle company is owned and funded (which will depend on the particular circumstances), it will ultimately be the lenders that control what it does once it has stepped-in.

[68] It can only be a probability because the direct agreement will not give the counterparty the right to require the lenders to exercise their step-in rights. All the counterparty has, therefore, is the knowledge that it is likely that if the project company cannot be made to continue to function in a way that will enable it to continue with the project, self interest will drive the lenders to exercise their option to do so.

security enforcement process) and the counterparties (who will want to impose as many restrictions as possible to minimize the risk of their technology being made available to actual or potential competitors).[69]

11.113 Direct agreements are usually structured in a way that allows the lenders to step-in either permanently (in which case the direct agreement will contain a novation mechanism such that the original project agreement is replaced altogether) or temporarily (in which case the parties rights and obligations under the original project agreement will be suspended until such time as the lenders exercise an option in the direct agreement to 'step-out' and thereby reactivate the original contract).

11.114 The main commercial points that will fall to be negotiated in relation to a direct agreement will be the matters mentioned in paragraphs 11.111–11.113 above, though of course there will be ancillary provisions such as covenants by the counterparty not to agree changes to the underlying project agreement without the lenders' approval and mutual confidentiality provisions.

Legal Opinions

Purpose

11.115 Legal opinions are included in this chapter because whilst they are not themselves finance documents (because they do not give rise to any rights or obligations between the project participants *inter se*), they both influence the terms of the finance documents and act as one of the key triggers in relation to the activation of the project participants' rights and obligations under the finance documents.

11.116 The issuance of formal legal opinions in relation to project financings serves as a confirmation to the lenders that:

(1) the project is being developed in accordance with the laws of the jurisdiction in which it is located; and

(2) the obligations that the various project participants have agreed to perform in connection with the furtherance of the development of the project, its financing, and its operation are binding obligations.

11.117 Formal legal opinions from local and international counsel are often the last of the conditions precedent that fall into place on the date of financial close, which is the date on which all parties accept that all (or at least virtually all) their obligations under all the project and financing agreements become unconditional. It is important, of course, to bear in mind that although formal opinions are issued at the end

---

[69] The extent of the lenders' ability freely to transfer their interests in the project to third parties should they need to enforce their security will form part of the overall risk matrix for the particular project.

of the process of documenting the development and financing arrangements for a project, the parties will require and receive legal advice on the different laws (in particular in the jurisdiction in which the project is located but elsewhere as well) that will or may have implications for their plans. Although in some ways the formal legal opinions issued at closing are a distillation of much of this historic legal advice, they should not be assumed to constitute the complete legal analysis of the project. That will be embodied primarily in the legal due diligence report (and supplemental opinions and memoranda relating to it) that will have been prepared for the transaction. An understanding of the full legal picture, therefore, requires a review of both the due diligence report and the formal closing opinions.

Although perhaps axiomatic, legal opinions are intended to deal with matters of **11.118** law and the legal consequences of documents and acts. They are not intended to confirm matters of fact. The project and financing agreements will contain representations as to matters of fact and as to matters of law because both are relevant as part of the risk allocation arrangements for the transaction. A lawyer (or a law firm) issuing an opinion can, of course, be requested to confirm, for example, that the relevant contracting party is not in the midst of litigation that might have an adverse impact on its creditworthiness or its ability to perform its obligations under the project documents, but such a confirmation is unlikely to be given. Even if given, it will achieve very little. If the confirmation is requested of an independent law firm, they will need to rely on a statement of the position made to them by the party on whose behalf they are issuing the opinion (because only that party will actually know the facts), so the addressees of the opinion will get nothing more than they get through the representations in the relevant contract. If it is requested of in-house counsel (and the circumstances are such that it is reasonable for him to be expected to know whether there is any such litigation), all the addressees of the opinion will gain over and above the representations in the relevant contract is a potential claim against the individual that issued the opinion (which it would be very surprising to see them pursue).

First in country

Although it might be more logical to include a discussion on legal opinions in **11.119** Chapter 4 on the basis that a legal analysis of the rules and regulations in the different jurisdictions relevant to the ownership, development, financing, and operation of a project is a key element of the overall assessment of the risks associated with (and therefore the risk allocation in relation to) the project, it is probably fair to say that it is only where a project is one of the first of its type in a particular country that legal opinions are key to the risk assessment with respect to a project. That is not to say that legal risks are unimportant in 'repeat' deals in the country. Rather it is to highlight the fact that in relation to transactions where there is an established precedent for dealing with identified legal risks, the risks blend into the background—they move naturally from being the brightly coloured new chair that needs to be moved around a room when it first arrives so that everyone can get used to it and decide where it should stay into being simply a part of the existing furniture in the room with which everyone is familiar (and therefore comfortable).

11.120   The local law legal opinions on 'first in country' deals will take time to finalize as counsel in the local jurisdiction develop their conclusions with respect to the rules that might affect the efficacy of different provisions of the project agreements and the financing agreements (and in particular the security documents).

11.121   Projects often raise novel and difficult technical legal questions in the jurisdictions in which they are located, not all of which will have clear-cut answers and many of which will require counsel to consider new rules and regulations. In many instances, these new rules and regulations are promulgated by newly appointed officials and regulators who are themselves developing their thinking on the best way to approach issues that they had not had to consider previously or which they had historically dealt with in a particular way. As a result, it is often the case that some elements of the laws that affect a project may actually be moulded to address issues identified in the course of the legal due diligence and opinion process and which are of particular concern, whether to the sponsors or the lenders (or both).

11.122   Issues raised by local counsel on 'first in country' deals will invariably lead to the inclusion of particular provisions in the project agreements in order to mitigate identified legal risks in an agreed way (or simply to ensure that the agreements make it clear how particular legal risks are being allocated among the parties).

Types of opinion

11.123   The classic opinions for project financing transactions are no different to the opinions seen in other types of financing transaction (with the 'usual' raft of assumptions, reservations and qualifications and, in the case of the opinions of counsel in the jurisdiction in which the project is located, whatever additional assumptions, reservations and qualifications are appropriate in the particular circumstances). Opinions broadly fall into three categories:

(1) corporate opinions;
(2) enforceability opinions; and
(3) combined corporate and enforceability opinions.

Corporate opinions

11.124   Corporate opinions are opinions from counsel in the jurisdiction of incorporation of the relevant[70] parties to the project and financing documents that confirm that

---

[70] Opinions are not normally sought in relation to the finance parties. However, in some instances it may be appropriate for an opinion to be issued in relation to the capacity of a finance party to enter into a particular arrangement. It would not be unusual, for example, to request a corporate opinion

those parties have the necessary corporate power to enter into and perform their obligations under the various agreements to which they are party and have done all that they need to do under the laws of their jurisdiction of incorporation and their constitutional documents to validly enter into those agreements.

Although addressed to the lenders, the corporate opinions relating to parties other **11.125** than the project company itself will generally be issued by counsel acting on behalf of the relevant contracting party. Most sponsors and contractors with internal legal departments would expect to satisfy the requirement for a corporate opinion by delivering an in-house opinion. The only point to note in this context is that some financing institutions might require an internal approval before they can agree to accept anything other than a legal opinion issued by an independent law firm.

The opinion from counsel to the project company in its jurisdiction of incorpora- **11.126** tion (which in almost all cases will be the jurisdiction in which the project is located) will deal with corporate matters, project matters (such as governmental consents and the like) and the enforceability of the contracts to which the project company is a party and which are governed by local law. The opinion from local counsel to the lenders will ordinarily cover the same ground as the opinions of counsel to the project company and counsel to any of the other project participants incorporated in the same jurisdiction.

Enforceability opinions

These opinions essentially confirm that the project and financing agreements **11.127** (including any security documents) as executed are 'legal, valid and binding'. These opinions also usually (and unsurprisingly) confirm that the relevant agreements are 'enforceable', although the use of the word 'enforceable' in this context is potentially confusing because, as mentioned in paragraph 11.62 above, it is more accurate to say that a contract is 'effective' rather than 'enforceable'.[71]

The normal English practice is for the enforceability opinions in relation to the **11.128** financing agreements (including security documents) that are governed by English law to be issued by English counsel to the lenders and (but with less uniformity from transaction to transaction) for the opinions in relation to the project agreements that are governed by English law to be issued by English counsel to the

---

in relation to a bank that is to issue a performance bond in favour of the authority responsible for granting the operating licence required by a project.

[71] What is meant by 'enforceable' in the context of a contract does not mean that a court will make an order requiring a party to perform its obligations under the contract but that it will make an order (i.e. an order requiring the payment of damages) that obliges a party that has failed to perform its obligations under a contract to pay monetary compensation to the innocent party for losses he (or she) has suffered as a result of that failure. At common law, the only obligation under a contract that a court will compel a party to perform is an obligation to pay a fixed sum of money. An order for specific performance of any other obligation is only available in equity, and as such is subject to limitations.

project company. The logic for this division is that whilst counsel to the lenders are heavily involved in the preparation and negotiation of the finance documents (even in cases where counsel to the project company has primary drafting responsibility for them), their more limited involvement in relation to the development and finalization of the project documents means that they are less well placed to issue an opinion that highlights any particular issues that, for the benefit of all concerned, is better raised and dealt with on a commercial level before financial close. However, this is not to say that counsel to the lenders are likely to miss things in the project agreements (and indeed it is not uncommon for counsel to the lenders to agree to opine on the project agreements even though they have not been directly involved in their preparation).

12

PROJECT FINANCE IN CIVIL LAW JURISDICTIONS

Antoine Maffei and Jean-Renaud Cazali, De Pardieu, Brocas, Maffei AARPI

Introduction

The origins of project financing under civil law

12.01 Civil law countries, such as France, have a long project financing history, having its roots in the concession system originated in Roman times up to and including the evolution of public private partnerships (PPPs) in the early twenty-first century.

12.02 However, notwithstanding this long history, the rules governing the concession system have never been comprehensively organized in many civil law jurisdictions. In France, despite the fact that the concession system was often used during the nineteenth century and that some important parts of the national infrastructure and of the national economy became dominated by the concession regime, no precise legal definition of the concession existed before the end of the nineteenth century. The concept of delegation of public service (*délégation de service public*) only became the basis of the concession system through administrative case law, practice, and doctrine at the end of the nineteenth century and beginning of the twentieth century.[1]

12.03 Nowadays, there is a major distinction between a number of different kinds of contracts entered into by the private sector and the public authorities. Two main categories of contract exist, the delegation of public services (concession or *affermage* of a public service) and the public procurement contract whether for public works, procurement or services (*marché public*) including PPP contracts.

12.04 The main characteristics and features of project financings were developed together with the implementation of public infrastructure projects through the concession system that allows the government to place the burden of the costs of investment on the private sector.

12.05 Typical projects in civil law countries are operated by the private sector on the basis of the following contracts.

Concession or affermage contract (conventions de délégation de service public)

12.06 The concession is an agreement under which a public authority grants to a private company (the *concessionaire*) the operation of a public service. The *concessionaire* is responsible for running the service within the framework settled by the public authority granting the concession and the service is typically paid for out of revenues received from the users of the service. The main characteristic of a concession is that the running of the service by the *concessionaire* is made at its own risk (*à ses*

---

[1] The *commissaire du gouvernement* defined the meaning of a concession in the leading case of *Gaz de Bordeaux* (CE 30 March 1916): 'the concession is a contract under which a public authority grants the responsibility for the construction of a public infrastructure or the operation of a public service to a person or a private company, at its own cost, with or without subsidies, and which is remunerated through the operation of the service out of the revenues received from the users of the service.'

risques et périls). This essentially means that the concessionaire recovers the costs of construction of the infrastructure and operation of the service from the revenues generated by the service and paid for by the users.

The distinction between a concession and *l'Affermage* lies essentially in the financ- **12.07** ing of the initial infrastructure. If the concessionaire has to finance the construction of the infrastructure used to render the delegated public service, the contract is a concession. In *l'Affermage*, the public authority finances and provides the infrastructure that the delegate operates. The public authority at the end of a concession often proposes an *Affermage* contract, as the investment to build the infrastructure has already been made.

Local transport services in France are typically operated by private companies which **12.08** have concessions from local municipalities to provide public transport in their area. Users of the transportation system pay these companies for the service. Although both operator and consumer are private persons and enter into private law contracts, the concession or *l'Affermage* itself is an administrative contract between the State, the local government ('*collectivités territoriales*') and the transport company.

Public Private Partnerships (contrats de partenariat public privé)

Based on the UK's Private Finance Initiative (PFI) model, France, like other civil **12.09** law jurisdictions, passed in 2004 general legislation relating to PPPs.[2] However, this legislation had to be amended several times to address certain difficulties which become apparent during the first years of PPPs, as the French government expressed the desire to 'make the partnership contract an instrument that fully finds its place in government administration, and not a simple tool of exception'.[3]

The two main differences between PPPs and concessions lie in (i) the way the project **12.10** is designed and (ii) the remuneration of the private company. In contrast to a concession, it is left to the private company to design the project according to the requirements of the public authority and the project company receives a pre-agreed remuneration over the life of the project covering investment costs (including the financing costs) and operating costs. The project company is therefore remunerated by the public authority rather than the users of the services.

Power Purchase Agreement—PPA

Simultaneously with the privatization of the energy sector and the separation **12.11** between the production and the distribution of electricity, the financing of

---

[2] Before the general regulation of 2004, only specific areas could be subject to public private contracts in relation to security or health matters (mainly projects related to the building of jails and hospitals). Since 2004, public private contracts can be used without limitation in respect of all areas, provided that the projects have a certain degree of urgency or complexity.

[3] Extract from the Council of Ministers report of 13 February 2008, on presentation of the law on public private partnership contracts.

power projects based on power purchase agreements has taken an important role in the energy sector. The PPA is a contract entered into between a private producer of electricity and the national electricity distribution company.

12.12 An example of this new approach in the power sector was the implementation in 2000 and 2001 of a general regulatory framework relating to the production and distribution of energy (including renewable energy). This framework is based on the obligation of the national electricity company (*Electricité de France* or EDF) to buy electricity generated from renewable sources, such as co-generation plants, wind turbines, or solar energy, under long-term power purchase contracts (with terms of between fifteen and twenty years) at tariffs set by the government. A key aspect of these kind of projects is that the project company does not bear the market risk as all electricity produced is mandatorily purchased at a pre-agreed tariff.

Public Projects and Tender Offers

12.13 In the framework of the EU regulations on public procurement, the award of public procurement contracts must comply with general principles set forth by the relevant EU directives.

EU Procurement Directives

12.14 The legal framework for public procurement in the EU is governed by the following EU Procurement Directives:

(1) Directive 2004/18/EC of the European Parliament and of the Council of 31 March 2004 on the coordination of procedures for the award of public works contracts, public supply contracts and public service contracts; and

(2) Directive 2004/17/EC of the European Parliament and of the Council of 31 March 2004 coordinating the procurement procedures of entities operating in the water and energy sectors.

12.15 These directives apply when public authorities and utilities seek to acquire supplies, services, or works (for example, civil engineering or construction) and provide that the awarding of public procurement contracts must comply with general principles of freedom of access to public bidding, non-discrimination, equal treatment of bidders, publicity and transparency of procedures, in order to ensure efficient competition between operators and the proper use of public funds. The EU directives apply to PPP contracts.

12.16 According to provisions of the EU Procurement Directives, public procurement contracts must generally be concluded after specific publication procedure has been complied with, and call for competition has been issued. This allows public bodies to tender to several competitors and choose their contracting partner through objective criteria, with strictly regulated exceptions.

Implementation in France—concessions and Public Private Partnerships

Under French national law, all PPP contracts must comply with a large number **12.17** of regulations and rules deriving from general administrative law and the EU Procurement Directives.

Each category of PPP contract is governed by specific internal French regulations. **12.18** However, these regulations have in common that they require a prior call for competition before awarding a contract.

The objective of requiring a prior call for competition is to award public contracts **12.19** on the basis of objective criteria which ensure compliance with the principles of transparency, non-discrimination, and equal treatment and which guarantee that tenders are assessed in conditions of effective competition.

In order to comply with the principle of equal treatment in the award of contracts, the **12.20** prior call for competition must ensure the necessary transparency to enable all tenderers to be reasonably informed of the criteria and arrangements which will be applied to identify the most economically advantageous tender. Therefore, the public authority must indicate the criteria for the award of the contract and the relative weighting given to each of those criteria in sufficient time for tenderers to be aware of them when preparing their tenders. In order to guarantee equal treatment, the criteria for the award of the contract should enable tenders to be compared and assessed objectively.

The main procedures to award public contracts are: **12.21**

(1) the call for tenders; and
(2) the competitive negotiation.

The call for tenders

The call for tenders is the procedure through which the public entity chooses the **12.22** economically most advantageous tender, without negotiation, on the basis of objective criteria brought to the prospective bidders' attention beforehand. This procedure is based exclusively on objective criteria mentioned in the publication notice, and the public body is not allowed to negotiate with tenderers.

As a result, only two award criteria are applied: 'the lowest price' and 'the most eco- **12.23** nomically advantageous tender'.

The competitive negotiation

In the case of particularly complex contracts, the public body can enter into com- **12.24** petitive negotiations with tenderers.

12.25 The purpose of the competitive negotiation is to discuss, on the basis of a functional plan (*programme fonctionnel*) that has already been drawn up, all aspects of the contract with the selected bidders (for example, technical/financial and legal aspects). During the negotiation, the public authority is obliged to ensure equality of treatment among the bidders. In particular, the public authority cannot give information to certain bidders which might give them an advantage over others and cannot reveal confidential information provided by other bidders. The final offer of the bidders is then submitted after the competitive negotiation.

12.26 Concession contracts are also subject to compliance with the general principles described above (transparency, non-discrimination, and equal treatment), although specific procedures may be implemented on a case-by-case basis. The public authority is entitled freely to organize such procedures without the formal requirements of a call for tenders or competitive negotiation provided that these rules ensure compliance with the general principles of transparency, non-discrimination, and equal treatment.

Consequences of breaches by the public authority of the prior call for competition

12.27 Non-compliance with the mandatory regulations prior to awarding a public contract may render the public contract null and void and therefore lead to its cancellation. The cancellation of the award of the '*Boulevard Périphérique Nord*' concession in the 1990s is a good example.

12.28 The nullity of a public contract is retroactive. The latter is therefore deemed to have never existed. The consequences of a public contract being declared a nullity includes financial implications which are of particular concern to the lenders (including the incurrence of hedging breakage costs).[4]

Creating and Perfecting Security Interests

Floating charges and pledges over business concerns in civil law jurisdictions

12.29 In civil law jurisdictions, no specific global security interests over assets can be perfected since the concept of the floating charge does not exist, subject to one exception: a pledge over a business concern. Therefore, the assets (taken as a whole) of a project company cannot be charged by way of security. Specific security interest instruments must be implemented for each type of asset, which requires the implementation of numerous security arrangements depending on the nature of the assets of the project company.

---

[4] See para. 12.149 et seq.

Civil law jurisdictions generally provide for a large range of security interests concerning specific assets (for example, cars, boats, aircraft, machines, inventory, etc.), to each of which specific legal provisions apply as regards the granting, registration (as the case may be), perfection and/or enforceability of the relevant security interest. **12.30**

Pledges over business concerns

The business concern of a company (which mainly comprises a range of intangible and tangible assets on the basis of which a commercial business is carried on) can be pledged in almost all civil law jurisdictions. However, the assets comprised in the business concern of a company which may be subject to this type of security are strictly limited and do not allow the creditors to perfect a security interest in some of the key assets of a project company. Adherence to the required formalities is also of key importance with respect to this type of security. **12.31**

Assets included in a pledge over a business concern

The pledge may solely cover the assets which are restrictively listed in the regulations governing this type of security. Assets which may generally be included in the pledge over business concern are: **12.32**

(1) the trade name ('*enseigne*');
(2) the corporate name ('*nom commercial*');
(3) the leasehold right ('*droit au bail*');
(4) the clientele and customers ('*achalandage*');
(5) the commercial equipment and tools used for the operation of the business concern; and
(6) the patents, licences, trademarks, industrial drawings and designs, and more generally the intellectual property rights attached thereto.

Some of the assets are by law included in the pledge over a business concern (i.e. trade and corporate, leasehold right, clientele and customers). The other assets are included in the scope of the pledge only if the parties elect to do so and expressly provide in the agreement itself a description of the relevant assets (i.e. patents, trademarks, equipment and tools). **12.33**

Consequently, the deed of pledge must precisely and expressly state the items of the business concern which are subject to the pledge. **12.34**

Assets excluded from the pledge over business concern

Most of the key assets of a project company are excluded from the scope of the pledge over the business concern. The following assets, which are of a particular relevance to creditors, cannot be pledged through this type of security: **12.35**

(1) inventory;
(2) property (buildings);

(3) receivables;

(4) rights arising from contracts (other than leasehold rights);

(5) bank accounts; and

(6) future assets (other than those replacing existing assets).

Formalism

12.36 In most of the civil law jurisdictions, a pledge over a business concern must be recorded in a notarial deed (*'acte authentique'*) or in a duly registered private instrument (*'acte sous seing privé, dûment enregistré'*).

12.37 The pledge deed (together with registration certificates (*'bordereaux d'inscription'*)) needs to be registered at a registry held with the clerk of the commercial court in whose jurisdiction the business is operated and, as the case may be, in which jurisdiction each of the branches of the business concern included in the pledge are located.

12.38 The rights resulting from the contractual pledge will be created by the registration and such registration date will determine the priority among the secured creditors.

12.39 Following the registration, the pledge over the business concern is generally valid for a limited period of time (ten years as far as pledges over business concerns governed by French law are concerned and five years as far as OHADA countries are concerned) unless the registration is renewed before the expiry of these deadlines.

Rights of creditors

12.40 The secured creditor benefits from a priority right (*'droit de priorité'*), which means that the secured creditor is entitled to be paid in priority from the sale of the business concern by preference over the unsecured creditors. The creditor's rights are linked to the secured assets so that the priority of the secured creditor follows the business concern into whichever hands it may pass.

12.41 The secured creditor does not benefit from a retention right (*'droit de rétention'*) or a right to require from a court that the business concern be transferred to him following foreclosure (*'droit d'attribution'*). The secured creditor has, however, the right to apply to a court to order the sale of the pledged business concern as a whole, eight days following notice to pay made to the debtor. A pledge over the business concern does not permit foreclosure over specific assets or types of assets included in the business concern subject to the pledge. From that perspective, it is essentially regarded as a defensive security which is rarely enforced but which puts the lenders in a strategic negotiation position in the framework of an insolvency proceeding.

Security interest by type of assets

12.42 In addition to special regimes applicable to specific types of assets (for example, cars, boats, aircraft, and business concerns), security can be classified in civil law jurisdictions in three categories:

(1) mortgages over real property;
(2) security over tangible moveable property; and
(3) security over intangible moveable property.

Mortgage over real property—mortgage and lender's purchase money security interest

Security interests which can be perfected over real property in civil law **12.43** jurisdictions are (i) mortgages and (ii) purchase money security interests (i.e. a lender's lien granted where the lender's claim results from a loan solely used by the borrower for the purpose of discharging the acquisition price of the relevant property). The latter is less likely to be used in the context of a project financing.

Mortgage

Nature and form of the mortgage

A mortgage is a lien granted over real property by the grantor of the mortgage to the **12.44** grantee of the mortgage as security for a debt owed typically by the mortgagor to the mortgagee. The mortgagor is left in possession. The mortgage grants in favour of the mortgagee:

(1) an ancillary right, which means that the security is linked to the debt itself and the mortgage is deemed extinguished if the debt is repaid;
(2) a right to pursue the forced sale of the real property in whatever hands the property is held ('*droit de suite*'); and
(3) a priority ('*droit de préférence*') over the sale proceeds of such real property provided that the mortgagor is not subject to an insolvency proceeding where special considerations apply.

A mortgage is intentionally created pursuant to a consensual deed executed by, **12.45** at least, the mortgagor and the mortgagee with the assistance of a notary.

In order for a mortgage to be valid, perfected, and enforceable and to have full **12.46** effect, it must:

(1) be drafted and executed by a notary and therefore drafted in the language of the relevant country where the real property is located;
(2) be executed in the country of location of the real property;
(3) describe the specific nature and location of the mortgaged property;
(4) provide for the amount secured; and
(5) be registered by the notary with the land registry.

The notary has sole responsibility *vis-à-vis* the lenders as regards the validity **12.47** and enforceability of these security interests thereby rendering title insurance unnecessary.

Enforcement of the mortgage

12.48 The registration of the mortgage in France is only valid for a limited time (up to thirty-five years as from the registration date, subject to renewal), which time limit must be specified in the notarized deed as well as in the registration application.

12.49 One of the requirements of a mortgage is that it has the 'virtue' of constituting *per se* an enforcement instrument ('*titre exécutoire*') which means that the mortgagee holding the instrument does not need to obtain from the court a recognition of legal title before implementing the enforcement of such mortgage. In other words, enforcement is not subject to litigation in respect of the secured claim. It is similar to a final judgment. Enforcement begins by a seizure procedure. However, before any seizure, the mortgagee must serve on the mortgagor a '*commandement*' (formal demand) to pay. This formal demand will have the effect of attaching the real property as well as all rents generated by it as from the day of the publication of the formal demand at the land registry. Filing of a '*cahier des charges*' (terms and conditions of foreclosure) is also required. Finally, an auction is carried out.

Costs of the mortgage

12.50 The mortgage is regarded as being an expensive security to record as taxes and fees to be paid in connection with this security are generally calculated on the basis of the amount secured by the mortgage. For example, the amount of taxes and fees to be paid in respect of French mortgages are approximately equal to 1.1 per cent of the amount of the secured loan. Depending on the amount of the financing and the value of the property, the amount of the taxes may be significant and should be taken into account in the financial model.

Purchase money security interest (lender's lien)

12.51 Civil law jurisdictions specifically define the purpose of the purchase money security interest ('*privilège de prêteur de deniers*') as the security used to secure a loan contracted to finance the acquisition of real property paid for through the lender's monies made available to the borrower, such monies being secured by a lien over the property so financed. This type of security interest may be of relevance in the context of the acquisition of existing assets for a project.

12.52 The legal principles applicable to the purchase money security interest are very similar to those applicable to the conventional mortgage, except for specific points mentioned below.

12.53 A purchase money security interest can be considered to be a specific type of mortgage in favour of the lenders when the loan granted by the latter is used by the borrower to purchase specific real property. A purchase money security interest is, by law, first ranking and has an initial duration expiring two years after the last contractual payment date. The lien can only be granted up to the purchase price of the real property financed out of the proceeds of the loan to be so secured. If excess moneys advanced need to be secured, a conventional mortgage would need to be granted to secure such excess.

Security over tangible moveable property

General provisions applicable to pledges of moveable tangible property

In civil law jurisdictions, all moveable tangible property may be subject to a pledge **12.54** pursuant to the general provisions of the laws applicable to pledges of moveable tangible property unless specific statutes apply with regard to certain assets such as vehicles or machinery and equipment ('*nantissement de materiel et outillage*'). Most of the civil law jurisdictions, under the influence of the French civil code, provide that the pledged property must be held by the pledgee or a third party pledgeholder to create a valid and enforceable pledge. Dispossession of the pledgor is therefore required to create a valid pledge in the OHADA countries and Belgium and was also required in France, until the legal reform of March 2006.[5]

In the circumstances where moveable property is to be pledged, such as machinery **12.55** and equipment necessary for the operation of the project, and dispossession cannot be implemented, a security interest over the equipment and machines would need to be implemented through a pledge over the project's business concern.[6]

Dispossession can, however, be facilitated through a third party pledgeholder **12.56** acting as custodian without disturbing the operations of the project company. This type of mechanism is often implemented in respect of pledges of inventory, although the reform of the law in 2006 has introduced flexibility in this respect and dispossession of the pledgor is no longer a condition to the validity of a pledge over moveable tangible property. If the pledge is made without dispossession, such pledge must be registered with the registrar of the commercial court. A number of civil law jurisdictions based on the French civil code system have yet to introduce this flexibility.

A secured creditor benefits from a retention right ('*droit de rétention*') and a right to **12.57** require from a court that the pledged property be transferred to him following foreclosure ('*droit d'attribution*'). The secured creditor also has the right to ask a court to order the sale of the pledged property.

---

[5] By ordinance n° 2006-346 dated 23 March 2006, France has implemented an important reform of the rules applicable to security interests and guarantees by, inter alia, introducing into its law the non-possessory pledge (perfection of which is made by registration of the pledge with a publicly available security registrar) or a special inventory pledge.

[6] See para. 12.31.

Pledge over machinery and equipment ('nantissement de materiel et outillage')

12.58 When machinery and equipment are not subject to a security interest through a pledge over a business concern (see paragraph 12.31) they may be subject to a pledge by separate written agreement governed by specific statutes.

12.59 The pledge over machinery and equipment (*'nantissement de materiel et outillage'*) is a purchase money security interest that may be created only in favour of lenders to secure the loans made available to purchase the relevant pledged machinery or equipment. The pledgee does not have to take possession of the pledged machinery or equipment.

12.60 This type of security may be difficult to implement in complex project financings with several groups of lenders as it obliges the lenders to segregate a tranche of financing dedicated to the purchase of the machinery and equipment so that the pledge secures this specific tranche only. It may also raise intercreditor issues as not necessarily all lenders to the project would participate in this tranche and therefore cannot benefit from the security on a *pari passu* basis.

Security over intangible moveable property

12.61 The main security interests over intangible moveable property in civil law jurisdictions comprise security interests over claims, over intellectual property rights, and security interests over shares.

Security interests over revenues: pledge over claims and pledge over bank accounts

12.62 In non-recourse project financings, the lenders mainly rely on the future revenues of the project company and therefore seek to take security interests over those revenues. Control of the cashflows of the project company is considered by the lenders as one of the key elements of their collateral and is achieved by taking security over revenues, by controlling both the use of revenues and the making of distributions by the project company to the shareholders.

12.63 Depending on the nature of the project and the debtors of the project company generating the revenues, different type of security interest can be implemented.

Security interest over claims

12.64 Two security instruments governed by the French civil code are available to all types of creditors to secure all types of obligations. These security instruments have been generally implemented in all civil law jurisdictions: i.e. the pledge over claims and the '*délégation*' (a type of assignment of receivables).

12.65 A third security instrument was introduced in the early 1980s in France. It is known as the '*cession Dailly*' (Dailly assignment) of receivables by way of security, the use of which is restricted to credit institutions for the purposes of securing credit transactions. This security instrument which is specific to the French legal system has no strict equivalent in any other civil law jurisdiction.[7]

As civil law jurisdictions do not recognize the floating charge concept, it should be noted that only identified or identifiable claims may be subject to a pledge or a *délégation*. Creditors may therefore take a security interest only over receivables, whether current or future, that arise under a contract existing at the time the security is granted. **12.66**

Pledge over claims

In civil law jurisdictions, a pledge over claims generally needs to be evidenced either by an agreement executed before a notary or by an agreement registered with the tax authority and notified to the debtor by a bailiff ('*huissier*') or acknowledged by the debtor in an instrument before a notary. **12.67**

This security is perceived as being impractical as a means to pledge receivables especially because of the cumbersome formalities and enforcement procedures applicable to it. For instance, such pledges often used to be subject to the prohibition of the '*pacte commissoire*' which prevents the secured creditor from enforcing the pledge without a prior court decision.[8] It used to be regarded by beneficiaries as more akin to a negative pledge, which would prevent the debtor from disposing of the receivables, rather than a security interest. **12.68**

This security is also impracticable when the number of relevant receivables and related debtors does not allow the project parties to identify the claims or the debtors and/or to notify the debtors of the existence of the pledge. This would be the case, for instance, in telecom projects or in relation to motorway concessions. **12.69**

Since the March 2006 law reform, the pledge over claims has become more attractive in France as the perfection formalities and the enforcement procedures have been simplified: **12.70**

(1) to be perfected, the pledge merely needs to be notified to the debtor or acknowledged by it in a private deed;
(2) the pledge may be enforced either by application to the court for an order transferring the pledged receivables to the secured creditors ('*attribution judiciaire*') or by agreement with the pledgor on any other method of transfer of the pledged receivables; and
(3) discharge of the payment obligations in respect of pledged claims can be effected by payment to the pledgee.

---

[7] See para. 12.93.
[8] The '*pacte commissoire*' prohibition has largely been removed by the March 2006 law reform in France.

12.71   Although the March 2006 law reform has not been exactly replicated in other civil law jurisdictions, a number of these jurisdictions have implemented similar provisions.

Délégation

12.72   The *'délégation'* involves a person (the debtor) undertaking an obligation upon the instructions of another person (the assignor), in favour of a third person (the assignee). In other words, upon the instruction of a creditor, the debtor agrees and undertakes to pay its debt incurred *vis-à-vis* such creditor to a third party. The consent of all the parties to the *'délégation'* must be obtained but no specific formality is required. A delegation is a tripartite arrangement.

12.73   The *'délégation'* is binding against third parties when it is entered into (i.e. as from the signature by the parties of the agreement setting up such *délégation*). The consent of the debtor is the main advantage of the *'délégation'* as the debtor acknowledges that it is obliged to pay the assignee. No notification is therefore required. However, the consent of the debtor may render this security impracticable when the number of relevant receivables and related debtors does not allow the project parties to identify the debtors and/or procure their consent, as would be the case in telecom projects or with respect to motorway concessions.

12.74   There are generally two kinds of delegation: the perfect delegation (*'délégation parfaite'*), which constitutes a novation pursuant to which the assignee (*'délégataire'*) has only a right of recourse against the debtor (*'délégué'*), and the imperfect delegation (*'délégation imparfaite'*) which does not constitute a novation pursuant to which the assignee maintains a right of recourse against both the assignor (*'délégant'*) and the debtor. The lenders will always ask for a *'délégation imparfaite'* to maintain its right of recourse against the project company.

12.75   Enforcement of a *'délégation'* does not require any specific enforcement procedure as the debtor undertakes *ab initio* to pay its debts directly to the assignee.

Security interest over bank accounts

12.76   When a pledge over claims or a *'délégation'* cannot be implemented for the reasons described above, for example as a result of the number of relevant receivables and related debtors, the alternative is to require the project company to have its revenues paid into one or several bank accounts pledged in favour of the lenders.

12.77   A pledge over a bank account in civil law jurisdictions actually constitutes a pledge over the balance standing to the credit of the bank account (current account) of the pledgor. This pledge does not technically relate to the cash itself, but rather to the contractual claim of the pledgor against the bank to recover the closing balance of its pledged bank account at the time the account is being closed. Such pledge is therefore governed by the provisions applicable to the pledge of claims described in paragraph 12.67 above.

The pledge of claims exists in most civil law jurisdictions following the French civil **12.78** code legal tradition. It is however possible in certain countries, typically in Africa, that the pledge over bank accounts using the mechanism of the pledge of claims is unknown and therefore not used in practice. One of the reasons may be that the banks benefit in certain countries such as Algeria from a statutory banker's lien over the account and the amounts standing to the credit of the bank accounts opened in their books so that they do not need to create additional security. However, this account bank privilege raises issues *vis-à-vis* the other lenders participating in the financing of the relevant project.

Security interests over intellectual property rights

If intellectual property rights such as trademarks, licences, software, or patents are **12.79** not subject to a security interest through the pledge over a business concern,[9] they may also be subject to a pledge by separate written agreement. The rules applicable to a pledge of intellectual property rights generally follow the rules applicable to the pledge of intangible assets. However, great care should be exercised in respect of the perfection formalities. In certain civil law jurisdictions such as France, registration of a pledge over intellectual property rights must be registered with a special intellectual property rights registrar.

Security interests over shares

Lenders customarily seek to perfect a security interest over the shares of the project **12.80** company. The purpose of the pledge over the project company shares is twofold:

(1) it entitles the lenders to control the shareholding of the project company as the shares cannot be assigned to third parties without the consent of the beneficiaries of pledge; and
(2) as the case may be, it entitles the lenders to take over management of the project company more quickly rather than enforcing their rights under the security interests taken over the assets of the project company and under the direct agreements.

However, depending on the nature of the project company's shares, enforcement of **12.81** a pledge over shares may be too slow to achieve due to certain cumbersome court procedures.

Rules relating to pledges over shares

Traditionally, the rules applicable to pledges over shares in most civil law jurisdic- **12.82** tions following the French civil code legal tradition requires the pledgee to take possession of the relevant share certificates. This is because the shares were considered to be moveable assets represented by share certificates. Dispossession is achieved

---

[9] See para. 12.31.

by delivery of the share certificates to the beneficiaries of the pledge or to a third party acting as custodian. This regime is still applicable in numerous civil law jurisdictions following the French civilian code legal tradition in which shares are materialized by share certificates.

12.83 In contrast, when the shares are not represented by shares certificates, the rules governing pledges over intangible moveable property are applicable. These rules generally require that the pledge needs to be evidenced by either: (i) an agreement executed before a notary; (ii) an agreement registered with the registrar of a commercial court or any other registrar having jurisdiction; or (iii) with the tax authority and notified to the debtor by a bailiff ('*huissier*') or accepted by the debtor in an instrument executed before a notary.

12.84 It should also be noted that certain jurisdictions such as France have significantly amended the law applicable to securities by introducing the principle of dematerialization of securities ('*valeurs mobilières*') and specific rules applicable to the granting of security over the shares of a joint stock company (such as '*société anonyme*' or '*société par actions simplifiée*'). Pursuant to a reform implemented in 1981[10] all securities ('*valeurs mobilières*') issued in whatever form in France and subject to French law are required to be registered in an account held by the issuer or by a financial intermediary. The particular effect of this reform was to render dematerialization compulsory and definitive and to phase out physical share certificates. These shares are held in book entry form in an account either with the issuer or with a financial intermediary. The pledge over these shares is granted through a pledge of the securities account to which the shares are recorded. No formalities are required other than mere execution of a pledge declaration by the pledgor. A number of civil law jurisdictions following the French civil code tradition such as Luxembourg have implemented the EU Collateral Directive with its absence of formalism and simplified enforcement in a manner which is creditor friendly. France exercised a partial opt-out when implementing the EU Collateral Directive since it implemented the Directive to its fullest extent only in respect of derivative transactions.

The pledge entitles the lenders to control the shareholding of the project company

12.85 Throughout the life of the project and until enforcement of the pledge over the project company shares, the pledge mainly entitles the lenders to prevent a change of control in the shareholding of the project company. As a result of this security, the sponsors cannot dispose of the shares of the project company without the prior consent of the lenders.

12.86 The inalienability of the project company shares raises concerns for sponsors who usually wish to maintain the right to dispose of their interest in the project by reducing their stake in the share capital of the project company. The problem is

---

[10] Law n° 81-1160 of 30 December 1981, which became effective on 3 November 1984.

exacerbated when the sponsors comprise financial investors such as investment funds. As a matter of principle, financial investors often do not intend to maintain their interest in the project until the end of its term.

A change of shareholding raises two issues for the lenders: 12.87

(1) the new shareholders will need to satisfy the 'kyc' (know your customer) requirements of the lenders; and
(2) the lenders will have to release and re-execute a pledge over the shares which are assigned to the new shareholder.

Great care needs to be exercised to ensure that the lenders do not lose their first 12.88 ranking security if for any reason there exist second ranking creditors. Lenders should also ensure that the new security, depending on the time of its granting, is not affected by, in the context of potential bankruptcy of the project company, possible preferences.

The enforcement procedure of the pledge may be cumbersome

Traditionally, the civil code provides that a creditor may not dispose of the pledged 12.89 assets upon the occurrence of an event of default (prohibition of the '*pacte commissoire*'). Foreclosure over shares needs to be authorized by the court either through a public sale or by allocation by the court up to the value of the pledged shares as determined by an expert. These types of procedures are cumbersome and take time. They are therefore not always going to facilitate the lenders' ability expeditiously to take over the management of the project company.

The prohibition of the '*pacte commissoire*' has recently been removed from French 12.90 law and the lenders are now entitled to use an alternative out-of-court enforcement process under which they can automatically be vested with title to property after an expert appraisal (the expert being appointed either by the court or the parties).

To mitigate the risks of this potentially lengthy enforcement procedure, lenders 12.91 may seek to take security over the shares of an offshore intermediary holding company owned by the sponsors and holding the share capital of the project company. Such a holding company can of course be incorporated in a more creditor-friendly jurisdiction which would enable the lenders to take over the management of the direct and sole shareholder of the project company. This solution may also be tax efficient if the tax regime applicable to the transfer of shares of the project company penalizes the lenders.

Limitation of the security by way of transfer of title

Some civil law jurisdictions outside the EU have taken a restrictive approach in 12.92 respect of the concept of transfer of title by way of security. Only a few exceptions have been implemented quite recently in France. Two have been implemented by law: (i) the assignment of receivables by way of transfer of title (the 'Dailly law assignment') in 1981 and (ii) the trust or '*fiducie*' in 2007. The third one has been developed by practice: the cash pledge. The EU Collateral Directive has introduced on an EU-wide basis the concept of transfer of title by way of security.

Dailly assignment

12.93 Even though the Dailly assignment is specific to France, it is interesting to note how this security instrument has become key in the financing of certain projects, and especially the financing of PPPs.

12.94 The Dailly assignment provides for a simplified method of assignment of receivables which enables their assignments by way of security through the mere remittance to the assignee of a transfer form ('*bordereau*') signed by the assignor, describing the amount and type of receivables to be assigned.

Nature of the parties

12.95 The assignment of receivables can only be granted by a legal entity (whether public or private) or by an individual, but in the latter case only if acting in a professional capacity. The beneficiary can only be a credit institution ('*établissement de crédit*').

12.96 The beneficiary of a Dailly assignment must be a French licensed credit institution or a European credit institution benefiting from the 'European passport' which authorizes it to conduct banking activity in France.

Consideration

12.97 The Dailly assignment must be granted in consideration of a facility granted by the beneficiary to the assignor. There are two possible ways of implementing this requirement:

(1) the Dailly assignment may be granted by way of security for the obligations of the assignor towards the beneficiary under a loan or other credit facility; or
(2) the Dailly assignment may be granted as an absolute assignment, against the payment by the beneficiary of an acquisition price. This would effectively be the case in the context of a discounting facility, whereby a bank agrees to purchase receivables at a discount reflecting, in particular, the net present value of the receivables (this form of Dailly assignment is known as a '*cession escompte sans recours*').

The type of receivables

12.98 Any type of receivable can be assigned, whether against private or public debtors and regardless of the origin of the receivable. The assigned receivables can be existing, contingent, and/or future receivables provided that they are sufficiently identified.

Form of the assignment

12.99 The Dailly assignment is created by the remittance to the beneficiary of a transfer form ('*bordereau*') listing the assigned receivables. The transfer form is signed by the assignor and dated by the beneficiary, upon which it takes effect between the parties and becomes binding against third parties.

Transferability

The transfer form may only be transferred by the beneficiary to another credit **12.100** institution. It can be stipulated that the transfer will be effected by endorsement of the transfer form, but in such case, it is thought that the endorsement can only be made for full value, and not for part of the transfer form.

Effects of the Dailly assignment

The Dailly assignment operates so as to transfer title to the assigned receivables to **12.101** the beneficiary as from the date on the transfer form, as well as all security interests, guarantees, and ancillary rights attached to each assigned receivable. As a result, the assignor cannot assign such receivables to any other person.

Notice of the Dailly assignment

Although the Dailly assignment is perfected by mere delivery of the transfer form **12.102** to the beneficiary and dating of that form by the beneficiary, notice of that assignment may be given by the beneficiary at its discretion. In that case assigned payment obligations can only be discharged by payment to the beneficiary. Pending delivery of that notice, collection of payments is made by the assignor on behalf of the beneficiary who holds those payments for the account of the beneficiary.

Acknowledgement of the Dailly assignment

The debtor may be required (but is not obliged) formally to acknowledge the **12.103** assignment. Following such acknowledgement, no defences can be raised by the debtor who is irrevocably committed to pay to the beneficiary unless the beneficiary knowingly acted to its detriment.

Application of the Dailly assignment in French PPPs

In 2004, the French legislature introduced a specific type of receivables assignment **12.104** which applies to receivables with respect to the remuneration payable by a public authority which has awarded a project in consideration of the investment costs incurred under PPP contracts and in hospital projects.[11] This mechanism, based on the Dailly assignment, allows the conversion of part of a project financing into a quasi-public financing. As a result, it reduces the costs of the project as the interest rate margins applicable to this quasi-public financing are significantly below the margins applicable to equivalent financings bearing project risk.

---

[11] Order (*Ordonnance*) n° 2004-559, dated 17 June 2004, further amended by law n° 2008-735 dated 28 July 2008 and law n° 2009-179 dated 19 February 2009.

Conditions to be met

12.105 Where all or part of the remuneration payable by the public authority to the project company under a PPP contract is assigned by the project company by way of a Dailly assignment, the beneficiary of the assignment can seek to have it formally acknowledged by the public authority for up to 80 per cent of the value of the assignment, subject to the following requirements:

(1) the remuneration must be in respect of investment costs relating to the project, which include design and development costs, construction costs, ancillary expenses, interest during construction, and financing costs; and

(2) the acknowledgement must be conditional upon the public authority being satisfied that the investments have been made in accordance with the provisions of the PPP contract (including, in any event, completion of the works).

Effect of the acknowledged Dailly assignment in French PPPs

12.106 Following the completion of the works, the acknowledgement of the assignment of receivables becomes irrevocable and the public authority is unconditionally committed to pay the amounts owed by it to the project company directly to the beneficiary and can no longer raise any defences based on its relationship with the project company (such as the cancellation or termination of the PPP contract, or the defence of set-off).

12.107 The only defence which can be validly raised against the beneficiary is the four-year statute of limitation period with respect to the limitation applicable to receivables held against the State or other public authorities.

12.108 Accordingly, the risk of the project company becoming insolvent and the receivables being claimed by other creditors of the project company is set aside since the cash no longer flows through the project company. The credit risk is taken by the lenders, as beneficiaries of the Dailly assignment, on the credit of the public authority, rather than on that of the project company.

12.109 The project company remains, however, liable for the payment of all amounts due by it to the public authority pursuant to any breach of its contractual obligations or any penalties owed by it (for example, due to lack of performance or late performance).

Transfer of risk and margins

12.110 The lenders' take risk on the performance of the project company during the construction phase of the project. Upon completion of the works, the acknowledgement of the Dailly assignment becomes irrevocable and the assigned cashflows become isolated from performance risk, the lenders' risk thereby shifts from the project company to the public authority.

Where the assignment has been effected as a Dailly assignment by way of security, **12.111** the lenders will have recourse against both the project company as borrower under the project facilities and the public authority pursuant to the acknowledged Dailly assignment.

It is possible that the lenders under an acknowledged Dailly assignment may agree **12.112** that they are actually providing financing to a public body and that recourse will only be possible against the relevant public authority. They would therefore waive their rights of recourse against the project company. In such a case, the lenders can be regarded as being no longer a project lender but effectively a lender to the public authority.

Given that the risk is mitigated by an acknowledged Dailly assignment, the margin **12.113** or interest rate payable following entry into force of the acknowledgement will usually decrease to reflect the new credit profile in line with the credit risk of the public authority. The costs of the project which are indirectly borne by the public authority are therefore decreased as it reduces the remuneration to be paid by the public authority to the project company under the PPP contract.

Cash collateral ('gage-espèces')

Cash collateral ('*gage-espèces*') is not governed by any specific provision of law. It has **12.114** been developed by practice and its validity (at least when it is held directly by the pledgee) has been confirmed by case law in certain jurisdictions even though the characterization of cash collateral as a pledge, instead of a transfer of ownership, is subject to debate among legal scholars in France. Under this type of security interest, a fixed amount of cash is transferred to the pledgee and co-mingled with its general cash funds. Such cash may be transferred into an account opened in the name of the pledgee or in the name of a third party acting as custodian of the pledgee.

Since it relates to fungible assets which cannot be segregated from the rest of the **12.115** secured party's assets, the cash collateral grants to the secured party the fiduciary ownership of the collateralized cash. Cash collateral can be used instead of a debt service reserve account, particularly when the amount to be cash collateralized does not change materially throughout the life of the financing. Debt service reserves in the form of cash collateral have been used in the financings of wind farms and photovoltaic power stations in the French market.

The cash collateral offers advantages from the perspective of enforcement. Indeed, **12.116** because of the fungible nature of cash, the pledgee is vested with the ownership of the collateralized cash. Under those circumstances, in the event of a default of the pledgor, the pledgee is entitled to set-off the sums owed by the pledgor against the obligation to return cash held by the pledgee pursuant to the cash pledge. Exercise of the right of set-off requires, however, mutuality of obligations. Therefore, this type of collateral may be impractical in the context of complex project financings involving several groups of lenders and multiple facilities.

12.117 Perfection of the cash collateral occurs upon transfer by the pledgor of the amount of the cash collateral to the account opened in the name of the pledgee or in the name of a third party acting as custodian of the pledgee.

12.118 It may not be possible to create and perfect this type of security developed in France in civil law jurisdictions other than France. The only alternative to taking a security over cash is to take a pledge over a blocked bank account.

Civil law fiducie (trust)

French fiducie

12.119 Under the Law of 19 February 2007,[12] France has adopted a *fiducie* regime designed to institute a mechanism making it possible to compete with the common law trust. Its introduction was the culmination of a debate in France over a period of almost thirty years. The regime has already been supplemented on several occasions mainly to widen its scope and clarify its effects in the event of insolvency proceedings.

12.120 The *fiducie* is a civil law tripartite contractual mechanism whereby a settlor transfers to a fiduciary the ownership of rights, assets, or security interests. The fiduciary then has the responsibility of administrating them in the interests of the beneficiaries and in accordance with the terms and conditions of the *fiducie* contract.

12.121 This tool has multiple applications for financing, asset management, and mergers and acquisitions.

12.122 The French *fiducie* has equivalents in other legal systems, particularly fiduciary alienation under German law and, to a certain extent, the trust in countries whose legal system is based on common law. But it is also based on a concept that is very specific to French civil law, the 'estate' (*patrimoine*), and more particularly the 'allocated estate' (*patrimoine d'affectation*).

12.123 Unlike a common law trust, there is no division of the ownership of the assets entrusted in *fiducie* between the legal ownership granted to the fiduciary and the economic ownership belonging to the *fiducie*'s beneficiary. However, the ownership transferred is of a contractual type. The French *fiducie* is also necessarily express, written, and consensual, whereas the common law trust can be implicit, unwritten, and unilateral. A settlor may not create a French *fiducie* without a deed signed by the fiduciary and without the beneficiary's acceptance.

---

[12] Law n° 2007-211 dated 19 February 2007 relating to the *fiducie*.

Application of the French fiducie to security

The *fiducie,* as introduced into French law, allows the creation of two possible secu- **12.124**
rity interests. First, it enables the transfer of assets and rights for the purpose of
creating a security interest. Secondly, it is a tool that enables management of personal or real security interests by a fiduciary on behalf of creditors benefiting from
such security interests.

Since the availability of mechanisms to create and perfect a security interest had **12.125**
previously been limited, the introduction of collateral *fiducie* has been enthusiasti-
cally welcomed in the French project finance market and elsewhere.

The *fiducie* represents a security interest mechanism that is both very effective from **12.126**
a lenders' perspective, should the debtor-settlors be subject to insolvency proceedings, and in that it provides significant flexibility.

Direct Agreements and Step in Rights

Rationale for direct agreements

In non-recourse project financings, the security interests of the lenders during **12.127**
the construction phase are limited and the lenders rely on the future fixtures
and revenues of the project company as the core assets of the project company.
To mitigate that risk and because the most valuable assets of a project company
during the construction phase are its contractual rights to build and operate the
project, direct agreements, which entitle the lenders to take over the contractual
rights of the project company by transferring these rights for their own benefit
or for the benefit of a third party designated by the lenders, have become
customary.[13]

It is important to note that, as is the case in common law jurisdictions, under the **12.128**
civil law, the rights granted to the lenders under direct agreements are pure contractual undertakings. They do not create a security interest over the subcontracts or
the rights arising thereunder in favour of the lenders. The efficacy of such a mechanism, especially in the context of bankruptcy of the project company, is also
questionable.[14]

Direct agreements and stipulation pour autrui

In certain concession or PPP transactions in France, the public authority may refuse **12.129**
to enter into direct agreements with the lenders not because it refuses to grant
step-in rights to the lenders but because the public authority considers that there

---

[13] See also para. 11.105.
[14] See para. 12.169 et seq.

exist other means to achieve the same purpose. Indeed, in the absence of direct agreements, step-in rights may be structured through the *stipulation pour autrui* mechanism provided for in the French civil code and which exists in most civil law countries.

12.130   The *stipulation pour autrui* is a civil law mechanism whereby an obligor (*promettant*) undertakes *vis-à-vis* a stipulating party (*stipulant*) to do or not to do something in favour of a third party beneficiary (*bénéficiaire*). An interesting feature of the *stipulation pour autrui* is that the beneficiary does not need to be a party to the agreement between the obligor and the stipulating party. The third party beneficiary only has to accept by a simple notification to the obligor that the *stipulation pour autrui* has been made in its favour.

12.131   Under a *stipulation pour autrui* provided for in a concession agreement or PPP contract, the public authority, as obligor, undertakes *vis-à-vis* the project company as the stipulating party in favour of the lenders, to transfer the concession agreement or PPP contract to any party designated by the lenders. The lenders then accept, by executing a separate letter, the *stipulation pour autrui*, which entitles them to enforce the step in rights.

12.132   The *stipulation pour autrui* mechanism is frequently used to organize the step in rights of the lenders if and when a public authority is reluctant to enter into a direct agreement with the lenders.

Issues Arising from Secured Lending

Early termination or cancellation of project contracts

12.133   In project financings of public infrastructure, one of the main concerns of the lenders is the impact of early termination of the underlying project contracts (for example, concession contracts, *Affermage*, PPP contracts, and, in projects where power is purchased by a state utility, power purchase agreements) since the lenders are financing the project on the basis of the projected cashflows to be generated until the expiry date of the relevant project contract. The lenders typically have limited rights over the assets of the project since the project assets either belong to the public authority from the inception of the project or have to be returned to the public authority upon termination of the project contracts. The other assets of the project have generally little value and are unlikely to be sufficient to provide full repayment to the lenders.

12.134   Therefore, the objective of the lenders is to ensure that the project company will be fully compensated and will receive an indemnity from the public authority covering at least the amounts outstanding under the financing in case of early termination of the relevant project contract.

Circumstances leading to the early termination or cancellation of the project contracts

Each of the following events occurring throughout the life of the project may lead **12.135** to the early termination of the underlying project contracts.

Nullity of a project contract

Administrative contracts entered into between public authorities and the private **12.136** sector have over the years resulted in significant amounts of litigation. The risk of litigation and subsequent nullity of a project contract has increased since the adoption in France of a regulatory framework on the awarding of public procurement contracts, the procedure of which must comply with general principles of freedom of access to public procurement, non-discrimination and equal treatment of bidders, publicity and transparency of procedures (see paragraph 12.13 et seq).

Recourse by third parties against the award decision of the public authority is there- **12.137** fore frequent and leaves a risk for the project which may lead to the cancellation of the relevant project contract and the related project.

Force Majeure

A *force majeure* event is a supervening event. *Force majeure* is traditionally defined **12.138** in civil law jurisdictions as an event which is (i) beyond the control of either of the contracting parties to overcome ('*irresistible*'), (ii) unforeseeable ('*imprévisible*'), and (iii) not related to the contracting parties ('*extérieur aux parties*'). Upon the occurrence of a *force majeure* event, the parties are relieved from their obligations to perform the contract.

In France, the administrative courts have also developed the concept of administra- **12.139** tive *force majeure* based on the general concept of *force majeure*. The administrative *force majeure* has the same facets as the general *force majeure* without the 'unavoidable' test. Indeed, the administrative courts consider that in certain circumstances, even if the event could be overcome, the event has resulted in a fundamental change to the equilibrium or the object of the contract.[15]

Project contracts generally provide that if a *force majeure* event occurs and is con- **12.140** tinuing for a determined period, either party has the right to require early termination of the relevant project contract.

The *force majeure* event in civil law countries is different from the theory of **12.141** *Imprévision* and of *Sujétions Imprévues*. Under the *Imprévision* theory, if supervening

---

[15] In *Compagnie des Tramways de Cherbourg* (CE 9 December 1932) the concessionaire was on the verge of bankruptcy, but if the tram fares had been increased any more, the company would have lost its customers. The court decided that the object of the contract (to operate a tramway service at a reasonable price) had been negated.

circumstances have arisen after entering into a project contract for which no (or inadequate) provision has been made, leading to a deterioration of the private party's position and making it uneconomical to perform its part, the private party will not be allowed to terminate the contract but will have a right to compensation. The private party will be compelled to perform the project contract in question and will then be entitled to an indemnity from the public authority against its extra expenses. In the case of a concession, the indemnity may take the form of a right to increase the applicable tariffs for the services charged by the project company to the users of the services above the limits initially set forth in the relevant project contract.

12.142 Under French administrative law principles, *Sujétions Imprévues* are related to events or difficulties which have a material impact on construction, such as ground or climate risks. Unlike *force majeure*, *Sujétions Imprévues* do not excuse the project company from performing its contractual obligations but grant a right of compensation. In exceptional circumstances, *Sujétions Imprévues* may lead to the termination of a project contract, but only if it substantially changes the equilibrium of the relevant project contract.

Termination of a project contract in the public interest (résiliation pour motif d'intérêts général)

12.143 The rules on administrative contracts developed by French administrative law, as well as other civil law countries, have a number of differences in comparison with private law contracts. Those special rules mainly come from the predominance of the public interest, an interest which must prevail even to the extent of overruling the express terms of a project contract.

12.144 Therefore, the public authority entering into a concession agreement or a PPP contract with the private sector will always have the right unilaterally to decide at any time throughout the life of the project whether to require early termination of a project contract.

Termination of a contract by the public authority upon default of the project company

12.145 As in every contract, the public authority may also terminate a project contract due to the default of the project company. The events leading to the termination of a project contract must achieve a fair balance between the public authority's desire to be able to terminate a project contract for inadequate provision of service and the project company's and lenders' interest in limiting termination to substantial defaults when all other alternatives have been exhausted, including a reasonable grace period. In practice, the events of default leading to early termination will be limited to events such as:

(1) repeated breaches of the project contract which materially and adversely affect the performance of the service;

(2) winding up or bankruptcy of the co-contractor;

(3) abandonment of the project;

(4) failure to achieve completion by a pre-agreed completion date;

(5) accumulation of penalties;

(6) non-compliance with insurance requirements; and

(7) non-compliance with change of control provisions.

Indemnification of the project company and the rights of the lenders

Indemnification of the project company by the public authority

French administrative case law provides for general principles of indemnification **12.146** arising from the losses incurred by the project company in case of early termination of a project contract. The amount of the compensation also depends on the cause of the termination.

Lenders and sponsors usually accept the principles developed under the relevant **12.147** administrative case law to determine the compensation to be paid by the public authority to the project company in such circumstances. The sponsors and the lenders generally negotiate detailed indemnification provisions in each project contract to avoid uncertainties on the level of compensation and to ensure, as much as possible, that most of the costs will be indemnified.

In summary, the indemnification provisions in concessions or PPP contracts **12.148** customarily provide for the following principles:

(1) *Early termination for project company's default*: The indemnification is traditionally based on the amounts due to the sponsors with respect to the equity and/or financing which they have provided and the amounts due to the lenders. This is reduced by an amount attributable to the loss incurred by the public authority. As a result, the indemnification is often lower than the amount outstanding under the lenders' financing so that the lenders remain at risk in case of early termination for project company's default. The inclusion in the indemnification of the breakage costs relating to the hedging arrangements entered into for the purpose of the project is usually subject to some negotiation among the lenders, the public authority and the sponsors.

(2) *Early termination for force majeure*: The indemnification covers the amounts due to the sponsors for their equity contribution and the amounts due to the lenders (including the breakage costs arising under the hedging arrangements) but excludes any loss of profit. It may also include the breakage costs arising under the commercial contracts which have been entered into by the project company.

(3) *Early termination for public interest*: The indemnification is traditionally equal to the indemnification arising in the case of early termination for *force majeure*, but increased to account for the loss of profit of the sponsors so that all parties

are entirely indemnified with respect to the losses they have incurred as a result of the early termination by the public authority in the public interest.

Hedging breakage costs in PPP contracts

12.149   Due to the long-term nature of PPP projects (from fifteen to forty years), the lenders do not have the capacity to make available such long-term facilities to the project company at a fixed interest rate mainly because the lenders cannot fund the facilities with deposits having the same maturity. The profile and the cost of the financing made available to the project company by the lenders to finance the investments made under PPP contracts are directly reflected in the remuneration profile paid by the public authority to the project company. However, for various reasons including budget constraints, the public authorities are reluctant to bear interest rate risks. A public authority will therefore usually require that the project company enter into interest rate swaps so that the portion of remuneration paid to the project company in consideration of the investments is fixed and not subject to floating rate variations.

12.150   The main issue with respect to the hedging arrangements relates to the breakage costs arising upon early termination of a project contract. The hedging banks will agree to enter into the required interest rate swaps provided that the costs incurred upon termination of the swaps are adequately covered either by the public authority or by the sponsors. As discussed in paragraph 12.148 above, most of the PPP contracts provide that the public authority will indemnify the breakage costs incurred by the project company upon early termination of a project contract. The indemnification provisions are included in the relevant project contract itself.

12.151   However, the indemnification provisions would not be effective if the early termination of a project contract results from its nullity following, for instance, recourse by third parties.

12.152   To mitigate this risk, the commitment of the hedging banks to enter into hedging arrangements is customarily contingent upon the expiry of the recourse periods during which a third party might challenge the validity of the PPP contract. In certain circumstances, the public authority may however insist on fixing the interest rates on the date of execution of the PPP contract or during a period of time starting from that date. To cover the risk of the PPP contract being nullified and the consequent invalidation of the indemnification provisions benefitting the hedging banks in a PPP contract, the hedging banks might be able to enter into a direct agreement with the public authority or seek a sponsor guarantee.

12.153   The validity of direct agreements (the purpose of which would be to ensure the survival of the indemnification provisions set forth in the relevant project contract) in the event a project contract is nullified is not free from doubt under French administrative law. Indeed, such an agreement would need to be a collateral contract (i.e. distinct from the relevant project contract) to avoid the nullification of the latter resulting in the invalidity of the direct agreement. This matter has yet to be resolved in France and is still the subject of debate.

Insolvency of the project company and enforcement of security

The commencement of insolvency proceedings affecting the project company in civil law jurisdictions generally triggers an automatic stay of all actions by creditors subject to a few exceptions. The debtor is prohibited from paying any pre-filing claims arising before the insolvency proceedings and creditors are barred from enforcing their rights against the debtor including their rights under any security granted by the debtor. This means that pre-filing financial debts are immediately 'frozen'. **12.154**

It is important to note also that the insolvency proceeding cannot per se accelerate pre-filing claims which have yet to mature, such as the bank or other debt made available to the project company (except in a judicial liquidation scenario where pre-bankruptcy claims are automatically accelerated). Any contractual clause to the contrary is usually deemed null and void. **12.155**

As a matter of principle, the lenders are therefore not entitled to enforce the security granted by the project company, subject to a few exceptions. **12.156**

Security granted by third parties such as sponsors or banks are, however, enforceable provided of course that the grantor or guarantor itself does not file for bankruptcy proceedings. **12.157**

Security granted by the project company and direct agreements

Security interests with a retention right

Despite the fact that the lenders would not be entitled to enforce pledges granted by the project company following the commencement of insolvency proceedings (except in a liquidation scenario), a distinction can be made between pledges conferring a retention right and those which do not confer such right. **12.158**

Indeed, during the insolvency proceedings, at the request of the administrator of the insolvency proceedings, the judge supervising the proceedings may exceptionally authorize the payment of a pre-filing creditor in order to procure that such secured creditor surrenders the retained pledged asset to the estate of the project company. This can be authorized only if the pledged asset retained by the secured creditor is deemed necessary to the debtor's continuation of its activity. **12.159**

Security interests without a retention right

In relation to security interests without a retention right, if the pledged asset is sold by the administrator with the consent of the supervising judge, the sale proceeds are kept in escrow until the end of the proceedings and then allocated to the creditors depending on their respective rank/privileges. Secured creditors are traditionally **12.160** paid after creditors benefiting from a super-priority lien such as employees and the tax authorities.

12.161   In a liquidation scenario, creditors benefiting from a pledge are entitled to enforce their security interest.

Security by way of transfer of title

12.162   The main exception to the automatic stay arises in the context of security by way of transfer of title. As discussed in paragraph 12.92 et seq above, security by way of transfer of title is available within the limited scope of special statutes but offers a high degree of protection in the case of insolvency proceedings of the project company.

12.163   The use of the Dailly assignment in France, the cash transfer of title contemplated under the EU Collateral Directive and the trust put the lenders in a more favourable situation upon the bankruptcy of the project company.

Direct agreements and step in rights

12.164   As indicated above, the main purpose of direct agreements is to allow the lenders to appoint a replacement company or to assume themselves the responsibilities of the project company under the relevant project contracts by 'stepping into the shoes' of the project company if the latter is in default. The efficacy of direct agreements needs to be analysed from a bankruptcy law perspective as the project company may already be bankrupt when the lenders enforce their rights under the direct agreements or is likely to go into bankruptcy immediately after it is deprived of its contract rights.

12.165   Direct agreements are rooted in the Anglo-American legal tradition and are structured on the basis of insolvency laws applicable in jurisdictions following that legal tradition, which are often considered as more creditor friendly in comparison with the insolvency law applicable in civil law countries following the French civilian legal tradition.

12.166   For example, set forth below is an analysis under French law of the various obstacles to implementing step-in rights involving an insolvent French debtor. Direct agreements are designed to transfer the contract rights from the insolvent project company to a third party upon enforcement by the lenders and may be in conflict with the following mandatory principles of the French insolvency rules:

(1) the rule relating to the automatic stay of enforcement actions by creditors against the debtor;[16]
(2) the prohibition of the payment of pre-bankruptcy claims which are frozen;[17]
(3) the prohibition of the right to terminate ongoing contracts; and

---

[16] See para. 12.154 et seq.
[17] Ibid.

(4) the exclusive power granted to an administrator of the insolvency proceedings to assist in the management of the bankrupt company, and of the bankruptcy court to decide the outcome of the insolvency proceedings.

A purported substitution under a direct agreement may also be considered to violate the regulations governing the award of public procurement contracts. **12.167**

Automatic stay and prohibition of payment of pre-bankruptcy claims

Even if the right of substitution under a direct agreement does not technically constitute a security interest nor a procedure to obtain accelerated payments from the debtor, the substitution may be characterized as a quasi-security. If courts characterize direct agreements as security, the exercise of the lenders rights under direct agreements would therefore be contrary to the principle of automatic stay of all enforcement actions against the debtor. **12.168**

A question may also arise as to the compatibility of the substitution rights with the prohibition on making payments to pre-bankruptcy creditors. Indeed, if the substitution directly or indirectly enables the project company to reimburse the lenders, the rule prohibiting the payment of pre-bankruptcy claims may be violated since the lenders would receive their payments through the transfer of an asset of the project company. **12.169**

Prohibition on termination of ongoing contracts

As a matter of principle, any ongoing contract should be performed in accordance with its initial terms and conditions notwithstanding any payment default existing at the time insolvency proceedings are commenced. The administrator of the insolvency proceedings is the sole person entitled to terminate any ongoing contracts whose execution is pending upon commencement of insolvency proceedings. **12.170**

Therefore, co-contractors of the project company (such as the suppliers or the lenders) are barred from terminating the agreements entered into with the project company upon the sole occurrence of insolvency proceedings. Any clause to the contrary is likely to be deemed null and void. **12.171**

Management and outcome of the insolvency proceedings

The administrator of the insolvency proceedings customarily has the exclusive power to assist the management of the insolvent company and the bankruptcy court and the exclusive power eventually to decide the outcome of the insolvency proceedings. The bankruptcy court is empowered to approve a restructuring plan or, if the continuation of the business is not possible, order the liquidation of the project company (i.e. sale of all or part of the assets). **12.172**

The exercise of step-in rights by lenders could be deemed to be contrary to the rules governing insolvency proceedings relating to the administration of an insolvent **12.173** project company by the administrator and the bankruptcy court. This is because they would be hindered or prevented from controlling the sale or liquidation of the business, since key contracts would have automatically vested in the substituted entities.

Competition law

12.174 In respect of the step-in rights of the lenders relating to project contracts entered into with public authorities, the substitution entails a modification of the initial conditions of the concession or PPP contracts, consisting of a transfer of the rights and duties to another *concessionaire* or partner. Consequently, the issue is to determine whether the implementation of step-in rights amounts to a fundamental rewriting of the concession itself, thus rendering it necessary to comply with the obligations resulting from the regulations governing the award of public procurement contracts.

12.175 On the other hand, one could also argue that if the substitution entails the termination of a project contract, the new agreement should be entered into in strict compliance with applicable competition and procurement rules.

12.176 This issue, which is still subject to debate, should be carefully taken into consideration by the lenders at the time of enforcement of step-in rights.

Efficacy of direct agreements

12.177 Direct agreements indisputably raise many issues as to their validity and interface with the French bankruptcy rules. The Channel Tunnel case is a good example of the uncertainties relating to the validity of step-in rights. The Channel Tunnel concession was approved by the international Treaty of Canterbury between the French Republic and the United Kingdom on 12 February 1986. The Treaty of Canterbury was promulgated in France by an act of parliament of 14 June 1987 to approve 'in as much as necessary' the concession agreement. In 2004, when the Channel Tunnel concession company was on the verge of bankruptcy, the financial creditors envisaged exercising their step-in rights as stipulated in the concession agreement.

12.178 Despite the fact that the Channel Tunnel concession and the step-in rights provided for thereunder were approved by an international treaty and an internal law in France, the validity of the step-in rights was questioned. The consensual analysis concluded that the application of French domestic insolvency rules, even if they were to qualify as mandatory 'public policy' rules, could not be a valid obstacle to the implementation/enforcement by a French judge of the step-in rights only because they were approved by the Treaty of Canterbury and validated by the act of parliament of 15 June 1987.

Security granted by the sponsors

In non-recourse project financings, the financial obligations of the sponsors are **12.179** traditionally limited to their obligation to contribute their equity stake in the project company. However, the sponsors:

(1) often grant a security interest over the project company's shares; and
(2) depending on the project and the risks identified by the lenders, may grant limited guarantees such as completion guarantees, performance guarantees, cost overrun guarantees or grant offshore cash collateral.

As a matter of French law, most of the security interests granted by the project **12.180** company are likely to be frozen because of the automatic stay rule of enforcement actions by creditors against the debtor in a bankruptcy scenario of the project company.

Therefore, as a matter of principle, lenders would have immediate access only to **12.181** the security or guarantees granted by the sponsors which should not, subject to exceptions depending on the relevant jurisdictions, be affected by a bankruptcy of the project company.

Influence of Civil Code in African Countries: Organisation pour l'Harmonisation en Afrique du Droit des Affaires (OHADA)

Project financing techniques have spread from France and elsewhere into many **12.182** African countries, which have seen considerable development of their economies through the closing of project finance transactions in the mining, oil and gas, telecom, power, and infrastructure sectors. It is therefore important to have a thorough understanding of civil law jurisprudence when seeking to structure project financings in Francophone Africa.

In addition, in many African countries, it is also important to have a thorough **12.183** understanding of the OHADA. This is the French acronym for '*Organisation pour l'Harmonisation du Droit des Affaires en Afrique*' translated in English as the 'Organization for the Harmonization of Business Law in Africa'. OHADA is an organization which was created on 17 October 1993 in Port Louis (Mauritius) and was formed by an international treaty.

Seventeen African states are now party to the OHADA treaty. Initially fourteen **12.184** African countries signed the treaty, with two countries subsequently adhering to the treaty (Comoros and Guinea), and a third, the Democratic Republic of Congo, joining in 2010. However, the Treaty is open to all African countries, whether or not members of the Organization of African Unity (OAU).

Purpose of the OHADA

12.185   The objective of the OHADA is the harmonization of business laws in the contract-ing states by the elaboration and adoption of simple modern common rules adapted to their economies, by setting up appropriate judicial procedures, and by encourag-ing arbitration for the settlement of contractual disputes.

12.186   The origin of the OHADA was based on the wish of the OHADA nations to adopt a regime which would increase their attractiveness to foreign investment by materially changing the investment rules in West and Central Africa, with a view to enhancing local development.

12.187   For such purposes, the OHADA nations have agreed to give up some national sov-ereignty in order to establish a single, cross-border regime of uniform business laws. A particular feature of the OHADA laws is that they are immediately incorporated into the domestic laws of each OHADA nation. Therefore, the OHADA laws are somewhat comparable to EU regulations that become immediately enforceable as law in all EU member states simultaneously.

French civil law influence on the OHADA laws

12.188   Since most of the OHADA nations have been strongly influenced by the French civil code, the OHADA laws are based on the French legal system and are substan-tially influenced by the French-based laws that preceded them in most of the OHADA territories. The OHADA laws have, however, been adapted to the needs of these developing economies and updated.

12.189   It is also reasonable to assume that the French legal system will continue to influ-ence new OHADA laws, at least to some degree, even if the member states of OHADA may have a keen interest in welcoming Anglophone African countries and their common-law heritage and to cherry-pick from various systems when drafting new laws, rather than to follow solely the French civil law tradition.

Structure of the OHADA organization

Member states of the OHADA

12.190   The uniform OHADA business law is applicable in 17 sub-Saharan African states : Benin (1995), Burkina Faso (1995), Cameroon (1996), Central Africa (1995), Comoros (1995), Congo (1999), Ivory Coast (1996), Gabon (1998), Guinea (2000), Guinea Bissau (1996), Equatorial Guinea (1999), Mali (1995), Niger (1995), Senegal (1995), Chad (1996), Togo (1996), and the Democratic Republic of Congo (2010).

12.191   Pursuant to article 53 of the OHADA treaty, any member state of the African Union may become a member, if it wishes to do so. Other African countries are giving active consideration to joining the OHADA common system of business laws.

OHADA institutions

The OHADA includes four institutions: **12.192**

(1) the Council of Ministers of Justice and Finance, which is the organization's legislative body;
(2) the Common Court of Justice and Arbitration, based in Ivory Coast (Abidjan);
(3) the Permanent Secretariat, based in Cameroon (Yaounde); and
(4) the Regional Training School of the Judiciary, based in Benin (Porto Novo), administratively attached to the Permanent Secretariat.

The institutions of OHADA mean that the OHADA is not just a system of uniform   **12.193**
laws, it is a unified legal system. It encompasses an entire legislative and judicial structure that formulates and interprets the OHADA laws and allows for their enforcement.

Council of Ministers of Justice and Finance—Uniform Acts

Acts enacted for the adoption of common rules by OHADA are known as 'Uniform   **12.194**
Acts'. Uniform Acts are prepared by the Permanent Secretariat office in consultation with the governments of member states. They are to be debated and adopted by the Council of Ministers of Justice and Finance on consultation with the Common Court of Justice and Arbitration.

Adoption of the Uniform Acts requires unanimous approval of the representatives   **12.195**
of the member states who are present and who have exercised their voting rights. Uniform Acts are directly applicable in the member states notwithstanding any conflict they may give rise to in respect of previous or subsequent enactment of laws by member states.

Common Court of Justice and Arbitration

Even though the OHADA laws provide for a harmonized set of rules throughout   **12.196**
the member states, the OHADA laws would not be effective unless they are enforced without major variation between the member states. A harmonized enforcement mechanism is achieved because a law that OHADA adopts automatically and immediately becomes an internal law of each of OHADA's member states, coupled with the interpretive function of the Common Court of Justice and Arbitration ('*Cour Commune de Justice et d'Arbitrage*') which serves as the court of last resort for judgments rendered and arbitrations instituted within member states.

Regional Judiciary Training School of the Judiciary ('Ecole Régionale Supérieure de la Magistrature')

Another body that OHADA has established is a regional judiciary training school,   **12.197**
the *Ecole Régionale Supérieure de la Magistrature*, which is designed to educate the legal professionals of the OHADA member states.

Content of the OHADA laws

12.198 The OHADA laws are purely business-related laws. These texts lay down the common rules governing business. The following uniform laws have already been adopted by the Council of Ministers:

(1) Uniform Act relating to general commercial law;

(2) Uniform Act relating to commercial companies and economic interest groups;

(3) Uniform Act relating to security (guarantees and collaterals);

(4) (iv) Uniform Act relating to simplified recovery procedures and measures of execution;

(5) Uniform Act relating to bankruptcy;

(6) Uniform Act relating to arbitration;

(7) Uniform Act relating to accounting law; and

(8) Uniform Act relating to law regulating contracts for the carriage of goods by road.

12.199 In the context of project finance and banking transactions, it is worth noting that the security interests governed by the Uniform Act relating to security include all the traditional French civil code security interests. The security interests developed more recently under French law and practice during the last thirty years (i.e. security interests over receivables by way of transfer of title, trust (*fiducie*), cash collateral, and pledges over securities accounts) still need to be implemented in the OHADA legal system.

12.200 The concept of a floating charge does not exist (except for the pledge over business concerns), nor does the concept of creating a security interest over receivables by way of transfer of title.

12.201 The Uniform Act relating to security governs the following types of security interest whose main terms and conditions are substantially based on the traditional methods of creating security interests under French law:

(1) the pledge over business concern;

(2) the pledge over moveable tangible property;

(3) the pledge over moveable intangible property;

(4) the pledge over shares;

(5) the pledge of inventory;

(6) the pledge of equipment; and

(7) the mortgage.

13

DEFAULTS AND WORKOUTS: RESTRUCTURING PROJECT FINANCINGS

Nick Angel and Alistair Hill, Milbank, Tweed, Hadley & McCloy LLP

Introduction

What is a restructuring?

13.01 There is no specific legal definition of a restructuring (also referred to as, amongst other things, a workout, turnaround, or corporate rescue) and it is a term which is used to cover a number of transactions ranging from a solvent covenant reset through to a fundamental balance sheet restructuring, often in the form of a debt for equity swap, whereby the existing equity in an entity is taken over by its creditors in consideration for the partial or complete release of those creditors' debt claims. As a general statement, however, a restructuring is a reference to a process by which a company which is experiencing, or which will imminently experience, financial difficulties, negotiates an amendment or rescheduling of its financial obligations in order to avoid a liquidation or other form of 'terminal' insolvency and thereby continue as a going concern. A restructuring therefore attempts to match a company's financial obligations to its actual performance.

13.02 The economic rationale for a restructuring is clear: formal insolvency is likely to be value destructive for all stakeholders and therefore each stakeholder is likely to be better served by a restructuring which seeks to preserve the economic value of a company, albeit on different terms from that bargained for when the company was originally financed. This assumes of course that the entity to be restructured has inherent value, i.e. companies which are successfully restructured tend to have a good underlying business but an inappropriate balance sheet for the size and prospects of that business going forward. Bad balance sheets can be dealt with by a restructuring; fundamentally bad businesses cannot.

13.03 Restructurings can take place either on a fully consensual, out-of-court basis (i.e. freely negotiated and agreed by all relevant stakeholders) or can be implemented on a non-consensual basis (where not all stakeholders agree with the particular restructuring being proposed). Where a restructuring is implemented on a non-consensual basis it will usually be done so using some form of formal, court-supervised insolvency or 'cram-down' process in the relevant jurisdiction or jurisdictions in order forcibly to bind or disenfranchise the dissenting stakeholder(s). The insolvency process in such a case is not, however, a terminal process as its purpose will be to enable the company to continue to operate and trade on a restructured basis as opposed to it being the process by which the company is wound down and ceases to exist.

What is different about a project finance restructuring?

13.04 Whilst project finance restructurings share much in common with their corporate brethren they can also differ in significant ways as a result of the particular, highly structured features of a typical project finance transaction. Project finance depends on a fundamental alignment of the debt and equity financing arrangements with the terms of the project's underlying commercial contracts. Project finance is one of the few practice areas of financial law where finance lawyers are required to delve deep into the underlying commercial contracts of the business being financed. As a result, whereas many corporate restructurings can be classified as purely financial restructurings (i.e. affecting only financial creditors, whilst the debtor's underlying commercial and trading contracts and relationships are unaffected), project finance restructurings often involve not only a financial restructuring to resize and/or amend the terms of the project company's debt, but may also involve a restructuring of the key commercial contracts upon which its business depends. This can make a project finance restructuring even more complex and time-consuming than the restructuring of a non-project entity.

This being said, for the reasons explained in paragraph 13.94 below, the options available to creditors in a project finance restructuring are frequently more limited than those available to creditors in a corporate restructuring and, consequently, the fundamental balance sheet and 'loan-to-own'[1] restructurings which have been a feature of a number of recent leveraged finance restructurings are less common (although not unknown) in project financings.   **13.05**

With the above in mind, the purpose of this chapter is to provide the non-restructuring specialist reader with a general overview of the protagonists in a restructuring, their motivations and options, together with an overview of the restructuring process, noting, where relevant, the particular features of project financing which have an impact on these matters as compared with a 'standard', corporate restructuring. The references throughout to the 'debtor' or 'company' are references to, in a project finance context, the project company.   **13.06**

Why do projects need restructuring?

As explored in Chapters 4 and 5, project finance depends fundamentally on risk identification and the mitigation and allocation of those risks amongst the various project stakeholders. Project risks are numerous and varied and include construction costs, timing and completion risk, third party performance risk, political and regulatory risk, and market risk. The manifestation of these risks and the subsequent financial difficulties that they entail can occur during any stage of a typical project's life cycle: development, construction, or operation.   **13.07**

Projects, like other corporates, are vulnerable to a number of risks which challenge the economic assumptions upon which their financing was arranged, for example, mismanagement, the insolvency of key customers or suppliers and, more generally, changes in the macro economic climate. In addition, as projects are, by their very definition, single purpose, non-diversified undertakings, projects are particularly vulnerable to unexpected changes in the particular market which they operate and/ or unrealistic assumptions about the market on which the original financing was prefaced. A good example of the impact of changes in particular market conditions was the significant fall in prices (up to 40 per cent) in the UK wholesale electricity market between 1998 and 2002 which led to several high-profile restructurings in   **13.08**

---

[1] 'Loan-to-own' is a reference to a strategy, generally pursued by a number of specialised hedge funds/opportunity funds, whereby investors purchase the debt in a financially distressed enterprise at a significant discount, with the specific aim of implementing a fundamental balance sheet restructuring whereby some or all of that debt is converted into equity in the restructured company.

the energy sector, for example, the 2003 restructuring of Drax, the UK's largest coal-fired power station. For a relatively recent example of the effect of unsustainable market assumptions, the original financing for the Lane Cove Tunnel project in Sydney was based on an assumption that traffic usage would range from 90,000 to 110,000 car trips a day. In reality, an initial toll-free period resulted in 75,000 car trips a day and, following the introduction of a toll, 50,000 trips a day.[2] It is unsurprising therefore that the original project company which owned and operated the tunnel subsequently went into receivership.

13.09 Notwithstanding the inherent riskiness of single purpose, non-recourse project financings, it is notable, by reference to the financial and liquidity crisis of 2008–2009, that project finance transactions have, in the main, remained relatively immune to the need for the fundamental restructurings that have been seen in other product areas such as leveraged finance and CMBS transactions. This is perhaps testament to the thoroughness of the downside risk assessment of project financings (a virtue of their inherent riskiness) and the highly structured manner in which risks are identified and, to the greatest extent possible, isolated and mitigated. Not only does this mean that default rates are lower but, generally speaking, even following a default, recovery rates on project financings have historically tended to be higher than on other forms of leveraged and general corporate financing.[3] It is because of these fundamental structural features that project finance, although premised on high leverage levels, tends to have much lower margins than in the corporate leveraged market.

Restructuring Protagonists

Overview

13.10 The outcome of any particular restructuring will be determined, in large part, by four key factors:

(1) the prevailing economic and financial circumstances at the time of the restructuring;

(2) the causes and extent of the company's financial difficulties;

(3) the identity of the protagonists and their economic motivations; and

---

[2] Cited in Geoff Phillips, 'Analysis of Sydney Public-Private Partnership Road Tunnels', Paper for ASOR National Conference, 3–5 December 2007, available at <http://www.maths.usyd.edu.au/u/geoffp/melfinrv.pdf>.

[3] See, for example, Standard Poor's, 'Project Finance Consortium Study Reveals Credit Performance Trends Since the Early 1990s', 8 August 2007 (available at <http://www2.standardandpoors.com/spf/pdf/products/ProjectFinanceConsortiumStudy_09_26.pdf>).

(4) the protagonists' legal rights and obligations under both their existing contractual arrangements and as a matter of the general law in the relevant jurisdiction(s).[4]

Perhaps more than any other area of financial law it is this fourth element which makes restructuring such a fascinating practice area as the ultimate 'backdrop' to any restructuring will be the insolvency alternative (i.e. what would be the result if a restructuring is not concluded and the entity in question is liquidated/wound-up). In the words of Philip Wood: **13.11**

> Insolvency law is the root of commercial and financial law because it obliges the law to choose. There is not enough money to go round and so the law must choose who to pay. The choice cannot be avoided, compromised or fudged. On insolvency, commercial law is at its most ruthless: it must decide who is to bear the risk so that there is always a winner and a loser, a victor and a victim. On bankruptcy it is difficult to split the difference. That is why bankruptcy is the most crucial indicator of the attitudes of a legal system in its commercial aspects and arguably the most important of all commercial legal disciplines.[5]

The harsh reality of the 'zero-sum' nature of insolvency as described above means that each protagonist's economic motivations and aspirations in a restructuring will need to be tempered by their legitimate expectations of what will happen if the restructuring fails and a terminal insolvency is the result. Restructurings can therefore often resemble a very complicated game of poker as the various protagonists attempt to second guess each other stakeholder's 'hand' by reference to their rights on paper and their inclination and ability to exercise those rights in practice. Understanding the motivations of each participant is key to achieving a successful restructuring. **13.12**

Whilst the identity of the protagonists, their motivations and their legal rights and obligations will obviously differ in each particular case, it is instructive to summarize (by way of a generalization) the key protagonists in a restructuring and some of the legal issues, options, and motivations which will be relevant to them, with reference to the specific features of project finance. **13.13**

The debtor and its directors

The debtor (i.e. the project company in the case of a project financing) will be at the centre of the restructuring. Central to what the debtor does will be the actions of its directors and those actions will be determined in large part by the requirements of **13.14**

---

[4] Different jurisdictions take very different approaches to how creditors' and borrowers' rights are affected on an insolvency. The nature of the legal regime in the jurisdiction in which the debtor would undergo an insolvency will therefore be key. The specific cross-border issues relating to the recognition of insolvency proceedings across borders and the exceptions to that recognition in each jurisdiction in which the debtor may have assets is, however, beyond the scope of this chapter.

[5] Philip Wood, *Principles of International Insolvency* (2nd edn, Sweet & Maxwell, London 2007) p. 3.

the law relating to directors' duties in the relevant jurisdiction(s). These duties can be central to the outcome of any restructuring and can fundamentally dictate the timing and form of a restructuring. Any restructuring stakeholder is therefore well advised to understand at the outset what these duties may entail. As director liability in many jurisdictions will entail personal financial liability and, in some jurisdictions, criminal liability for the directors in question, the issue tends to focus directors' minds beyond mere commercial expediency.

13.15 The example which is often given with respect to different jurisdictions' approach to directors' duties and the impact this can have on a restructuring is the contrast between the wrongful trading regimes under English and German law. Under English law, a director will potentially be liable for wrongful trading if 'at some time before the commencement of the winding up of the company, that [director] knew or ought to have concluded that there was no reasonable prospect that the company would avoid going into insolvent liquidation'.[6] It is a defence to a claim for wrongful trading if, after the director knew or should have concluded that there was no reasonable prospect of avoiding an insolvent winding up, the director took every step with a view to minimizing the potential loss to the company's creditors as he ought to have taken.[7]

13.16 The impact of the wrongful trading regime in England is that, generally, it allows directors to continue to trade when facing financial difficulties provided that there is a reasonable prospect that restructuring negotiations will successfully conclude (even if in fact they do not). This therefore gives time for the relevant financial and business information to be produced and analysed, restructuring proposals to be formulated and restructuring negotiations to occur without the directors feeling compelled to file the debtor for insolvency for fear of their own personal liability.

13.17 The position under English law contrasts with the position in Germany where directors of German debtors face criminal sanctions if they fail to file the debtor for insolvency within twenty-one days of actual knowledge of the company's insolvency, measured on a cashflow (illiquidity) and/or balance sheet (overindebtedness) basis. The three-week 'grace' period, however, is not available if, and to the extent that, prior to the expiry of the period, it becomes apparent that the insolvency grounds (i.e. illiquidity and/or overindebtedness) cannot be cured within that period. The impact of this regime is that it can give German companies much less time to arrange a restructuring than that afforded to English companies.

13.18 Whilst a restructuring is rarely an event which any of the main protagonists will particularly enjoy (it is, after all, not something that people, other than those who make a living from investing in, or advising, financially distressed companies,

---

[6] Section 214(2)(b) of the Insolvency Act 1986.
[7] Section 214(3) of the Insolvency Act 1986.

voluntarily embark upon), the position of the directors can often be the most stressful. The Chairman of the English casinos company, Gala Coral, which underwent a significant restructuring in 2010, put it as follows:

> It's been the year from hell. I'm going to write a book about it. At one stage, the mezzanine lenders accused me of being in the pocket of the private equity players. The senior lenders accused me of being a mezzanine poodle. And my private equity players accused me of being too close to the senior lenders. . . . My view on that was I had to be doing it about right because everyone seemed to hate me.[8]

The position for directors of a project company who are also employees of the spon- **13.19**
sors (which is often the case) can be particularly fraught. Even though their legal duties will be relatively clear (i.e. as the company enters into the 'twilight zone' of financial distress, the focus of their duties shifts from the shareholders (as the embodiment of the company's interests) to the creditors of the company), their role as an employee of a sponsor will inevitably complicate their position in practice. It is not unusual for directors to obtain legal advice for themselves separately from their company in a restructuring.

Whilst for some creditors playing 'hardball' with existing management/directors **13.20**
will be part of their *modus operandi* in restructuring negotiations, ultimately the process is unlikely to be helped if a genuine attempt is not made to keep the directors 'on-side'. They will, after all, likely know the business better than anyone else and, whilst not always the case, existing management (or certain individuals within the existing management) may be fundamental to the likelihood of successfully executing the revised business plan upon which any restructuring will be based.

The financial creditors

The financing parties' obvious motivation in any restructuring will be to protect the **13.21**
value of their investment. Behind this statement of the obvious, however, is the reality that in complex, multi-creditor structures (on which project financings are often based), it is very rare that creditors will act as a homogenous group during a restructuring. Different financial creditors will have different priorities and motivations depending on a number of variables, for example, whether they are an original par investor or a distressed secondary market purchaser, where their debt ranks in any intercreditor arrangement, what price the debt is 'marked' at for their own internal reporting purposes, and the nature of the debt held (for example, bank or bond debt).

In a project finance context, other points of difference between creditors can **13.22**
include different approaches from bridge lenders who finance the construction of the project but who otherwise expect to be refinanced on or prior to the project's commencement of operations and the project's longer-term investors.

---

[8] Neil Goulden (Executive Chairman, Gala Coral), quoted in *The Guardian*, 'Gala Coral Chief Executive Dominic Harrison to Quit', 21 July 2010.

Commercial banks can also often have a very different approach to a project finance restructuring when compared with the development/export credit agencies, which often, together with the commercial banks, participate in cross-border project finance transactions.

13.23 As a general rule, it will be the senior creditors (often represented through a committee of the largest creditors—see paragraphs 13.46–13.50 below) who will be largely responsible for devising, in conjunction with the debtor, a restructuring proposal and then 'selling' that proposal to other stakeholders and implementing it. However, even amongst senior creditors there can be a divergence of interests. This divergence of interests will broadly be between those who may have opportunistically bought into the senior debt at a discount and who may be motivated to agitate for a fundamental balance sheet restructuring (with a concomitant permanent 'haircut' on the debt outstanding) and those original par creditors whose motivation may be simply to renegotiate covenants with a borrower and thereby avoid having to report a non-performing asset on their books.

13.24 The emergence in the past ten to fifteen years of specialized distressed debt investors has undoubtedly had a profound impact on the manner in which restructurings are conducted and the form they take. These investors are highly specialist and will look across a company's entire capital structure for opportunities to profit from a restructuring; usually they will be focused on exploiting a position as a 'fulcrum' creditor (see paragraph 13.75 below for a discussion of 'fulcrum' creditors). The common characterization of such investors as 'vultures' is often unfair. Whilst their presence can complicate restructurings, they can be a source of vital liquidity for banks to manage their positions and can help develop innovative restructuring solutions as well as sometimes being prepared to provide new money to distressed entities.

13.25 In an attempt to regulate the competing agendas of different creditors during complex multi-creditor workouts, INSOL International has promulgated a set of principles[9] which are designed to reflect a best-practice approach by creditors and debtors to achieve a successful restructuring. There are eight principles in total and they revolve around the application of three fundamental concepts during the restructuring period:

(1) creditors should not take action to reduce their exposure (for example, by cancelling facilities that would otherwise be available);

---

[9] INSOL International, 'Statement of Principles for a Global Approach to Multi-Creditor Workouts', October 2000. Available at <http://www.insol.org/pdf/Lenders.pdf>. INSOL International is a worldwide federation of national associations for accountants and lawyers who specialise in turnaround and insolvency.

(2) borrowers should not take action which would adversely impact on a creditor's return; and

(3) if any new money is advanced to the debtor, it should be granted priority status.

While the principles obviously have no force of law they are sound guidelines for **13.26**
the conduct of a restructuring, particularly in multi-jurisdictional, multi-facility
situations. In practice, however, it is not uncommon to find the principles quoted
selectively and paid no more than lip-service by some stakeholders.

The sponsors

The sponsors are, for obvious reasons, central to any restructuring. They will **13.27**
have provided a significant amount of the original financing for the deal (albeit
subordinated to the creditors' claims) and will also often have, particularly in a
project finance context, the expertise and specialized, technical personnel necessary
for a project's successful development and/or operation.

In addition, whilst project finance is in theory fundamentally structured on a **13.28**
'non-recourse' or 'limited recourse' basis, meaning that the financial creditors in a
project financing will usually have no or limited recourse to the sponsors of the
project, in practice sponsors often retain some residual 'credit support' liability to
the project's financial creditors. For example, some form of contingent equity support may have been provided when the transaction was originally financed to
mitigate the risk of cost overruns during the construction phase of the project.
Sponsors sometimes also provide a completion guarantee whereby they agree to
guarantee the completion of the construction of the project and/or the repayment
of the senior debt during the construction phase of the project or provide a more
limited guarantee relating to specific risks. Depending on the timing of a project's
financial distress, this residual liability will obviously focus the sponsors' minds
because if the project fails and this residual liability is called upon, their loss will
exceed their original equity investment.

In a project finance context, the significance of the sponsors in a restructuring **13.29**
often exceeds the (important) fact that they have provided a portion of the original
financing. This is because they often 'wear another hat' in that their original equity
investment in the project will often be allied with the provision of core construction, operations, or maintenance services to the project or as an offtaker or marketer
of the project's product. This can complicate the bargaining dynamic between debt
and equity in a restructuring and can give the sponsors additional leverage that they
may not otherwise have in, for example, a leveraged finance restructuring.

Creditors generally recognize that they are in the business of lending money, not **13.30**
running complex projects, and therefore will usually place a premium on having a
borrower (through its sponsors) which is experienced in the industry in question as

it will generally be in the best position to keep the project afloat and improve the project's financial position.

13.31 For all these reasons, the bargaining dynamic between debt and equity in a project finance restructuring will be absolutely key to its outcome. The approach of the sponsors to a restructuring will be largely driven by their expected financial return on a project; their willingness to commit any new funds which may be required as part of a restructuring will principally be determined by their own internal rate of return objectives and requirements.

The project parties

13.32 Whilst the dynamics and risk sharing between debt and equity are common to any form of financial restructuring, what can make project financing restructuring different is that, as noted in paragraph 13.04 above, the underlying project contracts may need restructuring as well. Where this is the case, the parties to those contracts will also be key players in any restructuring. This contrasts with, for example, a restructuring of a corporate leveraged finance transaction where trade creditors, suppliers, and customers are, whilst interested observers in the process (if it takes place in the public domain), unlikely to be key players in what will usually be solely a financial restructuring, often implemented at a holding company level and therefore removed from the day-to-day operations of the underlying business.[10]

13.33 The original project contracts, be they the long-term supply contracts, the construction contracts, or the offtake contracts, will have been scrutinized in considerable detail when the original deal was put together and, fundamental to that scrutiny, will have been the identification and allocation of risks amongst all the interested parties. A restructuring will very often mean a restructuring of the risk allocation upon which the original transaction was based not only as between the providers of the project's finance but also as between the other key project parties such as offtakers, construction contractors, and project operators.

13.34 The ability of a project company successfully to restructure will depend on the willingness of the various project counterparties to engage in such a restructuring. Where, as is often the case, the relevant project party is connected to the project company (as noted above, sponsors often provide key construction, operation, or maintenance services to a project or otherwise purchase or market its products), it is likely to be incentivized to be cooperative in the restructuring process in order to ensure the continued viability of the project. In the case of a non-connected party, their willingness to cooperate will be purely based on a commercial assessment of their interests as a third party although the fact that they are likely to be an unsecured

---

[10] There are notable exceptions to this. For example, in the corporate restructurings of several car parts manufacturers and suppliers in recent years, the involvement of, and financing from, the global vehicle manufacturers has been crucial.

creditor of a project company, and their returns on any unsecured claim are likely to be negligible if the project fails, means that they will frequently be prepared to compromise to make a restructuring work. Unless, that is, they have a contract which is 'out of money' in which case their motivation may be just the opposite.

The government/local authorities

Politics can be a crucial aspect in project restructurings. As projects are often based on state granted concessions this will give the relevant public authorities a direct, vested interest in any restructuring, particularly bearing in mind the conditions that may have been attached to such a concession. In addition, as project financings often concern critical infrastructure projects, even where the state, in whatever guise, does not have a direct method of influence, there may well still be political considerations for project restructurings which would be absent in the course of a normal, corporate restructuring. This is coupled with the fact that a number of jurisdictions have specially designed insolvency procedures for certain types of public/private project companies. For example, Metronet, one of the project companies formed in the UK with respect to the high-profile and controversial public-private partnership (PPP) for the maintenance and upgrade of the London Underground network, was in July 2007 placed into the special PPP administration procedure provided for in the Greater London Authority Act 1999.[11]

13.35

Other parties

Depending on the type of project and the manner it which it was financed, a number of other parties may be relevant. For example, a number of project financings have been financed in the past by 'wrapped' bond issues. This refers to project bonds which benefit from a guarantee given by one of the monoline insurers. MBIA was a crucial player in the Eurotunnel restructuring[12] as it had given a guarantee for a large number of the bonds issued in connection with the Eurotunnel project and therefore bore the largest credit exposure during the restructuring of that entity. MBIA also featured in respect of the attempted restructuring of the Lane Cove Tunnel in Sydney (referred to above) as it had also provided a 'wrapped' bond guarantee in respect of the bonds used to finance the original development and construction of the tunnel.

13.36

---

[11] Whereas the interests of the creditors as a whole lie at the heart of the purpose of a normal administration under English law, the purpose of a PPP administration differs from this in that primacy is given to continuing the services provided under the relevant PPP agreement. This has to be balanced against the duty of the PPP administrators to protect the interests of creditors.

[12] For a summary of the Eurotunnel restructuring, one of the largest project finance restructurings in history and often referred to as one of the most complex restructurings to ever to have been completed, see the INSOL International publication 'Eurotunnel plc and Eurotunnel S.A. and Associated Companies: 2 August 2006 and 15 January 2007', Case Study—1 November 2008, available at <http://www.rovigo.ro/images/INSOLInternationalTechnicalCaseStudy1.pdf>.

Process

Introduction

13.37 Each restructuring will have its own process-related idiosyncrasies but as a broad generalization it will follow these five chronological, process categories/stages (although with some inevitable timing overlap between them):

(1) the occurrence of a restructuring 'trigger';
(2) creditor organization and information gathering;
(3) standstill negotiations and formalization;
(4) restructuring negotiations and proposals; and
(5) restructuring implementation.

The restructuring 'trigger'

13.38 To state the obvious, a restructuring requires the debtor to engage and unless the creditors have some form of contractual leverage, a debtor and/or its owners are unlikely to be willing to do so. The contractual 'trigger' that enables financial creditors to force the process is usually the occurrence of an event of default or potential event of default under the relevant finance documentation.

13.39 Prior to the occurrence of an unambiguous event of default (for example, the breach of a financial covenant), there can occur an uneasy stand-off between the debtor/the sponsors and creditors. The creditors, knowing that the company faces difficulties, will be combing the documents for potential leverage, whilst the debtor will usually tread very carefully, often seeking to delay the trigger and, usually, loathe to admit readily to the occurrence of an event of default. Even in circumstances where the debtor wants to be proactive, the relevant credit documentation can often provide that the very act of approaching creditors generally, or a group of creditors specifically, with a view to discussing debt re-scheduling can, *per se*, be an event of default.[13] Debtors will be very wary of the cross-default implications of such a provision in their financing documentation even if they are minded to make a proactive approach to creditors.

13.40 In addition, in a project finance context, as the occurrence of an event of default will likely have certain automatic consequences on, for example, the movement of cash under the accounts agreement (as referred to at paragraph 13.98 below) combined with the fact that the absence of an event of default will be a condition to, for

---

[13] The Loan Market Association standard form credit agreement provides that it is an Event of Default if the relevant entity 'is unable or admits inability to pay its debts as they fall due, suspends making payments on any of its debts or, *by reason of actual or anticipated financial difficulties, commences negotiations with one or more of its creditors with a view to rescheduling any of its indebtedness*' (emphasis added).

example, the release of any contingent equity support provided by the sponsors at the end of the construction phase of a project, the borrower and the sponsors may go out of their way to delay the occurrence of an event of default if at all possible.

Immediately upon the occurrence of an event of default, it is highly advisable, even **13.41** if the creditors have no immediate intention of exercising any of the rights which may accrue to them as a result of that event of default occurring, to write to the company formally reserving all rights to ensure that the debtor is not able subsequently to argue that there has been an implied waiver of rights. This formal notice of an event of default will also have the virtue of unambiguously starting any 'cure' periods which may operate with respect to potential or actual events of default which can otherwise be cured within a certain period of time under the relevant finance documents.[14]

Project finance covenants

The timing and nature of the event of default which will act as the restructuring **13.42** 'trigger' will depend fundamentally on the covenants which were negotiated as part of the original financing. As explained in previous chapters, project financings are highly structured, principally because the financial creditors' prospects of repayment will depend solely on the revenue stream from the asset being financed which, more often than not, will not start generating theses revenues until some years after the creditors make available the bulk of the funds to finance the project. As a result, project finance documentation tends to contain numerous covenants and restrictions to provide financiers with protections and early warning signs of potential problems with the project's underlying economic assumptions. Well-designed project finance documentation will contain a plethora of reporting requirements, the 'intrusiveness' of which would make an ordinary corporate borrower wince. These requirements should allow the project's financial creditors continually to test the validity of the underlying economic assumptions against the actuality of the project's development and performance, thereby giving the creditors the ability to intervene at an early stage should the project run into problems.

The impact of covenant 'loosening'

Notwithstanding the extensiveness and 'intrusiveness' of project finance covenants **13.43** as compared with other forms of financing, during the heady years of the 'great moderation' and the ensuing liquidity in the credit markets which reached a peak in 2007, the project finance market was no less immune to the loosening of covenants that occurred in the leveraged and other financing markets as banks competed

---

[14] Cure periods are often expressed to run from the time the debtor actually became aware of the relevant event of default or from the day upon which the debtor received notice of the occurrence of an event of default from the creditors' agent/trustee.

on a lowest common denominator basis for financing mandates. The result of this is that a large amount of the project financing arranged in the period between 2004 and 2007 was done on 'looser' terms than has historically been the case. This loosening permitted, amongst other things, higher leverage ratios, lower debt service coverage ratios, and, generally, less strict reporting requirements. As a result, the ability of creditors to intervene early has been restricted and, even when they are able to, the result of permitting much higher leverage ratios is that the creditors' equity protection (i.e. the amount of the 'first loss' financing provided by the sponsors) is much less than it has been in the past, so on an enforcement and sale following an event of default, lenders are more likely to suffer a loss on their debt.

Material adverse change 'triggers'

13.44 As stated above, the usual trigger for a restructuring is the actual or imminent breach of a financial covenant ratio. These have the virtue of being relatively unambiguous[15] as either the borrower demonstrably and objectively has or hasn't met the relevant financial covenant as provided for in the credit agreement. Prior to the occurrence of a financial covenant breach, creditors may investigate their ability to rely on a material adverse change (MAC) provision either by reference to a standalone MAC event of default or by reference to some other representation or covenant which is nonetheless qualified in its application by reference to a MAC.

13.45 As a general statement, creditors are unlikely to receive sufficient legal succour from their counsel that would allow them to rely solely on a MAC as a restructuring trigger. This is because the drafting of MAC clauses always includes some element of subjectivity and therefore an inherent risk that relying on it as a sole event of default will lead to a damages claim for breach of contract and/or tortuous liability if it is subsequently established that a MAC had not in fact occurred. Whilst, in the context of English law governed loan agreements, the House of Lords judgment in *Concord Trust v Law Debenture Trust Corporation plc*[16] has given some comfort to

---

[15] The complexity of financial covenant definitions, particularly under leveraged loan documentation, can lead to disagreements about whether a particular covenant has been complied with or not. Following the downturn in financial markets after 2007, there have been several high-profile examples of disagreement between creditors and sponsors/debtors over financial covenant calculations, particularly in relation to the impact of gains under debt-buy back transactions and the impact this has on EBITDA, for example, Endemol and Mauser.

[16] [2005] UKHL 27. The House of Lords ruled, on the specific facts of this case, that the bond trustee could not be sued for damages (under contract or tort) for the losses suffered by an issuer as a result of wrongful acceleration (i.e. acceleration on the basis of an event of default that had not actually occurred). The reasoning given was that, absent an express term prohibiting the issue of an invalid notice of acceleration, such a term would not be implied into the agreement unless it was necessary to give business efficacy to the contract. The notice of acceleration was therefore simply ineffective. For a further discussion of this case and MAC clauses more generally see Suhrud Mehta, 'Material Adverse Change Clauses in Adverse Markets', 3 October 2008, available at <http://www.milbank.com/NR/rdonlyres/F6BDC4A0-B496-43D6-A1D2-74896FFB2563/0/Material_Adverse_Change_Clauses_Mehta.pdf>.

trustees, agents, and creditors that their liability for incorrectly calling an event of default may not be as great as previously feared, the reality is that it will remain only in the most clear cut cases that creditors will formally rely on a MAC-based event of default.[17] Creditors will, however, use the MAC informally to attempt to hasten the debtor into restructuring negotiations.

Creditor organization

Following or shortly before the occurrence of the relevant restructuring trigger, creditors will seek formally to organize themselves in preparation for any restructuring negotiations. Depending on the size of the lending syndicate, it will often be in the company's interests, as well as its creditors, to appoint a lead bank or banks as formal 'coordinators' of the restructuring as well as a coordinating or 'steering' committee of (usually) the largest creditors, who will act as the main channel of communication and 'sounding board' for the syndicate as a whole during the restructuring. The Loan Market Association (LMA) has produced standard form coordinator/coordinating committee appointment documentation[18] which covers (a) the relationship between the company and the coordinator(s)/the coordinating committee and (b) the relationship between the coordinator(s)/coordinating committee and the lending syndicate as a whole. It is important to note that the role of the coordinator(s)/coordinating committee is purely administrative; it does not have an advisory role and many of the provisions included in the LMA precedents are aimed at making this point clear, i.e. express acknowledgement that the coordinator(s) and coordinating committee members have no fiduciary duties or general duty of care to any person and are not responsible for the accuracy or adequacy of any information or advice received in connection with the restructuring. **13.46**

Whilst the identity of the coordinator(s) and the composition of the coordinating committee will usually be dictated by creditor exposure, other factors can be relevant, such as previous restructuring experience, geographic presence, and industry expertise. In smaller restructurings, particularly where the outstanding debt is predominantly held by one or two large institutions, it may not be necessary to have a coordinating committee and the organization of the restructuring will simply be conducted via one or two coordinating banks. Substantively however there is no difference between a coordinator's role and that of a coordinating committee. **13.47**

---

[17] See *BNP Paribas v Yukos Oil* [2005] EWHC 1321 for an example of where the lenders successfully established, following a challenge from the debtor, that a MAC had occurred.

[18] Available to Loan Market Association members at <http://www.loan-market-assoc.com>. Note that these documents (or documents based on these standard forms) are generally used for restructurings in the European bank loan market. Different approaches may be necessary where, for example, the project has been financed by institutional investors in the bond market.

13.48 Depending on the complexity of the project company's capital structure, it may be necessary to have more than one coordinating committee/coordinator. For example, in transactions which have been financed by a combination of bank and bond debt, there may well be a bank coordinator/coordinating committee and some form of ad hoc noteholder committee. Likewise, if the project has been financed with mezzanine debt, the mezzanine creditors will usually want to organize separately from the senior creditors and may therefore appoint their own coordinator/coordinating committee.

13.49 Each relevant committee/coordinator will appoint its own legal advisers and usually its own financial advisers. The company will be expected to reimburse the creditors for the costs of these advisers and the indemnity for this will be covered by the form of coordinating committee appointment letter referred to above and/ or by the standstill agreement referred to below.

13.50 Once the coordinator/committee infrastructure is in place, it will be the coordinators, committees and their advisers which assume primary responsibility for:

(1) negotiating the standstill arrangements with the company (see in paragraphs 13.61–13.65 below);

(2) leading substantive restructuring negotiations with the company and amongst the various stakeholders to determine the form of restructuring; and

(3) negotiating the actual documentation by which the restructuring is implemented.

Information gathering

13.51 When a company experiences, or is exhibiting signs of, financial distress, the creditors' immediate priority will be to gather and analyse as much relevant information as possible. Establishing the infrastructure for the flow of information, including appropriate confidentiality agreements, will therefore be the number one priority in the early stages of a restructuring.

13.52 Prior to engaging in substantive restructuring negotiations, all stakeholders (although in particular financial creditors who will not be as close to the distressed entity in comparison to its sponsors and directors) will want as much information as possible to understand (a) the causes of the financial distress and the future prospects of the company, including its fundamental debt service capacity and (b) their rights under the relevant transaction documents and the rights of other stakeholders. It is on the basis of this information that a determination will be made as to whether the company has any realistic prospect of being successfully restructured on acceptable terms or alternatively whether it is beyond salvation. This phase of a restructuring has been described as:

> . . . a time when the size of the problem is ascertained, the lending, asset and group structure charts are being prepared, the strategy of the business is re-evaluated, recent

trading is assessed, cashflow is analysed, a schedule of banking facilities is prepared, the recourse of creditors and the maturity of their credit lines are established, other non-bank creditors are contacted and intra-group positions are analysed.[19]

A restructuring will therefore often involve as much information gathering and **13.53** diligence (if not more) than when the original financing was put in place. As noted in paragraph 13.42 above, however, given that project finance covenants require extensive ongoing reporting and information provision, project finance creditors tend to be relatively well informed as to the state of a project and its underlying finances in comparison to the creditors in normal corporate financings.

Financial information

The typical financial information which creditors will request in a distressed **13.54** scenario consists of:

(1) rolling twelve-week cashflow forecasts delivered on a weekly basis, including a management commentary on any variances between actual cashflows and projections on a week-to-week basis;
(2) a revised business plan, included detailed financial projections; and
(3) a management explanation as to why the financial difficulties have occurred.

In order to assess the reliability of the financial information provided by a distressed **13.55** company, creditors will almost always commission a firm of independent reporting accountants or financial advisers. Creditors will want independent verification that the financial information and projections provided by the company as part of the restructuring negotiations are not over-optimistic (management denial of a business's fundamental problems is not uncommon) or, of equal concern, such information and forecasts are not subject to management/sponsors 'low-balling'.

'Low-balling' (or 'sandbagging') is a reference to the fact that, once having accepted **13.56** the reality that a restructuring is necessary, it is possible that sponsors and management may use that restructuring deliberately to understate the future prospects of the company in the hope that this may entice creditors to reduce the debt burden of the company more than they otherwise would be prepared to do. Another dynamic that can emerge in this respect is that management, whose performance incentives may be reset as a part of a restructuring, may have an in interest in deliberately underplaying the chances of the restructured entity's success so that their restructured management incentives are linked to more easily achievable targets. Whether to guard against over-optimism or the more cynical practice of 'low-balling', creditors will place significant reliance on the work of their own

---

[19] Chris Howard and Bob Hedger, *Restructuring Law and Practice* (Butterworths Lexis Nexis, London 2008) p. 17.

independent reporting accountants/financial advisers to give them a realistic view of the company's finances and future prospects.

13.57 Of particular relevance to a project financing, where the financial distress has been caused by a fundamentally incorrect assumption about the relevant market for the particular asset or otherwise as a result of a mismatch between the assumed economics of the project's offtake or other arrangements and the debt serviceability and profile of the originally financed debt, creditors will want to understand this and may commission new independent third party technical and/or market reports in order that the original assumptions can be re-set as part of the restructuring and a new financial model constructed on the basis of these revised assumptions.

Legal due diligence

13.58 Creditors will, as part of the information gathering process, seek legal advice on the scope of their security, the options for enforcing that security and the risks and limitations in pursuing such an enforcement. When embarking on a restructuring, whilst security enforcement will typically be considered a last recourse option for the reasons analysed in paragraphs 13.99–13.105 below, creditors will nonetheless want to establish at the outset their downside scenario in the event that consensual restructuring discussions fail (and a base case as to which consensual proposals can be measured against) and to establish the leverage their security will give them *vis-à-vis* the debtor and other stakeholders.

13.59 The legal due diligence for a project finance restructuring should also cover an examination of the change of control and other provisions in the key project contracts and/or project licences/concessions to determine what impact an actual enforcement will have on the project's underlying commercial contracts. This will include an assessment of any direct agreement arrangements which may have been put in place with the relevant project contract counterparties.

13.60 As explored in Chapter 11, direct agreements will include rights to transfer a project company's contracts to a creditor sponsored vehicle. These step-in rights are regarded as crucial in a project financing as they theoretically allow, when combined with the creditors' proprietary security rights, the ability of the creditors to take over the project, ensure that it is completed/operated, and therefore that the cashflow on which their repayment depends is generated and sustained. As explained in paragraphs 13.104–13.105 below, the contrast between the theoretical exercise of these rights as written in the various contracts and their operation in practice, means that direct agreements may be of limited utility in certain circumstances, particularly where the debtor enters some form of formal insolvency procedure.

The standstill agreement

13.61 Following the occurrence of, or immediately prior to, an event of default under its financing documentation, the distressed company will be anxious to secure a formal recognition that financial creditors will 'standstill' for a period of time, i.e. agree not to exercise any of the rights they may have under the relevant finance documents as a result of the occurrence of that event of default. Standstill agreements take many different forms but generally cover the items summarized under in paragraphs 13.66–13.73 below.

The standstill agreement will be particularly important when the directors of the **13.62** company are considering their potential liabilities under the law of the jurisdiction in which the company is incorporated (see paragraphs 13.14–13.20 above). A standstill agreement, whilst not a panacea, will often give directors significant comfort that they can continue to trade whilst restructuring negotiations take place. This will particularly be the case if the standstill agreement contains provisions relating to the formal deferment or waiver of interest payment obligations as this will mean that the directors will have some comfort that the company will not imminently become cash-flow insolvent (i.e. unable to pay debts as they fall due). In addition, the existence of a standstill agreement can be very helpful for the debtor to manage its day-to-day trading relationships with suppliers and customers; these third parties will take some comfort from the fact that financial creditors have agreed to standstill and hence that the debtor is not at imminent risk of a formal insolvency process. As a result, third parties may feel more comfortable in continuing to trade with the debtor company during the period in which restructuring negotiations take place.

In addition to the directors, a standstill agreement will give comfort to creditors **13.63** as a whole (and other interested stakeholders) that a single creditor will not take precipitative action and, in this respect, an all creditor standstill arrangement helps to create a level playing field and a framework in which information can be shared and discussions held without fear that one creditor (or a group of creditors) will seek to use their contractual leverage to their advantage during the restructuring negotiations.

In a project finance context, where it may also be necessary to restructure certain of **13.64** the project contracts, it may be necessary to bring any relevant counterparties to the project contracts into the standstill arrangements if, for example, there has been a payment default by the project company under an important supply contract.

If it is not possible to negotiate a standstill agreement during the initial stages of **13.65** a restructuring, the company may have no option but to file for some form of formal insolvency process in the relevant jurisdiction and, if possible, negotiate a restructuring from behind the protection of any statutory moratorium or 'stay' that insolvency process provides.[20] There are, however, plenty of examples of

---

[20] Whether or not the directors are able to remain *in situ* following the filing for formal insolvency proceedings will depend on the type of proceedings available in each particular jurisdiction. In a number of jurisdictions, the filing for a formal insolvency proceeding will lead to an insolvency

restructuring situations where for various reasons, usually related to the complexity of the capital structure, it has not been possible to formalize a standstill arrangement amongst creditors but nonetheless, without the sanctity of either a statutory or contractual stay or moratorium, the company has continued to operate for months with a *de facto* standstill whilst restructuring negotiations take place.

Contents of a standstill agreement

Overview

13.66   The general objective of a standstill agreement is to provide the company with guaranteed financial stability for a period of time (the 'standstill period') by preventing creditors taking any form of enforcement action or otherwise exercising their rights under the relevant finance documents against the company during that period. During the standstill period stakeholders will analyse the relevant information, conduct restructuring negotiations and, in the event an agreement is reached, enter into a formal restructuring agreement (see paragaph 13.84 below) which will contain the framework for implementing the restructuring as well as reflecting the economic terms of that restructuring.

Contractual 'moratorium'—the standstill

13.67   The key operative provision of a standstill agreement will therefore be the creditors' formal agreement and undertaking not to take any form of enforcement action or otherwise pursue available remedies against the company (either as a matter of general law or in accordance with the particular rights provided for in the finance documentation). This contractual moratorium will be drafted very widely to cover any and all rights, including the right to accelerate the facilities and/or place them on demand, set-off rights, and any statutory insolvency remedies, for example, the right to petition for a winding-up in respect of an unpaid debt.

13.68   Where there are already standstill provisions included in an existing intercreditor agreement as between senior and junior tranches of debt[21], consideration will need to be given to the operation of these provisions and their interaction with the general standstill provided for in the all creditor standstill agreement. For example, the senior creditors will want to ensure that the standstill period negotiated with the company as part of the standstill agreement does not, in the event that restructuring

---

practitioner or other court-appointed or supervised trustee assuming control of the company in place of the directors. This approach contrasts with, for example, the 'debtor in possession' characteristic of Chapter 11 in the United States.

[21] In senior/mezzanine financings, the mezzanine creditors are typically required under the intercreditor agreement to standstill for a period of time following the occurrence of an event of default. The typical formulation is ninety days for a payment event of default, 120 days for a financial covenant event of default and 150 days for any other event of default. The mezzanine standstill is subject to certain exceptions, for example, the mezzanine creditors are able to take enforcement action if the relevant obligor is subject to an insolvency event.

negotiations fail, prejudice the separate standstill provisions between the senior creditors and the junior creditors in the relevant intercreditor agreement.

Interest deferral

Depending on the circumstances, as mentioned above, a standstill agreement can **13.69** also include provisions whereby creditors will agree to defer or forego certain interest payments. This will obviously only be agreed to by creditors reluctantly and only where the alternative for the company is cashflow insolvency during the standstill period.

Continued access to facilities

Assuming that an event of default acts as a draw-stop to any existing facilities (see **13.70** paragraph 13.96 below), the standstill agreement may set out provisions regulating the continued ability of the borrower to draw down on the facilities. These drawings may attract 'super priority' status. If new facilities are to be made available by the creditors to the company to enable it to meet its liquidity requirements during the standstill period then the arrangements for the priority of this new funding can also be reflected in the standstill agreement.

Company undertakings

Creditors will expect a quid pro quo for their forbearance and a standstill agreement **13.71** will typically include new obligations on the company. Depending on the situation, these new obligations can include:

(1) granting new or additional security or improving or remedying any defects with the existing security;[22]
(2) new restrictions imposed on the company with respect to the use of any surplus cash (although, in a project finance context, the existing accounts agreement will already regulate all of the project's cashflows);
(3) an undertaking not to prefer one creditor (or group of creditors) over another by the repayment of individual debts or the grant of preferential security or other credit support;
(4) an undertaking to pay the fees of any advisers engaged by the creditors;

---

[22] In a project finance context, all relevant assets will usually already be secured. If any new security is given or amendments are made to the existing security, creditors should be aware that, depending on the jurisdiction, new or amended security may be subject to new hardening periods and/or otherwise be voidable in respect of the relevant jurisdiction's transactional avoidance provisions which apply in a subsequent insolvency. For example, in England new floating charge security which is granted for existing debts will generally be voidable if the company subsequently enters into liquidation or administration in the period of twelve months from the granting of that security and was unable to pay its debts at the time of giving the security or became so as a result of the transaction (s 245 of the Insolvency Act 1986).

(5) an agreement to cooperate with creditors and work towards a restructuring plan, including the provision to the creditors and their advisers of all necessary information;

(6) an obligation to provide certain deliverables by certain dates, for example, production and distribution of a new business plan and delivery of a comprehensive restructuring proposal and an undertaking to provide certain of the periodic information referred to in paragraph 13.54 above, for example, weekly twelve-week cashflow forecasts; and

(7) an obligation not to take action which may jeopardize the company's financial position.

The duration of the standstill period

13.72 The length of the standstill period will vary from case to case although typically creditors will not want the standstill period to be too long, with a view to 'keeping the debtor's feet to the fire'. It is usually the case that the initial standstill period will be extended a number of times during the course of the restructuring negotiations as circumstances dictate. In addition to a 'backstop' standstill expiration date, the standstill agreement will usually include a number of automatic termination events. These will include the occurrence of an insolvency event, the company failing to comply with the undertakings given by it in the standstill agreement, and the occurrence of any other event of default under the finance documents not otherwise specifically disclosed in the standstill agreement. In addition, the creditors (usually on a majority basis) may negotiate the right unilaterally to terminate the standstill agreement.

Reservation of rights

13.73 Even if the creditors have already issued a formal reservation of rights letter to the company on the occurrence of the first restructuring 'trigger', the standstill agreement will usually include a formal reservation of rights and will make clear that, immediately upon the expiration/termination of the standstill period, the rights the subject of the standstill will immediately become exercisable.

Restructuring negotiations

13.74 Whilst there may have been preliminary discussions about the actual substance of a restructuring during the time that the restructuring 'infrastructure' (appointment of advisers, coordinating committee documents, information gathering, standstill agreement, etc.) is being put in place, it is likely that the substantive restructuring negotiations will only begin in earnest once these processes have been finalized. Prior to engaging in substantive, all-stakeholder discussions, certain protagonists may have chosen to align themselves with other stakeholders. These groupings will vary from restructuring to restructuring; in recent leveraged restructurings a pattern has emerged of sponsors aligning themselves with the senior creditors in an attempt to disenfranchise mezzanine or other junior creditors. As a result of these groupings, often competing restructuring proposals will develop and central to each proposal will be the protagonists' views as to the ongoing debt capacity of the company and, most importantly, the appropriate valuation of the company, as explored below.

Restructuring valuations

The determination of who is 'in the money' and who is 'out of the money' depending on what valuation is applied to the company and in what context lies at the very heart of restructuring negotiations. Inevitably, a number of the different protagonists will have different and strong opinions on value depending on their position in the capital structure. The early positioning in restructuring negotiations will turn around a debate as to who the 'fulcrum' creditors are as it is likely to be the fulcrum creditors who will take pole position in driving forward the shape of any restructuring. The fulcrum creditor is a reference to those in the capital structure where value is deemed to 'break'. Those creditors who are completely 'in the money', whilst obviously interested in the outcome of a restructuring, have the comfort that they should not suffer a loss whilst those creditors who are completely 'out of the money', so the argument goes, should have no influence in the restructuring as they have no economic value left to protect. It is therefore those creditors whose debt is not entirely covered in accordance with the prevailing valuation but who still have an economic interest in the company who often take the lead in a restructuring. **13.75**

As valuation is often highly subjective and depends fundamentally on the assumptions used and valuation method adopted, the scope for argument and debate on this key issue is considerable. Whilst there are a number of complex nuances to the valuation debate in restructurings, the fundamental schism is between whether a liquidation/distressed sale valuation is the appropriate valuation technique for a financially distressed company or whether the valuation should be based on the going concern valuation of the entity assuming it has been successfully restructured.[23] As the range of valuations between a liquidation or 'fire-sale' approach (at the lower end) to a valuation based on the inherent, ongoing value of an entity post-restructuring (at the higher end) can be in the tens if not hundreds of millions (depending on the size of the company), the determination of the 'correct' approach can have a fundamental impact on determining the identity of the fulcrum creditors. The issue is further complicated by the complex, multi-tiered capital structures that have been adopted in the past decade as this further increases the scope for valuation arguments as between different tranches of debt. **13.76**

---

[23] See Michael Crystal QC and Rizwaan Jameel Mokal, 'The Valuation of Distressed Companies—A Conceptual Framework', 2006 (available at <http://papers.ssrn.com/sol3/papers.cfm?abstract_id=877155>) for a summary of a number of the valuation arguments in this respect.

An English lawyer's approach to valuation

13.77 Whilst the law relating to the valuation of distressed entities is well developed in some jurisdictions (for example, the US), in a number of other jurisdictions the issue has received limited judicial attention, if any. In England, the restructuring of MyTravel plc in 2005 brought the issue to the attention of practitioners and the courts alike although the subsequent litigation[24] relating to that case was not determinative. More recently, the English High Court gave a key judgment[25] on valuation issues in relation to the restructuring of the pan-European car wash company, IMO Car Wash. The case concerned a disagreement between senior creditors and mezzanine creditors as to the correct valuation method to be adopted in the context of a restructuring of the leveraged financing for certain companies in the IMO group, to be implemented by way of schemes of arrangement under the English Companies Act 2006.[26]

13.78 In seeking to argue that the proposed schemes of arrangement were unfair (and so should not be sanctioned by the court), the mezzanine creditors needed to establish that they had an economic interest in the companies' business and assets, i.e. that whilst they were not completely 'in the money' they were not completely 'out of the money' either.[27] In so doing, they argued that their valuation (based on a theoretical discounted cashflow (DCF) valuation which regarded the companies as income generating assets to be held over time) was the appropriate valuation. The judge rejected this argument. This was on the basis that the mezzanine debt was contractually subordinated to the senior debt and the intercreditor arrangements, as common in leveraged finance transactions, gave the senior creditors the right to enforce their security unfettered by the claims of the mezzanine creditors. In the absence of a consensual restructuring, such an enforcement was a very likely option and therefore the relevant basis for valuing the companies in this case was the value of the companies' business and assets on a sale in the current market (based on a combination of actual values received during a marketing of the business, an income approach (based on discounted cashflow), a multiples analysis, and a market

---

[24] *In re MyTravel Group plc* [2004] EWCH 2741 (Ch) and *Fidelity Investments International plc v MyTravel Group plc* [2004] EWCA 1734.

[25] *Re Bluebrook Ltd* [2009] EWHC 2114 (Ch).

[26] Part 26 of the Companies Act 2006 provides a statutory 'cram-down' procedure under which a company is able to make a compromise or arrangement with its creditors (or any class of them) provided that a requisite majority of creditors agree (being 75 per cent in value and 50 per cent in number of each class of creditors who vote in favour of the scheme) and the court subsequently sanctions the scheme as fair and reasonable. Once the court sanction is obtained, the scheme will bind all creditors (or, as relevant, all creditors within a particular class) that are a party to the scheme, irrespective of whether they voted in favour of the scheme.

[27] In the IMO case the mezzanine creditors were not actually party to the schemes of arrangement as the schemes did not purport to alter their legal rights. Nonetheless creditors who are not otherwise party to a scheme can still object to it at the court sanction hearing on the grounds of unfairness if the proposed scheme unfairly affects their interests in ways other than affecting their strict legal rights.

comparables approach) and not by reference to the theoretical, DCF-based valuation which the mezzanine creditors espoused and which showed that value 'broke' in the mezzanine debt. The schemes of arrangement were therefore sanctioned by the court and the mezzanine creditors were left, following their implementation, with valueless claims against a holding company in the IMO group.

The IMO Car Wash case is now frequently cited (by senior creditors and, sometimes, sponsors) to show dissenting junior creditors the 'abyss' in restructuring negotiations concerning English companies or overseas companies which are otherwise able to be subject to an English scheme of arrangement.[28] Whilst the case is no doubt helpful to senior creditors in restructuring negotiations, as with so much case law, it turns on its own facts. In a project finance scenario those facts may well be different, particularly because the enforcement of security is, for the reasons explained below, not a realistic alternative to a consensual restructuring and because the overwhelming focus of project finance investors is, in fact, the prospective future cashflow of the project company and not the market value of its assets. In addition, the approach of courts in other jurisdictions on this important issue is not as clear as it is in the US and, following the decision in the IMO Car Wash case, in England.   **13.79**

The amount of ongoing debt

In addition to the valuation issue, at the heart of the restructuring negotiations will be a discussion between the relevant parties in relation to the amount and revised economic terms for the restructured company's debt. This will involve an inevitable balancing act between the natural inclination of most creditors[29] to leave as much debt as possible on the company's balance sheet (to avoid too large a write down) whilst at the same time leaving the company with a sustainable debt level going forward, taking into account the revised business plan and Financial Model.   **13.80**

Restructuring agreement and implementation

As restructuring negotiations are conducted, alliances amongst stakeholders are formalized, and the requisite due diligence is completed, detailed restructuring proposals will begin to emanate from the debtor itself and/or from groups of creditors. In most cases, once the various merits of each of the proposals has been scrutinized   **13.81**

---

[28] English law provides that any company which can be wound up under the Insolvency Act 1986 can be subject to a scheme of arrangement. Companies which can be wound up under the Insolvency Act include unregistered companies and these include foreign companies provided that certain conditions are satisfied, including that they have sufficient connection with England (*Re Drax Holdings Ltd* [2003] EWHC 2743 (Ch)). Recently, the English High Court approved jurisdiction for a Spanish company to be subject to an English scheme of arrangement (see *Re La Seda de Barcelona SA* [2010] EWHC 1364 (Ch)).

[29] As noted in para. 13.23 above, some creditors may favour a more significant write-down of debt than others, particularly those creditors whose motivations are based around a 'loan-to-own' strategy.

and the impact on each stakeholder analysed, a consensus will begin to emerge around one or two proposals. Generally speaking, those protagonists who build a consensus around a particular restructuring proposal will place a premium on the proposal being implemented on a consensual basis. The reasons for this are that a non-consensual process will generally be more costly to implement (as it will likely involve some form of formal court involvement or cram-down procedure such as a scheme of arrangement as referred to in paragraph 13.77 above) and that any non-consensual process will carry an inevitable litigation risk in respect of the parties who are objecting to the particular proposal and implementation process. Whilst there are exceptions, most project finance restructurings are concluded on a fully consensual basis and therefore without recourse to a formal insolvency, the courts, and/or a 'cram down' process.

13.82 However, in circumstances where it is not possible to obtain the consent of each relevant party, those advocating a particular proposal which has sufficient consent amongst the stakeholders may have to make use of some form of insolvency process or statutory compromise or cram down to ensure that dissenting parties are bound to the agreement which the majority parties have made. The form of this will vary from jurisdiction to jurisdiction. Where there are dissenting stakeholders to a proposal which otherwise has broad consent from the stakeholders, it will be crucial to develop a fully worked out, credible alternative implementation mechanic (often referred to by practitioners as 'Plan B'). In the ordinary course, the approach will be to demonstrate to dissenting stakeholders the way in which 'Plan B' can be made to work in detail in order to convince them that the proposal can be implemented without their consent and hence why they should proceed on a consensual basis with the restructuring consideration that they are being offered as part of a consensual deal. The aim being to avoid the costs, execution, and litigation risk that actual implementation of 'Plan B' may entail.

Restructuring documentation

13.83 The documentation for the agreed restructuring will vary depending on the nature of the restructuring. Where it takes the form of a relatively simple covenant re-set, it will most likely be documented by a straightforward amendment and restatement agreement which will amend and restate the relevant existing financing documents. The documentation for a more fundamental restructuring, such as a debt for equity swap, will be significantly more complex, time-consuming, and expensive.

13.84 Where the restructuring is complex and there may be a number of steps to go through over a period of time in order successfully to complete the restructuring, it is common for the consenting parties to enter into a detailed restructuring and 'lock-up' agreement. This document will perpetuate the standstill period for the period of time necessary to implement the restructuring and will include an agreement on the detailed steps necessary to complete the restructuring. Where there are dissenting creditors, the restructuring agreement will usually be drafted in a way which allows for the implementation of the restructuring on a non-consensual basis, whilst leaving the door open for non-consenting stakeholders to agree to the restructuring on a consensual basis if they accede to the restructuring/lock-up agreement by a certain date. Often the restructuring agreement will be drafted to incentivize non-consenting or apathetic stakeholders to accede by a certain date by making clear that there will be 'step-downs' in the restructuring consideration they will receive as time elapses and, where the restructuring has to be implemented on a non-consensual basis, making clear that the dissenting stakeholders will receive nothing. The restructuring/lock-up agreement will also often prevent creditors from trading their debt during the restructuring implementation period or allow them to do so only if the transferee agrees to be bound to the form of restructuring set out in the restructuring agreement.

Restructuring Options

Introduction

Whilst each restructuring will be unique, the options generally available in a restructuring scenario can be broadly categorized as below.

13.85

Extension/amendment

At its simplest, a restructuring may consist of a re-setting of financial covenants, usually on the basis that they are 'loosened' for a period of time to accommodate the actual or projected underperformance compared with the original base case for the financing. A covenant re-set may be coupled with a rescheduling of indebtedness such that its maturity is extended but the overall principal debt burden remains the same (or is potentially increased by amending some of the cash pay debt so it is payment in kind, in order to reduce the immediate interest burden on the borrower). The *quid pro quo* for this flexibility by the creditors will often be increased pricing for the debt (if this is sustainable considering the overall debt capacity of the company) and/or the payment of a restructuring consent fee. In addition, a quid quo pro for any financial covenant 'loosening' will often be increased covenant restrictions on the company (for example, restrictions on the movement of cash or the payment of dividends).

13.86

An extension and amendment process may occur before, but in anticipation, of an actual event of default. Sponsors may be prepared to take remedial steps prior to the occurrence of an actual event of default in order to try and protect their investment. Lenders may also be motivated to renegotiate covenants to avoid having to report non-performing loans on their books.

13.87

This covenant re-set process has become a common feature of the restructuring of a number of the highly leveraged buy-outs which took place between 2005 and 2007

13.88

and has been labelled by some as 'extend and pretend' or 'delay and pray', the implication being that this form of restructuring is merely a temporary fix and will inevitably require some form of more fundamental restructuring at a later stage.

Additional equity and/or priority creditor financing

13.89 In addition to covenant re-sets and maturity extensions as described above, the 'price' for the creditors' consent to the amendments may be the provision of new equity by the sponsors to fund the liquidity requirements of the revised business plan. In addition, in certain circumstances existing creditors or new investors may be prepared to provide additional financing (usually on a super priority basis). In certain cases, what may start out as a potential restructuring turns into a refinancing, in which all of the existing creditors are refinanced by new investors.

Sale/foreclosure/security enforcement

13.90 Following the occurrence of an event of default, creditors always have the theoretical option of enforcing their security either as a means to sell the relevant assets/companies to a third party purchaser (in the hope that a third party purchaser will be prepared to pay an amount sufficient to discharge the existing debt) or as a means to take control of the company themselves.

13.91 As a rule, lenders generally, and project finance lenders in particular, will be loathe to enforce their security unless they have lost all confidence in the directors/the sponsors. In a project finance context if creditors are nonetheless seriously contemplating an enforcement of security it will usually be with a view to taking actual control of the project as opposed to selling it to a third party. This is because the fundamental economic assumptions upon which project financing is arranged is by reference to the project asset's cashflows and not the market price of those assets (which may not be enough to repay the debt in full). An enforcement strategy will therefore usually be designed with a view to the creditors taking control of the project in order to preserve the project's existing or expected cashflows as their ultimate source of full repayment.

Debt for equity swap

13.92 In certain circumstances, usually where specialist distressed funds have purchased a financially distressed company's debt, the creditors may agitate for a fundamental balance sheet restructuring of a company whereby their debt claims are converted, either partially or in full, into equity in the restructured entity. The economic motivation is to use their position in a company's debt to force a restructuring on favourable terms which will lead to a large return in a relatively short time frame on the equity they acquire in the restructured entity. This was the strategy followed by a number of distressed debt funds in relation to the restructuring of the Drax power station in 2003. The strategy was successful and a number of the funds involved made very large returns as wholesale electricity prices rose from their all-time low in

2002 and the company was subsequently listed on the London Stock Exchange in 2005. In other circumstances, a debt for equity swap may be, whilst not the creditors' favoured outcome, the only realistic way in which creditors can attempt to preserve their value if the debt burden on the company is fundamentally unsustainable and there is no market for the asset or near term refinancing options.

The implementation of a debt for equity swap can either be done on a consensual basis or a non-consensual basis. Where it is done on a non-consensual basis, it will usually involve some form of security enforcement or facilitating insolvency process. Debt for equity swaps are significant undertakings and will involve a whole range of considerations, including a detailed tax analysis (as the release of debt claims typically crystallizes a taxable gain for the company released), detailed negotiations around the form of the new shareholders' agreement that will be needed (including drag and tag rights and other minority shareholder protections and corporate governance generally), and, depending on the identity of the converting creditors, the size of their shareholdings, and their other interests, competition law issues. **13.93**

Project finance limitations on creditors' options

In a project finance scenario, creditors' options are circumscribed by certain features (as described below) of project financing which mean that, in most cases, a project finance restructuring will consist of amendments, covenant re-sets and maturity extensions as opposed to some of the more fundamental balance sheet restructurings where creditors swap their debt claims for equity or otherwise become owners of the project. **13.94**

(1) As noted above, project finance is fundamentally a cashflow finance, as opposed to an asset finance, technique and creditors make their assessment of whether they will be repaid by reference to the cashflow generating ability of the project's assets, not the underlying value of the collateral/the balance sheet of the borrower. As a result, creditors may have no option but to give the project borrower the covenant or other flexibility it needs to complete and operate the project, in order to generate the revenues upon which the creditors' chances of full repayment will ultimately depend.

(2) Even if creditors are minded to enforce their security because they have lost faith in the borrower and/or its sponsors, there can often be limited market appetite for the large-scale, capital-intensive infrastructure assets which are typically financed in the project finance market. As a result, even if the creditors have the inclination and ability to conduct an efficient security enforcement (as to which see paragraphs 13.99–13.105 below), it may mean there are no buyers for the assets in question or that the only buyers will be opportunistic infrastructure investors who will be unwilling to pay full value.

(3) A project's contractual infrastructure and, in the case of sensitive infrastructure and other 'public interest' assets, governmental licensing/concession arrangements

will mean that an aggressive creditor restructuring strategy based around some form of unilateral enforcement or other security right, will be less likely to work than it would in the case of, for example, the corporate restructuring of a retail or manufacturing company.

Creditors' rights under project finance documents

13.95 The starting point for the creditors' assessment of their options when a project company experiences signs of financial distress will be their contractual rights under the existing financing documents. The nature of the contractual rights which the creditors may have at any particular time will depend on when the distress first manifests itself in a project's development, construction, and operation cycle.

Defaults during development/construction

13.96 As a general matter, drawings under credit facilities for a project during the development and construction phase of a project tend to be highly regulated and each drawing will be conditional on standard and project-specific conditions precedent. The project specific conditions precedent are often in the form of construction milestones and can be subject to independent verification, for example, for each draw down, the lenders' technical adviser is required to confirm that completion/commencement of operations is on target for a certain date. In addition, drawings will be contingent on the standard requirements that there be no outstanding event of default. This 'draw-stop' therefore gives creditors the option to prevent 'throwing good money after bad' if they are still contractually committed to lend funds immediately prior to the event of default. In practice, however, without access to funds to ensure completion, a project may be doomed and so, unless the creditors have recourse to some form of contingent equity support or completion guarantee, a draw-stop may serve no useful purpose other than crystallizing a loss for creditors. However painful or unpalatable it may be to lend into a structure which has defaulted on the terms originally bargained for, the continued provision of funds to finance completion of the project may present creditors with the best opportunity for eventual repayment.

13.97 If creditors do determine, however, to 'draw-stop' a project borrower, the event of default upon which they base that 'draw-stop' needs to be clear and unambiguous. The dangers for creditors in draw-stopping a loan on the basis of an event of default which the borrower is able to argue has not in fact occurred is that creditors may be held responsible for the losses consequential upon incorrectly calling an event of default and denying the borrower funds when it was otherwise contractually entitled to them.

Defaults during operations

13.98 When a project has reached an operational phase, the occurrence of an event of default will usually act as a dividend 'blocker' so that the sponsors will be unable, whilst the event of default subsists, to access any further distributions from the project. Another common restriction relates to the project company's freedom with respect to the project accounts and creditors will have a greater say under the relevant accounts agreement in respect of the movement of funds and how monies in the project accounts are used or invested. Typically, following the occurrence of an event of default, the accounts agreement will provide that the project company's day-to-day ability to manage the revenue cash waterfall is curtailed and all payments become subject to approval by the intercreditor agent and/or the account bank acting on behalf of the lenders.

Enforcement of security

As explained in Chapter 11, project financings depend fundamentally on a robust **13.99** security package. Security will usually be on an all asset basis and will include security over the shares in the project company. The transaction security will often cover a number of jurisdictions and hence be governed by a variety of laws depending on the location of the relevant assets. Despite receiving an extensive security package, project finance creditors will typically consider the enforcement of that security as a last resort in a financially distressed situation. The principal reasons for this are summarized below.

Jurisdiction risk

Notwithstanding the extensive nature of the security as described in the various **13.100** security documents at the time the transaction was originated, in practice, particularly in emerging markets, there will be significant concerns, taking into account costs, timing, and process, as to the actual effectiveness of the security in a practical enforcement scenario.

Whilst English lawyers are used to the extensive 'self-help' remedies available to **13.101** secured creditors including the appointment of an administrative receiver in certain circumstances,[30] as explained in Chapter 12, civil law jurisdictions generally do not (a) allow for the all asset embracing composite debenture which English

---

[30] Under English law, whilst the Enterprise Act 2002 removed the ability of secured creditors in most cases to appoint an administrative receiver in respect of security entered into after 15 September 2003, project finance lenders retain the ability to appoint administrative receivers in certain circumstances pursuant to the project finance exception contained in s 72(E) of the Insolvency Act 1986. This provides that an administrative receiver can be appointed in respect of a 'project company' if the project is a 'financed' project and includes 'step-in rights'. A project is financed if, under an agreement relating to the project, a project company incurs or, when the agreement is entered into, is expected to incur, a debt of at least £50 million for the purposes of carrying out the project. A project has 'step-in rights' if a person who provides finance in connection with the project has a conditional entitlement under an agreement to assume sole or principal responsibility, or make arrangements, for carrying out all or part of the project. See the Court of Appeal decision in *Cabivision v Feetum* [2005] EWCA Civ 1601 for a discussion of the project finance exception. In this judgment the Court of Appeal made clear that the right to appoint administrative receivers could not, *per se*, constitute step-in rights.

lawyers will be familiar with or (b) permit the availability of 'self-help' remedies for secured creditors, meaning that security enforcement can be a time-consuming, expensive, and uncertain process, often subject to the vagaries of court procedure and timetables.

Project contract risk

13.102 A project company's key and most valuable assets usually consist of (a) a particular concession or licence to develop the asset being financed and (b) rights under the various project contracts. Taking this into account, enforcement of security is often a blunt instrument because:

(1) the enforcement of that security (or the taking of it in the first place) will be subject to, in the case of state granted concessions or licences, the approval of the relevant minister or public authority granting the concession/licence; and

(2) an enforcement resulting in a sale to a third party is likely to trigger change of control provisions in the key project contracts and licences/permits which the project company has.

13.103 As explained in Chapter 11, direct agreements, a particular feature of project and construction finance, are designed to mitigate this risk by enabling creditors effectively to 'step into the shoes' of the project company and thereby they provide a right for the creditors to assume both the project company's rights and its obligations.

13.104 In a distressed scenario, the practical use of direct agreement needs to be carefully considered, particularly if the project company is to undergo some form of insolvency event as part of a restructuring. As noted in Chapter 12, direct agreements are founded on an Anglo-American legal tradition and a number of commentators have pointed to the fact that in other jurisdictions, with a less creditor friendly tradition/philosophy, the utility of direct agreements in those jurisdictions, particularly following the actual insolvency of the project company, may be compromised.[31] Generally this is because the rights of the debtor under a project contract are considered to be fundamental assets of the debtor's estate on its insolvency and provisions which purport, at the option of certain secured creditors, automatically to transfer those rights to another entity can be challenged on a variety of grounds (see paragraphs 12.177–12.178 in Chapter 12 for further analysis of this in a civil law context).

13.105 Even in an English law context, there are grounds upon which other, unsecured creditors of a project company which undergoes an administration or liquidation could seek to challenge the transfer of rights provided for under a direct agreement.

---

[31] See, for example, Sabina Axelsson, 'Project Finance and the Efficiency of Direct Agreements under Swedish Law: The Treatment of the Debtor's Contracts in Bankruptcy', Spring 2006, available at <http://gupea.ub.gu.se/bitstream/2077/1891/1/200636.pdf>.

In theory, such a transfer could be subject to a challenge by a liquidator or administrator as a transaction at an undervalue under section 238 of the Insolvency Act 1986 or as a preference under section 239 of the Insolvency Act 1986. In addition, English law, in common with civil law jurisdictions, does have an anti-deprivation principle which provides that, as a matter of public policy, assets which are not otherwise subject to an *in rem* right cannot be the subject of an arrangement where they are constituted as part of a debtor's property but are subject to being taken away in the event of the debtor's insolvency.[32] The application of this principle in each particular case will depend on the facts and the drafting of the relevant contract being challenged as contrary to the principle.[33]

---

[32] Per Cotton LJ in *Ex parte Jay, In Re Harrison* (1880) 14 Ch D 19 at 26: 'there cannot be a valid contract that a man's property shall remain his until his bankruptcy, and on the happening of that event shall go over to someone else, and be taken away from his creditors.'

[33] See *Perpetual Trustee Company Ltd v BNY Corporate Trustee Services Ltd* [2009] EWCA Civ 1160 for a recent discussion of the application of the anti-deprivation principle under English law.

14

DISPUTE RESOLUTION IN PROJECT FINANCE TRANSACTIONS

Michael Nolan, Julian Stait, and Erin Culbertson, Milbank, Tweed, Hadley & McCloy LLP

Introduction

14.01 Dispute resolution mechanisms in the project finance context are a means of enforcing the allocation of risks among a project's many participants—sponsors, lenders, contractors and subcontractors, service providers, off-take-purchasers, and others. To the extent that a dispute resolution mechanism is swift, flexible, reliable, final, and enforceable, the project's intended allocation of risks can be maintained. This chapter identifies various dispute resolution mechanisms that are available to project participants and discusses their suitability for the maintenance of a project's intended risk allocation.

(1) Paragraphs 14.02–14.24 address the options, which are predominantly contractual, for the resolution of disputes about commercial risks. It examines two regimes for dispute resolution that are commonly specified in project finance contracts: litigation in national courts and international arbitration.

(2) Paragraphs 14.25–14.51 address options for the resolution of disputes about political risk. It describes the main political risk factors that cross-border projects frequently face, explains the traditional means by which project participants have addressed political risks, and sets forth how bilateral and multilateral investment protection treaties (and to a lesser extent domestic investment legislation) have provided additional options to protect participants over the past two decades.

(3) Paragraphs 14.52–14.62 address enforcement of arbitral awards and judgments. One of the main advantages of choosing international arbitration instead of litigation in national courts is that arbitral awards are more readily enforceable in a large number of jurisdictions. The section describes the main enforcement mechanisms for international arbitration awards, as well as how national court judgments can be 'domesticated' and relied upon in foreign jurisdictions.

(4) Paragraphs 14.63–14.97 provide a 'toolkit' for drafting dispute resolution provisions to achieve participants' goals. It also describes 'multi-tiered' dispute resolution, which may include, for example, referring a technical dispute to an expert to assist in settlement of the dispute before turning to litigation or arbitration. Finally, the section describes options that may be useful to protect participants once they become engaged in disputes.

Disputes Involving Commercial Risk

14.02 Major international projects invariably face commercial risks. These risks typically are allocated in separate agreements between the various project participants. This section focuses on how the resolution of disputes may be affected by the contractual selection of either litigation or arbitration. There are three subparts: (a) identification of commercial risks for which dispute resolution provisions are frequently invoked in project finance transactions, (b) identification of features of the litigation and arbitration frameworks that may be of particular relevance in project finance transactions, and (c) analysis of how the choice of litigation or arbitration may affect the resolution of commercial risks.

Commercial Risks that Frequently Result in Project Disputes

As described in more detail in Chapter 4, international projects inevitably face a **14.03** number of risks that generally fall into categories, such as:

(1) completion risk, including delays, cost overruns and technology risks;
(2) offtake or revenue risk;
(3) operating risk;
(4) supply risk;
(5) currency risk;
(6) environmental and social risk;
(7) *force majeure* events; and
(8) participant risk.

Generally, project risks are assigned to the stakeholder in the project that is best able **14.04** to manage the relevant risk or are allocated as much as possible to risk-absorbing third parties, such as insurers. It is a basic, but important, point that a party's preferences with regard to dispute resolution mechanisms will vary depending upon the risks allocated to it. A project participant bearing little or no project risk, but having significant payment risk—such as a subcontractor, or a material or service provider, and in some circumstances lenders—may prefer a fast, public dispute resolution mechanism to obtain rights to satisfy payment obligations as quickly as possible, no matter the impact on the overall project. In contrast, a project participant with significant project risk likely will prefer a private dispute resolution mechanism that postpones the payment of money as long as possible.

Each type of commercial risk can give rise to disputes. The most significant dis- **14.05** putes, in terms of claim value, typically arise when substantial project risks materialize, such as when a project cannot achieve commercial operation or does so belatedly,[1] or when a concessionaire and a governmental contracting authority

---

[1] Examples of such disputes reported by the American Lawyer 2009 Arbitration Scorecard are (1) *German Federal Ministry of Transport, Building and Housing v Toll Collect GbR (Germany), DaimlerChrysler Financial Services AG (Germany), and Deutsche Telekom AG (Germany)*, a US$7.6 billion dispute with regard to lost revenues and contractual penalties for the Toll Collect consortium's alleged delay in constructing and operating a high-tech toll-collection system for heavy trucks on German highways; (2) *Thai-Lao Lignite (Thailand) Co., Ltd. v Government of Laos*, a US$3 billion dispute relating to an alleged breach of a Build-Operate-Transfer contract to operate a mine and build a power generation facility in Laos to transmit power to Thailand; and (3) *AREVA-Siemens Consortium (France/Germany) v Teollisuuden Voima Oyj (Finland)*, a US$2.8 billion dispute arising from the

disagree on material payment terms once the project enters commercial operation.[2] But seemingly smaller disputes can balloon, particularly when they arise during the development phase. For example, a subcontractor may pull out of a project over a payment dispute with the turnkey contractor, and this in turn could jeopardize the completion of the project. Thus, even when an underlying dispute is comparatively small, its effects—depending in part upon the availability of viable dispute resolution mechanisms to prevent endangering the project at large—may not be.

The Choice between Litigation and Arbitration

14.06 Fundamentally, commercial disputes can be resolved in one of two legal frameworks: by means of litigation in national courts (of the host state or some other state) or by means of international arbitration. Although there are other dispute resolution mechanisms discussed below that can be used either alone or in conjunction with litigation or arbitration, the enforcement mechanisms in place throughout the world generally allow for enforcement of only court judgments or arbitral awards. Thus, to the extent that a dispute is not resolved through settlement, it will likely be resolved by the courts or in arbitration, if it is to be resolved at all.

14.07 This reality is reflected in project agreements. Project agreements contain either a forum selection clause (also referred to as a 'jurisdiction clause' if the parties have selected litigation as their preferred method of dispute resolution),[3] or an arbitration

---

delayed construction of a nuclear power plant in Finland, between the Finnish utility Teollisuuden Voima and a Franco-German construction consortium.

[2] Examples of such disputes reported by the American Lawyer 2009 Arbitration Scorecard are (1) *Anadarko Algeria Company LLC (US) v Sonatrach (Algeria)*, a US$18 billion dispute with regard to a long-term production sharing agreement, in connection with changes in 2005 and 2006 to the Algerian hydrocarbons law affecting the payment terms of the production sharing agreement; (2) *Yemen Exploration & Production Company (US) v Republic of Yemen*, a US$9.3 billion dispute with regard to the extension of an oil production agreement; and (3) *Metro Rail Transit Corporation Limited (Hong Kong) v Republic of the Philippines*, a US$2.2 billion dispute arising out of a 1997 agreement between Metro Rail Transit Corporation and the Philippines over the building, leasing, operation, and transfer of a light rail system in the greater Manila area.

[3] Forum selection clauses became a viable choice in contracts involving parties in or with contacts with the US after *M/S Bremen v Zapata Off-Shore Co.*, 407 US 1 (1972), which recognized the validity of such clauses. The validity of forum selection clauses was confirmed thereafter in *Scherk v Alberto-Culver Co.*, 417 US 506 (1974) and *Carnival Cruise Lines, Inc. v Shute*, 499 US 585 (1991), among other cases. In Europe, international forum selection clauses involving one or more parties domiciled in a country that is a member of the EU (excluding Denmark) are generally enforceable. (Council Regulation 44/2001EC of 22 December 2000 on jurisdiction and the recognition and enforcement of judgments in civil and commercial matters, art. 23 ('If the parties, one or more of whom is domiciled in a Member State, have agreed that a court or the courts of a Member State are to have jurisdiction to settle any disputes which have arisen or which may arise in connection with a particular legal relationship, that court or those courts shall have jurisdiction.').)

clause if the parties desire to submit their disputes to arbitration.[4] A forum selection or jurisdiction clause permits or requires parties to pursue claims in one or more national courts which the parties, typically, designate. An arbitration clause embodies the parties' agreement to submit disputes to final and binding determination by non-governmental decision-makers.[5] The framework for resolution of project-related disputes through litigation, like the framework for the same through arbitration, has key features that may bear upon both the ultimate outcome of a dispute and the effect of the dispute resolution process on the project.

Litigation in national courts

The framework for litigation varies from country to country. If the parties choose a litigation framework to resolve their disputes, it is important to look at each specific jurisdiction in order to understand how a dispute may be treated. The litigation framework discussed below is drawn largely from a common law perspective; it refers to key civil law jurisdictions and concepts when appropriate. **14.08**

When a dispute is litigated, the plaintiff (or 'claimant') must serve a complaint or other initial document on the defendant. Depending in part upon the jurisdiction, this document can contain a great deal of information, or comparatively little, about the parties' dispute.[6] The manner in which a document initiating suit may be filed is frequently subject both to the civil procedure rules of the court in which the suit is to be filed, as well as to international agreements.[7] Once this document is **14.09**

---

[4] See generally Gary B. Born, *International Arbitration and Forum Selection Agreements: Drafting and Enforcing* (3rd edn, Kluwer Law International, 2010).

[5] See Nigel Blackaby, Constantine Partasides, Alan Redfern, et al., *Redfern and Hunter on International Arbitration* § 1.02 (5th edn, Oxford University Press, Oxford 2009) (hereinafter 'Redfern and Hunter').

[6] In the US, cases (other than fraud cases) generally require well-pleaded facts that allege a plausible claim for relief. See *Ashcroft v Iqbal* 129 S Ct 1937, 1940 (2009). In England and Wales, a concise written statement of the facts relied upon by the claimant must be provided to the defendant within fourteen days of the claim being served (Part 16.4 of the Civil Procedure Rules 1998) and there are specific provisions as to other information which must be provided in the case of certain types of disputes. Civil law systems generally require more detail. See, for example, German ZPO §253; see also Baumbach, Lauterbach, Albers, et al., *Zivilprozessordnung* (68th edn, 2010) 934–53 (requiring specific requests and basis for the requests to be stated at the complaint stage as a matter of German law); compare Serge Guinchard (ed.), *Droit et Pratique de la Procedure Civile* (2004) 353–84 (requiring that the first pleading must identify specific facts with exhibits as well as legal argumentation supporting the requested relief).

[7] See Convention of 15 November 1965 on the Service Abroad of Judicial and Extrajudicial Documents in Civil or Commercial Matters. The Convention captures different approaches to service of pleadings in common law and civil law jurisdictions. See also generally Philipp A. Buhler, 'Transnational Service of Process and Discovery in Federal Court Proceedings: An Overview' (2002) 27 Tul Mar LJ 1; Charles B. Campbell, 'No Sirve: The Invalidity of Service of Process Abroad by Mail or Private Process Server on Parties in Mexico Under the Hague Service Convention' (2010) 19 Minn J Int'l L 107; Kenneth B. Reisenfeld, 'Service of United States Process Abroad: A Practical Guide to Service Under the Hague Service Convention and the Federal Rules of Civil Procedure' (1990) 24 Int'l L 55.

properly filed and served, judicial relief is available at least as a matter of principle. For example, courts can order attachments of property at a very early stage.[8] The availability of preliminary relief at an early stage is a significant benefit if the dispute in question requires fast action. This comes at a cost, however, because the judge with the ability to act immediately is assigned, not chosen by the parties based on relevant experience, insulation from political pressures, or other attributes.

14.10   Litigation is perceived as the dispute resolution mechanism that tends to provide quick provisional remedies and strict, literal enforcement of loan documents. For example, most jurisdictions make summary judicial procedures available to resolve cases in which the legal sufficiency of claims or defenses can be assessed at an early stage.[9] Summary procedures can be an efficient way to resolve business disputes involving, for example, questions of contractual interpretation without a heavy factual component. This benefit may be overstated in the project context, however, because project disputes frequently involve complicated factual issues that cannot be resolved through summary procedures.[10]

14.11   Most jurisdictions provide their courts with at least some ability to compel the disclosure of documentary evidence and the testimony of witnesses. In the US, broad discovery is permitted in civil litigation, with a range of pre-trial discovery methods available to each side pursuant to the US Federal Rules of Civil Procedure

---

[8] See, for example, NY CPLR § 6200 et seq. (permitting a New York court to grant an order of attachment in any action where the claimant has demanded and would be entitled to a money judgment against the defendant); see also *Mareva Compania Naviera S.A. v Int'l Bulkcarriers S.A.* [1975] 2 Lloyd's Rep. 509 at 510 (CA 1975) ('If it appears that [a] debt is due and owing—and there is a danger that the debtor may dispose of his assets so as to defeat it before judgment—the Court has jurisdiction in a proper case to grant an interlocutory judgment so as to prevent him [from] disposing of those assets.') (Given statutory force in England and Wales by the Supreme Court Act 1981, s 37(3).) See also Part 25 of the Civil Procedure Rules 1998 (England and Wales).

[9] In the US, motions to dismiss for insufficiency of the underlying legal theory can be made at the outset of the case, and motions for summary judgment may be made prior to trial for failure of proof. See, for example, Fed R Civ P 12(b)(1) (motion to dismiss for lack of subject-matter jurisdiction); Fed R Civ P 12(b)(2) (motion to dismiss for lack of personal jurisdiction); Fed R Civ P 12(b)(6) (motion to dismiss for failure to state a claim upon which relief can be granted); Fed R Civ P 56 (motion for summary judgment); NY CPLR § 3211 (listing grounds for motions to dismiss); NY CPLR § 3212 (motion for summary judgment); see generally 2 *Moore's Federal Practice* (3rd edn, Matthew Bender) § 12; 11 *Moore's Federal Practice* (3rd edn, Matthew Bender) § 56. In England and Wales, the Court has the ability to give summary judgment against a claimant or defendant on whole or part of a claim if (1) there is no reasonable prospect of that case (or part of it) succeeding and (2) there is no other compelling reason why the case should proceed to a full trial (Part 24.2 of the Civil Procedure Rules 1998). Less formal rules available in civil law jurisdictions may permit the judge, in certain circumstances, to dismiss a complaint on its face. Schlesinger, et al., *Comparative Law* (1988) 417.

[10] In a number of jurisdictions, a claim for a certain sum of money may not necessitate even a complaint. For example, under New York law, when an action is based upon an instrument for the payment of money only, the claimant may serve a summons, a notice of motion for summary judgment, and supporting papers in lieu of a complaint. See NY CPLR §3231.

and state procedural laws.[11] Depositions, or sworn oral examinations prior to trial, for example, can be taken of not only the opposing side, but also of non-party witnesses.[12] Other jurisdictions, although they make compelled disclosure of evidence possible to various extents, do not allow such broad 'US-style' pre-trial discovery. In England and Wales, parties are under a duty to disclose documents to their opponents as part of the litigation process. The documents to be disclosed are essentially those documents on which a party will rely and any documents which could support or adversely affect either party's case.[13] In Singapore, discovery is generally allowed by order of the court, and the scope of document discovery is similar to that provided for under English law.[14] Nevertheless, documents that are indirectly relevant, such as documents that have the potential to lead to the discovery of directly relevant evidence, are not typically discoverable in England and Wales[15] or Singapore.[16] In Germany, no party is under any obligation to make documents and other materials available to the other side in the absence of a specific statutory basis.[17] In France, it is possible to obtain disclosure of such documents that are 'indispensable to the discovery of the truth of the matter' where the underlying information cannot otherwise be obtained.[18]

A judgment rendered by a court is typically subject to appeal, which serves as a **14.12** check on the legal correctness of the initial determination and may contribute to rigorous determinations and discourage compromise rulings.[19] Once appeals are exhausted (whether by determination or because the time in which an appeal must

---

[11] See, for example, Fed R Civ P 30 (depositions); Fed R Civ P 33 (interrogatories); Fed R Civ P 34 (requests for document production); Fed R Civ P 36 (requests for admission); NY CPLR § 3102 (listing disclosure devices); see generally 7 *Moore's Federal Practice* (3rd edn, Matthew Bender) §§ 30, 31, 32, 33, 34, 35, 36.

[12] See, for example, Fed R Civ P 45 (subpoena to facilitate non-party discovery); NY CPLR § 3102 (subpoenas to compel disclosure listed among disclosure devices); 9 *Moore's Federal Practice* (3rd edn, Matthew Bender) § 45.

[13] Part 31.6 of the Civil Procedure Rules 1998.

[14] Tan Chuan Thye and John Choong, 'Disclosure of Documents in Singapore International Arbitrations: Time for a Reassessment' (2005) 1(1) Asian International Arbitration Journal 49–50.

[15] Parties may apply for specific disclosure of classes of documents that fall outside the scope of standard disclosure: Part 31.12 of the Civil Procedure Rules 1998.

[16] Tan Chuan Thye and John Choong, (2005) 1(1) Asian International Arbitration Journal 49–50.

[17] Klaus Peter Berger, 'The International Arbitrator's Dilemma: Transnational Procedure versus Home Jurisdiction' (2009) 25(2) Arbitration International 226.

[18] Serge Guinchard (ed.), *Droit et Pratique de la Procedure Civile* (2004) 678–82.

[19] The manner in which appeal is taken and the grounds upon which it can be taken vary significantly from jurisdiction to jurisdiction. For example, in the US a court can review a jury verdict for sufficiency of evidence, a trial court's findings of fact for clear error, and a conclusion of law for clear error. See, for example, 19 *Moore's Federal Practice* (3rd edn, Matthew Bender) § 206. In Germany, on the other hand, appeals typically arise if there has been legal error or if facts established by the appeals court following the relevant appellate procedure justify a different result. Baumbach, Lauterbach, Albers, et al., *Zivilprozessordnung* (68th edn, 2010) 1599–705. An appellate court in England and Wales will allow an appeal if the decision was 'wrong or unjust because of a serious procedural or other irregularity in the proceedings in the lower court'. Civil Procedure Rules 1998, Part 52.11(3).

be brought has expired) a judgment is final in the jurisdiction in which it was issued. If a party does not voluntarily satisfy an adverse judgment and assets are not available in the jurisdiction in which the judgment was made, the judgment may need to be enforced abroad. Enforcement against assets abroad, however, may be far from straightforward or quick, as discussed below.

14.13   Litigation is conducted in accordance with laws, rules, and practices appropriate for a wide range of disputes, and judges are public officials. Dispute resolution by means of litigation thus often lacks flexibility.[20] As a practical matter, it is not possible for project participants to specify the manner in which litigation will be conducted to the same extent as they can in arbitration, which may be customized to suit the parties' preferences and the project's particular circumstances. If project participants specify litigation as a means of dispute resolution, their most important choice may be of a particular judicial system that offers key attributes attractive to them under the circumstances, such as the presence or absence of a mechanism for the speedy resolution of issues. Accordingly, lenders in cross-border project financings historically have preferred access to courts in either their home jurisdictions or in financial hubs, such as New York, London, or Hong Kong.[21]

Arbitration

14.14   Arbitration often is said to have several advantages over national court litigation.[22] For example, arbitration traditionally has been described as offering quick and efficient resolution of disputes and lower legal fees.[23] In actual experience, however, arbitration can be just as expensive (sometimes more so) and lengthy as litigation (sometimes more so), especially in complex disputes in which parties and their counsel press for extensive proceedings and exchanges of evidence.[24]

14.15   Arbitration undoubtedly is more flexible than litigation. Arbitration exists by virtue of parties' consent.[25] Parties are free to choose from a large variety of institutions

---

[20] Litigation is not entirely inflexible. For example, parties can waive their right to a jury trial.

[21] See, for example, Christophe Dugué, 'Dispute Resolution in International Project Finance Transactions' (2001) 24 Fordham Int'l LJ 1064, 1072.

[22] See generally Paul D. Friedland, *Arbitration Clauses for International Contracts* (2nd edn, JurisNet LLC, 2007); Redfern and Hunter at 34.

[23] See, for example, UNCITRAL, Travaux Preparatoire, New York Convention, Doc. No. E/2822/ Add.3 – *General Considerations by the United States Chamber of Commerce and the International Institute for the Unification of Private Law*, at 2 ('The Chamber of Commerce of the United States strongly advocates arbitration as a desirable and economic method of settling disputes in international trade, and recommends the inclusion of properly drawn arbitration clauses in foreign trade contracts.').

[24] See Redfern and Hunter at 35–36; see also William W. Park, 'Arbitration of International Contract Disputes' (1983) 39 Bus L 1783 ('Hard tasks take a high toll, and arbitration thus may become a long and costly process.').

[25] W. Michael Reisman, 'The Supervisory Jurisdiction of the International Court of Justice: International Arbitration and International Adjudication' (1996) 258(9) Academie de Droit International, Recueil des Cours 39 ('Insofar as a legal system enables legal actors to conclude a private contract with respect to future behaviour, it should encounter no theoretical problem with allowing

and rules, or *ad hoc* arbitral proceedings pursuant to rules of the parties' own design, to which they can submit disputes.[26] Arbitral proceedings can be tailored by contract to modify these rules and to meet the particular needs and circumstances of a specific transaction.[27] Arbitral proceedings are perceived to be neutral and to give the parties the ability to require arbitrators of third-state nationality, to avoid host state procedures and requirements, and to designate a place of arbitration in order to minimize the prospect of interference through host state judicial proceedings.[28] In many circumstances, it also can be far easier for parties to enforce an arbitral award internationally due to the existence of broadly ratified international treaties, particularly the 1958 Convention on the Recognition and Enforcement of Foreign Arbitral Awards, known as the 'New York Convention'.[29] The following outline is intended to provide a basic understanding of how a 'typical' arbitration of a cross-border commercial dispute may unfold in the project finance context and to give a sense of the advantages and disadvantages of arbitration.

Arbitration proceedings commence with the submission of a request document, **14.16** informing the adversary party of the claim being asserted against it.[30] Such requests vary in length and complexity, but typically describe the nature of the dispute and

---

those actors to designate someone else to specify, under procedures and on contingencies agreed upon in the contract, certain obligations that will be deemed, in advance, to be part of the contract. . . . With the extraordinary growth of transnational trade and investment, arbitration has become de facto a basic and indispensable strut of the world economy.').

[26] The parties can choose institutional arbitration, *ad hoc*, or un-administered arbitration. *Ad hoc* arbitration generally specifies that the rules promulgated by UNCITRAL shall be applicable. In terms of institutional arbitration, choices abound. Institutional arbitration may be conducted through the following institutions, among many others: American Arbitration Association; the International Center for Dispute Resolution; International Chamber of Commerce; London Court of International Arbitration; Inter-American Commercial Arbitration Commission; Vienna International Arbitral Centre; British Columbia International Commercial Arbitration Centre; Australian Centre for International Commercial Arbitration; German Institution of Arbitration; Japan Commercial Arbitration Association; Singapore International Arbitration Centre; Hong Kong International Arbitration Centre; Chinese International Economic and Trade Association Center; Cairo Regional Centre for International Commercial Arbitration; Kuala Lumpur Regional Centre for Arbitration; Indian Council of Arbitration; Dubai International Arbitration Centre; Abu Dhabi Commercial Conciliation and Arbitration Center; Qatari International Center for Arbitration; Bahrain Center for Dispute Resolution.

[27] How arbitration agreements can be tailored to meet specific project needs is discussed below. See also William W. Park, 'Arbitration of International Contract Disputes' (1983) 39 Bus L 1783; Born (2010) 37–110.

[28] Park, 39 Bus L 1783 (stating, on the basis of a hypothetical: 'Neither the Swedish shipyard nor the Libyan government "chooses" arbitration. Rather, arbitration imposes itself for lack of an acceptable alternative.').

[29] See New York Convention, art. III. The enforcement mechanism is discussed in more detail below.

[30] ICC Arbitration Rules, art. 4(3); LCIA Arbitration Rules, art. 1; UNCITRAL Arbitration Rules art. 3. See generally Julian M. Lew, Loukas A. Mistelis, et al., *Comparative International Commercial Arbitration* (2003) 514–17.

key evidence supporting the claim.[31] In the request document, the claimant often nominates its chosen arbitrator when the arbitral tribunal will consist of three arbitrators, as is commonly the case for major disputes. One arbitrator will be appointed by each party and the third arbitrator will be chosen by agreement of the two party-appointed arbitrators.[32]

14.17 The parties' ability to choose arbitrators directly, and to have the arbitrators selected by them choose the third arbitrator (often in consultation with the parties), is an important feature of arbitration. It both enables parties to shape the qualifications of the tribunal that will hear their dispute and gives parties a direct responsibility for the arbitral process that may contribute to parties' respect for its outcome.[33] For example, if a technical matter of some kind is at the core of a dispute, parties can appoint arbitrators with the desired technical expertise.

14.18 One significant potential drawback of arbitration follows from the manner of selecting arbitrators. Because parties typically select two arbitrators who then must confer and agree upon a third arbitrator, there is no decision-maker immediately available to issue interim relief, such as orders temporarily restraining transactions or actions that may upset the status quo.[34] This distinction between arbitration and litigation can be significant if time is of the essence, such as when a dispute threatens to grind construction or operation to a halt, or when there is a risk of dissipation of assets. Depending upon the jurisdiction in which the project is located or in which the relevant project participants keep assets, it often is possible to apply to a

---

[31] See generally David Rivkin, 'Strategic Considerations in Developing an International Arbitration Case' in Doak Bishop and Edward Kehoe (eds), *The Art of Advocacy in International Arbitration* (2nd edn, 2010) 151–72; Julian M. Lew, Loukas A. Mistelis, et al., *Comparative International Commercial Arbitration* (2003) 505–20.

[32] For example, in one of the largest arbitral institutions, the Court of International Arbitration of the International Chamber of Commerce (ICC), parties have agreed to resolution of disputes by an arbitral tribunal consisting of three arbitrators. See ICC Arbitration Rules, art. 8(4); see also UNCITRAL Arbitration Rules, art. 7. This practice, however, is not universal. Thus, the London Court of International Arbitration (LCIA) uses appointment by the institution if the arbitration agreement is silent regarding the selection of arbitrators. See LCIA Arbitration Rules, art. 7. To the extent that an arbitrator is not appointed within the appropriate timeframe, arbitration rules generally call for appointment of the arbitrator by the arbitral institution in question or by a neutral appointing authority. See ICC Arbitration Rules, art. 9; LCIA Arbitration Rules, art. 5.5; UNCITRAL Arbitration Rules, art. 8-10. For a detailed comparison of different rules practices, see Julian M. Lew, Loukas A. Mistelis, et al., *Comparative International Commercial Arbitration* (Kluwer Law International, 2003) 223–53. For a critique of the prevalent appointment method, see Jan Paulsson, *Are Unilateral Appointments Defensible?*, available at <http://kluwerarbitrationblog.com/blog/2009/04/02/are-unilateral-appointments-defensible>.

[33] Rivkin, *The Art of Advocacy in International Arbitration* (2nd edn, 2010) 151–72; Lew, *Comparative International Commercial Arbitration* (2003) 505–520; see also Redfern and Hunter, §§ 4.14–4.17; Born at 70–78.

[34] For a discussion of interim measures in international arbitration, see Kaj Hobér, 'Interim Measures by Arbitrators' in Albert Jan van den Berg (ed.), *International Arbitration 2006: Back to Basics?* (ICCA Congress Series, Montreal 2006 Vol. 13) 721–50 (2007) (summarizing interim measures rules available in ICDR, AAA, ICC, LCIA, CIETAC and SCC arbitrations).

court to act until an arbitration panel can be appointed.[35] This remedy, while effective in many instances, is a realistic option only if the counterparty is subject to the jurisdiction of the court in question. In some instances, resorting to local courts will be less effective if one seeks to restrain the activities of prominent project participants of the host country.

International arbitration often is described as allowing more disclosure of evidence **14.19** than European civil law systems, but less than in litigation in the US.[36] Unless otherwise agreed, parties to an arbitration typically will be given access to documents that are relevant or important to the dispute.[37] This generalization, although true, reveals a further key issue for arbitration: the disclosure of evidence is largely dependent upon the arbitrators' perspective of what constitutes 'relevant and material' evidence.[38] Practice in international arbitration varies depending on the background of the arbitrators and lawyers, who usually are influenced by the legal values and principles of their home jurisdictions.[39] Typically a combination of procedures taken from common law and civil law systems is adopted.[40] This amalgam approach can leave users from either legal tradition unsatisfied.

Arbitration provisions can be drafted to make clear the parties' intention as to the **14.20** manner and extent of document disclosure and presentation. How extensive is document disclosure to be? Will parties be permitted to request documents prior to the submission of their principal written statements of position? Or will 'fishing expeditions' be prohibited, with each party being limited to document requests

---

[35] For a discussion on recent developments regarding the availability of courts to issue interim measures in aid of arbitration, see Luis Enrique Graham, 'Interim Measures: Ongoing Regulation and Practices (A View from the UNCITRAL Arbitration Regime)' in Albert Jan van den Berg (ed.), Years of the New York Convention: ICCA International Arbitration Conference, ICCA Congress Series, 2009 Dublin Volume 14, 539–69 (2009).

[36] See, for example, Redfern and Hunter at §§ 6.84-6.91.

[37] See, for example, IBA Rules on the Taking of Evidence in International Arbitration, art. 3 (requiring that documents must be described 'sufficient to identify it', 'relevant and material to the outcome of the case', and 'not in the possession, custody or control of the requesting Party'). For a discussion of the IBA Rules, see Hilmar Raeschke-Kessler, 'The Production of Documents in International Arbitration—A Commentary on Article 3 of the New IBA Rules of Evidence' (2002) 18 Arb. Int'l 411.

[38] See IBA Rules on the Taking of Evidence in International Arbitration, art. 3.

[39] Klaus Peter Berger, 'The International Arbitrator's Dilemma: Transnational Procedure versus Home Jurisdiction' (2009) 25(2) Arbitration International 216, 228.

[40] Tan Chuan Thye and John Choong, 'Disclosure of Documents in Singapore International Arbitrations: Time for a Reassessment?' (2005) 1(1) Asian International Arbitration Journal 51–2. The International Bar Association Rules on the Taking of Evidence in International Commercial Arbitration (the 'IBA Rules'), which set forth detailed procedures for, *inter alia*, the disclosure of documents, can provide a useful starting point or guideline for parties or tribunals. The IBA Rules have 'built-in flexibility', allowing the tribunal to exercise its discretion to suit the circumstances of each case. *Ibid.* at 58. Differences between the disclosure regimes of various countries, such as in the presentation of evidence and the scope of discovery, and the impact of those differences on as-yet unknown disputes, may be difficult to assess at the drafting stage of a dispute resolution clause. Friedland, at 26–35.

only to 'fill gaps' after each side has asserted its claims and defenses in its primary written submission on the basis of the information in its possession before the arbitration began?

14.21 A hallmark of litigation is that published precedent and/or consistent education and training of lawyers and judges tends to result in similar cases being decided in a similar way. In contrast, commercial disputes in arbitration tend to be resolved not by comparison to past cases (the resolution of which are not routinely reported), but rather on the strength of their individual facts.[41] One benefit of this approach is that arbitrators with particular expertise relevant to the project or the dispute may be in a better position than a judge to assess the facts at hand. One risk (and common fear) is that arbitrators will 'split the baby'—that is, the two party-appointed arbitrators will favour the parties that appointed them, and the third 'neutral' arbitrator will attempt to find a compromise between the two.[42]

14.22 Arbitral decisions usually cannot be appealed. Although post-award challenges are becoming more frequent, many courts will not review the substance or merits of an arbitrator's decision. This lack of a substantive review of arbitral awards is based on several international conventions that have greatly increased the ability of parties to enforce final arbitral awards. The New York Convention, discussed in more detail below, has been ratified by 144 countries and requires domestic courts to recognize and enforce international arbitration agreements and awards.[43] Some parties may view the absence of appeal as an advantage of arbitration, while others may

---

[41] Stanimir Alexandrov, Panel Discussion, in Ian Laird and Todd Weiler (eds), *Investment Treaty Arbitration and International Law* (2009) vol. 2, 205 ('the outcome of the case is determined by the facts. And I have said that at other forums, and I want to say it here again. Many of those who comment on awards focus on the legal conclusions of the tribunal and completely ignore the facts of the case.').

[42] Commentators point out, however, a lack of empirical support for the view that arbitrators ignore or misapply the law in favour of finding compromise, and in fact, judges and juries also might render 'compromise verdicts'. See Friedland, *Arbitration Clauses for International Contracts* 18. At least one study suggests that many arbitral awards are substantially in favour of one party. *Ibid.*; see also Stephanie E. Keer and Richard W. Naimark, *Arbitrators Do Not 'Split the Baby': Empirical Evidence from International Business Arbitrations* (2001), reprinted in Christopher R. Drahozal and Richard W. Naimark (eds), *Towards a Science of International Arbitration: Collected Empirical Research* (2005) 311, 316 ('there seems to be little factual support for the idea that arbitrators thoughtlessly split award amounts. It also suggests that there is work to be done on the decision-making process utilized by arbitrators . . . Nevertheless, the results from this study show emphatically that arbitrators did not engage in the practice of "splitting the baby."').

[43] See <http://www.uncitral.org/en/uncitral_texts/arbitration/NYConvention_status .html>. Other conventions, such as the Inter-American Convention on International Commercial Arbitration, which has been ratified by 19 countries including the US, Mexico, the Dominican Republic, and several Latin American and South American countries, and the European Convention on International Commercial Arbitration, which has more than 30 signatories, are similar to the New York Convention in their treatment of international arbitration agreements and awards.

conclude for the same reason that international arbitration is 'essentially free of the rule of law'.[44]

A principal concern arising out of the lack of an appeals process is decisional error **14.23** incapable of correction. Error can have significant costs for the project: namely that the contractual allocation of risks agreed upon at the outset of the project has been changed. If this happens, a party may become shouldered with expenses and risks that it did not originally agree to incur and consequently will be under-compensated by the agreement in dispute. Outside of the agreement in dispute, depending upon the risk that now has been reallocated, other project agreements interlocking with the contract in dispute may now be founded on an incorrect premise. Because there may be a web of contracts, rather than just one contract, affected by an arbitral decision, misallocation of risk in the project context may have an unanticipated ripple effect. This ripple effect may lead to additional disputes regarding the performance of various agreements. The main safeguard against error in arbitration is the expertise of the arbitrators chosen by the parties.

Project companies, contractors, and operators often favour arbitration, with its **14.24** perceived efficient and timely procedures and privacy. The interrelated, ongoing nature of relationships between the project parties may be better preserved by an arbitral decision-making process. Similarly, off-taker purchasers, and particularly governmental off-taker purchasers, frequently are asked to enter into arbitration clauses to avoid having to litigate disputes in their home courts. Some governmental agencies will resist such a request because they may not be free to agree to certain dispute settlement methods, such as arbitration.[45] This can be a highly important matter if the prospect of 'home cooking' causes a sponsor to fear that host state courts may rewrite off-take agreements, leaving the sponsors with no meaningful commercial or legal recourse to address a denial of justice.

---

[44] See Friedland at 16–17. It is of course possible for parties to an arbitration agreement to specify appellate review as part of their arbitration clauses. See Born at 101–102 ('such provisions raise significant enforceability issues, on the ground that they purportedly interfere with statutory regimes specifying the permissible grounds for judicial review of arbitral awards'). An example clause provides:

> The arbitrators' award shall be final and binding, but any party hereto shall have the right to seek judicial review of such award in the courts of the place where the award is made in accordance with the standards of appellate review applicable to decisions of courts of first instance in that place.

There is currently an ongoing initiative for arbitration rules for appeals at the AAA.

[45] *Ibid.* See also United Nations Commission on International Trade Law, *Privately financed infrastructure projects: draft chapters of a legislative guide on privately financed infrastructure projects*, A/CN.9/471/Add.7 (8 February 2000) at 4 (hereinafter, 'UNCITRAL Legislative Guide'). For example, the Law of Arbitration of Saudi Arabia states that '[g]overnment bodies may not resort to arbitration for the settlement of their disputes with third parties except after approval of the President of the Council of Ministers.' Under some civil law systems, project agreements are regarded as administrative contracts, thereby requiring that disputes arising under such agreements be settled through the judiciary or administrative courts of the host country.

Disputes Involving Political Risk

Contractual, regulatory, and tax risks

14.25 So far, this Chapter has discussed dispute resolution options for commercial differences between the various participants in a project. But these are not the only disputes that may arise in a project: project participants often find themselves in disputes with host-state governments regarding contract performance, legal requirements, regulation, taxes, and foreign exchange. Disputes relating to such matters may arise in connection with the issuance, renewal, and revocation of permits and licenses;[46] changes in the regulatory and tax environments in which a project must operate;[47] politically driven reopening of price adjustment formulae;[48] the repatriation of profits, and, in extreme cases, expropriations.[49] Although disputes over matters such as these may be brought within the ambit of contractual arbitration, if there is an agreement to which the relevant government agency or instrumentality is a party, these disputes also may fall within the ambit of investor-protection regimes existing separately from the project documents themselves.

Investment agreements

14.26 A very basic tool to protect projects against political risks is the conclusion of an investment agreement, including concession agreements (as discussed in greater detail in Chapter 5) with the host country, or with an agency of the host country responsible for the project. The host state in such agreements frequently agrees to 'stabilize' the regulatory and fiscal regime for the project.[50] Traditionally, this has meant a freeze of the regulatory and fiscal environment as it existed at the conclusion of the investment agreement.[51] Contemporary agreements frequently do not freeze the regulatory and fiscal environment, but instead set parameters within

---

[46] See, for example, *Lauder v Czech Republic,* Final Award, dated 3 September 2001, Ad hoc—UNCITRAL Arbitration Rules; IIC 205 (2001) (discussing changes in licensing requirements in the broadcasting industry).

[47] See, for example, *Duke Energy International Peru Investments No 1, Ltd v Peru,* Award and Partial Dissenting Opinions; ICSID Case No ARB/03/28; IIC 334 (2008).

[48] See, for example, *Azurix Corp v Argentina,* Award, dated 23 June 2006, ICSID Case No ARB/01/12; IIC 24 (2006).

[49] See, for example, *Compañía del Desarrollo de Santa Elena SA v Costa Rica,* Final Award, dated 17 February 2000, ICSID Case No ARB/96/1, IIC 73 (2000).

[50] On the other hand, such agreements frequently also impose 'performance requirements' on the project participants such as a minimum capital investment, minimum project production, or minimal employment of host state nationals, to name a few.

[51] For example, Peru enters into legal stability agreements at the level of the investor and at the enterprise level. These agreements give contractual assurances for ten years (or, in the case of concessions, the entire period of the concession) of protection from any change in certain key policies. See United Nations Conference on Trade and Development, Investment Policy Review, Peru, UNCTAD/ITE/IIP/Misc.19 (2000).

which both may change in case of larger market shifts. To the extent that the government is a customer of the project or regulates prices for the project, investment agreements also may contain formulae for the determination of prices for the life of the project.

Frequently, investment agreements with the host state or with an agency of the host state contain arbitration clauses.[52] The inclusion of arbitration clauses historically was to avoid resolving disputes with the host state in the state's own courts. Even with arbitration clauses in place, however, host states frequently refused to enforce adverse arbitral awards by reference to public policy grounds or by reference to the alleged incapacity of state parties to enter into such agreements in the first place.[53] Partly in order to address these concerns, the World Bank in the 1960s took on the task to create, by way of the so-called Washington Convention, an international arbitration institution for the resolution of investment disputes between host states and nationals of third party states, creating the International Centre for the Settlement of Investment Disputes, or ICSID.[54]   **14.27**

ICSID provides a forum for dispute settlement, setting forth detailed rules of procedure and institutional support for investor-state disputes.[55] The ICSID process is 'entirely self-contained and hence delocalized'.[56] It provides a strong enforcement mechanism expressly adopted to avoid the prior enforcement problems in arbitrations to which a state was a (losing) party.[57] Further, pursuant to Article 25 of the Washington Convention, which defines the scope of ICSID jurisdiction, in order   **14.28**

---

[52] See, for example, Bishop, *Foreign Investment Disputes: Cases, Materials and Commentary* 225–313.

[53] See, for example, Sébastien Manciaux, *Investissement étrangers et Arbitrage entre états Ressortissants D'Autres états* (2004) 122; A. Broches, 'Note transmitted to the Executive Directors, Settlement of Disputes between Governments and Private Parties' dated 28 August 1961, in *History of the ICSID Convention II-1 2* (1970).

[54] John T. Schmidt provides a list of cases in which states have effectively reneged on their arbitration consent in an investment dispute with an international investor between 1930 and 1963. He list the following cases: *Anglo-Iranian Oil Co. Case*, I.C.J. Pleadings 11, 40, 258, 267–68 (1952); *British Petroleum Exploration Co. (Libya), Ltd. v. Government of the Libyan Arab Republic*, Unpublished Private Arbitral Award (1973); *Sapphire International Petroleums Ltd. v. National Iranian Oil Co., Private Arbitral Award* (1963); *Société Européene d'Etudes et d'Entreprise v. People's Federal Republic of Yugoslavia*, Private Arbitral Award (1956); *Lena Goldfields, Ltd. v. Government of the Soviet Union*, Private Arbitral Award (1930). See John T. Schmidt, 'Arbitration under the Auspices of the International Centre for the Settlement of Investment Disputes (ICSID): Implications of the Decision on Jurisdiction in Alcoa Minerals of Jamaica, Inc. v. Government of Jamaica' (1976) 17 Harv Int'l L J 90, n. 1. See also A. Broches, 'Note transmitted to the Executive Directors, Settlement of Disputes between Governments and Private Parties' dated 28 August 1961, in *History of the ICSID Convention II-1* (1970) 3. In national court proceedings, similar principles have become known as the 'act of state doctrine.' See Andreas Lowenfeld, *International Economic Law* (2002) 439–54.

[55] Rudolf Dolzer and Christoph Schreuer, *Principles of International Investment Law* (Oxford University Press, 2008) 223.

[56] Lucy Reed, Jan Paulsson, and Nigel Blackaby, *Guide to ICSID Arbitration* 8 (Kluwer Law International, 2004).

[57] Guide to ICSID Arbitration at 96.

to be eligible for ICSID arbitration, a dispute must (1) arise out of an investment; (2) involve a country that is a signatory to the Washington Convention and a national of another country that is a signatory to the Washington Convention; and (3) all parties to the dispute must consent to ICSID arbitration.[58] Other than that, the ICSID arbitral process is similar to the contractual arbitration process discussed above.

14.29 Many investment agreements contain arbitration clauses consenting to ICSID arbitration. Such consents have generally survived challenges by host states once an investor needed to commence an arbitration proceeding.[59] ICSID arbitration clauses therefore have become a safer option for investment agreements. Alternatively, ICC arbitration has been a typical choice in investment agreements, especially where the host country of the project is not a party to the Washington Convention.[60]

Treaty-based political risk protections

14.30 Another means of political risk protection exists in the form of international treaties. Although the scope and content of bilateral investment treaties (BITs) and multilateral investment treaties (MITs) varies considerably, most contain similar substantive protections.

Political risks covered by investment treaties and statutes

Expropriation

14.31 BITs and MITs oblige a host government to compensate foreign investors in the event of an expropriation, regardless of whether the expropriation resulted from a direct act of taking, such as nationalization, or an indirect taking that substantially deprived the investor of the use or enjoyment of its investment.[61] An expropriation

---

[58] Guide to the ICSID Convention at 14; Dolzer and Schreuer at 223. Article 25 of The Washington Convention provides in relevant part: '(1) The jurisdiction of the Centre shall extend to any legal dispute arising directly out of an investment, between a Contracting State (or any constituent subdivision or agency of a Contracting State designated to the Centre by that State) and a national of another Contracting State, which the parties to the dispute consent in writing to submit to the Centre. When the parties have given their consent, no party may withdraw its consent unilaterally.'

[59] See *Société Ouest Africaine des Bétons Industriels v Senegal*, ICSID Case No. ARB/82/1 (1991) ICSID Review—Foreign Investment Law Journal 125, award (25 February 1988).

[60] Although approximately 144 countries are parties to the Washington Convention, countries that are not parties to the Washington Convention include Russia, Brazil, and India, as well as Canada and Mexico. The list of contracting states is available at <http://icsid.worldbank.org/ICSID/Front Servlet?requestType=ICSIDDocRH&actionVal=ContractingStates&ReqFrom=Main>. China is a party, but issued a reservation that indicates that China will consider submitting to the jurisdiction of ICSID with respect to disputes arising in limited circumstances. China issued a Notification on 7 January 1993 stating that: '[P]ursuant to Article 25(4) of the Convention, the Chinese Government would only consider submitting to the jurisdiction of the International Centre for Settlement of Investment Disputes disputes over compensation resulting from expropriation and nationalization.'

[61] Guide to ICSID Arbitration at 52.

can be 'creeping' when the host government takes a foreign investment in stages or through a series of acts collectively tantamount to expropriation.[62] Clauses in a BIT typically address 'only the conditions and consequences of an expropriation, leaving the right to expropriate as such unaffected'.[63] Most treaties provide that a legal expropriatory measure must: (1) serve a public purpose; (2) not be arbitrary and discriminatory; (3) follow the principles of due process; and (4) be accompanied by prompt, adequate, and effective compensation.[64]

Regulatory risk (fair and equitable treatment)

Most investment treaties also provide for fair and equitable treatment of foreign investments.[65] Fair and equitable treatment has diverse manifestations, depending in part upon the wording of the specific clause in a treaty. Much debate has focused on whether the fair and equitable treatment standard to which BITs and MITs refer reflects a minimum standard of treatment, as required by customary international law, or whether it is an independent treaty standard that exists in addition to customary international law.[66] For example, Article 1105(1) of the North American Free Trade Agreement (NAFTA) requires that: 'Each Party shall accord to investments of investors of another Party treatment in accordance with international law, including fair and equitable treatment and full protection and security.'[67] The NAFTA Free Trade Commission and subsequent NAFTA tribunals have accepted the interpretation that Article 1105(1) reflects customary international law and does not require additional treatment.[68] In contrast, arbitral tribunals interpreting other treaties have attempted to provide more specific definitions for fair and equitable treatment, based on the specific wording of the treaty.[69]

14.32

---

[62] Dolzer and Schreuer at 114-15. For example, in *Siemens v Argentina*, ICSID Case No. ARB/02/8, Award, 6 February 2007, Argentina had taken a series of adverse measures, including postponements and suspensions of the investor's profitable activities, renegotiations, and cancellation of the project, which the tribunal found amounted to a creeping expropriation.

[63] Dolzer and Schreuer at 89.

[64] Dolzer and Schreuer at 91. Historically this formulation was contested, but it currently has achieved significant global acceptance. On the historical origins of expropriation, see Andreas Lowenfeld, *International Economic Law* (2002) 392–414.

[65] Dolzer and Schreuer at 119, 149. For a detailed discussion of fair and equitable treatment, see Ioana Tudor, *The Fair and Equitable Treatment Standard in International Foreign Investment Law* (2008).

[66] Dolzer and Schreuer at 124.

[67] (1993) 32 ILM 639.

[68] Dolzer and Schreuer at 125. The scope of international custom similarly has led to some debate. A narrower view is currently supported by the recent award in *Glamis Gold Ltd v United States*, Award, dated 14 May 2009, Ad hoc—UNCITRAL Arbitration Rules; IIC 380 (2009); a broader conception has been adopted by *Merrill & Ring Forestry LP v Canada*, Award, dated 31 March 2010, Ad hoc—UNCITRAL Arbitration Rules; IIC 427 (2010).

[69] See, for example, *MTD Equity Sdn Bhd and MTD Chile SA v Chile*, Award, dated 25 May 2004, ICSID Case No ARB/01/7; IIC 174 (2004); Dolzer and Schreuer at 126.

14.33   In general, countries are required to maintain stable and predictable investment environments consistent with the reasonable investment-backed expectations of foreign investors.[70] For example, the tribunal in *Saluka v Czech Republic* described the requirements of fair and equitable treatment as follows:

> A foreign investor whose interests are protected under the Treaty is entitled to expect that the [host state] will not act in a way that is manifestly inconsistent, non-transparent, unreasonable (i.e. unrelated to some rational policy), or discriminatory (i.e. based on unjustifiable distinctions).[71]

14.34   A protection conceptually linked to fair and equitable treatment is 'full protection and security'. This standard has been applied primarily in situations of physical protection of real and tangible property, but it has been extended to apply to other circumstances, such as the withdrawal of a vital governmental authorization.[72]

Non-discrimination

14.35   The host country usually is under a legal obligation not to impair the management or operation of an investment by 'arbitrary or discriminatory measures'.[73] Arbitrariness has been viewed as a 'wilful disregard of due process of law'.[74] There is a partial overlap between the arbitrary and non-discriminatory standard and the fair and equitable treatment standard, as an arbitrary action arguably is not fair or equitable treatment. Although some tribunals have found that the standards are merged, other tribunals have evaluated the two standards separately.[75] A discriminatory measure treats an investor differently than other similarly situated investors.[76] Under a 'national treatment' standard, a host country must treat foreign investors 'no less favourably' than national investors.[77] Under the 'most favoured nation'

---

[70] *Técnicas Medioambientales Tecmed S.A. v Mexico*, ARB(AF)/00/2, IIC 247 (2003), 10 *ICSID Report* 130, at 154, award (29 May 2003); *EDF (Services) Limited v Romania*, award, at 216; *Waguih Elie George Siag and Clorinda Vecchi v Egypt*, award, op. cit. at 450.

[71] *Saluka v Czech Republic*, Partial Award, 17 March 2006.

[72] See, for example, *Waguih Elie George Siag and Clorinda Vecchi v Egypt*, award, at 447; see also Guide to ICSID Arbitration at 50.

[73] See, for example, Agreement Between the Government of the Kingdom of Sweden and the Government of the Republic of Estonia on the Promotion and Reciprocal Protection of Investments, 2 May 1992, art. 2(2); see also Guide to ICSID Arbitration at 50.

[74] *Case Concerning Elettronica Sicula SpA (ELSI) (United States v Italy)*, Judgment (20 July 1989) (1989) ICJ Reports 15 at 76.

[75] Compare *Saluka Investments BV (The Netherlands) v The Czech Republic*, Partial Award, 17 March 2006, para. 460 with *Siemens v Argentina*, Award, 6 February 2007, at paras 310–21.

[76] Guide to ICSID Arbitration at 50.

[77] For example, art. 2(1) of the Treaty Between the Government of the United States and the Government of the State of Bahrain Concerning the Encouragement and Reciprocal Protection of Investment (the 'US-Bahrain BIT') provides: 'With respect to the establishment, acquisition, expansion, management, conduct, operation and sale or other disposition of covered investments, each Party shall accord treatment no less favourable than that it accords, in like situations, to investments in its territory of its own nationals or companies (hereinafter "national treatment") or to investments in its territory of nationals or companies of a third country (hereinafter "most favoured nation treatment"), whichever is most favourable (hereinafter "national and most favoured nation treatment").

standard, a host country may not treat one foreign investor less favourably than another foreign investor from a different country.[78] The inclusion of a 'most favoured nation' clause in a BIT may have broad implications. Some tribunals have ruled on the basis of a 'most favoured nation' clause that a foreign investor may rely on broader treaty protections available to investors, from different states, under different BITs.[79]

Contract risk (umbrella clauses)

Umbrella clauses are blanket provisions in a BIT that require the host government **14.36** to observe, or guarantee the observance of, specific promises and obligations towards investors, such as investor-state contracts or national investment laws.[80] It has been argued that umbrella clauses import arbitration into a contract that does not include an arbitration clause. The effect of umbrella clauses is to 'blur the distinction between investment arbitration and commercial arbitration'.[81] One of the most contentious issues with regard to umbrella clauses is 'whether, and under what circumstances, they place investment agreements, that is, contracts between the host state and the investor, under the treaty's protection'.[82] Tribunal decisions have been divided on the interpretation of the purpose, meaning and scope of umbrella

---

Each Party shall ensure that its state enterprises, in the provision of their goods or services, accord national and most favoured nation treatment to covered investments.'

See also Model UK Bilateral Investment Treaty, art. 3. In some European BITs, the national treatment clauses state that the foreign investor and his investments are 'accorded treatment no less favourable than that which the host state accords its own investors.' See R. Dolzer and M. Stevens, *Bilateral Investment Treaties* (1995) 63–5; see also Dolzer and Schreuer at 178; Guide to ICSID Arbitration at 50.

[78] See Model UK Bilateral Investment Treaty, art. 3:
  (1) Neither Contracting Party shall in its territory subject investments or returns of nationals or companies of the other Contracting Party to treatment less favourable than that which it accords to investments or returns of its own nationals or companies or to investments or returns of nationals or companies of any third State.
  (2) Neither Contracting Party shall in its territory subject nationals or companies of the other Contracting Party, as regards their management, maintenance, use, enjoyment or disposal of their investments, to treatment less favourable than that which it accords to its own nationals or companies or to nationals or companies of any third State.
  See also US-Bahrain BIT, art. 2(1); see generally Guide to ICSID Arbitration at 50.

[79] See, for example, *AAPL v Sri Lanka* ICSID/ARB/87/3; *Maffezini v Spain* ICSID/ARB/97/7; *Suez & Interaguas v Argentina* ICSID/ARB/03/17; and *CMS Gas Transmission Company v Argentina* ICSID/ARB/01/8.

[80] See Model UK Bilateral Investment Treaty, art. 2(2): 'Each Contracting Party shall observe any obligation it may have entered into with regard to investments of nationals or companies of the other Contracting Party.'; see also Switzerland-Pakistan BIT, art. 11: 'Either Contracting Party shall constantly guarantee the observance of the commitments it has entered into with respect to the investments of the investors of the other Contracting Party.'; see generally Guide to ICSID Arbitration at 55.

[81] Dolzer and Schreuer at 155.

[82] See, for example, Michael D. Nolan and Edward G. Baldwin, *The Treatment of Contract-Related Claims in Treaty-Based Arbitration*, Mealey's International Arbitration Report (June 2006); see generally Dolzer and Schreuer at 153.

clauses. In *SGS v Philippines*, for example, the tribunal adhered to the conventional view of umbrella clauses when it ruled that in the presence of an umbrella clause, a violation of an investment agreement leads to a violation of an investment treaty.[83] In *SGS v Pakistan*, on the other hand, the tribunal interpreted the investment treaty narrowly and concluded that the conventional understanding of umbrella clauses would have a 'far-reaching impact' on the sovereignty of the host country.[84] Subsequent tribunals have attempted to distinguish between 'sovereign' and 'commercial' acts when interpreting the scope and impact of umbrella clauses.[85]

Potentially eligible project participants with treaty protections

14.37 To have access to various protections under national legislation and treaties, an 'investment' (as defined in the relevant investment treaties or statutes) must have been made. Some tribunals have held projects or transactions to qualify as investments when the project or transaction:

> (a) had a significant duration; (b) provided a measurable return to the investor; (c) involved an element of risk on both sides; (d) involved a substantial commitment on the part of the investor; and (e) was significant to the [host country's] development.[86]

As a general matter, tribunals 'have not entertained doubts' that construction and infrastructure projects are investments.[87]

Sponsors

14.38 BITs typically include shares of stock in a company or the commitment of capital in the definition of investment. For example, the BIT between Argentina and the US defines 'investment' to include 'a company or shares of stock or other interests in a company or interests in the assets thereof'.[88] The BIT between the US and Chile defines 'investment' broadly:

> Investment means every asset that an investor owns or controls, directly or indirectly, that has the characteristics of an investment, including such characteristics as the commitment of capital or other resources, the expectation of gain or profit, or the assumption of risk.[89]

Thus a sponsor, who directly or indirectly owns or controls the project, typically has committed capital, expects a profit and has assumed risk.

---

[83] *SGS v Philippines*, Decision on Jurisdiction, 29 January 2004, 8 ICSID Reports (2005) 518.

[84] *SGS v Pakistan*, Decision on Jurisdiction, 6 August 2003, 42 ILM (2003) 1290.

[85] Dolzer and Schreuer at 158–60.

[86] Guide to ICSID Arbitration at 15.

[87] Christoph Schreuer, et al., *The ICSID Convention: A Commentary* (2nd edn, Cambridge University Press, 2009) 127 (citing arbitral decisions).

[88] Dolzer and Schreuer at 63.

[89] Article 10.27 of the Free Trade Agreement between the Government of the United States of America and the Government of the Republic of Chile, 6 June 2003.

Lenders

Financial instruments such as loans and other credit facilities have been repeatedly **14.39** recognized by arbitral tribunals as investments.[90] Therefore, lenders who extend loans and credit facilities in order to finance projects generally are 'investors' entitled to certain treaty protections.

Contractors

Most treaties and national legislation include rights under contract as an **14.40** 'investment'.[91] For example, the US Model BIT of 2004 provides that an investment may take the form of 'turnkey, construction, management, production, concession, revenue-sharing, and other similar contracts'.[92] Thus, a contractor on a project typically also is an 'investor' entitled to certain treaty protections.

Operators

Contribution to a host country's development has been identified as a feature of an **14.41** investment.[93] To the extent an operator of a project contributes to a country's GDP or to the 'development of human potential, political and social development and the protection of the local and the global environment',[94] the operator may well be an 'investor' entitled to certain treaty protections.

Consent to arbitration in investment treaties

One of the main benefits of BITs and MITs is that private investors frequently can **14.42** initiate arbitration even in the absence of a contractual arbitration agreement. Investors can seek relief when host state consent for such proceedings is given by means of multi-lateral investment protection treaties, such as NAFTA,[95] the Energy

---

[90] ICSID Commentary at 126; see *Fedax v Venezuela*, Decision on Jurisdiction, 11 July 1997, paras 18–43 (concluding that loans and other credit facilities were within the jurisdiction of the Centre); *CSOB v Slovakia*, Decision on Jurisdiction, 24 May 1999, paras 76–91 (holding that the broad meaning of investment included a loan, especially if the loan contributed substantially to the host country's economic development); *Sempra v Argentina*, Award, 28 September 2007, paras 214–16 (accepting loans as an investment and noting that the loans were part of the overall investment's continuing financing arrangement).

[91] ICSID Commentary at 126 ('It is also well established that rights arising from contracts may amount to investments.').

[92] The full text of the 2004 US Model BIT is available at <http://www.state.gov/documents/organization/117601.pdf>.

[93] ICSID Commentary at 128–34.

[94] *Ibid.* at 134.

[95] NAFTA, art. 1116. For a recent discussion of the jurisdictional scope of NAFTA, see *Theodorus de Boer*, et al. *(Canadian Cattlemen for Fair Trade) v United States,* Ad hoc UNCITRAL Arbitration Rules, IIC 316 (2008), award on jurisdiction (28 January 2008).

Charter Treaty,[96] or the ASEAN Treaty,[97] or by means of bilateral investment treaties, which by some estimates had increased from 385 in 1989 to approximately 2,300 in 2003.[98] These consents frequently are to arbitration pursuant to ICSID or, alternatively, *ad hoc* arbitration or national court litigation.

14.43 In such non-contractual arbitration, consent generally is expressed in two steps.[99] First, the host country expresses its consent by including in a treaty its standing, unilateral offer to submit to arbitration.[100] Secondly, the investor subsequently matches that free-standing consent either in writing to the host government at the time of the investment, or by filing a request to arbitrate with the designated tribunal.[101] It is advisable to consult a specialist to determine whether consent was actually given. A mere reference to arbitration as a dispute resolution mechanism may not actually be consent. Once the consent of the host state has been engaged, the arbitration proceeding follows rules that are relatively similar to the arbitral process discussed above.

Political risk insurance

14.44 As further described in paragraph 4.60, another means to protect against political risk is the purchase of political risk insurance. Political risk insurance is likely to be available from public sources from the home states of project participants. Commercial political risk insurers also offer political risk coverage to investors in emerging market projects.[102] In addition, the World Bank makes available political risk guarantees through the Multilateral Investment Guarantee Agency (MIGA).

14.45 A related coverage offered by the Overseas Private Investment Corporation (OPIC) is coverage for failure to pay an arbitral award or, alternatively, to perform an arbitration agreement.[103] In the first case, an arbitral award must actually have been obtained. In the second case, it is necessary to show only that the respondent

---

[96] Energy Charter Treaty, art. 26. For a recent discussion of jurisdiction pursuant to the ECT, see, for example, *AMTO LLC v Ukraine*, Final Award, dated 26 March 2008, SCC Case No 080/2005; IIC 346 (2008); *Hulley Enterprises Ltd v Russian Federation*, Interim Award on Jurisdiction and Admissibility, dated 30 November 2009, PCA Case No AA 226; IIC 415 (2009).

[97] For a discussion of the ASEAN framework, see *Yaung Chi Oo Trading Pte Ltd v Myanmar*, Award, dated 31 March 2003, ASEAN Case No ARB/01/1; IIC 278 (2003); (2003) 42 ILM 540.

[98] UNCTAD, Quantitative data on bilateral investment treaties and double taxation treaties, available at <http://www.unctad.org/Templates/WebFlyer.asp?intItemID=3150&lang=1>.

[99] For a full discussion of the operation of consent instruments in investor-state arbitration, see Michael D. Nolan and Frédéric G. Sourgens, *The Interplay Between State Consent to ICSID Arbitration and Denunciation of the ICSID Convention: The (Possible) Venezuelan Case Study, Transnational Dispute Management* (2007); Michael D. Nolan and Frédéric G. Sourgens, *Limits Of Consent—Arbitration Without Privity And Beyond, in Liber Amicorum Bernardo Cremades* (2010) [843].

[100] *Ibid.*

[101] *Ibid.*

[102] *Ibid.*

[103] See *MidAmerican Energy Holdings Company* (Indonesia: 1999), (partly relying on failure to arbitrate coverage for its claim).

government should have gone to arbitration but frustrated its own arbitral undertaking. In that case, it is necessary to show only the plausibility of success on the merits.[104]

Political risk insurance historically was one of the main tools to protect against political risk. With the increased use of other protections such as treaty arbitration, it is no longer as prominent a tool. Yet, political risk insurance remains an important component in political risk structuring, even where investors also have structured their investments to benefit from international treaty protections.[105] Political risk insurance can in many instances be a faster and more reliable means to obtain redress with regard to clear-cut political risks—as evidenced in the context of the Enron decision. Yet the correct mix of investment treaty and insurance protection remains for each project participant to consider on a project-by-project basis. In addition, political risk insurance determinations provide important insight into the scope of proper government conduct and how investors can protect themselves against political risk. These mechanisms continue to have significant importance. **14.46**

Although coverage may differ, political risk insurance is available for currency inconvertibility, expropriation, and political violence.[106] Other specialized coverage is available for certain kinds of breaches of contract or breaches of an arbitration agreement or failure to enforce arbitration awards.[107] The coverage generally does not cover the entire loss, but only a fraction of the loss, with the project participant effectively paying a deductible. **14.47**

OPIC and MIGA also make available insurance for the breach of certain types of investment agreements. For example, MIGA may require a determination that the contract has in fact been breached in order to pay a claim through an arbitral proceeding or a local court judgment.[108] In those instances, investment insurance coverage in the project context is available only to the extent that the dispute resolution provisions discussed above have already resulted in a favourable result for the insured investor. **14.48**

---

[104] See *Construction Aggregates Corporation* (Dominica: 1977) (arbitration proceedings were commenced but not pursued when the government failed to participate in the arbitration proceedings).

[105] See *Enron Corporation and Ponderosa Assets, LP v Argentina*, Award, ICSID Case No. ARB/01/3; IIC 292 (2007), at 235.

[106] See, for example, OPIC Handbook 16 (2010 version).

[107] See, for example, <http://www.opic.gov>.

[108] See, for example, MIGA, *Types of Coverage*, available at <http://www.miga.org/guarantees/index_sv.cfm?stid=1547> (stating with regard to breach of contract coverage that: '[i]n the event of an alleged breach or repudiation, the investor should invoke a dispute resolution mechanism set out in the underlying contract and obtain a final arbitral award or judicial decision for damages.').

Structuring investments to optimize political risk protections

14.49   Not all investment structures make available the same political risk protections. Some may make available different insurance protection options; others may make available treaty protections. For projects in which political risk is a major concern, political risk structuring may be a worthwhile and long-term cost-saving exercise. In many instances, this structuring could be done in tandem with international tax structure concerns in order to optimize both the political risk protection and fiscal profile of a project.[109]

14.50   The key in structuring for political risk is to understand the scope of treaty protections available for the host country through different structures. Online databases such as <http://www.investmentclaims.com> and UNCTAD's treaty website[110] currently make available many international investment-protection treaties. The substantive protections and arbitration consents of each can be mapped out relatively easily. With these differences in protection in hand, it should be possible to compare the relative tax advantages and disadvantages of the different jurisdictions through which an investment could be structured. It thus is possible to understand fully the indirect costs of each investment structure and proceed accordingly.

14.51   'Nationality planning', 'forum shopping', or 'treaty shopping' is typically accomplished through the establishment of a company in a country that has favourable treaty relations with the host country.[111] 'That company will then be used as a conduit for the investment.'[112] Such structuring at the beginning of a project generally has been recognized as acceptable thus far.[113] Once a dispute is brewing, restructuring an investment in order to benefit from such treaty protections is another matter: depending upon the specific facts, such restructurings may or may not survive scrutiny.[114]

Enforcement of Judgments and Awards

14.52   Dispute resolution mechanisms often are only as good as the reliability of the enforcement of their final results. In the project context, project participants will

---

[109] Dolzer and Schreuer at 54.

[110] <http://www.unctadxi.org/templates/DocSearch_779.aspx>.

[111] Dolzer and Schreuer at 54.

[112] Ibid. For example, the tribunal in *Aguas del Tunari v Bolivia* stated: 'It is not uncommon in practice, and—absent a particular limitation—not illegal to locate one's operations in a jurisdiction perceived to provide a beneficial regulatory and legal environment in terms, for examples, of taxation or the substantive law of the jurisdiction . . .' *Aguas del Tunari v Bolivia*, Decision on Jurisdiction, 21 October 2005.

[113] See Alison Ross, 'Brigitte in Brazil', Global Arbitration Review, 22 June 2010, available at <http://www.globalarbitrationreview.com/journal/article/28562/brigitte-brazil>.

[114] Ibid; see also *Phoenix Action Ltd v Czech Republic*, ICSID Case No. ARB/06/5 (15 April 2009).

come from many different countries and generally will not have a reliable large asset base in the same place. This means that the result of the dispute resolution mechanism—awards and judgments—will have to travel. As mentioned above and discussed below, arbitral awards in general travel far more easily than court judgments do. Repeat users of international arbitration value this benefit of international arbitration perhaps the most.

Enforcement of judgments

Court judgments frequently face cross-border enforcement issues. Many jurisdictions treat foreign money judgments as presumptively enforceable. But judgments generally will be reviewed in detail by the enforcing courts, frequently leading to an effective re-litigation of a dispute at the enforcement stage. **14.53**

For example, in the US most states have adopted the Uniform Foreign Money Judgments Recognition Act (UFMJRA), under which foreign monetary judgments are presumptively enforceable under the principle of comity.[115] The UFMJRA allows significant procedural review of the underlying judgment.[116] **14.54**

The ease with which a foreign judgment can be enforced in England and Wales is largely dependent upon where the judgment originated. If it originated from a jurisdiction which has entered into reciprocal enforcement arrangements with the UK, enforcement is typically by way of a registration process.[117] If, however, the judgment originates from a jurisdiction which has no such reciprocal arrangement, then it will ordinarily be necessary for the party seeking to enforce the judgment to bring fresh proceedings before the English courts, seeking to recover the foreign judgment as a debt. The claimant would normally seek summary judgment at an early stage. There are a number of potential defences open to a party wishing to challenge such proceedings. These defences include, amongst others, lack of jurisdiction on the part of the foreign court, the judgment not being final and conclusive on the issue, the judgment being obtained by fraud, and the judgment conflicting with a prior judgment of the English court. **14.55**

---

[115] UFMJRA, 13 ULA Supp 89 (West Supp 2000).

[116] The UFMJRA provides a list of mandatory and discretionary grounds for non-enforcement of a judgment. The mandatory grounds for non-enforcement are limited to (1) the judgment was rendered under a system that does not provide impartial tribunals or procedures compatible with due process, or (2) the foreign court did not have personal or subject matter jurisdiction over the defendant or the subject matter. UFMJRA, § 4(a). In several situations, however, US courts have the option to decide not to recognize the foreign judgment even where these mandatory grounds were not present, including situations in which US courts deemed that the foreign court was a seriously inconvenient forum. UFMJRA, § 4(b).

[117] See Part 74 of the Civil Procedure Rules 1998; Council Regulation 44/2001/EC; the Administration of Justice Act 1920; and the Foreign Judgments (Reciprocal Enforcement) Act 1933, in particular.

14.56 The German civil procedure code (ZPO) on its face grants courts a measure of discretion in enforcing foreign judgments. It states that foreign judgments shall not be enforced if, as a matter of German law, the foreign court lacked jurisdiction over the dispute, there has been a failure of service, there is a conflict between the judgment and a German proceeding, the foreign judgment violates German public policy, or if there has been a failure of due process.[118] One potential issue that is frequently overlooked is service: some countries may take particularly strong opposition to service by mail even where the jurisdiction in which a judgment is rendered allows for it.[119] Depending on how the forum selection clause is drafted, such service issues can make a judgment effectively unenforceable.

14.57 There are international attempts to regulate cross-border enforcement of international judgments. One such international regime that has greatly facilitated cross-border enforcement is the Brussels Regulation applicable in the EU (the 'EU').[120] It mandates cross-border enforcement, subject only to limited challenges by a party opposing enforcement.[121] To the extent that a European judgment is sought to be enforced in another EU state, this regime will greatly facilitate the portability of judgments. That said, in the project context, it is likely that project participants will hail from both inside and outside the EU, meaning that the Brussels Regulation will have limited relevance as a practical matter.

14.58 A new development that may support greater enforceability of judicial decisions is the Hague Convention on Choice of Court Agreements (the 'Choice of Court Convention'). The Choice of Court Convention generally applies to forum selection (jurisdiction) clauses. It has been described as making litigation a 'more viable alternative to arbitration', because the Choice of Court Convention 'ensures the enforcement of forum selection clauses just like the New York Convention guarantees the enforcement of arbitration clauses'.[122] So far, the signatories to the Choice of Court Convention are the US and the EU, and Mexico

---

[118] ZPO, § 328.

[119] See Philipp A. Buhler, 'Transnational Service of Process and Discovery in Federal Court Proceedings: An Overview' (2002) 27 Tul Mar LJ 1; Charles B. Campbell, 'No Sirve: The Invalidity of Service of Process Abroad by Mail or Private Process Server on Parties in Mexico Under the Hague Service Convention' (2010) 19 Minn J Int'l L 107; Kenneth B. Reisenfeld, 'Service of United States Process Abroad: A Practical Guide to Service Under the Hague Service Convention and the Federal Rules of Civil Procedure' (1990) 24 Int'l L 55.

[120] See Council Regulation 44/2001/EC.

[121] *Ibid.*

[122] Louise Ellen Teitz, 'The Hague Choice of Court Convention: Validating Party Autonomy and Providing an Alternative to Arbitration' (2005) 53 Am J Comp L 543 at 557. Article 6, Choice of Courts Convention, provides:

> A court of a Contracting State other than that of the chosen court shall suspend or dismiss proceedings to which an exclusive choice of court agreement applies unless
>
> (a) the agreement is null and void under the law of the State of the chosen court;
> (b) a party lacked the capacity to conclude the agreement under the law of the State of the court seised;

is the only country that has acceded to the Choice of Court Convention.[123] The application of the Choice of Court Convention in practice has not yet been tested.

Enforcement of arbitral awards

Arbitration, on the other hand, is a tested international dispute resolution mecha- **14.59** nism with a long history of relatively consistent international enforcement. There are two important international conventions governing enforcement of arbitral awards: the New York Convention and the Washington Convention.

New York Convention

The New York Convention is the main mechanism for enforcement of commercial **14.60** awards. To date, it has 144 state parties.[124] It requires that 'each Contracting State shall recognize arbitral awards as binding and enforce them'.[125] Awards may be refused enforcement only in certain limited circumstances regarding the proce- dural propriety of awards—that is, was the question at issue in an award properly submitted to a neutral arbitral tribunal and did the parties have a fair and equal opportunity to present their case?[126] To the extent that these questions are answered

---

(c) giving effect to the agreement would lead to a manifest injustice or would be manifestly contrary to the public policy of the state of the court seised;
(d) for exceptional reasons beyond the control of the parties, the agreement cannot reasonably be performed; or
(e) the chosen court has decided not to hear the case.

Similarly, if either party to an agreement containing a forum selection clause attempts to file a lawsuit in a court that was *not* designated as a chosen forum, that court must, under nearly all circumstances, suspend or dismiss proceedings.

[123] See Status Table, Convention of 30 June 2005 on Choice of Court Agreements, available at <http://www.hcch.net/index_en.php?act=conventions.statusprint&cid=98>.

[124] UNCITRAL, New York Convention, status, available at <http://www.uncitral.org/uncitral/ en/uncitral_texts/arbitration/NYConvention_status.html>. Note that the convention allows states to ratify its terms subject to certain reservations; these are typically referred to as the 'reciprocity reservation' (in essence, that an award will only be enforced if it has been rendered from another Convention state) and the 'commercial reservation' (that the state will enforce only awards relating to commercial matters).

[125] New York Convention, art. III.

[126] New York Convention, art. V: 'I. Recognition and enforcement of the award may be refused, at the request of the party against whom it is invoked, only if that party furnishes to the competent authority where the recognition and enforcement is sought, proof that:
(a) The parties to the agreement referred to in article II were, under the law applicable to them, under some incapacity, or the said agreement is not valid under the law to which the parties have subjected it or, failing any indication thereon, under the law of the country where the award was made; or
(b) The party against whom the award is invoked was not given proper notice of the appoint- ment of the arbitrator or of the arbitration proceedings or was otherwise unable to present his case; or
(c) The award deals with a difference not contemplated by or not falling within the terms of the submission to arbitration, or it contains decisions on matters beyond the scope of the

in the affirmative, it is difficult, barring exceptional circumstances, to challenge and set aside an arbitral award.

14.61 The main risk to enforcement in the context of the New York Convention is an action to set aside the award at the seat of the arbitration. Such challenges can be broader than those listed in the New York Convention itself, depending on the jurisdiction.[127] Jurisdictions differ significantly in terms of whether they will enforce an award which has been set aside, with the US having expressed some concerns with regard to enforcement and France having a strong pro-enforcement point of view where the setting-aside decision itself is dubious.[128]

---

submission to arbitration, provided that, if the decisions on matters submitted to arbitration can be separated from those not so submitted, that part of the award which contains decisions on matters submitted to arbitration may be recognized and enforced; or

(d) The composition of the arbitral authority or the arbitral procedure was not in accordance with the agreement of the parties, or, failing such agreement, was not in accordance with the law of the country where the arbitration took place; or

(e) The award has not yet become binding on the parties, or has been set aside or suspended by a competent authority of the country in which, or under the law of which, that award was made.'

Recognition and enforcement of an arbitral award may also be refused if the competent authority in the country where recognition and enforcement is sought finds that:

(a) The subject matter of the difference is not capable of settlement by arbitration under the law of that country; or

(b) The recognition or enforcement of the award would be contrary to the public policy of that country.'

See also *Admart AG v Stephen & Mary Birch Found., Inc.*, 457 F.3d 302 (3d Cir. 2006) (explaining that 'to carry out the policy favouring enforcement of foreign arbitral awards, courts have strictly applied the Article V defenses and generally view them narrowly').

[127] Compare *Caja Nacional De Ahorro Y Seguros in Liquidation v Deutsche Ruckversicherung AG*, 2007 US Dist LEXIS 56197 (SDNY 1 August 2007) (limiting review in a set aside action to egregious procedural issues) and *Saipem SpA v Bangladesh*, Decision on jurisdiction and recommendation on provisional measures, ICSID Case No. ARB/05/07; IIC 280 (2007) (describing Bangladeshi set aside proceeding on relatively minor procedural grounds).

[128] See, for example, *Judgment of 9 October 1984, Pabalk Ticaret Limited Sirketi v Norsolor SA*, XI YB Comm Arb 484 (French *Cour de cassation civ Le*) (1986) (reversing lower court judgment denying recognition to an arbitral award that had been made, and then annulled, in Austria, the arbitral seat); *Judgment of 29 September 2005*, XXXI YB Comm Arb 629 (Paris *Cour d'appel*) (2006) (recognizing award annulled in arbitral seat); *Judgment of 6 December 1988, Société Nationale pour la Recherche, le Transport et la commercialization des Hydrocarbures (Sonatrach) v Ford, Bacon & Davis, Inc.*, XV YB Comm Arb 370 (Brussels *Tribunal de Premiere Instance*) (1990) (recognizing award annulled in Algeria); *Judgment of 20 October 1993, Radenska v Kajo*, XXVIa YB Comm Arb 919 (Austrian *Oberster Gerichtshof*) (1999) (reversing lower court decision refusing to recognize an award that was made and then annulled on public policy grounds in Belgrade); *Chromalloy Gas Turbine Corp v Arab Republic of Egypt*, 939 F Supp 907 (DDCs 1996) (recognizing an arbitral award made in Egypt, notwithstanding the fact that an Egyptian court had subsequently annulled the award on the grounds that the arbitrators had misapplied Egyptian law); *Baker Marine Ltd v Chevron Ltd*, 191 F3d 194, 197 n.3 (2d Cir., 1999) (refusing to recognize an arbitral award that had been annulled in Nigeria due to excess of authority and procedural misconduct); *Termorio SA v Electranta SP*, 487 F3d 928 (DC Cir., 2007) (holding that an arbitral award made by a Colombian tribunal could not be enforced in the US, because Colombia's highest administrative court nullified the award on the ground that the arbitration clause violated Colombian law).

Washington Convention

As noted above, The Washington Convention is applicable to investor-state dis- **14.62**
putes arbitrated at ICSID. One advantage to ICSID arbitration is the enforcement
mechanism available under the Washington Convention. 'One of the greatest
strengths' of the Washington Convention is that it is 'even more favourable to recognition and enforcement than the New York Convention', because the Washington
Convention 'accepts no grounds whatsoever' for refusal to recognize and enforce
ICSID tribunal awards.[129] ICSID awards are considered binding and final. They are
not subject to review except under certain limited conditions outlined in the
Washington Convention—on restricted grounds before a three-member *ad hoc*
committee that may only interpret, revise, or annul the award.[130] Generally, an
ICSID award is therefore more readily enforceable than a New York Convention
award. An ICSID award avoids local set aside actions, and replaces such actions
with specialized review by a panel chosen by the ICSID itself. Despite a current
surge in attempts to set aside a number of ICSID awards rendered in the context of
the Argentine Peso crisis in the early 2000s, the efficacy of ICSID awards remains
significant.

Dispute Resolution 'Toolkit'

Previous sections discussed key risks and benefits of different dispute resolution **14.63**
mechanisms and investment structures. This section identifies tools which are available to structure around some of the risks discussed above, as well as the costs those
structures may entail.[131] These tools generally need to be employed at the drafting
stage, rather than after a dispute has already developed.

Dispute resolution clauses, common components

If the parties to a project finance transaction choose arbitration as the method to **14.64**
resolve disputes, consideration of the various types of disputes that may arise is vital
in addressing the political and commercial risks that are inherent in a multi-party,
multi-contract transaction. It is important to remember that disputes to which an

---

[129] Guide to ICSID Arbitration at 96.
[130] Dolzer and Schreuer at 224; Guide to ICSID Arbitration at 96; but see E. Baldwin, M. Kantor,
and M. Nolan, 'Limits to Enforcement of ICSID Awards', (2006) 23 J of Int'l Arb 1 (identifying possible ways to avoid ICSID Awards).
[131] For more detailed discussion of the following section, see generally Born; Friedland.

arbitration clause applies frequently arise years after it has been drafted.[132] As one influential treatise explains:

> Most international commercial arbitration takes place pursuant to an arbitration clause in a commercial contract. These clauses are often 'midnight clauses', i.e. the last clauses to be considered in contract negotiations, sometimes late at night or in the early hours of the morning. Insufficient thought is given as to how disputes are to be resolved (possibly because the parties are reluctant to contemplate falling into dispute) and an inappropriate and unwieldy compromise is often adopted. . . . If a dispute arises, and arbitration proceedings begin, these matters must be dealt with before any progress can be made with the real issues.[133]

14.65 Below is a list of the various components of an arbitration clause.

Exclusivity

Unilateral option clauses

14.66 Typically an arbitration clause states that arbitration is the sole method of dispute resolution. Situations may arise, however, in which the parties to a project finance agreement would like the option of choosing either arbitration or litigation, depending on the type of dispute that arises. Currently, courts in the US 'are not aligned on whether "unilateral option clauses" are enforceable in the arbitration context'.[134] Hybrid clauses that allow one or more parties to choose between litigation or arbitration is an attempt to permit parties to select the most appropriate type of dispute resolution *after* a dispute has arisen. Such clauses have become increasingly popular in Asia, the Middle East, and Saudi Arabia. A well-drafted clause that presents just one of the parties with the option to refer a dispute to arbitration, if and when such a dispute arises, will typically be upheld as a matter of English law.[135]

Scope of arbitration

14.67 The range of disputes or claims that will be subject to arbitration is critical. Most arbitration clauses are drafted broadly to encompass 'all disputes, claims, controversies and disagreements' that are 'arising under', 'arising out of', 'in connection with', or 'relating to' the agreement or the 'subject matter of the agreement'.[136] Questions arise as to whether non-contractual claims, such as tort claims, 'arise

---

[132] Alternatively, parties can enter into a 'submission agreement'—an agreement to arbitrate that is made after a dispute has actually arisen. See Redfern and Hunter at § 1.39.

[133] See Redfern and Hunter, *Law and Practice of International Commercial Arbitration* (2004) 3–302.

[134] Scott L. Hoffman, *The Law and Business of International Project Finance* (3rd edn, Cambridge University Press, 2007) 406.

[135] See *NB Three Shipping Ltd v Harebell Shipping Ltd* [2005] 1 All ER 200 and *Law Debenture Trust Corporation PLC v Elektrim Finance BV and others* [2005] 2 All ER 476.

[136] See generally Born at 39–41; Friedland at 61.

under' an agreement. Courts in the US, for example, look to the terms of the clause to determine whether the parties intended the clause to be broad or narrow.[137] Therefore, the broader phrases of 'relating to' or 'in connection with' may be preferable. The position under English law was clarified and modernized by the House of Lords in the case of *Premium Nafta Products Ltd v Fili Shipping Ltd*. In the words of Lord Hoffmann:

> . . . the construction of an arbitration clause should start from the assumption that the parties, as rational businessmen, are likely to have intended any dispute arising out of the relationship into which they have entered or purported to enter to be decided by the same tribunal. The clause should be construed in accordance with this presumption unless the language makes it clear that certain questions were intended to be excluded from the arbitrator's jurisdiction . . .[138]

Institution selected for arbitration

Institutional arbitration is conducted pursuant to procedural rules of the selected arbitration institution. Choosing among the established arbitral institutions requires considering the parties' transaction, identities, and respective interests, as well as the likely nature of future disputes.[139] Once an arbitral institution has been selected, it is important to incorporate the institution's rules. Keep in mind that it is usually possible to modify aspects of an institution's arbitration rules (although, if this is done, such modifications should be drafted with great care). Institutional arbitration may be the most useful for project financing because the complexity of transactions as well as multiple parties and interests may need an experienced panel acting under well-developed rules.[140]   **14.68**

By contrast, *ad hoc* arbitration is conducted without an administering authority and generally without the aid of institutional procedural rules. The United Nations Commission for International Trade Law (UNCITRAL) Arbitration Rules were approved by the UN General Assembly, thus making them more acceptable to parties from all regions. Moreover, there is a substantial body of reported interpretations using UNCITRAL Rules. The CPR Institute for Dispute Resolution also has published procedural rules for *ad hoc* international arbitrations. *Ad hoc* arbitration is appropriate when all parties to the transaction are experienced with international   **14.69**

---

[137] See, for example, *Vetco Sales, Inc. v Vinar*, 98 F. App'x 264, 266-67 (5th Cir., 2004) (finding that 'arising out of' language in arbitration clause indicated that 'the parties intended to limit the applicability of this clause', and holding that claims for breach of a related agreement were outside the scope of the arbitration clause).

[138] [2008] 1 Lloyd's Rep 254.

[139] See Born at 57.

[140] See Hoffman at 412; see also Born at 44 (institutional arbitration offers heightened predictability, stability, and international expertise). Refer to footnote 26 above for a non-exclusive list of arbitral institutions.

arbitration and are cooperating. It also may be attractive for disputes for which parties wish to avoid paying fees to an arbitral institution.

Selection of arbitration panel

14.70 The selection of the arbitral tribunal, whose members will serve as the judges in the case, is one of the most important aspects of the arbitral process. The number of arbitrators should be determined in advance and should depend on cost, speed, expertise, consistency, and efficiency. The most common way to select arbitrators is to include an 'appointing authority' (as set out in the institutional arbitration rules) which will select either a sole arbitrator or a presiding arbitrator (if the parties chose three arbitrators as the number to sit on the panel). When three arbitrators are selected, each party usually selects one arbitrator and the third arbitrator is selected by the two party-nominated arbitrators or by the 'appointing authority'.

14.71 The nationality of the arbitrator can be a particularly important factor in choosing, or objecting to, an arbitrator. Different arbitration rules deal with the question of nationality differently.[141] Many commercial arbitration rules do *not* prohibit the appointment by a party of an arbitrator who has the same nationality as the party itself. Many institutional rules require, however, that the presiding arbitrator should not have the same nationality as any of the parties. For example, the 1998 ICC Arbitration Rules provide that 'the sole arbitrator or the chairman of the Arbitral Tribunal shall be of a nationality other than those of the parties'.

14.72 Finally, arbitrators should be 'independent' and 'impartial' of the parties—that is, arbitrators should not have direct financial, business, or professional relationships with any of the parties. Arbitrators may be required to submit statements, which should be updated in the light of any material developments, certifying their independence.

Severability

14.73 Most jurisdictions treat an arbitration clause contained in a larger transactional agreement as a separate contract from the remainder of the transaction. For example, the House of Lords in *Fiona Trust and Holding Corp. v Privalov*[142] (also reported

---

[141] See, for example, ICSID Arbitration Rules:

> The majority of the arbitrators shall be nationals of States other than the State party to the dispute and of the State whose national is a party to the dispute, unless the sole arbitrator or each individual member of the Tribunal is appointed by agreement of the parties. Where the Tribunal is to consist of three members, a national of either of these States may not be appointed as an arbitrator by a party without the agreement of the other party to the dispute. Where the Tribunal is to consist of five or more members, nationals of either of these States may not be appointed as arbitrators by a party if appointment by the other party of the same number of arbitrators of either of these nationalities would result in a majority of arbitrators of these nationalities.

[142] [2007] UKHL 40.

sub nom. Premium Nafta Products Ltd v Fili Shipping Co. Ltd) confirmed that, as a matter of English law, an agreement to arbitrate is separable from the underlying contract, even in the face of allegations that the entire contract was induced by bribery.[143] Therefore, challenges against the transaction or the contract will not necessarily defeat the arbitration clause.

Language of arbitration

An easily overlooked, yet significant, matter is the language for the conduct of the arbitration. It is common for the language of the arbitration to be the same language that governs the contract. Some arbitration clauses, however, may require that arbitrators be fluent in a second language or that witnesses be permitted to testify in their native languages. Choosing two or more languages may burden the arbitral proceedings and increase the time and cost for translation and interpreters.[144]   **14.74**

Seat of arbitration

The law governing the arbitral proceedings—the *lex arbitri*—is normally determined by the seat of the arbitration. It can be a different law altogether from the law that governs the underlying contract. The choice of an appropriate seat can have significant implications for an international arbitration. The seat of arbitration is the place where the formal arbitral award will be made and the jurisdiction whose laws will ordinarily govern the arbitral proceedings and actions to vacate the award. Moreover, the arbitral seat could have a material effect on the selection of the arbitrators, arbitral procedures, and other substantive and procedural issues. The procedural rules of an arbitration will be affected to some extent by the choice of an arbitral institution, as each of the institutions and *ad hoc* arbitrations have formulated different rules.   **14.75**

It is key to designate the arbitral seat to be a state that is a party to one of the international enforcement conventions (i.e. the New York Convention, the Panama Convention, or the European Convention). Similarly, the arbitral seat should have national arbitration legislation and national courts that are 'hospitable to and supportive of' international arbitration, such as legislation based on the UNCITRAL Model Law on International Commercial Arbitration.[145]   **14.76**

Unless, as is usually the case, the parties agree on the seat of the arbitration, the rules of the various institutions typically empower the tribunal to make   **14.77**

---

[143] See Mark S. McNeill and Ben Juratowitch, 'Agora: Thoughts on Fiona Trust—The Doctrine of Separability and Consent to Arbitrate' (2008) 24(3) Arbitration International 475.

[144] See Friedland at 70.

[145] The purpose of the UNCITRAL Model Law is to make international arbitration agreements and awards more 'readily, predictably, and uniformly enforceable'. See Born at 65, 107.

that determination. Various factual and legal factors influence the choice of place of arbitration, such as: (1) the suitability of the law on arbitral procedure of the place of arbitration; (2) whether there is a multilateral or bilateral treaty on enforcement of arbitral awards between the state where the arbitration takes place and the state or states where the award may have to be enforced (as described above); (3) the convenience of the parties and the arbitrators; (4) the availability and cost of support services; and (5) the location of the subject matter in dispute and the location of evidence.[146]

Scope of disclosure

14.78 International arbitration lacks a fixed legal regime governing discovery; therefore, a party that desires expressly to permit or prohibit certain types of discovery may do so through the arbitration clause. The efficacy and application of discovery provisions may be affected by the national law in the seat of arbitration, the institutional rules, the nationalities and legal backgrounds of the arbitrators, and the availability of remedies or sanctions for non-compliance.[147] As discussed above, broad disclosure of documents is not embraced by some arbitrators.

Privacy and/or confidentiality

14.79 Arbitration proceedings are generally less public than litigation proceedings. Such privacy does not, however, keep the submissions or the proceedings confidential. Confidentiality provisions in, or parallel with, the parties' arbitration agreement can supplement the privacy or confidentiality provided by institutional rules.

Jurisdiction

14.80 Jurisdictional objections can be raised in court proceedings or with the arbitral tribunal. The manner and timing of such challenges will depend on the respective legal system in which the proceedings are taking place, as well as the arbitral clause. For example, in some countries, such as the US, courts have the first turn at deciding jurisdictional issues *unless* a clause in the arbitration agreement gives the arbitral tribunal the power to decide such issues.[148] Other countries, however, may have different default rules with respect to jurisdictional objections.[149]

---

[146] UNCITRAL Notes on the Organization of Arbitral Proceedings (1996).

[147] See, for example, Born at 80-81.

[148] See, for example, *China Minmetals Materials Import and Export Co. v Chi Mei Corp.*, 334 F.3d 274 (3d Cir., 2003).

[149] For example, in Germany an arbitral tribunal may rule on its own jurisdiction. See § 1040 (1) Code of Civil Procedure. Objections to the jurisdiction of the arbitral tribunal must be raised within certain time-limits. See § 1040 (2) Code of Civil Procedure. In England and Wales, the tribunal is able to rule on its own jurisdiction, unless the parties have agreed otherwise. Section 30(1) of the Arbitration Act 1996. Further, a challenge to a tribunal's jurisdiction should typically be made to the tribunal itself, rather than the court, unless (1) all parties consent to the court hearing the issue or

Entry of judgment, judgment currency, and manner of payment

An arbitration clause can limit the remedial powers of the arbitrator by stating a **14.81** range of monetary awards (a 'high-low' arbitration clause) or by providing that the arbitrators must select a proposal submitted by one of the parties (sometimes called, 'baseball arbitration', especially in the United States). The purpose of such provisions is to provide a financial incentive for compromise and negotiation.[150]

An 'entry of judgment' clause ensures the enforceability of arbitral awards in **14.82** the United States. Although other legal systems generally do not require such provisions for enforcement, it may be prudent to consider such a clause when a U.S.-related party or transaction is involved.[151]

Final and binding arbitration

The clause should state that the arbitration award will be final and binding on all **14.83** parties.

Payment of costs and legal fees

Under most institutional arbitration rules, parties pay their own litigation expenses **14.84** and share payment of the arbitrators' and the institution's fees and costs.[152] This initial payment, however, usually is subsequently reallocated to the unsuccessful party.[153]

Choice of law

A choice of law clause specifying the substantive law applicable to the underlying **14.85** contract should be in a separate provision in the contract, not in the dispute resolution clause. A different law, however, may apply to the arbitration agreement, because most legal systems deem the arbitration agreement to be a separable contract.[154] Regardless, the law governing the proceedings will be the law of the seat of arbitration. Parties can include a choice of law provision that designates the law governing future arbitral proceedings.[155] If the parties do not select a governing law,

---

(2) the permission of the tribunal is first obtained and the court is satisfied that the application was made without delay, will result in a substantial saving in costs, and there is good reason why the court should hear the issue (s 32 of the Arbitration Act 1996). Note that time-limits apply to any challenge to jurisdiction: see, in particular, s 73 of the Arbitration Act 1996.

[150] See Born at 105–6.
[151] *Ibid.* at 86.
[152] See *ibid.* at 82–4. Note also that should one party fail to pay its initial share of the tribunal's or the arbitration centre's costs, the other (innocent) party will likely have to pay the defaulting party's share as well and then seek to recover those costs by way of a costs award from the tribunal.
[153] See *ibid.*
[154] See *ibid.* at 79–80.
[155] See *ibid.*

then the decision is left to the arbitrators, who typically choose the law of the location of the arbitration.

14.86 Parties can explicitly consent to release arbitrators from their obligation to apply substantive law. Such *ex aequo et bono* and *amiable compositeur* arbitrations are based in equity and fairness, similar to a mediation or conciliation, rather than on a substantive application of the law.[156] The concepts were developed with the aim of restoring harmony and achieving a workable legal relationship between the parties.[157]

Reducing disruption—multi-tiered dispute resolution

14.87 Drawn out disputes are inherently disruptive to ongoing projects. Given the collaborative nature of a typical project, it may be preferable to avoid formal confrontation from a business perspective. Further, there are often significant and negative implications associated with the publicity of court cases and arbitrations that can have a further damaging impact on the project.

14.88 Court hearings and the court file, including pleadings and exhibits, are open to the public and press in many countries. Such disclosure could impede negotiations as well as the broader progress on the project due to bad publicity. For some participants in certain projects, 'transparency'—and in particular, the desire to avoid being publicly perceived as being non-transparent—is important. Other parties may desire for the proceeding and the outcome to become public, in order to raise public awareness or to generate binding precedent. By contrast, arbitral proceedings typically are private, a characteristic that appeals to lenders and host governments which may want to avoid publicity of their disputes. Arbitral hearings and parties submissions are almost always private.[158] Arbitrations, however, appear to be moving in the direction of more transparency, not less.

14.89 Although there is an expectation and tradition that arbitration proceedings are confidential in addition to being private,[159] that expectation is not entirely accurate. Arbitration permits, not imposes, confidentiality. Different countries have different legal regimes respecting arbitral confidentiality. For example, Singapore recognizes an implied duty of confidentiality in arbitration proceedings, although

---

[156] Karl-Heinz Bockstiegel, Stefan Michael Kroll, and Patricia Nacimiento (eds), *Arbitration in Germany: The Model Law in Practice* (Kluwer Law International, 2007) 359.

[157] See *ibid*.

[158] There is a distinction between contractual and treaty-based arbitration. For example, the Central American Free Trade Agreement guarantees the transparency of arbitral proceedings by requiring the respondent to make submissions available to the public and the tribunal to conduct hearings open to the public. (Dominican Republic—Central America—United States Free Trade Agreement, 2004, Article 10.21.)

[159] See, for example, Friedland at 20–1 ('Notwithstanding the usual absence of prohibitions on party disclosure, there is an expectation and tradition of confidentiality in arbitration, which a party violates at its own peril vis-à-vis the arbitrators.').

disclosures can be made in certain circumstances.[160] Under Swedish law, on the other hand, parties in arbitration proceedings are not bound by a duty of confidentiality unless the parties have entered into an express agreement regarding confidentiality.[161] The differences in laws regarding confidentiality illustrate the importance of the seat of arbitration (as discussed above). Confidentiality agreements or provisions still must be expressly negotiated and executed, either at the contracting stage or when a dispute arises and arbitration has commenced.

A tool that can help avoid drawn-out and costly disputes is the use of different forms of alternative dispute resolution (ADR) prior to engaging in arbitration or litigation. 'Escalation' or multi-tiered dispute resolution clauses are an example. Such clauses require the exhaustion of specified dispute resolution mechanisms prior to the institution of the 'formal' and final form of dispute resolution. The main benefit is the ability to settle a dispute at an early stage. The main drawbacks include the time and resources it takes to complete such preliminary steps of dispute resolution (especially if it seems unlikely in a particular circumstance that success will result) and the strategic withholding of key positions and information that parties may be tempted to engage in order to improve their positions should preliminary efforts and dispute resolution fail. Problems and satellite disputes can occur if the drafting of the multi-tier dispute resolution provisions do not make it entirely clear which steps in the process are optional and which are mandatory. Care should be taken to ensure that, by agreeing to ADR as part of a mandatory escalation procedure, the parties have not prevented themselves from seeking urgent precautionary or protective relief from a court while the ADR process runs its course. **14.90**

Typical means of ADR

Mediation and conciliation

Non-binding forms of dispute resolution include mediation and conciliation, in which an independent third party or panel assists the parties in dispute to reach an amicable settlement.[162] The terms 'mediation' and 'conciliation' often are used interchangeably as synonyms, although there are distinctions. A mediator listens to the outline of a dispute, meets with each party separately, and tries to 'persuade the parties to moderate their respective positions'.[163] A conciliator makes proposals for a settlement, and if no settlement is reached during the conciliation proceedings, **14.91**

---

[160] Michael Young and Simon Chapman, 'Confidentiality in International Arbitration: Does the Exception Prove the Rule? Where Now for the Implied Duty of Confidentiality Under English Law?' (2009) 27(1) ASA Bulletin 41 (citing *Myanma Yaung Chi Oo Co. v Win Win Nu* [2003] 2 SLR 547).

[161] Young and Chapman, at 43–4 (citing *Bulgarian Foreign Trade Bank Ltd. v A.I. Trade Finance Inc.*, an English translation of which can be found in A.J. van den Berg (ed.), *Yearbook of Commercial Arbitration*, Vol. XXVI (2001) 291–8).

[162] See Redfern and Hunter at 46; see also UNCITRAL Legislative Guide at 6–7.

[163] See *ibid.*

the conciliator may formulate the terms of a possible settlement and submit the terms to the parties for acceptance or rejection.[164]

14.92   Mediation and conciliation procedures typically are confidential, informal, easily pursued, quick, and inexpensive.[165] Both mediation and conciliation end when there is a settlement of the dispute or if the process is unsuccessful in reaching a settlement.[166] Mediation and conciliation may be particularly useful when there are many parties involved and it would be difficult to achieve a settlement by direct negotiations between the parties.[167] As with all dispute resolution methods, conciliation and mediation raise issues that parties should consider. For example, parties may be reluctant to present, at an early stage in a dispute, a well-developed statement of position for fear of providing 'informal discovery' or some type of advantage to the other side. Parties may perceive that agreeing to conciliation or mediation before commencing arbitration or litigation is a wasted expense, particularly if the parties believe that the dispute ultimately will go to arbitration or litigation. But the International Chamber of Commerce has had success with ADR, with many cases leading to a settlement before resorting to arbitration.

14.93   If parties provide for mediation or conciliation in the project agreements, they should consider a number of procedural questions. For example, parties should consider whether a mediator should be permitted to become an arbitrator. This may increase the efficiency of the process, because the individual will already be familiar will all of the issues. But it may undermine the arbitral process and its requirements of impartiality and a fair hearing.[168] The UNCITRAL Conciliation Rules and the ICC ADR Rules are a popular means of pre-arbitration mediation.[169] Further, the parties should ensure, to the extent possible, that material created for the purposes of any mediation or conciliation are protected from subsequent use in any arbitration or litigation. It is important to bear in mind that, in some jurisdictions, such as the United Arab Emirates, the protection which is afforded in other jurisdictions to 'without prejudice' communications is not, *prima facie* respected.

Expert determination

14.94   Disputes arising from a project financing may involve highly technical matters. Disputes also may need to be resolved quickly in order not to disrupt the construction or the operation of the facility.[170] In those circumstances, parties may wish to consider selecting mechanisms that allow for the choice of competent experts to

---

[164] *Ibid.* at 46–7.
[165] UNCITRAL Legislative Guide at 4.
[166] *Ibid.* at 6.
[167] *Ibid.* at 7.
[168] Redfern and Hunter at 48.
[169] ICC ADR Rules, available at <http://www.iccwbo.org/drs/english/adr/pdf_documents/adr_rules.pdf>.
[170] See UNCITRAL Legislative Guide at 4.

assist in the settlement of disputes.[171] Expert determination may be useful in international contracts relating to energy, mining, and telecommunication projects.

An agreement can specify that certain disputes, such as taxation issues, should be presented for expert determination, while other disputes should be resolved by arbitration or some other dispute resolution method. An expert determination clause should include, among other things: (i) the issue to be determined; (ii) the qualifications of the expert; (iii) the methodology for appointing the expert; and (iv) the conditions under which the expert's decision will be final and binding.[172]   **14.95**

Dispute boards

Another form of dispute resolution is a dispute resolution board, which under some circumstances may offer advantages over both arbitration and litigation, including speed, cost and simplicity.[173] Dispute boards historically have been used almost exclusively in connection with construction contracts, but they have become more widely used over time. The boards typically are established at the beginning of a project and remain in place throughout its duration. The members of these boards or panels—which can be companies or organizations, as well as individuals—are chosen for their expertise in a certain area. For certain disputes, it will be more useful to have decision-makers with technical expertise rather than legal expertise. In other cases, it may be useful for a dispute resolution board to be located on the site of a large-scale construction project in order to immediately address problems as they arise.[174] In some large infrastructure projects, more than one review board may be established—for example, one board may deal exclusively with disputes regarding matters of a technical nature, while another board may deal with disputes of a contractual or financial nature.[175] The ICC has adopted simple and proven rules for different types of boards that can be established for any type of contract.[176]   **14.96**

Management resolution

Another form of dispute resolution is management resolution, requiring that high-level decision-makers for the disputing parties become involved in the resolution of   **14.97**

---

[171] *Ibid.* at 4, 8.
[172] See Friedland at 150–1.
[173] See *ibid.* at 143.
[174] See UNCITRAL Legislative Guide, p. 9.
[175] *Ibid.* at 8–9.
[176] A Dispute Review Board issues recommendations with which the parties agree to comply if no party expresses dissatisfaction within a given time period. A Dispute Adjudication Board issues decisions with which the parties must comply immediately. A Combined Dispute Board typically issues recommendations, but it can issue decisions upon a party's request. Even if a contract contains a clause designating a Dispute Resolution Board, arbitration or litigation can be preserved as option that a party may elect if the party is dissatisfied with the decisions or recommendations of the board. See <http://www.iccwbo.org/court/dispute_boards/id4529/index.html>.

disputes generally or, alternatively, in relation to specific types of dispute. This usually is included as a preliminary step in an escalation clause with other ADR mechanisms, followed by arbitration or litigation. This dispute resolution mechanism has gained more prominence recently.

Reducing the Chance for Error: Qualification Requirements and Appeals

Limited flexibility in litigation

14.98 There are limited ways in which to affect the qualifications or rights to appeal in the litigation context. The only true choice that a party has to affect such risks in litigation is in the choice of forum or jurisdiction.

Qualification requirements in arbitral clauses

14.99 Arbitration agreements also can specify certain qualifications and characteristics of prospective arbitrators. In anticipating project finance disputes, whether an arbitrator is well suited to the case may depend upon the arbitrator's ability to understand technical or legal issues that are crucial to the case. For example, the agreement could require the appointment of an accountant as an arbitrator.[177] It is also possible to designate arbitrators in advance, but parties should be aware that a pre-designated arbitrator may become unavailable or conflicted by the time a dispute arises.[178]

Appeals rules in arbitral clauses

14.100 Some arbitral institutions have instituted arbitral rules for appeals of arbitral awards. Given the flexibility of arbitral clauses, it is possible to include a provision in an arbitration clause allowing for an arbitral appeal. In the projects context, this is not industry practice. Including appeals rules therefore should be carefully considered on a case-by-case basis.

Consolidation of Potential Disputes by Agreement

14.101 Other than litigation, arbitration exists only on the basis of the consent of the parties to a dispute. This requirement of consent means that non-parties to a specific

---

[177] But see Friedland at 71 (cautioning that it is unwise to specify any qualifications for arbitrators in advance because the parties may find it difficult to identify an arbitrator who fulfills the contractual criteria and also is available and unconflicted and because the parties rarely know in advance of a dispute what qualifications may be appropriate).
[178] See Born at 70–1.

dispute resolution clause cannot be joined to an arbitration without their express subsequent consent, no matter how instrumental they are to the dispute itself, whereas such joinder may be possible in the litigation context.[179] Especially in the early stages of a project, there may be significant overlap between project agreements and between different participants. A dispute regarding one contract may impact the entire project, given the transactional unity of project financings.[180] This may lead to a significant risk of contribution suits between the different affected parties to other agreements in order to allocate the costs of an adverse decision correctly between themselves.[181]

Structuring for permissive joinder in litigation

A second procedural complexity may arise when parallel proceedings are com- **14.102** menced at different times under related contracts as discussed above.[182] In litigation, joinder of parties can be relatively simple if all parties are generally subject to the jurisdiction of the court before which a dispute is pending. Further, it may be helpful to include waiver clauses in an arbitration agreement stating that no

---

[179] In litigation, mechanisms generally are available for the joinder of necessary third parties. For example, as a matter of US civil procedure, a party can be joined to an ongoing proceeding, if but for the joinder, the court could not accord complete relief among existing parties. Fed R Civ P 19(a) (1)(A). Problematically, the ability of courts to join parties to an ongoing dispute will depend upon whether the court has personal jurisdiction over the additional party. In the context of projects, this frequently may not be the case. It will be especially difficult in the context of certain special-purpose vehicles incorporated in tax-favourable jurisdictions or of certain host state project participants. The typical means employed by an arbitral tribunal to join a non-signatory, which are much more limited than those available in litigation, include agency theories or, in a parent-subsidiary relationship, some form of piercing of the corporate veil. Some jurisdictions also recognize a group of companies theory to join a non-signatory to an arbitration proceeding, but this is availing only if the companies to be joined are in the same corporate family. See, for example, *Dow Chemical case*, ICC Case No. 4131 (1982), (1984) 9 YB Com Arb 136. Thus, little to no means exists to add true third parties to an arbitration proceeding, unless consent to such joinder can be obtained after a dispute arises. To the extent that certain groups of contracts with different project participants would likely lead to a cluster of disputes relating to the same underlying occurrence, it may therefore be worthwhile to keep this risk in mind at the drafting stage.

[180] See Dugué at 1064.

[181] There may be many hidden costs associated with the inability to join all relevant parties in an arbitration. In some instances, a prospective claimant may conclude that without the ability to claim against multiple parties in a single proceeding, claims are not worth pursing in multiple arbitrations or with the prospect of, at most, incomplete relief. Another hidden cost is the possibility of contribution suits. Thus, when one party is saddled with a risk that is covered by a third agreement, this party will have to commence suit anew. This need for duplicative dispute resolution has both immediate costs and long-term project costs. Most immediately, multiple disputes likely will impose greater burden and distraction upon management of the claimant, as well as higher counsel fees and multiple arbitration or litigation costs. Less immediate, but perhaps more importantly, such disputes involve project risks that project participants will continuously be in litigation or arbitration with one another as adversaries rather than partners.

[182] IBA Guidelines for Drafting International Arbitration Clauses, Final Draft for Consultation, 9 March 2009, at 105.

objection would be made to joinder in any ongoing proceeding between other project participants in the underlying project agreements.

Structuring for multi-party arbitration

14.103 If parties desire the consolidation of related arbitral proceedings, the arbitration clause in each underlying contract should be drafted to permit consolidation.[183] A master agreement, which is incorporated by reference into the individual project contracts, is one means of providing a single contractual dispute resolution mechanism.[184] When drafting, one should consider whether the following elements should be included in such clauses: (i) equality among all parties in the appointment of arbitrators; (ii) parties' consent to the participation of third parties to future arbitrations; and (iii) consolidation of possible parallel arbitration proceedings.[185] Keep in mind that although the prospect of multiple arbitral proceedings can be addressed through multi-party, multiple-contract arbitration agreements, *all* parties must consent to such agreements.

Increasing Effectiveness: Early Remedies and Final Enforcement

Waiver of defenses to enforcement of judgments

14.104 It may be possible to include waivers to objections, immunities or defenses with regard to enforcement in the forum selection clause. One such typical waiver is included if a party to an agreement might enjoy sovereign immunity.[186] The enforceability of such waivers will differ from jurisdiction to jurisdiction. These issues will be of particular importance if the civil procedure rules of a country in which enforcement would likely be sought require *sua sponte*[187] determinations by the court with regard to the underlying judgments.

Early relief in arbitration

14.105 One of the key problems with regard to the choice of arbitration of disputes requiring the availability of quick interim relief was that such relief traditionally was not available. Some arbitral institutions have worked on introducing emergency arbitrators who are available to resolve such interim relief issues if empowered by

---

[183] *Ibid.* at 106.
[184] A multi-party agreement might permit any party to assert claims against any other party, for any respondent to add additional parties or for any party to have the right to intervene. See Born at 98–9.
[185] See Dugué at 1078.
[186] Care must be taken to ensure that the waiver is effectively drafted, because the requirements of an effective waiver may go beyond a simple statement of intention, as is the case in connection with the waiver of sovereign immunity under English law.
[187] I.e. of the court's own volition.

an arbitration clause.[188] Parties electing arbitration may agree to the availability of courts prior to the empanelment of an arbitral tribunal. In some jurisdictions, the parties may also agree to the availability of urgent relief from the court before the arbitral tribunal has been established will be assumed in the absence of the parties' express agreement to the contrary.[189]

Limiting recourse to set aside actions

Depending on the jurisdiction, it may be possible further to reduce the ability of **14.106** parties to seek to set aside an arbitral award. A waiver of this kind should be agreed to in the underlying transaction documents. If justified concerns about the suitability of the seat of jurisdiction necessitate a waiver clause, the courts of the seat of the arbitration of course may be more likely to ignore such provisions. Such a waiver clause may nevertheless help protect the award against the consequences of proceedings in a different jurisdiction aimed at setting aside the award.[190]

---

[188] See American Arbitration Association, Commercial Arbitration Rules and Mediation Procedures, Optional Rules for Emergency Measures for Protection. Where parties by special agreement or in their arbitration clause have adopted the AAA's rules for emergency measures of protection, a party in need of emergency relief prior to the constitution of the arbitral panel shall notify the AAA and all other parties in writing of the nature of the relief sought and the reasons why such relief is required on an emergency basis. Within one business day of receipt of notice, the AAA shall appoint a single emergency arbitrator from a special AAA panel of emergency arbitrators designated to rule on emergency applications.

[189] See, for example, in England and Wales, s 44 of the Arbitration Act 1996.

[190] See, for example, *In the Matter of the Arbitration of Certain Controversies Between Chromalloy Aeroservices and the Arab Republic of Egypt*, 939 F Supp 907 (D DC, 1996).

APPENDIX 1

Checklist of Conditions Precedent, Representations, Covenants, and Events of Default for inclusion in Finance Documents

This checklist sets out, in abbreviated form, sample provisions for conditions precedent, representations and warranties, covenants and events of default that are frequently encountered in finance documents, regardless of the nature of the asset or project being financed. Not all of these sample provisions will be relevant for all transactions, and materiality and other exclusions will be the subject of negotiation. The specific terms will also vary dramatically from transaction to transaction to reflect the source of financing. For instance, capital markets terms are usually less restrictive in nature.

As in all financings, the finance documentation will additionally provide for loan and other credit mechanics that are specific to the transaction, as well as yield protection and provisions that are specific to the project or asset being financed.

1. Conditions Precedent

1.1 Conditions Precedent to Closing and First Drawdown under the Finance Documents

The following conditions precedent will be required to be met to the satisfaction of the lenders:

(a) Execution of the credit agreement and all other related financing and security documents.

(b) Execution of the principal project documents. For instance, the construction contract, ground lease, supply contracts, transportation agreement, offtake contracts, technology/operational licenses and operations and management contract.

(c) Delivery of appropriate consents, and the making of appropriate filings and recordings in each jurisdiction, as necessary.

(d) Receipt of certified copies of the organizational documents (such as the memorandum and articles of association/charter, certificate of incorporation or partnership agreement) of, and evidence of all corporate or partnership action taken by, the project company and the other principal project participants (referred to collectively as the Obligors). The identity of the entities included as Obligors are often the subject of negotiation and may include the affiliates of the project company, the equity participants, the subordinated lenders, the offtaker, the operator, the construction contractor, the feedstock supplier and each person providing credit support for the obligations of these parties.

(e) Receipt and approval by the lenders of the most recent financial statements of the Obligors.

(f) The absence of any material adverse change in the financial condition of any Obligor, or any person providing credit support for the obligations of such Obligor, and receipt of a certificate of an authorized officer of each Obligor certifying the same.

(g) Receipt of a satisfactory report from the technical adviser that addresses the technical and economic viability of the project. It will, among other things, touch on the project's capital budget, construction plan, equipment selection, expected performance, development and production costs, operating costs, the operator's experience and the plan by which the project and, as applicable, the fuel or feedstock source will be operated.

(h) Receipt of a satisfactory report from the environmental consultant providing an environmental and geotechnical risk assessment, as well as a permit review and an analysis of how environmental risks can be mitigated.

(i) Receipt of the environmental and social management plan (ESMP) outlining the environmental and social management system to be put in place for the project.

(j) Receipt of a certificate of an internationally recognized insurance broker stating that all required insurance policies are in full force and effect, are not subject to cancellation without prior notice, and otherwise conform with the requirements specified in the insurance provisions of the credit agreement.

(k) Receipt of certified copies of all governmental actions, licenses, permits and approvals (collectively, the Governmental Approvals), together with copies of all applications required for the construction and operation of the project. These Governmental Approvals will, of course, be specific to each project and the jurisdiction in which it is located. Governmental Approvals required for construction or operation that cannot reasonably be obtained, or are customarily not obtained or required, until a later stage in the project's construction or after operation has commenced, will not be included unless there is reason to expect they might not be obtained when required. The project company will typically provide a certificate stating that all such Governmental Approvals are final, binding and non-appealable.

(l) Receipt of customary land surveys and satisfactory title reports or title insurance.

(m) Receipt of a construction budget and construction drawdown schedule that is prepared and certified by the project company as well as verified by the technical adviser.

(n) Receipt of a base case financial model (including a capital expenditure schedule) that is prepared and certified by the project company and verified by the technical adviser showing a loan life coverage ratio of at least [1.___:1] and minimum annual debt service coverage of [1.___:1].

(o) Absence of any defaults under any project documents.

(p) Procurement of acceptable credit support, if required, for the contractor's obligations under the construction contract, the supplier's obligations under the supply contracts, the subordinated lenders' or equity participants' obligations under the finance documents and for each other Obligor under the project documents to which it is a party.

(q) Issuance of the notice to proceed under the construction contract.

(r) Receipt of a letter from the process agent confirming it has accepted its appointment as process agent for the project company and the other Obligors.

(s) Receipt of satisfactory legal opinions of counsel for the various parties as to the matters customarily covered in project financings. These opinions are typically delivered by special financing and special local counsel to the project company, counsel to each Obligor and special financing and special local counsel to the lenders' agent/lenders.

(t) Receipt of any other documents, opinions or representations relating to the foregoing as the agent or, depending on the nature of the financing arrangements, a lender or the majority lenders, may reasonably request.

1.2 Conditions Precedent to Initial and Subsequent Loan Drawings

The following conditions precedent will be required to be met to the satisfaction of the lenders' agent and the lenders:

(a) The representations and warranties contained in the credit agreement are true and correct in all material respects.

(b) No default or event of default shall have occurred and be continuing.

(c) Reports have been received from the project company detailing the use of proceeds and showing there is no material variance between the construction status and the construction schedule that has not been addressed by the project company to the satisfaction of the lenders' agent. These reports must have been verified by the technical adviser and address all aspects of design, construction, and procurement as well as any other relevant factors required by the lenders' agent.

(d) The project company shall be deemed to have certified to the lenders' agent and the lenders, as of the date of each loan drawing, the correctness of the matters specified in paragraphs (a) through (c) above.

1.3 Conditions Precedent to Term Loan Conversion/ Project Completion

The following conditions precedent shall be met to the satisfaction of the lenders:

(a) The representations and warranties contained in the credit agreement are true and correct in all material respects.

(b) No default or event of default shall have occurred and be continuing.

(c) The technical adviser shall have certified that the requirements for 'Final Performance Acceptance' have occurred under the construction contract.

(d) All project documents are in full force and effect.

(e) No material adverse change has occurred in the project company's or any Obligor's financial condition, business or operations and which can reasonably be expected to result in a material adverse effect on the project or on their ability to perform their obligations under the project documents.

(f) No party to any project document is in default thereunder.

(g) Certified copies of all Governmental Approvals required for the construction, operation and maintenance of the project that have not been previously delivered to the lenders' agent shall have been received by the agent, together with a certificate of the project company to the effect that all such Governmental Approvals are final, binding and non-appealable.

(h) A survey of the project shall demonstrate that, as built, the project conforms with the specifications of the project documents.

(i) Such other documents, opinions or representations relating to the foregoing as the agent or the lenders may have reasonably requested shall have been received by the agent and the lenders. The project company shall be deemed to have certified to the lenders' agent and the lenders as of the date of term loan conversion/project completion the correctness of the matters specified in paragraphs (a), (b), (d), (e) and (f) above, or in such other paragraphs as are appropriate.

2. Representations and Warranties of the Project Company

The project company will make the following representations and warranties (subject to customary exceptions and materiality standards):

(a) The project company is a validly existing corporation (or, as relevant, partnership) with the power and authority to carry out its business and to perform its obligations.

(b) The project company has authority to enter into all documentation relating to the credit agreement and the project documents, and all such documentation is binding on the project company.

(c) The execution, delivery and performance by the project company of the credit agreement and the project documents will not violate or conflict with its organizational documents, any law, rule or regulation, any Governmental Approval or any material agreement to which it is a party.

(d) The project company possesses title to, or valid leasehold interest in, all property it purports to own (or lease) free and clear of liens, but subject to any agreed exceptions and liens created under the security documents (collectively, the Permitted Security Interests).

(e) The project company is, and the project will be, in compliance in all material respects with all laws, rules, regulations and zoning requirements, and the requirements set forth in the project documents.

(f) All Governmental Approvals required for the financing, construction and operation of the project, in accordance with the plans and specifications for the project, have been duly obtained and are not subject to appeal and do not contain any conditions that are not reasonably capable of being satisfied by the project company in a manner consistent with the funds available to it and without materially and adversely affecting the project. This shall not include such Government Approvals for construction or operation that cannot reasonably be, or are not required or customarily obtained, until a later stage of construction or after commercial operation has commenced, provided that there is no reason to expect they will not be obtained when required.

(g) No litigation exists against the project company, or with respect to the project, the Obligors, the project documents, or the transactions contemplated thereby, which if adversely determined would have a material adverse effect on the project, unless such action or proceeding is unlikely to be adversely determined against the project company or such Obligor.

(h) No potential default or event of default has occurred or is continuing.

(i) The project company's latest financial statements, copies of which shall have been delivered to the agent, have been prepared in conformity with generally accepted accounting principles and fairly present the financial condition of the project company as of the date thereof and the results of its operations for the period then ended, and since such date there has been no material adverse change in its financial condition, business or operations.

(j)   The project company will use the proceeds of the credit facility in accordance with the terms of the finance documentation.

(k)   The project company is in compliance in all material respects with the ESMP and all applicable environmental laws.

(l)   The budgets and projections of the project are reasonable.

(m)   The security arrangements contemplated in the finance documents and project documents, and the priorities established therein, are effective and fully enforceable against the project company.

(n)   The project company has filed or caused to be filed all tax returns required to be filed by it and paid all taxes imposed upon it by a governmental authority, other than those it is contesting in good faith and for which adequate reserves are maintained.

(o)   The project company has not engaged in any material business activities, and is not a party to any material agreements, except in connection with the project and related matters.

(p)   The project company has no subsidiaries.

(q)   No information exists, unless otherwise disclosed by the project company to the agent, that would cause the information set forth in the offering/syndication information memorandum or in other specified documents supplied to the agent in conjunction with the credit agreement as of the closing date to be materially incorrect or misleading.

(r)   The services to be performed, the materials to be supplied and the property rights to be granted pursuant to the project documents assigned to the lenders comprise all of the property rights and interests necessary for the construction, operation and maintenance of the project and provide adequate ingress and egress for any reasonable purpose in connection with the construction, operation and maintenance of the project.

(s)   There are no undisclosed material liabilities.

3. Covenants

3.1 Affirmative Covenants of the Project Company

The project company will covenant that, unless waived by the agent and the lenders representing a [__] per cent interest (and subject to customary exceptions and materiality standards), it will:

(a)   Preserve its existence, rights and franchises.

(b)   Permit inspection of its accounting records, and maintain such accounting records in accordance with generally accepted accounting principles.

(c)   Promptly invoice and collect for products/services.

(d)   Maintain the project in accordance with prudent applicable industry practices.

(e)   Perform all actions required of it to enter into, comply with its obligations under, and maintain in full force and effect the project documents.

(f)   Furnish annual audited financial statements, certified by an accounting firm acceptable to the agent, within [__] days of the end of the year, semi-annual unaudited statements certified by an appropriate corporate officer within [__] days of the end of the second quarter, together with other required information concerning the construction, operating and financial status of the project.

(g)   Diligently complete the project in accordance with the original design specifications approved by the agent.

(h)   Comply with all Governmental Approvals, laws, rules and regulations.

(i)   Maintain insurance cover over its assets and undertakings and all other insurances required in the insurance section of the credit agreement.

(j)   Give prompt notice of any litigation and defaults or events of default under the credit agreement or any other project document.

(k)   Perform and observe all of its material covenants under the project documents.

(l)   Permit the lenders' agent or its representatives at any reasonable time, and from time to time upon reasonable notice, to visit and inspect the project.

(m)   Apply the proceeds of each loan disbursement to its specified purpose.

(n)   Take all action reasonably necessary to meet performance benchmarks and other requirements by the dates originally scheduled therefor.

(o) Obtain and maintain, or cause to be obtained and maintained, in full force and effect all Governmental Approvals that may from time to time become necessary or advisable in connection with (i) the execution, delivery and performance in accordance with their respective terms of the credit agreement and the project documents, (ii) the taking of any action contemplated thereby, (iii) the timely achievement of the final completion date and (iv) the operation of the project.

(p) Ensure the presence at the project site, throughout the construction period, of a full-time authorized representative of the project company.

(q) Advise the lenders' agent as soon as possible of the occurrence of a force majeure event as well as the date that such force majeure event ends.

(r) Pay and discharge all taxes, assessments and governmental charges or levies imposed prior to the date on which penalties are attached thereto, and all lawful claims which, if unpaid, might adversely affect the security.

(s) Maintain title to all material property the project company purports to own.

(t) Take all action required or desirable to maintain and to preserve the liens/security interests created by the security documents and the priority thereof.

(u) Adopt an operating budget, which shall be subject to the prior approval of the lenders' agent, covering the project's operation and maintenance expenses for each calendar year.

(v) Establish control account(s) with the lenders' agent/account bank through which all revenues of the project will be deposited and all disbursements of funds processed.

(w) Apply all revenues in the following order of priority:
   (i) Payment of operation and maintenance expenses;
   (ii) Payment of debt service;
   (iii) Funding of the capital replacement/maintenance reserve account;
   (iv) Funding of the debt service reserve account;
   (v) Funding of subordinated debt service; and
   (vi) Funding of distributions to, as relevant, the project's shareholders or partners.[1]

(x) Enter into interest rate protection and currency/other hedging programmes with terms and conditions satisfactory to the lenders.

3.2 Reporting Covenants

The project company will covenant that, unless waived by the agent and the lenders representing a [__] per cent interest (and subject to customary exceptions and materiality standards), it will:

(a) Provide the agent and the lenders copies of all material documents furnished (i) to the project company by any governmental authority or Obligor or (ii) to any governmental authority or Obligor by the project company.

(b) Furnish the lenders' agent with a copy of any material revision to the plans and specifications and any change orders under the construction contract.

(c) Furnish the lenders' agent with any material revisions of construction schedules, expenditure drawdowns and any other financial report regarding the project as may be reasonably requested.

(d) Furnish the lenders' agent with copies of each Governmental Approval received after the closing date and advise the lenders' agent of any change in the status of any Governmental Approval.

(e) Furnish the agent with copies of all receipts for taxes paid and for all payments made in lieu of taxes.

(f) Provide quarterly/semi-annual operating statements.

3.3 Negative Covenants of the Project Company

The project company will covenant, unless waived by the lenders' agent and, as appropriate, the majority lenders or all the lenders, that it will not (subject to customary exceptions and materiality standards):

(a) Increase, assume, incur, permit or suffer to exist any security interest over any of the project property, whether now owned or hereafter acquired, except for Permitted Security Interests.

---

[1] A project's revenue waterfall will need to be tailored to that particular project and the priorities within the waterfall will be the subject of negotiation.

(b) Declare or pay any dividends or make any other distribution to, as appropriate the shareholders or partners, unless the following conditions are satisfied:
  (i) The first repayment date has occurred and all amounts due on such date have been repaid;
  (ii) No event of default or potential event of default has occurred or would result from the proposed distribution;
  (iii) The project's debt service coverage ratio is at least [__];
  (iv) The debt service reserve account balance is not less than [__]; and
  (v) The project completion date has occurred.[2]

(c) Guarantee obligations of others except (i) those guarantees contained in the project documents, (ii) those indemnities in respect of unfiled mechanics' liens not to exceed an aggregate agreed amount and (iii) those indemnities to appropriate governmental bodies for the benefit of the project.

(d) Undertake the sale of assets, other than in the ordinary course of business, in excess of an agreed amount per event and/or an agreed amount in aggregate per annum.

(e) (i) Take any action to terminate, amend or modify, or waive timely performance under the project documents, or other documents if such termination, amendment, modification or waiver would have a material adverse effect on the project; (ii) enter into any new project document without the prior written consent of the majority lenders; or (iii) revise the construction budget.[3]

(f) Suffer to exist any indebtedness (including capital leases, discounted receivables, current borrowings, guarantees, secured non-recourse debt, subordinated debt and trade debt) except:
  (i) Indebtedness under the finance documents;
  (ii) Indebtedness under any subordinated debt agreements;
  (iii) Current accounts and other amounts payable in the ordinary course of business to the extent incurred for the construction or operation of the project, and amounts payable as contemplated by the operating agreement;
  (iv) Other debt not to exceed at any one time [__];
  (v) Other unsecured debt, in an aggregate amount not to exceed [__], expressly subordinated to all other commitments of the project company pursuant to subordination provisions satisfactory to the agent;
  (vi) Non-recourse debt to the extent such debt is secured solely by Permitted Security Interests; and
  (vii) Loans by the shareholders or partners, unsecured and subordinated to the satisfaction of the agent.

(g) Merge with or into, or consolidate with, any person or acquire all or substantially all of the assets or stock of any class of, or any partnership or joint venture interest in, any person, or create or acquire any subsidiary.

(h) Engage in any business unrelated to the ownership and operation of the project.

(i) Make any capital expenditures other than those contemplated by the plans and specifications for the project. However, in some transactions, the project company may be permitted to make capital expenditures which are intended to enhance or to repair the project and which would not have a material adverse effect on the project or on the project company's ability to perform its obligations under the finance documents or the project documents.

(j) Enter into any transaction with any affiliate on a basis materially less favourable to the project company than would be the case if such transaction had been effected with a person other than

---

[2] It should also be noted that the definition of the relevant debt coverage ratio will substantially affect the consequences of this clause and are often negotiated at the term sheet stage.

[3] It should be noted that the issue of amendments or modifications is often negotiated in the context of the materiality (i.e. the contractual value) of such amendments or modifications or the materiality of the documents to which such amendments or modifications are to be made. In addition, issues regarding entering into new project documents without the prior written consent of the majority lenders are often negotiated in the context of the materiality of the additional project documents into which the project company desires to enter.

an affiliate, except with respect to agreements with affiliates in effect on the closing date details of which have been previously disclosed in writing to the lenders' agent.

(k) Make any investments other than permitted investments.

(l) Permit or consent to the transfer (by assignment, sale or otherwise) of any equity in the project company or issue new stock or other equity interests in the project company.

(m) Enter into change orders pursuant to the construction contract without giving [__] days prior written notice to the lenders' agent and only if such change orders do not provide for an increase in construction costs by an aggregate amount exceeding [__] and do not provide for a material change to, or amendment of, the project or the construction schedule.

4. Events of Default

Events of default will include:

(a) Failure to make any payment of scheduled principal under the credit agreement when due; or make any payment of interest or commitment fee payable under the credit agreement for [__] days beyond the date when due.[4]

(b) The final performance acceptance date of the project not having occurred on or before the [*date certain*].

(c) Failure to perform or to observe a covenant set forth under [*specified covenants*] or failure to perform or to observe any other covenant or obligation under the finance documents that has not been cured within [__] days after notice of such failure (or, if the project company is diligently attempting to cure the same, such longer period of time that may, in the reasonable opinion of the agent, be necessary to effect the cure, but in no event to exceed [__] days).

(d) Any representation or warranty made by the project company in any of the finance or project documents to which it is a party or any representation or warranty or statement contained in any other document provided to the lendes' agent on behalf of any other Obligor proving to have been false or misleading in any respect as of the time made, confirmed or furnished. This may be qualified by the requirement that, at the time of discovery thereof, such false or misleading representation, warranty or statement had or was reasonably expected to have a material adverse effect on the project or on the project company's ability to perform its obligations under the finance documents or the project documents.

(e) Any Obligor filing a petition in bankruptcy or taking similar action. Depending on the nature of the transaction, it may be the case that the bankruptcy of any person other than the project company will not be deemed an event of default unless it can reasonably be expected to result in a material adverse effect on the project or on the project company's ability to perform its obligations under the finance documents or the project documents.

(f) The commencement of an insolvency proceeding against any Obligor, or the issuance of a warrant of attachment or execution or similar process against property of such Obligor having a value in excess of [__], and such proceeding continuing undismissed for more than [__] days. Depending on the transaction, if such an event affects any Obligor other than the project company, it may not be deemed an event of default unless it can reasonably be expected to result in a material adverse effect on the project or on the project company's ability to perform its obligations under the finance documents or the project documents.

(g) Final judgments in excess of [__] being rendered against the project company or any other Obligor and remaining unstayed or unsatisfied for more than [__] consecutive days. Depending on the transaction, if such an event affects any Obligor other than the project company, it may not be deemed an event of default unless it can reasonably be expected to result in a material adverse effect on the project or on the project company's ability to perform its obligations under the finance documents or the project documents.

(h) The project company failing to obtain, renew, maintain or comply in all material respects with all Governmental Approvals which are at the time necessary for the continued operation of

---

[4] If a grace period is agreed, it may be linked to delays in payment caused by administrative errors or similar events.

the project in the manner contemplated under the finance documents. In certain transactions, this may be limited to events where such failure can reasonably be expected to have a material adverse effect on the project or on the project company's ability to perform its obligations under the credit agreement or under the project documents.

(i) Any action being taken by any person to terminate any project document by reason of a default by the project company; or any project document prior to its stated termination date, ceasing to be in full force and effect. In certain transactions, this may be limited to events where such occurrence can reasonably be expected to have a material adverse effect on the project or on the project company's ability to perform its obligations under the credit agreement or under the project documents.

(j) Abandonment or condemnation of the project.

(k) The corporate parent/lead shareholders of the project company directly or through wholly owned subsidiaries ceasing to own or to exercise control over a majority of the voting capital stock of the project company.

(l) A default by any party under any project document, which default is not remedied within applicable grace periods. In certain transactions, this may be limited to events where such default can reasonably be expected to have a material adverse effect on the project or on the project company's ability to perform its obligations under the credit agreement or under the project documents.

(m) Any Obligor defaulting in the payment when due of any debt of such person in excess of [__]. Depending on the transaction, if such an event affects any Obligor other than the project company, it may not be deemed an event of default unless it can reasonably be expected to result in a material adverse effect on the project or on the project company's ability to perform its obligations under the credit agreement or under the project documents.

(n) Any subordinated lender or equity participant failing to make, when due, any subordinated loan or equity contribution required under the finance documents.

(o) Any security document ceasing to be in full force and effect, any party thereto so asserting in writing or any security document ceasing to be effective to create a first priority perfected security interest in any of the collateral to which it relates.

(p) Failure to comply with the minimum loan life or senior debt service coverage ratios.

(q) A material portion of the plant or the property on which the project is situated is permanently or temporarily condemned or seized or taken by any government authority under power of eminent domain or otherwise and such action could reasonably be expected to have a material adverse effect.

APPENDIX 2

Environmental Due Diligence Checklist

The development of large infrastructure projects may raise significant issues regarding environmental liability. The following is a checklist of questions that should be posed and answered in order to evaluate the environmental risks involved in a particular project.

1. International Requirements

1.1 Sources of law: What treaties (e.g. international, regional, bilateral) or customary international legal principles apply to the proposed project? Are these independently enforceable against the project or its sponsors, or are they required to be implemented through national legislation?

1.2 Administrative: How are the obligations imposed by such sources of law enforced (e.g. only by governments or by individuals as well, and through what institutions)?

2. National Requirements

2.1 What categories of environmental laws (and regulations) exist in the country (e.g. those directly applicable, those governing major site or project approval, those dealing with specific permits, common law principles)?

2.2 How are they enforced or effectuated?

(a) What is the regulatory authority (if any) that administers major site or project approvals (e.g. environmental impact statement preparation and review) and what are its procedures? What are the substantive criteria, if any, under which it makes its evaluation?

(b) What are the regulatory authorities (if any) that administer specific permits and what are their procedures? What are the substantive criteria under which these authorities determine permit conditions (e.g. governing disposal of solid wastes, discharges to water or emissions to air)?

(c) What mechanisms, if any, are used to obtain public input to these approval processes (e.g. notice, hearings, informal public meetings, appellate review), on either an administrative or judicial level?

(d) What remedies exist for violations of laws, regulations and permit terms (e.g. administrative enforcement, permit revocation or non-renewal, judicial enforcement or independent citizens' lawsuits)?

(e) What is the legal significance of information provided to governmental authorities in permit applications, environmental impact statements, registrations, reports and correspondence (e.g. binding obligations under law or not)?

2.3 Are there any legal requirements concerning the cleanup of site conditions, whether originating from historical operations on the site or from the proposed activity? How are such requirements enforced (e.g. through administrative enforcement, judicial enforcement instigated by governmental authorities or by aggrieved parties)?

2.4 Is the proposed project subject to different regulatory treatment (e.g. expedited or longer review, greater or lesser public participation requirements, exemptions or additional requirements) under the statutes or programmes authorizing such projects (e.g. build-own-transfer, or build-own operate legislation)?

2.5 What is the nature of co-ordination and co-operation that must be achieved among government agencies in order to obtain the approvals under national law and how does such interaction work in practice?

2.6 Is there any basis under national law for holding shareholders, parent corporations or lenders liable for violations of environmental law or for the cleanup of contamination associated with a project?

2.7 Are there any proposed laws or regulations, or any provisions of existing laws or regulations, that are not yet effective, that are reasonably likely to affect environmental requirements applicable to the project?

3. Local Requirements

3.1 Is there a local agency that plays a role in either major site or project approval or in developing specific permit requirements for the project?

3.2 What are its procedures (e.g. opportunities for public participation, comment or appeal) and substantive criteria?

3.3 How are these procedures and criteria integrated into the national level process (e.g. is local procedure controlling or merely advisory; do local and national agencies act jointly)?

4. Privately-imposed or Informal Environmental and Social Requirements

4.1 Are there entities participating in the project's financing that impose environmental and social requirements independent of those imposed by international, national or local law (e.g. Equator Principles financing institutions, export credit agencies, bilateral agencies, commercial lenders or World Bank affiliates)?

4.2 Can such requirements be, or have they been, addressed in the same proceedings and with the same information as are required in connection with compliance with national or other laws?

4.3 Do these entities impose requirements in addition to those imposed by national law (e.g. consideration of climate change, public participation, evaluation of resettlement issues)?

4.4 If there are multiple entities with such requirements, can their procedural and substantive requirements be met through coordinated efforts directed at meeting all such requirements?

4.5 Is the financing subject to the Equator Principles (e.g. project with a capital value greater than US$10M financed by an Equator Principles financing institution)?
  (a) If so, what is the environmental and social risk category of the project (Category A, B or C)?
  (b) Has the sponsor prepared a Social and Environmental Assessment and Social and Environmental Management Plan?
  (c) Are there action items that need to be addressed? Note that the level of review under the Equator Principles depends on whether the project is located in a non-OECD country or country that is not classified as high income by the OECD (in which case the IFC and World Bank Performance Standards and Guidelines apply) or is considered high-income by the OECD (in which case the assessment is whether the project complies with host country laws and requirements).

5. Pragmatic Questions

5.1 Are national or local environmental standards set subjectively, based on the political connections of the sponsors?

5.2 Is there any expectation of public opposition and, if so, from whom in general? How organized is the opposition and how influential are its leaders? To which participants in the project is such opposition directed?

5.3 Can project economics support the more restrictive environmental regulatory options when a particular standard or requirement is contested or otherwise in doubt?

6. Business Issues

6.1 Is there sufficient technical information upon which to assess the risks to the project under the legal (and political) framework outlined above?

6.2 Are the post-closing regulatory risks (e.g. outstanding permit applications, pending or prospective appeals and applicable regulatory requirements) understood and acceptable?

7. Documentation Issues

7.1 Do the project company's representations, covenants, conditions to closing, defaults and remedies set forth in the loan documents contemplate the different sources of environmental requirements (e.g. treaties, laws, regulations, permits, informal guidelines, representations to the government)?

7.2 Are the administrative processes for obtaining approvals adequately reflected in the loan documentation (e.g. are the national and local approvals included, and have the notices been given and hearings held as required)?

7.3 Is the project, as proposed and described in the project documents, consistent with the regulatory approvals and requirements that will be applicable to the project after completion (e.g. do the guarantees in the construction contract match the permit limits)?

7.4 Are private or informal environmental guidelines, such as the Equator Principles, applicable to the project clearly set out or otherwise incorporated by reference in the loan documents (e.g. if a set of guidelines is specified, is there agreement on such specification)?

8. Risk Allocation

8.1 Do the representations, warranties and covenants in the loan documents clearly and precisely cover the applicable environmental requirements?

8.2 Can the project company financially support the reasonably foreseeable environmental compliance costs and liabilities associated with its project?

8.3 Have other creditworthy entities assumed risks that would reasonably be allocated to them (e.g. is the construction contractor accepting the risk of the project's capability to comply)?

8.4 Are the remaining risks to the lenders—either through financial effects on the project company or direct effects on the lenders—quantifiable and reasonably well understood?

APPENDIX 3

Checklist of Key Provisions of a Joint Venture or Partnership Agreement

The following checklist highlights some of the more significant provisions and issues that should be considered in finalizing or reviewing the agreement under which the vehicle undertaking the project is to be organized.

1. Capital Contributions

(a) With respect to initial capital contributions, the agreement will set out any conditions to funding by the participants. This will include an obligation to fund on a date certain (regardless of completion) or only upon achievement of satisfactory completion. Certain participants may also contribute property or services and will expect that this will be appropriately valued in the agreement.

(b) The agreement will also provide for additional contributions in the event of construction shortfalls or post-completion operating deficits and set out in detail how they will be funded.

(c) In the event the required capital contributions are not made, remedies may include a squeeze-down of interests, a right to buy out, a right to take over control, and a right to bring in new shareholders.

2. Compensation of Participants

In some cases equity interests may be offered on a 'carried' basis for no monetary consideration, compensating participants for specific contributions.

3. Allocation of Cash and Tax Benefits

The agreement will allocate both cash distributions and tax benefits, typically by taking into account the percentage interests of the parties. A mechanism is typically included, so that in the event there are changes in such percentage interests, cash and tax benefits will be allocated accordingly.

4. Participants' Area of Responsibility

The roles of the participants should be clearly defined and the agreement will ideally govern conflicts of interest by excluding shareholders from votes when they are conflicted.

5. Management of the Venture

(a) Typically, one shareholder will control the venture as the managing shareholder. The agreement should clearly establish the managing shareholder's role, as well as that of the other parties.

(b) Voting procedures are typically established for major decisions between the shareholders. These will specifically cover major issues such as:
  (i) Dissolution and winding up of the vehicle;
  (ii) Admission of any new or additional shareholders;
  (iii) Removal of any shareholder;
  (iv) Election of a 'liquidating shareholder'; and
  (v) Preparation of tax returns.

(c) Other major issues will often include:
  (i) Financing—whether to incur indebtedness;
  (ii) Security—whether to sell, pledge, mortgage, grant of security interest in, or transfer company assets;

    (iii) Budgets—whether to adopt or materially modify the development budget or annual operations budget;

    (iv) Major contracts—whether the company should execute material amendments, terminate, or grant a material waiver of any major contract (including major change orders);

    (v) Capital expenditures—whether any expenditure should be made in excess of specified amounts in settlement of claims; and

    (vi) Day-to-day operations—whether decision making procedures should be changed (e.g. governing the organization of the management committee) and decisions with respect to interim and annual reporting requirements.

6. Expansion

(a) The agreement may anticipate expansions of the project and govern the rights of shareholders to enter into such expansions. In lieu of a right to participate, a shareholder may sell its existing rights in order to take part in the project expansion.

(b) The criteria, implementation and cost of an anticipated expansion should be set out in advance and for those shareholders who fund the project expansion, the agreement should ensure that the benefits of the expansion are allocated accordingly.

7. Events of Default and Remedies

Events of default and applicable cure periods will be included, along with appropriate remedies which will typically range from damages to the more drastic granting of buy-out rights, changes of management, changes of voting rights and even election to wind up the company.

8. Restrictions on Rights to Transfer

(a) Any transfer of rights will usually be subject to the transferee having the requisite expertise, financial responsibility and compatibility with the project and the shareholders.

(b) The shareholders may also seek to place a cap on the number of shareholders and/or have rights of pre-emption/first refusal or first offer to any transfer.

(c) The agreement may also seek to address the tax consequences of transfers.

(d) In the event unrestricted transfers are permitted, the agreement may allow for termination following certain transfers.

(e) Other considerations the parties may wish to address, include compliance with applicable law as well as with the loan and other agreements.

9. Dissolution and Liquidation

(a) There are number of circumstances in which the participants may wish to dissolve the entity, including upon its insolvency. Dissolution may also be provided to occur on an agreed-upon date.

(b) The agreement should provide for management during winding up and the balancing of capital accounts for tax purposes.

10. Governing Law

While a partnership, joint venture or shareholders' agreement may be governed by the law of the 'host' jurisdiction, where that law is not well developed or when the participants are based in a number of different jurisdictions, the choice of a 'neutral' law may be more appropriate.

11. Dispute Resolution

Most agreements will provide for disputes to be settled in a neutral forum. This will often involve some form of binding arbitration.

APPENDIX 4

Checklist of Key Provisions in a Concession Agreement

In projects relating to a natural resource, such as minerals extraction and oil and gas or in relation to the provision of public infrastructure, such as a toll road, bridge or tunnel project, the government will usually enter into a concession agreement with the project company that sets out the responsibilities and liabilities of each party and provides the necessary legal framework to make the project viable.

The nature of a concession agreement varies from project to project depending on a number of factors including:

  (i) the type of project in question (for instance whether it is a Build, Own, Transfer (BOT) or Build, Own, Operate (BOO) structure);
 (ii) the natural resource being exploited or the infrastructure being developed; and
(iii) the degree to which the government is to be involved in the project.

Whether the government or the sponsors have leverage in negotiating a concession agreement depends largely on the market and the nature of the project. On the one hand, the government may select a bidder and award the concession following a competitive procurement process. In such cases, the government may be less likely to yield on issues and, as a result, the bidders may have to accept less favourable terms. In other cases, the sponsors may have greater negotiating power. As a result, whilst there is no single standard form concession agreement, developed forms of concession agreements have emerged in certain jurisdictions which include commonly accepted terms.

The following checklist examines the more significant provisions and issues that should be considered when negotiating or reviewing concession agreements.

1. Objectives

The objectives of a concession agreement are to set out (a) the rights and obligations of the project company and the government in respect of the project and (b) the ownership rights to the assets of the project.

2. Scope, Duration and Termination

A concession agreement is the foundation of a project and, as such, the provisions setting out the scope, duration and the conditions for its termination should be clearly stated.

2.1 Scope

The agreement should (a) define the period for which the concession is being granted and (b) include a specific description of the physical area and rights that it covers.

2.2 Duration

The concession should be valid at least for the life of the project and, from a lenders' perspective, it should extend beyond the term of the loans by an agreed period or 'tail'.

2.3 Termination

(a) The concession agreement will typically contain provisions which enable the agreement to be terminated upon:
   (i) breach of any material term of the agreement;
  (ii) insolvency of the project company;

    (iii) intentional and material misrepresentation by the project company in procuring the government's execution of the concession agreement;

    (iv) assignment of an interest in the concession agreement by the project company without prior government consent;

    (v) payment default under the concession agreement by the government or the project company; and

    (vi) failure by the government or the project company to comply with a final determination or arbitral award.

(b) The concession should not automatically terminate upon the enforcement of security by the lenders and the circumstances under which the government may terminate the concession should not be expropriatory in nature. In many cases, there will be compensation payable upon termination of the concession agreement, the quantum of which usually varies depending upon the nature of the relevant termination event. If the government elects to take ownership of the assets following a project company default, termination compensation is often sized to enable repayment of the outstanding debt owed to the lenders. If termination arises due to government default, the termination compensation is usually increased to include an amount to compensate the sponsors (i.e. returning their equity investment plus an amount reflecting, e.g., the net present value of the profits they would otherwise have made had the concession not terminated).

3. Rights and Obligations

3.1 Government obligations

The government's obligations often include:

(a) to grant the right to access and (if applicable) exploit a resource, infrastructure and/or service in a specified area for a specified period. However, governments will often reserve the right to offer access to other parties, provided it does not interfere with the concession holder's use of their right;

(b) provide the project with the requisite licences and permits and assist in acquiring any necessary approvals from other government ministries;

(c) to provide assistance in procuring leases, easements and other rights of way, if necessary;

(d) to complete any infrastructure necessary for the project to be successful;

(e) to provide assistance in procuring, amongst other things, security protection (although this is often at the project company's cost);

(f) to pass any necessary legislation to enable the project to progress; and

(g) to guarantee the provision of any necessary feedstock supplies, e.g., fuel gas for LNG projects and feedstock for petrochemical projects.

3.2 Project Company obligations

There should not be any unduly onerous terms imposed on the project company, such as high levels of liquidated damages if the completion of the project is not achieved by a scheduled date and to the extent that the project company is unable to pass-through all such liquidated damages to its own contractor. Customary project company obligations include:

(a) to finance, construct, operate and maintain the project to the schedule and specifications set forth in the concession;

(b) to comply with all applicable legislation, in particular environmental and social regulations;

(c) to use its best efforts to avoid obstructing or interfering with the operations of any third party;

(d) to undertake to employ a minimum number of host country citizens for the purposes of constructing and operating the project; in addition, the government may require the project company to offer a mutually agreed number of nationals from the host country an opportunity for on-the-job training and practical experience; and

(e) to pay concession fees where appropriate—such payments are ordinarily facilitated through the payment of royalties from profits and lease and other payments to the government or government bodies.

4. Force Majeure

This clause addresses material risks that are generally acknowledged to be beyond the control of either party. This sort of clause often includes the following elements:

(a) a general description of events constituting force majeure;

(b) force majeure is stated to be a risk shared by the parties;

(c) no party should be unduly prevented from claiming a force majeure event has taken place;

(d) the party claiming force majeure should be required to use reasonable efforts to overcome or mitigate the effects of such force majeure, and the burden of proving such force majeure should fall upon the claiming party;

(e) a concession is often extended by a period equal to the duration of any force majeure event, with consideration given to whether any caps to such extensions are applicable; and

(f) force majeure events arising from government action or inaction—circumstances where the government takes certain actions or fails to take actions which impact upon the project and are out of the control of the other party, may be subject to a compensation regime to ensure that the project company is not unfairly disadvantaged by the government.

5. Change in Law and Government Action

These provisions usually address material governmental actions that could alter the economics of the project.

(a) The concession agreement should set out arrangements relating to a change in law. Ideally, such arrangement should, at the least, stipulate that the concession period will be extended if the construction of the project is delayed because new regulations come into force requiring, e.g., a reworking of the design or the re-fitting of new environmental protection equipment.

(b) There may be a grace period for a change in law to allow the project to adapt and there may be an obligation on the government to provide assistance to the project in such circumstances. In certain projects there can be a large amount of time between winning a bid and the start of the project's operation. The sponsors will seek to ensure any change of law during the bid process will be covered by such a provision.

(c) Whilst it is accepted that in order effectively to run the state, governments must be free to implement necessary laws, such laws may at times be detrimental to the project. Similarly, a government cannot bind its successor not to change the law. It is for these reasons that the concession agreement may contain 'stabilization' provisions requiring the government to 'freeze' the law in respect of the project, or, to the extent this is not possible, pay compensation for such changes in law.

(d) Where the concession is granted in an emerging market and if project revenues are received in local currency, it will be important to have assurances from the government regarding the convertibility of such revenues to meet the foreign currency obligations of the project, such as debt service, operating costs (e.g. for the importation of spare parts) and the distribution of dividends to foreign shareholders. Equally important will be assurances as to the transferability of such funds and the ability to operate foreign bank accounts.

6. Tax Issues

A concession agreement may contain assurances about the granting of subsidies and tax concessions, such as tax holidays, necessary for the project to be economically attractive to investors. It is important to ensure, at a minimum, certainty as to the level of withholdings on the repatriation of profits generated from the project or on interest paid to lenders.

7. Dispute Resolution and Governing Law

(a) Because concession agreements are agreements with governments, they are most often governed by the laws of the jurisdiction of the state in which the project is situated.

(b) In many jurisdictions, a concession agreement may be promulgated into law and the statute will govern the project. Any amendment or change in arrangements may not be valid unless also made as law, and in certain circumstances may require governmental approval.

(c) It may be preferable to seek an arbitration agreement, calling for the venue to be located in a 'neutral' country. Consideration should be given as to whether arbitration under the auspices of the International Centre for the Settlement of Investment Disputes (ICSID), which was established by the Washington Convention of 1965, may be appropriate. ICSID jurisdiction applies in relation to disputes between a contracting state (or any constituent subdivision or agency designated by the contracting state) and a national of another contracting state. The convention calls for the direct enforcement of awards against the contracting state without the range of exceptions contemplated by, e.g., the 1958 New York Convention on the Recognition of Foreign Arbitral Awards.

APPENDIX 5

Checklist of Key Provisions in Turnkey Construction/EPC Contracts

The following checklist sets forth the key provisions in a turnkey construction contract that are typically required by the project company (Owner) and its lenders. The list, however, is by no means exhaustive; each project will have its own special requirements that will need to be addressed after consultation and negotiation among the Owner, the lenders, their engineers and the contractor (Contractor).

1. Project Design

The design of a project is generally determined by the nature and complexity of the project's technology and should be provided by the Contractor after consultation with the Owner and its advisers (note that the design is often included as part of the Contractor's 'scope of work' to prevent the Contractor from shifting performance or warranty-related liability to a third party, such as a technology provider which may not be creditworthy).[1] The economics, feasibility and efficiency of the design are usually reviewed and approved by the lenders' technical adviser as part of its due diligence.

2. Scope of Work

The 'scope of work' sets out the Contractor's responsibilities for all aspects of design, engineering, procurement, construction and equipping of the project.

3. Contract Price

The contract price is generally a fixed price, subject to mutually agreed changes. The price should include all taxes (although in many cases, any sales tax on equipment used for construction will be excluded from the contract price and paid directly by the Owner), insurance costs, and other costs incurred during the project's construction phase. Pricing on a 'time and material' or 'cost-plus' basis is generally resisted by Owners, although some contracts may provide for a cost escalation mechanism tied to the cost of equipment integral to the project (e.g. a turbine) in the event that the placing of orders for such equipment is delayed through no fault of the Contractor or its subcontractors. Additionally, the construction contract may provide for a 'bonus' payment to the Contractor in the event of early completion and acceptance. The argument for such a payment is that early operation enables the Owner to enjoy earlier than anticipated revenues as well as savings of construction period interest, and the Contractor should therefore share in the benefit.

4. Payment Schedule

The payment schedule is usually based on the Owner's 'notice to proceed' and construction milestones that have been achieved. Payments are made for work actually completed and for materials actually purchased and incorporated in such work. Title to the work and materials purchased often vests in

---

[1] In some projects, such as certain projects in the process industries, this may not be possible, in which case the risk will need to be mitigated, e.g., through completion support.

the Owner upon payment, although risk of loss should remain with the Contractor until the final completion of the project. The contract may provide for a retention from each payment, with any retained amount to be paid upon final acceptance. In some contracts, in lieu of a cash retention, the Contractor is obliged to post a retention bond issued by a bank having a prescribed credit rating and this allows the Contractor to be paid in full for each milestone which is achieved.

5. Performance Security

Both the Owner and the lenders customarily require the obligations of the Contractor to be appropriately credit enhanced. Therefore, it may be necessary for the Contractor to provide a parent guarantee of its performance and payment obligations. In addition, the Contractor will be obliged to furnish a performance bond with a face value of, e.g., 25 per cent of the contract price. In addition, it is likely that the Contractor will be entitled to a sizeable 'advance payment' when the Owner issues the 'notice to proceed'. In such instances, it is common for the Contractor to provide an advance payment bond with a face value equating the relevant advance payment. As the project proceeds, the face amount of the bond reduces in stages to zero. In addition, during the warranty period,[2] the Contractor is usually obliged to post a warranty bond with a face value of around 5 per cent of the contract price.

6. Completion Schedule

The contract typically provides for a 'date certain' scheduled completion date for the project. The Contractor will often be required to pay liquidated damages for delays not required pursuant to a change order or arising from a force majeure event, and is given a limited time to cure any failure to pass agreed upon performance tests before paying additional 'buy-down' or performance liquidated damages as a result of having under performed.

7. Mechanical Completion

Mechanical completion occurs when the project and all related facilities and systems are completed in accordance with the design specifications, irrespective of whether in fact it will satisfy the performance guarantees. The Owner and the lenders will require the Contractor unconditionally to agree to cause mechanical completion to occur.

8. Performance Tests and Guarantees

Performance tests, together with acceptable test procedures and assumptions for the evaluation of such performance tests, are carefully assessed and approved by the lenders' technical adviser. The tests typically cover (i) efficiency (in a power project measured in terms of heat rate, which assesses the project's consumption of energy and raw materials); (ii) compliance with applicable environmental and other governmental requirements; (iii) net capacity (e.g., a minimum daily production level); and (iv) reliability (e.g., ability to operate at the guaranteed capacity over a specified period of time). The performance tests must be satisfied while the plant complies with all laws, rules, regulations and permits applicable to the plant. The Contractor (or, if the Contractor is not sufficiently creditworthy, the Contractor's parent or an acceptable guarantor) is required to guarantee that if the performance tests are not satisfied, it will pay damages sufficient to enable the Owner to prepay or 'buy-down' the project debt to a level that can be serviced and retired on the basis of an amortization schedule which takes into account the project's impaired performance.

9. Substantial Completion

Substantial completion occurs upon the successful completion of all performance tests or payment of appropriate buy-down or liquidated damages.

---

[2] See paragraph 5–14 below.

10. Final Completion

Final completion occurs upon the satisfactory completion of all 'punch-list' items that include non-essential finishing items, like painting and landscaping. Some contracts provide that final completion does not occur until the lapse of all warranty periods.

11. Liquidated Damages

These are generally divided into two categories: delay damages and performance damages. Delay damages should be payable for each day during the cure period which applies should the Contractor fail to complete the works by the scheduled date. These damages need to be calculated to cover debt service (which typically includes only interest) and the Owner's fixed operating expenses, together with any damages payable to the offtaker/purchaser of the project's product or services during such period, after which the Contractor must demonstrate satisfaction of the performance guarantees or pay the applicable performance or 'buy-down' liquidated damages.

12. Force Majeure

From the Owner's and the lenders' perspective, the definition of this term should not be overly broad. Although it is often difficult to avoid the ever present phrase 'including, but not limited to', the definition generally excludes strikes affecting only the Contractor, its employees or its onsite subcontractors, and any other event that is within the control of the Contractor. It will be important to ensure that the force majeure provisions 'mesh' with those to be found in the project's concession agreement or offtake contract.

13. Change Orders

Material change orders generally require the approval of the lenders, acting on the advice of their technical adviser. The lenders will not wish to allow change orders other than as the result of events of force majeure or unless otherwise agreed to by the Owner and the lenders.

14. Warranties

The Contractor should provide equipment that is 'new and clean' and should be prepared to warrant against deficiencies or breakdown for a period of at least one to two years after final completion (it is common to provide for an 'evergreen warranty' that renews the warranty period for any part or component that needs to be repaired or replaced).

15. Indemnity

The Contractor typically agrees to indemnify the Owner, the lenders and their representatives and agents from any third party claims arising out of the acts or omissions of the Contractor, its employees or agents in connection with the performance of the construction contract, including claims for personal injury, property damage, regulatory penalties, fines and patent infringement.

16. Subcontractors

The construction contract often defines subcontractors broadly to include offsite suppliers of specially manufactured equipment. The Owner and the lenders may seek to restrict the Contractor's right to subcontract and, in certain instances, the Owner and/or the lenders may require 'direct' rights vis-à-vis key subcontractors which may, e.g., allow a transfer of the relevant subcontract to the Owner or its designee following default by the Contractor.

17. Limitation on Liability

There is generally an overall cap on the liability of the Contractor under the construction contract, and specified sub-limits for liquidated damages. Indemnities and certain other obligations are sometimes excluded from such limitations.

18. Termination or Suspension

The lenders will seek to limit the Contractor's right to terminate the construction contract or suspend performance in the case of non-payment.

19. Insurance

A typical insurance package (obtained preferably by the Owner) will include: employer's liability, workmen's compensation, comprehensive auto liability, comprehensive general liability, delay in start-up and builder's all-risk coverage.

20. Dispute Resolution

The Contractor often agrees to continue to perform during the pendency of a dispute, which is to be ultimately resolvable by arbitration or judicial process. Arbitration procedures should be clearly articulated to avoid unnecessary delay and expense in resolving disputes.

21. Assignment

The construction contract should be assignable as collateral security to the lenders, and the Contractor usually agrees to execute a consent to such assignment (or direct agreement) in form and substance reasonably satisfactory to the lenders. The direct agreement typically approves the lenders' further assignment of the construction contract upon foreclosure by the lenders.

APPENDIX 6

Checklist of Key Provisions in Feedstock Supply Contracts

Feedstock supply contracts in an energy or a process industry project ensure that the project will have a sufficient amount of feedstock (typically this includes, in the case of a power project, fuels such as coal, oil and/or gas or, e.g., in the case of a petrochemical project, feedstock such as ethylene) to operate the facility. If the feedstock supply contract does not provide for delivery of feedstock to the facility site, transportation arrangements need to be made for delivery. The purpose of the feedstock supply contract is to guarantee the project a steady, uninterrupted supply of its entire requirements for feedstock at fixed or predictable prices for the entire life of the debt. While these contracts are usually negotiated and executed prior to or at the time the debt financing closes, full scale deliveries will not start until the project is ready for commercial operation, which may be two or three years later.

The following list outlines key provisions in a feedstock supply contract that are typically required by the project company (Owner) and its lenders. This list is by no means exhaustive as each project will have its own special requirements that will need to be addressed after consultation and negotiation among the Owner, the lenders, their technical advisers and the feedstock supplier (Feedstock Supplier).

1. Types of Feedstock Supply Contracts

1.1 Requirements Contracts

(a) The Owner may be obliged to purchase all, or a large portion of, the feedstock required by the project from the Feedstock Supplier.
(b) The Feedstock Supplier is obliged to supply a corresponding amount of the project's feedstock requirements.

1.2 Output Contracts

(a) The Feedstock Supplier may be obliged to sell its entire output to the project company (such as gas from a dedicated gas field).
(b) The Owner may be obliged to purchase the entire output of the Feedstock Supplier.

1.3 Take-or-pay Contracts

(a) The Owner is obliged to purchase a specified volume of feedstock or make minimum periodic payments to the Feedstock Supplier even if feedstock is not being taken by the Owner. In the event that feedstock is paid for, but not taken, the Owner typically has the right to take a corresponding amount of additional feedstock in succeeding years.
(b) The Feedstock Supplier is obliged to supply a specified volume of feedstock.

2. Term of Contract

(a) The term of the feedstock supply contract should be structured to correlate with that of the project loans, often with an option for the Owner to extend it for successive terms.
(b) The term usually begins contemporaneously with the commencement of commercial operations, but should also provide for the supply of feedstock during the commissioning and performance testing of the project.

3. Quantities Delivered

(a) The total quantity of feedstock to be delivered under the feedstock supply contract must be sufficient to operate the project facility at anticipated levels of operation. The Owner will seek feedstock supply flexibility during the commissioning period of the project facilities and there may be a 'ramp up' phase during which feedstock supply is increased in line with the requirements of the project facilities.

(b) Delivery schedules must accommodate the project facility's consumption and storage capacity.

(c) The Owner will seek to have the flexibility to adjust the delivery schedule according to the project facility's consumption.

(d) The Feedstock Supplier typically measures the quantities delivered, while the Owner requests the right to inspect the measuring devices used.

4. Quality of Feedstock

(a) The Feedstock Supplier should agree to deliver feedstock that conforms to the specifications required by the project facility (such specifications are usually part of the performance warranties in the construction and operating contracts).

(b) Feedstock that reduces only the efficiency and output of the project facility may be acceptable at a reduced price that is calculated to compensate the Owner for any loss of revenue or increase in costs caused by, e.g., substandard fuel.

(c) Feedstock that will damage the project facility or cannot be used for technical, environmental or economic reasons may be rejected by the Owner.

(d) In power projects, regular fuel samples may be taken for analysis. Typically, one sample is tested and one sample is kept by each of the Feedstock Supplier and the Owner to assist in resolving any future disputes.

5. Transportation/Place of Delivery

(a) The Owner will seek to: (i) be a third party beneficiary under any transportation contracts, (ii) have a right to receive any notices of default and (iii) have a right to cure any such default.

(b) If the Feedstock Supplier is not itself obliged to deliver feedstock to the project facility, one or more long term transportation contracts may need to be negotiated.

(c) Title to feedstock will often pass to the Owner upon delivery to the project facility. If title passes earlier, it will be necessary to ensure that insurance is in place and to assess which party bears the liability for the period in which the feedstock is in transit.

6. Price

(a) Price may be fixed for a period of time or the entire term (the latter is unusual in longer term contracts) or may fluctuate based on price escalators or deflators. A portion of the price may be fixed and the other portion variable.

(b) Examples of escalators include: the Consumer Price Index, the GNP price deflator, various labour cost indices, raw material price indices, or changes in average prices paid by representative feedstock purchasers similar to the project.

(c) It is important that the indices are readily ascertainable and estimated with accuracy. Ideally, this would include a cap on price increases during the term of the feedstock supply contract, although this is often difficult to achieve.

(d) In the context of power projects, the price escalation formulae in the fuel supply contract should correlate with the price escalation formulae in the power purchase agreement so that higher feedstock costs correspond to higher project revenues under the power purchase agreement.

7. Force Majeure

(a) The force majeure provision allocates economic risk for unforeseen events outside of the control of the parties to the contract. Negotiations usually centre around:
  (i) who can best control the risk; and
  (ii) who can insure against the risk.
(b) Force majeure events usually excuse performance for a specified time, after which the feedstock supply contract can be terminated.
(c) In the event the Feedstock Supplier claims a force majeure event has occurred (or is ongoing), the Owner often has the right to purchase feedstock elsewhere.

8. Representations and Warranties

(a) The Feedstock Supplier typically represents and warrants to the Owner that:
  (i) it has sufficient feedstock to satisfy the Owner's requirements, which usually means up to the maximum projected requirement to operate the project facility at the output used for the project's financial forecasts;
  (ii) the quality of feedstock will conform to the required specifications; and
  (iii) the Feedstock Supplier has all required permits and authorizations and will comply with all such permits and applicable law.
(b) The lenders will often require that the Feedstock Supplier provide either dedicated reserves or a guarantee from a corporate parent to ensure that it will perform its obligations. If gas reserves are dedicated to the project, the lenders may also request that ongoing evidence of the adequacy of the relevant reserves be furnished periodically (e.g. reserve reports or revalidations thereof).

9. Indemnification

(a) The indemnification provision typically covers the project company against a breach by the Feedstock Supplier of the feedstock supply contract and covers losses and expenses resulting from third party litigation.
(b) Environmental liability should also be addressed.

10. Assignments

Assignment provisions will allow for collateral assignment to actual and potential lenders. The lenders are usually entitled to notice of any defaults and the right to cure such defaults within an extended cure period. The Feedstock Supplier typically executes a consent to assignment (or direct agreement), which often approves the lenders' further assignment of the contract following foreclosure.

11. Governing Law and Dispute Resolution

In many cases, the feedstock supply contract will be governed by the law of the host jurisdiction. However, because feedstock supply often involves trans-border shipments, the contract may be governed by the law of a 'neutral' jurisdiction. Difficulties may arise where the governing law, or the forum for dispute settlement, differs as between the feedstock supply contract and the project's offtake contract. It is preferable, where issues of fact or law may be common to a dispute among the parties (e.g., whether an interruption in feedstock supply is excusable by force majeure), to ensure that the issue is resolved in a single proceeding with the goal of a common resolution among the parties.

APPENDIX 7

Checklist of Key Provisions in Offtake/Power Purchase Agreements

Since the power purchase agreement (the PPA) is the principal revenue source in a power generation project, it is one of the most significant contracts for the project company (the Owner) and its lenders. PPAs are usually negotiated very early in the development process and tend to be substantially completed by the time the Owner seeks debt financing. Many of the principles and provisions described below will equally apply in other offtake contracts for other types of projects.

Not all PPAs are 'bankable' or financeable, and consequently, the lenders may seek amendments, either directly to the PPA or in the consent to assignment (or direct agreement) entered into by the relevant utility. However, utilities may be required, or at least inclined, to use contract forms that have previously been approved or accepted by their management and, in some cases, the applicable regulatory authority. In such cases it may be difficult to negotiate or obtain amendments to a PPA that differ substantially from such forms.

The following outline highlights some of the more significant provisions and issues that should be considered in negotiating or reviewing PPAs.

1. Types of PPAs

(a) The need for power in a utility's service area is not constant. It will fluctuate at any given time depending on a number of factors, including the season, the temperature and the time of day or night. A utility must therefore be in a position to deliver power when needed and as efficiently as possible.

(b) To accomplish this objective, utilities own, or purchase, electricity from different types of generating facilities some of which run constantly (referred to as 'base-load' or 'must-run' facilities) and others that only cover 'high peak' demands and are easily and economically turned on and off (referred to as 'peaking' or 'despatchable' facilities).

(c) PPAs take different forms depending on the type of generating facility involved. With respect to a 'must-run' facility, the utility will purchase a fixed amount of energy and capacity. With respect to a 'peaker' facility, the utility will purchase, in effect, the right to a fixed amount of capacity, but may not be obliged to purchase any actual power.

2. Term

(a) The customary term of a PPA runs from 10 to 20 years or more from the date at which the 'initial operations' of the facility are commenced. There are often renewal options.

(b) The lenders will typically structure the term of the debt so that the final payment under the loan agreement occurs substantially prior to the termination of the PPA. In practice, this means anywhere from 2 to 10 years, which ensures that there is a cushion or 'tail' between the final payment under the credit facility and the termination of the revenue source (the PPA) in the event that the debt is not repaid as originally scheduled for any reason, including force majeure.

3. Price

(a) Pricing often equals some percentage of 'avoided cost', which means the cost the purchasing utility would incur to generate or otherwise acquire the power if it did not purchase electricity from the project company under the PPA. As part of this calculation, there is typically a pricing adjustment mechanism linked to an index such as inflation.

(b) Pricing in PPAs typically consists of either (i) capacity payments and energy payments (a Capacity PPA) or (ii) energy payments only (an Energy Only PPA).

(c) A capacity payment is a price paid to reserve the available capacity of the facility, regardless of whether the utility actually purchases any electricity.

(d) An energy payment is the price paid for the actual power delivered. The Owner and the lenders will want these energy payments to correlate as closely as possible to the anticipated fuel costs of the project, with appropriate escalators to reflect any increases in such fuel costs. They will also want the right to renegotiate the energy payments if the energy payments and the actual fuel costs no longer correlate.

(e) It is essential that the revenue of any PPA, whether a Capacity PPA or an Energy Only PPA, be adequate to cover the cost of operating the facility, repaying the debt and providing a reasonable return on equity.

(f) In international projects, where the currency of payment between (i) the utility and its consumer and (ii) the Owner and the lenders, are different, the Owner is exposed to currency risk. Accordingly, the Owner may seek pricing under the PPA to be linked to the exchange rate of the currency of the project debt.

(g) Bonus payments may be included with respect to available capacity above the originally stated available capacity, while a reduction in capacity will often lead to substantial penalty payments to the utility. The proposed capacity must therefore be realistic and attainable.

(h) In many instances, the PPA is structured so that the project receives payment for capacity and/or energy in excess of the utility's 'avoided cost' (e.g. the utility's hypothetical cost of purchasing alternative capacity) during the early years, and payments which are less than the 'avoided cost' during the latter years. Over the full term of the PPA, the average of the payments made for capacity and/or energy will equal the tariff (the Tariff).

(i) These early payments are often referred to as 'front-loaded' payments and may facilitate the financing of the project by providing early additional revenue in order to amortise the debt incurred to finance the project.

(j) While utilities may be willing to provide for such 'front-loaded' payments, they will be concerned about the project having been paid in excess of the Tariff if the PPA is terminated prior to its expected term. To cover this risk, the utility may require that an energy bank account or suspense account be established, although not necessarily funded. Such accounts are used to keep track of the incremental payments being made in excess of the average Tariff.

(k) If the PPA is terminated prior to its expected term, the project may be obliged to repay the incremental excess, which is the difference between the amount the utility would have paid if it had paid the Tariff, and the amount actually received by the utility.

4. Conditions Precedent

(a) All PPAs will have a variety of conditions precedent that need to be satisfied before the utility is obliged to purchase power. In certain instances, failure to satisfy the conditions precedent by a date certain may entitle the utility to terminate the PPA. Since many of these conditions precedent are related to the safety of the system or are mandated by regulators, utilities may not be willing to modify these conditions precedent.

(b) Typical conditions precedent are:
  (i) commencement of construction by a specified date;
  (ii) achieving further construction milestones by specified dates;
  (iii) commencement of initial operations by a specified date;
  (iv) obtaining certain permits by specified dates;
  (v) execution of fuel supply contracts that conform to certain criteria;
  (vi) construction of the facility in accordance with the design approved by the utility; and
  (vii) initial synchronization of the facility with the utility's system.

(c) In reviewing the conditions precedent, the lenders and the Owner must be satisfied that each can be accomplished as and when required. To the extent possible, the time when any condition precedent must be satisfied should be extended in the event of force majeure.

(d) An ultimate 'hell or high water' date (meaning the last date upon which initial operations must occur regardless of any delay, including force majeure) may, however, be acceptable if sufficient time is afforded to cover all reasonable contingencies.

5. Force Majeure and Regulatory Considerations

(a) The lenders and the Owner will seek the broadest definition of force majeure in order to protect against (i) the Owner becoming obliged to pay delay or performance damages and/or (ii) the termination of the PPA. The utility may demand the right to terminate the PPA in the event of an extended force majeure event.

(b) The force majeure definition customarily includes:
   (i) natural disasters;
   (ii) war and terrorism;
   (iii) governmental actions;
   (iv) system emergencies; and
   (v) labour strikes.

(c) If the project's capacity is unavailable due to force majeure events, the utility will sometimes agree to continue the capacity payments for a limited period of time and if the relevant circumstances constitute 'political force majeure' (e.g. arising from a change in law) the utility may agree to continue making capacity payments during the subsistence of such an event.

6. Security

(a) It is not unusual for a utility to require security in connection with (i) a delay in initial operations after a specified date, and (ii) the performance obligations of the Owner under the PPA.

(b) In satisfaction of such security obligations, utilities have required letters of credit, corporate guarantees and second mortgages on the facilities. The second mortgage may raise concern for the lenders who will often object to sharing the only collateral securing their debt and may be uneasy about the various and sometimes conflicting rights of the lenders and the utility in connection with the collateral.

(c) A utility may also require a step-in right in the event of a default (especially a performance default) under the PPA. With such a right, a utility could 'step-in' and operate the facility itself. The lenders may be concerned about this risk unless the utility also assumes all of the Owner's obligations to the lenders and others under the loan agreement and the other project documents.

7. Curtailment of Electricity Deliveries

(a) A PPA that does not provide a certain stream of revenue (with limited exceptions) may not be financeable. The right of the utility to curtail its purchase of power should be strictly limited unless the PPA is structured so that the capacity payment component is sufficient to satisfy fixed operating costs and debt service.

(b) Utilities will usually be permitted to curtail for:
   (i) utility maintenance, within defined limits of days/hours per month/year and with appropriate notice to the project; and
   (ii) in the event of an emergency shutdown (although in this context the definition of emergency should be narrow).

(c) Capacity payments should continue to be made if the utility reduces its consumption of power below the level specified in the PPA, whether due to forced outages or otherwise.

(d) In a cogeneration project, the requirements of the steam host must also be considered. If the electric output of the facility must be curtailed due to the utility's requirements, the cost of producing steam to satisfy the requirements of the steam host will be substantially increased. To address this concern, the force majeure definition in the steam sales agreement might include facility shutdowns caused by the utility.

8. Interconnection

(a) The Owner is typically responsible for delivering its power to the utility's existing power lines.

(b) The utility may agree to provide the necessary interconnection facilities. However, in a number of projects, the Owner is obliged to finance and construct such facilities and, at project completion, transfer such 'special facilities' to the utility, which then takes responsibility for the ongoing operation and maintenance of the interconnection facilities.

9. Line Upgrades

(a) The Owner may be asked to pay for upgrades to the utility's existing power lines in order to handle the increased load resulting from the project becoming operational.

(b) In this event, it is usually prudent to:
    (i)   avoid open-ended commitments;
    (ii) negotiate up-front cost sharing to be made with other users;
    (iii) consider the tax benefits associated with the upgrades when negotiating the payments; and
    (iv) specify additional operating costs, if any.

10. Assignment

(a) The PPA should allow for the assignment of collateral to the lenders as well as the right of the lenders to receive notice of any default and the right to cure such default.

(b) Assignment conditions and the lenders' rights to notice and cure rights for default are typically set out in a separate consent to assignment (or direct agreement). Sometimes a utility has its own form of consent that it prefers to execute.

11. Termination

(a) The PPA should set out clearly the basis on which either party may terminate the agreement. Termination by the utility may leave the project with no access to the market and thus should be limited to significant events. The project company will want meaningful grace periods and cure rights while the lenders will insist upon step in rights.

(b) In emerging market PPAs, there are often detailed provisions relating to the payment of termination amounts, the size of which varies depending on the nature of the termination event. There is typically no buyout unless the utility wants to purchase the project. On the other hand, if a termination event occurs following breach by the utility, the termination amount could be sized to cover the repayment of debt and may also contain an equity component which includes returning the investment made by the shareholders of the project company and a return on equity based on the net present value of the potential revenue stream from the project (which is determined based on the return on equity that would have otherwise been made over life of the project).

12. Governing Law

In most cases, the PPA will be governed by the law of the host jurisdiction, but where that law is not well developed, it may be preferable to select a well recognized governing law.

13. Dispute Settlement

Most Owners will wish disputes to be settled in a neutral forum. In many cases this will involve binding arbitration.

APPENDIX 8

Checklist of Key Provisions in Operation and Maintenance Agreements

This checklist sets forth lists key provisions typically contained in an Operation and Maintenance Agreement (O&M Agreement). The list, however, is by no means exhaustive. Each project will have its own unique requirements that will need to be provided for after consultation and negotiation among the project company (the Owner), the lenders, the lenders' technical adviser and the operator (Operator).

1. Objectives

The objectives of an O&M Agreement include:

(a) Ensuring the Operator meets performance guarantees tied to maximizing revenues under the project's offtake agreements.
(b) Allocating the risk of any operational deficiencies of the facility.
(c) Managing the cost of operating the facility and, in particular, ensuring that project revenues will cover all operational and other costs.

2. Structure of Contracts

There are three basic structures for an O&M Agreement:

2.1 Cost Plus Structure

Under a cost plus contract, the Owner pays the costs reasonably incurred by the Operator in the operation and management of the facility, including a provision for overhead and a fixed fee.

(a) Most risks associated with the performance of the facility during its commercial operations remain with the Owner, thereby reducing both the Operator's fee and its profits.
(b) A broad termination provision minimizes the risk to the Owner of excessive costs and deficient performance by the Operator.
(c) The lenders may resist cost plus contracts that do not adequately mitigate the risk of cost overruns, which in turn could reduce the net revenues from which debt service is paid.

2.2 Bonus/Penalty Structure

This contractual structure measures the Operator's compensation through incentives tied to the facility's output and/or the Operator's ability to meet the operating budget. The Operator is provided with incentives to maximize facility output and minimize operational costs. For instance:

(a) Bonuses and penalties may be based upon agreed operational performance levels for output. Projected levels of facility output and efficiency should be set according to the performance capability achieved during the facility's completion testing, as required by the construction contract.
(b) If projected output is reached and all efficiency, pollution and other governmental standards are met, incentive compensation may be paid to the Operator as a percentage of cashflow, generally from revenues attributable to performance above guaranteed levels.
(c) In the case of deficient performance, the Operator may be required to compensate the Owner for any non-operational periods and/or the cost of the repair and replacement of parts. However, the Operator may resist such penalties in the case of output deficiencies caused by events beyond the Operator's control, such as equipment failure, fuel supply interruptions and force majeure events.

(d) Bonuses and penalties may also be based on deviations from the project's operating budget.
(e) The project's operating budget is typically negotiated annually between the Owner, the Operator and the lenders (through the exercise of their rights under the finance documents).
(f) The operating budget should include all major costs within the Operator's control, including labour and general administrative expenses. Costs such as spare parts, consumables and minor equipment repairs may also be included.
(g) Maximum penalties and bonuses are often capped.

2.3 Fixed Price Structure

Under this structure, the Owner and the Operator agree to a fixed price for the operation of the facility. The Operator's profit is measured by the difference between the total costs incurred to operate the facility and the contract price. This structure is usually the most costly to the Owner because the Operator charges a premium for its assumption of the project's operational risks. This form is most commonly applied when the Operator is an affiliate of the Owner or of the construction contractor.

3. Term

The term of the contract varies by transaction, but typically correlates with the term of the project loans.

4. Scope of Work

(a) The actual obligations delegated to the Operator will depend on the technology of the project, the expertise of the Owner and the nature of the fuel or feedstock supply arrangements. The O&M Agreement should always clearly define the Operator's duties and responsibilities.
(b) The Operator's duties generally include:
    (i) provision of all necessary personnel and services for the operation, maintenance and repair of the facility, including the preparation of an annual budget, operating procedures and a maintenance program; and
    (ii) monitoring compliance with all other project contracts, government permits, licenses, applicable industry standards and good engineering practices.
(c) The Operator's duties may include the procurement of fuel or feedstock depending, of course, on whether a fuel or feedstock supply contract has been entered into by the Owner.
(d) Warranties received from outside vendors or subcontractors are generally passed through to the Owner, but maintained and administered by the Operator.

5. Force Majeure

(a) Lenders and Owners prefer that the definition of force majeure be narrow and include a 'closed' or exhaustive list of events permitting a claim of force majeure. If it is necessary to broaden the term, specific 'events' or 'occurrences' will be added to the list.
(b) The definition will generally state that force majeure events are causes outside the control of the parties that cannot be avoided by the exercise of due care.

6. Authority of Operator

The Owner must determine the scope of the Operator's authority to enter into contracts on behalf of the Owner.

7. Termination

(a) Lenders and Owners prefer that the grounds for termination of the O&M Agreement by the Operator be extremely limited and, if any are agreed, that they be carefully defined.
(b) Generally, the Owner's ability to terminate or replace the Operator is limited to a material breach of contract (which will include failure to meet performance guarantees over a set period) by the Operator, or the Operator's bankruptcy or insolvency, except in the case of a 'cost plus' agreement, where termination rights may be broader.

(c) The lenders will often prevent the Owner from terminating or replacing the Operator without giving their own consent to the change.

8. Insurance

(a) The Operator is generally required to carry insurance, including worker's compensation, comprehensive general liability, comprehensive auto liability and excess umbrella liability coverage.
(b) Usually, the Owner will carry the necessary property and business interruption insurance.

9. Warranties

The Operator may give the following warranties:

(a) the project's operations will be performed 'in accordance with applicable industry standards and good engineering practices';
(b) all equipment or parts will be new and free of all material defects and utilized according to manufacturer and supplier recommendations; and
(c) operating personnel will be appropriately trained and have relevant experience.

10. Indemnity

(a) The Operator may agree to indemnify the Owner, the lenders and their representatives and agents from any third party claims arising out of the acts or omissions of the Operator, its employees or agents in connection with the performance of the O&M Agreement, including claims for personal injury, property damage, regulatory penalties, and fines.
(b) The O&M Agreement sometimes provides an indemnity by the Operator to the Owner for any liability to the offtakers (e.g. the purchasing utility) arising from the fault of the Operator.

11. Assignment

(a) The Operator is usually prohibited from assigning its rights or obligations under the O&M Agreement without the Owner's consent.
(b) The O&M Agreement should allow for collateral assignment to lenders, with the right to receive notice of any default and the right to cure the Owner's defaults.
(c) Assignment conditions and cure rights are typically set out in a separate consent to assignment (or direct agreement).

INDEX